# Game Engine Architecture

# Game Engine Architecture

## Jason Gregory

A K Peters, Ltd.
Natick, Massachusetts

Editorial, Sales, and Customer Service Office

A K Peters, Ltd.
5 Commonwealth Road, Suite 2C
Natick, Massachusetts
www.akpeters.com

**Library of Congress Cataloging-in-Publication Data**

Gregory, Jason, 1970-
 Game engine architecture / Jason Gregory.
   p. cm.
 Includes bibliographical references and index.
 ISBN 978-1-56881-413-1 (alk. paper)
 1. Computer games--Programming. 2. Computer architecture. I. Title.
 QA76.76.C672G77 2009
 794.8'1526--dc22

                                                      2009013092

Havok Physics (TM) is a trademark of Havok.

Printed in the United States of America
13  12  11  10  09                        10 9 8 7 6 5 4 3 2

Dedicated to
Trina, Evan and Quinn Gregory,

in memory of our heros,
Joyce Osterhus and Kenneth Gregory.

# Contents

Foreword                                                          xiii

Preface                                                           xvii

## 1   Foundations                                                  1

### 1   Introduction                                                3

   1.1    Structure of a Typical Game Team             5
   1.2    What Is a Game?                              8
   1.3    What Is a Game Engine?                       11
   1.4    Engine Differences Across Genres             13
   1.5    Game Engine Survey                           25
   1.6    Runtime Engine Architecture                  28
   1.7    Tools and the Asset Pipeline                 49

### 2   Tools of the Trade                                          57

   2.1    Version Control                              57
   2.2    Microsoft Visual Studio                      66
   2.3    Profiling Tools                              85

2.4    Memory Leak and Corruption Detection              87
2.5    Other Tools                                       88

3    Fundamentals of Software
     Engineering for Games                               91
     3.1    C++ Review and Best Practices                91
     3.2    Data, Code, and Memory in C/C++              98
     3.3    Catching and Handling Errors                 128

4    3D Math for Games                                  137
     4.1    Solving 3D Problems in 2D                    137
     4.2    Points and Vectors                           138
     4.3    Matrices                                     151
     4.4    Quaternions                                  169
     4.5    Comparison of Rotational Representations     177
     4.6    Other Useful Mathematical Objects            181
     4.7    Hardware-Accelerated SIMD Math               185
     4.8    Random Number Generation                     192

II   Low-Level Engine Systems                           195

5    Engine Support Systems                             197
     5.1    Subsystem Start-Up and Shut-Down             197
     5.2    Memory Management                            205
     5.3    Containers                                   223
     5.4    Strings                                      242
     5.5    Engine Configuration                         252

6    Resources and the File System                      261
     6.1    File System                                  262
     6.2    The Resource Manager                         272

7    The Game Loop and Real-Time Simulation             303
     7.1    The Rendering Loop                           303
     7.2    The Game Loop                                304

|  | 7.3 | Game Loop Architectural Styles | 307 |
|  | 7.4 | Abstract Timelines | 310 |
|  | 7.5 | Measuring and Dealing with Time | 312 |
|  | 7.6 | Multiprocessor Game Loops | 324 |
|  | 7.7 | Networked Multiplayer Game Loops | 333 |

| 8 | Human Interface Devices (HID) | | 339 |
|---|---|---|---|
|  | 8.1 | Types of Human Interface Devices | 339 |
|  | 8.2 | Interfacing with a HID | 341 |
|  | 8.3 | Types of Inputs | 343 |
|  | 8.4 | Types of Outputs | 348 |
|  | 8.5 | Game Engine HID Systems | 349 |
|  | 8.6 | Human Interface Devices in Practice | 366 |

| 9 | Tools for Debugging and Development | | 367 |
|---|---|---|---|
|  | 9.1 | Logging and Tracing | 367 |
|  | 9.2 | Debug Drawing Facilities | 372 |
|  | 9.3 | In-Game Menus | 379 |
|  | 9.4 | In-Game Console | 382 |
|  | 9.5 | Debug Cameras and Pausing the Game | 383 |
|  | 9.6 | Cheats | 384 |
|  | 9.7 | Screen Shots and Movie Capture | 384 |
|  | 9.8 | In-Game Profiling | 385 |

| III | Graphics and Motion | | 397 |
|---|---|---|---|

| 10 | The Rendering Engine | | 399 |
|---|---|---|---|
|  | 10.1 | Foundations of Depth-Buffered Triangle Rasterization | 400 |
|  | 10.2 | The Rendering Pipeline | 444 |
|  | 10.3 | Advanced Lighting and Global Illumination | 469 |
|  | 10.4 | Visual Effects and Overlays | 481 |

| 11 | Animation Systems | | 491 |
|---|---|---|---|
|  | 11.1 | Types of Character Animation | 491 |
|  | 11.2 | Skeletons | 496 |

| | | |
|---|---|---:|
| 11.3 | Poses | 499 |
| 11.4 | Clips | 504 |
| 11.5 | Skinning and Matrix Palette Generation | 518 |
| 11.6 | Animation Blending | 523 |
| 11.7 | Post-Processing | 542 |
| 11.8 | Compression Techniques | 545 |
| 11.9 | Animation System Architecture | 552 |
| 11.10 | The Animation Pipeline | 553 |
| 11.11 | Action State Machines | 568 |
| 11.12 | Animation Controllers | 593 |

## 12   Collision and Rigid Body Dynamics                          595

| | | |
|---|---|---:|
| 12.1 | Do You Want Physics in Your Game? | 596 |
| 12.2 | Collision/Physics Middleware | 601 |
| 12.3 | The Collision Detection System | 603 |
| 12.4 | Rigid Body Dynamics | 630 |
| 12.5 | Integrating a Physics Engine into Your Game | 666 |
| 12.6 | A Look Ahead: Advanced Physics Features | 684 |

# IV   Gameplay                                                      687

## 13   Introduction to Gameplay Systems                            689

| | | |
|---|---|---:|
| 13.1 | Anatomy of a Game World | 690 |
| 13.2 | Implementing Dynamic Elements: Game Objects | 695 |
| 13.3 | Data-Driven Game Engines | 698 |
| 13.4 | The Game World Editor | 699 |

## 14   Runtime Gameplay Foundation Systems                         711

| | | |
|---|---|---:|
| 14.1 | Components of the Gameplay Foundation System | 711 |
| 14.2 | Runtime Object Model Architectures | 715 |
| 14.3 | World Chunk Data Formats | 734 |
| 14.4 | Loading and Streaming Game Worlds | 741 |
| 14.5 | Object References and World Queries | 750 |
| 14.6 | Updating Game Objects in Real Time | 757 |

14.7    Events and Message-Passing                      773
14.8    Scripting                                       794
14.9    High-Level Game Flow                            817

V    Conclusion                                         819

15   You Mean There's More?                             821
15.1    Some Engine Systems We Didn't Cover             821
15.2    Gameplay Systems                                823

References                                              827

Index                                                   831

# Foreword

The very first video game was built entirely out of hardware, but rapid advancements in microprocessors have changed all that. These days, video games are played on versatile PCs and specialized video game consoles that use software to make it possible to offer a tremendous variety of gaming experiences. It's been 50 years since those first primitive games, but the industry is still considered by many to be immature. It may be young, but when you take a closer look, you will find that things have been developing rapidly. Video games are now a multibillion-dollar industry covering a wide range of demographics.

Video games come in all shapes and sizes, falling into categories or "genres" covering everything from solitaire to massively multiplayer online role-playing games, and these games are played on virtually anything with a microchip in it. These days, you can get games for your PC, your cell phone, as well as a number of different specialized gaming consoles—both handheld and those that connect to your home TV. These specialized home consoles tend to represent the cutting edge of gaming technology, and the pattern of these platforms being released in cycles has come to be called console "generations." The powerhouses of this latest generation are Microsoft's Xbox 360 and Sony's PLAYSTATION 3, but the ever-present PC should never be overlooked, and the extremely popular Nintendo Wii represents something new this time around.

The recent explosion of downloadable and casual games has added even more complexity to the diverse world of commercial video games. Even so, big games are still big business. The incredible computing power available on today's complicated platforms has made room for increased complexity in the software. Naturally, all this advanced software has to be created by someone, and that has driven up the size of development teams—not to mention development costs. As the industry matures, we're always looking for better, more efficient ways to build our products, and development teams have begun compensating for the increased complexity by taking advantage of things like reusable software and middleware.

With so many different styles of game on such a wide array of platforms, there cannot be any single ideal software solution. However, certain patterns have developed, and there is a vast menu of potential solutions out there. The problem today is choosing the right solution to fit the needs of the particular project. Going deeper, a development team must consider all the different aspects of a project and how they fit together. It is rare to find any one software package that perfectly suits every aspect of a new game design.

Those of us who are now veterans of the industry found ourselves pioneering unknown territory. Few programmers of our generation have Computer Science degrees (Matt's is in Aeronautical Engineering, and Jason's is in Systems Design Engineering), but these days many colleges are starting to programs and degrees in video games. The students and developers of today need a good place to turn to for solid game-development information. For pure high-end graphics, there are a lot of sources of very good information from research to practical jewels of knowledge. However, these sources are often not directly applicable to production game environments or suffer from not having actual production-quality implementations. For the rest of game development, there are so-called beginner books that so gloss over the details and act as if they invented everything without giving references that they are just not useful or often even accurate. Then there are high-end specialty books for various niches like physics, collision, AI, etc. But these can be needlessly obtuse or too high level to be understood by all, or the piecemeal approach just doesn't all fit together. Many are even so directly tied to a particular piece of technology as to become rapidly dated as the hardware and software change.

Then there is the Internet, which is an excellent supplementary tool for knowledge gathering. However, broken links, widely inaccurate data, and variable-to-poor quality often make it not useful at all unless you know exactly what you are after.

Enter Jason Gregory, himself an industry veteran with experience at Naughty Dog—one of the most highly regarded video game studios in the world. While teaching a course in game programming at USC, Jason found himself facing a shortage of textbooks covering the fundamentals of video-game architecture. Luckily for the rest of us, he has taken it upon himself to fill that gap.

What Jason has done is pull together production-quality knowledge actually used in shipped game projects and bring together the entire game-development picture. His experience has allowed him to bring together not only the ideas and techniques but also actual code samples and implementation examples to show you how the pieces come together to actually make a game. The references and citations make it a great jumping-off point to dig deeper into any particular aspect of the process. The concepts and techniques are the actual ones we use to create games, and while the examples are often grounded in a technology, they extend way beyond any particular engine or API.

This is the kind of book we wanted when we were getting started, and we think it will prove very instructive to people just starting out as well as those with experience who would like some exposure to the larger context.

Jeff Lander
Matthew Whiting

# Preface

Welcome to *Game Engine Architecture*. This book aims to present a complete discussion of the major components that make up a typical commercial game engine. Game programming is an immense topic, so we have a lot of ground to cover. Nevertheless, I trust you'll find that the depth of our discussions is sufficient to give you a solid understanding of both the theory and the common practices employed within each of the engineering disciplines we'll cover. That said, this book is really just the beginning of a fascinating and potentially life-long journey. A wealth of information is available on all aspects of game technology, and this text serves both as a foundation-laying device and as a jumping-off point for further learning.

Our focus in this book will be on game engine technologies and architecture. This means we'll cover both the theory underlying the various subsystems that comprise a commercial game engine and also the data structures, algorithms, and software interfaces that are typically used to implement them. The line between the game engine and the game is rather blurry. We'll focus primarily on the engine itself, including a host of low-level foundation systems, the rendering engine, the collision system, the physics simulation, character animation, and an in-depth discussion of what I call the *gameplay foundation layer*. This layer includes the game's object model, world editor, event system, and scripting system. We'll also touch on some aspects of gameplay programming, including player mechanics, cameras, and AI. However, by necessity, the scope of these discussions will be limited mainly to the ways in which gameplay systems interface with the engine.

This book is intended to be used as a course text for a two- or three-course college-level series in intermediate game programming. Of course, it can also be used by amateur software engineers, hobbyists, self-taught game programmers, and existing members of the game industry alike. Junior engineers can use this text to solidify their understanding of game mathematics, engine architecture, and game technology. And some senior engineers who have devoted their careers to one particular specialty may benefit from the bigger picture presented in these pages, as well.

To get the most out of this book, you should have a working knowledge of basic object-oriented programming concepts and at least some experience programming in C++. Although a host of new and exciting languages are beginning to take hold within the game industry, industrial-strength 3D game engines are still written primarily in C or C++, and any serious game programmer needs to know C++. We'll review the basic tenets of object-oriented programming in Chapter 3, and you will no doubt pick up a few new C++ tricks as you read this book, but a solid foundation in the C++ language is best obtained from [39], [31], and [32]. If your C++ is a bit rusty, I recommend you refer to these or similar books to refresh your knowledge as you read this text. If you have no prior C++ experience, you may want to consider reading at least the first few chapters of [39], or working through a few C++ tutorials online, before diving into this book.

The best way to learn computer programming of any kind is to actually write some code. As you read through this book, I strongly encourage you to select a few topic areas that are of particular interest to you and come up with some projects for yourself in those areas. For example, if you find character animation interesting, you could start by installing Ogre3D and exploring its skinned animation demo. Then you could try to implement some of the animation blending techniques described in this book, using Ogre. Next you might decide to implement a simple joypad-controlled animated character that can run around on a flat plane. Once you have something relatively simple working, expand upon it! Then move on to another area of game technology. Rinse and repeat. It doesn't particularly matter what the projects are, as long as you're *practicing* the art of game programming, not just reading about it.

Game technology is a living, breathing thing that can never be entirely captured within the pages of a book. As such, additional resources, errata, updates, sample code, and project ideas will be posted from time to time on this book's website at http://gameenginebook.com.

# Acknowledgments

No book is created in a vacuum, and this one is certainly no exception. This book would not have been possible without the help of my family, friends, and colleagues in the game industry, and I'd like to extend warm thanks to everyone who helped me to bring this project to fruition.

Of course, the ones most impacted by a project like this one are invariably the author's family. So I'd like to start by offering a special thank-you to my wife Trina, who has been a pillar of strength during this difficult time, taking care of our two boys Evan (age 5) and Quinn (age 3) day after day (and night after night!) while I holed myself up to get yet another chapter under my belt, forgoing her own plans to accommodate my schedule, doing my chores as well as her own (more often than I'd like to admit), and always giving me kind words of encouragement when I needed them the most. I'd also like to thank my eldest son Evan for being patient as he endured the absence of his favorite video game playing partner, and his younger brother Quinn for always welcoming me home after a long day's work with huge hugs and endless smiles.

I would also like to extend special thanks to my editors, Matt Whiting and Jeff Lander. Their insightful, targeted, and timely feedback was always right on the money, and their vast experience in the game industry has helped to give me confidence that the information presented in these pages is as accurate and up-to-date as humanly possible. Matt and Jeff were both a pleasure to work with, and I am honored to have had the opportunity to collaborate with such consummate professionals on this project. I'd like to thank Jeff in particular for putting me in touch with Alice Peters and helping me to get this project off the ground in the first place.

A number of my colleagues at Naughty Dog also contributed to this book, either by providing feedback or by helping me with the structure and topic content of one of the chapters. I'd like to thank Marshall Robin and Carlos Gonzalez-Ochoa for their guidance and tutelage as I wrote the rendering chapter, and Pål-Kristian Engstad for his excellent and insightful feedback on the text and content of that chapter. I'd also like to thank Christian Gyrling for his feedback on various sections of the book, including the chapter on animation (which is one of his many specialties). My thanks also go to the entire Naughty Dog engineering team for creating all of the incredible game engine systems that I highlight in this book. Special thanks go to Keith Schaeffer of Electronic Arts for providing me with much of the raw content regarding the impact of physics on a game, found in Section 12.1. I'd also like to thank Paul Keet of Electronic Arts and Steve Ranck, the lead engineer on the *Hydro Thunder* project at Midway San Diego, for their mentorship and guidance over the years. While they did not contribute to the book directly, their influences are echoed on virtually every page in one way or another.

This book arose out of the notes I developed for a course called *ITP-485: Programming Game Engines*, which I have been teaching under the auspices of the Information Technology Program at the University of Southern California for approximately three years now. I would like to thank Dr. Anthony Borquez, the director of the ITP department at the time, for hiring me to develop the ITP-485 course curriculum in the first place. I'd also like to extend warm thanks to Ashish Soni, the current ITP director, for his continued support and encouragement as ITP-485 continues to evolve.

My extended family and friends also deserve thanks, in part for their unwavering encouragement, and in part for entertaining my wife and our two boys on so many occasions while I was working. I'd like to thank my sister- and brother-in-law, Tracy Lee and Doug Provins, my cousin-in-law Matt Glenn, and all of our incredible friends, including: Kim and Drew Clark, Sherilyn and Jim Kritzer, Anne and Michael Scherer, and Kim and Mike Warner. My father Kenneth Gregory wrote a book on investing in the stock market when I was a teenager, and in doing so he inspired me to write a book. For this and so much more, I am eternally grateful to him. I'd also like to thank my mother Erica Gregory, in part for her insistence that I embark on this project, and in part for spending countless hours with me when I was a child, beating the art of writing into my cranium — I owe my writing skills (not to mention my work ethic… and my rather twisted sense of humor…) entirely to her!

Last but certainly not least, I'd like to thank Alice Peters and Kevin Jackson-Mead, as well as the entire A K Peters staff, for their Herculean efforts in publishing this book. Alice and Kevin have both been a pleasure to work with, and I truly appreciate both their willingness to bend over backwards to get this book out the door under very tight time constraints, and their infinite patience with me as a new author.

Jason Gregory
*April 2009*

# I
# Foundations

# 1
# Introduction

When I got my first game console in 1979—a way-cool Intellivision system by Mattel—the term "game engine" did not exist. Back then, video and arcade games were considered by most adults to be nothing more than toys, and the software that made them tick was highly specialized to both the game in question and the hardware on which it ran. Today, games are a multi-billion-dollar mainstream industry rivaling Hollywood in size and popularity. And the software that drives these now-ubiquitous three-dimensional worlds—*game engines* like id Software's Quake and Doom engines, Epic Games' Unreal Engine 3 and Valve's Source engine—have become fully featured reusable software development kits that can be licensed and used to build almost any game imaginable.

While game engines vary widely in the details of their architecture and implementation, recognizable coarse-grained patterns are emerging across both publicly licensed game engines and their proprietary in-house counterparts. Virtually all game engines contain a familiar set of core components, including the rendering engine, the collision and physics engine, the animation system, the audio system, the game world object model, the artificial intelligence system, and so on. Within each of these components, a relatively small number of semi-standard design alternatives are also beginning to emerge.

There are a great many books that cover individual game engine subsystems, such as three-dimensional graphics, in exhaustive detail. Other books cobble together valuable tips and tricks across a wide variety of game technology areas. However, I have been unable to find a book that provides its reader with a reasonably complete picture of the entire gamut of components that make up a modern game engine. The goal of this book, then, is to take the reader on a guided hands-on tour of the vast and complex landscape of game engine architecture.

In this book you will learn

- how real industrial-strength production game engines are architected;
- how game development teams are organized and work in the real world;
- which major subsystems and design patterns appear again and again in virtually every game engine;
- the typical requirements for each major subsystem;
- which subsystems are genre- or game-agnostic, and which ones are typically designed explicitly for a specific genre or game;
- where the engine normally ends and the game begins.

We'll also get a first-hand glimpse into the inner workings of some popular game engines, such as Quake and Unreal, and some well-known middleware packages, such as the Havok Physics library, the OGRE rendering engine, and Rad Game Tools' Granny 3D animation and geometry management toolkit.

Before we get started, we'll review some techniques and tools for large-scale software engineering in a game engine context, including

- the difference between logical and physical software architecture;
- configuration management, revision control, and build systems;
- some tips and tricks for dealing with one of the common development environments for C and C++, Microsoft Visual Studio.

In this book I assume that you have a solid understanding of C++ (the language of choice among most modern game developers) and that you understand basic software engineering principles. I also assume you have some exposure to linear algebra, three-dimensional vector and matrix math, and trigonometry (although we'll review the core concepts in Chapter 4). Ideally you should have some prior exposure to the basic concepts of real-time and event-driven programming. But never fear—I will review these topics briefly, and I'll also point you in the right direction if you feel you need to hone your skills further before we embark.

# 1.1.  Structure of a Typical Game Team

Before we delve into the structure of a typical game engine, let's first take a brief look at the structure of a typical game development team. Game studios are usually composed of five basic disciplines: engineers, artists, game designers, producers, and other management and support staff (marketing, legal, information technology/technical support, administrative, etc.). Each discipline can be divided into various subdisciplines. We'll take a brief look at each below.

## 1.1.1.  Engineers

The engineers design and implement the software that makes the game, and the tools, work. Engineers are often categorized into two basic groups: *runtime* programmers (who work on the engine and the game itself) and *tools* programmers (who work on the off-line tools that allow the rest of the development team to work effectively). On both sides of the runtime/tools line, engineers have various specialties. Some engineers focus their careers on a single engine system, such as rendering, artificial intelligence, audio, or collision and physics. Some focus on gameplay programming and scripting, while others prefer to work at the systems level and not get too involved in how the game actually plays. Some engineers are generalists—jacks of all trades who can jump around and tackle whatever problems might arise during development.

Senior engineers are sometimes asked to take on a technical leadership role. Lead engineers usually still design and write code, but they also help to manage the team's schedule, make decisions regarding the overall technical direction of the project, and sometimes also directly manage people from a human resources perspective.

Some companies also have one or more technical directors (TD), whose job it is to oversee one or more projects from a high level, ensuring that the teams are aware of potential technical challenges, upcoming industry developments, new technologies, and so on. The highest engineering-related position at a game studio is the chief technical officer (CTO), if the studio has one. The CTO's job is to serve as a sort of technical director for the entire studio, as well as serving a key executive role in the company.

## 1.1.2.  Artists

As we say in the game industry, "content is king." The artists produce all of the visual and audio content in the game, and the quality of their work can literally make or break a game. Artists come in all sorts of flavors:

- *Concept artists* produce sketches and paintings that provide the team with a vision of what the final game will look like. They start their work early in the concept phase of development, but usually continue to provide visual direction throughout a project's life cycle. It is common for screen shots taken from a shipping game to bear an uncanny resemblance to the concept art.

- *3D modelers* produce the three-dimensional geometry for everything in the virtual game world. This discipline is typically divided into two subdisciplines: foreground modelers and background modelers. The former create objects, characters, vehicles, weapons, and the other objects that populate the game world, while the latter build the world's static background geometry (terrain, buildings, bridges, etc.).

- *Texture artists* create the two-dimensional images known as textures, which are applied to the surfaces of 3D models in order to provide detail and realism.

- *Lighting artists* lay out all of the light sources in the game world, both static and dynamic, and work with color, intensity, and light direction to maximize the artfulness and emotional impact of each scene.

- *Animators* imbue the characters and objects in the game with motion. The animators serve quite literally as actors in a game production, just as they do in a CG film production. However, a game animator must have a unique set of skills in order to produce animations that mesh seamlessly with the technological underpinnings of the game engine.

- *Motion capture actors* are often used to provide a rough set of motion data, which are then cleaned up and tweaked by the animators before being integrated into the game.

- *Sound designers* work closely with the engineers in order to produce and mix the sound effects and music in the game.

- *Voice actors* provide the voices of the characters in many games.

- Many games have one or more *composers*, who compose an original score for the game.

As with engineers, senior artists are often called upon to be team leaders. Some game teams have one or more *art directors*—very senior artists who manage the look of the entire game and ensure consistency across the work of all team members.

### 1.1.3. Game Designers

The game designers' job is to design the interactive portion of the player's experience, typically known as *gameplay*. Different kinds of designers work at different levels of detail. Some (usually senior) game designers work at the macro level, determining the story arc, the overall sequence of chapters or levels, and the high-level goals and objectives of the player. Other designers work on individual levels or geographical areas within the virtual game world, laying out the static background geometry, determining where and when enemies will emerge, placing supplies like weapons and health packs, designing puzzle elements, and so on. Still other designers operate at a highly technical level, working closely with gameplay engineers and/or writing code (often in a high-level scripting language). Some game designers are ex-engineers, who decided they wanted to play a more active role in determining how the game will play.

Some game teams employ one or more *writers*. A game writer's job can range from collaborating with the senior game designers to construct the story arc of the entire game, to writing individual lines of dialogue.

As with other disciplines, some senior designers play management roles. Many game teams have a game director, whose job it is to oversee all aspects of a game's design, help manage schedules, and ensure that the work of individual designers is consistent across the entire product. Senior designers also sometimes evolve into producers.

### 1.1.4. Producers

The role of producer is defined differently by different studios. In some game companies, the producer's job is to manage the schedule and serve as a human resources manager. In other companies, producers serve in a senior game design capacity. Still other studios ask their producers to serve as liaisons between the development team and the business unit of the company (finance, legal, marketing, etc.). Some smaller studios don't have producers at all. For example, at Naughty Dog, literally everyone in the company, including the two co-presidents, play a direct role in constructing the game; team management and business duties are shared between the senior members of the studio.

### 1.1.5. Other Staff

The team of people who directly construct the game is typically supported by a crucial team of support staff. This includes the studio's executive management team, the marketing department (or a team that liaises with an external marketing group), administrative staff, and the IT department, whose job is to purchase, install, and configure hardware and software for the team and to provide technical support.

### 1.1.6.  Publishers and Studios

The marketing, manufacture, and distribution of a game title are usually handled by a *publisher*, not by the game studio itself. A publisher is typically a large corporation, like Electronic Arts, THQ, Vivendi, Sony, Nintendo, etc. Many game studios are not affiliated with a particular publisher. They sell each game that they produce to whichever publisher strikes the best deal with them. Other studios work exclusively with a single publisher, either via a long-term publishing contract, or as a fully owned subsidiary of the publishing company. For example, THQ's game studios are independently managed, but they are owned and ultimately controlled by THQ. Electronic Arts takes this relationship one step further, by directly managing its studios. *First-party developers* are game studios owned directly by the console manufacturers (Sony, Nintendo, and Microsoft). For example, Naughty Dog is a first-party Sony developer. These studios produce games exclusively for the gaming hardware manufactured by their parent company.

## 1.2.    What Is a Game?

We probably all have a pretty good intuitive notion of what a game is. The general term "game" encompasses board games like chess and *Monopoly*, card games like poker and blackjack, casino games like roulette and slot machines, military war games, computer games, various kinds of play among children, and the list goes on. In academia we sometimes speak of "game theory," in which multiple agents select strategies and tactics in order to maximize their gains within the framework of a well-defined set of game rules. When used in the context of console or computer-based entertainment, the word "game" usually conjures images of a three-dimensional virtual world featuring a humanoid, animal, or vehicle as the main character under player control. (Or for the old geezers among us, perhaps it brings to mind images of two-dimensional classics like *Pong, Pac-Man,* or *Donkey Kong*.)  In his excellent book, *A Theory of Fun for Game Design*, Raph Koster defines a "game" to be an interactive experience that provides the player with an increasingly challenging sequence of patterns which he or she learns and eventually masters [26]. Koster's assertion is that the activities of learning and mastering are at the heart of what we call "fun," just as a joke becomes funny at the moment we "get it" by recognizing the pattern.

For the purposes of this book, we'll focus on the subset of games that comprise two- and three-dimensional virtual worlds with a small number of players (between one and 16 or thereabouts). Much of what we'll learn can also be applied to Flash games on the Internet, pure puzzle games like *Tetris*, or massively multiplayer online games (MMOG). But our primary focus will be on game engines capable of producing first-person shooters, third-person action/platform games, racing games, fighting games, and the like.

## 1.2.1. Video Games as Soft Real-Time Simulations

Most two- and three-dimensional video games are examples of what computer scientists would call *soft real-time interactive agent-based computer simulations*. Let's break this phrase down in order to better understand what it means.

In most video games, some subset of the real world—or an imaginary world—is *modeled* mathematically so that it can be manipulated by a computer. The model is an approximation to and a simplification of reality (even if it's an *imaginary* reality), because it is clearly impractical to include every detail down to the level of atoms or quarks. Hence, the mathematical model is a *simulation* of the real or imagined game world. Approximation and simplification are two of the game developer's most powerful tools. When used skillfully, even a greatly simplified model can sometimes be almost indistinguishable from reality—and a lot more fun.

An *agent-based* simulation is one in which a number of distinct entities known as "agents" interact. This fits the description of most three-dimentsional computer games very well, where the agents are vehicles, characters, fireballs, power dots, and so on. Given the agent-based nature of most games, it should come as no surprise that most games nowadays are implemented in an object-oriented, or at least loosely object-based, programming language.

All interactive video games are *temporal simulations*, meaning that the virtual game world model is *dynamic*—the state of the game world changes over time as the game's events and story unfold. A video game must also respond to unpredictable inputs from its human player(s)—thus *interactive temporal simulations*. Finally, most video games present their stories and respond to player input in real-time, making them *interactive real-time simulations*. One notable exception is in the category of turn-based games like computerized chess or non-real-time strategy games. But even these types of games usually provide the user with some form of real-time graphical user interface. So for the purposes of this book, we'll assume that all video games have at least *some* real-time constraints.

At the core of every real-time system is the concept of a *deadline*. An obvious example in video games is the requirement that the screen be updated at least 24 times per second in order to provide the illusion of motion. (Most games render the screen at 30 or 60 frames per second because these are multiples of an NTSC monitor's refresh rate.) Of course, there are many other kinds of deadlines in video games as well. A physics simulation may need to be updated 120 times per second in order to remain stable. A character's artificial intelligence system may need to "think" at least once every second to prevent the appearance of stupidity. The audio library may need to be called at least once every 1/60 second in order to keep the audio buffers filled and prevent audible glitches.

A "soft" real-time system is one in which missed deadlines are not catastrophic. Hence all video games are *soft real-time systems*—if the frame rate dies, the human player generally doesn't! Contrast this with a *hard real-time system*, in which a missed deadline could mean severe injury to or even the death of a human operator. The avionics system in a helicopter or the control-rod system in a nuclear power plant are examples of hard real-time systems.

Mathematical models can be *analytic* or *numerical*. For example, the analytic (closed-form) mathematical model of a rigid body falling under the influence of constant acceleration due to gravity is typically written as follows:

$$y(t) = \tfrac{1}{2} g\, t^2 + v_0\, t + y_0. \tag{1.1}$$

An analytic model can be evaluated for any value of its independent variables, such as the time $t$ in the above equation, given only the initial conditions $v_0$ and $y_0$ and the constant $g$. Such models are very convenient when they can be found. However many problems in mathematics have no closed-form solution. And in video games, where the user's input is unpredictable, we cannot hope to model the entire game analytically.

A numerical model of the same rigid body under gravity might be

$$y(t + \Delta t) = F(y(t), \dot{y}(t), \ddot{y}(t), \ldots). \tag{1.2}$$

That is, the height of the rigid body at some future time $(t + \Delta t)$ can be found as a function of the height and its first and second time derivatives at the current time $t$. Numerical simulations are typically implemented by running calculations repeatedly, in order to determine the state of the system at each discrete time step. Games work in the same way. A main "game loop" runs repeatedly, and during each iteration of the loop, various game systems such as artificial intelligence, game logic, physics simulations, and so on are given a chance to calculate or update their state for the next discrete time step. The results are then "rendered" by displaying graphics, emitting sound, and possibly producing other outputs such as force feedback on the joypad.

# 1.3.  What Is a Game Engine?

The term "game engine" arose in the mid-1990s in reference to first-person shooter (FPS) games like the insanely popular *Doom* by id Software. *Doom* was architected with a reasonably well-defined separation between its core software components (such as the three-dimensional graphics rendering system, the collision detection system, or the audio system) and the art assets, game worlds, and rules of play that comprised the player's gaming experience. The value of this separation became evident as developers began licensing games and re-tooling them into new products by creating new art, world layouts, weapons, characters, vehicles, and game rules with only minimal changes to the "engine" software. This marked the birth of the "mod community"—a group of individual gamers and small independent studios that built new games by modifying existing games, using free toolkits provided by the original developers. Towards the end of the 1990s, some games like *Quake III Arena* and *Unreal* were designed with reuse and "modding" in mind. Engines were made highly customizable via scripting languages like id's Quake C, and engine licensing began to be a viable secondary revenue stream for the developers who created them. Today, game developers can license a game engine and reuse significant portions of its key software components in order to build games. While this practice still involves considerable investment in custom software engineering, it can be much more economical than developing all of the core engine components in-house.

The line between a game and its engine is often blurry. Some engines make a reasonably clear distinction, while others make almost no attempt to separate the two. In one game, the rendering code might "know" specifically how to draw an orc. In another game, the rendering engine might provide general-purpose material and shading facilities, and "orc-ness" might be defined entirely in data. No studio makes a perfectly clear separation between the game and the engine, which is understandable considering that the definitions of these two components often shift as the game's design solidifies.

Arguably a *data-driven architecture* is what differentiates a game engine from a piece of software that is a game but not an engine. When a game contains hard-coded logic or game rules, or employs special-case code to render specific types of game objects, it becomes difficult or impossible to reuse that software to make a different game. We should probably reserve the term "game engine" for software that is extensible and can be used as the foundation for many different games without major modification.

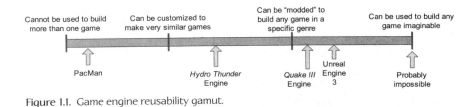

Figure 1.1. Game engine reusability gamut.

Clearly this is not a black-and-white distinction. We can think of a gamut of reusability onto which every engine falls. Figure 1.1 takes a stab at the locations of some well-known games/engines along this gamut.

One would think that a game engine could be something akin to Apple QuickTime or Microsoft Windows Media Player—a general-purpose piece of software capable of playing virtually *any* game content imaginable. However this ideal has not yet been achieved (and may never be). Most game engines are carefully crafted and fine-tuned to run a particular game on a particular hardware platform. And even the most general-purpose multiplatform engines are really only suitable for building games in one particular genre, such as first-person shooters or racing games. It's safe to say that the more general-purpose a game engine or middleware component is, the less optimal it is for running a particular game on a particular platform.

This phenomenon occurs because designing any efficient piece of software invariably entails making trade-offs, and those trade-offs are based on assumptions about how the software will be used and/or about the target hardware on which it will run. For example, a rendering engine that was designed to handle intimate indoor environments probably won't be very good at rendering vast outdoor environments. The indoor engine might use a BSP tree or portal system to ensure that no geometry is drawn that is being occluded by walls or objects that are closer to the camera. The outdoor engine, on the other hand, might use a less-exact occlusion mechanism, or none at all, but it probably makes aggressive use of level-of-detail (LOD) techniques to ensure that distant objects are rendered with a minimum number of triangles, while using high resolution triangle meshes for geometry that is close to the camera.

The advent of ever-faster computer hardware and specialized graphics cards, along with ever-more-efficient rendering algorithms and data structures, is beginning to soften the differences between the graphics engines of different genres. It is now possible to use a first-person shooter engine to build a real-time strategy game, for example. However, the trade-off between gener-

ality and optimality still exists. A game can always be made more impressive by fine-tuning the engine to the specific requirements and constraints of a particular game and/or hardware platform.

## 1.4.    Engine Differences Across Genres

Game engines are typically somewhat genre specific. An engine designed for a two-person fighting game in a boxing ring will be very different from a massively multiplayer online game (MMOG) engine or a first-person shooter (FPS) engine or a real-time strategy (RTS) engine. However, there is also a great deal of overlap—all 3D games, regardless of genre, require some form of low-level user input from the joypad, keyboard, and/or mouse, some form of 3D mesh rendering, some form of heads-up display (HUD) including text rendering in a variety of fonts, a powerful audio system, and the list goes on. So while the Unreal Engine, for example, was designed for first-person shooter games, it has been used successfully to construct games in a number of other genres as well, including the wildly popular third-person shooter *Gears of War* by Epic Games; the character-based action-adventure game *Grimm,* by American McGee's Shanghai-based development studio, Spicy Horse; and *Speed Star,* a futuristic racing game by South Korea-based Acro Games.

Let's take a look at some of the most common game genres and explore some examples of the technology requirements particular to each.

### 1.4.1.   First-Person Shooters (FPS)

The first-person shooter (FPS) genre is typified by games like *Quake, Unreal Tournament, Half-Life, Counter-Strike,* and *Call of Duty* (see Figure 1.2). These games have historically involved relatively slow on-foot roaming of a potentially large but primarily corridor-based world. However, modern first-person shooters can take place in a wide variety of virtual environments including vast open outdoor areas and confined indoor areas. Modern FPS traversal mechanics can include on-foot locomotion, rail-confined or free-roaming ground vehicles, hovercraft, boats, and aircraft. For an overview of this genre, see http://en.wikipedia.org/wiki/First-person_shooter.

First-person games are typically some of the most technologically challenging to build, probably rivaled in complexity only by third-person shooter/action/platformer games and massively multiplayer games. This is because first-person shooters aim to provide their players with the illusion of being immersed in a detailed, hyperrealistic world. It is not surprising that many of the game industry's big technological innovations arose out of the games in this genre.

Figure 1.2. *Call of Duty 2* (Xbox 360/PLAYSTATION 3).

First-person shooters typically focus on technologies, such as

- efficient rendering of large 3D virtual worlds;
- a responsive camera control/aiming mechanic;
- high-fidelity animations of the player's virtual arms and weapons;
- a wide range of powerful hand-held weaponry;
- a forgiving player character motion and collision model, which often gives these games a "floaty" feel;
- high-fidelity animations and artificial intelligence for the non-player characters (the player's enemies and allies);
- small-scale online multiplayer capabilities (typically supporting up to 64 simultaneous players), and the ubiquitous "death match" gameplay mode.

The rendering technology employed by first-person shooters is almost always highly optimized and carefully tuned to the particular type of envi-

ronment being rendered. For example, indoor "dungeon crawl" games often employ binary space partitioning (BSP) trees or portal-based rendering systems. Outdoor FPS games use other kinds of rendering optimizations such as occlusion culling, or an offline sectorization of the game world with manual or automated specification of which target sectors are visible from each source sector.

Of course, immersing a player in a hyperrealistic game world requires much more than just optimized high-quality graphics technology. The character animations, audio and music, rigid-body physics, in-game cinematics, and myriad other technologies must all be cutting-edge in a first-person shooter. So this genre has some of the most stringent and broad technology requirements in the industry.

## 1.4.2. Platformers and Other Third-Person Games

"Platformer" is the term applied to third-person character-based action games where jumping from platform to platform is the primary gameplay mechanic. Typical games from the 2D era include *Space Panic*, *Donkey Kong*, *Pitfall!*, and

Figure 1.3. *Jak & Daxter: The Precursor Legacy.*

*Super Mario Brothers*. The 3D era includes platformers like *Super Mario 64, Crash Bandicoot, Rayman 2, Sonic the Hedgehog*, the *Jak and Daxter* series (Figure 1.3), the *Ratchet & Clank* series, and more recently *Super Mario Galaxy*. See http://en.wikipedia.org/wiki/Platformer for an in-depth discussion of this genre.

In terms of their technological requirements, platformers can usually be lumped together with third-person shooters and third-person action/adventure games, like *Ghost Recon, Gears of War* (Figure 1.4), and *Uncharted: Drake's Fortune*.

Third-person character-based games have a lot in common with first-person shooters, but a great deal more emphasis is placed on the main character's abilities and locomotion modes. In addition, high-fidelity full-body character animations are required for the player's avatar, as opposed to the somewhat less-taxing animation requirements of the "floating arms" in a typical FPS game. It's important to note here that almost all first-person shooters have an online multiplayer component, so a full-body player avatar must be rendered in addition to the first-person arms. However the fidelity of these FPS player avatars is usually not comparable to the fidelity of the non-player characters

Figure 1.4. *Gears of War*.

in these same games; nor can it be compared to the fidelity of the player avatar in a third-person game.

In a platformer, the main character is often cartoon-like and not particularly realistic or high-resolution. However, third-person shooters often feature a highly realistic humanoid player character. In both cases, the player character typically has a very rich set of actions and animations.

Some of the technologies specifically focused on by games in this genre include

- moving platforms, ladders, ropes, trellises, and other interesting locomotion modes;
- puzzle-like environmental elements;
- a third-person "follow camera" which stays focused on the player character and whose rotation is typically controlled by the human player via the right joypad stick (on a console) or the mouse (on a PC—note that while there are a number of popular third-person shooters on PC, the platformer genre exists almost exclusively on consoles);
- a complex camera collision system for ensuring that the view point never "clips" through background geometry or dynamic foreground objects.

### 1.4.3. Fighting Games

Fighting games are typically two-player games involving humanoid characters pummeling each other in a ring of some sort. The genre is typified by games like *Soul Calibur* and *Tekken* (see Figure 1.5). The Wikipedia page http://en.wikipedia.org/wiki/Fighting_game provides an overview of this genre.

Traditionally games in the fighting genre have focused their technology efforts on

- a rich set of fighting animations;
- accurate hit detection;
- a user input system capable of detecting complex button and joystick combinations;
- crowds, but otherwise relatively static backgrounds.

Since the 3D world in these games is small and the camera is centered on the action at all times, historically these games have had little or no need for world subdivision or occlusion culling. They would likewise not be expected to employ advanced three-dimensional audio propagation models, for example.

Figure 1.5. *Tekken 3* (PlayStation).

State-of-the-art fighting games like EA's *Fight Night Round 3* (Figure 1.6) have upped the technological ante with features like

- high-definition character graphics, including realistic skin shaders with subsurface scattering and sweat effects;
- high-fidelity character animations;
- physics-based cloth and hair simulations for the characters.

It's important to note that some fighting games like *Heavenly Sword* take place in a large-scale virtual world, not a confined arena. In fact, many people consider this to be a separate genre, sometimes called a *brawler*. This kind of fighting game can have technical requirements more akin to those of a first-person shooter or real-time strategy game.

**Figure 1.6.** *Fight Night Round 3* (PLAYSTATION 3).

### 1.4.4. Racing Games

The racing genre encompasses all games whose primary task is driving a car or other vehicle on some kind of track. The genre has many subcategories. Simulation-focused racing games ("sims") aim to provide a driving experience that is as realistic as possible (e.g., *Gran Turismo*). Arcade racers favor over-the-top fun over realism (e.g., *San Francisco Rush, Cruisin' USA, Hydro Thunder*). A relatively new subgenre explores the subculture of street racing with tricked out consumer vehicles (e.g., *Need for Speed, Juiced*). Kart racing is a subcategory in which popular characters from platformer games or cartoon characters from TV are re-cast as the drivers of whacky vehicles (e.g., *Mario Kart, Jak X, Freaky Flyers*). "Racing" games need not always involve time-based competition. Some kart racing games, for example, offer modes in which players shoot at one another, collect loot, or engage in a variety of other timed and untimed tasks. For a discussion of this genre, see http://en.wikipedia.org/wiki/Racing_game.

A racing game is often very linear, much like older FPS games. However, travel speed is generally much faster than in a FPS. Therefore more focus is placed on very long corridor-based tracks, or looped tracks, sometimes with various alternate routes and secret short-cuts. Racing games usually focus all their graphic detail on the vehicles, track, and immediate surroundings. However, kart racers also devote significant rendering and animation bandwidth to the characters driving the vehicles. Figure 1.7 shows a screen shot from the latest installment in the well-known *Gran Turismo* racing game series, *Gran Turismo 5*.

Some of the technological properties of a typical racing game include the following techniques.

- Various "tricks" are used when rendering distant background elements, such as employing two-dimensional cards for trees, hills, and mountains.

- The track is often broken down into relatively simple two-dimensional regions called "sectors." These data structures are used to optimize rendering and visibility determination, to aid in artificial intelligence and path finding for non-human-controlled vehicles, and to solve many other technical problems.

Figure 1.7. *Gran Turismo 5* (PLAYSTATION 3).

- The camera typically follows behind the vehicle for a third-person perspective, or is sometimes situated inside the cockpit first-person style.

- When the track involves tunnels and other "tight" spaces, a good deal of effort is often put into ensuring that the camera does not collide with background geometry.

### 1.4.5. Real-Time Strategy (RTS)

The modern real-time strategy (RTS) genre was arguably defined by *Dune II: The Building of a Dynasty* (1992). Other games in this genre include *Warcraft, Command & Conquer, Age of Empires,* and *Starcraft.* In this genre, the player deploys the battle units in his or her arsenal strategically across a large playing field in an attempt to overwhelm his or her opponent. The game world is typically displayed at an oblique top-down viewing angle. For a discussion of this genre, see http://en.wikipedia.org/wiki/Real-time_strategy.

The RTS player is usually prevented from significantly changing the viewing angle in order to see across large distances. This restriction permits

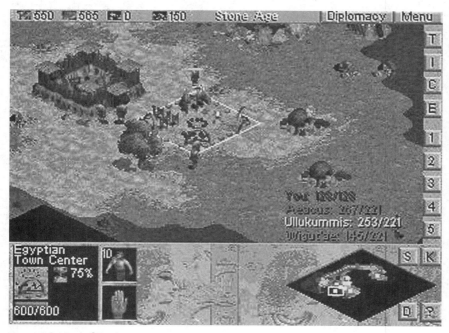

Figure 1.8. *Age of Empires.*

developers to employ various optimizations in the rendering engine of an RTS game.

Older games in the genre employed a grid-based (cell-based) world construction, and an orthographic projection was used to greatly simplify the renderer. For example, Figure 1.8 shows a screen shot from the classic RTS *Age of Empires*.

Modern RTS games sometimes use perspective projection and a true 3D world, but they may still employ a grid layout system to ensure that units and background elements, such as buildings, align with one another properly. A popular example, *Command & Conquer 3*, is shown in Figure 1.9.

Some other common practices in RTS games include the following techniques.

**Figure 1.9.** *Command & Conquer 3.*

- Each unit is relatively low-res, so that the game can support large numbers of them on-screen at once.

- Height-field terrain is usually the canvas upon which the game is designed and played.

- The player is often allowed to build new structures on the terrain in addition to deploying his or her forces.

- User interaction is typically via single-click and area-based selection of units, plus menus or toolbars containing commands, equipment, unit types, building types, etc.

## 1.4.6. Massively Multiplayer Online Games (MMOG)

The massively multiplayer online game (MMOG) genre is typified by games like *Neverwinter Nights*, *EverQuest*, *World of Warcraft*, and *Star Wars Galaxies*, to name a few. An MMOG is defined as any game that supports huge numbers of simultaneous players (from thousands to hundreds of thousands), usually all

Figure 1.10. *World of Warcraft*.

playing in one very large, *persistent* virtual world (i.e., a world whose internal state persists for very long periods of time, far beyond that of any one player's gameplay session). Otherwise, the gameplay experience of an MMOG is often similar to that of their small-scale multiplayer counterparts. Subcategories of this genre include MMO role-playing games (MMORPG), MMO real-time strategy games (MMORTS), and MMO first-person shooters (MMOFPS). For a discussion of this genre, see http://en.wikipedia.org/wiki/MMOG. Figure 1.10 shows a screen shot from the hugely popular MMORPG *World of Warcraft*.

At the heart of all MMOGs is a very powerful battery of servers. These servers maintain the authoritative state of the game world, manage users signing in and out of the game, provide inter-user chat or voice-over-IP (VoIP) services, etc. Almost all MMOGs require users to pay some kind of regular subscription fee in order to play, and they may offer micro-transactions within the game world or out-of-game as well. Hence, perhaps the most important role of the central server is to handle the billing and micro-transactions which serve as the game developer's primary source of revenue.

Graphics fidelity in an MMOG is almost always lower than its non-massively multiplayer counterparts, as a result of the huge world sizes and extremely large numbers of users supported by these kinds of games.

### 1.4.7.   Other Genres

There are of course many other game genres which we won't cover in depth here. Some examples include

- sports, with subgenres for each major sport (football, baseball, soccer, golf, etc.);
- role-playing games (RPG);
- God games, like *Populus* and *Black & White*;
- environmental/social simulation games, like *SimCity* or *The Sims*;
- puzzle games like *Tetris*;
- conversions of non-electronic games, like chess, card games, go, etc.;
- web-based games, such as those offered at Electronic Arts' Pogo site;
- and the list goes on.

We have seen that each game genre has its own particular technological requirements. This explains why game engines have traditionally differed quite a bit from genre to genre. However, there is also a great deal of technological overlap between genres, especially within the context of a single hardware platform. With the advent of more and more powerful hardware, differences between genres that arose because of optimization concerns are beginning to evaporate. So it is becoming increasingly possible to reuse the same engine technology across disparate genres, and even across disparate hardware platforms.

## 1.5.   Game Engine Survey

### 1.5.1.   The Quake Family of Engines

The first 3D first-person shooter (FPS) game is generally accepted to be *Castle Wolfenstein 3D* (1992). Written by id Software of Texas for the PC platform, this game led the game industry in a new and exciting direction. Id Software went on to create *Doom, Quake, Quake II,* and *Quake III.* All of these engines are very similar in architecture, and I will refer to them as the Quake family of engines. Quake technology has been used to create many other games and even other engines. For example, the lineage of *Medal of Honor* for the PC platform goes something like this:

- *Quake III* (Id);
- *Sin* (Ritual);
- *F.A.K.K. 2* (Ritual);
- *Medal of Honor: Allied Assault* (2015 & Dreamworks Interactive);
- *Medal of Honor: Pacific Assault* (Electronic Arts, Los Angeles).

Many other games based on Quake technology follow equally circuitous paths through many different games and studios. In fact, Valve's Source engine (used to create the *Half-Life* games) also has distant roots in Quake technology.

The *Quake* and *Quake II* source code is freely available, and the original Quake engines are reasonably well architected and "clean" (although they are of course a bit outdated and written entirely in C). These code bases serve as great examples of how industrial-strength game engines are built. The full source code to *Quake* and *Quake II* is available on id's website at http://www.idsoftware.com/business/techdownloads.

If you own the Quake and/or Quake II games, you can actually build the code using Microsoft Visual Studio and run the game under the debugger using the real game assets from the disk. This can be incredibly instructive. You can set break points, run the game, and then analyze how the engine actually works by stepping through the code. I highly recommend downloading one or both of these engines and analyzing the source code in this manner.

### 1.5.2. The Unreal Family of Engines

Epic Games Inc. burst onto the FPS scene in 1998 with its legendary game *Unreal*. Since then, the Unreal Engine has become a major competitor to Quake technology in the FPS space. Unreal Engine 2 (UE2) is the basis for *Unreal Tournament 2004* (UT2004) and has been used for countless "mods," university projects, and commercial games. Unreal Engine 3 (UE3) is the next evolutionary step, boasting some of the best tools and richest engine feature sets in the industry, including a convenient and powerful graphical user interface for creating shaders and a graphical user interface for game logic programming called Kismet. Many games are being developed with UE3 lately, including of course Epic's popular *Gears of War*.

The Unreal Engine has become known for its extensive feature set and cohesive, easy-to-use tools. The Unreal Engine is not perfect, and most developers modify it in various ways to run their game optimally on a particular hardware platform. However, Unreal is an incredibly powerful prototyping tool and commercial game development platform, and it can be used to build virtually any 3D first-person or third-person game (not to mention games in other genres as well).

The Unreal Developer Network (UDN) provides a rich set of documentation and other information about the various versions of the Unreal Engine (see http://udn.epicgames.com). Some of the documentation on Unreal Engine 2 is freely available, and "mods" can be constructed by anyone who owns a copy of UT2004. However, access to the balance of the UE2 docs and all of the UE3 docs are restricted to licensees of the engine. Unfortunately, licenses are extremely expensive, and hence out of reach for all independent game developers and most small studios as well. But there are plenty of other useful websites and wikis on Unreal. One popular one is http://www.beyondunreal.com.

### 1.5.3. The Half Life Source Engine

Source is the game engine that drives the smash hit *Half-Life 2* and its sequels *HL2: Episode One*, *HL2: Episode Two*, *Team Fortress 2*, and *Portal* (shipped together under the title *The Orange Box*). Source is a high-quality engine, rivaling Unreal Engine 3 in terms of graphics capabilities and tool set.

### 1.5.4. Microsoft's XNA Game Studio

Microsoft's XNA Game Studio is an easy-to-use and highly accessible game development platform aimed at encouraging players to create their own games and share them with the online gaming community, much as YouTube encourages the creation and sharing of home-made videos.

XNA is based on Microsoft's C# language and the Common Language Runtime (CLR). The primary development environment is Visual Studio or its free counterpart, Visual Studio Express. Everything from source code to game art assets are managed within Visual Studio. With XNA, developers can create games for the PC platform and Microsoft's Xbox 360 console. After paying a modest fee, XNA games can be uploaded to the Xbox Live network and shared with friends. By providing excellent tools at essentially zero cost, Microsoft has brilliantly opened the floodgates for the average person to create new games. XNA clearly has a bright and fascinating future ahead of it.

### 1.5.5. Other Commercial Engines

There are lots of other commercial game engines out there. Although indie developers may not have the budget to purchase an engine, many of these products have great online documentation and/or wikis that can serve as a great source of information about game engines and game programming in general. For example, check out the C4 Engine by Terathon Software (http://www.terathon.com), a company founded by Eric Lengyel in 2001. Documentation for the C4 Engine can be found on Terathon's website, with additional details on the C4 Engine wiki (http://www.terathon.com/wiki/index.php?title=Main_Page).

### 1.5.6. Proprietary in-House Engines

Many companies build and maintain proprietary in-house game engines. Electronic Arts built many of its RTS games on a proprietary engine called SAGE, developed at Westwood Studios. Naughty Dog's *Crash Bandicoot*, *Jak and Daxter* series, and most recently *Uncharted: Drake's Fortune* franchises were each built on in-house engines custom-tailored to the PlayStation, PlayStation 2, and PLAYSTATION 3 platforms, respectively. And of course, most commercially licensed game engines like Quake, Source, or the Unreal Engine started out as proprietary in-house engines.

### 1.5.7. Open Source Engines

Open source 3D game engines are engines built by amateur and professional game developers and provided online for free. The term "open source" typically implies that source code is freely available and that a somewhat open development model is employed, meaning almost anyone can contribute code. Licensing, if it exists at all, is often provided under the Gnu Public License (GPL) or Lesser Gnu Public License (LGPL). The former permits code to be freely used by anyone, as long as their code is also freely available; the latter allows the code to be used even in proprietary for-profit applications. Lots of other free and semi-free licensing schemes are also available for open source projects.

There are a staggering number of open source engines available on the web. Some are quite good, some are mediocre, and some are just plain awful! The list of game engines provided online at http://cg.cs.tu-berlin.de/~ki/engines.html will give you a feel for the sheer number of engines that are out there.

OGRE 3D is a well-architected, easy-to-learn, and easy-to-use 3D rendering engine. It boasts a fully featured 3D renderer including advanced lighting and shadows, a good skeletal character animation system, a two-dimensional overlay system for heads-up displays and graphical user interfaces, and a post-processing system for full-screen effects like bloom. OGRE is, by its authors' own admission, not a full game engine, but it does provide many of the foundational components required by pretty much any game engine.

Some other well-known open source engines are listed here.

- Panda3D is a script-based engine. The engine's primary interface is the Python custom scripting language. It is designed to make prototyping 3D games and virtual worlds convenient and fast.

- Yake is a relatively new fully featured game engine built on top of OGRE.

- Crystal Space is a game engine with an extensible modular architecture.

- Torque and Irrlicht are also well-known and widely used engines.

## 1.6.   Runtime Engine Architecture

A game engine generally consists of a tool suite and a runtime component. We'll explore the architecture of the runtime piece first and then get into tools architecture in the following section.

Figure 1.11 shows all of the major runtime components that make up a typical 3D game engine. Yeah, it's *big!* And this diagram doesn't even account for all the tools. Game engines are definitely large software systems.

Like all software systems, game engines are built in *layers*. Normally upper layers depend on lower layers, but not vice versa. When a lower layer depends upon a higher layer, we call this a *circular dependency*. Dependency cycles are to be avoided in any software system, because they lead to undesirable coupling between systems, make the software untestable, and inhibit code reuse. This is especially true for a large-scale system like a game engine.

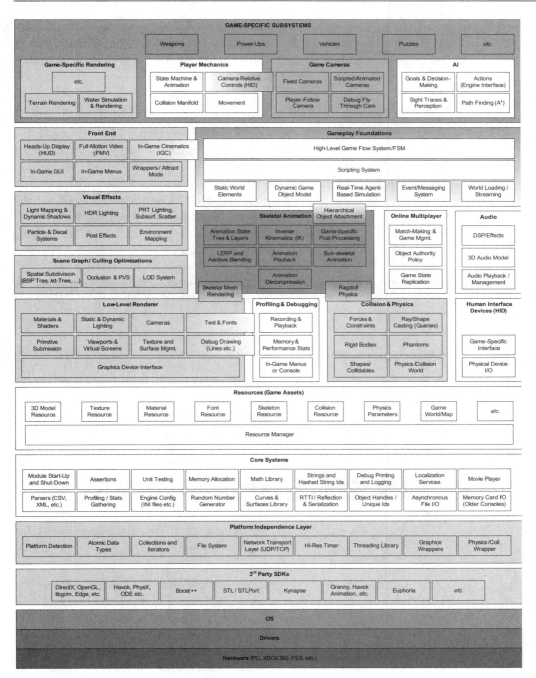

**Figure 1.11.** Runtime game engine architecture.

What follows is a brief overview of the components shown in the diagram in Figure 1.11. The rest of this book will be spent investigating each of these components in a great deal more depth and learning how these components are usually integrated into a functional whole.

### 1.6.1.   Target Hardware

The target hardware layer, shown in isolation in Figure 1.12, represents the computer system or console on which the game will run. Typical platforms include Microsoft Windows- and Linux-based PCs, the Apple iPhone and Macintosh, Microsoft's Xbox and Xbox 360, Sony's PlayStation, PlayStation 2, PlayStation Portable (PSP), and PLAYSTATION 3, and Nintendo's DS, Game-Cube, and Wii. Most of the topics in this book are platform-agnostic, but we'll also touch on some of the design considerations peculiar to PC or console development, where the distinctions are relevant.

Hardware (PC, XBOX360, PS3, etc.)

**Figure 1.12.** Hardware layer.

### 1.6.2.   Device Drivers

As depicted in Figure 1.13, device drivers are low-level software components provided by the operating system or hardware vendor. Drivers manage hardware resources and shield the operating system and upper engine layers from the details of communicating with the myriad variants of hardware devices available.

Drivers

**Figure 1.13.** Device driver layer.

### 1.6.3.   Operating System

On a PC, the operating system (OS) is running all the time. It orchestrates the execution of multiple programs on a single computer, one of which is your game. The OS layer is shown in Figure 1.14. Operating systems like Microsoft Windows employ a time-sliced approach to sharing the hardware with multiple running programs, known as pre-emptive multitasking. This means that a PC game can never assume it has full control of the hardware—it must "play nice" with other programs in the system.

| OS |
| --- |

Figure 1.14. Operating system layer.

On a console, the operating system is often just a thin library layer that is compiled directly into your game executable. On a console, the game typically "owns" the entire machine. However, with the introduction of the Xbox 360 and PLAYSTATION 3, this is no longer strictly the case. The operating system on these consoles can interrupt the execution of your game, or take over certain system resources, in order to display online messages, or to allow the player to pause the game and bring up the PS3's Xross Media Bar or the Xbox 360's dashboard, for example. So the gap between console and PC development is gradually closing (for better or for worse).

### 1.6.4. Third-Party SDKs and Middleware

Most game engines leverage a number of third-party software development kits (SDKs) and middleware, as shown in Figure 1.15. The functional or class-based interface provided by an SDK is often called an application programming interface (API). We will look at a few examples.

| 3rd Party SDKs | | | | | | | |
| --- | --- | --- | --- | --- | --- | --- | --- |
| DirectX, OpenGL, libgcm, Edge, etc. | Havok, PhysX, ODE etc. | Boost++ | STL / STLPort | Kynapse | Granny, Havok Animation, etc. | Euphoria | etc. |

Figure 1.15. Third-party SDK layer.

#### 1.6.4.1. Data Structures and Algorithms

Like any software system, games depend heavily on collection data structures and algorithms to manipulate them. Here are a few examples of third-party libraries which provide these kinds of services.

- *STL.* The C++ standard template library provides a wealth of code and algorithms for managing data structures, strings, and stream-based I/O.
- *STLport.* This is a portable, optimized implementation of STL.
- *Boost.* Boost is a powerful data structures and algorithms library, designed in the style of STL. (The online documentation for Boost is also a great place to learn a great deal about computer science!)
- *Loki.* Loki is a powerful generic programming template library which is exceedingly good at making your brain hurt!

Game developers are divided on the question of whether to use template libraries like STL in their game engines. Some believe that the memory allocation patterns of STL, which are not conducive to high-performance programming and tend to lead to memory fragmentation (see Section 5.2.1.4), make STL unusable in a game. Others feel that the power and convenience of STL outweigh its problems, and that most of the problems can in fact be worked around anyway. My personal belief is that STL is all right for use on a PC, because its advanced virtual memory system renders the need for careful memory allocation a bit less crucial (although one must still be very careful). On a console, with limited or no virtual memory facilities and exorbitant cache miss costs, you're probably better off writing custom data structures that have predictable and/or limited memory allocation patterns. (And you certainly won't go far wrong doing the same on a PC game project either.)

### 1.6.4.2.  Graphics

Most game rendering engines are built on top of a hardware interface library, such as the following:

- *Glide* is the 3D graphics SDK for the old Voodoo graphics cards. This SDK was popular prior to the era of hardware transform and lighting (hardware T&L) which began with DirectX 8.
- *OpenGL* is a widely used portable 3D graphics SDK.
- *DirectX* is Microsoft's 3D graphics SDK and primary rival to OpenGL.
- *libgcm* is a low-level direct interface to the PLAYSTATION 3's RSX graphics hardware, which was provided by Sony as a more efficient alternative to OpenGL.
- *Edge* is a powerful and highly-efficient rendering and animation engine produced by Naughty Dog and Sony for the PLAYSTATION 3 and used by a number of first- and third-party game studios.

### 1.6.4.3.  Collision and Physics

Collision detection and rigid body dynamics (known simply as "physics" in the game development community) are provided by the following well-known SDKs.

- *Havok* is a popular industrial-strength physics and collision engine.
- *PhysX* is another popular industrial-strength physics and collision engine, available for free download from NVIDIA.
- *Open Dynamics Engine (ODE)* is a well-known open source physics/collision package.

### I.6.4.4.  Character Animation

A number of commercial animation packages exist, including but certainly not limited to the following.

- *Granny.* Rad Game Tools' popular Granny toolkit includes robust 3D model and animation exporters for all the major 3D modeling and animation packages like Maya, 3D Studio MAX, etc., a runtime library for reading and manipulating the exported model and animation data, and a powerful runtime animation system. In my opinion, the Granny SDK has the best-designed and most logical animation API of any I've seen, commercial or proprietary, especially its excellent handling of time.

- *Havok Animation.* The line between physics and animation is becoming increasingly blurred as characters become more and more realistic. The company that makes the popular Havok physics SDK decided to create a complimentary animation SDK, which makes bridging the physics-animation gap much easier than it ever has been.

- *Edge.* The Edge library produced for the PS3 by the ICE team at Naughty Dog, the Tools and Technology group of Sony Computer Entertainment America, and Sony's Advanced Technology Group in Europe includes a powerful and efficient animation engine and an efficient geometry-processing engine for rendering.

### I.6.4.5.  Artificial Intelligence

- *Kynapse.* Until recently, artificial intelligence (AI) was handled in a custom manner for each game. However, a company called Kynogon has produced a middleware SDK called Kynapse. This SDK provides low-level AI building blocks such as path finding, static and dynamic object avoidance, identification of vulnerabilities within a space (e.g., an open window from which an ambush could come), and a reasonably good interface between AI and animation.

### I.6.4.6.  Biomechanical Character Models

- *Endorphin and Euphoria.* These are animation packages that produce character motion using advanced biomechanical models of realistic human movement.

As we mentioned above, the line between character animation and physics is beginning to blur. Packages like Havok Animation try to marry physics and animation in a traditional manner, with a human animator providing the majority of the motion through a tool like Maya and with physics augmenting that motion at runtime. But recently a firm called Natural Motion Ltd. has produced a product that attempts to redefine how character motion is handled in games and other forms of digital media.

Its first product, Endorphin, is a Maya plug-in that permits animators to run full biomechanical simulations on characters and export the resulting animations as if they had been hand-animated. The biomechanical model accounts for center of gravity, the character's weight distribution, and detailed knowledge of how a real human balances and moves under the influence of gravity and other forces.

Its second product, Euphoria, is a real-time version of Endorphin intended to produce physically and biomechanically accurate character motion at runtime under the influence of unpredictable forces.

### 1.6.5.   Platform Independence Layer

Most game engines are required to be capable of running on more than one hardware platform. Companies like Electronic Arts and Activision/Blizzard, for example, always target their games at a wide variety of platforms, because it exposes their games to the largest possible market. Typically, the only game studios that do not target at least two different platforms per game are first-party studios, like Sony's Naughty Dog and Insomniac studios. Therefore, most game engines are architected with a platform independence layer, like the one shown in Figure 1.16. This layer sits atop the hardware, drivers, operating system, and other third-party software and shields the rest of the engine from the majority of knowledge of the underlying platform.

By wrapping or replacing the most commonly used standard C library functions, operating system calls, and other foundational application programming interfaces (APIs), the platform independence layer ensures consistent behavior across all hardware platforms. This is necessary because there is a good deal of variation across platforms, even among "standardized" libraries like the standard C library.

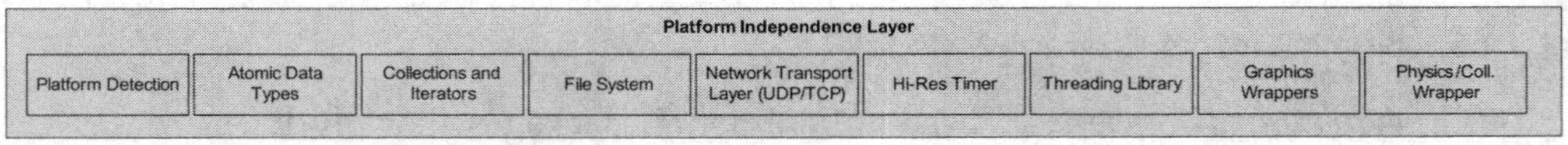

| Platform Independence Layer | | | | | | | | |
|---|---|---|---|---|---|---|---|---|
| Platform Detection | Atomic Data Types | Collections and Iterators | File System | Network Transport Layer (UDP/TCP) | Hi-Res Timer | Threading Library | Graphics Wrappers | Physics/Coll. Wrapper |

**Figure 1.16.**  Platform independence layer.

### 1.6.6.   Core Systems

Every game engine, and really every large, complex C++ software application, requires a grab bag of useful software utilities. We'll categorize these under the label "core systems." A typical core systems layer is shown in Figure 1.17. Here are a few examples of the facilities the core layer usually provides.

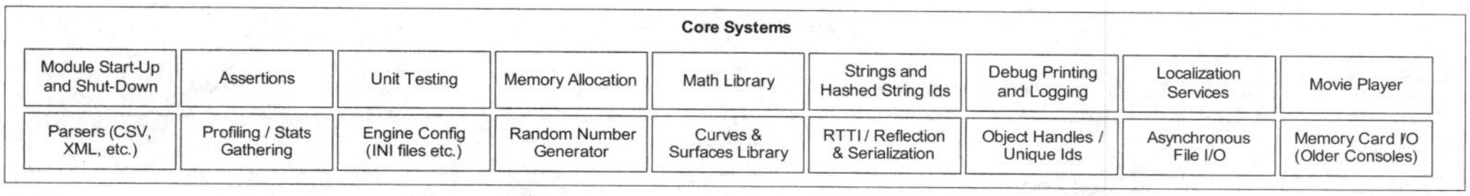

| Core Systems | | | | | | | | | |
|---|---|---|---|---|---|---|---|---|---|
| Module Start-Up and Shut-Down | Assertions | Unit Testing | Memory Allocation | Math Library | Strings and Hashed String Ids | Debug Printing and Logging | Localization Services | Movie Player | |
| Parsers (CSV, XML, etc.) | Profiling / Stats Gathering | Engine Config (INI files etc.) | Random Number Generator | Curves & Surfaces Library | RTTI / Reflection & Serialization | Object Handles / Unique Ids | Asynchronous File I/O | Memory Card I/O (Older Consoles) | |

Figure 1.17. Core engine systems.

- *Assertions* are lines of error-checking code that are inserted to catch logical mistakes and violations of the programmer's original assumptions. Assertion checks are usually stripped out of the final production build of the game.

- *Memory management.* Virtually every game engine implements its own custom memory allocation system(s) to ensure high-speed allocations and deallocations and to limit the negative effects of memory fragmentation (see Section 5.2.1.4).

- *Math library.* Games are by their nature highly mathematics-intensive. As such, every game engine has at least one, if not many, math libraries. These libraries provide facilities for vector and matrix math, quaternion rotations, trigonometry, geometric operations with lines, rays, spheres, frusta, etc., spline manipulation, numerical integration, solving systems of equations, and whatever other facilities the game programmers require.

- *Custom data structures and algorithms.* Unless an engine's designers decided to rely entirely on a third-party package such as STL, a suite of tools for managing fundamental data structures (linked lists, dynamic arrays, binary trees, hash maps, etc.) and algorithms (search, sort, etc.) is usually required. These are often hand-coded to minimize or eliminate dynamic memory allocation and to ensure optimal runtime performance on the target platform(s).

A detailed discussion of the most common core engine systems can be found in Part II.

## 1.6.7. Resource Manager

Present in every game engine in some form, the resource manager provides a unified interface (or suite of interfaces) for accessing any and all types of game assets and other engine input data. Some engines do this in a highly centralized and consistent manner (e.g., Unreal's packages, OGRE 3D's `ResourceManager` class). Other engines take an ad hoc approach, often leaving it up to the game programmer to directly access raw files on disk or within compressed archives such as Quake's PAK files. A typical resource manager layer is depicted in Figure 1.18.

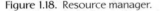

Figure 1.18. Resource manager.

### 1.6.8.   Rendering Engine

The rendering engine is one of the largest and most complex components of
any game engine. Renderers can be architected in many different ways. There
is no one accepted way to do it, although as we'll see, most modern rendering
engines share some fundamental design philosophies, driven in large part by
the design of the 3D graphics hardware upon which they depend.

One common and effective approach to rendering engine design is to employ a layered architecture as follows.

#### 1.6.8.1.   Low-Level Renderer

The *low-level renderer*, shown in Figure 1.19, encompasses all of the raw rendering facilities of the engine. At this level, the design is focused on rendering
a collection of geometric primitives as quickly and richly as possible, without
much regard for which portions of a scene may be visible. This component is
broken into various subcomponents, which are discussed below.

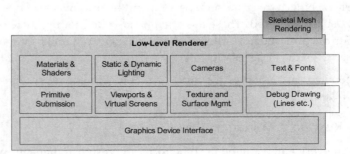

Figure 1.19. Low-level rendering engine.

*Graphics Device Interface*

Graphics SDKs, such as DirectX and OpenGL, require a reasonable amount of
code to be written just to enumerate the available graphics devices, initialize
them, set up render surfaces (back-buffer, stencil buffer etc.), and so on. This

is typically handled by a component that I'll call the *graphics device interface* (although every engine uses its own terminology).

For a PC game engine, you also need code to integrate your renderer with the Windows message loop. You typically write a "message pump" that services Windows messages when they are pending and otherwise runs your render loop over and over as fast as it can. This ties the game's keyboard polling loop to the renderer's screen update loop. This coupling is undesirable, but with some effort it is possible to minimize the dependencies. We'll explore this topic in more depth later.

*Other Renderer Components*

The other components in the low-level renderer cooperate in order to collect submissions of *geometric primitives* (sometimes called *render packets*), such as meshes, line lists, point lists, particles, terrain patches, text strings, and whatever else you want to draw, and render them as quickly as possible.

The low-level renderer usually provides a viewport abstraction with an associated camera-to-world matrix and 3D projection parameters, such as field of view and the location of the near and far clip planes. The low-level renderer also manages the state of the graphics hardware and the game's shaders via its *material system* and its *dynamic lighting system*. Each submitted primitive is associated with a material and is affected by $n$ dynamic lights. The material describes the texture(s) used by the primitive, what device state settings need to be in force, and which vertex and pixel shader to use when rendering the primitive. The lights determine how dynamic lighting calculations will be applied to the primitive. Lighting and shading is a complex topic, which is covered in depth in many excellent books on computer graphics, including [14], [42], and [1].

### 1.6.8.2. Scene Graph/Culling Optimizations

The low-level renderer draws all of the geometry submitted to it, without much regard for whether or not that geometry is actually visible (other than back-face culling and clipping triangles to the camera frustum). A higher-level component is usually needed in order to limit the number of primitives submitted for rendering, based on some form of visibility determination. This layer is shown in Figure 1.20.

For very small game worlds, a simple *frustum cull* (i.e., removing objects that the camera cannot "see") is probably all that is required. For larger game worlds, a more advanced *spatial subdivision* data structure might be used to improve rendering efficiency, by allowing the potentially visible set (PVS) of objects to be determined very quickly. Spatial subdivisions can take many

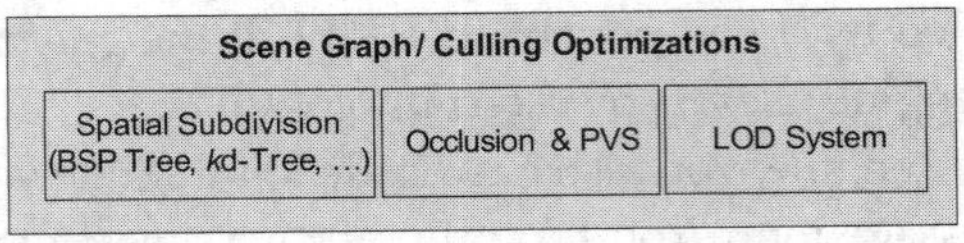

| Scene Graph / Culling Optimizations | | |
|---|---|---|
| Spatial Subdivision (BSP Tree, kd-Tree, ...) | Occlusion & PVS | LOD System |

Figure 1.20. A typical scene graph/spatial subdivision layer, for culling optimization.

forms, including a binary space partitioning (BSP) tree, a quadtree, an octree, a kd-tree, or a sphere hierarchy. A spatial subdivision is sometimes called a scene graph, although technically the latter is a particular kind of data structure and does not subsume the former. Portals or occlusion culling methods might also be applied in this layer of the rendering engine.

Ideally, the low-level renderer should be completely agnostic to the type of spatial subdivision or scene graph being used. This permits different game teams to reuse the primitive submission code, but craft a PVS determination system that is specific to the needs of each team's game. The design of the OGRE 3D open source rendering engine (http://www.ogre3d.org) is a great example of this principle in action. OGRE provides a plug-and-play scene graph architecture. Game developers can either select from a number of pre-implemented scene graph designs, or they can provide a custom scene graph implementation.

### 1.6.8.3. Visual Effects

Modern game engines support a wide range of visual effects, as shown in Figure 1.21, including

- particle systems (for smoke, fire, water splashes, etc.);
- decal systems (for bullet holes, foot prints, etc.);
- light mapping and environment mapping;
- dynamic shadows;
- full-screen post effects, applied after the 3D scene has been rendered to an offscreen buffer.

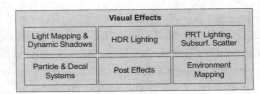

Figure 1.21. Visual effects.

Some examples of full-screen post effects include

- high dynamic range (HDR) lighting and bloom;
- full-screen anti-aliasing (FSAA);
- color correction and color-shift effects, including bleach bypass, saturation and de-saturation effects, etc.

It is common for a game engine to have an *effects system* component that manages the specialized rendering needs of particles, decals, and other visual effects. The particle and decal systems are usually distinct components of the rendering engine and act as inputs to the low-level renderer. On the other hand, light mapping, environment mapping, and shadows are usually handled internally within the rendering engine proper. Full-screen post effects are either implemented as an integral part of the renderer or as a separate component that operates on the renderer's output buffers.

### 1.6.8.4. Front End

Most games employ some kind of 2D graphics overlaid on the 3D scene for various purposes. These include

- the game's *heads-up display* (HUD);
- in-game menus, a console, and/or other *development tools*, which may or may not be shipped with the final product;
- possibly an in-game *graphical user interface* (GUI), allowing the player to manipulate his or her character's inventory, configure units for battle, or perform other complex in-game tasks.

This layer is shown in Figure 1.22. Two-dimensional graphics like these are usually implemented by drawing textured quads (pairs of triangles) with an orthographic projection. Or they may be rendered in full 3D, with the quads bill-boarded so they always face the camera.

We've also included the *full-motion video* (FMV) system in this layer. This system is responsible for playing full-screen movies that have been recorded

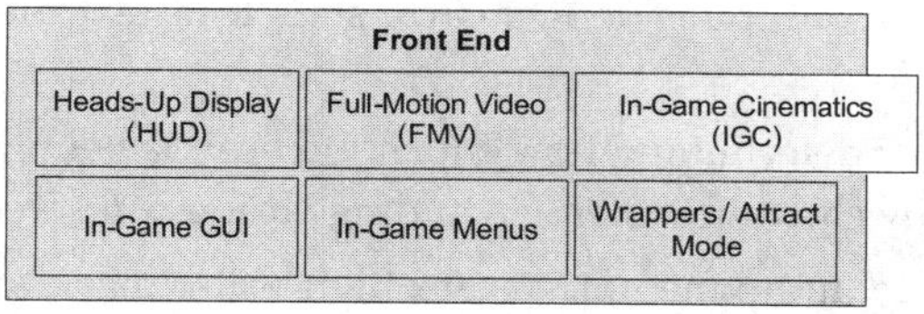

| Front End | | |
|---|---|---|
| Heads-Up Display (HUD) | Full-Motion Video (FMV) | In-Game Cinematics (IGC) |
| In-Game GUI | In-Game Menus | Wrappers / Attract Mode |

Figure 1.22. Front end graphics.

earlier (either rendered with the game's rendering engine or using another rendering package).

A related system is the *in-game cinematics* (IGC) system. This component typically allows cinematic sequences to be choreographed within the game itself, in full 3D. For example, as the player walks through a city, a conversation between two key characters might be implemented as an in-game cinematic. IGCs may or may not include the player character(s). They may be done as a deliberate cut-away during which the player has no control, or they may be subtly integrated into the game without the human player even realizing that an IGC is taking place.

### 1.6.9. Profiling and Debugging Tools

Figure 1.23. Profiling and debugging tools.

Games are real-time systems and, as such, game engineers often need to profile the performance of their games in order to optimize performance. In addition, memory resources are usually scarce, so developers make heavy use of memory analysis tools as well. The profiling and debugging layer, shown in Figure 1.23, encompasses these tools and also includes in-game debugging facilities, such as debug drawing, an in-game menu system or console, and the ability to record and play back gameplay for testing and debugging purposes.

There are plenty of good general-purpose software profiling tools available, including

- Intel's *VTune*,
- IBM's *Quantify* and *Purify* (part of the *PurifyPlus* tool suite),
- Compuware's *Bounds Checker*.

However, most game engines also incorporate a suite of custom profiling and debugging tools. For example, they might include one or more of the following:

- a mechanism for manually instrumenting the code, so that specific sections of code can be timed;
- a facility for displaying the profiling statistics on-screen while the game is running;
- a facility for dumping performance stats to a text file or to an Excel spreadsheet;
- a facility for determining how much memory is being used by the engine, and by each subsystem, including various on-screen displays;
- the ability to dump memory usage, high-water mark, and leakage stats when the game terminates and/or during gameplay;

- tools that allow debug print statements to be peppered throughout the code, along with an ability to turn on or off different categories of debug output and control the level of verbosity of the output;
- the ability to record game events and then play them back. This is tough to get right, but when done properly it can be a very valuable tool for tracking down bugs.

## 1.6.10. Collision and Physics

Collision detection is important for every game. Without it, objects would interpenetrate, and it would be impossible to interact with the virtual world in any reasonable way. Some games also include a realistic or semi-realistic dynamics simulation. We call this the "physics system" in the game industry, although the term *rigid body dynamics* is really more appropriate, because we are usually only concerned with the motion (kinematics) of rigid bodies and the forces and torques (dynamics) that cause this motion to occur. This layer is depicted in Figure 1.24.

Collision and physics are usually quite tightly coupled. This is because when collisions are detected, they are almost always resolved as part of the physics integration and constraint satisfaction logic. Nowadays, very few game companies write their own collision/physics engine. Instead, a third-party SDK is typically integrated into the engine.

- *Havok* is the gold standard in the industry today. It is feature-rich and performs well across the boards.
- *PhysX* by NVIDIA is another excellent collision and dynamics engine. It was integrated into Unreal Engine 3 and is also available for free as a standalone product for PC game development. PhysX was originally designed as the interface to Ageia's new physics accelerator chip. The

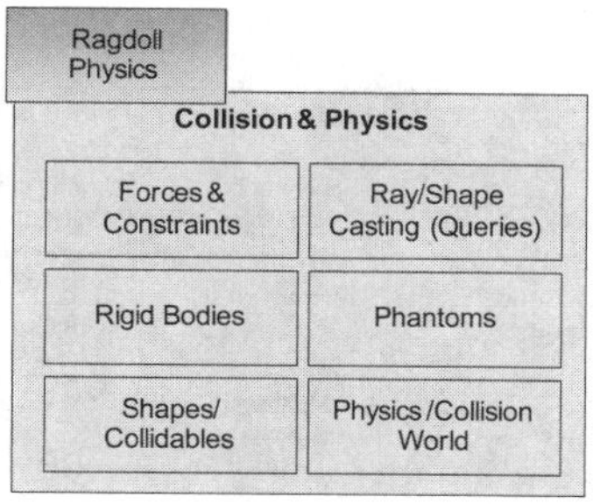

Figure 1.24. Collision and physics subsystem.

SDK is now owned and distributed by NVIDIA, and the company is adapting PhysX to run on its latest GPUs.

Open source physics and collision engines are also available. Perhaps the best-known of these is the Open Dynamics Engine (ODE). For more information, see http://www.ode.org. I-Collide, V-Collide, and RAPID are other popular non-commercial collision detection engines. All three were developed at the University of North Carolina (UNC). For more information, see http://www.cs.unc.edu/~geom/I_COLLIDE/index.html, http://www.cs.unc.edu/~geom/V_COLLIDE/index.html, and http://www.cs.unc.edu/~geom/OBB/OBBT.html.

## 1.6.11. Animation

Any game that has organic or semi-organic characters (humans, animals, cartoon characters, or even robots) needs an animation system. There are five basic types of animation used in games:

- sprite/texture animation,
- rigid body hierarchy animation,
- skeletal animation,
- vertex animation, and
- morph targets.

Skeletal animation permits a detailed 3D character mesh to be posed by an animator using a relatively simple system of bones. As the bones move, the vertices of the 3D mesh move with them. Although morph targets and vertex animation are used in some engines, skeletal animation is the most prevalent animation method in games today; as such, it will be our primary focus in this book. A typical skeletal animation system is shown in Figure 1.25.

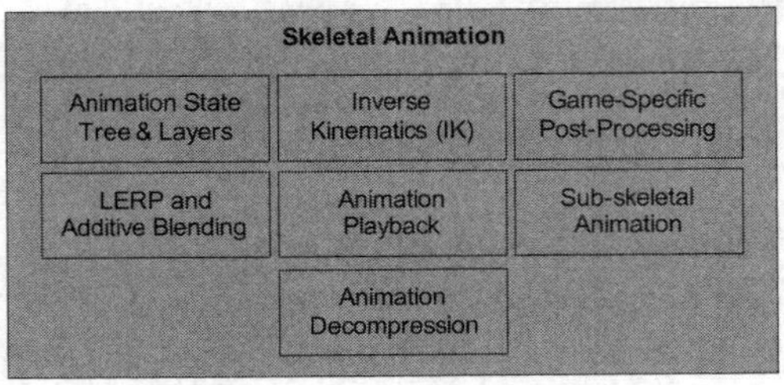

Figure 1.25. Skeletal animation subsystem.

You'll notice in Figure 1.11 that Skeletal Mesh Rendering is a component that bridges the gap between the renderer and the animation system. There is a tight cooperation happening here, but the interface is very well defined. The animation system produces a pose for every bone in the skeleton, and then these poses are passed to the rendering engine as a palette of matrices. The renderer transforms each vertex by the matrix or matrices in the palette, in order to generate a final blended vertex position. This process is known as *skinning*.

There is also a tight coupling between the animation and physics systems, when *rag dolls* are employed. A rag doll is a limp (often dead) animated character, whose bodily motion is simulated by the physics system. The physics system determines the positions and orientations of the various parts of the body by treating them as a constrained system of rigid bodies. The animation system calculates the palette of matrices required by the rendering engine in order to draw the character on-screen.

## 1.6.12. Human Interface Devices (HID)

Every game needs to process input from the player, obtained from various *human interface devices* (HIDs) including

- the keyboard and mouse,
- a joypad, or
- other specialized game controllers, like steering wheels, fishing rods, dance pads, the WiiMote, etc.

We sometimes call this component the *player I/O* component, because we may also provide *output* to the player through the HID, such as force feedback/rumble on a joypad or the audio produced by the WiiMote. A typical HID layer is shown in Figure 1.26.

The HID engine component is sometimes architected to divorce the low-level details of the game controller(s) on a particular hardware platform from the high-level game controls. It massages the raw data coming from the hardware, introducing a dead zone around the center point of each joypad stick, de-bouncing button-press inputs, detecting button-down and button-up events, interpreting and smoothing accelerometer inputs (e.g., from the PLAYSTATION 3 Sixaxis controller), and more. It often provides a mechanism allowing the player to customize the mapping between physical controls and logical game functions. It sometimes also includes a system for detecting chords (multiple buttons pressed together), sequences (buttons pressed in sequence within a certain time limit), and gestures (sequences of inputs from the buttons, sticks, accelerometers, etc.).

Figure 1.26. The player input/output system. also known as the human interface device (HID) layer.

### 1.6.13. Audio

Audio is just as important as graphics in any game engine. Unfortunately, audio often gets less attention than rendering, physics, animation, AI, and gameplay. Case in point: Programmers often develop their code with their speakers turned off! (In fact, I've known quite a few game programmers who didn't even *have* speakers or headphones.) Nonetheless, no great game is complete without a stunning audio engine. The audio layer is depicted in Figure 1.27.

| Audio |
|-------|
| DSP/Effects |
| 3D Audio Model |
| Audio Playback / Management |

**Figure 1.27.** Audio subsystem.

Audio engines vary greatly in sophistication. Quake's and Unreal's audio engines are pretty basic, and game teams usually augment them with custom functionality or replace them with an in-house solution. For DirectX platforms (PC and Xbox 360), Microsoft provides an excellent audio tool suite called XACT. Electronic Arts has developed an advanced, high-powered audio engine internally called SoundR!OT. In conjunction with first-party studios like Naughty Dog, Sony Computer Entertainment America (SCEA) provides a powerful 3D audio engine called Scream, which has been used on a number of PS3 titles including Naughty Dog's *Uncharted: Drake's Fortune*. However, even if a game team uses a pre-existing audio engine, every game requires a great deal of custom software development, integration work, fine-tuning, and attention to detail in order to produce high-quality audio in the final product.

### 1.6.14. Online Multiplayer/Networking

Many games permit multiple human players to play within a single virtual world. Multiplayer games come in at least four basic flavors.

- *Single-screen multiplayer.* Two or more human interface devices (joypads, keyboards, mice, etc.) are connected to a single arcade machine, PC, or console. Multiple player characters inhabit a single virtual world, and a single camera keeps all player characters in frame simultaneously. Examples of this style of multiplayer gaming include *Smash Brothers*, *Lego Star Wars*, and *Gauntlet*.

- *Split-screen multiplayer.* Multiple player characters inhabit a single virtual world, with multiple HIDs attached to a single game machine, but each with its own camera, and the screen is divided into sections so that each player can view his or her character.

- *Networked multiplayer.* Multiple computers or consoles are networked together, with each machine hosting one of the players.

- *Massively multiplayer online games (MMOG).* Literally hundreds of thousands of users can be playing simultaneously within a giant, persistent, online virtual world hosted by a powerful battery of central servers.

The multiplayer networking layer is shown in Figure 1.28.

Multiplayer games are quite similar in many ways to their single-player counterparts. However, support for multiple players can have a profound impact on the design of certain game engine components. The game world object model, renderer, human input device system, player control system, and animation systems are all affected. Retrofitting multiplayer features into a pre-existing single-player engine is certainly not impossible, although it can be a daunting task. Still, many game teams have done it successfully. That said, it is usually better to design multiplayer features from day one, if you have that luxury.

It is interesting to note that going the other way—converting a multi-player game into a single-player game—is typically trivial. In fact, many game engines treat single-player mode as a special case of a multiplayer game, in which there happens to be only one player. The Quake engine is well known for its *client-on-top-of-server* mode, in which a single executable, running on a single PC, acts both as the client and the server in single-player campaigns.

| Online Multiplayer |
| --- |
| Match-Making & Game Mgmt. |
| Object Authority Policy |
| Game State Replication |

Figure 1.28. Online multiplayer subsystem.

### 1.6.15. Gameplay Foundation Systems

The term *gameplay* refers to the action that takes place in the game, the rules that govern the virtual world in which the game takes place, the abilities of the player character(s) (known as *player mechanics*) and of the other characters and objects in the world, and the goals and objectives of the player(s). Game-play is typically implemented either in the native language in which the rest of the engine is written, or in a high-level scripting language—or sometimes both. To bridge the gap between the gameplay code and the low-level engine systems that we've discussed thus far, most game engines introduce a layer

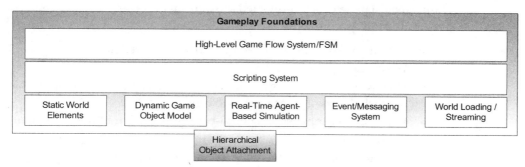

Figure 1.29. Gameplay foundation systems.

that I'll call the *gameplay foundations* layer (for lack of a standardized name). Shown in Figure 1.29, this layer provides a suite of core facilities, upon which game-specific logic can be implemented conveniently.

### 1.6.15.1. Game Worlds and Object Models

The gameplay foundations layer introduces the notion of a game world, containing both static and dynamic elements. The contents of the world are usually modeled in an object-oriented manner (often, but not always, using an object-oriented programming language). In this book, the collection of object types that make up a game is called the *game object model*. The game object model provides a real-time simulation of a heterogeneous collection of objects in the virtual game world.

Typical types of game objects include

- static background geometry, like buildings, roads, terrain (often a special case), etc.;
- dynamic rigid bodies, such as rocks, soda cans, chairs, etc.;
- player characters (PC);
- non-player characters (NPC);
- weapons;
- projectiles;
- vehicles;
- lights (which may be present in the dynamic scene at run time, or only used for static lighting offline);
- cameras;
- and the list goes on.

The game world model is intimately tied to a *software object model*, and this model can end up pervading the entire engine. The term software object model refers to the set of language features, policies, and conventions used to implement a piece of object-oriented software. In the context of game engines, the software object model answers questions, such as:

- Is your game engine designed in an object-oriented manner?
- What language will you use? C? C++? Java? OCaml?
- How will the static class hierarchy be organized? One giant monolithic hierarchy? Lots of loosely coupled components?
- Will you use templates and policy-based design, or traditional polymorphism?
- How are objects referenced? Straight old pointers? Smart pointers? Handles?

- How will objects be uniquely identified? By address in memory only? By name? By a global unique identifier (GUID)?
- How are the lifetimes of game objects managed?
- How are the states of the game objects simulated over time?

We'll explore software object models and game object models in considerable depth in Section 14.2.

### 1.6.15.2. Event System

Game objects invariably need to communicate with one another. This can be accomplished in all sorts of ways. For example, the object sending the message might simply call a member function of the receiver object. An event-driven architecture, much like what one would find in a typical graphical user interface, is also a common approach to inter-object communication. In an event-driven system, the sender creates a little data structure called an *event* or *message*, containing the message's type and any argument data that are to be sent. The event is passed to the receiver object by calling its *event handler function*. Events can also be stored in a queue for handling at some future time.

### 1.6.15.3. Scripting System

Many game engines employ a scripting language in order to make development of game-specific gameplay rules and content easier and more rapid. Without a scripting language, you must recompile and relink your game executable every time a change is made to the logic or data structures used in the engine. But when a scripting language is integrated into your engine, changes to game logic and data can be made by modifying and reloading the script code. Some engines allow script to be reloaded while the game continues to run. Other engines require the game to be shut down prior to script recompilation. But either way, the turn-around time is still much faster than it would be if you had to recompile and relink the game's executable.

### 1.6.15.4. Artificial Intelligence Foundations

Traditionally, artificial intelligence (AI) has fallen squarely into the realm of game-specific software—it was usually not considered part of the game engine per se. More recently, however, game companies have recognized patterns that arise in almost every AI system, and these foundations are slowly starting to fall under the purview of the engine proper.

A company called Kynogon has developed a commercial AI engine called Kynapse, which acts as an "AI foundation layer" upon which game-specific AI logic can be quite easily developed. Kynapse provides a powerful suite of features, including

- a network of path nodes or roaming volumes, that defines areas or paths where AI characters are free to move without fear of colliding with static world geometry;
- simplified collision information around the edges of each free-roaming area;
- knowledge of the entrances and exits from a region, and from where in each region an enemy might be able to see and/or ambush you;
- a path-finding engine based on the well-known A* algorithm;
- hooks into the collision system and world model, for line-of-sight (LOS) traces and other perceptions;
- a custom world model which tells the AI system where all the entities of interest (friends, enemies, obstacles) are, permits dynamic avoidance of moving objects, and so on.

Kynapse also provides an architecture for the AI decision layer, including the concept of *brains* (one per character), *agents* (each of which is responsible for executing a specific task, such as moving from point to point, firing on an enemy, searching for enemies, etc.), and *actions* (responsible for allowing the character to perform a fundamental movement, which often results in playing animations on the character's skeleton).

## 1.6.16. Game-Specific Subsystems

On top of the gameplay foundation layer and the other low-level engine components, gameplay programmers and designers cooperate to implement the features of the game itself. Gameplay systems are usually numerous, highly varied, and specific to the game being developed. As shown in Figure 1.30, these systems include, but are certainly not limited to the mechanics of the player character, various in-game camera systems, artificial intelligence for the control of non-player characters (NPCs), weapon systems, vehicles, and

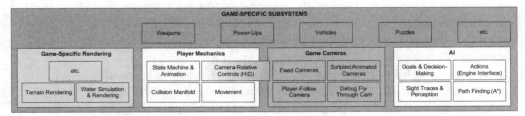

Figure 1.30. Game-specific subsystems.

the list goes on. If a clear line could be drawn between the engine and the game, it would lie between the game-specific subsystems and the gameplay foundations layer. Practically speaking, this line is never perfectly distinct. At least some game-specific knowledge invariably seeps down through the gameplay foundations layer and sometimes even extends into the core of the engine itself.

# 1.7.    Tools and the Asset Pipeline

Any game engine must be fed a great deal of data, in the form of game assets, configuration files, scripts, and so on. Figure 1.31 depicts some of the types of game assets typically found in modern game engines. The thicker dark-grey arrows show how data flows from the tools used to create the original source assets all the way through to the game engine itself. The thinner light-grey arrows show how the various types of assets refer to or use other assets.

## 1.7.1.    Digital Content Creation Tools

Games are multimedia applications by nature. A game engine's input data comes in a wide variety of forms, from 3D mesh data to texture bitmaps to animation data to audio files. All of this source data must be created and manipulated by artists. The tools that the artists use are called *digital content creation* (DCC) applications.

   A DCC application is usually targeted at the creation of one particular type of data—although some tools can produce multiple data types. For example, Autodesk's Maya and 3ds Max are prevalent in the creation of both 3D meshes and animation data. Adobe's Photoshop and its ilk are aimed at creating and editing bitmaps (textures). SoundForge is a popular tool for creating audio clips. Some types of game data cannot be created using an off-the-shelf DCC app. For example, most game engines provide a custom editor for laying out game worlds. Still, some engines do make use of pre-existing tools for game world layout. I've seen game teams use 3ds Max or Maya as a world layout tool, with or without custom plug-ins to aid the user. Ask most game developers, and they'll tell you they can remember a time when they laid out terrain height fields using a simple bitmap editor, or typed world layouts directly into a text file by hand. Tools don't have to be pretty—game teams will use whatever tools are available and get the job done. That said, tools must be relatively *easy to use*, and they absolutely must be *reliable*, if a game team is going to be able to develop a highly polished product in a timely manner.

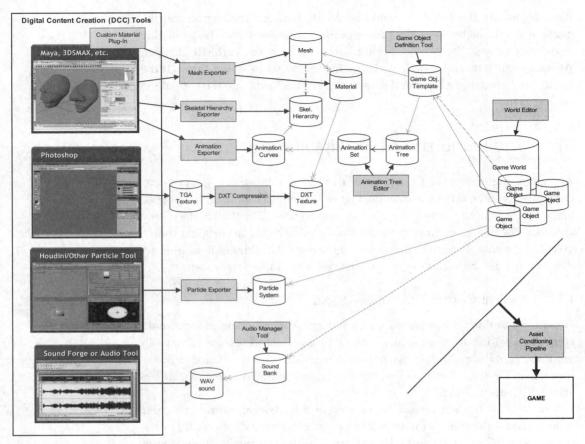

Figure 1.31. Tools and the asset pipeline.

## 1.7.2. Asset Conditioning Pipeline

The data formats used by digital content creation (DCC) applications are rarely suitable for direct use in-game. There are two primary reasons for this.

1.  The DCC app's in-memory model of the data is usually much more complex than what the game engine requires. For example, Maya stores a directed acyclic graph (DAG) of scene nodes, with a complex web of interconnections. It stores a history of all the edits that have been performed on the file. It represents the position, orientation, and scale of every object in the scene as a full hierarchy of 3D transformations, decomposed into translation, rotation, scale, and shear components. A

game engine typically only needs a tiny fraction of this information in order to render the model in-game.

2. The DCC application's file format is often too slow to read at run time, and in some cases it is a closed proprietary format.

Therefore, the data produced by a DCC app is usually exported to a more accessible standardized format, or a custom file format, for use in-game.

Once data has been exported from the DCC app, it often must be further processed before being sent to the game engine. And if a game studio is shipping its game on more than one platform, the intermediate files might be processed differently for each target platform. For example, 3D mesh data might be exported to an intermediate format, such as XML or a simple binary format. Then it might be processed to combine meshes that use the same material, or split up meshes that are too large for the engine to digest. The mesh data might then be organized and packed into a memory image suitable for loading on a specific hardware platform.

The pipeline from DCC app to game engine is sometimes called the *asset conditioning pipeline*. Every game engine has this in some form.

## 1.7.3. 3D Model/Mesh Data

The visible geometry you see in a game is typically made up of two kinds of data.

### 1.7.3.1. Brush Geometry

Brush geometry is defined as a collection of convex hulls, each of which is defined by multiple planes. Brushes are typically created and edited directly in the game world editor. This is what some would call an "old school" approach to creating renderable geometry, but it is still used.

Pros:

- fast and easy to create;
- accessible to game designers — often used to "block out" a game level for prototyping purposes;
- can serve both as collision volumes and as renderable geometry.

Cons:

- low-resolution – difficult to create complex shapes;
- cannot support articulated objects or animated characters.

### 1.7.3.2. 3D Models (Meshes)

For detailed scene elements, 3D *models* (also referred to as *meshes*) are superior to brush geometry. A mesh is a complex shape composed of triangles and vertices. (A mesh might also be constructed from quads or higher-order subdivision surfaces. But on today's graphics hardware, which is almost exclusively geared toward rendering rasterized triangles, all shapes must eventually be translated into triangles prior to rendering.) A mesh typically has one or more *materials* applied to it, in order to define visual surface properties (color, reflectivity, bumpiness, diffuse texture, etc.). In this book, I will use the term "mesh" to refer to a single renderable shape, and "model" to refer to a composite object that may contain multiple meshes, plus animation data and other metadata for use by the game.

Meshes are typically created in a 3D modeling package such as 3ds Max, Maya, or SoftImage. A relatively new tool called ZBrush allows ultra high-resolution meshes to be built in a very intuitive way and then down-converted into a lower-resolution model with normal maps to approximate the high-frequency detail.

Exporters must be written to extract the data from the digital content creation (DCC) tool (Maya, Max, etc.) and store it on disk in a form that is digestible by the engine. The DCC apps provide a host of standard or semi-standard export formats, although none are perfectly suited for game development (with the possible exception of COLLADA). Therefore, game teams often create custom file formats and custom exporters to go with them.

## 1.7.4.  Skeletal Animation Data

A *skeletal mesh* is a special kind of mesh that is bound to a skeletal hierarchy for the purposes of articulated animation. Such a mesh is sometimes called a *skin*, because it forms the skin that surrounds the invisible underlying skeleton. Each vertex of a skeletal mesh contains a list of indices indicating to which joint(s) in the skeleton it is bound. A vertex usually also includes a set of joint weights, specifying the amount of influence each joint has on the vertex.

In order to render a skeletal mesh, the game engine requires three distinct kinds of data.

1.  the mesh itself,

2.  the skeletal hierarchy (joint names, parent-child relationships and the base pose the skeleton was in when it was originally bound to the mesh), and

3.  one or more animation clips, which specify how the joints should move over time.

The mesh and skeleton are often exported from the DCC application as a single data file. However, if multiple meshes are bound to a single skeleton, then it is better to export the skeleton as a distinct file. The animations are usually exported individually, allowing only those animations which are in use to be loaded into memory at any given time. However, some game engines allow a bank of animations to be exported as a single file, and some even lump the mesh, skeleton, and animations into one monolithic file.

An unoptimized skeletal animation is defined by a stream of $4 \times 3$ matrix samples, taken at a frequency of at least 30 frames per second, for each of the joints in a skeleton (of which there are often 100 or more). Thus animation data is inherently memory-intensive. For this reason, animation data is almost always stored in a highly compressed format. Compression schemes vary from engine to engine, and some are proprietary. There is no one standardized format for game-ready animation data.

## 1.7.5.    Audio Data

Audio clips are usually exported from Sound Forge or some other audio production tool in a variety of formats and at a number of different data sampling rates. Audio files may be in mono, stereo, 5.1, 7.1, or other multichannel configurations. Wave files (.wav) are common, but other file formats such as PlayStation ADPCM files (.vag and .xvag) are also commonplace. Audio clips are often organized into banks for the purposes of organization, easy loading into the engine, and streaming.

## 1.7.6.    Particle Systems Data

Modern games make use of complex particle effects. These are authored by artists who specialize in the creation of visual effects. Third-party tools, such as Houdini, permit film-quality effects to be authored; however, most game engines are not capable of rendering the full gamut of effects that can be created with Houdini. For this reason, many game companies create a custom particle effect editing tool, which exposes only the effects that the engine actually supports. A custom tool might also let the artist see the effect exactly as it will appear in-game.

## 1.7.7.    Game World Data and the World Editor

The game world is where everything in a game engine comes together. To my knowledge, there are no commercially available game world editors (i.e., the game world equivalent of Maya or Max). However, a number of commercially available game engines provide good world editors.

- Some variant of the *Radiant* game editor is used by most game engines based on Quake technology;
- The *Half-Life 2* Source engine provides a world editor called *Hammer*;
- *UnrealEd* is the Unreal Engine's world editor. This powerful tool also serves as the asset manager for all data types that the engine can consume.

Writing a good world editor is difficult, but it is an extremely important part of any good game engine.

## 1.7.8.  Some Approaches to Tool Architecture

A game engine's tool suite may be architected in any number of ways. Some tools might be standalone pieces of software, as shown in Figure 1.32. Some tools may be built on top of some of the lower layers used by the runtime engine, as Figure 1.33 illustrates. Some tools might be built into the game itself. For example, Quake- and Unreal-based games both boast an in-game console that permits developers and "modders" to type debugging and configuration commands while running the game.

As an interesting and unique example, Unreal's world editor and asset manager, UnrealEd, is built right into the runtime game engine. To run the editor, you run your game with a command-line argument of "editor." This unique architectural style is depicted in Figure 1.34. It permits the tools to have total access to the full range of data structures used by the engine and

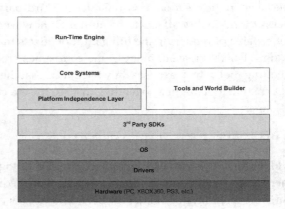

**Figure 1.32.** Standalone tools architecture.

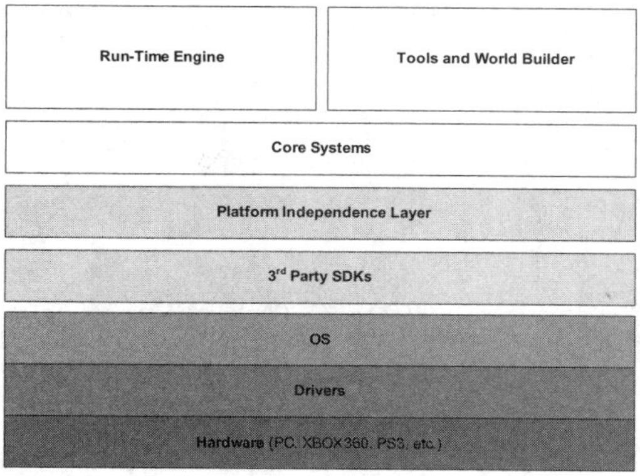

**Figure 1.33.** Tools built on a framework shared with the game.

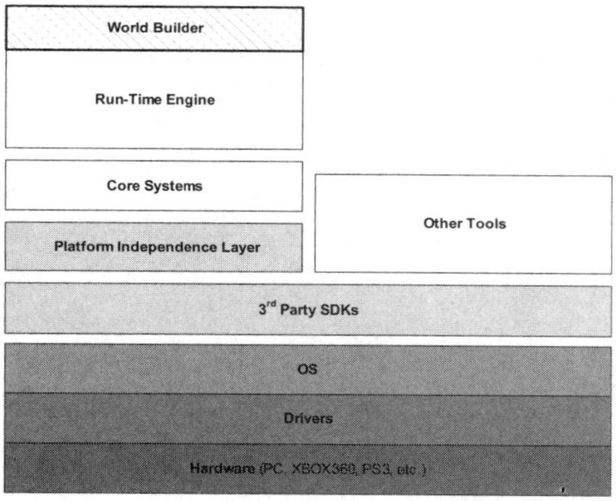

**Figure 1.34.** UnrealEngine's tool architecture.

avoids a common problem of having to have two representations of every data structure – one for the runtime engine and one for the tools. It also means that running the game from within the editor is very fast (because the game is actually already running). Live in-game editing, a feature that is normally very tricky to implement, can be developed relatively easily when the editor is a part of the game. However, an in-engine editor design like this does have its share of problems. For example, when the engine is crashing, the tools become unusable as well. Hence a tight coupling between engine and asset creation tools can tend to slow down production.

# 2
# Tools of the Trade

Before we embark on our journey across the fascinating landscape of game engine architecture, it is important that we equip ourselves with some basic tools and provisions. In the next two chapters, we will review the software engineering concepts and practices that we will need during our voyage. In Chapter 2, we'll explore the tools used by the majority of professional game engineers. Then in Chapter 3, we'll round out our preparations by reviewing some key topics in the realms of object-oriented programming, design patterns, and large-scale C++ programming.

Game development is one of the most demanding and broad areas of software engineering, so believe me, we'll want to be well equipped if we are to safely navigate the sometimes-treacherous terrain we'll be covering. For some readers, the contents of this chapter and the next will be very familiar. However, I encourage you not to skip these chapters entirely. I hope that they will serve as a pleasant refresher; and who knows—you might even pick up a new trick or two.

## 2.1. Version Control

A *version control* system is a tool that permits multiple users to work on a group of files collectively. It maintains a history of each file, so that changes can be tracked and reverted if necessary. It permits multiple users to modify files—even the same file—simultaneously, without everyone stomping on each other's work. Version control gets its name from its ability to track the version history of files. It is sometimes called *source control*, because it is primarily used by computer programmers to manage their source code. However, version control can be used for other kinds of files as well. Version control systems are usually best at managing text files, for reasons we will discover below. However, many game studios use a single version control system to manage both source code files (which are text) and game assets like textures, 3D meshes, animations, and audio files (which are usually binary).

### 2.1.1.    Why Use Version Control?

Version control is crucial whenever software is developed by a team of multiple engineers. Version control

- provides a central repository from which engineers can share source code;
- keeps a history of the changes made to each source file;
- provides mechanisms allowing specific versions of the code base to be tagged and later retrieved;
- permits versions of the code to be branched off from the main development line, a feature often used to produce demos or make patches to older versions of the software.

A source control system can be useful even on a single-engineer project. Although its multiuser capabilities won't be relevant, its other abilities, such as maintaining a history of changes, tagging versions, creating branches for demos and patches, tracking bugs, etc., are still invaluable.

### 2.1.2.    Common Version Control Systems

Here are the most common source control systems you'll probably encounter during your career as a game engineer.

- *SCCS and RCS.* The Source Code Control System (SCCS) and the Revision Control System (RCS) are two of the oldest version control systems. Both employ a command-line interface. They are prevalent primarily on UNIX platforms.
- *CVS.* The Concurrent Version System (CVS) is a heavy-duty professional-grade command-line-based source control system, originally built on top of RCS (but now implemented as a standalone tool). CVS is preva-

lent on UNIX systems but is also available on other development platforms such as Microsoft Windows. It is open source and licensed under
the Gnu General Public License (GPL). CVSNT (also known as WinCVS)
is a native Windows implementation that is based on, and compatible
with, CVS.

- *Subversion.* Subversion is an open source version control system aimed
  at replacing and improving upon CVS. Because it is open source and
  hence free, it is a great choice for individual projects, student projects,
  and small studios.

- *Git.* This is an open source revision control system that has been
  used for many venerable projects, including the Linux kernel. In the
  git development model, the programmer makes changes to files and
  commits the changes to a branch. The programmer can then merge
  his changes into any other code branch quickly and easily, because git
  "knows" how to rewind a sequence of diffs and reapply them onto
  a new base revision—a process git calls *rebasing*. The net result is a
  revision control system that is highly efficient and fast when dealing
  with multiple code branches. More information on git can be found at
  http://git-scm.com/.

- *Perforce.* Perforce is a professional-grade source control system, with
  both text-based and GUI interfaces. One of Perforce's claims to fame is
  its concept of *change lists*. A change list is a collection of source files that
  have been modified as a logical unit. Change lists are checked into the
  repository atomically – either the entire change list is submitted, or none
  of it is. Perforce is used by many game companies, including *Naughty
  Dog* and *Electronic Arts*.

- *NxN Alienbrain.* Alienbrain is a powerful and feature-rich source control
  system designed explicitly for the game industry. Its biggest claim to
  fame is its support for very large databases containing both text source
  code files and binary game art assets, with a customizable user interface
  that can be targeted at specific disciplines such as artists, producers, or
  programmers.

- *ClearCase.* ClearCase is professional-grade source control system aimed
  at very large-scale software projects. It is powerful and employs a
  unique user interface that extends the functionality of Windows Explorer. I haven't seen ClearCase used much in the game industry, perhaps
  because it is one of the more expensive version control systems.

- *Microsoft Visual SourceSafe.* SourceSafe is a light-weight source control
  package that has been used successfully on some game projects.

### 2.1.3.   Overview of Subversion and TortoiseSVN

I have chosen to highlight Subversion in this book for a few reasons. First off, it's free, which is always nice. It works well and is reliable, in my experience. A Subversion central repository is quite easy to set up; and as we'll see, there are already a number of free repository servers out there, if you don't want to go to the trouble of setting one up yourself. There are also a number of good Windows and Mac Subversion clients, such as the freely available TortoiseSVN for Windows. So while Subversion may not be the best choice for a large commercial project (I personally prefer Perforce for that purpose), I find it perfectly suited to small personal and educational projects. Let's take a look at how to set up and use Subversion on a Microsoft Windows PC development platform. As we do so, we'll review core concepts that apply to virtually any version control system.

Subversion, like most other version control systems, employs a client-server architecture. The server manages a central repository, in which a version-controlled directory hierarchy is stored. Clients connect to the server and request operations, such as checking out the latest version of the directory tree, committing new changes to one or more files, tagging revisions, branching the repository, and so on. We won't discuss setting up a server here; we'll assume you have a server, and instead we will focus on setting up and using the client. You can learn how to set up a Subversion server by reading Chapter 6 of [37]. However you probably will never need to do so, because you can always find free Subversion servers. For example, Google provides free Subversion code hosting at http://code.google.com/.

### 2.1.4.   Setting up a Code Repository on Google

The easiest way to get started with Subversion is to visit http://code.google.com/ and set up a free Subversion repository. Create a Google user name and password if you don't already have one, then navigate to Project Hosting under Developer Resources (see Figure 2.1). Click "Create a new project," then enter a suitable unique project name, like "*mygoogleusername*-code." You can enter a summary and/or description if you like, and even provide tags so that other users all over the world can search for and find your repository. Click the "Create Project" button and you're off to the races.

Once you've created your repository, you can administer it on the Google Code website. You can add and remove users, control options, and perform a wealth of advanced tasks. But all you really need to do next is set up a Subversion client and start using your repository.

**Figure 2.1.** Google Code home page, Project Hosting link.

### 2.1.5. Installing TortoiseSVN

TortoiseSVN is a popular front-end for Subversion. It extends the functionality of the Microsoft Windows Explorer via a convenient right-click menu and overlay icons to show you the status of your version-controlled files and folders.

To get TortoiseSVN, visit http://tortoisesvn.tigris.org/. Download the latest version from the download page. Install it by double-clicking the .msi file that you've downloaded and following the installation wizard's instructions.

Once TortoiseSVN is installed, you can go to any folder in Windows Explorer and right-click—TortoiseSVN's menu extensions should now be visible. To connect to an existing code repository (such as one you created on Google Code), create a folder on your local hard disk and then right-click and select "SVN Checkout...." The dialog shown in Figure 2.2 will appear. In the "URL of repository" field, enter your repository's URL. If you are using Google Code, it should be https://*myprojectname*.googlecode.com/svn/trunk, where *myprojectname* is whatever you named your project when you first created it (e.g., "*mygoogleusername*-code").

If you forget the URL of your repository, just log in to http://code.google. com/, go to "Project Hosting" as before, sign in by clicking the "Sign in" link in the upper right-hand corner of the screen, and then click the Settings link, also found in the upper right-hand corner of the screen. Click the "My Profile" tab, and you should see your project listed there. Your project's URL is https:// *myprojectname*.googlecode.com/svn/trunk, where *myprojectname* is whatever name you see listed on the "My Profile" tab.

You should now see the dialog shown in Figure 2.3. The user name should be your Google login name. The password is *not* your Google login

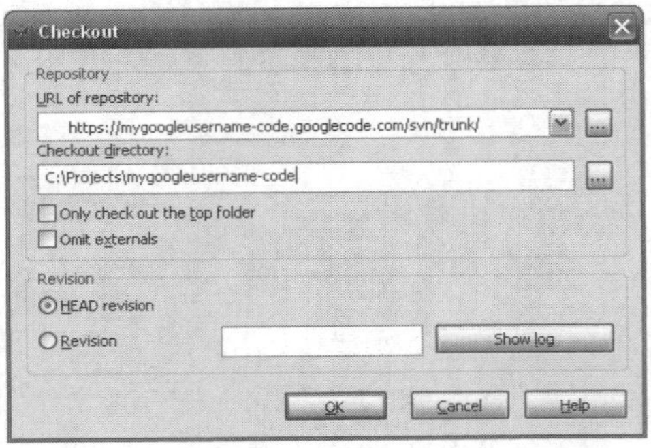

Figure 2.2. TortoiseSVN initial check-out dialog.

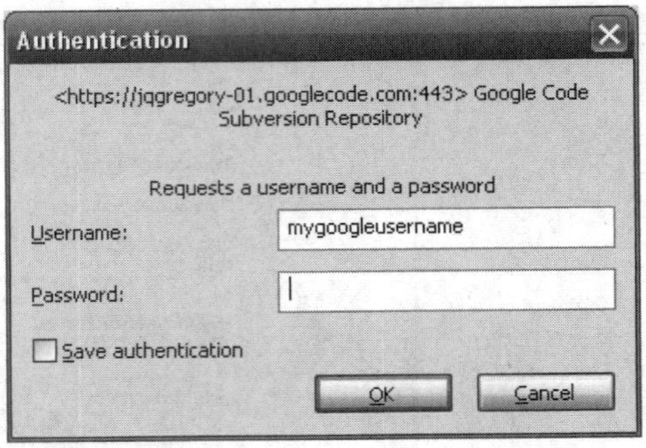

Figure 2.3. TortoiseSVN user authentication dialog.

password—it is an automatically generated password that can be obtained by signing in to your account on Goggle's "Project Hosting" page and clicking on the "Settings" link. (See above for details.) Checking the "Save authentication" option on this dialog allows you to use your repository without ever having to log in again. Only select this option if you are working on your own personal machine—never on a machine that is shared by many users.

Once you've authenticated your user name, TortoiseSVN will download ("check out") the entire contents of your repository to your local disk. If you just set up your repository, this will be … nothing! The folder you created will still be empty. But now it is connected to your Subversion repository on Google (or wherever your server is located). If you refresh your Windows Explorer window (hit F5), you should now see a little green and white check-mark on your folder. This icon indicates that the folder is connected to a Subversion repository via TortoiseSVN and that the local copy of the repository is up-to-date.

## 2.1.6.   File Versions, Updating, and Committing

As we've seen, one of the key purposes of any source control system like Subversion is to allow multiple programmers to work on a single software code base by maintaining a central repository or "master" version of all the source code on a server. The server maintains a version history for each file, as shown in Figure 2.4. This feature is crucial to large-scale multiprogrammer software development. For example, if someone makes a mistake and checks in code that "breaks the build," you can easily go back in time to undo those changes (and check the log to see who the culprit was!). You can also grab a snapshot of the code as it existed at any point in time, allowing you to work with, demonstrate, or patch previous versions of the software.

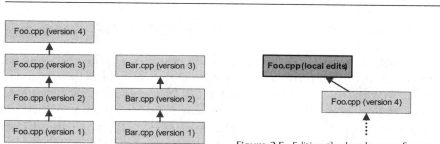

**Figure 2.4.** File version histories.

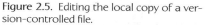

**Figure 2.5.** Editing the local copy of a version-controlled file.

Each programmer gets a local copy of the code on his or her machine. In the case of TortoiseSVN, you obtain your initial working copy by "checking out" the repository, as described above. Periodically you should update your local copy to reflect any changes that may have been made by other programmers. You do this by right-clicking on a folder and selecting "SVN Update" from the pop-up menu.

You can work on your local copy of the code base without affecting the other programmers on the team (Figure 2.5). When you are ready to share your changes with everyone else, you *commit* your changes to the repository (also known as *submitting* or *checking in*). You do this by right-clicking on the folder you want to commit and selecting "SVN Commit…" from the pop-up

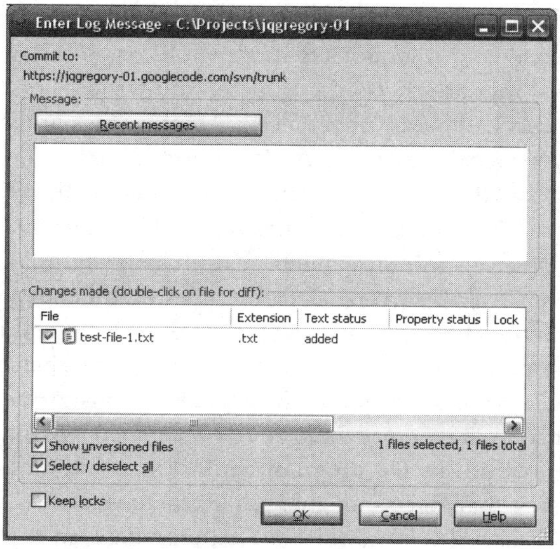

**Figure 2.6.** TortoiseSVN Commit dialog.

menu. You will get a dialog like the one shown in Figure 2.6, asking you to confirm the changes.

During a commit operation, Subversion generates a *diff* between your local version of each file and the latest version of that same file in the repository. The term "diff" means difference, and it is typically produced by performing a line-by-line comparison of the two versions of the file. You can double-click on any file in the TortoiseSVN Commit dialog (Figure 2.6) to see the diffs between your version and the latest version on the server (i.e., the changes you made). Files that have changed (i.e., any files that "have diffs") are committed. This replaces the latest version in the repository with your local version, adding a new entry to the file's version history. Any files that have not changed (i.e., your local copy is identical to the latest version in the repository) are ignored by default during a commit. An example commit operation is shown in Figure 2.7.

**Figure 2.7.** Committing local edits to the repository.

If you created any new files prior to the commit, they will be listed as "non-versioned" in the Commit dialog. You can check the little check boxes beside them in order to add them to the repository. Any files that you deleted locally will likewise show up as "missing"—if you check their check boxes, they will be deleted from the repository. You can also type a comment in the Commit dialog. This comment is added to the repository's history log, so that you and others on your team will know why these files were checked in.

### 2.1.7.   Multiple Check-Out, Branching, and Merging

Some version control systems require *exclusive check-out*. This means that you must first indicate your intentions to modify a file by *checking it out* and *locking* it. The file(s) that are checked out to you are writable on your local disk and cannot be checked out by anyone else. All other files in the repository are read-only on your local disk. Once you're done editing the file, you can check it in, which releases the lock and commits the changes to the repository for everyone else to see. The process of exclusively locking files for editing ensures that no two people can edit the same file simultaneously.

Subversion, CVS, Perforce, and many other high-quality version control systems also permit *multiple check-out.*; i.e., you can be editing a file while someone else is editing that same file. Whichever user's changes are committed first become the latest version of the file in the repository. Any subsequent commits by other users require that programmer to merge his or her changes with the changes made by the programmer(s) who committed previously.

Because more than one set of changes (diffs) have been made to the same file, the version control system must *merge* the changes in order to produce a final version of the file. This is often not a big deal, and in fact many conflicts

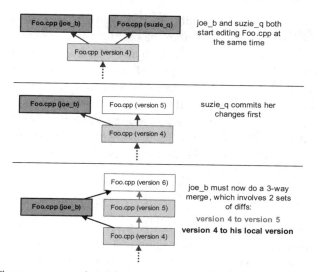

**Figure 2.8.** Three-way merge due to local edits by two different users.

can be resolved automatically by the version control system. For example, if you changed function `f()` and another programmer changed function `g()`, then your edits would have been to a different range of lines in the file than those of the other programmer. In this case, the merge between your changes and his or her changes will usually resolve automatically without any conflicts. However, if you were both making changes to the same function `f()`, then the second programmer to commit his or her changes will need to do a *three-way merge* (see Figure 2.8).

For three-way merges to work, the version control server has to be smart enough to keep track of which version of each file you currently have on your local disk. That way, when you merge the files, the system will know which version is the base version (the common ancestor, such as version 4 in Figure 2.8).

Subversion permits multiple check-out, and in fact it doesn't require you to check out files explicitly at all. You simply start editing the files locally—all files are writable on your local disk at all times. (By the way, this is one reason that Subversion doesn't scale well to large projects, in my opinion. To determine which files you have changed, Subversion must search the entire tree of source files, which can be slow. Version control systems like Perforce, which explicitly keep track of which files you have modified, are usually easier to work with when dealing with large amounts of code. But for small projects, Subversion's approach works just fine.)

When you perform a commit operation by right-clicking on any folder and selecting "SVN Commit…" from the pop-up menu, you may be prompted to *merge* your changes with changes made by someone else. But if no one has changed the file since you last updated your local copy, then your changes will be committed without any further action on your part. This is a very convenient feature, but it can also be dangerous. It's a good idea to always check your commits carefully to be sure you aren't committing any files that you didn't intend to modify. When TortoiseSVN displays its Commit Files dialog, you can double-click on an individual file in order to see the diffs you made prior to hitting the "OK" button.

### 2.1.8.  Deleting Files

When a file is deleted from the repository, it's not really gone. The file still exists in the repository, but its latest version is simply marked "deleted" so that users will no longer see the file in their local directory trees. You can still see and access previous versions of a deleted file by right-clicking on the folder in which the file was contained and selecting "Show log" from the TortoiseSVN menu.

You can undelete a deleted file by updating your local directory to the version immediately before the version in which the file was marked deleted. Then simply commit the file again. This replaces the latest deleted version of the file with the version just prior to the deletion, effectively undeleting the file.

## 2.2.  Microsoft Visual Studio

Compiled languages, such as C++, require a *compiler* and *linker* in order to transform source code into an executable program. There are many compilers/linkers available for C++, but for the Microsoft Windows platform the most commonly used package is probably Microsoft Visual Studio. The fully featured Professional Edition of the product can be purchased at any store that sells Windows software. And Visual Studio Express, its lighter-weight cousin, is available for free download at http://www.microsoft.com/express/download/. Documentation on Visual Studio is available online at the Microsoft Developer's Network (MSDN) site (http://msdn.microsoft.com/en-us/library/52f3sw5c.aspx).

Visual Studio is more than just a compiler and linker. It is an *integrated development environment* (IDE), including a slick and fully featured *text editor* for source code and a powerful source-level and machine-level *debugger*. In this book, our primary focus is the Windows platform, so we'll investigate Visual Studio in some depth. Much of what you learn below will be applicable to other compilers, linkers, and debuggers, so even if you're not planning on ever using Visual Studio, I suggest you skim this section for useful tips on using compilers, linkers, and debuggers in general.

### 2.2.1.  Source Files, Headers, and Translation Units

A program written in C++ is comprised of *source files*. These typically have a .c, .cc, .cxx, or .cpp extension, and they contain the bulk of your program's source code. Source files are technically known as *translation units,* because the compiler *translates* one source file at a time from C++ into machine code.

A special kind of source file, known as a *header file*, is often used in order to share information, such as type declarations and function prototypes, between translation units. Header files are not seen by the compiler. Instead, the C++ *preprocessor* replaces each #include statement with the contents of the corresponding header file prior to sending the translation unit to the compiler. This is a subtle but very important distinction to make. Header files exist as distinct files from the point of view of the programmer—but thanks to the preprocessor's header file expansion, all the compiler ever sees are translation units.

### 2.2.2.  Libraries, Executables, and Dynamic Link Libraries

When a translation unit is compiled, the resulting machine code is placed in an object file (files with a .obj extension under Windows, or .o under UNIX-based operating systems). The machine code in an object file is

- *relocatable,* meaning that the memory addresses at which the code resides have not yet been determined, and
- *unlinked,* meaning that any external references to functions and global data that are defined outside the translation unit have not yet been resolved.

Object files can be collected into groups called *libraries.* A library is simply an archive, much like a Zip or tar file, containing zero or more object files. Libraries exist merely as a convenience, permitting a large number of object files to be collected into a single easy-to-use file.

Object files and libraries are *linked* into an executable by the linker. The executable file contains fully resolved machine code that can be loaded and run by the operating system. The linker's jobs are

- to calculate the final relative addresses of all the machine code, as it will appear in memory when the program is run, and

- to ensure that all external references to functions and global data made by each translation unit (object file) are properly resolved.

It's important to remember that the machine code in an executable file is still relocatable, meaning that the addresses of all instructions and data in the file are still *relative* to an arbitrary base address, not absolute. The final absolute base address of the program is not known until the program is actually loaded into memory, just prior to running it.

A *dynamic link library* (DLL) is a special kind of library that acts like a hybrid between a regular static library and an executable. The DLL acts like a library, because it contains functions that can be called by any number of different executables. However, a DLL also acts like an executable, because it can be loaded by the operating system independently, and it contains some start-up and shut-down code that runs much the way the `main()` function in a C++ executable does.

The executables that use a DLL contain *partially linked* machine code. Most of the function and data references are fully resolved within the final executable, but any references to external functions or data that exist in a DLL remain unlinked. When the executable is run, the operating system resolves the addresses of all unlinked functions by locating the appropriate DLLs, loading them into memory if they are not already loaded, and patching in the necessary memory addresses. Dynamically linked libraries are a very useful operating system feature, because individual DLLs can be updated without changing the executable(s) that use them.

### 2.2.3. Projects and Solutions

Now that we understand the difference between libraries, executables, and dynamic link libraries (DLLs), let's see how to create them. In Visual Studio, a *project* is a collection of *source files* which, when compiled, produce a library, an executable, or a DLL. Projects are stored in project files with a .vcproj extension. In Visual Studio .NET 2003 (version 7), Visual Studio 2005 (version 8), and Visual Studio 2008 (version 9), .vcproj files are in XML format, so they are reasonably easy for a human to read and even edit by hand if necessary.

All versions of Visual Studio since version 7 (Visual Studio 2003) employ *solution files* (files with a *.sln* extension) as a means of containing and managing collections of projects. A solution is a collection of dependent and/or independent projects intended to build one or more libraries, executables and/or DLLs. In the Visual Studio graphical user interface, the *Solution Explorer* is usually displayed along the right or left side of the main window, as shown in Figure 2.9.

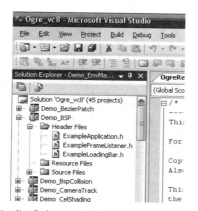

Figure 2.9. The VisualStudio Solution Explorer window.

The Solution Explorer is a tree view. The solution itself is at the root, with the projects as its immediate children. Source files and headers are shown as children of each project. A project can contain any number of user-defined folders, nested to any depth. Folders are for organizational purposes only and have nothing to do with the folder structure in which the files may reside on-disk. However it is common practice to mimic the on-disk folder structure when setting up a project's folders.

## 2.2.4. Build Configurations

The C/C++ preprocessor, compiler, and linker offer a wide variety of options to control how your code will be built. These options are normally specified on the command line when the compiler is run. For example, a typical command to build a single translation unit with the Microsoft compiler might look like this:

```
C:\> cl /c foo.cpp /Fo foo.obj /Wall /Od /Zi
```

This tells the compiler/linker to compile but not link (/c) the translation unit named foo.cpp, output the result to an object file named foo.obj (/Fo foo.obj), turn on all warnings (/Wall), turn off all optimizations (/Od), and generate debugging information (/Zi).

Modern compilers provide so many options that it would be impractical and error prone to specify all of them every time you build your code. That's where *build configurations* come in. A build configuration is really just a collection of preprocessor, compiler, and linker options associated with a particular project in your solution. You can define any number of build configurations, name them whatever you want, and configure the preprocessor, compiler, and linker options differently in each configuration. By default, the same options are applied to every translation unit in the project, although you can override the global project settings on an individual translation unit basis. (I recommend avoiding this if at all possible, because it becomes difficult to tell which .cpp files have custom settings and which do not.)

Most projects have at least two build configurations, typically called "Debug" and "Release." The release build is for the final shipping software, while the debug build is for development purposes. A debug build runs more slowly than a release build, but it provides the programmer with invaluable information for developing and debugging the program.

### 2.2.4.1.   Common Build Options

This section lists some of the most common options you'll want to control via build configurations for a game engine project.

*Preprocessor Settings*

The C++ preprocessor handles the expansion of #included files and the definition and substitution of #defined macros. One extremely powerful feature of all modern C++ preprocessors is the ability to define preprocessor macros via command-line options (and hence via build configurations). Macros defined in this way act as though they had been written into your source code with a #define statement. For most compilers, the command line option for this is -D or /D, and any number of these directives can be used.

This feature allows you to communicate various build options to your code, without having to modify the source code itself. As a ubiquitous example, the symbol _DEBUG is always defined for a debug build, while in release builds the symbol NDEBUG is defined instead. The source code can check these flags and in effect "know" whether it is being built in debug or release mode. This is known as *conditional compilation*. For example:

```
void f()
{
#ifdef _DEBUG
    printf("Calling function f()\n");
#endif
    // ...
}
```

The compiler is also free to introduce "magic" preprocessor macros into your code, based on its knowledge of the compilation environment and target platform. For example, the macro __cplusplus is defined by most C/C++

compilers when compiling a C++ file. This allows code to be written that automatically adapts to being compiled for C or C++.

As another example, every compiler identifies itself to the source code via a "magic" preprocessor macro. When compiling code under the Microsoft compiler, the macro _MSC_VER is defined; when compiling under the GNU compiler (gcc), the macro _GNUC_ is defined instead, and so on for the other compilers. The target platform on which the code will be run is likewise identified via macros. For example, when building for a 32-bit Windows machine, the symbol _WIN32 is always defined. These key features permit cross-platform code to be written, because they allow your code to "know" what compiler is compiling it and on which target platform it is destined to be run.

*Compiler Settings*

One of the most common compiler options controls whether or not the compiler should include *debugging information* with the object files it produces. This information is used by debuggers to step through your code, display the values of variables, and so on. Debugging information makes your executables larger on disk and also opens the door for hackers to reverse-engineer your code. So, it is always stripped from the final shipping version of your executable. However, during development, debugging information is invaluable and should always be included in your builds.

The compiler can also be told whether or not to expand *inline functions*. When inline function expansion is turned off, every inline function appears only once in memory, at a distinct address. This makes the task of tracing through the code in the debugger much simpler, but obviously comes at the expense of the execution speed improvements normally achieved by inlining.

Inline function expansion is but one example of generalized code transformations known as *optimizations*. The aggressiveness with which the compiler attempts to optimize your code, and the kinds of optimizations its uses, can be controlled via compiler options. Optimizations have a tendency to re-order the statements in your code, and they also cause variables to be stripped out of the code altogether, or moved around, and can cause CPU registers to be reused for new purposes later in the same function. Optimized code usually confuses most debuggers, causing them to "lie" to you in various ways, and making it difficult or impossible to see what's really going on. As a result, all optimizations are usually turned off in a debug build. This permits every variable and every line of code to be scrutinized as it was originally coded. But, of course, such code will run much more slowly than its fully optimized counterpart.

*Linker Settings*

The linker also exposes a number of options. You can control what type of output file to produce—an executable or a DLL. You can also specify which external libraries should be linked into your executable, and which directory paths to search in order to find them. A common practice is to link with debug libraries when building a debug executable and with optimized libraries when building in release mode.

Linker options also control things like stack size, the preferred base address of your program in memory, what type of machine the code will run on (for machine-specific optimizations), and a host of other minutia with which we will not concern ourselves here.

### 2.2.4.2. Typical Build Configurations

Game projects often have more than just two build configurations. Here are a few of the common configurations I've seen used in game development.

- *Debug.* A debug build is a very slow version of your program, with all optimizations turned off, all function inlining disabled, and full debugging information included. This build is used when testing brand new code and also to debug all but the most trivial problems that arise during development.

- *Release.* A release build is a faster version of your program, but with debugging information and assertions still turned on. (See Section 3.3.3.3 for a discussion of assertions.) This allows you to see your game running at a speed representative of the final product, but still gives you some opportunity to debug problems.

- *Production.* A production configuration is intended for building the final game that you will ship to your customers. It is sometimes called a "Final" build or "Disk" build. Unlike a release build, all debugging information is stripped out of a production build, all assertions are usually turned off, and optimizations are cranked all the way up. A production build is very tricky to debug, but it is the fastest and leanest of all build types.

- *Tools.* Some game studios utilize code libraries that are *shared* between offline tools and the game itself. In this scenario, it often makes sense to define a "Tools" build, which can be used to conditionally compile shared code for use by the tools. The tools build usually defines a preprocessor macro (e.g., `TOOLS_BUILD`) that informs the code that it is being built for use in a tool. For example, one of your tools might require certain C++ classes to expose editing functions that are not needed by the game. These functions could be wrapped in an `#ifdef TOOLS_`

`BUILD` directive. Since you usually want both debug and release versions of your tools, you will probably find yourself creating *two* tools builds, named something like "ToolsDebug" and "ToolsRelease."

### Hybrid Builds

A hybrid build is a build configuration in which the majority of the translation units are built in release mode, but a small subset of them is built in debug mode. This permits the segment of code that is currently under scrutiny to be easily debugged, while the rest of the code continues to run at full speed.

With a text-based build system like `make`, it is quite easy to set up a hybrid build which permits users to specify the use of debug mode on a per-translation-unit basis. In a nutshell, we define a make variable called something like `$HYBRID_SOURCES`, which lists the names of all translation units (.cpp files) that should be compiled in debug mode for our hybrid build. We set up build rules for compiling both debug and release versions of every translation unit, and arrange for the resulting object files (.obj/.o) to be placed into two different folders, one for debug and one for release. The final link rule is set up to link with the debug versions of the object files listed in `$HYBRID_SOURCES` and with the release versions of all other object files. If we've set it up properly, `make`'s dependency rules will take care of the rest.

Unfortunately, this is not so easy to do in Visual Studio, because its build configurations are designed to be applied on a per-project basis, not per translation unit. The crux of the problem is that we cannot easily define a list of the translation units that we want to build in debug mode. However, if your source code is already organized into libraries, you *can* set up a "Hybrid" build configuration at the solution level, which picks and chooses between debug and release builds on a per-project (and hence per-*library*) basis. This isn't as flexible as having control on a per-translation-unit basis, but it does work reasonably well if your libraries are sufficiently granular.

### Build Configurations and Testability

The more build configurations your project supports, the more difficult testing becomes. Although the differences between the various configurations may be slight, there's a finite probability that a critical bug may exist in one of them but not in the others. Therefore, each build configuration must be tested equally thoroughly. Most game studios do not formally test their debug builds, because the debug configuration is primarily intended for internal use during initial development of a feature and for the debugging of problems found in one of the other configurations. However, if your testers spend most of their time testing your release configuration, then you cannot simply make a production build of your game the night before Gold Master and expect it to have an identical bug profile to that of the release build. Practically speaking, the test team must test both your release and production builds equally throughout alpha and beta, to ensure that there aren't any nasty surprises lurking in your production build. In terms of testability, there is a clear advantage to keeping your build configurations to a minimum, and in fact some studios have no production build for this reason—they simply ship their release build once it has been thoroughly tested.

### 2.2.4.3. Project Configuration Tutorial

Right-clicking on any project in the Solution Explorer and selecting "Properties…" from the menu brings up the project's "Property Pages" dialog. The tree view on the left shows various categories of settings. Of these, the three we will use most are

- Configuration Properties/General,
- Configuration Properties/Debugging,
- Configuration Properties/C++,
- Configuration Properties/Linker.

*Configurations Drop-Down Combo Box*

Notice the drop-down combo box labeled "Configuration:" at the top-left corner of the window. All of the properties displayed on these property pages apply separately to each build configuration. If you set a property for the debug configuration, this does not necessarily mean that the same setting exists for the release configuration.

If you click on the combo box to drop down the list, you'll find that you can select a single configuration or multiple configurations, including "All configurations." As a rule of thumb, try to do most of your build configuration editing with "All configurations" selected. That way, you won't have to make the same edits multiple times, once for each configuration—and you don't risk setting things up incorrectly in one of the configurations by accident. However, be aware that some settings *need* to be different between the debug and release configurations. For example, function inlining and code optimization settings should of course be different between debug and release builds.

*General Tab*

On the General tab, shown in Figure 2.10, the most useful fields are the following.

- *Output directory.* This defines where the final product(s) of the build will go—namely the executable, library, or DLL that the compiler/linker ultimately outputs.

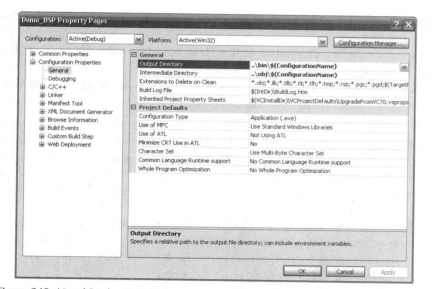

**Figure 2.10.** Visual Studio project property pages—General page.

- *Intermediate directory.* This defines where intermediate files, primarily object files (.obj extension), are placed during a build. Intermediate files are never shipped with your final program—they are only required during the process of building your executable, library, or DLL. Hence, it is a good idea to place intermediate files in a different directory than the final products (.exe, .lib or .dll files).

Note that VisualStudio provides a macro facility which may be used when specifying directories and other settings in the "Project Property Pages" dialog. A *macro* is essentially a named variable that contains a global value and that can be referred to in your project configuration settings.

Macros are invoked by writing the name of the macro enclosed in parentheses and prefixed with a dollar sign (e.g., $(ConfigurationName)). Some commonly used macros are listed below.

- $(TargetFileName). The name of the final executable, library, or DLL file being built by this project.

- $(TargetPath). The full path of the folder containing the final executable, library, or DLL.

- $(ConfigurationName). The name of the build config, typically "Debug" or "Release."

- `$(OutDir)`. The value of the "Output Directory" field specified in this dialog.
- `$(IntDir)`. The value of the "Intermediate Directory" field in this dialog.
- `$(VCInstallDir)`. The directory in which Visual Studio's standard C library is currently installed.

The benefit of using macros instead of hard-wiring your configuration settings is that a simple change of the global macro's value will automatically affect all configuration settings in which the macro is used. Also, some macros like `$(ConfigurationName)` automatically change their values depending on the build configuration, so using them can permit you to use identical settings across all your configurations.

To see a complete list of all available macros, click in either the "Output Directory" field or the "Intermediate Directory" field on the "General" tab, click the little arrow to the right of the text field, select "Edit…" and then click the "Macros" button in the dialog that comes up.

### Debugging Tab

The "Debugging" tab is where the name and location of the executable to debug is specified. On this page, you can also specify the command-line argument(s) that should be passed to the program when it runs. We'll discuss debugging your program in more depth below.

### C/C++ Tab

The C/C++ tab controls compile-time language settings—things that affect how your source files will be compiled into object files (.obj extension). The settings on this page do *not* affect how your object files are linked into a final executable or DLL.

You are encouraged to explore the various subpages of the C/C++ tab to see what kinds of settings are available. Some of the most commonly used settings include the following.

- *General Tab/Include Directories.* This field lists the on-disk directories that will be searched when looking for #included header files.
  **Important**: It is always best to specify these directories using *relative paths* and/or with Visual Studio macros like `$(OutDir)` or `$(IntDir)`. That way, if you move your build tree to a different location on disk or to another computer with a different root folder, everything will continue to work properly.
- *General Tab/Debug Information.* This field controls whether or not debug information is generated. Typically both debug and release configura-

tions include debugging information so that you can track down problems during development of your game. The final production build will have all the debug info stripped out to prevent hacking.

- *Preprocessor Tab/Preprocessor Definitions.* This very handy field lists any number of C/C++ preprocessor symbols that should be defined in the code when it is compiled. See *Preprocessor Settings* in Section 2.2.4.1 for a discussion of preprocessor-defined symbols.

### Linker Tab

The "Linker" tab lists properties that affect how your object code files will be linked into an executable or DLL. Again, you are encouraged to explore the various subpages. Some commonly used settings follow.

- *General Tab/Output File.* This setting lists the name and location of the final product of the build, usually an executable or DLL.
- *General Tab/Additional Library Directories.* Much like the C/C++ Include Directories field, this field lists zero or more directories that will be searched when looking for libraries and object files to link into the final executable.
- *Input Tab/Additional Dependencies.* This field lists external libraries that you want linked into your executable or DLL. For example, the Ogre libraries would be listed here if you are building an Ogre-enabled application.

Note that Visual Studio employs various "magic spells" to specify libraries that should be linked into an executable. For example, a special #pragma instruction in your source code can be used to instruct the linker to automatically link with a particular library. For this reason, you may not see all of the libraries you're actually linking to in the "Additional Dependencies" field. (In fact, that's why they are called *additional* dependencies.) You may have noticed, for example, that Direct X applications do not list all of the DirectX libraries manually in their "Additional Dependencies" field. Now you know why.

### 2.2.4.4. Creating New .vcproj Files

With so many preprocessor, compiler, and linker options, all of which must be set properly, creating a new project may seem like an impossibly daunting task. I usually take one of the following two approaches when creating a new Visual Studio project.

### Use a Wizard

Visual Studio provides a wide variety of wizards to create new projects of various kinds. If you can find a wizard that does what you want, this is the easiest way to create a new project.

*Copy an Existing Project*

If I am creating a project that is similar to an existing project that I know already works, I'll often just copy that .vcproj file and then modify it as necessary. In Visual Studio 2005, this is very easy. You simply copy the .vcproj file on disk, then add the newly copied project to your solution by right-clicking the solution in the Solution Explorer and selecting "Add…" and "Existing project…" from the pop-up menus.

One caveat when copying project files is that the name of the project is stored inside the .vcproj file itself. So when you load up the new project for the first time in Visual Studio 2005, it will still have the original name. To rectify this, you can simply select the project in the Solution Explorer window, and hit F2 to rename it appropriately.

Another problem arises when the name of the executable, library, or DLL that the project creates is specified *explicitly* in the .vcproj file. For example, the executable might be specified as "`C:\MyGame\bin\MyGame.exe`" or "`$(OutDir)\MyGame.exe`." In this case, you'll need to open the .vcproj file and do a global search-and-replace of the executable, library, or DLL name and/or its directory path. This is not too difficult. Project files are XML, so you can rename your copied .vcproj file to have an ".xml" extension and then open it in Visual Studio (or any other XML or raw text editor). One elegant solution to this problem is to use Visual Studio's macro system when specifying all output files in your project. For example, if you specify the output executable as "`$(OutDir)\$(ProjectName).exe`", then the project's name will automatically be reflected in the name of the output executable file.

I should mention that using a text editor to manipulate .vcproj files is not always to be avoided. In fact, the practice is quite common, at least in my experience. For example, let's say you decided to move the folder containing all of your graphics header files to a new path on disk. Rather than manually open each project in turn, open the Project Property Pages window, navigate to the C/C++ tab, and finally update the include path manually, it's much easier and less error-prone to edit the files as XML text and do a search-and-replace. You can even do a "Replace in files" operation in Visual Studio for mass edits.

## 2.2.5. Debugging Your Code

One of the most important skills any programmer can learn is how to effectively debug code. This section provides some useful debugging tips and tricks. Some are applicable to any debugger and some are specific to Microsoft Visual Studio. However, you can usually find an equivalent to Visual Studio's debugging features in other debuggers, so this section should prove useful even if you don't use Visual Studio to debug your code.

### 2.2.5.1. The Start-Up Project

A Visual Studio solution can contain more than one project. Some of these projects build executables, while others build libraries or DLLs. It's possible to have more than one project that builds an executable in a single solution. However, you cannot debug more than one program at a time. For this reason, Visual Studio provides a setting known as the "Start-Up Project." This is the project that is considered "current" for the purposes of the debugger.

The start-up project is highlighted in bold in the Solution Explorer. Hitting F5 to run your program in the debugger will run the .exe built by the start-up project (if the start-up project builds an executable).

### 2.2.5.2. Break Points

*Break points* are the bread and butter of code debugging. A break point instructs the program to stop at a particular line in your source code so that you can inspect what's going on.

In Visual Studio, select a line and hit F9 to toggle a break point. When you run your program and the line of code containing the break point is about to be executed, the debugger will stop the program. We say that the break point has been "hit." A little arrow will show you which line of code the CPU's program counter is currently on. This is shown in Figure 2.11.

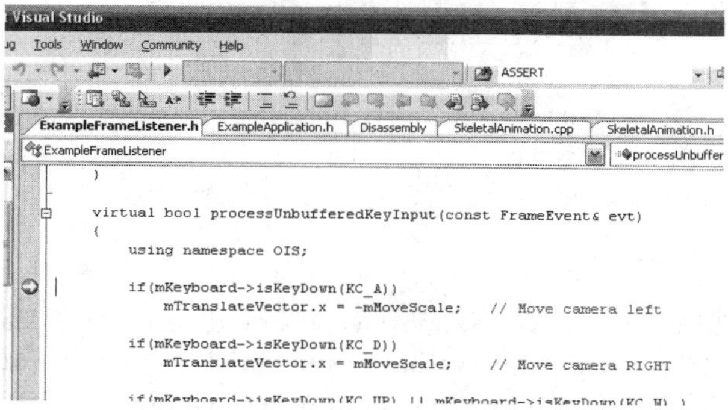

Figure 2.11. Setting a break point in Visual Studio.

### 2.2.5.3. Stepping through Your Code

Once a break point has been hit, you can single-step your code by hitting the F10 key. The yellow program-counter arrow moves to show you the lines as they execute. Hitting F11 steps *into* a function call (i.e., the next line of code you'll see is the first line of the called function), while F10 steps *over* that function call (i.e., the debugger calls the function at full speed and then breaks again on the line right after the call).

### 2.2.5.4. The Call Stack

The *call stack* window, shown in Figure 2.12, shows you the stack of functions that have been called at any given moment during the execution of your code. To display the call stack (if it is not already visible), go to the "Debug" menu on the main menu bar, select "Windows," and then "Call Stack."

Once a break point has been hit (or the program is manually paused), you can move up and down the call stack by double-clicking on entries in the "Call Stack" window. This is very useful for inspecting the chain of function calls that were made between main() and the current line of code. For example, you might trace back to the root cause of a bug in a parent function which has manifested itself in a deeply nested child function.

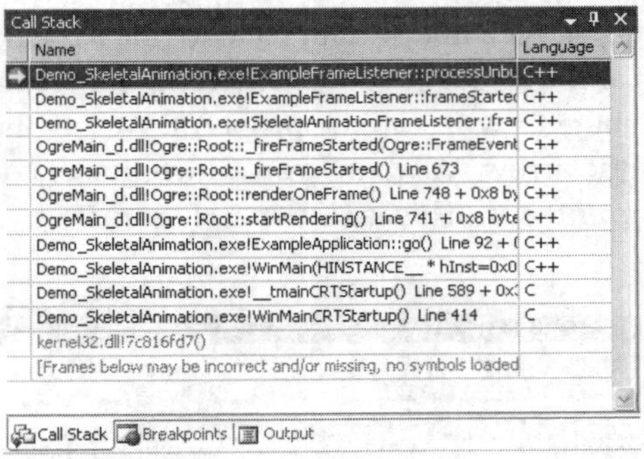

Figure 2.12. The call stack window.

### 2.2.5.5. The Watch Window

As you step through your code and move up and down the call stack, you will want to be able to inspect the values of the variables in your program. This is what *watch windows* are for. To open a watch window, go to the "Debug" menu, select "Windows...," then select "Watch...," and finally select one of "Watch 1" through "Watch 4." (Visual Studio allows you to open up to four watch windows simultaneously.) Once a watch window is open, you can type the names of variables into the window or drag expressions in directly from your source code.

As you can see in Figure 2.13, variables with simple data types are shown with their values listed immediately to the right of their names. Complex data types are shown as little tree views that can be easily expanded to "drill

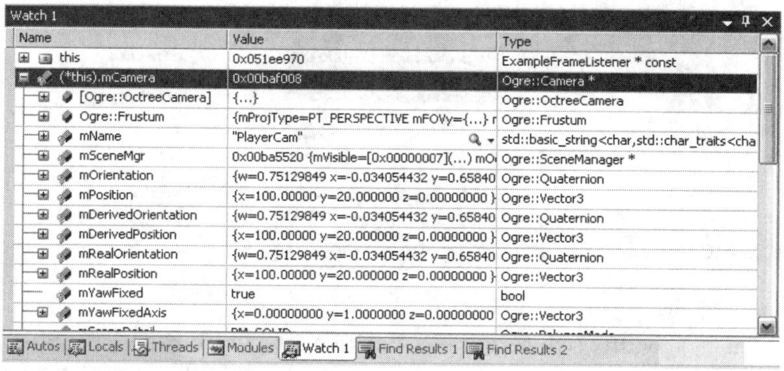

**Figure 2.13.** Visual Studio's watch window.

down" into virtually any nested structure. The base class of a class is always shown as the first child of an instance of a derived class. This allows you to inspect not only the class' data members, but also the data members of its base class(es).

You can type virtually any valid C/C++ *expression* into the watch window, and Visual Studio will evaluate that expression and attempt to display the resulting value. For example, you could type "5+3" and Visual Studio will display "8." You can cast variables from one type to another by using C or C++ casting syntax. For example, typing "(float)myIntegerVariable * 0.5f" in the watch window will display the value of myIntegerVariable divided by two, as a floating-point value.

You can even *call functions in your program* from within the watch window. Visual Studio re-evaluates the expressions typed into the watch window(s) automatically, so if you invoke a function in the watch window, it will be called every time you hit a break point or single-step your code. This allows you to leverage the functionality of your program in order to save yourself work when trying to interpret the data that you're inspecting in the debugger. For example, let's say that your game engine provides a function called quatToAngleDeg() which converts a quaternion to an angle of rotation in degrees. You can call this function in the watch window in order to easily inspect the rotation angle of any quaternion from within the debugger.

You can also use various suffixes on the expressions in the watch window in order to change the way Visual Studio displays the data, as shown in Figure 2.14.

- The ",d" suffix forces values to be displayed in decimal notation.
- The ",x" suffix forces values to be displayed in hexadecimal notation.

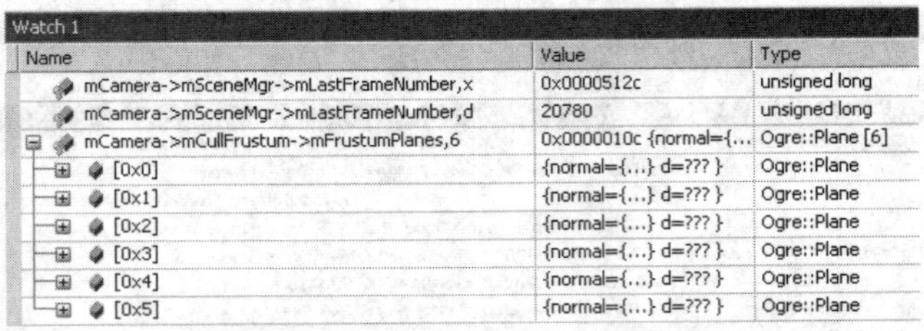

| Watch 1 | | |
|---|---|---|
| Name | Value | Type |
| mCamera->mSceneMgr->mLastFrameNumber,x | 0x0000512c | unsigned long |
| mCamera->mSceneMgr->mLastFrameNumber,d | 20780 | unsigned long |
| ⊟ mCamera->mCullFrustum->mFrustumPlanes,6 | 0x0000010c {normal={... | Ogre::Plane [6] |
| ⊞ [0x0] | {normal={...} d=??? } | Ogre::Plane |
| ⊞ [0x1] | {normal={...} d=??? } | Ogre::Plane |
| ⊞ [0x2] | {normal={...} d=??? } | Ogre::Plane |
| ⊞ [0x3] | {normal={...} d=??? } | Ogre::Plane |
| ⊞ [0x4] | {normal={...} d=??? } | Ogre::Plane |
| ⊞ [0x5] | {normal={...} d=??? } | Ogre::Plane |

Figure 2.14. Comma suffixes in the Visual Studio watch window.

- The ",$n$" suffix (where $n$ is any positive integer) forces Visual Studio to treat the value as an array with $n$ elements. This allows you to expand array data that is referenced through a pointer.

Be careful when expanding very large data structures in the watch window, because it can sometimes slow the debugger down to the point of being unusable.

### 2.2.5.6.  Data Break Points

Regular break points trip when the CPU's program counter hits a particular machine instruction or line of code. However, another incredibly useful feature of modern debuggers is the ability to set a break point that trips whenever a specific memory address is *written to* (i.e., changed). These are called *data break points*, because they are triggered by changes to data, or sometimes *hardware break points*, because they are implemented via a special feature of the CPU's hardware—namely the ability to raise an interrupt when a predefined memory address is written to.

Here's how data break points are typically used. Let's say you are tracking down a bug that manifests itself as a zero (0.0f) value mysteriously appearing inside a member variable of a particular object called m_angle that *should* always contain a nonzero angle. You have no idea which function might be writing that zero into your variable. However, you do know the address of the variable. (You can just type "&object.m_angle" into the watch window to find its address.) To track down the culprit, you can set a data break point on the address of object.m_angle, and then simply let the program run. When the value changes, the debugger will stop automatically. You can then inspect the call stack to catch the offending function red-handed.

To set a data break point in Visual Studio, take the following steps.

- Bring up the "Breakpoints" window found on the "Debug" menu under "Windows" and then "Breakpoints" (Figure 2.15).
- Select the "New" drop-down button in the upper-left corner of the window.

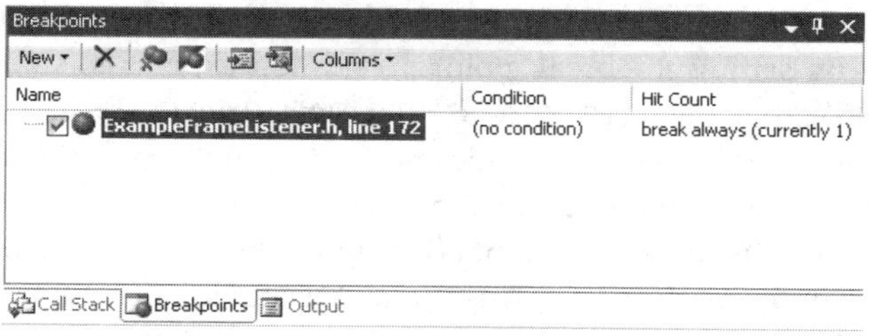

Figure 2.15. The Visual Studio break points window.

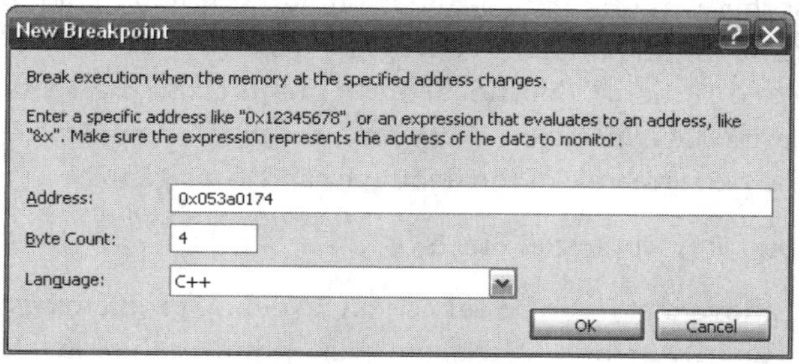

Figure 2.16. Defining a data break point.

- Select "New Data Breakpoint."
- Type in the raw address or an address-valued expression, such as "&myVariable" (Figure 2.16).

The "Byte count" field should almost always contain the value 4. This is because 32-bit Pentium CPUs can really only inspect 4-byte (32-bit) values natively. Specifying any other data size requires the debugger to do some trickery which tends to slow your program's execution to a crawl (if it works at all).

### 2.2.5.7. Conditional Break Points

You'll also notice in the "Break Points" window that you can set conditions and hit counts on any type break point—data break points or regular line-of-code break points.

A *conditional break point* causes the debugger to evaluate the C/C++ expression you provide every time the break point is hit. If the expression is true, the debugger stops your program and gives you a chance to see what's going on. If the expression is false, the break point is ignored and the program continues. This is very useful for setting break points that only trip when a function is called on a particular instance of a class. For example, let's say you have a game level with 20 tanks on-screen, and you want to stop your program when the third tank, whose memory address you know to be 0x12345678, is running. By setting the break point's condition express to something like "(unsigned)this == 0x12345678", you can restrict the break point only to the class instance whose memory address (this pointer) is 0x12345678.

Specifying a *hit count* for a break point causes the debugger to decrement a counter every time the break point is hit, and only actually stop the program when that counter reaches zero. This is really useful for situations where your break point is inside a loop, and you need to inspect what's happening during the 376th iteration of the loop (e.g., the 376th element in an array). You can't very well sit there and hit the F5 key 375 times! But you *can* let the hit count feature of Visual Studio do it for you.

One note of caution: Conditional break points cause the debugger to evaluate the conditional expression every time the break point is hit, so they can bog down the performance of the debugger and your game.

### 2.2.5.8. Debugging Optimized Builds

I mentioned above that it can be very tricky to debug problems using a release build, due primarily to the way the compiler optimizes the code. Ideally, every programmer would prefer to do all of his or her debugging in a debug build. However, this is often not possible. Sometimes a bug occurs so rarely that you'll jump at any chance to debug the problem, even if it occurs in a release build on someone else's machine. Other bugs only occur in your release build, but magically disappear whenever you run the debug build. These dreaded *release-only bugs* are sometimes caused by uninitialized variables, because variables and dynamically allocated memory blocks are often set to zero in debug mode, but are left containing garbage in a release build. Other common causes of release-only bugs include code that has been accidentally omitted from the release build (e.g., when important code is erroneously placed inside an assertion statement), data structures whose size or data member packing changes between debug and release builds, bugs that are only triggered by inlining or compiler-introduced optimizations, and (in rare cases) bugs in the compiler's optimizer itself, causing it to emit incorrect code in a fully optimized build.

Clearly, it behooves every programmer to be capable of debugging problems in a release build, unpleasant as it may seem. The best ways to reduce the pain of debugging optimized code is to practice doing it and to expand your skill set in this area whenever you have the opportunity. Here are a few tips.

- *Learn to read and step through disassembly in the debugger.* In a release build, the debugger often has trouble keeping track of which line of source code is currently being executed. Thanks to instruction reordering, you'll often see the program counter jump around erratically within the function when viewed in source code mode. However, things become sane again when you work with the code in disassembly mode (i.e., step through the assembly language instructions individually). Every C/C++ programmer should be at least a little bit familiar with the architecture and assembly language of their target CPU(s). That way, even if the debugger is confused, you won't be.

- *Use registers to deduce variables' values or addresses.* The debugger will sometimes be unable to display the value of a variable or the contents of an object in a release build. However, if the program counter is not too far away from the initial use of the variable, there's a good chance its address or value is still stored in one of the CPU's registers. If you can trace back through the disassembly to where the variable is first loaded into a register, you can often discover its value or its address by inspecting that register. Use the register window, or type the name of the register into a watch window, to see its contents.

- *Inspect variables and object contents by address.* Given the address of a variable or data structure, you can usually see its contents by casting the address to the appropriate type in a watch window. For example, if we know that an instance of the Foo class resides at address 0x1378A0C0, we can type "(Foo*)0x1378A0C0" in a watch window, and the debugger will interpret that memory address as if it were a pointer to a Foo object.

- *Leverage static and global variables.* Even in an optimized build, the debugger can usually inspect global and static variables. If you cannot deduce the address of a variable or object, keep your eye open for a static or global that might contain its address, either directly or indirectly. For example, if we want to find the address of an internal object within the physics system, we might discover that it is in fact stored in a member variable of the global PhysicsWorld object.

- *Modify the code.* If you can reproduce a release-only bug relatively easily, consider modifying the source code to help you debug the problem. Add print statements so you can see what's going on. Introduce a global variable to make it easier to inspect a problematic variable or object in the debugger. Add code to detect a problem condition or to isolate a particular instance of a class.

## 2.3.   Profiling Tools

Games are typically high-performance real-time programs. As such, game engine programmers are always looking for ways to speed up their code. There is a well-known, albeit rather unscientific, rule of thumb known as the *Pareto principle* (see http://en.wikipedia.org/wiki/Pareto_principle). It is also known as the *80-20 rule*, because it states that in many situations, 80% of the effects of some event come from only 20% of the possible causes. In computer science, we often use a variant of this principle known as the *90-10 rule*, which states that 90% of the wall clock time spent running any piece of software is accounted for by only 10% of the code. In other words, if you optimize 10% of your code, you can potentially realize 90% of all the gains in execution speed you'll ever realize.

So, how do you know *which* 10% of your code to optimize? For that, you need a *profiler*. A profiler is a tool that measures the execution time of your code. It can tell you how much time is spent in each function. You can then direct your optimizations toward only those functions that account for the lion's share of the execution time.

Some profilers also tell you how many *times* each function is called. This is an important dimension to understand. A function can eat up time for two reasons: (a) it takes a long time to execute on its own, or (b) it is called frequently. For example, a function that runs an A* algorithm to compute the optimal paths through the game world might only be called a few times each frame, but the function itself may take a significant amount of time to run. On the other hand, a function that computes the dot product may only take a few cycles to execute, but if you call it hundreds of thousands of times per frame, it might drag down your game's frame rate.

Even more information can be obtained, if you use the right profiler. Some profilers report the call graph, meaning that for any given function, you can see which functions called it (these are known as *parent functions*) and which functions it called (these are known as *child functions* or *descendants*). You can even see what *percentage* of the function's time was spent calling each of its descendants and the percentage of the overall running time accounted for by each individual function.

Profilers fall into two broad categories.

1. *Statistical profilers.* This kind of profiler is designed to be unobtrusive, meaning that the target code runs at almost the same speed, whether or not profiling is enabled. These profilers work by sampling the CPU's program counter register periodically and noting which function is currently running. The number of samples taken within each function yields an approximate percentage of the total running time that is eaten up by that function. Intel's *VTune* is the gold standard in statistical profilers for Windows machines employing Intel Pentium processors, and it is now also available for Linux. See http://www.

intel.com/cd/software/products/asmo-na/eng/vtune/239144.htm    for details.

2. *Instrumenting profilers.* This kind of profiler is aimed at providing the most accurate and comprehensive timing data possible, but at the expense of real-time execution of the target program—when profiling is turned on, the target program usually slows to a crawl. These profilers work by preprocessing your executable and inserting special prologue and epilogue code into every function. The prologue and epilogue code calls into a profiling library, which in turn inspects the program's call stack and records all sorts of details, including which parent function called the function in question and how many times that parent has called the child. This kind of profiler can even be set up to monitor every line of code in your source program, allowing it to report how long each line is taking to execute. The results are stunningly accurate and comprehensive, but turning on profiling can make a game virtually unplayable. IBM's Rational Quantify, available as part of the Rational Purify Plus tool suite, is an excellent instrumenting profiler. See http://www. ibm.com/developerworks/rational/library/957.html for an introduction to profiling with Quantify.

Microsoft has also published a profiler that is a hybrid between the two approaches. It is called LOP, which stands for low-overhead profiler. It uses a statistical approach, sampling the state of the processor periodically, which means it has a low impact on the speed of the program's execution. However, with each sample it analyzes the call stack, thereby determining the chain of parent functions that resulted in each sample. This allows LOP to provide information normally not available with a statistical profiler, such as the distribution of calls across parent functions.

### 2.3.1. List of Profilers

There are a great many profiling tools available. See http://en.wikipedia.org/ wiki/List_of_performance_analysis_tool for a reasonably comprehensive list.

## 2.4. Memory Leak and Corruption Detection

Two other problems that plague C and C++ programmers are memory leaks and memory corruption. A memory leak occurs when memory is allocated but never freed. This wastes memory and eventually leads to a potentially fatal out-of-memory condition. Memory corruption occurs when the program inadvertently writes data to the wrong memory location, overwriting the important data that was there—while simultaneously failing to update the memory location where that data *should* have been written. Blame for both of these problems falls squarely on the language feature known as the *pointer*.

A pointer is a powerful tool. It can be an agent of good when used properly—but it can also be all-too-easily transformed into an agent of evil. If a pointer points to memory that has been freed, or if it is accidentally assigned a nonzero integer or floating-point value, it becomes a dangerous tool for corrupting memory, because data written through it can quite literally end up anywhere. Likewise, when pointers are used to keep track of allocated memory, it is all too easy to forget to free the memory when it is no longer needed. This leads to memory leaks.

Clearly good coding practices are one approach to avoiding pointer-related memory problems. And it is certainly possible to write solid code that essentially never corrupts or leaks memory. Nonetheless, having a tool to help you detect potential memory corruption and leak problems certainly can't hurt. Thankfully, many such tools exist.

My personal favorite is IBM's Rational Purify, which comes as part of the Purify Plus tool kit. Purify instruments your code prior to running it, in order to hook into all pointer dereferences and all memory allocations and deallocations made by your code. When you run your code under Purify, you get a live report of the problems—real and potential—encountered by your code. And when the program exits, you get a detailed memory leak report. Each problem is linked directly to the source code that caused the problem, making tracking down and fixing these kinds of problems relatively easy. You can find more information on Purify at http://www-306.ibm.com/software/awdtools /purify.

Another popular tool is Bounds Checker by CompuWare. It is similar to Purify in purpose and functionality. You can find more information on Bounds Checker at http://www.compuware.com/products/devpartner/visualc .htm.

## 2.5.   Other Tools

There are a number of other commonly used tools in a game programmer's toolkit. We won't cover them in any depth here, but the following list will make you aware of their existence and point you in the right direction if you want to learn more.

- *Difference tools.* A difference tool, or *diff tool*, is a program that compares two versions of a text file and determines what has changed between them. (See http://en.wikipedia.org/wiki/Diff for a discussion of diff tools.) Diffs are usually calculated on a line-by-line basis, although modern diff tools can also show you a range of characters on a changed line that have been modified. Most version control systems come with a diff tool. Some programmers like a particular diff tool and configure their version control software to use the tool of their choice. Popular tools include ExamDiff (http://www.prestosoft.com/edp_examdiff.asp), AraxisMerge (http://www.araxis.com), WinDiff (available in the Options Packs for most Windows versions and available from many independent websites as well), and the GNU diff tools package (http://www.gnu.org/software/diffutils/diffutils.html).

- *Three-way merge tools.* When two people edit the same file, two independent sets of diffs are generated. A tool that can merge two sets of diffs into a final version of the file that contains both person's changes is called a three-way merge tool. The name "three-way" refers to the fact that three versions of the file are involved: the original, user A's version, and user B's version. (See http://en.wikipedia.org/wiki/3-way_merge#Three-way_merge for a discussion of two-way and three-way merge technologies.) Many merge tools come with an associated diff tool. Some popular merge tools include AraxisMerge (http://www.araxis.com) and WinMerge (http://winmerge.org). Perforce also comes with an excellent three-way merge tool (http://www.perforce.com/perforce/products/merge.html).

- *Hex editors.* A hex editor is a program used for inspecting and modifying the contents of binary files. The data are usually displayed as integers in hexadecimal format, hence the name. Most good hex editors can display data as integers from one byte to 16 bytes each, in 32- and 64-bit floating point format and as ASCII text. Hex editors are particularly useful when tracking down problems with binary file formats or when reverse-engineering an unknown binary format—both of which are relatively common endeavors in game engine development circles. There are quite literally a million different hex editors out there; I've had good luck with HexEdit by Expert Commercial Software (http://www.expertcomsoft.com/index.html), but your mileage may vary.

As a game engine programmer you will undoubtedly come across other tools that make your life easier, but I hope this chapter has covered the main tools you'll use on a day-to-day basis.

# 3
# Fundamentals of Software Engineering for Games

In this chapter, we'll briefly review the basic concepts of object-oriented programming and then delve into some advanced topics which should prove invaluable in any software engineering endeavor (and especially when creating games). As with Chapter 2, I hope you will not to skip this chapter entirely; it's important that we all embark on our journey with the same set of tools and supplies.

## 3.1.  C++ Review and Best Practices

### 3.1.1.  Brief Review of Object-Oriented Programming

Much of what we'll discuss in this book assumes you have a solid understanding of the principles of object-oriented design. If you're a bit rusty, the following section should serve as a pleasant and quick review. If you have no idea what I'm talking about in this section, I recommend you pick up a book or two on object-oriented programming (e.g., [5]) and C++ in particular (e.g., [39] and [31]) before continuing.

#### 3.1.1.1.  Classes and Objects

A *class* is a collection of attributes (data) and behaviors (code) which together form a useful, meaningful whole. A class is a *specification* describing how individual *instances* of the class, known as *objects,* should be constructed. For example, your pet Rover is an instance of the class "dog." Thus there is a one-to-many relationship between a class and its instances.

### 3.1.1.2.  Encapsulation

*Encapsulation* means that an object presents only a limited interface to the outside world; the object's internal state and implementation details are kept hidden. Encapsulation simplifies life for the user of the class, because he or she need only understand the class' limited interface, not the potentially intricate details of its implementation. It also allows the programmer who wrote the class to ensure that its instances are always in a logically consistent state.

### 3.1.1.3.  Inheritance

*Inheritance* allows new classes to be defined as *extensions* to pre-existing classes. The new class modifies or extends the data, interface, and/or behavior of the existing class. If class Child extends class Parent, we say that Child *inherits from* or is *derived from* Parent. In this relationship, the class Parent is known as the *base class* or *superclass,* and the class Child is the *derived class* or *subclass.* Clearly, inheritance leads to hierarchical (tree-structured) relationships between classes.

Inheritance creates an "is-a" relationship between classes. For example, a circle *is a* type of shape. So if we were writing a 2D drawing application, it would probably make sense to derive our Circle class from a base class called Shape.

We can draw diagrams of class hierarchies using the conventions defined by the Unified Modeling Language (UML). In this notation, a rectangle represents a class, and an arrow with a hollow triangular head represents inheritance. The inheritance arrow points from child class to parent. See Figure 3.1 for an example of a simple class hierarchy represented as a UML *static class diagram.*

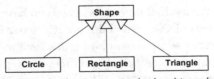

Figure 3.1. UML static class diagram depicting a simple class hierarchy.

#### Multiple Inheritance

Some languages support *multiple inheritance* (MI), meaning that a class can have more than one parent class. In theory MI can be quite elegant, but in

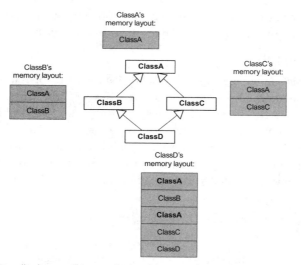

Figure 3.2. "Deadly diamond" in a multiple inheritance hierarchy.

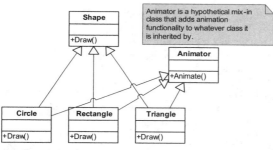

Figure 3.3. Example of a mix-in class.

practice this kind of design usually gives rise to a lot of confusion and technical difficulties (see http://en.wikipedia.org/wiki/Multiple_inheritance). This is because multiple inheritance transforms a simple *tree* of classes into a potentially complex *graph*. A class graph can have all sorts of problems that never plague a simple tree—for example, the *deadly diamond* (http://en.wikipedia.org/wiki/Diamond_problem), in which a derived class ends up containing *two copies* of a grandparent base class (see Figure 3.2). In C++, *virtual inheritance* allows one to avoid this doubling of the grandparent's data.

Most C++ software developers avoid multiple inheritance completely or only permit it in a limited form. A common rule of thumb is to allow only simple, parentless classes to be multiply inherited into an otherwise strictly single-inheritance hierarchy. Such classes are sometimes called *mix-in classes* because they can be used to introduce new functionality at arbitrary points in a class tree. See Figure 3.3 for a somewhat contrived example of a mix-in class.

### 3.1.1.4.   Polymorphism

*Polymorphism* is a language feature that allows a collection of objects of different types to be manipulated through a single *common interface*. The common interface makes a heterogeneous collection of objects *appear* to be homogeneous, from the point of view of the code using the interface.

For example, a 2D painting program might be given a list of various shapes to draw on-screen. One way to draw this heterogeneous collection of shapes is to use a switch statement to perform different drawing commands for each distinct type of shape.

```cpp
void drawShapes(std::list<Shape*> shapes)
{
    std::list<Shape*>::iterator pShape = shapes.begin();
    std::list<Shape*>::iterator pEnd = shapes.end();

    for ( ; pShape != pEnd; ++pShape)
    {
        switch (pShape->mType)
        {
        case CIRCLE:
            // draw shape as a circle
            break;

        case RECTANGLE:
            // draw shape as a rectangle
            break;

        case TRIANGLE:
            // draw shape as a triangle
            break;
        //...
        }
    }
}
```

The problem with this approach is that the drawShapes() function needs to "know" about all of the kinds of shapes that can be drawn. This is fine in a simple example, but as our code grows in size and complexity, it can become difficult to add new types of shapes to the system. Whenever a new shape type is added, one must find every place in the code base where knowledge of the set of shape types is embedded—like this switch statement—and add a case to handle the new type.

The solution is to insulate the majority of our code from any knowledge of the types of objects with which it might be dealing. To accomplish this, we can define classes for each of the types of shapes we wish to support. All of these classes would inherit from the common base class Shape. A *virtual function*—the C++ language's primary polymorphism mechanism—would be defined called Draw(), and each distinct shape class would implement this function in a different way. Without "knowing" what specific types of shapes it has been given, the drawing function can now simply call each shape's Draw() function in turn.

```cpp
struct Shape
{
    virtual void Draw() = 0;    // pure virtual function
};

struct Circle : public Shape
{
    virtual void Draw()
    {
        // draw shape as a circle
    }
};

struct Rectangle : public Shape
{
    virtual void Draw()
    {
        // draw shape as a rectangle
    }
};

struct Triangle : public Shape
{
    void Draw()
    {
        // draw shape as a triangle
    }
};

void drawShapes(std::list<Shape*> shapes)
{
    std::list<Shape*>::iterator pShape = shapes.begin();
    std::list<Shape*>::iterator pEnd = shapes.end();

    for ( ; pShape != pEnd; ++pShape)
    {
        pShape->Draw();
    }
}
```

### 3.1.1.5.  Composition and Aggregation

*Composition* is the practice of using a *group* of *interacting* objects to accomplish a high-level task. Composition creates a "has-a" or "uses-a" relationship between classes. (Technically speaking, the "has-a" relationship is called *composition*, while the "uses-a" relationship is called *aggregation*.) For example, a space ship *has an* engine, which in turn *has a* fuel tank. Composition/aggregation usually results in the individual classes being simpler and more focused. Inexperienced object-oriented programmers often rely too heavily on inheritance and tend to underutilize aggregation and composition.

As an example, imagine that we are designing a graphical user interface for our game's front end. We have a class `Window` that represents any rectangular GUI element. We also have a class called `Rectangle` that encapsulates the mathematical concept of a rectangle. A naïve programmer might derive the `Window` class from the `Rectangle` class (using an "is-a" relationship). But in a more flexible and well-encapsulated design, the `Window` class would *refer to* or *contain* a `Rectangle` (employing a "has-a" *or* "uses-a" relationship). This makes both classes simpler and more focused and allows the classes to be more easily tested, debugged, and reused.

### 3.1.1.6.  Design Patterns

When the same type of problem arises over and over, and many different programmers employ a very similar solution to that problem, we say that a *design pattern* has arisen. In object-oriented programming, a number of common design patterns have been identified and described by various authors. The most well-known book on this topic is probably the "Gang of Four" book [17].

Here are a few examples of common general-purpose design patterns.

- *Singleton.* This pattern ensures that a particular class has only one instance (the *singleton instance*) and provides a global point of access to it.
- *Iterator.* An iterator provides an efficient means of accessing the individual elements of a collection, without exposing the collection's underlying implementation. The iterator "knows" the implementation details of the collection, so that its users don't have to.
- *Abstract factory.* An abstract factory provides an interface for creating families of related or dependent classes without specifying their concrete classes.

The game industry has its own set of design patterns, for addressing problems in every realm from rendering to collision to animation to audio. In a sense, this book is all about the high-level design patterns prevalent in modern 3D game engine design.

## 3.1.2. Coding Standards: Why and How Much?

Discussions of coding conventions among engineers can often lead to heated "religious" debates. I do not wish to spark any such debate here, but I will go so far as to suggest that following at least some minimal coding standards is a good idea. Coding standards exist for two primary reasons.

1. Some standards make the code more readable, understandable, and maintainable.

2. Other conventions help to prevent programmers from shooting themselves in the foot. For example, a coding standard might encourage the programmer to use only a smaller, more testable, and less error-prone subset of the whole language. The C++ language is rife with possibilities for abuse, so this kind of coding standard is particularly important when using C++.

In my opinion, the most important things to achieve in your coding conventions are the following.

- *Interfaces are king.* Keep your interfaces (.h files) clean, simple, minimal, easy to understand, and well-commented.

- *Good names encourage understanding and avoid confusion.* Stick to intuitive names that map directly to the purpose of the class, function, or variable in question. Spend time up-front identifying a good name. Avoid a naming scheme that requires programmers to use a look-up table in order to decipher the meaning of your code. Remember that high-level programming languages like C++ are intended for *humans* to read. (If you disagree, just ask yourself why you don't write all your software directly in machine language.)

- *Don't clutter the global namespace.* Use C++ namespaces or a common naming prefix to ensure that your symbols don't collide with symbols in other libraries. (But be careful not to overuse namespaces, or nest them too deeply.) Name #defined symbols with extra care; remember that C++ preprocessor macros are really just text substitutions, so they cut across all C/C++ scope and namespace boundaries.

- *Follow C++ best practices.* Books like the *Effective C++* series by Scott Meyers [31, 32], Meyers' *Effective STL* [33], and *Large-Scale C++ Software Design* by John Lakos [27] provide excellent guidelines that will help keep you out of trouble.

- *Be consistent.* The rule I try to use is as follows: If you're writing a body of code from scratch, feel free to invent any convention you like—then stick to it. When editing pre-existing code, try to follow whatever conventions have already been established.

- *Make errors stick out.* Joel Spolsky wrote an excellent article on coding conventions, which can be found at http://www.joelonsoftware.com/ articles/Wrong.html. Joel suggests that the "cleanest" code is not necessarily code that looks neat and tidy on a superficial level, but rather the code that is written in a way that makes common programming errors *easier to see.* Joel's articles are always fun and educational, and I highly recommend this one.

## 3.2.    Data, Code, and Memory in C/C++

### 3.2.1.    Numeric Representations

Numbers are at the heart of everything that we do in game engine development (and software development in general). Every software engineer should understand how numbers are represented and stored by a computer. This section will provide you with the basics you'll need throughout the rest of the book.

#### 3.2.1.1.    Numeric Bases

People think most naturally in *base ten*, also known as *decimal notation*. In this notation, ten distinct digits are used (0 through 9), and each digit from right to left represents the next highest power of 10. For example, the number 7803 = $(7 \times 10^3) + (8 \times 10^2) + (0 \times 10^1) + (3 \times 10^0) = 7000 + 800 + 0 + 3$.

In computer science, mathematical quantities such as integers and real-valued numbers need to be stored in the computer's memory. And as we know, computers store numbers in *binary* format, meaning that only the two digits 0 and 1 are available. We call this a *base-two* representation, because each digit from right to left represents the next highest power of 2. Computer scientists sometimes use a prefix of "0b" to represent binary numbers. For example, the binary number 0b1101 is equivalent to decimal 13, because 0b1101 = $(1 \times 2^3) + (1 \times 2^2) + (0 \times 2^1) + (1 \times 2^0) = 8 + 4 + 0 + 1 = 13$.

Another common notation popular in computing circles is *hexadecimal*, or *base 16*. In this notation, the 10 digits 0 through 9 and the six letters A through F are used; the letters A through F replace the decimal values 10 through 15, respectively. A prefix of "0x" is used to denote hex numbers in the C and C++ programming languages. This notation is popular because computers generally store data in groups of 8 bits known as *bytes*, and since a single hexadecimal digit represents 4 bits exactly, a *pair* of hex digits represents a byte. For example, the value 0xFF = 0b11111111 = 255 is the largest number that can be stored in 8 bits (1 byte). Each digit in a hexadecimal number, from right to left, represents the next power of 16. So, for example, 0xB052 = $(11 \times 16^3) + (0 \times 16^2) + (5 \times 16^1) + (2 \times 16^0) = (11 \times 4096) + (0 \times 256) + (5 \times 16) + (2 \times 1) = 45,138$.

### 3.2.1.2.  Signed and Unsigned Integers

In computer science, we use both signed and unsigned integers. Of course, the term "unsigned integer" is actually a bit of a misnomer—in mathematics, the *whole numbers* or *natural numbers* range from 0 (or 1) up to positive infinity, while the *integers* range from negative infinity to positive infinity. Nevertheless, we'll use computer science lingo in this book and stick with the terms "signed integer" and "unsigned integer."

Most modern personal computers and game consoles work most easily with integers that are 32 bits or 64 bits wide (although 8- and 16-bit integers are also used a great deal in game programming as well). To represent a 32-bit unsigned integer, we simply encode the value using binary notation (see above). The range of possible values for a 32-bit unsigned integer is 0x00000000 (0) to 0xFFFFFFFF (4,294,967,295).

To represent a *signed* integer in 32 bits, we need a way to differentiate between positive and negative vales. One simple approach would be to reserve the most significant bit as a *sign bit*—when this bit is zero the value is positive, and when it is one the value is negative. This gives us 31 bits to represent the magnitude of the value, effectively cutting the range of possible magnitudes in half (but allowing both positive and negative forms of each distinct magnitude, including zero).

Most microprocessors use a slightly more efficient technique for encoding negative integers, called *two's complement* notation. This notation has only one representation for the value zero, as opposed to the two representations possible with simple sign bit (positive zero and negative zero). In 32-bit two's complement notation, the value 0xFFFFFFFF is interpreted to mean −1, and negative values count down from there. Any value with the most significant bit set is considered negative. So values from 0x00000000 (0) to 0x7FFFFFFF (2,147,483,647) represent positive integers, and 0x80000000 (−2,147,483,648) to 0xFFFFFFFF (−1) represent negative integers.

### 3.2.1.3.  Fixed-Point Notation

Integers are great for representing whole numbers, but to represent fractions and irrational numbers we need a different format that expresses the concept of a decimal point.

One early approach taken by computer scientists was to use *fixed-point* notation. In this notation, one arbitrarily chooses how many bits will be used to represent the whole part of the number, and the rest of the bits are used to represent the fractional part. As we move from left to right (i.e., from the most significant bit to the least significant bit), the magnitude bits represent decreasing powers of two (…, 16, 8, 4, 2, 1), while the fractional bits represent

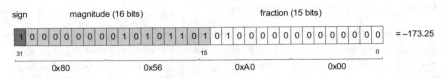

Figure 3.4. Fixed-point notation with l6-bit magnitude and l6-bit fraction.

decreasing *inverse* powers of two ($\frac{1}{2}$, $\frac{1}{4}$, $\frac{1}{8}$, $\frac{1}{16}$, ...). For example, to store the number −173.25 in 32-bit fixed-point notation, with one sign bit, 16 bits for the magnitude and 15 bits for the fraction, we first convert the sign, the whole part and fractional part into their binary equivalents individually (negative = 0b1, 173 = 0b0000000010101101, and 0.25 = 1/4 = 0b010000000000000). Then we pack those values together into a 32-bit integer. The final result is 0x8056A000. This is illustrated in Figure 3.4.

The problem with fixed-point notation is that it constrains both the range of magnitudes that can be represented and the amount of precision we can achieve in the fractional part. Consider a 32-bit fixed-point value with 16 bits for the magnitude, 15 bits for the fraction, and a sign bit. This format can only represent magnitudes up to ±65,535, which isn't particularly large. To overcome this problem, we employ a *floating-point* representation.

### 3.2.1.4. Floating-Point Notation

In floating-point notation, the position of the decimal place is arbitrary and is specified with the help of an exponent. A floating-point number is broken into three parts: the *mantissa*, which contains the relevant digits of the number on both sides of the decimal point, the *exponent*, which indicates where in that string of digits the decimal point lies, and a *sign bit*, which of course indicates whether the value is positive or negative. There are all sorts of different ways to lay out these three components in memory, but the most common standard is IEEE-754. It states that a 32-bit floating-point number will be represented with the sign in the most significant bit, followed by 8 bits of exponent, and finally 23 bits of mantissa.

The value $v$ represented by a sign bit $s$, an exponent $e$ and a mantissa $m$ is $v = s \times 2^{(e-127)} \times (1 + m)$.

The sign bit $s$ has the value +1 or −1. The exponent $e$ is biased by 127 so that negative exponents can be easily represented. The mantissa begins with an implicit 1 that is not actually stored in memory, and the rest of the bits are interpreted as inverse powers of two. Hence the value represented is really 1 + $m$, where $m$ is the fractional value stored in the mantissa.

Figure 3.5. IEEE-754 32-bit floating-point format.

For example, the bit pattern shown in Figure 3.5 represents the value 0.15625, because $s = 0$ (indicating a positive number), $e = 0b01111100 = 124$, and $m = 0b0100\ldots = 0\times2^{-1} + 1\times2^{-2} = \frac{1}{4}$. Therefore,

$$
\begin{aligned}
v &= s \times 2^{(e-127)} \times (1+m) \\
&= (+1) \times 2^{(124-127)} \times (1 + \tfrac{1}{4}) \\
&= 2^{-3} \times \tfrac{5}{4} \\
&= \tfrac{1}{8} \times \tfrac{5}{4} \\
&= 0.125 \times 1.25 = 0.15625.
\end{aligned}
\tag{3.1}
$$

### The Trade-Off between Magnitude and Precision

The *precision* of a floating-point number increases as the *magnitude* decreases, and vice versa. This is because there are a fixed number of bits in the mantissa, and these bits must be shared between the whole part and the fractional part of the number. If a large percentage of the bits are spent representing a large magnitude, then a small percentage of bits are available to provide fractional precision. In physics the term *significant digits* is typically used to describe this concept (http://en.wikipedia.org/wiki/Significant_digits).

To understand the trade-off between magnitude and precision, let's look at the largest possible floating-point value, FLT_MAX $\approx 3.403\times10^{38}$, whose representation in 32-bit IEEE floating-point format is 0x7F7FFFFF. Let's break this down:

- The largest absolute value that we can represent with a 23-bit mantissa is 0x00FFFFFF in hexadecimal, or 24 consecutive binary ones—that's 23 ones in the mantissa, plus the implicit leading one.

- An exponent of 255 has a special meaning in the IEEE-754 format—it is used for values like not-a-number (NaN) and infinity—so it cannot be used for regular numbers. Hence the maximum 8-bit exponent is actually 254, which translates into 127 after subtracting the implicit bias of 127.

So FLT_MAX is 0x00FFFFFF$\times2^{127}$ = 0xFFFFFF00000000000000000000000000. In other words, our 24 binary ones were shifted up by 127 bit positions, leaving $127 - 23 = 104$ binary zeros (or $104/4 = 26$ hexadecimal zeros) after the least significant digit of the mantissa. Those trailing zeros don't correspond to any actual bits in our 32-bit floating-point value—they just appear out of thin air because of the exponent. If we were to subtract a small number (where "small" means any number composed of fewer than 26 hexadecimal digits) from FLT_MAX, the result would still be FLT_MAX, because those 26 least significant hexadecimal digits don't really exist!

The opposite effect occurs for floating-point values whose magnitudes are much less than one. In this case, the exponent is large but negative, and the significant digits are shifted in the opposite direction. We trade the ability to represent large magnitudes for high precision. In summary, we always have the same number of *significant digits* (or really *significant bits*) in our floating-point numbers, and the exponent can be used to shift those significant bits into higher or lower ranges of magnitude.

Another subtlety to notice is that there is a finite gap between zero and the smallest nonzero value we can represent with any floating-point notation. The smallest nonzero magnitude we can represent is FLT_MIN $= 2^{-126} \approx 1.175 \times 10^{-38}$, which has a binary representation of 0x00800000 (i.e., the exponent is 0x01, or −126 after subtracting the bias, and the mantissa is all zeros, except for the implicit leading one). There is no way to represent a nonzero magnitude that is smaller than $1.175 \times 10^{-38}$, because the next smallest valid value is zero. Put another way, the real number line is *quantized* when using a floating-point representation.

For a particular floating-point representation, the *machine epsilon* is defined to be the smallest floating-point value $\varepsilon$ that satisfies the equation, $1 + \varepsilon \neq 1$. For an IEEE-754 floating-point number, with its 23 bits of precision, the value of $\varepsilon$ is $2^{-23}$, which is approximately $1.192 \times 10^{-7}$. The most significant digit of $\varepsilon$ falls *just inside* the range of significant digits in the value 1.0, so adding any value smaller than $\varepsilon$ to 1.0 has no effect. In other words, any new bits contributed adding a value smaller than $\varepsilon$ will get "chopped off" when we try to fit the sum into a mantissa with only 23 bits.

The concepts of limited precision and the machine epsilon have real impacts on game software. For example, let's say we use a floating-point variable to track absolute game time in seconds. How long can we run our game before the magnitude of our clock variable gets so large that adding 1/30th of a second to it no longer changes its value? The answer is roughly 12.9 days. That's longer than most games will be left running, so we can probably get away with using a 32-bit floating-point clock measured in seconds in a game. But clearly it's important to understand the limitations of the floating-point format, so that we can predict potential problems and take steps to avoid them when necessary.

*IEEE Floating-Point Bit Tricks*

See [7], Section 2.1, for a few really useful IEEE floating-point "bit tricks" that can make floating-point calculations lightning-fast.

### 3.2.1.5.   Atomic Data Types

As you know, C and C++ provide a number of atomic data types. The C and C++ standards provide guidelines on the relative sizes and signedness of these data types, but each compiler is free to define the types slightly differently in order to provide maximum performance on the target hardware.

- `char`. A `char` is usually 8 bits and is generally large enough to hold an ASCII or UTF-8 character (see Section 5.4.4.1). Some compilers define `char` to be signed, while others use unsigned `chars` by default.
- `int`, `short`, `long`. An `int` is supposed to hold a signed integer value that is the most efficient size for the target platform; it is generally defined to be 32 bits wide on Pentium class PCs. A `short` is intended to be smaller than an `int` and is 16 bits on many machines. A `long` is as large as or larger than an `int` and may be 32 or 64 bits, depending on the hardware.
- `float`. On most modern compilers, a `float` is a 32-bit IEEE-754 floating-point value.
- `double`. A `double` is a double-precision (i.e., 64-bit) IEEE-754 floating-point value.
- `bool`. A `bool` is a true/false value. The size of a `bool` varies widely across different compilers and hardware architectures. It is never implemented as a single bit, but some compilers define it to be 8 bits while others use a full 32 bits.

*Compiler-Specific Sized Types*

The standard C/C++ atomic data types were designed to be portable and therefore nonspecific. However, in many software engineering endeavors, including game engine programming, it is often important to know exactly how wide a particular variable is. The Visual Studio C/C++ compiler defines the following extended keywords for declaring variables that are an explicit number of bits wide: `__int8`, `__int16`, `__int32`, and `__int64`.

*SIMD Types*

The CPUs on many modern computers and game consoles have a specialized type of arithmetic logic unit (ALU) referred to as a *vector processor* or *vector unit*. A vector processor supports a form of parallel processing known as *single instruction, multiple data* (SIMD), in which a mathematical operation is performed on multiple quantities in parallel, using a single machine instruction. In order to be processed by the vector unit, two or more quantities are packed into a 64- or 128-bit CPU register. In game programming, the most commonly used SIMD register format packs four 32-bit IEEE-754 floating-point quantities into a 128-bit SIMD register. This format allows us to perform calculations such as vector dot products and matrix multiplications much more efficiently than would be possible with a SISD (single instruction, single data) ALU.

Each microprocessor has a different name for its SIMD instruction set, and the compilers that target those microprocessors use a custom syntax to declare SIMD variables. For example, on a Pentium class CPU, the SIMD instruction set is known as *SSE* (streaming SIMD extensions), and the Microsoft Visual Studio compiler provides the built-in data type `__m128` to represent a four-float SIMD quantity. The PowerPC class of CPUs used on the PLAYSTATION 3 and Xbox 360 calls its SIMD instruction set *Altivec*, and the Gnu C++ compiler uses the syntax `vector float` to declare a packed four-float SIMD variable. We'll discuss how SIMD programming works in more detail in Section 4.7.

### Portable Sized Types

Most other compilers have their own "sized" data types, with similar semantics but slightly different syntax. Because of these differences between compilers, most game engines achieve source code portability by defining their own custom atomic data types. For example, at Naughty Dog we use the following atomic types:

- `F32` is a 32-bit IEEE-754 floating-point value.

- `U8`, `I8`, `U16`, `I16`, `U32`, `I32`, `U64`, and `I64` are unsigned and signed 8-, 16-, 32-, and 64-bit integers, respectively.

- `U32F` and `I32F` are "fast" unsigned and signed 32-bit values, respectively. Each of these data types acts as though it contains a 32-bit value, but it actually occupies 64 bits in memory. This permits the PS3's central PowerPC-based processor (called the PPU) to read and write these variables directly into its 64-bit registers, providing a significant speed boost over reading and writing 32-bit variables.

- `VF32` represents a packed four-float SIMD value.

### OGRE's Atomic Data Types

OGRE defines a number of atomic types of its own. `Ogre::uint8`, `Ogre::uint16` and `Ogre::uint32` are the basic unsigned sized integral types.

`Ogre::Real` defines a real floating-point value. It is usually defined to be 32 bits wide (equivalent to a `float`), but it can be redefined globally to be 64 bits wide (like a `double`) by defining the preprocessor macro `OGRE_DOU-BLE_PRECISION` to `1`. This ability to change the meaning of `Ogre::Real` is generally only used if one's game has a particular requirement for double-precision math, which is rare. Graphics chips (GPUs) always perform their math with 32-bit or 16-bit floats, the CPU/FPU is also usually faster when working in single-precision, and SIMD vector instructions operate on 128-bit registers that contain four 32-bit floats each. Hence most games tend to stick to single-precision floating-point math.

The data types `Ogre::uchar`, `Ogre::ushort`, `Ogre::uint` and `Ogre::ulong` are just shorthand notations for C/C++'s `unsigned char`, `unsigned short`, and `unsigned long`, respectively. As such, they are no more or less useful than their native C/C++ counterparts.

The types `Ogre::Radian` and `Ogre::Degree` are particularly interesting. These classes are wrappers around a simple `Ogre::Real` value. The primary role of these types is to permit the angular units of hard-coded literal constants to be documented and to provide automatic conversion between the two unit systems. In addition, the type `Ogre::Angle` represents an angle in the current "default" angle unit. The programmer can define whether the default will be radians or degrees when the OGRE application first starts up.

Perhaps surprisingly, OGRE does not provide a number of sized atomic data types that are commonplace in other game engines. For example, it defines no signed 8-, 16-, or 64-bit integral types. If you are writing a game engine on top of OGRE, you will probably find yourself defining these types manually at some point.

### 3.2.1.6. Multi-Byte Values and Endianness

Values that are larger than eight bits (one byte) wide are called *multi-byte quantities*. They're commonplace on any software project that makes use of integers and floating-point values that are 16 bits or wider. For example, the integer value 4660 = 0x1234 is represented by the two bytes 0x12 and 0x34. We call 0x12 the most significant byte (MSB) and 0x34 the least significant byte (LSB). In a 32-bit value, such as 0xABCD1234, the MSB is 0xAB and the LSB is 0x34. The same concepts apply to 64-bit integers and to 32- and 64-bit floating-point values as well.

Multi-byte integers can be stored into memory in one of two ways, and different microprocessors may differ in their choice of storage method (see Figure 3.6).

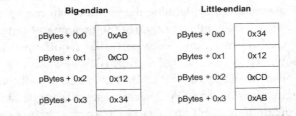

```
U32 value  = 0xABCD1234;
U8* pBytes = (U8*)&value;
```

**Big-endian**

| pBytes + 0x0 | 0xAB |
| pBytes + 0x1 | 0xCD |
| pBytes + 0x2 | 0x12 |
| pBytes + 0x3 | 0x34 |

**Little-endian**

| pBytes + 0x0 | 0x34 |
| pBytes + 0x1 | 0x12 |
| pBytes + 0x2 | 0xCD |
| pBytes + 0x3 | 0xAB |

**Figure 3.6.** Big- and little-endian representations of the value 0xABCD1234.

- *Little-endian.* If a microprocessor stores the least significant byte (LSB) of a multi-byte value at a lower memory address than the most significant byte (MSB), we say that the processor is *little-endian*. On a little-endian machine, the number 0xABCD1234 would be stored in memory using the consecutive bytes 0x34, 0x12, 0xCD, 0xAB.

- *Big-endian.* If a microprocessor stores the most significant byte (MSB) of a multi-byte value at a lower memory address than the least significant byte (LSB), we say that the processor is *big-endian*. On a big-endian machine, the number 0xABCD1234 would be stored in memory using the bytes 0xAB, 0xCD, 0x12, 0x34.

Most programmers don't need to think much about endianness. However, when you're a game programmer, endianness can become a bit of a thorn in your side. This is because games are usually *developed* on a PC or Linux machine running an Intel Pentium processor (which is little-endian), but *run* on a console such as the Wii, Xbox 360, or PLAYSTATION 3—all three of which utilize a variant of the PowerPC processor (which can be configured to use either endianness, but is big-endian by default). Now imagine what happens when you generate a data file for consumption by your game engine on an Intel processor and then try to load that data file into your engine running on a PowerPC processor. Any multi-byte value that you wrote out into that data file will be stored in little-endian format. But when the game engine reads the file, it expects all of its data to be in big-endian format. The result? You'll write 0xABCD1234, but you'll read 0x3412CDAB, and that's clearly not what you intended!

There are at least two solutions to this problem.

1. You could write all your data files as text and store all multi-byte numbers as sequences of decimal digits, one character (one byte) per digit. This would be an inefficient use of disk space, but it would work.

2. You can have your tools endian-swap the data prior to writing it into a binary data file. In effect, you make sure that the data file uses the endianness of the target microprocessor (the game console), even if the tools are running on a machine that uses the opposite endianness.

*Integer Endian-Swapping*

Endian-swapping an integer is not conceptually difficult. You simply start at the most significant byte of the value and swap it with the least significant byte; you continue this process until you reach the half-way point in the value. For example, 0xA7891023 would become 0x231089A7.

The only tricky part is knowing *which bytes* to swap. Let's say you're writing the contents of a C struct or C++ class from memory out to a file. To properly endian-swap this data, you need to keep track of the locations and sizes of each data member in the struct and swap each one appropriately based on its size. For example, the structure

```
struct Example
{
    U32    m_a;
    U16    m_b;
    U32    m_c;
};
```

might be written out to a data file as follows:

```
void writeExampleStruct(Example& ex, Stream& stream)
{
    stream.writeU32(swapU32(ex.m_a));
    stream.writeU16(swapU16(ex.m_b));
    stream.writeU32(swapU32(ex.m_c));
}
```

and the swap functions might be defined like this:

```
inline U16 swapU16(U16 value)
{
    return ((value & 0x00FF) << 8)
         | ((value & 0xFF00) >> 8);
}

inline U32 swapU32(U32 value)
{
    return ((value & 0x000000FF) << 24)
         | ((value & 0x0000FF00) << 8)
         | ((value & 0x00FF0000) >> 8)
         | ((value & 0xFF000000) >> 24);
}
```

You cannot simply cast the `Example` object into an array of bytes and blindly swap the bytes using a single general-purpose function. We need to know both *which data members* to swap and *how wide* each member is; and each data member must be swapped individually.

*Floating-Point Endian-Swapping*

Let's take a brief look at how floating-point endian-swapping differs from integer endian-swapping. As we've seen, an IEEE-754 floating-point value has a detailed internal structure involving some bits for the mantissa, some bits for the exponent, and a sign bit. However, you can endian-swap it just as if it were an integer, because bytes are bytes. You can reinterpret floats as integers by using C++'s `reinterpret_cast` operator on a pointer to the float; this is known as *type punning*. But punning can lead to optimization bugs when strict aliasing is enabled. (See http://cocoawithlove.com/2008/04/using-pointers-to-recast-in-c-is-bad.html for an excellent description of this problem.) One convenient approach is to use a union, as follows:

```cpp
union U32F32
{
    U32     m_asU32;
    F32     m_asF32;
};

inline F32 swapF32(F32 value)
{
    U32F32 u;
    u.m_asF32 = value;

    // endian-swap as integer
    u.m_asU32 = swapU32(u.m_asU32);

    return u.m_asF32;
}
```

## 3.2.2. Declarations, Definitions, and Linkage

### 3.2.2.1. Translation Units Revisited

As we saw in Chapter 2, a C or C++ program is comprised of *translation units*. The compiler translates one .cpp file at a time, and for each one it generates an output file called an object file (.o or .obj). A .cpp file is the smallest unit of translation operated on by the compiler; hence, the name "translation unit." An object file contains not only the compiled machine code for all of the functions defined in the .cpp file, but also all of its global and static variables. In addition, an object file may contain *unresolved references* to functions and global variables defined in *other* .cpp files.

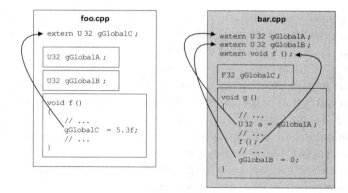

**Figure 3.7.** Unresolved external references in two translation units.

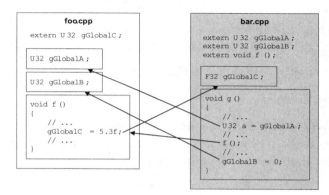

**Figure 3.8.** Fully resolved external references after successful linking.

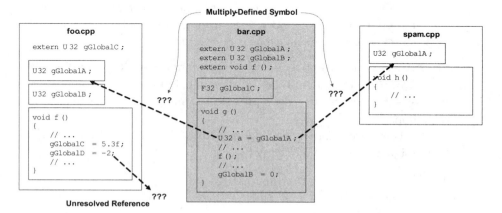

**Figure 3.9.** The two most common linker errors.

The compiler only operates on one translation unit at a time, so whenever it encounters a reference to an external global variable or function, it must "go on faith" and assume that the entity in question really exists, as shown in Figure 3.7. It is the linker's job to combine all of the object files into a final executable image. In doing so, the linker reads all of the object files and attempts to resolve all of the unresolved cross-references between them. If it is successful, an executable image is generated containing all of the functions, global variables, and static variables, with all cross-translation-unit references properly resolved. This is depicted in Figure 3.8.

The linker's primary job is to resolve external references, and in this capacity it can generate only two kinds of errors:

1. The target of an `extern` reference might not be found, in which case the linker generates an "unresolved symbol" error.

2. The linker might find more than one variable or function with the same name, in which case it generates a "multiply defined symbol" error.

These two situations are shown in Figure 3.9.

3.2.2.2.   Declaration versus Definition

In the C and C++ languages, variables and functions must be *declared* and *defined* before they can be used. It is important to understand the difference between a declaration and a definition in C and C++.

- A *declaration* is a description of a data object or function. It provides the compiler with the *name* of the entity and its *data type* or *function signature* (i.e., return type and argument type(s)).

- A *definition,* on the other hand, describes a unique region of memory in the program. This memory might contain a variable, an instance of a struct or class, or the machine code of a function.

In other words, a declaration is a *reference to an entity,* while a definition is the *entity itself.* A definition is always a declaration, but the reverse is not always the case—it is possible to write a pure declaration in C and C++ that is not a definition.

Functions are *defined* by writing the body of the function immediately after the signature, enclosed in curly braces:

*foo.cpp*

```
// definition of the max() function
int max(int a, int b)
{
```

```
    return (a > b) ? a : b;
}

// definition of the min() function
int min(int a, int b)
{
    return (a <= b) ? a : b;
}
```

A pure declaration can be provided for a function so that it can be used in other translation units (or later in the same translation unit). This is done by writing a function signature followed by a semicolon, with an optional prefix of extern:

*foo.h*

```
extern int max(int a, int b); // a function declaration

int min(int a, int b);        // also a declaration (the
                              // 'extern' is optional/
                              // assumed)
```

Variables and instances of classes and structs are defined by writing the data type followed by the name of the variable or instance, and an optional array specifier in square brackets:

*foo.cpp*

```
// All of these are variable definitions:
U32 gGlobalInteger = 5;
F32 gGlobalFloatArray[16];
MyClass gGlobalInstance;
```

A global variable defined in one translation unit can optionally be *declared* for use in other translation units by using the extern keyword:

*foo.h*

```
// These are all pure declarations:
extern U32 gGlobalInteger;
extern F32 gGlobalFloatArray[16];
extern MyClass gGlobalInstance;
```

### Multiplicity of Declarations and Definitions

Not surprisingly, any particular data object or function in a C/C++ program can have multiple identical *declarations*, but each can have only one *definition*. If two or more identical definitions exist in a single translation unit, the compiler will notice that multiple entities have the same name and flag an error. If two or more identical definitions exist in *different* translation units, the compiler will not be able to identify the problem, because it operates on one translation unit at a time. But in this case, the linker will give us a "multiply defined symbol" error when it tries to resolve the cross-references.

### Definitions in Header Files and Inlining

It is usually dangerous to place *definitions* in header files. The reason for this should be pretty obvious: If a header file containing a *definition* is #included into more than one *.cpp* file, it's a sure-fire way of generating a "multiply de-fined symbol" linker error.

Inline function definitions are an exception to this rule, because each in-vocation of an inline function gives rise to a brand new copy of that function's machine code, embedded directly into the calling function. In fact, inline func-tion definitions *must* be placed in header files if they are to be used in more than one translation unit. Note that it is *not* sufficient to tag a function *declara-tion* with the inline keyword in a *.h* file and then place the body of that func-tion in a *.cpp* file. The compiler must be able to "see" the body of the function in order to inline it. For example:

*foo.h*

```
// This function definition will be inlined properly.
inline int max(int a, int b)
{
    return (a > b) ? a : b;

}

// This declaration cannot be inlined because the
// compiler cannot "see" the body of the function.
inline int min(int a, int b);
```

*foo.cpp*

```
// The body of min() is effectively "hidden" from the
// compiler, and so it can ONLY be inlined within
// foo.cpp.
int min(int a, int b)
{
    return (a <= b) ? a : b;
}
```

The inline keyword is really just a hint to the compiler. It does a cost/benefit analysis of each inline function, weighing the size of the function's code versus the potential performance benefits of inling it, and the compiler gets the final say as to whether the function will really be inlined or not. Some compilers provide syntax like __forceinline, allowing the programmer to bypass the compiler's cost/benefit analysis and control function inlining directly.

### 3.2.2.3. Linkage

Every definition in C and C++ has a property known as *linkage*. A definition with *external linkage* is visible to and can be referenced by translation units other than the one in which it appears. A definition with *internal linkage* can only be "seen" inside the translation unit in which it appears and thus cannot be referenced by other translation units. We call this property *linkage* because it dictates whether or not the linker is permitted to cross-reference the entity in question. So, in a sense, linkage is the translation unit's equivalent of the `public:` and `private:` keywords in C++ class definitions.

By default, definitions have external linkage. The `static` keyword is used to change a definition's linkage to internal. Note that two or more identical `static` definitions in two or more different *.cpp* files are considered to be *distinct entities* by the linker (just as if they had been given different names), so they will *not* generate a "multiply defined symbol" error. Here are some examples:

*foo.cpp*

```
// This variable can be used by other .cpp files
// (external linkage).
U32 gExternalVariable;

// This variable is only usable within foo.cpp (internal
// linkage).
static U32 gInternalVariable;

// This function can be called from other .cpp files
// (external linkage).
void externalFunction()
{
    // ...
}

// This function can only be called from within foo.cpp
// (internal linkage).
static void internalFunction()
{
    // ...
}
```

*bar.cpp*

```
// This declaration grants access to foo.cpp's variable.
extern U32 gExternalVariable;
```

```
    // This 'gInternalVariable' is distinct from the one
    // defined in foo.cpp - no error. We could just as
    // well have named it gInternalVariableForBarCpp - the
    // net effect is the same.
    static U32 gInternalVariable;

    // This function is distinct from foo.cpp's
    // version - no error. It acts as if we had named it
    // internalFunctionForBarCpp().
    static void internalFunction()
    {
        // ...
    }

    // ERROR - multiply defined symbol!
    void externalFunction()
    {
        // ...
    }
```

Technically speaking, *declarations* don't have a linkage property at all, because they do not allocate any storage in the executable image; therefore, there is no question as to whether or not the linker should be permitted to cross-reference that storage. A declaration is merely a reference to an entity defined elsewhere. However, it is sometimes convenient to speak about declarations as having internal linkage, because a declaration only applies to the translation unit in which it appears. If we allow ourselves to loosen our terminology in this manner, then declarations *always* have internal linkage—there is no way to cross-reference a single declaration in multiple .cpp files. (If we put a declaration in a header file, then multiple .cpp files can "see" that declaration, but they are in effect each getting a distinct *copy* of the declaration, and each copy has internal linkage within that translation unit.)

This leads us to the real reason why inline function definitions are permitted in header files: It is because inline functions have *internal linkage* by default, just as if they had been declared static. If multiple *.cpp* files #include a header containing an inline function definition, each translation unit gets a private copy of that function's body, and no "multiply defined symbol" errors are generated. The linker sees each copy as a distinct entity.

### 3.2.3. C/C++ Memory Layout

A program written in C or C++ stores its data in a number of different places in memory. In order to understand how storage is allocated and how the various types of C/C++ variables work, we need to understand the memory layout of a C/C++ program.

### 3.2.3.1. Executable Image

When a C/C++ program is built, the linker creates an executable file. Most UNIX-like operating systems, including many game consoles, employ a popular executable file format called the *executable and linking format* (ELF). Executable files on those systems therefore have an *.elf* extension. The Windows executable format is similar to the ELF format; executables under Windows have an *.exe* extension. Whatever its format, the executable file always contains a partial *image* of the program as it will exist in memory when it runs. I say a "partial" image because the program generally allocates memory at runtime in addition to the memory laid out in its executable image.

The executable image is divided into contiguous blocks called *segments* or *sections*. Every operating system lays things out a little differently, and the layout may also differ slightly from executable to executable on the same operating system. But the image is usually comprised of at least the following four segments:

1. *Text segment.* Sometimes called the *code segment,* this block contains executable machine code for all functions defined by the program.

2. *Data segment.* This segment contains all *initialized* global and static variables. The memory needed for each global variable is laid out exactly as it will appear when the program is run, and the proper initial values are all filled in. So when the executable file is loaded into memory, the initialized global and static variables are ready to go.

3. *BSS segment.* "BSS" is an outdated name which stands for "block started by symbol." This segment contains all of the *uninitialized* global and static variables defined by the program. The C and C++ languages explicitly define the initial value of any uninitialized global or static variable to be zero. But rather than storing a potentially very large block of zeros in the BSS section, the linker simply stores a *count* of how many zero bytes are required to account for all of the uninitialized globals and statics in the segment. When the executable is loaded into memory, the operating system reserves the requested number of bytes for the BSS section and fills it with zeros prior to calling the program's entry point (e.g. `main()` or `WinMain()`).

4. *Read-only data segment.* Sometimes called the *rodata* segment, this segment contains any read-only (constant) global data defined by the program. For example, all floating-point constants (e.g., `const float kPi`

= 3.141592f;) and all global object instances that have been declared with the const keyword (e.g., const Foo gReadOnlyFoo;) reside in this segment. Note that integer constants (e.g., const int kMaxMonsters = 255;) are often used as *manifest constants* by the compiler, meaning that they are inserted directly into the machine code wherever they are used. Such constants occupy storage in the text segment, but they are not present in the read-only data segment.

Global variables, i.e., variables defined at *file scope* outside any function or class declaration, are stored in either the data or BSS segments, depending on whether or not they have been initialized. The following global will be stored in the data segment, because it has been initialized:

*foo.cpp*

```
F32 gInitializedGlobal = -2.0f;
```

and the following global will be allocated and initialized to zero by the operating system, based on the specifications given in the BSS segment, because it has not been initialized by the programmer:

*foo.cpp*

```
F32 gUninitializedGlobal;
```

We've seen that the static keyword can be used to give a global variable or function definition *internal linkage,* meaning that it will be "hidden" from other translation units. The static keyword can also be used to declare a global variable *within a function.* A function-static variable is *lexically scoped* to the function in which it is declared (i.e., the variable's name can only be "seen" inside the function). It is initialized the first time the function is called (rather than before main() is called as with file-scope statics). But in terms of memory layout in the executable image, a function-static variable acts identically to a file-static global variable—it is stored in either the data or BSS segment based on whether or not it has been initialized.

```
void readHitchhikersGuide(U32 book)
{
    static U32 sBooksInTheTrilogy = 5;   // data segment
    static U32 sBooksRead;               // BSS segment
    // ...
}
```

### 3.2.3.2. Program Stack

When an executable program is loaded into memory and run, the operating system reserves an area of memory for the *program stack.* Whenever a function is called, a contiguous area of stack memory is pushed onto the stack—we call this block of memory a *stack frame.* If function a() calls another function b(), a new stack frame for b() is pushed on top of a()'s frame. When b() returns, its stack frame is popped, and execution continues wherever a() left off.

A stack frame stores three kinds of data:

1. It stores the *return address* of the calling function, so that execution may continue in the calling function when the called function returns.

2. The contents of all relevant *CPU registers* are saved in the stack frame. This allows the new function to use the registers in any way it sees fit, without fear of overwriting data needed by the calling function. Upon return to the calling function, the state of the registers is restored so that execution of the calling function may resume. The return value of the called function, if any, is usually left in a specific register so that the calling function can retrieve it, but the other registers are restored to their original values.

3. The stack frame also contains all *local variables* declared by the function; these are also known as *automatic variables*. This allows each distinct function invocation to maintain its own private copy of every local variable, even when a function calls itself recursively. (In practice, some local variables are actually allocated to CPU registers rather than being stored in the stack frame but, for the most part, such variables operate as if they were allocated within the function's stack frame.) For example:

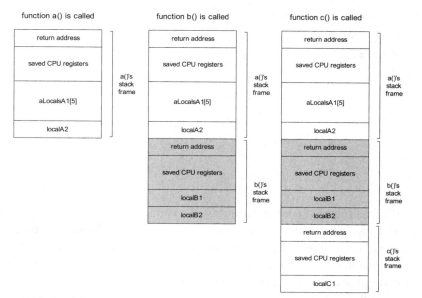

Figure 3.10. Stack frames.

```
void someFunction()
{
    U32 anInteger;
    // ...
}
```

Pushing and popping stack frames is usually implemented by adjusting the value of a single register in the CPU, known as the stack pointer. Figure 3.10 illustrates what happens when the functions shown below are executed.

```
void c()
{
    U32 localC1;
    // ...
}

F32 b()
{
    F32 localB1;
    I32 localB2;

    // ...

    c();   // call function c()

    // ...

    return localB1;
}

void a()
{
    U32 aLocalsA1[5];

    // ...

    F32 localA2 = b();       // call function b()

    // ...
}
```

When a function containing automatic variables returns, its stack frame is abandoned and all automatic variables in the function should be treated as if they no longer exist. Technically, the memory occupied by those variables is still there in the abandoned stack frame—but that memory will very likely be overwritten as soon as another function is called. A common error involves returning the address of a local variable, like this:

```
U32* getMeaningOfLife()
{
    U32 anInteger = 42;
    return &anInteger;
}
```

You *might* get away with this if you use the returned pointer immediately and don't call any other functions in the interim. But more often than not, this kind of code will crash—in ways that can be difficult to debug.

### 3.2.3.3. Dynamic Allocation Heap

Thus far, we've seen that a program's data can be stored as global or static variables or as local variables. The globals and statics are allocated within the executable image, as defined by the data and BSS segments of the executable file. The locals are allocated on the program stack. Both of these kinds of storage are *statically* defined, meaning that the size and layout of the memory is known when the program is compiled and linked. However, a program's memory requirements are often not fully known at compile time. A program usually needs to allocate additional memory *dynamically*.

To allow for dynamic allocation, the operating system maintains a block of memory that can be allocated by a running program by calling `malloc()` and later returned to the pool for use by other programs by calling `free()`. This memory block is known as *heap memory,* or the *free store*. When we allocate memory dynamically, we sometimes say that this memory resides *on the heap*.

In C++, the global `new` and `delete` operators are used to allocate and free memory to and from the heap. Be wary, however—individual classes may overload these operators to allocate memory in custom ways, and even the *global* `new` and `delete` operators can be overloaded, so you cannot simply assume that `new` is always allocating from the heap.

We will discuss dynamic memory allocation in more depth in Chapter 6. For additional information, see http://en.wikipedia.org/wiki/Dynamic_memory_allocation.

## 3.2.4. Member Variables

C `structs` and C++ `classes` allow variables to be grouped into logical units. It's important to remember that a `class` or `struct` *declaration* allocates no memory. It is merely a description of the layout of the data—a cookie cutter which can be used to stamp out *instances* of that `struct` or `class` later on. For example:

```
struct Foo        // struct declaration
{
    U32     mUnsignedValue;
    F32     mFloatValue;
    bool    mBooleanValue;
};
```

Once a struct or class has been declared, it can be allocated (defined) in any of the ways that an atomic data type can be allocated, for example,

- as an automatic variable, on the program stack;

```
void someFunction()
{
    Foo localFoo;
    // ...
}
```

- as a global, file-static or function-static;

```
Foo gFoo;
static Foo sFoo;

void someFunction()
{
    static Foo sLocalFoo;
    // ...
}
```

- dynamically allocated from the heap. In this case, the pointer or reference variable used to hold the address of the data can itself be allocated as an automatic, global, static, or even dynamically.

```
Foo* gpFoo = NULL; // global pointer to a Foo

void someFunction()
{
    // allocate a Foo instance from the heap
    gpFoo = new Foo;

    // ...

    // allocate another Foo, assign to local
    // pointer
    Foo* pAnotherFoo = new Foo;

    // ...

    // allocate a POINTER to a Foo from the heap
    Foo** ppFoo = new Foo*;
    (*ppFoo) = pAnotherFoo;
}
```

### 3.2.4.1. Class-Static Members

As we've seen, the `static` keyword has many different meanings depending on context:

- When used at file scope, `static` means "restrict the visibility of this variable or function so it can only be seen inside this .cpp file."
- When used at function scope, `static` means "this variable is a global, not an automatic, but it can only be seen inside this function."
- When used inside a `struct` or `class` declaration, `static` means "this variable is not a regular member variable, but instead acts just like a global."

Notice that when `static` is used inside a class declaration, it does not control the *visibility* of the variable (as it does when used at file scope)—rather, it differentiates between regular per-instance member variables and per-class variables that act like globals. The *visibility* of a class-static variable is determined by the use of `public:`, `protected:` or `private:` keywords in the class declaration. Class-static variables are automatically included within the namespace of the `class` or `struct` in which they are declared. So the name of the `class` or `struct` must be used to disambiguate the variable whenever it is used outside that `class` or `struct` (e.g., `Foo::sVarName`).

Like an `extern` declaration for a regular global variable, the declaration of a class-static variable within a class allocates no memory. The memory for the class-static variable must be defined in a *.cpp* file. For example:

*foo.h*

```
class Foo
{
public:
    static F32 sClassStatic;    // allocates no
                                // memory!
};
```

*foo.cpp*

```
F32 Foo::sClassStatic = -1.0f;   // define memory and
                                 // init
```

## 3.2.5. Object Layout in Memory

It's useful to be able to visualize the memory layout of your classes and structs. This is usually pretty straightforward—we can simply draw a box for the struct or class, with horizontal lines separating data members. An

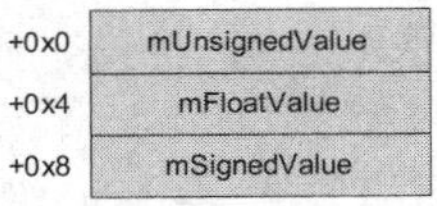

+0x0 | mUnsignedValue
+0x4 | mFloatValue
+0x8 | mSignedValue

**Figure 3.11.** Memory layout of a simple struct.

example of such a diagram for the struct Foo listed below is shown in Figure 3.11.

```
struct Foo
{
    U32   mUnsignedValue;
    F32   mFloatValue;
    I32   mSignedValue;
};
```

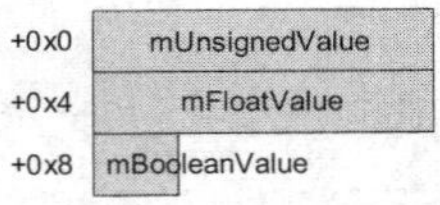

The sizes of the data members are important and should be represented in your diagrams. This is easily done by using the width of each data member to indicate its size in bits—i.e., a 32-bit integer should be roughly four times the width of an 8-bit integer (see Figure 3.12).

+0x0 | mUnsignedValue
+0x4 | mFloatValue
+0x8 | mBooleanValue

**Figure 3.12.** A memory layout using width to indicate member sizes.

```
struct Bar
{
    U32   mUnsignedValue;
    F32   mFloatValue;
    bool  mBooleanValue; // diagram assumes this is 8 bits

};
```

### 3.2.5.1. Alignment and Packing

As we start to think more carefully about the layout of our structs and classes in memory, we may start to wonder what happens when small data members are interspersed with larger members. For example:

```
struct InefficientPacking
{
    U32    mU1;    // 32 bits
    F32    mF2;    // 32 bits
    U8     mB3;    // 8 bits
    I32    mI4;    // 32 bits
    bool   mB5;    // 8 bits
    char*  mP6;    // 32 bits
};
```

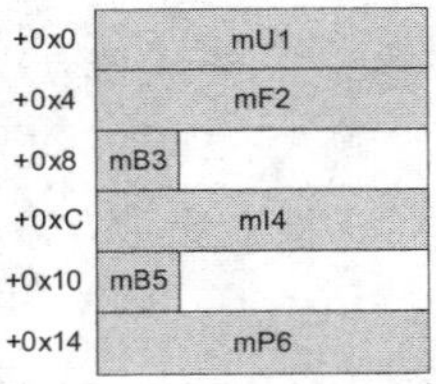

+0x0 | mU1
+0x4 | mF2
+0x8 | mB3
+0xC | mI4
+0x10 | mB5
+0x14 | mP6

**Figure 3.13.** Inefficient struct packing due to mixed data member sizes.

You might imagine that the compiler simply packs the data members into memory as tightly as it can. However, this is not usually the case. Instead, the compiler will typically leave "holes" in the layout, as depicted in Figure 3.13. (Some compilers can be requested not to leave these holes by using a preprocessor directive like #pragma pack, or via command-line options; but the default behavior is to space out the members as shown in Figure 3.13.)

Why does the compiler leave these "holes?" The reason lies in the fact that every data type has a natural *alignment* which must be respected in order to permit the CPU to read and write memory effectively. The *alignment* of a data object refers to whether its *address in memory* is a multiple of its *size* (which is generally a power of two):

- An object with one-byte alignment resides at any memory address.
- An object with two-byte alignment resides only at even addresses (i.e., addresses whose least significant nibble is 0x0, 0x2, 0x4, 0x8, 0xA, 0xC, or 0xE).
- An object with four-byte alignment resides only at addresses that are a multiple of four (i.e., addresses whose least significant nibble is 0x0, 0x4, 0x8, or 0xC).
- A 16-byte aligned object resides only at addresses that are a multiple of 16 (i.e., addresses whose least significant nibble is 0x0).

Alignment is important because many modern processors can actually only read and write properly aligned blocks of data. For example, if a program requests that a 32-bit (four-byte) integer be read from address 0x6A341174, the memory controller will load the data happily because the address is four-byte aligned (in this case, its least significant nibble is 0x4). However, if a request is made to load a 32-bit integer from address 0x6A341173, the memory controller now has to read *two* four-byte blocks: the one at 0x6A341170 and the one at 0x6A341174. It must then mask and shift the two parts of the 32-bit integer and logically OR them together into the destination register on the CPU. This is shown in Figure 3.14.

Some microprocessors don't even go this far. If you request a read or write of unaligned data, you might just get garbage. Or your program might just crash altogether! (The PlayStation 2 is a notable example of this kind of intolerance for unaligned data.)

Different data types have different alignment requirements. A good rule of thumb is that a data type should be aligned to a boundary equal to the width of the data type in bytes. For example, 32-bit values generally have a four-byte alignment requirement, 16-bit values should be two-byte aligned, and 8-bit values can be stored at any address (one-byte aligned). On CPUs that support SIMD vector math, the SIMD registers each contain four 32-bit floats, for a total of 128 bits or 16 bytes. And as you would guess, a four-float SIMD vector typically has a 16-byte alignment requirement.

This brings us back to those "holes" in the layout of struct Ineffi-cientPacking shown in Figure 3.13. When smaller data types like 8-bit bools are interspersed with larger types like 32-bit integers or floats in a structure

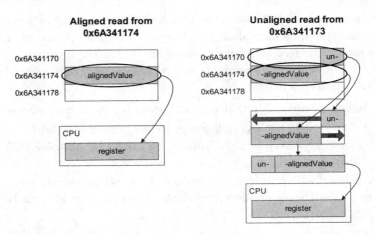

**Figure 3.14.** Aligned and unaligned reads of a 32-bit integer.

| | |
|---|---|
| +0x0 | mU1 |
| +0x4 | mF2 |
| +0x8 | mI4 |
| +0xC | mP6 |
| +0x10 | mB3 \| mB5 \| (pad) |

**Figure 3.15.** More efficient packing by grouping small members together.

or class, the compiler introduces padding (holes) in order to ensure that everything is properly aligned. It's a good idea to think about alignment and packing when declaring your data structures. By simply rearranging the members of struct InefficientPacking from the example above, we can eliminate some of the wasted padding space, as shown below and in Figure 3.15:

```
struct MoreEfficientPacking
{
    U32     mU1;    // 32 bits (4-byte aligned)
    F32     mF2;    // 32 bits (4-byte aligned)
    I32     mI4;    // 32 bits (4-byte aligned)
    char*   mP6;    // 32 bits (4-byte aligned)
    U8      mB3;    // 8 bits (1-byte aligned)
    bool    mB5;    // 8 bits (1-byte aligned)
};
```

You'll notice in Figure 3.15 that the size of the structure as a whole is now 20 bytes, not 18 bytes as we might expect, because it has been padded by two bytes at the end. This padding is added by the compiler to ensure proper alignment of the structure in an *array context*. That is, if an array of these structs is defined and the first element of the array is aligned, then the padding at the end guarantees that *all subsequent elements* will also be aligned properly.

The alignment of a structure as a whole is equal to the largest alignment requirement among its members. In the example above, the largest member alignment is four-byte, so the structure as a whole should be four-byte aligned. I usually like to add explicit padding to the end of my structs, to make the wasted space visible and explicit, like this:

```
struct BestPacking
{
    U32      mU1;      // 32 bits (4-byte aligned)
    F32      mF2;      // 32 bits (4-byte aligned)
    I32      mI4;      // 32 bits (4-byte aligned)
    char*    mP6;      // 32 bits (4-byte aligned)
    U8       mB3;      // 8 bits (1-byte aligned)
    bool     mB5;      // 8 bits (1-byte aligned)
    U8       _pad[2];  // explicit padding
};
```

### 3.2.5.2. Memory Layout of C++ Classes

Two things make C++ classes a little different from C structures in terms of memory layout: *inheritance* and *virtual functions.*

When class B inherits from class A, B's data members simply appear immediately after A's in memory, as shown in Figure 3.16. Each new derived class simply tacks its data members on at the end, although alignment requirements may introduce padding between the classes. (Multiple inheritance does some whacky things, like including multiple copies of a single base class in the memory layout of a derived class. We won't cover the details here, because game programmers usually prefer to avoid multiple inheritance altogether anyway.)

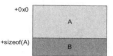

Figure 3.16. Effect of inheritance on class layout.

If a class contains or inherits one or more *virtual functions,* then four additional bytes (or however many bytes a pointer occupies on the target hardware) are added to the class layout, typically at the very beginning of the class' layout. These four bytes are collectively called the *virtual table pointer* or *vpointer,* because they contain a pointer to a data structure known as the *virtual function table* or *vtable.* The vtable for a particular class contains pointers to all the virtual functions that it declares or inherits. Each concrete class has its own virtual table, and every instance of that class has a pointer to it, stored in its vpointer.

The virtual function table is at the heart of polymorphism, because it allows code to be written that is ignorant of the specific concrete classes it is dealing with. Returning to the ubiquitous example of a Shape base class with derived classes for Circle, Rectangle, and Triangle, let's imagine that Shape defines a virtual function called Draw(). The derived classes all override this function, providing distinct implementations named Circle::Draw(), Rectangle::Draw(), and Triangle::Draw(). The virtual table for any class derived from Shape will contain an entry for the Draw() function, but that entry will point to different function implementations, depending on the

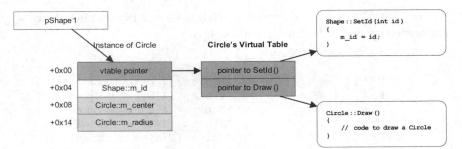

Figure 3.17. pShape1 points to an instance of class Circle.

concrete class. `Circle`'s vtable will contain a pointer to `Circle::Draw()`, while `Rectangle`'s virtual table will point to `Rectangle::Draw()`, and `Triangle`'s vtable will point to `Triangle::Draw()`. Given an arbitrary pointer to a `Shape` (`Shape* pShape`), the code can simply dereference the vtable pointer, look up the `Draw()` function's entry in the vtable, and call it. The result will be to call `Circle::Draw()` when `pShape` points to an instance of `Circle`, `Rectangle::Draw()` when `pShape` points to a `Rectangle`, and `Triangle::Draw()` when `pShape` points to a `Triangle`.

These ideas are illustrated by the following code excerpt. Notice that the base class `Shape` defines two virtual functions, `SetId()` and `Draw()`, the latter of which is declared to be *pure virtual.* (This means that `Shape` provides no default implementation of the `Draw()` function, and derived classes *must* override it if they want to be instantiable.) Class `Circle` derives from `Shape`, adds some data members and functions to manage its center and radius, and overrides the `Draw()` function; this is depicted in Figure 3.17. Class `Triangle` also derives from `Shape`. It adds an array of `Vector3` objects to store its three vertices and adds some functions to get and set the individual vertices. Class `Triangle` overrides `Draw()` as we'd expect, and for illustrative purposes it also overrides `SetId()`. The memory image generated by the `Triangle` class is shown in Figure 3.18.

```
class Shape
{
public:
    virtual void SetId(int id) { m_id = id; }
    int          GetId() const { return m_id; }
    virtual void Draw() = 0; // pure virtual - no impl.

private:
    int          m_id;
};
```

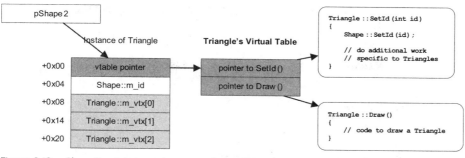

Figure 3.18. pShape2 points to an instance of class Triangle.

```cpp
class Circle : public Shape
{
public:
    void      SetCenter(const Vector3& c) { m_center=c; }
    Vector3   GetCenter() const { return m_center; }

    void      SetRadius(float r) { m_radius = r; }
    float     GetRadius() const { return m_radius; }

virtual void Draw()
    {
        // code to draw a circle
    }

private:
    Vector3       m_center;
    float         m_radius;
};

class Triangle : public Shape
{
public:
    void      SetVertex(int i, const Vector3& v);
    Vector3   GetVertex(int i) const { return m_vtx[i]; }
    virtual void Draw()
    {
        // code to draw a triangle
    }

    virtual void SetId(int id)
    {
        Shape::SetId(id);
```

```
        // do additional work specific to Triangles...
    }

private:
    Vector3          m_vtx[3];
};

// ------------------------------

void main(int, char**)
{
Shape* pShape1 = new Circle;
    Shape* pShape2 = new Triangle;

    // ...

    pShape1->Draw();
    pShape2->Draw();

    // ...
}
```

## 3.3. Catching and Handling Errors

There are a number of ways to catch and handle error conditions in a game engine. As a game programmer, it's important to understand these different mechanisms, their pros and cons, and when to use each one.

### 3.3.1. Types of Errors

In any software project there are two basic kinds of error conditions: *user errors* and *programmer errors*. A user error occurs when the user of the program does something incorrect, such as typing an invalid input, attempting to open a file that does not exist, etc. A programmer error is the result of a *bug* in the code itself. Although it may be triggered by something the user has done, the essence of a programmer error is that the problem could have been avoided if the programmer had not made a mistake, and the user has a reasonable expectation that the program *should* have handled the situation gracefully.

Of course, the definition of "user" changes depending on context. In the context of a game project, user errors can be roughly divided into two categories: errors caused by the person playing the game and errors caused by the people who are making the game during development. It is important to keep track of which type of user is affected by a particular error and handle the error appropriately.

There's actually a third kind of user—the other programmers on your team. (And if you are writing a piece of game middleware software, like Havok or OpenGL, this third category extends to other programmers all over the world who are using your library.) This is where the line between *user errors* and *programmer errors* gets blurry. Let's imagine that programmer A writes a function f(), and programmer B tries to call it. If B calls f() with invalid arguments (e.g., a NULL pointer, or an out-of-range array index), then this could be seen as a user error by programmer A, but it would be a programmer error from B's point of view. (Of course, one can also argue that programmer A should have anticipated the passing of invalid arguments and should have handled them gracefully, so the problem really is a programmer error, on A's part.) The key thing to remember here is that the line between user and programmer can shift depending on context—it is rarely a black-and-white distinction.

## 3.3.2. Handling Errors

When handling errors, the requirements differ significantly between the two types. It is best to handle *user errors* as gracefully as possible, displaying some helpful information to the user and then allowing him or her to continue working—or in the case of a game, to continue playing. Programmer errors, on the other hand, should *not* be handled with a graceful "inform and continue" policy. Instead, it is usually best to halt the program and provide detailed low-level debugging information, so that a programmer can quickly identify and fix the problem. In an ideal world, *all* programmer errors would be caught and fixed before the software ships to the public.

### 3.3.2.1. Handling Player Errors

When the "user" is the person playing your game, errors should obviously be handled within the context of gameplay. For example, if the player attempts to reload a weapon when no ammo is available, an audio cue and/or an animation can indicate this problem to the player without taking him or her "out of the game."

### 3.3.2.2. Handling Developer Errors

When the "user" is someone who is making the game, such as an artist, animator or game designer, errors may be caused by an invalid asset of some sort. For example, an animation might be associated with the wrong skeleton, or a texture might be the wrong size, or an audio file might have been sampled at an unsupported sample rate. For these kinds of *developer errors,* there are two competing camps of thought.

On the one hand, it seems important to prevent bad game assets from persisting for too long. A game typically contains literally thousands of assets, and a problem asset might get "lost," in which case one risks the possibility of the bad asset surviving all the way into the final shipping game. If one takes this point of view to an extreme, then the best way to handle bad game assets is to prevent the entire game from running whenever even a single problematic asset is encountered. This is certainly a strong incentive for the developer who created the invalid asset to remove or fix it immediately.

On the other hand, game development is a messy and iterative process, and generating "perfect" assets the first time around is rare indeed. By this line of thought, a game engine should be robust to almost any kind of problem imaginable, so that work can continue even in the face of totally invalid game asset data. But this too is not ideal, because the game engine would become bloated with error-catching and error-handling code that won't be needed once the development pace settles down and the game ships. And the probability of shipping the product with "bad" assets becomes too high.

In my experience, the best approach is to find a middle ground between these two extremes. When a developer error occurs, I like to *make the error obvious* and then allow the team to continue to work in the presence of the problem. It is extremely costly to prevent all the other developers on the team from working, just because one developer tried to add an invalid asset to the game. A game studio pays its employees well, and when multiple team members experience downtime, the costs are multiplied by the number of people who are prevented from working. Of course, we should only handle errors in this way when it is practical to do so, without spending inordinate amounts of engineering time, or bloating the code.

As an example, let's suppose that a particular mesh cannot be loaded. In my view, it's best to draw a big red box in the game world at the places that mesh would have been located, perhaps with a text string hovering over each one that reads, "Mesh *blah-dee-blah* failed to load." This is superior to printing an easy-to-miss message to an error log. And it's *far* better than just crashing the game, because then no one will be able to work until that one mesh reference has been repaired. Of course, for particularly egregious problems it's fine to just spew an error message and crash. There's no silver bullet for all kinds of problems, and your judgment about what type of error handling approach to apply to a given situation will improve with experience.

### 3.3.2.3.  Handling Programmer Errors

The best way to detect and handle programmer errors (a.k.a. bugs) is often to embed error-checking code into your source code and arrange for failed error checks to halt the program. Such a mechanism is known as an *assertion system;* we'll investigate assertions in detail in Section 3.3.3.3. Of course, as we said above, one programmer's user error is another programmer's bug; hence, assertions are not always the right way to handle every programmer error. Making a judicious choice between an assertion and a more graceful error handling technique is a skill that one develops over time.

## 3.3.3. Implementation of Error Detection and Handling

We've looked at some philosophical approaches to handling errors. Now let's turn our attention to the choices we have as programmers when it comes to implementing error detection and handling code.

### 3.3.3.1. Error Return Codes

A common approach to handling errors is to return some kind of failure code from the function in which the problem is first detected. This could be a Boolean value indicating success or failure or it could be an "impossible" value, one that is outside the range of normally returned results. For example, a function that returns a positive integer or floating-point value could return a negative value to indicate that an error occurred. Even better than a Boolean or an "impossible" return value, the function could be designed to return an enumerated value to indicate success or failure. This clearly separates the error code from the output(s) of the function, and the exact nature of the problem can be indicated on failure (e.g., enum `Error { kSuccess, kAssetNot-Found, kInvalidRange, ... };`).

The calling function should intercept error return codes and act appropriately. It might handle the error immediately. Or it might work around the problem, complete its own execution, and then pass the error code on to whatever function called *it*.

### 3.3.3.2. Exceptions

Error return codes are a simple and reliable way to communicate and respond to error conditions. However, error return codes have their drawbacks. Perhaps the biggest problem with error return codes is that the function that detects an error may be totally unrelated to the function that is capable of handling the problem. In the worst-case scenario, a function that is 40 calls deep in the call stack might detect a problem that can only be handled by the top-level game loop, or by `main()`. In this scenario, every one of the 40 functions on the call stack would need to be written so that it can pass an appropriate error code all the way back up to the top-level error-handling function.

One way to solve this problem is to throw an exception. *Structured exception handling* (SEH) is a very powerful feature of C++. It allows the function that detects a problem to communicate the error to the rest of the code without knowing anything about which function might handle the error. When an exception is thrown, relevant information about the error is placed into a data object of the programmer's choice known as an *exception object.* The call stack is then automatically unwound, in search of a calling function that wrapped its call in a try-catch block. If a try-catch block is found, the exception object is matched against all possible catch blocks and if a match is found, the corresponding catch block's code is executed. The destructors of any automatic variables are called as needed during the stack unwinding.

The ability to separate error detection from error handling in such a clean way is certainly attractive, and exception handling is an excellent choice for some software projects. However, SEH adds a lot of overhead to the program. Every stack frame must be augmented to contain additional information required by the stack unwinding process. Also, the stack unwind is usually very slow—on the order of two to three times more expensive than simply returning from the function. Also, if even one function in your program (or a library that your program links with) uses SEH, your *entire program* must use SEH. The compiler can't know which functions might be above you on the call stack when you throw an exception.

Therefore, there's a pretty strong argument for turning *off* structured exception handling in your game engine altogether. This is the approach employed at Naughty Dog and also on most of the projects I've worked on at Electronic Arts and Midway. Console game engines should probably never use SEH, because of a console's limited memory and processing bandwidth. However, a game engine that is intended to be run on a personal computer might be able to use SEH without any problems.

There are many interesting articles on this topic on the web. Here are links to a few of them:

- http://www.joelonsoftware.com/items/2003/10/13.html
- http://www.nedbatchelder.com/text/exceptions-vs-status.html
- http://www.joelonsoftware.com/items/2003/10/15.html

### 3.3.3.3.  Assertions

An *assertion* is a line of code that checks an expression. If the expression evaluates to true, nothing happens. But if the expression evaluates to false, the program is stopped, a message is printed, and the debugger is invoked if possible. Steve Maguire provides an in-depth discussion of assertions in his must-read book, *Writing Solid Code* [30].

Assertions check a programmer's assumptions. They act like *land mines* for bugs. They check the code when it is first written to ensure that it is functioning properly. They also ensure that the original assumptions continue to hold for long periods of time, even when the code around them is constantly changing and evolving. For example, if a programmer changes code that used to work, but accidentally violates its original assumptions, they'll hit the land mine. This immediately informs the programmer of the problem and permits him or her to rectify the situation with minimum fuss. Without assertions, bugs have a tendency to "hide out" and manifest themselves later in ways that are difficult and time-consuming to track down. But with assertions embedded in the code, bugs announce themselves the moment they are introduced—which is usually the best moment to fix the problem, while the code changes that caused the problem are fresh in the programmer's mind.

Assertions are implemented as a #define macro, which means that the assertion checks can be stripped out of the code if desired, by simply changing the #define. The cost of the assertion checks can usually be tolerated during development, but stripping out the assertions prior to shipping the game can buy back that little bit of crucial performance if necessary.

*Assertion Implementation*

Assertions are usually implemented via a combination of a #defined macro that evaluates to an if/else clause, a function that is called when the assertion fails (the expression evaluates to false), and a bit of assembly code that halts the program and breaks into the debugger when one is attached. Here's a typical implementation:

```
#if ASSERTIONS_ENABLED
    // define some inline assembly that causes a break
    // into the debugger - this will be different on each
    // target CPU
    #define debugBreak() asm { int 3 }

    // check the expression and fail if it is false
    #define ASSERT(expr) \
        if (expr) { } \
        else \
        { \
            reportAssertionFailure(#expr, \
                                    __FILE__, \
                                    __LINE__); \
            debugBreak(); \
        }
```

```
#else
   #define ASSERT(expr)        // evaluates to nothing
#endif
```

Let's break down this definition so we can see how it works:

- The outer `#if/#else/#endif` is used to strip assertions from the code base. When `ASSERTIONS_ENABLED` is nonzero, the `ASSERT()` macro is defined in its fully glory, and all assertion checks in the code will be included in the program. But when assertions are turned off, `ASSERT(expr)` evaluates to nothing, and all instances of it in the code are effectively removed.

- The `debugBreak()` macro evaluates to whatever assembly-language instructions are required in order to cause the program to halt and the debugger to take charge (if one is connected). This differs from CPU to CPU, but it is usually a single assembly instruction.

- The `ASSERT()` macro itself is defined using a full `if/else` statement (as opposed to a lone `if`). This is done so that the macro can be used in any context, even within *other* unbracketed `if/else` statements.

  Here's an example of what would happen if `ASSERT()` were defined using a solitary `if`:

```
#define ASSERT(expr)  if (!(expr)) debugBreak()

void f()
{
    if (a < 5)
        ASSERT(a >= 0);
    else
        doSomething(a);
}
```

  This expands to the following incorrect code:

```
void f()
{

    if (a < 5)
        if (!(a >= 0))
            debugBreak();
        else   // Oops! Bound to the wrong if()!
            doSomething(a);
}
```

- The `else` clause of an `ASSERT()` macro does two things. It displays some kind of message to the programmer indicating what went wrong, and then it breaks into the debugger. Notice the use of #expr as the first argument to the message display function. The pound (#) preprocessor operator causes the expression expr to be turned into a string, thereby allowing it to be printed out as part of the assertion failure message.

- Notice also the use of __FILE__ and __LINE__. These compiler-defined macros magically contain the *.cpp* file name and line number of the line of code on which they appear. By passing them into our message display function, we can print the exact location of the problem.

I highly recommend the use of assertions in your code. However, it's important to be aware of their performance cost. You may want to consider defining two kinds of assertion macros. The regular ASSERT() macro can be left active in *all* builds, so that errors are easily caught even when not running in debug mode. A second assertion macro, perhaps called SLOW_ASSERT(), could be activated only in debug builds. This macro could then be used in places where the cost of assertion checking is too high to permit inclusion in release builds. Obviously SLOW_ASSERT() is of lower utility, because it is stripped out of the version of the game that your testers play every day. But at least these assertions become active when programmers are debugging their code.

It's also extremely important to use assertions properly. They should be used to catch bugs in the program itself—*never* to catch user errors. Also, assertions should always cause the entire game to halt when they fail. It's usually a bad idea to allow assertions to be skipped by testers, artists, designers, and other non-engineers. (This is a bit like the boy who cried wolf: if assertions can be skipped, then they cease to have any significance, rendering them ineffective.) In other words, assertions should only be used to catch fatal errors. If it's OK to continue past an assertion, then it's probably better to notify the user of the error in some other way, such as with an on-screen message, or some ugly bright-orange 3D graphics. For a great discussion on the proper usage of assertions, see http://www.wholesalealgorithms.com/blog9.

# 4

# 3D Math for Games

A game is a mathematical model of a virtual world simulated in real-time on a computer of some kind. Therefore, mathematics pervades everything we do in the game industry. Game programmers make use of virtually all branches of mathematics, from trigonometry to algebra to statistics to calculus. However, by far the most prevalent kind of mathematics you'll be doing as a game programmer is 3D vector and matrix math (i.e., 3D *linear algebra*).

Even this one branch of mathematics is very broad and very deep, so we cannot hope to cover it in any great depth in a single chapter. Instead, I will attempt to provide an overview of the mathematical tools needed by a typical game programmer. Along the way, I'll offer some tips and tricks which should help you keep all of the rather confusing concepts and rules straight in your head. For an excellent in-depth coverage of 3D math for games, I highly recommend Eric Lengyel's book on the topic [28].

## 4.1. Solving 3D Problems in 2D

Many of the mathematical operations we're going to learn about in the following chapter work equally well in 2D and 3D. This is very good news, because it means you can *sometimes* solve a 3D vector problem by thinking and drawing pictures in 2D (which is considerably easier to do!) Sadly, this equivalence between 2D and 3D does not hold all the time. Some operations, like the cross product, are only defined in 3D, and some problems only make sense when all three dimensions are considered. Nonetheless, it almost never hurts to start by thinking about a simplified two-dimensional version of the problem at hand. Once you understand the solution in 2D, you can think about how the problem extends into three dimensions. In some cases, you'll happily discover that your 2D result works in 3D as well. In others, you'll be able to find a coordinate system in which the problem really *is* two-dimensional. In this book, we'll employ two-dimensional diagrams wherever the distinction between 2D and 3D is not relevant.

## 4.2. Points and Vectors

The majority of modern 3D games are made up of three-dimensional objects in a virtual world. A game engine needs to keep track of the positions, orientations, and scales of all these objects, animate them in the game world, and transform them into screen space so they can be rendered on screen. In games, 3D objects are almost always made up of triangles, the vertices of which are represented by points. So before we learn how to represent whole objects in a game engine, let's first take a look the point and its closely related cousin, the vector.

### 4.2.1. Points and Cartesian Coordinates

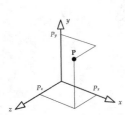

Figure 4.1. A point represented in Cartesian coordinates.

Technically speaking, a *point* is a location in *n*-dimensional space. (In games, *n* is usually equal to 2 or 3.) The Cartesian coordinate system is by far the most common coordinate system employed by game programmers. It uses two or three mutually perpendicular axes to specify a position in 2D or 3D space. So a point $\mathbf{P}$ is represented by a pair or triple of real numbers, $(P_x, P_y)$ or $(P_x, P_y, P_z)$.

Of course, the Cartesian coordinate system is not our only choice. Some other common systems include:

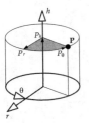

Figure 4.2. A point represented in cylindrical coordinates.

- *Cylindrical coordinates.* This system employs a vertical "height" axis $h$, a radial axis $r$ emanating out from the vertical, and a yaw angle *theta* ($\theta$). In cylindrical coordinates, a point $\mathbf{P}$ is represented by the triple of numbers $(P_h, P_r, P_\theta)$. This is illustrated in Figure 4.2.
- *Spherical coordinates.* This system employs a pitch angle phi ($\phi$), a yaw angle theta ($\theta$), and a radial measurement $r$. Points are therefore represented by the triple of numbers $(P_r, P_\phi, P_\theta)$. This is illustrated in Figure 4.3.

Cartesian coordinates are by far the most widely used coordinate system in game programming. However, always remember to select the coordinate system that best maps to the problem at hand. For example, in the game *Crank the Weasel* by Midway Home Entertainment, the main character Crank runs around an art-deco city picking up loot. I wanted to make the items of loot swirl around Crank's body in a spiral, getting closer and closer to him until they disappeared. I represented the position of the loot in cylindrical coordinates relative to the Crank character's current position. To implement the spiral animation, I simply gave the loot a constant angular speed in $\theta$, a small constant linear speed inward along its radial axis $r$, and a very slight constant linear speed upward along the $h$-axis so the loot would gradually rise up to the level of Crank's pants pockets. This extremely simple animation looked great, and it was much easier to model using cylindrical coordinates than it would have been using a Cartesian system.

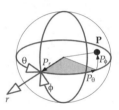

Figure 4.3. A point represented in spherical coordinates.

### 4.2.2. Left-Handed vs. Right-Handed Coordinate Systems

In three-dimensional Cartesian coordinates, we have two choices when arranging our three mutually perpendicular axes: right-handed (RH) and left-handed (LH). In a right-handed coordinate system, when you curl the fingers of your right hand around the $z$-axis with the thumb pointing toward positive $z$ coordinates, your fingers point from the $x$-axis toward the $y$-axis. In a left-handed coordinate system the same thing is true using your left hand.

The only difference between a left-handed coordinate system and a right-handed coordinate system is the direction in which one of the three axes is pointing. For example, if the $y$-axis points upward and $x$ points to the right, then $z$ comes toward us (out of the page) in a right-handed system, and away from us (into the page) in a left-handed system. Left- and right-handed Cartesian coordinate systems are depicted in Figure 4.4.

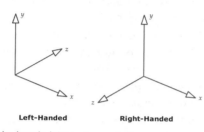

Figure 4.4. Left- and right-handed Cartesian coordinate systems.

It is easy to convert from LH to RH coordinates and vice-versa. We simply flip the direction of any one axis, leaving the other two axes alone. It's important to remember that the rules of mathematics do not change between LH and RH coordinate systems. Only our *interpretation* of the numbers—our mental image of how the numbers map into 3D space—changes. Left-handed and right-handed conventions apply to visualization only, not to the underlying mathematics. (Actually, handedness does matter when dealing with cross products in physical simulations, but we can safely ignore these subtleties for the majority of our game programming tasks. For more information, see http://en.wikipedia.org/wiki/Pseudovector.)

The mapping between the numerical representation and the visual representation is entirely up to us as mathematicians and programmers. We could choose to have the $y$-axis pointing up, with $z$ forward and $x$ to the left (RH) or right (LH). Or we could choose to have the $z$-axis point up. Or the $x$-axis could point up instead—or down. All that matters is that we decide upon a mapping, and then stick with it consistently.

That being said, some conventions do tend to work better than others for certain applications. For example, 3D graphics programmers typically work with a left-handed coordinate system, with the $y$-axis pointing up, $x$ to the right and positive $z$ pointing away from the viewer (i.e., in the direction the virtual camera is pointing). When 3D graphics are rendered onto a 2D screen using this particular coordinate system, increasing $z$-coordinates correspond to increasing *depth* into the scene (i.e., increasing distance away from the virtual camera). As we will see in subsequent chapters, this is exactly what is required when using a $z$-buffering scheme for depth occlusion.

### 4.2.3. Vectors

A *vector* is a quantity that has both a *magnitude* and a *direction* in $n$-dimensional space. A vector can be visualized as a *directed line segment* extending from a point called the *tail* to a point called the *head*. Contrast this to a *scalar* (i.e., an ordinary real-valued number), which represents a magnitude but has no direction. Usually scalars are written in italics (e.g., $v$) while vectors are written in boldface (e.g., **v**).

A 3D vector can be represented by a triple of scalars $(x, y, z)$, just as a point can be. The distinction between points and vectors is actually quite subtle. Technically, a vector is just an offset *relative to* some known point. A vector can be moved anywhere in 3D space—as long as its magnitude and direction don't change, it is the same vector.

A vector can be used to represent a point, provided that we fix the tail of the vector to the origin of our coordinate system. Such a vector is sometimes called a *position vector* or *radius vector*. For our purposes, we can interpret any triple of scalars as either a point or a vector, provided that we remember that a *position vector* is constrained such that its tail remains at the origin of the chosen coordinate system. This implies that points and vectors are treated in subtly different ways mathematically. One might say that points are *absolute*, while vectors are *relative*.

The vast majority of game programmers use the term "vector" to refer both to points (position vectors) and to vectors in the strict linear algebra sense (purely directional vectors). Most 3D math libraries also use the term "vector" in this way. In this book, we'll use the term "direction vector" or just "direction" when the distinction is important. Be careful to always keep the difference between points and directions clear in your mind (even if your math library doesn't). As we'll see in Section 4.3.6.1, directions need to be treated differently from points when converting them into homogeneous coordinates for manipulation with 4 × 4 matrices, so getting the two types of vector mixed up can and will lead to bugs in your code.

#### 4.2.3.1. Cartesian Basis Vectors

It is often useful to define three *orthogonal unit vectors* (i.e., vectors that are mutually perpendicular and each with a length equal to one), corresponding to the three principal Cartesian axes. The unit vector along the $x$-axis is typically called $\mathbf{i}$, the $y$-axis unit vector is called $\mathbf{j}$, and the $z$-axis unit vector is called $\mathbf{k}$. The vectors $\mathbf{i}$, $\mathbf{j}$, and $\mathbf{k}$ are sometimes called Cartesian *basis vectors*.

Any point or vector can be expressed as a sum of scalars (real numbers) multiplied by these unit basis vectors. For example,

$$(5, 3, -2) = 5\mathbf{i} + 3\mathbf{j} - 2\mathbf{k}.$$

### 4.2.4. Vector Operations

Most of the mathematical operations that you can perform on scalars can be applied to vectors as well. There are also some new operations that apply only to vectors.

#### 4.2.4.1. Multiplication by a Scalar

Multiplication of a vector $\mathbf{a}$ by a scalar $s$ is accomplished by multiplying the individual components of $\mathbf{a}$ by $s$:

$$s\mathbf{a} = (\, sa_x, sa_y, sa_z \,).$$

Multiplication by a scalar has the effect of scaling the magnitude of the vector, while leaving its direction unchanged, as shown in Figure 4.5. Multiplication by $-1$ flips the direction of the vector (the head becomes the tail and vice-versa).

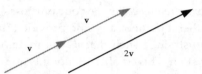

Figure 4.5. Multiplication of a vector by the scalar 2.

The scale factor can be different along each axis. We call this *nonuniform scale*, and it can be represented as the *component-wise product* of a scaling vector **s** and the vector in question, which we'll denote with the $\otimes$ operator. Technically speaking, this special kind of product between two vectors is known as the *Hadamard product*. It is rarely used in the game industry—in fact, nonuniform scaling is one of its *only* commonplace uses in games:

$$\mathbf{s} \otimes \mathbf{a} = (s_x a_x, s_y a_y, s_z a_z). \tag{4.1}$$

As we'll see in Section 4.3.7.3, a scaling vector **s** is really just a compact way to represent a $3 \times 3$ diagonal scaling matrix **S**. So another way to write Equation (4.1) is as follows:

$$\mathbf{aS} = \begin{bmatrix} a_x & a_y & a_z \end{bmatrix} \begin{bmatrix} s_x & 0 & 0 \\ 0 & s_y & 0 \\ 0 & 0 & s_z \end{bmatrix} = \begin{bmatrix} s_x a_x & s_y a_y & s_z a_z \end{bmatrix}.$$

### 4.2.4.2. Addition and Subtraction

The addition of two vectors **a** and **b** is defined as the vector whose components are the sums of the *components* of **a** and **b**. This can be visualized by placing the head of vector **a** onto the tail of vector **b**—the sum is then the vector from the tail of **a** to the head of **b**:

$$\mathbf{a} + \mathbf{b} = [\ (a_x + b_x),\ (a_y + b_y),\ (a_z + b_z)\ ].$$

Vector subtraction $\mathbf{a} - \mathbf{b}$ is nothing more than addition of **a** and $-\mathbf{b}$ (i.e., the result of scaling **b** by $-1$, which flips it around). This corresponds to the vector

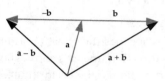

Figure 4.6. Vector addition and subtraction.

whose components are the difference between the components of **a** and the components of **b**:

$$\mathbf{a} - \mathbf{b} = [\ (a_x - b_x),\ (a_y - b_y),\ (a_z - b_z)\ ].$$

Vector addition and subtraction are depicted in Figure 4.6.

*Adding and Subtracting Points and Directions*

You can add and subtract direction vectors freely. However, technically speaking, points cannot be added to one another—you can only add a direction vector to a point, the result of which is another point. Likewise, you can take the difference between two points, resulting in a direction vector. These operations are summarized below:

- direction + direction = direction
- direction − direction = direction
- point + direction = point
- point − point = direction
- point + point = *nonsense* (don't do it!)

### 4.2.4.3. Magnitude

The magnitude of a vector is a scalar representing the length of the vector as it would be measured in 2D or 3D space. It is denoted by placing vertical bars around the vector's boldface symbol. We can use the Pythagorean theorem to calculate a vector's magnitude, as shown in Figure 4.7:

$$|\mathbf{a}| = \sqrt{a_x^2 + a_y^2 + a_z^2}.$$

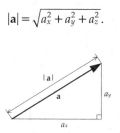

Figure 4.7. Magnitude of a vector (shown in 2D for ease of illustration).

### 4.2.4.4. Vector Operations in Action

Believe it or not, we can already solve all sorts of real-world game problems given just the vector operations we've learned thus far. When trying to solve a problem, we can use operations like addition, subtraction, scaling, and magnitude to generate new data out of the things we already know. For example,

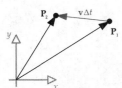

**Figure 4.8.** Simple vector addition can be used to find a character's position in the next frame, given her position and velocity in the current frame.

if we have the current position vector of an A.I. character $P_1$, and a vector $\mathbf{v}$ representing her current velocity, we can find her position on the next frame $P_2$ by scaling the velocity vector by the frame time interval $\Delta t$, and then adding it to the current position. As shown in Figure 4.8, the resulting vector equation is $P_2 = P_1 + (\Delta t)\mathbf{v}$. (This is known as *explicit Euler integration*—it's actually only valid when the velocity is constant, but you get the idea.)

As another example, let's say we have two spheres, and we want to know whether they intersect. Given that we know the center points of the two spheres, $C_1$ and $C_2$, we can find a direction vector between them by simply subtracting the points, $\mathbf{d} = C_2 - C_1$. The magnitude of this vector $d = |\mathbf{d}|$ determines how far apart the spheres' centers are. If this distance is less than the sum of the spheres' radii, they are intersecting; otherwise they're not. This is shown in Figure 4.9.

Square roots are expensive to calculate on most computers, so game programmers should always use the *squared magnitude* whenever it is valid to do so:

$$|\mathbf{a}|^2 = \left(a_x^2 + a_y^2 + a_z^2\right).$$

Using the squared magnitude is valid when comparing the *relative lengths* of two vectors ("is vector $\mathbf{a}$ longer than vector $\mathbf{b}$?"), or when comparing a vector's magnitude to some other (squared) scalar quantity. So in our sphere-sphere intersection test, we should calculate $d^2 = |\mathbf{d}|^2$ and compare this to the squared sum of the radii, $(r_1 + r_2)^2$ for maximum speed. When writing high-performance software, never take a square root when you don't have to!

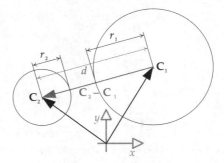

**Figure 4.9.** A sphere-sphere intersection test involves only vector subtraction, vector magnitude, and floating-point comparison operations.

### 4.2.4.5. Normalization and Unit Vectors

A *unit vector* is a vector with a magnitude (length) of one. Unit vectors are very useful in 3D mathematics and game programming, for reasons we'll see below.

Given an arbitrary vector $\mathbf{v}$ of length $v = |\mathbf{v}|$, we can convert it to a unit vector $\mathbf{u}$ that points in the same direction as $\mathbf{v}$, but has unit length. To do this, we simply multiply $\mathbf{v}$ by the reciprocal of its magnitude. We call this *normalization*:

$$\mathbf{u} = \frac{\mathbf{v}}{|\mathbf{v}|} = \frac{1}{v}\mathbf{v}.$$

### 4.2.4.6. Normal Vectors

A vector is said to be *normal* to a surface if it is *perpendicular* to that surface. Normal vectors are highly useful in games and computer graphics. For example, a *plane* can be defined by a point and a normal vector. And in 3D graphics, lighting calculations make heavy use of normal vectors to define the direction of surfaces relative to the direction of the light rays impinging upon them.

Normal vectors are usually of unit length, but they do not need to be. Be careful not to confuse the term "normalization" with the term "normal vector." A normalized vector is any vector of unit length. A normal vector is any vector that is perpendicular to a surface, whether or not it is of unit length.

### 4.2.4.7. Dot Product and Projection

Vectors can be multiplied, but unlike scalars there are a number of different kinds of vector multiplication. In game programming, we most often work with the following two kinds of multiplication:

- the *dot product* (a.k.a. scalar product or inner product), and
- the *cross product* (a.k.a. vector product or outer product).

The dot product of two vectors yields a scalar; it is defined by adding the products of the individual components of the two vectors:

$$\mathbf{a} \cdot \mathbf{b} = a_x b_x + a_y b_y + a_z b_z = d \quad \text{(a scalar)}.$$

The dot product can also be written as the product of the magnitudes of the two vectors and the cosine of the angle between them:

$$\mathbf{a} \cdot \mathbf{b} = |\mathbf{a}|\,|\mathbf{b}|\,\cos(\theta).$$

The dot product is *commutative* (i.e., the order of the two vectors can be reversed) and *distributive* over addition:

$$\mathbf{a} \cdot \mathbf{b} = \mathbf{b} \cdot \mathbf{a};$$

$$\mathbf{a} \cdot (\mathbf{b} + \mathbf{c}) = \mathbf{a} \cdot \mathbf{b} + \mathbf{a} \cdot \mathbf{c}.$$

And the dot product combines with scalar multiplication as follows:

$$s\mathbf{a} \cdot \mathbf{b} = \mathbf{a} \cdot s\mathbf{b} = s(\mathbf{a} \cdot \mathbf{b}).$$

## Vector Projection

If **u** is a unit vector ($|\mathbf{u}| = 1$), then the dot product ($\mathbf{a} \cdot \mathbf{u}$) represents the length of the *projection* of vector **a** onto the infinite line defined by the direction of **u**, as shown in Figure 4.10. This projection concept works equally well in 2D or 3D and is highly useful for solving a wide variety of three-dimensional problems.

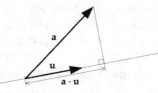

**Figure 4.10.** Vector projection using the dot product.

## Magnitude as a Dot Product

The squared magnitude of a vector can be found by taking the dot product of that vector with itself. Its magnitude is then easily found by taking the square root:

$$|\mathbf{a}|^2 = \mathbf{a} \cdot \mathbf{a};$$

$$|\mathbf{a}| = \sqrt{\mathbf{a} \cdot \mathbf{a}}.$$

This works because the cosine of zero degrees is 1, so all that is left is $|\mathbf{a}| \, |\mathbf{a}| = |\mathbf{a}|^2$.

## Dot Product Tests

Dot products are great for testing if two vectors are collinear or perpendicular, or whether they point in roughly the same or roughly opposite directions. For any two arbitrary vectors **a** and **b**, game programmers often use the following tests, as shown in Figure 4.11:

- *Collinear.* ($\mathbf{a} \cdot \mathbf{b}$) = $|\mathbf{a}| \, |\mathbf{b}|$ = $ab$ (i.e., the angle between them is exactly 0 degrees—this dot product equals +1 when **a** and **b** are *unit vectors*).

- *Collinear but opposite.* ($\mathbf{a} \cdot \mathbf{b}$) = $-ab$ (i.e., the angle between them is 180 degrees—this dot product equals −1 when **a** and **b** are unit vectors).

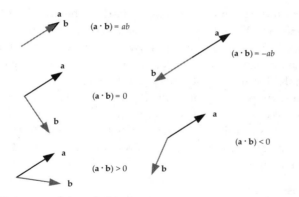

**Figure 4.11.** Some common dot product tests.

- *Perpendicular.* $(\mathbf{a} \cdot \mathbf{b}) = 0$ (i.e., the angle between them is 90 degrees).
- *Same direction.* $(\mathbf{a} \cdot \mathbf{b}) > 0$ (i.e., the angle between them is less than 90 degrees).
- *Opposite directions.* $(\mathbf{a} \cdot \mathbf{b}) < 0$ (i.e., the angle between them is greater than 90 degrees).

### Some Other Applications of the Dot Product

Dot products can be used for all sorts of things in game programming. For example, let's say we want to find out whether an enemy is in front of the player character or behind him. We can find a vector from the player's position $\mathbf{P}$ to the enemy's position $\mathbf{E}$ by simple vector subtraction ($\mathbf{v} = \mathbf{E} - \mathbf{P}$). Let's assume we have a vector $\mathbf{f}$ pointing in the direction that the player is *facing*. (As we'll see in Section 4.3.10.3, the vector $\mathbf{f}$ can be extracted directly from the player's model-to-world matrix.) The dot product $d = \mathbf{v} \cdot \mathbf{f}$ can be used to test whether the enemy is in front of or behind the player—it will be positive when the enemy is in front and negative when the enemy is behind.

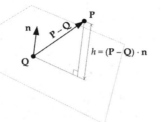

**Figure 4.12.** The dot product can be used to find the height of a point above or below a plane.

The dot product can also be used to find the height of a point above or below a plane (which might be useful when writing a moon-landing game for example). We can define a plane with two vector quantities: a point $\mathbf{Q}$ lying anywhere on the plane, and a unit vector $\mathbf{n}$ that is perpendicular (i.e., normal) to the plane. To find the height $h$ of a point $\mathbf{P}$ above the plane, we first calculate a vector from any point on the plane ($\mathbf{Q}$ will do nicely) to the point in question $\mathbf{P}$. So we have $\mathbf{v} = \mathbf{P} - \mathbf{Q}$. The dot product of vector $\mathbf{v}$ with the unit-length normal vector $\mathbf{n}$ is just the projection of $\mathbf{v}$ onto the line defined by $\mathbf{n}$. But that is exactly the height we're looking for. Therefore, $h = \mathbf{v} \cdot \mathbf{n} = (\mathbf{P} - \mathbf{Q}) \cdot \mathbf{n}$. This is illustrated in Figure 4.12.

### 4.2.4.8. Cross Product

The *cross product* (also known as the *outer product* or *vector product*) of two vectors yields another *vector* that is *perpendicular* to the two vectors being multiplied, as shown in Figure 4.13. The cross product operation is only defined in three dimensions:

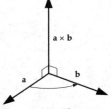

**Figure 4.13.** The cross product of vectors a and b (right-handed).

$$\mathbf{a} \times \mathbf{b} = [(a_y b_z - a_z b_y), \quad (a_z b_x - a_x b_z), \quad (a_x b_y - a_y b_x)]$$
$$= (a_y b_z - a_z b_y)\mathbf{i} + (a_z b_x - a_x b_z)\mathbf{j} + (a_x b_y - a_y b_x)\mathbf{k}.$$

### Magnitude of the Cross Product

The magnitude of the cross product vector is the product of the magnitudes of the two vectors and the sine of the angle between them. (This is similar to the definition of the dot product, but it replaces the cosine with the sine.)

$$|\mathbf{a} \times \mathbf{b}| = |\mathbf{a}|\,|\mathbf{b}|\,\sin(\theta).$$

The magnitude of the cross product $|\mathbf{a} \times \mathbf{b}|$ is equal to the area of the parallelogram whose sides are $\mathbf{a}$ and $\mathbf{b}$, as shown in Figure 4.14. Since a triangle is one-half of a parallelogram, the area of a triangle whose vertices are specified by the position vectors $\mathbf{V}_1$, $\mathbf{V}_2$, and $\mathbf{V}_3$ can be calculated as one-half of the magnitude of the cross product of any two of its sides:

$$A_{\text{triangle}} = \tfrac{1}{2}\left|(\mathbf{V}_2 - \mathbf{V}_1) \times (\mathbf{V}_3 - \mathbf{V}_1)\right|.$$

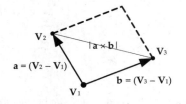

**Figure 4.14.** Area of a parallelogram expressed as the magnitude of a cross product.

## Direction of the Cross Product

When using a right-handed coordinate system, you can use the *right-hand rule* to determine the direction of the cross product. Simply cup your fingers such that they point in the direction you'd rotate vector **a** to move it on top of vector **b**, and the cross product (**a** × **b**) will be in the direction of your thumb.

Note that the cross product is defined by the *left-hand rule* when using a left-handed coordinate system. This means that the direction of the cross product changes depending on the choice of coordinate system. This might seem odd at first, but remember that the handedness of a coordinate system does *not* affect the mathematical calculations we carry out—it only changes our *visualization* of what the numbers look like in 3D space. When converting from a RH system to a LH system or vice-versa, the numerical representations of all the points and vectors stay the same, but one axis flips. Our visualization of everything is therefore mirrored along that flipped axis. So if a cross product just happens to align with the axis we're flipping (e.g., the z-axis), it needs to flip when the axis flips. If it didn't, the mathematical definition of the cross product itself would have to be changed so that the z-coordinate of the cross product comes out negative in the new coordinate system. I wouldn't lose too much sleep over all of this. Just remember: when *visualizing* a cross product, use the right-hand rule in a right-handed coordinate system and the left-hand rule in a left-handed coordinate system.

## Properties of the Cross Product

The cross product is *not commutative* (i.e., order matters):

$$\mathbf{a} \times \mathbf{b} \neq \mathbf{b} \times \mathbf{a}.$$

However, it is *anti-commutative:*

$$\mathbf{a} \times \mathbf{b} = -\mathbf{b} \times \mathbf{a}.$$

The cross product is distributive over addition:

$$\mathbf{a} \times (\mathbf{b} + \mathbf{c}) = (\mathbf{a} \times \mathbf{b}) + (\mathbf{a} \times \mathbf{c}).$$

And it combines with scalar multiplication as follows:

$$(s\mathbf{a}) \times \mathbf{b} = \mathbf{a} \times (s\mathbf{b}) = s(\mathbf{a} \times \mathbf{b}).$$

The Cartesian basis vectors are related by cross products as follows:

$$(\mathbf{i} \times \mathbf{j}) = -(\mathbf{j} \times \mathbf{i}) = \mathbf{k},$$
$$(\mathbf{j} \times \mathbf{k}) = -(\mathbf{k} \times \mathbf{j}) = \mathbf{i},$$
$$(\mathbf{k} \times \mathbf{i}) = -(\mathbf{i} \times \mathbf{k}) = \mathbf{j}.$$

These three cross products define the direction of *positive rotations* about the Cartesian axes. The positive rotations go from $x$ to $y$ (about $z$), from $y$ to $z$ (about $x$) and from $z$ to $x$ (about $y$). Notice how the rotation about the $y$-axis "reversed" alphabetically, in that it goes from $z$ to $x$ (not from $x$ to $z$). As we'll see below, this gives us a hint as to why the matrix for rotation about the $y$-axis looks *inverted* when compared to the matrices for rotation about the $x$- and $z$-axes.

### The Cross Product in Action

The cross product has a number of applications in games. One of its most common uses is for finding a vector that is perpendicular to two other vectors. As we'll see in Section 4.3.10.2, if we know an object's local unit basis vectors, ($i_{local}$, $j_{local}$, and $k_{local}$), we can easily find a matrix representing the object's orientation. Let's assume that all we know is the object's $k_{local}$ vector—i.e., the direction in which the object is facing. If we assume that the object has no roll about $k_{local}$, then we can find $i_{local}$ by taking the cross product between $k_{local}$ (which we already know) and the world-space up vector $j_{world}$ (which equals [0  1  0]). We do so as follows: $i_{local}$ = normalize($j_{world} \times k_{local}$). We can then find $j_{local}$ by simply crossing $i_{local}$ and $k_{local}$ as follows: $j_{local} = k_{local} \times i_{local}$.

A very similar technique can be used to find a unit vector normal to the surface of a triangle or some other plane. Given three points on the plane $P_1$, $P_2$, and $P_3$, the normal vector is just $n$ = normalize$[(P_2 - P_1) \times (P_3 - P_1)]$.

Cross products are also used in physics simulations. When a force is applied to an object, it will give rise to rotational motion if and only if it is applied off-center. This rotational force is known as a *torque*, and it is calculated as follows. Given a force $F$, and a vector $r$ from the center of mass to the point at which the force is applied, the torque $N = r \times F$.

## 4.2.5. Linear Interpolation of Points and Vectors

In games, we often need to find a vector that is midway between two known vectors. For example, if we want to smoothly animate an object from point $A$ to point $B$ over the course of two seconds at 30 frames per second, we would need to find 60 intermediate positions between $A$ and $B$.

A *linear interpolation* is a simple mathematical operation that finds an intermediate point between two known points. The name of this operation is often shortened to LERP. The operation is defined as follows, where $\beta$ ranges from 0 to 1 inclusive:

$$\mathbf{L} = \mathbf{LERP}(\mathbf{A}, \mathbf{B}, \beta) = (1 - \beta)\mathbf{A} + \beta\mathbf{B}$$
$$= [(1 - \beta)A_x + \beta B_x, \quad (1 - \beta)A_y + \beta B_y, \quad (1 - \beta)A_z + \beta B_z].$$

Geometrically, $\mathbf{L} = \mathbf{LERP}(\mathbf{A}, \mathbf{B}, \beta)$ is the position vector of a point that lies $\beta$ percent of the way along the line segment from point $\mathbf{A}$ to point $\mathbf{B}$, as shown in Figure 4.15. Mathematically, the **LERP** function is just a *weighted average* of the two input vectors, with weights $(1 - \beta)$ and $\beta$, respectively. Notice that the weights always add to 1, which is a general requirement for any weighted average.

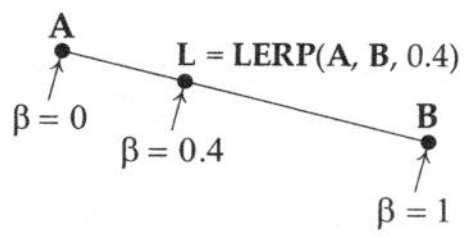

Figure 4.15. Linear interpolation (LERP) between points A and B, with $\beta = 0.4$.

## 4.3. Matrices

A *matrix* is a rectangular array of $m \times n$ scalars. Matrices are a convenient way of representing linear transformations such as translation, rotation, and scale.

A matrix $\mathbf{M}$ is usually written as a grid of scalars $M_{rc}$ enclosed in square brackets, where the subscripts $r$ and $c$ represent the row and column indices of the entry, respectively. For example, if $\mathbf{M}$ is a $3 \times 3$ matrix, it could be written as follows:

$$\mathbf{M} = \begin{bmatrix} M_{11} & M_{12} & M_{13} \\ M_{21} & M_{22} & M_{23} \\ M_{31} & M_{32} & M_{33} \end{bmatrix}.$$

We can think of the rows and/or columns of a $3 \times 3$ matrix as 3D vectors. When all of the row and column vectors of a $3 \times 3$ matrix are of unit magnitude, we call it a *special orthogonal* matrix. This is also known as an *isotropic* matrix, or an *orthonormal* matrix. Such matrices represent pure rotations.

Under certain constraints, a $4 \times 4$ matrix can represent arbitrary 3D *transformations*, including *translations, rotations,* and changes in *scale*. These are called *transformation matrices,* and they are the kinds of matrices that will be most useful to us as game engineers. The transformations represented by a matrix are applied to a point or vector via matrix multiplication. We'll investigate how this works below.

An *affine* matrix is a $4 \times 4$ transformation matrix that preserves parallelism of lines and relative distance ratios, but not necessarily absolute lengths and angles. An affine matrix is any combination of the following operations: rotation, translation, scale and/or shear.

### 4.3.1. Matrix Multiplication

The product $\mathbf{P}$ of two matrices $\mathbf{A}$ and $\mathbf{B}$ is written $\mathbf{P} = \mathbf{AB}$. If $\mathbf{A}$ and $\mathbf{B}$ are transformation matrices, then the product $\mathbf{P}$ is another transformation matrix that performs *both* of the original transformations. For example, if $\mathbf{A}$ is a scale matrix and $\mathbf{B}$ is a rotation, the matrix $\mathbf{P}$ would both scale *and* rotate the points or vectors to which it is applied. This is particularly useful in game programming, because we can precalculate a single matrix that performs a whole sequence of transformations and then apply all of those transformations to a large number of vectors efficiently.

To calculate a matrix product, we simply take dot products between the rows of the $n_A \times m_A$ matrix $\mathbf{A}$ and the columns of the $n_B \times m_B$ matrix $\mathbf{B}$. Each dot product becomes one component of the resulting matrix $\mathbf{P}$. The two matrices can be multiplied as long as the *inner dimensions* are equal (i.e., $m_A = n_B$). For example, if $\mathbf{A}$ and $\mathbf{B}$ are $3 \times 3$ matrices, then

$$\mathbf{P} = \mathbf{AB},$$

$$
\begin{aligned}
P_{11} &= \mathbf{A}_{\text{row1}} \cdot \mathbf{B}_{\text{col1}}; & P_{12} &= \mathbf{A}_{\text{row1}} \cdot \mathbf{B}_{\text{col2}}; & P_{13} &= \mathbf{A}_{\text{row1}} \cdot \mathbf{B}_{\text{col3}}; \\
P_{21} &= \mathbf{A}_{\text{row2}} \cdot \mathbf{B}_{\text{col1}}; & P_{22} &= \mathbf{A}_{\text{row2}} \cdot \mathbf{B}_{\text{col2}}; & P_{23} &= \mathbf{A}_{\text{row2}} \cdot \mathbf{B}_{\text{col3}}; \\
P_{31} &= \mathbf{A}_{\text{row3}} \cdot \mathbf{B}_{\text{col1}}; & P_{32} &= \mathbf{A}_{\text{row3}} \cdot \mathbf{B}_{\text{col2}}; & P_{33} &= \mathbf{A}_{\text{row3}} \cdot \mathbf{B}_{\text{col3}}.
\end{aligned}
$$

Matrix multiplication is not commutative. In other words, the order in which matrix multiplication is done matters:

$$\mathbf{AB} \neq \mathbf{BA}.$$

We'll see exactly why this matters in Section 4.3.2.

Matrix multiplication is often called *concatenation*, because the product of $n$ transformation matrices is a matrix that concatenates, or chains together, the original sequence of transformations in the order the matrices were multiplied.

## 4.3.2.  Representing Points and Vectors as Matrices

Points and vectors can be represented as *row matrices* ($1 \times n$) or *column matrices* ($n \times 1$), where $n$ is the dimension of the space we're working with (usually 2 or 3). For example, the vector $\mathbf{v} = (3, 4, -1)$ can be written either as

$$\mathbf{v}_1 = [3 \quad 4 \quad -1],$$

or as

$$\mathbf{v}_2 = \begin{bmatrix} 3 \\ 4 \\ -1 \end{bmatrix} = \mathbf{v}_1^{\text{T}}.$$

The choice between column and row vectors is a completely arbitrary one, but it does affect the order in which matrix multiplications are written. This happens because when multiplying matrices, the inner dimensions of the two matrices must be equal, so:

- to multiply a $1 \times n$ row vector by an $n \times n$ matrix, the vector must appear to the *left* of the matrix ( $\mathbf{v}'_{1 \times n} = \mathbf{v}_{1 \times n} \mathbf{M}_{n \times n}$ ), whereas
- to multiply an $n \times n$ matrix by an $n \times 1$ column vector, the vector must appear to the *right* of the matrix ( $\mathbf{v}'_{n \times 1} = \mathbf{M}_{n \times n} \mathbf{v}_{n \times 1}$ ).

If multiple transformation matrices $\mathbf{A}$, $\mathbf{B}$, and $\mathbf{C}$ are applied in order to a vector $\mathbf{v}$, the transformations "read" from *left to right* when using *row* vectors, but from *right to left* when using column vectors. The easiest way to remember this is to realize that the matrix *closest* to the vector is applied first. This is illustrated by the parentheses below:

$$\mathbf{v}' = (((\mathbf{v}\mathbf{A})\mathbf{B})\mathbf{C}) \quad \text{Row vectors: read left-to-right;}$$

$$\mathbf{v}' = (\mathbf{C}(\mathbf{B}(\mathbf{A}\mathbf{v}))) \quad \text{Column vectors: read right-to-left.}$$

In this book we'll adopt the *row vector convention,* because the left-to-right order of transformations is most intuitive to read for English-speaking people. That said, be very careful to check which convention is used by your game engine, and by other books, papers, or web pages you may read. You can usually tell by seeing whether vector-matrix multiplications are written with the vector on the left (for row vectors) or the right (for column vectors) of the matrix. When using column vectors, you'll need to *transpose* all the matrices shown in this book.

### 4.3.3. The Identity Matrix

The *identity matrix* is a matrix that, when multiplied by any other matrix, yields the very same matrix. It is usually represented by the symbol $\mathbf{I}$. The identity matrix is always a square matrix with 1's along the diagonal and 0's everywhere else:

$$\mathbf{I}_{3 \times 3} = \begin{bmatrix} 1 & 0 & 0 \\ 0 & 1 & 0 \\ 0 & 0 & 1 \end{bmatrix};$$

$$\mathbf{A}\mathbf{I} = \mathbf{I}\mathbf{A} \equiv \mathbf{A}.$$

### 4.3.4. Matrix Inversion

The *inverse* of a matrix $\mathbf{A}$ is another matrix (denoted $\mathbf{A}^{-1}$) that *undoes* the effects of matrix $\mathbf{A}$. So, for example, if $\mathbf{A}$ rotates objects by 37 degrees about the $z$-axis, then $\mathbf{A}^{-1}$ will rotate by $-37$ degrees about the $z$-axis. Likewise, if $\mathbf{A}$ scales objects to be twice their original size, then $\mathbf{A}^{-1}$ scales objects to be half-sized. When a matrix is multiplied by its own inverse, the result is *always* the identity matrix, so

$\mathbf{A}(\mathbf{A}^{-1}) \equiv (\mathbf{A}^{-1})\mathbf{A} \equiv \mathbf{I}$. Not all matrices have inverses. However, all *affine* matrices (combinations of pure rotations, translations, scales, and shears) do have inverses. Gaussian elimination or LU decomposition can be used to find the inverse, if one exists.

Since we'll be dealing with matrix multiplication a lot, it's important to note here that the inverse of a sequence of concatenated matrices can be written as the *reverse concatenation* of the individual matrices' inverses. For example,

$$(\mathbf{ABC})^{-1} = \mathbf{C}^{-1}\mathbf{B}^{-1}\mathbf{A}^{-1}.$$

### 4.3.5. Transposition

The *transpose* of a matrix $\mathbf{M}$ is denoted $\mathbf{M}^{\mathrm{T}}$. It is obtained by reflecting the entries of the original matrix across its diagonal. In other words, the rows of the original matrix become the columns of the transposed matrix, and vice-versa:

$$\begin{bmatrix} a & b & c \\ d & e & f \\ g & h & i \end{bmatrix}^{\mathrm{T}} = \begin{bmatrix} a & d & g \\ b & e & h \\ c & f & i \end{bmatrix}.$$

The transpose is useful for a number of reasons. For one thing, the inverse of an orthonormal (pure rotation) matrix is exactly equal to its transpose—which is good news, because it's much cheaper to transpose a matrix than it is to find its inverse in general. Transposition can also be important when moving data from one math library to another, because some libraries use column vectors while others expect row vectors. The matrices used by a row-vector-based library will be *transposed* relative to those used by a library that employs the column vector convention.

As with the inverse, the transpose of a sequence of concatenated matrices can be rewritten as the reverse concatenation of the individual matrices' transposes. For example,

$$(\mathbf{ABC})^{\mathrm{T}} = \mathbf{C}^{\mathrm{T}}\mathbf{B}^{\mathrm{T}}\mathbf{A}^{\mathrm{T}}.$$

This will prove useful when we consider how to apply transformation matrices to points and vectors.

### 4.3.6. Homogeneous Coordinates

You may recall from high-school algebra that a $2 \times 2$ matrix can represent a rotation in two dimensions. To rotate a vector $\mathbf{r}$ through an angle of $\phi$ degrees (where positive rotations are counter-clockwise), we can write

$$[r'_x \quad r'_y] = [r_x \quad r_y] \begin{bmatrix} \cos\phi & \sin\phi \\ -\sin\phi & \cos\phi \end{bmatrix}.$$

It's probably no surprise that rotations in three dimensions can be represented by a $3 \times 3$ matrix. The two-dimensional example above is really just a three-dimensional rotation about the $z$-axis, so we can write

$$[r'_x \quad r'_y \quad r'_z] = [r_x \quad r_y \quad r_z] \begin{bmatrix} \cos\phi & \sin\phi & 0 \\ -\sin\phi & \cos\phi & 0 \\ 0 & 0 & 1 \end{bmatrix}.$$

The question naturally arises: Can a $3 \times 3$ matrix be used to represent *translations*? Sadly, the answer is no. The result of translating a point $\mathbf{r}$ by a translation $\mathbf{t}$ requires adding the components of $\mathbf{t}$ to the components of $\mathbf{r}$ individually:

$$\mathbf{r} + \mathbf{t} = [(r_x + t_x) \quad (r_y + t_y) \quad (r_z + t_z)].$$

Matrix multiplication involves multiplication and addition of matrix elements, so the idea of using multiplication for translation seems promising. But, unfortunately, there is no way to arrange the components of $\mathbf{t}$ within a $3 \times 3$ matrix such that the result of multiplying it with the column vector $\mathbf{r}$ yields sums like $(r_x + t_x)$.

The good news is that we *can* obtain sums like this if we use a $4 \times 4$ matrix. What would such a matrix look like? Well, we know that we don't want any rotational effects, so the upper $3 \times 3$ should contain an identity matrix. If we arrange the components of $\mathbf{t}$ across the bottom-most row of the matrix and set the fourth element of the $\mathbf{r}$ vector (usually called $w$) equal to 1, then taking the dot product of the vector $\mathbf{r}$ with column 1 of the matrix will yield $(1 \times r_x) + (0 \times r_y) + (0 \times r_z) + (t_x \times 1) = (r_x + t_x)$, which is exactly what we want. If the bottom right-hand corner of the matrix contains a 1 and the rest of the fourth column contains zeros, then the resulting vector will also have a 1 in its $w$ component. Here's what the final $4 \times 4$ translation matrix looks like:

$$\mathbf{r} + \mathbf{t} = [r_x \quad r_y \quad r_z \quad 1] \begin{bmatrix} 1 & 0 & 0 & 0 \\ 0 & 1 & 0 & 0 \\ 0 & 0 & 1 & 0 \\ t_x & t_y & t_z & 1 \end{bmatrix}$$

$$= [(r_x + t_x) \quad (r_y + t_y) \quad (r_z + t_z) \quad 1].$$

When a point or vector is extended from three dimensions to four in this manner, we say that it has been written in *homogeneous coordinates*. A point in homogeneous coordinates always has $w = 1$. Most of the 3D matrix math done by game engines is performed using $4 \times 4$ matrices with four-element points and vectors written in homogeneous coordinates.

### 4.3.6.1. Transforming Direction Vectors

Mathematically, points (position vectors) and direction vectors are treated in subtly different ways. When transforming a point by a matrix, the translation, rotation, and scale of the matrix are all applied to the point. But when transforming a direction by a matrix, the *translational* effects of the matrix are ignored. This is because direction vectors have no translation per se—applying a translation to a direction would alter its magnitude, which is usually not what we want.

In homogeneous coordinates, we achieve this by defining points to have their $w$ components equal to one, while direction vectors have their $w$ components equal to *zero*. In the example below, notice how the $w = 0$ component of the vector **v** multiplies with the **t** vector in the matrix, thereby eliminating translation in the final result:

$$[\mathbf{v} \quad 0] \begin{bmatrix} \mathbf{U} & \mathbf{0} \\ \mathbf{t} & 1 \end{bmatrix} = [(\mathbf{v}\mathbf{U} + 0\mathbf{t}) \quad 0] = [\mathbf{v}\mathbf{U} \quad 0].$$

Technically, a point in homogeneous (four-dimensional) coordinates can be converted into non-homogeneous (three-dimensional) coordinates by dividing the $x$, $y$, and $z$ components by the $w$ component:

$$[x \quad y \quad z \quad w] \equiv \begin{bmatrix} \dfrac{x}{w} & \dfrac{y}{w} & \dfrac{z}{w} \end{bmatrix}.$$

This sheds some light on why we set a point's $w$ component to one and a vector's $w$ component to zero. Dividing by $w = 1$ has no effect on the coordinates of a point, but dividing a pure direction vector's components by $w = 0$ would yield infinity. A point at infinity in 4D can be rotated but not translated, because no matter what translation we try to apply, the point will remain at infinity. So in effect, a pure direction vector in three-dimensional space acts like a point at infinity in four-dimensional homogeneous space.

## 4.3.7. Atomic Transformation Matrices

Any affine transformation matrix can be created by simply concatenating a sequence of 4×4 matrices representing pure translations, pure rotations, pure scale operations, and/or pure shears. These atomic transformation building blocks are presented below. (We'll omit shear from these discussions, as it tends to be used only rarely in games.)

Notice that all affine $4 \times 4$ transformation matrices can be partitioned into four components:

$$\begin{bmatrix} \mathbf{U}_{3\times3} & \mathbf{0}_{3\times1} \\ \mathbf{t}_{1\times3} & 1 \end{bmatrix}.$$

- the upper $3 \times 3$ matrix $\mathbf{U}$, which represents the rotation and/or scale,
- a $1 \times 3$ translation vector $\mathbf{t}$,
- a $3 \times 1$ vector of zeros $\mathbf{0} = [\,0\,0\,0\,]^T$, and
- a scalar 1 in the bottom-right corner of the matrix.

When a point is multiplied by a matrix that has been partitioned like this, the result is as follows:

$$[\mathbf{r}'_{1\times3} \quad 1] = [\mathbf{r}_{1\times3} \quad 1] \begin{bmatrix} \mathbf{U}_{3\times3} & \mathbf{0}_{3\times1} \\ \mathbf{t}_{1\times3} & 1 \end{bmatrix} = [(\mathbf{r}\mathbf{U}+\mathbf{t}) \quad 1].$$

### 4.3.7.1. Translation

The following matrix translates a point by the vector $\mathbf{t}$:

$$\mathbf{r} + \mathbf{t} = [r_x \quad r_y \quad r_z \quad 1] \begin{bmatrix} 1 & 0 & 0 & 0 \\ 0 & 1 & 0 & 0 \\ 0 & 0 & 1 & 0 \\ t_x & t_y & t_z & 1 \end{bmatrix}$$

$$= [(r_x+t_x) \quad (r_y+t_y) \quad (r_z+t_z) \quad 1],$$

or in partitioned shorthand:

$$[\mathbf{r} \quad 1] \begin{bmatrix} \mathbf{I} & \mathbf{0} \\ \mathbf{t} & 1 \end{bmatrix} = [(\mathbf{r}+\mathbf{t}) \quad 1].$$

To invert a pure translation matrix, simply negate the vector $\mathbf{t}$ (i.e., negate $t_x$, $t_y$, and $t_z$).

### 4.3.7.2. Rotation

All $4 \times 4$ pure rotation matrices have the form:

$$[\mathbf{r} \quad 1] \begin{bmatrix} \mathbf{R} & \mathbf{0} \\ \mathbf{0} & 1 \end{bmatrix} = [\mathbf{r}\mathbf{R} \quad 1].$$

The $\mathbf{t}$ vector is zero and the upper $3 \times 3$ matrix $\mathbf{R}$ contains cosines and sines of the rotation angle, measured in radians.

The following matrix represents rotation about the $x$-axis by an angle $\phi$:

$$\text{rotate}_x(\mathbf{r},\phi) = [r_x \quad r_y \quad r_z \quad 1] \begin{bmatrix} 1 & 0 & 0 & 0 \\ 0 & \cos\phi & \sin\phi & 0 \\ 0 & -\sin\phi & \cos\phi & 0 \\ 0 & 0 & 0 & 1 \end{bmatrix}.$$

The matrix below represents rotation about the $y$-axis by an angle $\theta$. Notice that this one is *transposed* relative to the other two—the positive and negative sine terms have been reflected across the diagonal:

$$\text{rotate}_y(\mathbf{r}, \theta) = \begin{bmatrix} r_x & r_y & r_z & 1 \end{bmatrix} \begin{bmatrix} \cos\theta & 0 & -\sin\theta & 0 \\ 0 & 1 & 0 & 0 \\ \sin\theta & 0 & \cos\theta & 0 \\ 0 & 0 & 0 & 1 \end{bmatrix}.$$

This matrix represents rotation about the $z$-axis by an angle $\gamma$:

$$\text{rotate}_z(\mathbf{r}, \gamma) = \begin{bmatrix} r_x & r_y & r_z & 1 \end{bmatrix} \begin{bmatrix} \cos\gamma & \sin\gamma & 0 & 0 \\ -\sin\gamma & \cos\gamma & 0 & 0 \\ 0 & 0 & 1 & 0 \\ 0 & 0 & 0 & 1 \end{bmatrix}.$$

Here are a few observations about these matrices:

- The 1 within the upper $3 \times 3$ always appears on the axis we're rotating about, while the sine and cosine terms are off-axis.

- Positive rotations go from $x$ to $y$ (about $z$), from $y$ to $z$ (about $x$), and from $z$ to $x$ (about $y$). The $z$ to $x$ rotation "wraps around," which is why the rotation matrix about the $y$-axis is transposed relative to the other two. (Use the right-hand or left-hand rule to remember this.)

- The inverse of a pure rotation is just its transpose. This works because inverting a rotation is equivalent to rotating by the negative angle. You may recall that $\cos(-\theta) = \cos(\theta)$ while $\sin(-\theta) = -\sin(\theta)$, so negating the angle causes the two sine terms to effectively switch places, while the cosine terms stay put.

### 4.3.7.3. Scale

The following matrix scales the point $\mathbf{r}$ by a factor of $s_x$ along the $x$-axis, $s_y$ along the $y$-axis, and $s_z$ along the $z$-axis:

$$\mathbf{r}\,\mathbf{S} = \begin{bmatrix} r_x & r_y & r_z & 1 \end{bmatrix} \begin{bmatrix} s_x & 0 & 0 & 0 \\ 0 & s_y & 0 & 0 \\ 0 & 0 & s_z & 0 \\ 0 & 0 & 0 & 1 \end{bmatrix}$$

$$= \begin{bmatrix} s_x r_x & s_y r_y & s_z r_z & 1 \end{bmatrix}.$$

or in partitioned shorthand:

$$[\mathbf{r} \quad 1] \begin{bmatrix} \mathbf{S}_{3\times3} & 0 \\ 0 & 1 \end{bmatrix} = [\mathbf{r}\,\mathbf{S}_{3\times3} \quad 1].$$

Here are some observations about this kind of matrix:

- To invert a scaling matrix, simply substitute $s_x$, $s_y$, and $s_z$ with their reciprocals (i.e., $1/s_x$, $1/s_y$, and $1/s_z$).

- When the scale factor along all three axes is the same ($s_x = s_y = s_z$), we call this *uniform scale*. Spheres remain spheres under uniform scale, whereas under nonuniform scale they become ellipsoids. To keep the mathematics of bounding sphere checks simple and fast, many game engines impose the restriction that only uniform scale may be applied to renderable geometry or collision primitives.

- When a uniform scale matrix $\mathbf{S}_u$ and a rotation matrix $\mathbf{R}$ are concatenated, the order of multiplication is unimportant (i.e., $\mathbf{S}_u\mathbf{R} = \mathbf{R}\mathbf{S}_u$). This only works for *uniform* scale!

### 4.3.8.  4 × 3 Matrices

The rightmost column of an affine $4 \times 4$ matrix always contains the vector $[\,0 \quad 0 \quad 0 \quad 1\,]^{T}$. As such, game programmers often omit the fourth column to save memory. You'll encounter $4 \times 3$ affine matrices frequently in game math libraries.

### 4.3.9.  Coordinate Spaces

We've seen how to apply transformations to points and direction vectors using $4 \times 4$ matrices. We can extend this idea to rigid objects by realizing that such an object can be thought of as an infinite collection of points. Applying a transformation to a rigid object is like applying that same transformation to every point within the object. For example, in computer graphics an object is usually represented by a mesh of triangles, each of which has three vertices represented by points. In this case, the object can be transformed by applying a transformation matrix to all of its vertices in turn.

We said above that a point is a vector whose tail is fixed to the origin of some coordinate system. This is another way of saying that a point (position vector) is always expressed *relative* to a set of coordinate axes. The triplet of numbers representing a point changes numerically whenever we select a new set of coordinate axes. In Figure 4.16, we see a point P represented by two different position vectors—the vector $\mathbf{P}_A$ gives the position of P relative to the

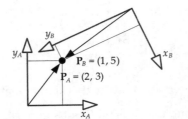

**Figure 4.16.** Position vectors for the point P relative to different coordinate axes.

"A" axes, while the vector $\mathbf{P}_B$ gives the position of that same point relative to a different set of axes "B."

In physics, a set of coordinate axes represents a frame of reference, so we sometimes refer to a set of axes as a *coordinate frame* (or just a *frame*). People in the game industry also use the term *coordinate space* (or simply *space*) to refer to a set of coordinate axes. In the following sections, we'll look at a few of the most common coordinate spaces used in games and computer graphics.

#### 4.3.9.1. Model Space

When a triangle mesh is created in a tool such as Maya or 3DStudioMAX, the positions of the triangles' vertices are specified relative to a Cartesian coordinate system which we call *model space* (also known as *object space* or *local space*). The model space origin is usually placed at a central location within the object, such as at its center of mass, or on the ground between the feet of a humanoid or animal character.

Most game objects have an inherent directionality. For example, an airplane has a nose, a tail fin, and wings that correspond to the front, up, and left/right directions. The model space axes are usually aligned to these natural directions on the model, and they're given intuitive names to indicate their directionality as illustrated in Figure 4.17.

- *Front.* This name is given to the axis that points in the direction that the object naturally travels or faces. In this book, we'll use the symbol $\mathbf{F}$ to refer to a unit basis vector along the front axis.

- *Up.* This name is given to the axis that points towards the top of the object. The unit basis vector along this axis will be denoted $\mathbf{U}$.

- *Left or right.* The name "left" or "right" is given to the axis that points toward the left or right side of the object. Which name is chosen depends on whether your game engine uses left-handed or right-handed

Figure 4.17. One possible choice of the model-space front, left and up axis basis vectors for an airplane.

coordinates. The unit basis vector along this axis will be denoted **L** or **R**, as appropriate.

The mapping between the (*front, up, left*) labels and the (*x, y, z*) axes is completely arbitrary. A common choice when working with right-handed axes is to assign the label *front* to the positive *z*-axis, the label *left* to the positive *x*-axis, and the label *up* to the positive *y*-axis (or in terms of unit basis vectors, **F** = **k**, **L** = **i**, and **U** = **j**). However, it's equally common for +*x* to be *front* and +*z* to be right (**F** = **i**, **R** = **k**, **U** = **j**). I've also worked with engines in which the *z*-axis is oriented vertically. The only real requirement is that you stick to one convention consistently throughout your engine.

As an example of how intuitive axis names can reduce confusion, consider *Euler angles* (pitch, yaw, roll), which are often used to describe an aircraft's orientation. It's not possible to define pitch, yaw, and roll angles in terms of the (**i, j, k**) basis vectors because their orientation is arbitrary. However, we *can* define pitch, yaw, and roll in terms of the (**L, U, F**) basis vectors, because their orientations are clearly defined. Specifically,

- *pitch* is rotation about **L** or **R**,
- *yaw* is rotation about **U**, and
- *roll* is rotation about **F**.

### 4.3.9.2. World Space

*World space* is a fixed coordinate space, in which the positions, orientations, and scales of all objects in the game world are expressed. This coordinate space ties all the individual objects together into a cohesive virtual world.

The location of the world-space origin is arbitrary, but it is often placed near the center of the playable game space to minimize the reduction in floating-point precision that can occur when (*x, y, z*) coordinates grow very large. Likewise, the orientation of the *x-, y-,* and *z*-axes is arbitrary, although most

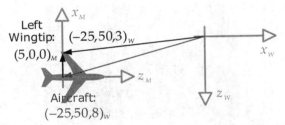

**Figure 4.18.** A lear jet whose left wingtip is at (5, 0, 0) in model space. If the jet is rotated by 90 degrees about the world-space *y*-axis, and its model-space origin translated to (–25, 50, 8) in world space, then its left wingtip would end up at (–25, 50, 3) when expressed in world space coordinates.

of the engines I've encountered use either a *y*-up or a *z*-up convention. The *y*-up convention was probably an extension of the two-dimensional convention found in most mathematics textbooks, where the *y*-axis is shown going up and the *x*-axis going to the right. The *z*-up convention is also common, because it allows a top-down orthographic view of the game world to look like a traditional two-dimensional *xy*-plot.

As an example, let's say that our aircraft's left wingtip is at (5, 0, 0) in model space. (In our game, front vectors correspond to the positive *z*-axis in model space with *y* up, as shown in Figure 4.17.) Now imagine that the jet is facing down the positive *x*-axis in world space, with its model-space origin at some arbitrary location, such as (–25, 50, 8). Because the **F** vector of the airplane, which corresponds to +*z* in model space, is facing down the +*x*-axis in world space, we know that the jet has been rotated by 90 degrees about the world *y*-axis. So if the aircraft were sitting at the world space origin, its left wingtip would be at (0, 0, –5) in world space. But because the aircraft's origin has been translated to (–25, 50, 8), the final position of the jet's left wingtip in model space is (–25, 50, [8 – 5]) = (–25, 50, 3). This is illustrated in Figure 4.18.

We could of course populate our friendly skies with more than one Lear jet. In that case, all of their left wingtips would have coordinates of (5, 0, 0) in model space. But in world space, the left wingtips would have all sorts of interesting coordinates, depending on the orientation and translation of each aircraft.

### 4.3.9.3. View Space

*View space* (also known as *camera space*) is a coordinate frame fixed to the camera. The view space origin is placed at the focal point of the camera. Again, any axis orientation scheme is possible. However, a *y*-up convention with *z*

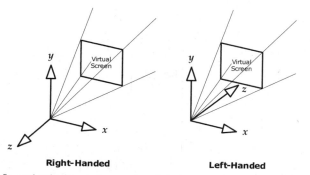

Figure 4.19. Left- and right-handed examples of view space, also known as camera space.

increasing in the direction the camera is facing (left-handed) is typical because it allows $z$ coordinates to represent depths into the screen. Other engines and APIs, such as OpenGL, define view space to be right-handed, in which case the camera faces towards *negative z*, and $z$ coordinates represent negative depths.

## 4.3.10. Change of Basis

In games and computer graphics, it is often quite useful to convert an object's position, orientation, and scale from one coordinate system into another. We call this operation a *change of basis*.

### 4.3.10.1. Coordinate Space Hierarchies

Coordinate frames are relative. That is, if you want to quantify the position, orientation, and scale of a set of axes in three-dimensional space, you must specify these quantities *relative to* some other set of axes (otherwise the numbers would have no meaning). This implies that coordinate spaces form a *hierarchy*—every coordinate space is a *child* of some other coordinate space, and the other space acts as its *parent*. World space has no parent; it is at the root of the coordinate-space tree, and all other coordinate systems are ultimately specified relative to it, either as direct children or more-distant relatives.

### 4.3.10.2. Building a Change of Basis Matrix

The matrix that transforms points and directions from any child coordinate system C to its parent coordinate system P can be written $\mathbf{M}_{C \to P}$ (pronounced "C to P"). The subscript indicates that this matrix transforms points and directions from child space to parent space. Any child-space position vector $\mathbf{P}_C$ can be transformed into a parent-space position vector $\mathbf{P}_P$ as follows:

$$\mathbf{P}_P = \mathbf{P}_C \, \mathbf{M}_{C \to P};$$

$$\mathbf{M}_{C \to P} = \begin{bmatrix} \mathbf{i}_C & 0 \\ \mathbf{j}_C & 0 \\ \mathbf{k}_C & 0 \\ \mathbf{t}_C & 0 \end{bmatrix}$$

$$= \begin{bmatrix} i_{Cx} & i_{Cy} & i_{Cz} & 0 \\ j_{Cx} & j_{Cy} & j_{Cz} & 0 \\ k_{Cx} & k_{Cy} & k_{Cz} & 0 \\ t_{Cx} & t_{Cy} & t_{Cz} & 1 \end{bmatrix}.$$

In this equation,

- $\mathbf{i}_C$ is the unit basis vector along the child space $x$-axis, expressed in parent space coordinates;
- $\mathbf{j}_C$ is the unit basis vector along the child space $y$-axis, in parent space;
- $\mathbf{k}_C$ is the unit basis vector along the child space $z$-axis, in parent space;
- $\mathbf{t}_C$ is the translation of the child coordinate system relative to parent space.

This result should not be too surprising. The $\mathbf{t}_C$ vector is just the translation of the child space axes relative to parent space, so if the rest of the matrix were identity, the point $(0, 0, 0)$ in child space would become $\mathbf{t}_C$ in parent space, just as we'd expect. The $\mathbf{i}_C$, $\mathbf{j}_C$, and $\mathbf{k}_C$ unit vectors form the upper $3 \times 3$ of the matrix, which is a pure rotation matrix because these vectors are of unit length. We can see this more clearly by considering a simple example, such as a situation in which child space is rotated by an angle $\gamma$ about the $z$-axis, with no translation. The matrix for such a rotation is given by

$$\text{rotate}_z(\mathbf{r}, \gamma) = \begin{bmatrix} r_x & r_y & r_z & 1 \end{bmatrix} \begin{bmatrix} \cos\gamma & \sin\gamma & 0 & 0 \\ -\sin\gamma & \cos\gamma & 0 & 0 \\ 0 & 0 & 1 & 0 \\ 0 & 0 & 0 & 1 \end{bmatrix}. \tag{4.2}$$

But in Figure 4.20, we can see that the coordinates of the $\mathbf{i}_C$ and $\mathbf{j}_C$ vectors, expressed in parent space, are $\mathbf{i}_C = [\cos\gamma \ \sin\gamma \ 0]$ and $\mathbf{j}_C = [-\sin\gamma \ \cos\gamma \ 0]$. When we plug these vectors into our formula for $\mathbf{M}_{C \to P}$, with $\mathbf{k}_C = [0 \ 0 \ 1]$, it exactly matches the matrix $\text{rotate}_z(\mathbf{r}, \gamma)$ from Equation (4.2).

### Scaling the Child Axes

Scaling of the child coordinate system is accomplished by simply scaling the unit basis vectors appropriately. For example, if child space is scaled up by a

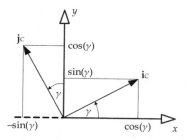

Figure 4.20. Change of basis when child axes are rotated by an angle γ relative to parent.

factor of two, then the basis vectors $\mathbf{i}_C$, $\mathbf{j}_C$, and $\mathbf{k}_C$ will be of length 2 instead of unit length.

### 4.3.10.3. Extracting Unit Basis Vectors from a Matrix

The fact that we can build a change of basis matrix out of a translation and three Cartesian basis vectors gives us another powerful tool: Given *any* affine $4 \times 4$ transformation matrix, we can go in the other direction and extract the child-space basis vectors $\mathbf{i}_C$, $\mathbf{j}_C$, and $\mathbf{k}_C$ from it by simply isolating the appropriate rows of the matrix (or columns if your math library uses column vectors).

This can be incredibly useful. Let's say we are given a vehicle's model-to-world transform as an affine $4 \times 4$ matrix (a very common representation). This is really just a change of basis matrix, transforming points in model space into their equivalents in world space. Let's further assume that in our game, the positive z-axis always points in the direction that an object is facing. So, to find a unit vector representing the vehicle's facing direction, we can simply extract $\mathbf{k}_C$ directly from the model-to-world matrix (by grabbing its third row). This vector will already be normalized and ready to go.

### 4.3.10.4. Transforming Coordinate Systems versus Vectors

We've said that the matrix $\mathbf{M}_{C \to P}$ transforms points and directions from child space into parent space. Recall that the fourth row of $\mathbf{M}_{C \to P}$ contains $\mathbf{t}_C$, the translation of the child coordinate axes relative to the world space axes. Therefore, another way to visualize the matrix $\mathbf{M}_{C \to P}$ is to imagine it taking the parent *coordinate axes* and transforming them *into* the child axes. This is the reverse of what happens to points and direction vectors. In other words, if a matrix transforms *vectors* from child space to parent space, then it also transforms *coordinate axes* from parent space to child space. This makes sense when you think about it—moving a point 20 units to the right with the coordinate axes fixed is the same as moving the coordinate axes 20 units to the left with the point fixed. This concept is illustrated in Figure 4.21.

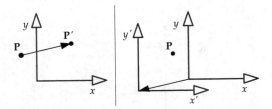

**Figure 4.21.** Two ways to interpret a transformation matrix. On the left, the point moves against a fixed set of axes. On the right, the axes move in the opposite direction while the point remains fixed.

Of course, this is just another point of potential confusion. If you're thinking in terms of coordinate axes, then transformations go in one direction, but if you're thinking in terms of points and vectors, they go in the other direction! As with many confusing things in life, your best bet is probably to choose a single "canonical" way of thinking about things and stick with it. For example, in this book we've chosen the following conventions:

- Transformations apply to vectors (not coordinate axes).
- Vectors are written as rows (not columns).

Taken together, these two conventions allow us to read sequences of matrix multiplications from left to right and have them make sense (e.g., $\mathbf{P}_D = \mathbf{P}_A \, \mathbf{M}_{A \to B} \, \mathbf{M}_{B \to C} \, \mathbf{M}_{C \to D}$ ). Obviously if you start thinking about the coordinate axes moving around rather than the points and vectors, you either have to read the transforms from right to left, or flip one of these two conventions around. It doesn't really matter what conventions you choose as long as *you* find them easy to remember and work with.

That said, it's important to note that certain problems are easier to think about in terms of vectors being transformed, while others are easier to work with when you imagine the coordinate axes moving around. Once you get good at thinking about 3D vector and matrix math, you'll find it pretty easy to flip back and forth between conventions as needed to suit the problem at hand.

## 4.3.11.  Transforming Normal Vectors

A *normal vector* is a special kind of vector, because in addition to (usually!) being of unit length, it carries with it the additional requirement that it should always remain *perpendicular* to whatever surface or plane it is associated with. Special care must be taken when transforming a normal vector, to ensure that both its length and perpendicularity properties are maintained.

In general, if a point or (non-normal) vector can be rotated from space A to space B via the $3 \times 3$ marix $\mathbf{M}_{A \to B}$ , then a normal vector $\mathbf{n}$ will be transformed from space A to space B via the *inverse transpose* of that matrix, $(\mathbf{M}_{A \to B}^{-1})^{\mathrm{T}}$ . We will not prove or derive this result here (see [28], Section 3.5 for an excellent derivation). However, we will observe that if the matrix $\mathbf{M}_{A \to B}$ contains only uniform scale and no shear, then the angles between all surfaces and vectors in space B will be the same as they were in space A. In this case, the matrix $\mathbf{M}_{A \to B}$ will actually work just fine for any vector, normal or non-normal. However, if $\mathbf{M}_{A \to B}$ contains nonuniform scale or shear (i.e., is *non-orthogonal*), then the angles between surfaces and vectors are *not* preserved when moving from space A to space B. A vector that was normal to a surface in space A will not necessarily be perpendicular to that surface in space B. The inverse transpose operation accounts for this distortion, bringing normal vectors back into perpendicularity with their surfaces even when the transformation involves non-uniform scale or shear.

## 4.3.12. Storing Matrices in Memory

In the C and C++ languages, a two-dimensional array is often used to store a matrix. Recall that in C/C++ two-dimensional array syntax, the first subscript is the row and the second is the column, and that the column index varies fastest as you move through memory sequentially.

```
float m[4][4]; // [row][col], col varies fastest

// "flatten" the array to demonstrate ordering
float* pm = &m[0][0];
ASSERT( &pm[0] == &m[0][0] );
ASSERT( &pm[1] == &m[0][1] );
ASSERT( &pm[2] == &m[0][2] );
// etc.
```

We have two choices when storing a matrix in a two-dimensional C/C++ array. We can either

1. store the vectors ($\mathbf{i}_C$, $\mathbf{j}_C$, $\mathbf{k}_C$, $\mathbf{t}_C$) *contiguously* in memory (i.e., each row contains a single vector), or

2. store the vectors *strided* in memory (i.e., each column contains one vector).

The benefit of approach (1) is that we can address any one of the four vectors by simply indexing into the matrix and interpreting the four contiguous values we find there as a 4-element vector. This layout also has the benefit of matching up exactly with *row vector* matrix equations (which is another reason why I've selected row vector notation for this book). Approach (2) is sometimes necessary when doing fast matrix-vector multiplies using a vector-enabled (SIMD) microprocessor, as we'll see later in this chapter. In most game engines I've personally encountered, matrices are stored using approach (1), with the *vectors* in the *rows* of the two-dimensional C/C++ array. This is shown below:

```
float M[4][4];

M[0][0]=ix;   M[0][1]=iy;   M[0][2]=iz;   M[0][3]=0.0f;
M[1][0]=jx;   M[1][1]=jy;   M[1][2]=jz;   M[1][3]=0.0f;
M[2][0]=kx;   M[2][1]=ky;   M[2][2]=kz;   M[2][3]=0.0f;
M[3][0]=tx;   M[3][1]=ty;   M[3][2]=tz;   M[3][3]=1.0f;
```

The matrix M looks like this when viewed in a debugger:

```
M[][]
    [0]
        [0] ix
        [1] iy
        [2] iz
        [3] 0.0000

    [1]
        [0] jx
        [1] jy
        [2] jz
        [3] 0.0000

    [2]
        [0] kx
        [1] ky
        [2] kz
        [3] 0.0000

    [3]
        [0] tx
        [1] ty
        [2] tz
        [3] 1.0000
```

One easy way to determine which layout your engine uses is to find a function that builds a 4 × 4 translation matrix. (Every good 3D math library provides such a function.) You can then inspect the source code to see where the elements of the **t** vector are being stored. If you don't have access to the source code of your math library (which is pretty rare in the game industry), you can always call the function with an easy-to-recognize translation like (4, 3, 2), and then inspect the resulting matrix. If row 3 contains the values 4.0, 3.0, 2.0, 1.0, then the vectors are in the rows, otherwise the vectors are in the columns.

# 4.4.   Quaternions

We've seen that a $3 \times 3$ matrix can be used to represent an arbitrary rotation in three dimensions. However, a matrix is not always an ideal representation of a rotation, for a number of reasons:

1.  We need nine floating-point values to represent a rotation, which seems excessive considering that we only have three degrees of freedom—pitch, yaw, and roll.

2.  Rotating a vector requires a vector-matrix multiplication, which involves three dot products, or a total of nine multiplications and six additions. We would like to find a rotational representation that is less expensive to calculate, if possible.

3.  In games and computer graphics, it's often important to be able to find rotations that are some percentage of the way between two known rotations. For example, if we are to smoothly animate a camera from some starting orientation A to some final orientation B over the course of a few seconds, we need to be able to find lots of intermediate rotations between A and B over the course of the animation. It turns out to be difficult to do this when the A and B orientations are expressed as matrices.

Thankfully, there is a rotational representation that overcomes these three problems. It is a mathematical object known as a *quaternion*. A quaternion looks a lot like a four-dimensional vector, but it *behaves* quite differently. We usually write quaternions using non-italic, non-boldface type, like this: $q = [\, q_x \ q_y \ q_z \ q_w \,]$.

Quaternions were developed by Sir William Rowan Hamilton in 1843 as an extension to the complex numbers. They were first used to solve problems in the area of mechanics. Technically speaking, a quaternion obeys a set of rules known as a four-dimensional *normed division algebra* over the real numbers. Thankfully, we won't need to understand the details of these rather esoteric algebraic rules. For our purposes, it will suffice to know that the *unit-length* quaternions (i.e., all quaternions obeying the constraint $q_x^2 + q_y^2 + q_z^2 + q_w^2 = 1$) represent three-dimensional rotations.

There are a lot of great papers, web pages, and presentations on quaternions available on the web, for further reading. Here's one of my favorites: http://graphics.ucsd.edu/courses/cse169_w05/CSE169_04.ppt.

## 4.4.1.   Unit Quaternions as 3D Rotations

A unit quaternion can be visualized as a three-dimensional vector plus a fourth scalar coordinate. The vector part $\mathbf{q}_V$ is the unit axis of rotation, scaled by the sine of the half-angle of the rotation. The scalar part $q_S$ is the cosine of the half-angle. So the unit quaternion q can be written as follows:

$$q = [\mathbf{q}_V \quad q_S]$$
$$= [\mathbf{a} \sin\tfrac{\theta}{2} \quad \cos\tfrac{\theta}{2}],$$

where $\mathbf{a}$ is a unit vector along the axis of rotation, and $\theta$ is the angle of rotation. The direction of the rotation follows the *right-hand rule,* so if your thumb points in the direction of $\mathbf{a}$, positive rotations will be in the direction of your curved fingers.

Of course, we can also write q as a simple four-element vector:

$$q = [q_x \quad q_y \quad q_z \quad q_w], \text{ where}$$
$$q_x = q_{Vx} = a_x \sin\tfrac{\theta}{2},$$
$$q_y = q_{Vy} = a_y \sin\tfrac{\theta}{2},$$
$$q_z = q_{Vz} = a_z \sin\tfrac{\theta}{2},$$
$$q_w = q_S \quad = \cos\tfrac{\theta}{2}.$$

A unit quaternion is very much like an axis+angle representation of a rotation (i.e., a four-element vector of the form [ $\mathbf{a}$ $\theta$ ]). However, quaternions are more convenient mathematically than their axis+angle counterparts, as we shall see below.

## 4.4.2.  Quaternion Operations

Quaternions support some of the familiar operations from vector algebra, such as magnitude and vector addition. However, we must remember that the sum of two unit quaternions does not represent a 3D rotation, because such a quaternion would not be of unit length. As a result, you won't see any quaternion sums in a game engine, unless they are scaled in some way to preserve the unit length requirement.

### 4.4.2.1.  Quaternion Multiplication

One of the most important operations we will perform on quaternions is that of multiplication. Given two quaternions p and q representing two rotations $\mathbf{P}$ and $\mathbf{Q}$, respectively, the product pq represents the composite rotation (i.e., rotation $\mathbf{Q}$ followed by rotation $\mathbf{P}$). There are actually quite a few different kinds of quaternion multiplication, but we'll restrict this discussion to the variety used in conjunction with 3D rotations, namely the Grassman product. Using this definition, the product pq is defined as follows:

$$pq = \Big[ (p_S \mathbf{q}_V + q_S \mathbf{p}_V + \mathbf{p}_V \times \mathbf{q}_V) \quad (p_S q_S - \mathbf{p}_V \cdot \mathbf{q}_V) \Big].$$

Notice how the Grassman product is defined in terms of a vector part, which ends up in the $x$, $y$, and $z$ components of the resultant quaternion, and a scalar part, which ends up in the $w$ component.

### 4.4.2.2. Conjugate and Inverse

The *inverse* of a quaternion q is denoted $q^{-1}$ and is defined as a quaternion which, when multiplied by the original, yields the scalar 1 (i.e., $qq^{-1} = 0i + 0j + 0k + 1$). The quaternion $[\,0\ \ 0\ \ 0\ \ 1\,]$ represents a zero rotation (which makes sense since $\sin(0) = 0$ for the first three components, and $\cos(0) = 1$ for the last component).

In order to calculate the inverse of a quaternion, we must first define a quantity known as the *conjugate*. This is usually denoted $q^*$ and it is defined as follows:

$$q^* = [-\mathbf{q}_V \quad q_S].$$

In other words, we negate the vector part but leave the scalar part unchaged.

Given this definition of the quaternion conjugate, the inverse quaternion $q^{-1}$ is defined as follows:

$$q^{-1} = \frac{q^*}{|q|^2}.$$

Our quaternions are always of unit length (i.e., $|q| = 1$), because they represent 3D rotations. So, for our purposes, the inverse and the conjugate are identical:

$$q^{-1} = q^* = [-\mathbf{q}_V \quad q_S] \quad \text{when} \quad |q| = 1.$$

This fact is incredibly useful, because it means we can always avoid doing the (relatively expensive) division by the squared magnitude when inverting a quaternion, as long as we know a priori that the quaternion is normalized. This also means that inverting a quaternion is generally much faster than inverting a 3 × 3 matrix—a fact that you may be able to leverage in some situations when optimizing your engine.

#### Conjugate and Inverse of a Product

The conjugate of a quaternion product (pq) is equal to the reverse product of the conjugates of the individual quaternions:

$$(pq)^* = q^* p^*.$$

Likewise the inverse of a quaternion product is equal to the reverse product of the inverses of the individual quaternions:

$$(pq)^{-1} = q^{-1} p^{-1}. \tag{4.3}$$

This is analogous to the reversal that occurs when transposing or inverting matrix products.

### 4.4.3.  Rotating Vectors with Quaternions

How can we apply a quaternion rotation to a vector? The first step is to rewrite the vector in *quaternion form*. A vector is a sum involving the unit basis vectors $\mathbf{i}$, $\mathbf{j}$, and $\mathbf{k}$. A quaternion is a sum involving $\mathbf{i}$, $\mathbf{j}$, and $\mathbf{k}$, but with a fourth scalar term as well. So it makes sense that a vector can be written as a quaternion with its scalar term $q_S$ equal to zero. Given the vector $\mathbf{v}$, we can write a corresponding quaternion $v = [\ \mathbf{v}\ \ 0\ ] = [\ v_x\ \ v_y\ \ v_z\ \ 0\ ]$.

In order to rotate a vector $\mathbf{v}$ by a quaternion q, we pre-multiply the vector (written in its quaternion form v) by q and then post-multiply it by the *inverse* quaternion, $q^{-1}$. Therefore, the rotated vector $\mathbf{v}'$ can be found as follows:

$$v' = \text{rotate}(q, \mathbf{v}) = qvq^{-1}.$$

This is equivalent to using the quaternion conjugate, because our quaternions are always unit length:

$$v' = \text{rotate}(q, \mathbf{v}) = qvq^{*}. \tag{4.4}$$

The rotated vector $\mathbf{v}'$ is obtained by simply extracting it from its quaternion form v'.

Quaternion multiplication can be useful in all sorts of situations in real games. For example, let's say that we want to find a unit vector describing the direction in which an aircraft is flying. We'll further assume that in our game, the positive z-axis always points toward the front of an object by convention. So the forward unit vector of any object *in model space* is always $\mathbf{F}_M \equiv [\ 0\ \ 0\ \ 1\ ]$ by definition. To transform this vector into world space, we can simply take our aircraft's orientation quaternion q and use it with Equation (4.4) to rotate our model-space vector $\mathbf{F}_M$ into its world space equivalent $\mathbf{F}_W$ (after converting these vectors into quaternion form, of course):

$$F_W = qF_Mq^{-1} = q\ [0\ \ \ 0\ \ \ 1\ \ \ 0]\ q^{-1}.$$

#### 4.4.3.1.  Quaternion Concatenation

Rotations can be *concatenated* in exactly the same way that matrix-based transformations can, by multiplying the quaternions together. For example, consider three distinct rotations, represented by the quaternions $q_1$, $q_2$, and $q_3$, with matrix equivalents $\mathbf{R}_1$, $\mathbf{R}_2$, and $\mathbf{R}_3$. We want to apply rotation 1 first, followed by rotation 2 and finally rotation 3. The composite rotation matrix $\mathbf{R}_{net}$ can be found and applied to a vector $\mathbf{v}$ as follows:

$$\mathbf{R}_{net} = \mathbf{R}_1\mathbf{R}_2\mathbf{R}_3;$$

$$\mathbf{v}' = \mathbf{v}\mathbf{R}_1\mathbf{R}_2\mathbf{R}_3 = \mathbf{v}\mathbf{R}_{net}.$$

Likewise, the composite rotation quaternion $q_{net}$ can be found and applied to vector **v** (in its quaternion form, v) as follows:

$$q_{net} = q_3 q_2 q_1;$$

$$v' = q_3 q_2 q_1 v q_1^{-1} q_2^{-1} q_3^{-1} = q_{net} v q_{net}^{-1}.$$

Notice how the quaternion product must be performed in an order *opposite* to that in which the rotations are applied ($q_3 q_2 q_1$). This is because quaternion rotations always multiply on *both* sides of the vector, with the uninverted quaternions on the left and the inverted quaternions on the right. As we saw in Equation (4.3), the inverse of a quaternion product is the reverse product of the individual inverses, so the uninverted quaternions read right-to-left while the inverted quaternions read left-to-right.

### 4.4.4. Quaternion-Matrix Equivalence

We can convert any 3D rotation freely between a $3 \times 3$ matrix representation **R** and a quaternion representation q. If we let $q = [\ \mathbf{q}_V\ q_S\ ] = [\ q_{Vx}\ q_{Vy}\ q_{Vz}\ q_S\ ] = [\ x\ y\ z\ w\ ]$, then we can find **R** as follows:

$$\mathbf{R} = \begin{bmatrix} 1-2y^2-2z^2 & 2xy+2zw & 2xz-2yw \\ 2xy-2zw & 1-2x^2-2z^2 & 2yz+2xw \\ 2xz+2yw & 2yz-2xw & 1-2x^2-2y^2 \end{bmatrix}.$$

Likewise, given **R** we can find q as follows (where q[0] = $q_{Vx}$, q[1] = $q_{Vy}$, q[2] = $q_{Vz}$, and q[3] = $q_S$). This code assumes that we are using row vectors in C/C++ (i.e., that the rows of matrix R[row][col] correspond to the rows of the matrix **R** shown above). The code was adapted from a *Gamasutra* article by Nick Bobic, published on July 5, 1998, which is available here: http://www.gamasutra.com/view/feature/3278/rotating_objects_using_quaternions.php. For a discussion of some even faster methods for converting a matrix to a quaternion, leveraging various assumptions about the nature of the matrix, see http://www.euclideanspace.com/maths/geometry/rotations/conversions/matrixToQuaternion/index.htm.

```
void matrixToQuaternion(
    const float R[3][3],
    float       q[/*4*/])
{
    float trace = R[0][0] + R[1][1] + R[2][2];
```

```
                // check the diagonal
                if (trace > 0.0f)
                {
                    float s = sqrt(trace + 1.0f);
                    q[3] = s * 0.5f;

                    float t = 0.5f / s;
                    q[0] = (R[2][1] - R[1][2]) * t;
                    q[1] = (R[0][2] - R[2][0]) * t;
                    q[2] = (R[1][0] - R[0][1]) * t;
                }
                else
                {
                    // diagonal is negative
                    int i = 0;
                    if (R[1][1] > R[0][0]) i = 1;
                    if (R[2][2] > R[i][i]) i = 2;

                    static const int NEXT[3] = {1, 2, 0};
                    j = NEXT[i];
                    k = NEXT[j];

                    float s = sqrt ((R[i][i]
                                    -(R[j][j] + R[k][k]))
                                    + 1.0f);

                    q[i] = s * 0.5f;

                    float t;
                    if (s != 0.0)    t = 0.5f / s;
                    else             t = s;

                    q[3] = (R[k][j] - R[j][k]) * t;
                    q[j] = (R[j][i] + R[i][j]) * t;
                    q[k] = (R[k][i] + R[i][k]) * t;
                }
            }
```

## 4.4.5. Rotational Linear Interpolation

Rotational interpolation has many applications in the animation, dynamics and camera systems of a game engine. With the help of quaternions, rotations can be easily interpolated just as vectors and points can.

The easiest and least computationally intensive approach is to perform a four-dimensional vector LERP on the quaternions you wish to interpolate. Given two quaternions $q_A$ and $q_B$ representing rotations A and B, we can find an intermediate rotation $q_{LERP}$ that is $\beta$ percent of the way from A to B as follows:

$$q_{\mathrm{LERP}} = \mathrm{LERP}(q_A, q_B, \beta) = \frac{(1-\beta)q_A + \beta q_B}{\left|(1-\beta)q_A + \beta q_B\right|}$$

$$= \mathrm{normalize}\left(\begin{bmatrix} (1-\beta)q_{Ax} + \beta q_{Bx} \\ (1-\beta)q_{Ay} + \beta q_{By} \\ (1-\beta)q_{Az} + \beta q_{Bz} \\ (1-\beta)q_{Aw} + \beta q_{Bw} \end{bmatrix}^T\right).$$

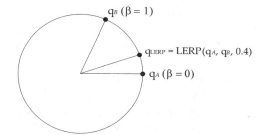

**Figure 4.22.** Linear interpolation (LERP) between quaternions $q_A$ and $q_B$.

Notice that the resultant interpolated quaternion had to be renormalized. This is necessary because the LERP operation does not preserve a vector's length in general.

Geometrically, $q_{\mathrm{LERP}} = \mathrm{LERP}(q_A, q_B, \beta)$ is the quaternion whose orientation lies $\beta$ percent of the way from orientation A to orientation B, as shown (in two dimensions for clarity) in Figure 4.22. Mathematically, the LERP operation results in a *weighed average* of the two quaternions, with weights $(1 - \beta)$ and $\beta$ (notice that $(1 - \beta) + \beta = 1$).

### 4.4.5.1. Spherical Linear Interpolation

The problem with the LERP operation is that it does not take account of the fact that quaternions are really points on a four-dimensional *hypersphere*. A LERP effectively interpolates along a *chord* of the hypersphere, rather than along the surface of the hypersphere itself. This leads to rotation animations that do not have a constant angular speed when the parameter $\beta$ is changing at a constant rate. The rotation will appear slower at the end points and faster in the middle of the animation.

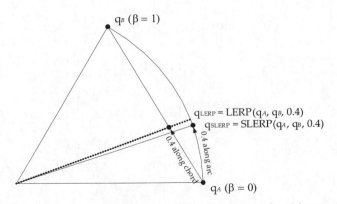

Figure 4.23. Spherical linear interpolation along a great circle arc of a 4D hypersphere.

To solve this problem, we can use a variant of the LERP operation known as *spherical linear interpolation*, or SLERP for short. The SLERP operation uses sines and cosines to interpolate along a *great circle* of the 4D hypersphere, rather than along a chord, as shown in Figure 4.23. This results in a constant angular speed when $\beta$ varies at a constant rate.

The formula for SLERP is similar to the LERP formula, but the weights $(1 - \beta)$ and $\beta$ are replaced with weights $w_p$ and $w_q$ involving sines of the angle between the two quaternions.

$$\text{SLERP}(\mathrm{p}, \mathrm{q}, \beta) = w_p\, \mathrm{p} + w_q\, \mathrm{q},$$

where

$$w_p = \frac{\sin((1 - \beta)\theta)}{\sin(\theta)},$$

$$w_q = \frac{\sin(\beta\theta)}{\sin(\theta)}.$$

The cosine of the angle between any two unit-length quaternions can be found by taking their four-dimensional dot product. Once we know $\cos(\theta)$, we can calculate the angle $\theta$ and the various sines we need quite easily:

$$\cos(\theta) = \mathrm{p} \cdot \mathrm{q} = p_x q_x + p_y q_y + p_z q_z + p_w q_w;$$

$$\theta = \cos^{-1}(\mathrm{p} \cdot \mathrm{q}).$$

### 4.4.5.2. To SLERP or Not to SLERP (That's Still the Question)

The jury is still out on whether or not to use SLERP in a game engine. Jonathan Blow wrote a great article positing that SLERP is too expensive, and LERP's quality is not really that bad—therefore, he suggests, we should understand SLERP but avoid it in our game engines (see http://number-none.com/product/Understanding%20Slerp,%20Then%20Not%20Using%20It/index.html). On the other hand, some of my colleagues at Naughty Dog have found that a good SLERP implementation performs nearly as well as LERP. (For example, on the PS3's SPUs, Naughty Dog's Ice team's implementation of SLERP takes 20 cycles per joint, while its LERP implementation takes 16.25 cycles per joint.) Therefore, I'd personally recommend that you profile your SLERP and LERP implementations before making any decisions. If the performance hit for SLERP isn't unacceptable, I say go for it, because it may result in slightly better-looking animations. But if your SLERP is slow (and you cannot speed it up, or you just don't have the time to do so), then LERP is usually good enough for most purposes.

## 4.5.   Comparison of Rotational Representations

We've seen that rotations can be represented in quite a few different ways. This section summarizes the most common rotational representations and outlines their pros and cons. No one representation is ideal in all situations. Using the information in this section, you should be able to select the best representation for a particular application.

### 4.5.1.   Euler Angles

We briefly explored *Euler angles* in Section 4.3.9.1. A rotation represented via Euler angles consists of three scalar values: yaw, pitch, and roll. These quantities are sometimes represented by a 3D vector [ $\theta_Y$ $\theta_P$ $\theta_R$ ].

The benefits of this representation are its simplicity, its small size (three floating-point numbers), and its intuitive nature—yaw, pitch, and roll are easy to visualize. You can also easily interpolate simple rotations about a single axis. For example, it's trivial to find intermediate rotations between two distinct yaw angles by linearly interpolating the scalar $\theta_Y$. However, Euler angles cannot be interpolated easily when the rotation is about an arbitrarily-oriented axis.

In addition, Euler angles are prone to a condition known as *gimbal lock*. This occurs when a 90-degree rotation causes one of the three principal axes to "collapse" onto another principal axis. For example, if you rotate by 90 degrees about the $x$-axis, the $y$-axis collapses onto the $z$-axis. This prevents any further rotations about the original $y$-axis, because rotations about $y$ and $z$ have effectively become equivalent.

Another problem with Euler angles is that the order in which the rotations are performed around each axis matters. The order could be PYR, YPR, RYP, and so on, and each ordering may produce a different composite rotation. No one standard rotation order exists for Euler angles across all disciplines (although certain disciplines do follow specific conventions). So the rotation angles [ $\theta_Y$ $\theta_P$ $\theta_R$ ] do not uniquely define a particular rotation—you need to know the rotation order to interpret these numbers properly.

A final problem with Euler angles is that they depend upon the mapping from the $x$-, $y$-, and $z$-axes onto the natural *front*, *left/right*, and *up* directions for the object being rotated. For example, yaw is always defined as rotation about the *up* axis, but without additional information we cannot tell whether this corresponds to a rotation about $x$, $y$, or $z$.

### 4.5.2.  3×3 Matrices

A $3 \times 3$ matrix is a convenient and effective rotational representation for a number of reasons. It does not suffer from gimbal lock, and it can represent arbitrary rotations uniquely. Rotations can be applied to points and vectors in a straightforward manner via matrix multiplication (i.e., a series of dot products). Most CPUs and all GPUs now have built-in support for hardware-accelerated dot products and matrix multiplication. Rotations can also be reversed by finding an inverse matrix, which for a pure rotation matrix is the same thing as finding the transpose—a trivial operation. And $4 \times 4$ matrices offer a way to represent arbitrary affine transformations—rotations, translations, and scaling—in a totally consistent way.

However, rotation matrices are not particularly intuitive. Looking at a big table of numbers doesn't help one picture the corresponding transformation in three-dimensional space. Also, rotation matrices are not easily interpolated. Finally, a rotation matrix takes up a lot of storage (nine floating-point numbers) relative to Euler angles.

### 4.5.3.  Axis + Angle

We can represent rotations as a unit vector defining the axis of rotation plus a scalar for the angle of rotation. This is known as an *axis+angle* representation, and it is sometimes denoted by the four-dimensional vector [ **a** $\theta$ ], where **a** is the axis of rotation and $\theta$ the angle in radians. In a right-handed coordinate system, the direction of a positive rotation is defined by the right-hand rule, while in a left-handed system we use the left-hand rule instead.

The benefits of the axis+angle representation are that it is reasonably intuitive and also compact (only requires four floating-point numbers, as opposed to the nine required for a $3 \times 3$ matrix).

One important limitation of the axis+angle representation is that rotations cannot be easily interpolated. Also, rotations in this format cannot be applied to points and vectors in a straightforward way—one needs to convert the axis+angle representation into a matrix or quaternion first.

### 4.5.4. Quaternions

As we've seen, a unit-length quaternion can represent 3D rotations in a manner analogous to the axis+angle representation. The primary difference between the two representations is that a quaternion's axis of rotation is scaled by the sine of the half angle of rotation, and instead of storing the angle in the fourth component of the vector, we store the cosine of the half angle.

The quaternion formulation provides two immense benefits over the axis+angle representation. First, it permits rotations to be concatenated and applied directly to points and vectors via quaternion multiplication. Second, it permits rotations to be easily interpolated via simple LERP or SLERP operations. Its small size (four floating-point numbers) is also a benefit over the matrix formulation.

### 4.5.5. SQT Transformations

By itself, a quaternion can only represent a rotation, whereas a $4 \times 4$ matrix can represent an arbitrary affine transformation (rotation, translation, and scale). When a quaternion is combined with a *translation vector* and a *scale factor* (either a scalar for uniform scaling or a vector for nonuniform scaling), then we have a viable alternative to the $4 \times 4$ matrix representation of affine transformations. We sometimes call this an *SQT transform*, because it contains a *s*cale factor, a *q*uaternion for rotation, and a *t*ranslation vector.

$$\text{SQT} = [s \quad q \quad t] \quad \text{(uniform scale } s\text{),}$$

or

$$\text{SQT} = [s \quad q \quad t] \quad \text{(non-uniform scale vector } s\text{).}$$

SQT transforms are widely used in computer animation because of their smaller size (eight floats for uniform scale, or ten floats for nonuniform scale, as opposed to the 12 floating-point numbers needed for a $4 \times 3$ matrix) and their ability to be easily interpolated. The translation vector and scale factor are interpolated via LERP, and the quaternion can be interpolated with either LERP or SLERP.

### 4.5.6. Dual Quaternions

Complete transformations involving rotation, translation, and scale can be represented using a mathematical object known as a *dual quaternion*. A dual quaternion is like an ordinary quaternion, except that its four components are *dual numbers* instead of regular real-valued numbers. A dual number can be written as the sum of a non-dual part and a dual part as follows: $\hat{a} = a_0 + \varepsilon a_\varepsilon$. Here $\varepsilon$ is a magical number called the *dual unit*, defined as $\varepsilon^2 = 0$. (This is analogous to the imaginary number $i = \sqrt{-1}$ used when writing a complex number as the sum of a real and an imaginary part: $c = a + ib$.)

Because each dual number can be represented by two real numbers (the non-dual and dual parts), a dual quaternion can be represented by an eight-element vector. It can also be represented as the sum of two ordinary quaternions, where the second one is multiplied by the dual unit, as follows: $\hat{q} = q_0 + \varepsilon q_\varepsilon$.

A full discussion of dual numbers and dual quaternions is beyond our scope here. However, a number of excellent articles on them exist online and in the literature. I recommend starting with https://www.cs.tcd.ie/publications/tech-reports/reports.06/TCD-CS-2006-46.pdf.

### 4.5.7. Rotations and Degrees of Freedom

The term *"degrees of freedom"* (or *DOF* for short) refers to the number of mutually-independent ways in which an object's physical state (position and orientation) can change. You may have encountered the phrase "six degrees of freedom" in fields such as mechanics, robotics, and aeronautics. This refers to the fact that a three-dimensional object (whose motion is not artificially constrained) has three degrees of freedom in its translation (along the $x$-, $y$-, and $z$-axes) and three degrees of freedom in its rotation (about the $x$-, $y$-, and $z$-axes), for a total of six degrees of freedom.

The DOF concept will help us to understand how different rotational representations can employ different numbers of floating-point parameters, yet all specify rotations with only three degrees of freedom. For example, Euler angles require three floats, but axis+angle and quaternion representations use four floats, and a $3 \times 3$ matrix takes up nine floats. How can these representations all describe 3-DOF rotations?

The answer lies in *constraints*. All 3D rotational representations employ three or more floating-point parameters, but some representations also have one or more constraints on those parameters. The constraints indicate that the parameters are not *independent*—a change to one parameter induces changes to the other parameters in order to maintain the validity of the constraint(s).

If we subtract the number of constraints from the number of floating-point parameters, we arrive at the number of degrees of freedom—and this number should always be three for a 3D rotation:

$$N_{\text{DOF}} = N_{\text{parameters}} - N_{\text{constraints}}. \tag{4.5}$$

The following list shows Equation (4.5) in action for each of the rotational representations we've encountered in this book.

- *Euler Angles.* 3 parameters – 0 constraints = 3 DOF.
- *Axis+Angle.* 4 parameters – 1 constraint = 3 DOF.
  Constraint: Axis is constrained to be unit length.
- *Quaternion.* 4 parameters – 1 constraint = 3 DOF.
  Constraint: Quaternion is constrained to be unit length.
- *3 × 3 Matrix.* 9 parameters – 6 constraints = 3 DOF.
  Constraints: All three rows and all three columns must be of unit length (when treated as three-element vectors).

## 4.6. Other Useful Mathematical Objects

As game engineers, we will encounter a host of other mathematical objects, in addition to points, vectors, matrices and quaternions. This section briefly outlines the most common of these.

### 4.6.1. Lines, Rays, and Line Segments

An infinite line can be represented by a point $\mathbf{P}_0$ plus a unit vector $\mathbf{u}$ in the direction of the line. A *parametric equation* of a line traces out every possible point $\mathbf{P}$ along the line by starting at the initial point $\mathbf{P}_0$ and moving an arbitrary distance $t$ along the direction of the unit vector $\mathbf{u}$. The infinitely large set of points $\mathbf{P}$ becomes a *vector function* of the scalar parameter $t$:

$$\mathbf{P}(t) = \mathbf{P}_0 + t\,\mathbf{u}, \quad \text{where} \quad -\infty < t < +\infty. \tag{4.73}$$

This is depicted in Figure 4.24.

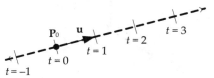

Figure 4.24. Parametric equation of a line.

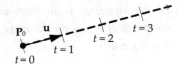

**Figure 4.25.** Parametric equation of a ray.

A *ray* is a line that extends to infinity in only one direction. This is easily expressed as $\mathbf{P}(t)$ with the constraint $t \geq 0$, as shown in Figure 4.25.

A *line segment* is bounded at both ends by $\mathbf{P}_0$ and $\mathbf{P}_1$. It too can be represented by $\mathbf{P}(t)$, in either one of the following two ways (where $\mathbf{L} = \mathbf{P}_1 - \mathbf{P}_0$ and $L = |\mathbf{L}|$ is the length of the line segment):

1. $\mathbf{P}(t) = \mathbf{P}_0 + t\mathbf{u}$, where $0 \leq t \leq L$, or

2. $\mathbf{P}(t) = \mathbf{P}_0 + t\mathbf{L}$, where $0 \leq t \leq 1$.

The latter format, depicted in Figure 4.26, is particularly convenient because the parameter $t$ is normalized; in other words, $t$ always goes from zero to one, no matter which particular line segment we are dealing with. This means we do not have to store the constraint $L$ in a separate floating-point parameter; it is already encoded in the vector $\mathbf{L} = L\mathbf{u}$ (which we have to store anyway).

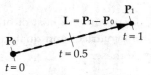

**Figure 4.26.** Parametric equation of a line segment, with normalized parameter t.

### 4.6.2. Spheres

Spheres are ubiquitous in game engine programming. A sphere is typically defined as a center point $\mathbf{C}$ plus a radius $r$, as shown in Figure 4.27. This packs

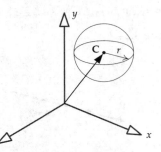

**Figure 4.27.** Point-radius representation of a sphere.

nicely into a four-element vector, $[\ C_x\ C_y\ C_z\ r\ ]$. As we'll see below when we discuss SIMD vector processing, there are distinct benefits to being able to pack data into a vector containing four 32-bit floats (i.e., a 128-bit package).

### 4.6.3. Planes

A *plane* is a 2D surface in 3D space. As you may recall from high school algebra, the equation of a plane is often written as follows:

$$Ax + By + Cz + D = 0.$$

This equation is satisfied only for the locus of points $\mathbf{P} = [\ x\ \ y\ \ z\ ]$ that lie on the plane.

Planes can be represented by a point $\mathbf{P}_0$ and a unit vector $\mathbf{n}$ that is normal to the plane. This is sometimes called *point-normal form*, as depicted in Figure 4.28.

It's interesting to note that when the parameters $A$, $B$, and $C$ from the traditional plane equation are interpreted as a 3D vector, that vector lies in the direction of the plane normal. If the vector $[\ A\ B\ C\ ]$ is normalized to unit length, then the normalized sub-vector $[\ a\ b\ c\ ] = \mathbf{n}$, and the normalized parameter $d = D/\sqrt{A^2 + B^2 + C^2}$ is just the distance from the plane to the origin. The sign of $d$ is positive if the plane's normal vector ($\mathbf{n}$) is pointing toward the origin (i.e., the origin is on the "front" side of the plane) and negative if the normal is pointing away from the origin (i.e., the origin is "behind" the plane). In fact, the normalized equation $ax + by + cz + d = 0$ is just another way of writing $(\mathbf{n} \cdot \mathbf{P}) = -d$, which means that when any point $\mathbf{P}$ on the plane is projected onto the plane normal $\mathbf{n}$, the length of that projection will be $-d$.

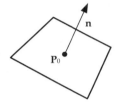

Figure 4.28. A plane in point-normal form.

A plane can actually be packed into a four-element vector, much like a sphere can. To do so, we observe that to describe a plane uniquely, we need only the normal vector $\mathbf{n} = [\ a\ b\ c\ ]$ and the distance from the origin $d$. The four-element vector $\mathbf{L} = [\ \mathbf{n}\ d\ ] = [\ a\ b\ c\ d\ ]$ is a compact and convenient way to represent and store a plane in memory. Note that when $\mathbf{P}$ is written in homogeneous coordinates with $w = 1$, the equation $(\mathbf{L} \cdot \mathbf{P}) = 0$ is yet another way of writing $(\mathbf{n} \cdot \mathbf{P}) = -d$. (These equations are satisfied for all points $\mathbf{P}$ that lie on the plane $\mathbf{L}$.)

Planes defined in four-element vector form can be easily transformed from one coordinate space to another. Given a matrix $\mathbf{M}_{A \to B}$ that transforms points and (non-normal) vectors from space A to space B, we already know that to transform a *normal vector* such as the plane's $\mathbf{n}$ vector, we need to use the inverse transpose of that matrix, $\left(\mathbf{M}_{A \to B}^{-1}\right)^T$. So it shouldn't be a big surprise to learn that applying the inverse transpose of a matrix to a four-element plane vector $\mathbf{L}$ will, in fact, correctly transform that plane from space A to space B.

We won't derive or prove this result any further here, but a thorough explanation of why this little "trick" works is provided in Section 4.2.3 of [28].

### 4.6.4. Axis-Aligned Bounding Boxes (AABB)

An axis-aligned bounding box (AABB) is a 3D *cuboid* whose six rectangular faces are aligned with a particular coordinate frame's mutually orthogonal axes. As such, an AABB can be represented by a six-element vector containing the minimum and maximum coordinates along each of the 3 principal axes, [ $x_{min}$ , $x_{max}$ , $y_{min}$ , $y_{max}$ , $z_{min}$ , $z_{max}$ ], or two points $\mathbf{P}_{min}$ and $\mathbf{P}_{max}$.

This simple representation allows for a particularly convenient and inexpensive method of testing whether a point $\mathbf{P}$ is inside or outside any given AABB. We simply test if all of the following conditions are true:

$$P_x \geq x_{min} \text{ and } P_x \leq x_{max} \text{ and }$$
$$P_y \geq y_{min} \text{ and } P_y \leq y_{max} \text{ and }$$
$$P_z \geq z_{min} \text{ and } P_z \leq z_{max}.$$

Because intersection tests are so speedy, AABBs are often used as an "early out" collision check; if the AABBs of two objects do not intersect, then there is no need to do a more detailed (and more expensive) collision test.

### 4.6.5. Oriented Bounding Boxes (OBB)

An oriented bounding box (OBB) is a *cuboid* that has been oriented so as to align in some logical way with the object it bounds. Usually an OBB aligns with the local-space axes of the object. Hence it acts like an AABB in local space, although it may not necessarily align with the world space axes.

Various techniques exist for testing whether or not a point lies within an OBB, but one common approach is to transform the point into the OBB's "aligned" coordinate system and then use an AABB intersection test as presented above.

### 4.6.6. Frusta

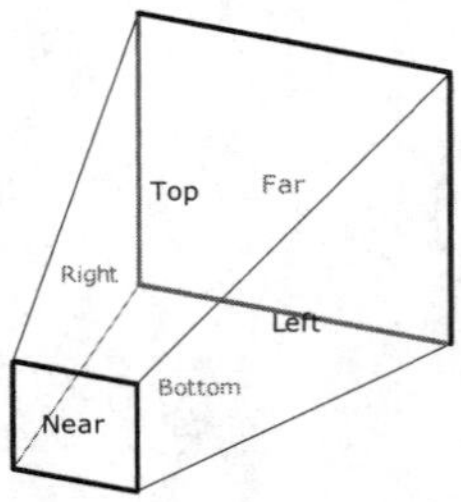

Figure 4.29. A frustum.

As shown in Figure 4.29, a *frustum* is a group of six planes that define a *truncated pyramid* shape. Frusta are commonplace in 3D rendering because they conveniently define the viewable region of the 3D world when rendered via a perspective projection from the point of view of a virtual camera. Four of the planes bound the edges of the screen space, while the other two planes represent the the near and far clipping planes (i.e., they define the minimum and maximum z coordinates possible for any visible point).

One convenient representation of a frustum is as an array of six planes, each of which is represented in point-normal form (i.e., one point and one normal vector per plane).

Testing whether a point lies inside a frustum is a bit involved, but the basic idea is to use dot products to determine whether the point lies on the front or back side of each plane. If it lies inside all six planes, it is inside the frustum.

A helpful trick is to transform the world-space point being tested, by applying the camera's perspective projection to it. This takes the point from world space into a space known as *homogeneous clip space*. In this space, the frustum is just an axis-aligned cuboid (AABB). This permits much simpler in/out tests to be performed.

### 4.6.7. Convex Polyhedral Regions

A *convex polyhedral region* is defined by an arbitrary set of planes, all with normals pointing inward (or outward). The test for whether a point lies inside or outside the volume defined by the planes is relatively straightforward; it is similar to a frustum test, but with possibly more planes. Convex regions are very useful for implementing arbitrarily-shaped trigger regions in games. Many engines employ this technique; for example, the Quake engine's ubiquitous *brushes* are just volumes bounded by planes in exactly this way.

# 4.7.  Hardware-Accelerated SIMD Math

SIMD stands for "single instruction multiple data." This refers to the ability of most modern microprocessors to perform a single mathematical operation on multiple data items *in parallel,* using a single machine instruction. For example, the CPU might multiply four pairs of floating-point numbers in parallel with a single instruction. SIMD is widely used in game engine math libraries, because it permits common vector operations such as dot products and matrix multiplication to be performed extremely rapidly.

Intel first introduced MMX instructions with their Pentium line of CPUs in 1994. These instructions permitted SIMD calculations to be performed on 8-, 16-, and 32-bit integers packed into special 64-bit MMX registers. Intel followed this up with various revisions of an extended instruction set called Streaming SIMD Extensions, or SSE, the first version of which appeared in the Pentium III processor. The SSE instruction set utilizes 128-bit registers that can contain integer or IEEE floating-point data.

The SSE mode most commonly used by game engines is called *packed 32-bit floating-point mode.* In this mode, four 32-bit `float` values are packed into a single 128-bit register; four operations such as additions or multiplications are performed in parallel on four pairs of floats using a single instruction. This is just what the doctor ordered when multiplying a four-element vector by a $4 \times 4$ matrix!

### 4.7.1.1. SSE Registers

In packed 32-bit floating-point mode, each 128-bit SSE register contains four 32-bit floats. The individual floats within an SSE register are conveniently referred to as $[\, x \;\; y \;\; z \;\; w \,]$, just as they would be when doing vector/matrix math in homogeneous coordinates on paper (see Figure 4.30). To see how the SSE registers work, here's an example of a SIMD instruction:

```
addps xmm0, xmm1
```

The `addps` instruction adds the four floats in the 128-bit XMM0 register with the four floats in the XMM1 register, and stores the four results back into XMM0. Put another way:

$$xmm0.x = xmm0.x + xmm1.x;$$
$$xmm0.y = xmm0.y + xmm1.y;$$
$$xmm0.z = xmm0.z + xmm1.z;$$
$$xmm0.w = xmm0.w + xmm1.w.$$

The four floating-point values stored in an SSE register can be extracted to or loaded from memory or registers individually, but such operations tend to be comparatively slow. Moving data between the x87 FPU registers and the SSE registers is particularly bad, because the CPU has to wait for either the x87 or the SSE unit to spit out its pending calculations. This stalls out the CPU's entire instruction execution pipeline and results in a lot of wasted cycles. In a nutshell, code that mixes regular `float` mathematics with SSE mathematics should be avoided like the plague.

To minimize the costs of going back and forth between memory, x87 FPU registers, and SSE registers, most SIMD math libraries do their best to leave data in the SSE registers for as long as possible. This means that even scalar values are left in SSE registers, rather than transferring them out to `float` variables. For example, a dot product between two vectors produces a scalar result, but if we leave that result in an SSE register it can be used later in other

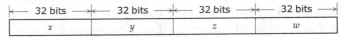

Figure 4.30. The four components of an SSE register in 32-bit floating-point mode.

vector calculations without incurring a transfer cost. Scalars are represented by duplicating the single floating-point value across all four "slots" in an SSE register. So to store the scalar $s$ in an SSE register, we'd set $x = y = z = w = s$.

### 4.7.1.2. The __m128 Data Type

Using one of these magic SSE 128-bit values in C or C++ is quite easy. The Microsoft Visual Studio compiler provides a predefined data type called __m128. This data type can be used to declare global variables, automatic variables, and even class and structure members. In many cases, variables of this type will be stored in RAM. But when used in calculations, __m128 values are manipulated directly in the CPU's SSE registers. In fact, declaring automatic variables and function arguments to be of type __m128 often results in the compiler storing those values directly in SSE registers, rather than keeping them in RAM on the program stack.

#### Alignment of __m128 Variables

When an __m128 variable is stored in RAM, it is the programmer's responsibility to ensure that the variable is *aligned* to a 16-byte address boundary. This means that the hexadecimal address of an __m128 variable must always end in the nibble 0x0. The compiler will automatically pad structures and classes so that if the entire struct or class is aligned to a 16-byte boundary, all of the __m128 data members within it will be properly aligned as well. If you declare an automatic or global struct/class containing one or more __m128s, the compiler will align the object for you. However, it is still your responsibility to align dynamically allocated data structures (i.e., data allocated with new or malloc()); the compiler can't help you there.

### 4.7.1.3. Coding with SSE Intrinsics

SSE mathematics can be done in raw assembly language, or via inline assembly in C or C++. However, writing code like this is not only non-portable, it's also a big pain in the butt. To make life easier, modern compilers provide *intrinsics*—special commands that look and behave like regular C functions, but are really boiled down to inline assembly code by the compiler. Many intrinsics translate into a single assembly language instruction, although some are *macros* that translate into a sequence of instructions.

In order to use the __m128 data type and SSE intrinsics, your .cpp file must #include <xmmintrin.h>.

As an example, let's take another look at the addps assembly language instruction. This instruction can be invoked in C/C++ using the intrinsic _mm _add_ps(). Here's a side-by-side comparison of what the code would look like with and without the use of the intrinsic.

```
__m128 addWithAssembly(           __m128 addWithIntrinsics(
    __m128 a,                         __m128 a,
    __m128 b)                         __m128 b)
{                                 {
    __m128 r;                         __m128 r =
    __asm                               _mm_add_ps(a, b);
    {                                 return r;
        movaps xmm0,              }
          xmmword ptr [a]
        movaps xmm1,
          xmmword ptr [b]
        addps  xmm0, xmm1
        movaps xmmword ptr [r],
          xmm0
    }
    return r;
}
```

In the assembly language version, we have to use the __asm keyword to invoke inline assembly instructions, and we must create the linkage between the input parameters a and b and the SSE registers xmm0 and xmm1 manually, via movaps instructions. On the other hand, the version using intrinsics is much more intuitive and clear, and the code is smaller. There's no inline assembly, and the SSE instruction looks just like a regular function call.

If you'd like to experiment with these example functions, they can be invoked via the following test bed main() function. Notice the use of another intrinsic, _mm_load_ps(), which loads values from an in-memory array of floats into an __m128 variable (i.e., into an SSE register). Also notice that we are forcing our four global float arrays to be 16-byte aligned via the __declspec(align(16)) directive—if we omit these directives, the program will crash.

```
#include <xmmintrin.h>

// ... function definitions from above ...

__declspec(align(16)) float A[]={2.0f,-1.0f,3.0f,4.0f};
__declspec(align(16)) float B[]={-1.0f,3.0f,4.0f,2.0f};
__declspec(align(16)) float C[]={0.0f,0.0f,0.0f,0.0f};
__declspec(align(16)) float D[]={0.0f,0.0f,0.0f,0.0f};

int main(int argc, char* argv[])
{
    // load a and b from floating-point data arrays above
    __m128 a = _mm_load_ps(&A[0]);
    __m128 b = _mm_load_ps(&B[0]);
```

```
// test the two functions
__m128 c = addWithAssembly(a, b);
__m128 d = addWithIntrinsics(a, b);

// store the original values back to check that they
// weren't overwritten
_mm_store_ps(&A[0], a);
_mm_store_ps(&B[0], b);

// store results into float arrays so we can print
// them
_mm_store_ps(&C[0], c);
_mm_store_ps(&D[0], d);

// inspect the results
printf("%g %g %g %g\n", A[0], A[1], A[2], A[3]);
printf("%g %g %g %g\n", B[0], B[1], B[2], B[3]);
printf("%g %g %g %g\n", C[0], C[1], C[2], C[3]);
printf("%g %g %g %g\n", D[0], D[1], D[2], D[3]);

return 0;
}
```

#### 4.7.1.4. Vector-Matrix Multiplication with SSE

Let's take a look at how vector-matrix multiplication might be implemented using SSE instructions. We want to multiply the $1 \times 4$ vector $\mathbf{v}$ with the $4 \times 4$ matrix $\mathbf{M}$ to generate a result vector $\mathbf{r}$.

$$\mathbf{r} = \mathbf{v}\mathbf{M};$$

$$[r_x \quad r_y \quad r_z \quad r_w] = [v_x \quad v_y \quad v_z \quad v_w] \begin{bmatrix} M_{11} & M_{12} & M_{13} & M_{14} \\ M_{21} & M_{22} & M_{23} & M_{24} \\ M_{31} & M_{32} & M_{33} & M_{34} \\ M_{41} & M_{42} & M_{43} & M_{44} \end{bmatrix}$$

$$= \begin{bmatrix} (v_x M_{11} & (v_x M_{12} & (v_x M_{13} & (v_x M_{14} \\ +v_y M_{21} & +v_y M_{22} & +v_y M_{23} & +v_y M_{24} \\ +v_z M_{31} & +v_z M_{32} & +v_z M_{33} & +v_z M_{34} \\ +v_w M_{41}) & +v_w M_{42}) & +v_w M_{43}) & +v_w M_{44}) \end{bmatrix}.$$

The multiplication involves taking the dot product of the *row* vector $\mathbf{v}$ with the *columns* of matrix $\mathbf{M}$. So to do this calculation using SSE instructions, we might first try storing $\mathbf{v}$ in an SSE register (__m128), and storing each of the *columns* of $\mathbf{M}$ in SSE registers as well. Then we could calculate all of the products $v_k M_{ij}$ in parallel using only four mulps instructions, like this:

```
__m128 mulVectorMatrixAttempt1(__m128 v,
    __m128 Mcol1, __m128 Mcol2,
    __m128 Mcol3, __m128 Mcol4)
{
    __m128 vMcol1 = _mm_mul_ps(v, Mcol1);
    __m128 vMcol2 = _mm_mul_ps(v, Mcol2);
    __m128 vMcol3 = _mm_mul_ps(v, Mcol3);
    __m128 vMcol4 = _mm_mul_ps(v, Mcol4);
    // ... then what?
}
```

The above code would yield the following intermediate results:

$$\text{vMcol1} = [\, v_x M_{11} \quad v_y M_{21} \quad v_z M_{31} \quad v_w M_{41} \,];$$
$$\text{vMcol2} = [\, v_x M_{12} \quad v_y M_{22} \quad v_z M_{32} \quad v_w M_{42} \,];$$
$$\text{vMcol3} = [\, v_x M_{13} \quad v_y M_{23} \quad v_z M_{33} \quad v_w M_{43} \,];$$
$$\text{vMcol4} = [\, v_x M_{14} \quad v_y M_{24} \quad v_z M_{34} \quad v_w M_{44} \,].$$

But the problem with doing it this way is that we now have to add "across the registers" in order to generate the results we need. For example, $r_x = (v_x M_{11} + v_y M_{21} + v_z M_{31} + v_w M_{41})$, so we'd need to add the four components of vMcol1 together. Adding across a register like this is difficult and inefficient, and moreover it leaves the four components of the result in four separate SSE registers, which would need to be combined into the single result vector **r**. We can do better.

The "trick" here is to multiply with the *rows* of **M**, not its columns. That way, we'll have results that we can add in parallel, and the final sums will end up in the four components of a *single* SSE register representing the output vector **r**. However, we don't want to multiply **v** as-is with the rows of **M**—we want to multiply $v_x$ with all of row 1, $v_y$ with all of row 2, $v_z$ with all of row 3, and $v_w$ with all of row 4. To do this, we need to *replicate* a single component of **v**, such as $v_x$, across a register to yield a vector like [ $v_x$ $v_x$ $v_x$ $v_x$ ]. Then we can multiply the *replicated* component vectors by the appropriate *rows* of **M**.

Thankfully there's a powerful SSE instruction which can replicate values like this. It is called shufps, and it's wrapped by the intrinsic _mm_shuffle_ps(). This beast is a bit complicated to understand, because it's a general-purpose instruction that can shuffle the components of an SSE register around in arbitrary ways. However, for our purposes we need only know that the following macros replicate the *x, y, z* or *w* components of a vector across an entire register:

```
#define SHUFFLE_PARAM(x, y, z, w) \
    ((x) | ((y) << 2) | ((z) << 4) | ((w) << 6))
```

```
#define    _mm_replicate_x_ps(v) \
   _mm_shuffle_ps((v), (v), SHUFFLE_PARAM(0, 0, 0, 0))

#define    _mm_replicate_y_ps(v) \
   _mm_shuffle_ps((v), (v), SHUFFLE_PARAM(1, 1, 1, 1))

#define    _mm_replicate_z_ps(v) \
   _mm_shuffle_ps((v), (v), SHUFFLE_PARAM(2, 2, 2, 2))

#define    _mm_replicate_w_ps(v) \
   _mm_shuffle_ps((v), (v), SHUFFLE_PARAM(3, 3, 3, 3))
```

Given these convenient macros, we can write our vector-matrix multiplication function as follows:

```
__m128 mulVectorMatrixAttempt2(__m128 v,
   __m128 Mrow1, __m128 Mrow2,
   __m128 Mrow3, __m128 Mrow4)
{
   __m128 xMrow1 = _mm_mul_ps(_mm_replicate_x_ps(v),
                              Mrow1);
   __m128 yMrow2 = _mm_mul_ps(_mm_replicate_y_ps(v),
                              Mrow2);
   __m128 zMrow3 = _mm_mul_ps(_mm_replicate_z_ps(v),
                              Mrow3);
   __m128 wMrow4 = _mm_mul_ps(_mm_replicate_w_ps(v),
                              Mrow4);

   __m128 result = _mm_add_ps(xMrow1, yMrow2);
   result        = _mm_add_ps(result, zMrow3);
   result        = _mm_add_ps(result, wMrow4);

   return result;
}
```

This code produces the following intermediate vectors:

$$\text{xMrow1} = [\ v_x M_{11}\ \ v_x M_{12}\ \ v_x M_{13}\ \ v_x M_{14}\ ];$$
$$\text{yMrow2} = [\ v_y M_{21}\ \ v_y M_{22}\ \ v_y M_{23}\ \ v_y M_{24}\ ];$$
$$\text{zMrow3} = [\ v_z M_{31}\ \ v_z M_{32}\ \ v_z M_{33}\ \ v_z M_{34}\ ];$$
$$\text{wMrow4} = [\ v_w M_{41}\ \ v_w M_{42}\ \ v_w M_{43}\ \ v_w M_{44}\ ].$$

Adding these four vectors in parallel produces our result $\mathbf{r}$:

$$\mathbf{r} = \begin{bmatrix} (v_x M_{11} & (v_x M_{12} & (v_x M_{13} & (v_x M_{14} \\ +v_y M_{21} & +v_y M_{22} & +v_y M_{23} & +v_y M_{24} \\ +v_z M_{31} & +v_z M_{32} & +v_z M_{33} & +v_z M_{34} \\ +v_w M_{41}) & +v_w M_{42}) & +v_w M_{43}) & +v_w M_{44}) \end{bmatrix}.$$

On some CPUs, the code shown above can be optimized even further by using a rather handy *multiply-and-add* instruction, usually denoted madd. This instruction multiplies its first two arguments and then adds the result to its third argument. Unfortunately SSE doesn't support a madd instruction, but we can fake it reasonably well with a macro like this:

```
#define _mm_madd_ps(a, b, c) \
    _mm_add_ps(_mm_mul_ps((a), (b)), (c))


__m128 mulVectorMatrixFinal(__m128 v,
    __m128 Mrow1, __m128 Mrow2,
    __m128 Mrow3, __m128 Mrow4)
{
    __m128 result;
    result = _mm_mul_ps (_mm_replicate_x_ps(v), Mrow1);
    result = _mm_madd_ps(_mm_replicate_y_ps(v), Mrow2,
                         result);
    result = _mm_madd_ps(_mm_replicate_z_ps(v), Mrow3,
                         result);
    result = _mm_madd_ps(_mm_replicate_w_ps(v), Mrow4,
                         result);
    return result;
}
```

We can of course perform matrix-matrix multiplication using a similar approach. Check out http://msdn.microsoft.com for a full listing of the SSE intrinsics for the Microsoft Visual Studio compiler.

## 4.8. Random Number Generation

Random numbers are ubiquitous in game engines, so it behooves us to have a brief look at the two most common random number generators, the linear congruential generator and the Mersenne Twister. It's important to realize that random number generators are just very complicated but totally deterministic pre-defined sequences of numbers. For this reason, we call the sequences they produce *pseudo-random*. What differentiates a good generator from a bad one is how long the sequence of numbers is before it repeats (its *period*), and how well the sequences hold up under various well-known randomness tests.

### 4.8.1. Linear Congruential Generators

Linear congruential generators are a very fast and simple way to generate a sequence of pseudo-random numbers. Depending on the platform, this algorithm is sometimes used in the standard C library's rand() function. However, your mileage may vary, so don't count on `rand()` being based on any particular algorithm. If you want to be sure, you'll be better off implementing your own random number generator.

The linear congruential algorithm is explained in detail in the book *Numerical Recipes in C,* so I won't go into the details of it here.

What I will say is that this random number generator does not produce particularly high-quality pseudo-random sequences. Given the same initial seed value, the sequence is always exactly the same. The numbers produced do not meet many of the criteria widely accepted as desirable, such as a long period, low- and high-order bits that have similarly-long periods, and absence of sequential or spatial correlation between the generated values.

### 4.8.2. Mersenne Twister

The Mersenne Twister pseudo-random number generator algorithm was designed specifically to improve upon the various problems of the linear congruential algorithm. Wikipedia provides the following description of the benefits of the algorithm:

1. It was designed to have a colossal period of $2^{19937} - 1$ (the creators of the algorithm proved this property). In practice, there is little reason to use larger ones, as most applications do not require $2^{19937}$ unique combinations ($2^{19937} \approx 4.3 \times 10^{6001}$).

2. It has a very high order of dimensional equidistribution (see linear congruential generator). Note that this means, by default, that there is negligible serial correlation between successive values in the output sequence.

3. It passes numerous tests for statistical randomness, including the stringent Diehard tests.

4. It is fast.

Various implementations of the Twister are available on the web, including a particularly cool one that uses SIMD vector instructions for an extra speed boost, called *SFMT* (SIMD-oriented fast Mersenne Twister). SFMT can be downloaded from http://www.math.sci.hiroshima-u.ac.jp/~m-mat/MT/ SFMT/index.html.

### 4.8.3. Mother-of-All and Xorshift

In 1994, George Marsaglia, a computer scientist and mathematician best known for developing the Diehard battery of tests of randomness (http://www.stat. fsu.edu/pub/diehard), published a pseudo-random number generation algorithm that is much simpler to implement and runs faster than the Mersenne Twister algorithm. He claimed that it could produce a sequence of 32-bit pseudo-random numbers with a period of non-repetition of $2^{250}$. It passed all of the Diehard tests and still stands today as one of the best pseudo-random number generators for high-speed applications. He called his algorithm the *Mother of All Pseudo-Random Number Generators*, because it seemed to him to be the only random number generator one would ever need.

Later, Marsaglia published another generator called Xorshift, which is between Mersenee and Mother-of-All in terms of randomness, but runs slightly faster than Mother.

You can read about George Marsaglia at http://en.wikipedia.org/wiki/George_Marsaglia, and about the Mother-of-All generator at ftp://ftp.forth.org/pub/C/mother.c and at http://www.agner.org/random. You can download a PDF of George's paper on Xorshift at http://www.jstatsoft.org/v08/i14/paper.

# Part II
# Low-Level
# Engine Systems

# 5

# Engine Support Systems

E very game engine requires some low-level support systems that manage
mundane but crucial tasks, such as starting up and shutting down the engine, configuring engine and game features, managing the engine's memory
usage, handling access to file system(s), providing access to the wide range of
heterogeneous asset types used by the game (meshes, textures, animations,
audio, etc.), and providing debugging tools for use by the game development
team. This chapter will focus on the lowest-level support systems found in
most game engines. In the chapters that follow, we will explore some of the
larger core systems, including resource management, human interface devices, and in-game debugging tools.

## 5.1.    Subsystem Start-Up and Shut-Down

A game engine is a complex piece of software consisting of many interacting
subsystems. When the engine first starts up, each subsystem must be configured and initialized in a specific order. Interdependencies between subsystems implicitly define the order in which they must be started—i.e., if subsystem B depends on subsystem A, then A will need to be started up before B
can be initialized. Shut-down typically occurs in the reverse order, so B would
shut down first, followed by A.

### 5.1.1.   C++ Static Initialization Order (or Lack Thereof)

Since the programming language used in most modern game engines is C++, we should briefly consider whether C++'s native start-up and shut-down semantics can be leveraged in order to start up and shut down our engine's subsystems. In C++, global and static objects are constructed before the program's entry point (`main()`, or `WinMain()` under Windows) is called. However, these constructors are called in a totally unpredictable order. The destructors of global and static class instances are called after `main()` (or `WinMain()`) returns, and once again they are called in an unpredictable order. Clearly this behavior is not desirable for initializing and shutting down the subsystems of a game engine, or indeed any software system that has interdependencies between its global objects.

This is somewhat unfortunate, because a common design pattern for implementing major subsystems such as the ones that make up a game engine is to define a *singleton class* (often called a *manager*) for each subsystem. If C++ gave us more control over the order in which global and static class instances were constructed and destroyed, we could define our singleton instances as globals, without the need for dynamic memory allocation. For example, we could write:

```
class RenderManager
{
public:
    RenderManager()
    {
        // start up the manager...
    }

    ~RenderManager()
    {
        // shut down the manager...
    }

    // ...
};

// singleton instance
static RenderManager gRenderManager;
```

Alas, with no way to directly control construction and destruction order, this approach won't work.

#### 5.1.1.1.   Construct On Demand

There is one C++ "trick" we can leverage here. A static variable that is declared within a function will not be constructed before `main()` is called, but rather on the first invocation of that function. So if our global singleton is function-static, we can control the order of construction for our global singletons.

```cpp
class RenderManager
{
public:

    // Get the one and only instance.
    static RenderManager& get()
    {
        // This function-static will be constructed on the
        // first call to this function.
        static RenderManager sSingleton;
        return sSingleton;
    }

    RenderManager()
    {
        // Start up other managers we depend on, by
        // calling their get() functions first...
        VideoManager::get();
        TextureManager::get();

        // Now start up the render manager.
        // ...
    }

    ~RenderManager()
    {
        // Shut down the manager.
        // ...
    }
};
```

You'll find that many software engineering textbooks suggest this design, or a variant that involves dynamic allocation of the singleton as shown below.

```cpp
static RenderManager& get()
{
    static RenderManager* gpSingleton = NULL;
    if (gpSingleton == NULL)
    {
        gpSingleton = new RenderManager;
    }
    ASSERT(gpSingleton);
    return *gpSingleton;
}
```

Unfortunately, this still gives us no way to control destruction order. It is possible that C++ will destroy one of the managers upon which the `RenderManager` depends for its shut-down procedure, prior to the `RenderManager`'s destructor being called. In addition, it's difficult to predict exactly when the `RenderManager` singleton will be constructed, because the construction will happen on the first call to `RenderManager::get()` — and who knows when that might be? Moreover, the programmers using the class may not be expecting an innocuous-looking `get()` function to do something expensive, like allocating and initializing a heavy-weight singleton. This is an unpredictable and dangerous design. Therefore we are prompted to resort to a more direct approach that gives us greater control.

## 5.1.2. A Simple Approach That Works

Let's presume that we want to stick with the idea of singleton managers for our subsystems. In this case, the simplest "brute-force" approach is to define explicit start-up and shut-down functions for each singleton manager class. These functions take the place of the constructor and destructor, and in fact we should arrange for the constructor and destructor to do *absolutely nothing*. That way, the start-up and shut-down functions can be explicitly called *in the required order* from within `main()` (or from some over-arching singleton object that manages the engine as a whole). For example:

```
class RenderManager
{
public:
    RenderManager()
    {
        // do nothing
    }

    ~RenderManager()
    {
        // do nothing
    }

    void startUp()
    {
        // start up the manager...
    }

    void shutDown()
    {
        // shut down the manager...
    }
```

```
      // ...
   };

   class PhysicsManager     { /* similar... */ };

   class AnimationManager   { /* similar... */ };

   class MemoryManager      { /* similar... */ };

   class FileSystemManager  { /* similar... */ };

   // ...

   RenderManager           gRenderManager;
   PhysicsManager          gPhysicsManager;
   AnimationManager        gAnimationManager;
   TextureManager          gTextureManager;

   VideoManager            gVideoManager;
   MemoryManager           gMemoryManager;
   FileSystemManager       gFileSystemManager;
   // ...

   int main(int argc, const char* argv)
   {
       // Start up engine systems in the correct order.
       gMemoryManager.startUp();
       gFileSystemManager.startUp();
       gVideoManager.startUp();
       gTextureManager.startUp();
       gRenderManager.startUp();
       gAnimationManager.startUp();
       gPhysicsManager.startUp();
       // ...

       // Run the game.
       gSimulationManager.run();

       // Shut everything down, in reverse order.
       // ...
       gPhysicsManager.shutDown();
       gAnimationManager.shutDown();
       gRenderManager.shutDown();
       gFileSystemManager.shutDown();
       gMemoryManager.shutDown();

       return 0;
   }
```

There are "more elegant" ways to accomplish this. For example, you could have each manager register itself into a global priority queue and then walk this queue to start up all the managers in the proper order. You could define the manger-to-manager dependency graph by having each manager explicitly list the other managers upon which it depends and then write some code to calculate the optimal start-up order given their interdependencies. You could use the construct-on-demand approach outlined above. In my experience, the brute-force approach always wins out, because:

- It's simple and easy to implement.
- It's explicit. You can see and understand the start-up order immediately by just looking at the code.
- It's easy to debug and maintain. If something isn't starting early enough, or is starting too early, you can just move one line of code.

One minor disadvantage to the brute-force manual start-up and shut-down method is that you might accidentally shut things down in an order that isn't strictly the reverse of the start-up order. But I wouldn't lose any sleep over it. As long as you can start up and shut down your engine's subsystems successfully, you're golden.

### 5.1.3.   Some Examples from Real Engines

Let's take a brief look at some examples of engine start-up and shut-down taken from real game engines.

#### 5.1.3.1.   Ogre3D

Ogre3D is by its authors' admission a rendering engine, not a game engine per se. But by necessity it provides many of the low-level features found in full-fledged game engines, including a simple and elegant start-up and shut-down mechanism. Everything in Ogre is controlled by the singleton object `Ogre::Root`. It contains pointers to every other subsystem in Ogre and manages their creation and destruction. This makes it very easy for a programmer to start up Ogre—just `new` an instance of `Ogre::Root` and you're done.

Here are a few excerpts from the Ogre source code so we can see what it's doing:

*OgreRoot.h*

```
class _OgreExport Root : public Singleton<Root>
{
    // <some code omitted...>

    // Singletons
    LogManager* mLogManager;
```

```
        ControllerManager* mControllerManager;
        SceneManagerEnumerator* mSceneManagerEnum;
        SceneManager* mCurrentSceneManager;
        DynLibManager* mDynLibManager;
        ArchiveManager* mArchiveManager;
        MaterialManager* mMaterialManager;
        MeshManager* mMeshManager;
        ParticleSystemManager* mParticleManager;
        SkeletonManager* mSkeletonManager;
        OverlayElementFactory* mPanelFactory;
        OverlayElementFactory* mBorderPanelFactory;
        OverlayElementFactory* mTextAreaFactory;
        OverlayManager* mOverlayManager;
        FontManager* mFontManager;
        ArchiveFactory *mZipArchiveFactory;
        ArchiveFactory *mFileSystemArchiveFactory;
        ResourceGroupManager* mResourceGroupManager;
        ResourceBackgroundQueue* mResourceBackgroundQueue;
        ShadowTextureManager* mShadowTextureManager;

        // etc.
    };
```

*OgreRoot.cpp*

```
    Root::Root(const String& pluginFileName,
               const String& configFileName,
               const String& logFileName) :
            mLogManager(0),
            mCurrentFrame(0),
            mFrameSmoothingTime(0.0f),
            mNextMovableObjectTypeFlag(1),
            mIsInitialised(false)
    {
        // superclass will do singleton checking
        String msg;

        // Init
        mActiveRenderer = 0;
        mVersion
            = StringConverter::toString(OGRE_VERSION_MAJOR)
            + "."
            + StringConverter::toString(OGRE_VERSION_MINOR)
            + "."
            + StringConverter::toString(OGRE_VERSION_PATCH)
            + OGRE_VERSION_SUFFIX + " "
            + "(" + OGRE_VERSION_NAME + ")";
        mConfigFileName = configFileName;

        // Create log manager and default log file if there
        // is no log manager yet
```

```
if(LogManager::getSingletonPtr() == 0)
{
    mLogManager = new LogManager();
    mLogManager->createLog(logFileName, true, true);
}

// Dynamic library manager
mDynLibManager = new DynLibManager();
mArchiveManager = new ArchiveManager();

// ResourceGroupManager
mResourceGroupManager = new ResourceGroupManager();

// ResourceBackgroundQueue
mResourceBackgroundQueue
    = new ResourceBackgroundQueue();

// and so on...
```

Ogre provides a templated `Ogre::Singleton` base class from which all of its singleton (manager) classes derive. If you look at its implementation, you'll see that `Ogre::Singleton` does not use deferred construction, but instead relies on `Ogre::Root` to explicitly new each singleton. As we discussed above, this is done to ensure that the singletons are created and destroyed in a well-defined order.

### 5.1.3.2. Naughty Dog's *Uncharted: Drake's Fortune*

The *Uncharted: Drake's Fortune* engine created by Naughty Dog Inc. uses a similar explicit technique for starting up its subsystems. You'll notice by looking at the following code that engine start-up is not always a simple sequence of allocating singleton instances. A wide range of operating system services, third party libraries, and so on must all be started up during engine initialization. Also, dynamic memory allocation is avoided wherever possible, so many of the singletons are statically-allocated objects (e.g., `g_fileSystem`, `g_languageMgr`, etc.) It's not always pretty, but it gets the job done.

```
Err BigInit()
{
    init_exception_handler();

    U8* pPhysicsHeap = new(kAllocGlobal, kAlign16)
        U8[ALLOCATION_GLOBAL_PHYS_HEAP];
    PhysicsAllocatorInit(pPhysicsHeap,
        ALLOCATION_GLOBAL_PHYS_HEAP);

    g_textDb.Init();
    g_textSubDb.Init();
```

```
g_spuMgr.Init();

g_drawScript.InitPlatform();

PlatformUpdate();

thread_t init_thr;
thread_create(&init_thr, threadInit, 0, 30,
    64*1024, 0, "Init");

char masterConfigFileName[256];
snprintf(masterConfigFileName,
    sizeof(masterConfigFileName),
    MASTER_CFG_PATH);
{
    Err err = ReadConfigFromFile(
        masterConfigFileName);
    if (err.Failed())
    {
        MsgErr("Config file not found (%s).\n",
            masterConfigFileName);
    }
}

memset(&g_discInfo, 0, sizeof(BootDiscInfo));
int err1 = GetBootDiscInfo(&g_discInfo);
Msg("GetBootDiscInfo() : 0x%x\n", err1);
if(err1 == BOOTDISCINFO_RET_OK)
{
    printf("titleId       : [%s]\n",
        g_discInfo.titleId);
    printf("parentalLevel : [%d]\n",
        g_discInfo.parentalLevel);
}

g_fileSystem.Init(g_gameInfo.m_onDisc);

g_languageMgr.Init();
if (g_shouldQuit) return Err::kOK;

// and so on...
```

## 5.2.  Memory Management

As game developers, we are always trying to make our code run more quickly.
The performance of any piece of software is dictated not only by the algorithms it employs, or the efficiency with which those algorithms are coded,

but also by how the program *utilizes memory* (RAM). Memory affects performance in two ways:

1. *Dynamic memory allocation* via `malloc()` or C++'s global `operator new` is a very slow operation. We can improve the performance of our code by either avoiding dynamic allocation altogether or by making use of custom memory allocators that greatly reduce allocation costs.

2. On modern CPUs, the performance of a piece of software is often dominated by its *memory access patterns.* As we'll see, data that is located in small, *contiguous* blocks of memory can be operated on much more efficiently by the CPU than if that same data were to be spread out across a wide range of memory addresses. Even the most efficient algorithm, coded with the utmost care, can be brought to its knees if the data upon which it operates is not laid out efficiently in memory.

In this section, we'll learn how to optimize our code's memory utilization along these two axes.

### 5.2.1. Optimizing Dynamic Memory Allocation

Dynamic memory allocation via `malloc()` and `free()` or C++'s global `new` and `delete` operators—also known as *heap allocation*—is typically very slow. The high cost can be attributed to two main factors. First, a heap allocator is a general-purpose facility, so it must be written to handle any allocation size, from one byte to one gigabyte. This requires a lot of management overhead, making the `malloc()` and `free()` functions inherently slow. Second, on most operating systems a call to `malloc()` or `free()` must first context-switch from user mode into kernel mode, process the request, and then context-switch back to the program. These context switches can be extraordinarily expensive. One rule of thumb often followed in game development is:

> Keep heap allocations to a minimum, and never allocate from the heap within a tight loop.

Of course, no game engine can entirely avoid dynamic memory allocation, so most game engines implement one or more custom allocators. A custom allocator can have better performance characteristics than the operating system's heap allocator for two reasons. First, a custom allocator can satisfy requests from a preallocated memory block (itself allocated using `malloc()` or `new`, or declared as a global variable). This allows it to run in user mode and entirely avoid the cost of context-switching into the operating system. Second, by making various assumptions about its usage patterns, a custom allocator can be much more efficient than a general-purpose heap allocator.

In the following sections, we'll take a look at some common kinds of custom allocators. For additional information on this topic, see Christian Gyrling's excellent blog post, http://www.swedishcoding.com/2008/08/31/are-we-out-of-memory.

### 5.2.1.1. Stack-Based Allocators

Many games allocate memory in a stack-like fashion. Whenever a new game level is loaded, memory is allocated for it. Once the level has been loaded, little or no dynamic memory allocation takes place. At the conclusion of the level, its data is unloaded and all of its memory can be freed. It makes a lot of sense to use a stack-like data structure for these kinds of memory allocations.

A *stack allocator* is very easy to implement. We simply allocate a large contiguous block of memory using `malloc()` or global `new`, or by declaring a global array of bytes (in which case the memory is effectively allocated out of the executable's BSS segment). A pointer to the top of the stack is maintained. All memory addresses below this pointer are considered to be in use, and all addresses above it are considered to be free. The top pointer is initialized to the lowest memory address in the stack. Each allocation request simply moves the pointer up by the requested number of bytes. The most-recently allocated block can be freed by simply moving the top pointer back down by the size of the block.

It is important to realize that with a stack allocator, memory cannot be freed in an arbitrary order. All frees must be performed in an order opposite to that in which they were allocated. One simple way to enforce these restrictions is to disallow individual blocks from being freed at all. Instead, we can provide a function that rolls the stack top back to a previously-marked location, thereby freeing all blocks between the current top and the roll-back point.

It's important to always roll the top pointer back to a point that lies at the boundary between two allocated blocks, because otherwise new allocations would overwrite the tail end of the top-most block. To ensure that this is done properly, a stack allocator often provides a function that returns a *marker* representing the current top of the stack. The roll-back function then takes one of these markers as its argument. This is depicted in Figure 5.1. The interface of a stack allocator often looks something like this.

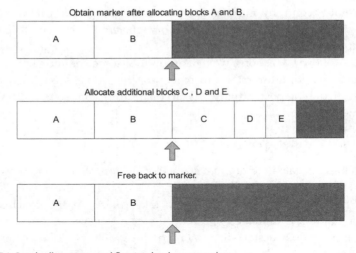

Figure 5.1. Stack allocation, and freeing back to a marker.

```
class StackAllocator
{
public:
    // Stack marker: Represents the current top of the
    // stack. You can only roll back to a marker, not to
    // arbitrary locations within the stack.
    typedef U32 Marker;

    // Constructs a stack allocator with the given total
    // size.
    explicit StackAllocator(U32 stackSize_bytes);

    // Allocates a new block of the given size from stack
    // top.
    void* alloc(U32 size_bytes);

    // Returns a marker to the current stack top.
    Marker getMarker();

    // Rolls the stack back to a previous marker.
    void freeToMarker(Marker marker);

    // Clears the entire stack (rolls the stack back to
    // zero).
    void clear();
```

```
private:
    // ...
};
```

*Double-Ended Stack Allocators*

A single memory block can actually contain two stack allocators—one which allocates up from the bottom of the block and one which allocates down from the top of the block. A double-ended stack allocator is useful because it uses memory more efficiently by allowing a trade-off to occur between the memory usage of the bottom stack and the memory usage of the top stack. In some situations, both stacks may use roughly the same amount of memory and meet in the middle of the block. In other situations, one of the two stacks may eat up a lot more memory than the other stack, but all allocation requests can still be satisfied as long as the total amount of memory requested is not larger than the block shared by the two stacks. This is depicted in Figure 5.2.

In Midway's *Hydro Thunder* arcade game, all memory allocations are made from a single large block of memory managed by a double-ended stack allocator. The bottom stack is used for loading and unloading levels (race tracks), while the top stack is used for temporary memory blocks that are allocated and freed every frame. This allocation scheme worked extremely well and ensured that *Hydro Thunder* never suffered from memory fragmentation problems (see Section 5.2.1.4). Steve Ranck, *Hydro Thunder*'s lead engineer, describes this allocation technique in depth in [6], Section 1.9.

Figure 5.2. A double-ended stack allocator.

### 5.2.1.2.   Pool Allocators

It's quite common in game engine programming (and software engineering in general) to allocate lots of small blocks of memory, each of which are the same size. For example, we might want to allocate and free matrices, or iterators, or links in a linked list, or renderable mesh instances. For this type of memory allocation pattern, a *pool allocator* is often the perfect choice.

A pool allocator works by preallocating a large block of memory whose size is an exact multiple of the size of the elements that will be allocated. For example, a pool of 4 × 4 matrices would be an exact multiple of 64 bytes (16 elements per matrix times four bytes per element). Each element within the pool is added to a linked list of free elements; when the pool is first initialized, the free list contains all of the elements. Whenever an allocation request is made, we simply grab the next free element off the free list and return it. When an element is freed, we simply tack it back onto the free list. Both allocations and frees are $O(1)$ operations, since each involves only a couple of pointer manipulations, no matter how many elements are currently free. (The notation $O(1)$ is an example of big "O" notation. In this case it means that the execution time of both allocations and frees are roughly constant and do not depend on things like the number of elements currently in the pool. See Section 5.3.3 for an explanation of big "O" notation.)

The linked list of free elements can be a singly-linked list, meaning that we need a single pointer (four bytes on most machines) for each free element. Where should we obtain the memory for these pointers? Certainly they could be stored in a separate preallocated memory block, occupying `(sizeof(void*) * numElementsInPool)` bytes. However, this is unduly wasteful. We need only realize that the blocks on the free list are, by definition, free memory blocks. So why not use the free blocks themselves to store the free list's "next" pointers? This little "trick" works as long as `elementSize >= sizeof(void*)`.

If each element is smaller than a pointer, then we can use pool element indices instead of pointers to implement our linked list. For example, if our pool contains 16-bit integers, then we can use 16-bit indices as the "next pointers" in our linked list. This works as long as the pool doesn't contain more than $2^{16}$ = 65,536 elements.

### 5.2.1.3.   Aligned Allocations

As we saw in Section 3.2.5.1, every variable and data object has an alignment requirement. An 8-bit integer variable can be aligned to any address, but a 32-bit integer or floating-point variable must be 4-byte aligned, meaning its address can only end in the nibbles 0x0, 0x4, 0x8 or 0xC. A 128-bit SIMD vector value generally has a 16-byte alignment requirement, meaning that its memory address can end only in the nibble 0x0. On the PS3, memory blocks that are to be transferred to an SPU via the direct memory access (DMA) controller should be 128-bit aligned for maximum DMA throughput, meaning they can only end in the bytes 0x00 or 0x80.

All memory allocators must be capable of returning aligned memory blocks. This is relatively straightforward to implement. We simply allocate a little bit more memory than was actually requested, adjust the address of the memory block upward slightly so that it is aligned properly, and then return the adjusted address. Because we allocated a bit more memory than was requested, the returned block will still be large enough, even with the slight upward adjustment.

In most implementations, the number of additional bytes allocated is equal to the alignment. For example, if the request is for a 16-byte aligned memory block, we would allocate 16 additional bytes. This allows for the worst-case address adjustment of 15 bytes, plus one extra byte so that we can use the same calculations even if the original block is already aligned. This simplifies and speeds up the code at the expense of one wasted byte per allocation. It's also important because, as we'll see below, we'll need those extra bytes to store some additional information that will be used when the block is freed.

We determine the amount by which the block's address must be adjusted by masking off the least-significant bits of the original block's memory address, subtracting this from the desired alignment, and using the result as the adjustment offset. The alignment should always be a *power of two* (four-byte and 16-byte alignments are typical), so to generate the mask we simply subtract one from the alignment. For example, if the request is for a 16-byte aligned block, then the mask would be (16 − 1) = 15 = 0x0000000F. Taking the bitwise AND of this mask and any misaligned address will yield the amount by which the address is misaligned. For example, if the originally-allocated block's address is 0x50341233, ANDing this address with the mask 0x0000000F yields 0x00000003, so the address is misaligned by three bytes. To align the address, we add (alignment − misalignment) = (16 − 3) = 13 = 0xD bytes to it. The final aligned address is therefore 0x50341233 + 0xD = 0x50341240.

Here's one possible implementation of an aligned memory allocator:

```
// Aligned allocation function. IMPORTANT: 'alignment'
// must be a power of 2 (typically 4 or 16).
void* allocateAligned(U32 size_bytes, U32 alignment)
{
    // Determine total amount of memory to allocate.
    U32 expandedSize_bytes = size_bytes + alignment;

    // Allocate an unaligned block & convert address to a
    // U32.
    U32 rawAddress
        = (U32)allocateUnaligned(expandedSize_bytes);

    // Calculate the adjustment by masking off the lower
    // bits of the address, to determine how "misaligned"
    // it is.
    U32 mask = (alignment - 1);
    U32 misalignment = (rawAddress & mask);
    U32 adjustment = alignment - misalignment;
```

```
    // Calculate the adjusted address, and return as a
    // pointer.
    U32 alignedAddress = rawAddress + adjustment;
    return (void*)alignedAddress;
}
```

When this block is later freed, the code will pass us the adjusted address, not the original address we allocated. How, then, do we actually free the memory? We need some way to convert an adjusted address back into the original, possibly misaligned address.

To accomplish this, we simply store some meta-information in those extra bytes we allocated in order to align the data in the first place. The smallest adjustment we might make is one byte. That's enough room to store the number of bytes by which the address was adjusted (since it will never be more than 256). We always store this information in the byte immediately preceding the adjusted address (no matter how many bytes of adjustment we actually added), so that it is trivial to find it again, given the adjusted address. Here's how the modified allocateAligned() function would look.

```
// Aligned allocation function. IMPORTANT: 'alignment'
// must be a power of 2 (typically 4 or 16).
void* allocateAligned(U32 size_bytes, U32 alignment)
{
    // Clients must call allocateUnaligned() and
    // freeUnaligned() if alignment == 1.
    ASSERT(alignment > 1);

    // Determine total amount of memory to allocate.
    U32 expandedSize_bytes = size_bytes + alignment;

    // Allocate an unaligned block & convert address to a
    // U32.
    U32 rawAddress
        = (U32)allocateUnaligned(expandedSize_bytes);

    // Calculate the adjustment by masking off the lower
    // bits of the address, to determine how "misaligned"
    // it is.
    U32 mask = (alignment - 1);
    U32 misalignment = (rawAddress & mask);
    U32 adjustment = alignment - misalignment;

    // Calculate the adjusted address, and return as a
    // pointer.
    U32 alignedAddress = rawAddress + adjustment;
```

```
    // Store the adjustment in the four bytes immediately
    // preceding the adjusted address that we're
    // returning.

    U32* pAdjustment = (U32*)(alignedAddress - 4);
    *pAdjustment = adjustment;

    return (void*)alignedAddress;
}
```

And here's how the corresponding `freeAligned()` function would be implemented.

```
void freeAligned(void* p)
{
    U32 alignedAddress = (U32)p;
    U8* pAdjustment = (U8*)(alignedAddress - 4);
    U32 adjustment = (U32)*pAdjustment;

    U32 rawAddress = alignedAddress - adjustment;

    freeUnaligned((void*)rawAddress);
}
```

### 5.2.1.4. Single-Frame and Double-Buffered Memory Allocators

Virtually all game engines allocate at least some temporary data during the game loop. This data is either discarded at the end of each iteration of the loop or used on the next frame and then discarded. This allocation pattern is so common that many engines support *single-* and *double-buffered* allocators.

*Single-Frame Allocators*

A single-frame allocator is implemented by reserving a block of memory and managing it with a simple stack allocator as described above. At the beginning of each frame, the stack's "top" pointer is cleared to the bottom of the memory block. Allocations made during the frame grow toward the top of the block. Rinse and repeat.

```
StackAllocator g_singleFrameAllocator;

// Main Game Loop
while (true)
{
    // Clear the single-frame allocator's buffer every
    // frame.
    g_singleFrameAllocator.clear();
```

```
// ...

// Allocate from the single-frame buffer. We never
// need to free this data! Just be sure to use it
// only this frame.
void* p = g_singleFrameAllocator.alloc(nBytes);

// ...
}
```

One of the primary benefits of a single-frame allocator is that allocated memory needn't ever be freed—we can rely on the fact that the allocator will be cleared at the start of every frame. Single-frame allocators are also blindingly fast. The one big negative is that using a single-frame allocator requires a reasonable level of discipline on the part of the programmer. You need to realize that a memory block allocated out of the single-frame buffer will only be valid during the current frame. Programmers must *never* cache a pointer to a single-frame memory block across the frame boundary!

### Double-Buffered Allocators

A double-buffered allocator allows a block of memory allocated on frame *i* to be used on frame (*i* + 1). To accomplish this, we create two single-frame stack allocators of equal size and then ping-pong between them every frame.

```
class DoubleBufferedAllocator
{
    U32                 m_curStack;
    StackAllocator      m_stack[2];
public:

    void swapBuffers()
    {
        m_curStack = (U32)!m_curStack;
    }

    void clearCurrentBuffer()
    {
        m_stack[m_curStack].clear();
    }

    void* alloc(U32 nBytes)
    {
        return m_stack[m_curStack].alloc(nBytes);
    }

    // ...
};
```

```
// ...

DoubleBufferedAllocator g_doubleBufAllocator;

// Main Game Loop
while (true)
{
    // Clear the single-frame allocator every frame as
    // before.
    g_singleFrameAllocator.clear();

    // Swap the active and inactive buffers of the double
    // buffered allocator.
    g_doubleBufAllocator.swapBuffers();

    // Now clear the newly active buffer, leaving last
    // frame's buffer intact.
    g_doubleBufAllocator.clearCurrentBuffer();

    // ...

    // Allocate out of the current buffer, without
    // disturbing last frame's data. Only use this data
    // this frame or next frame. Again, this memory never
    // needs to be freed.
    void* p = g_doubleBufAllocator.alloc(nBytes);

    // ...
}
```

This kind of allocator is extremely useful for caching the results of asynchronous processing on a multicore game console like the Xbox 360 or the PLAYSTATION 3. On frame $i$, we can kick off an asynchronous job on one of the PS3's SPUs, handing it the address of a destination buffer that has been allocated from our double-buffered allocator. The job runs and produces its results some time before the end of frame $i$, storing them into the buffer we provided. On frame $(i + 1)$, the buffers are swapped. The results of the job are now in the inactive buffer, so they will not be overwritten by any double-buffered allocations that might be made during this frame. As long as we use the results of the job before frame $(i + 2)$, our data won't be overwritten.

## 5.2.2.  Memory Fragmentation

Another problem with dynamic heap allocations is that memory can become *fragmented* over time. When a program first runs, its heap memory is entirely free. When a block is allocated, a contiguous region of heap memory of the appropriate size is marked as "in use," and the remainder of the heap remains free. When a block is freed, it is marked as such, and adjacent free blocks are merged into a single, larger free block. Over time, as allocations and deallocations of various sizes occur in random order, the heap memory begins to look like a patchwork of free and used blocks. We can think of the free regions as "holes" in the fabric of used memory. When the number of holes becomes large, and/or the holes are all relatively small, we say the memory has become *fragmented*. This is illustrated in Figure 5.3.

The problem with memory fragmentation is that allocations may fail even when there are enough free bytes to satisfy the request. The crux of the problem is that allocated memory blocks must always be *contiguous*. For example, in order to satisfy a request of 128 kB, there must exist a free "hole" that is 128 kB or larger. If there are 2 holes, each of which is 64 kB in size, then enough bytes are available but the allocation fails because they are not *contiguous bytes*.

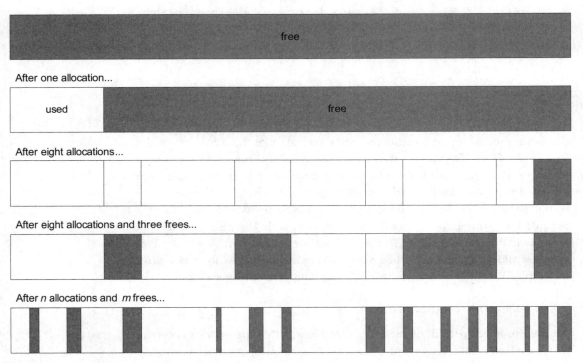

**Figure 5.3.** Memory fragmentation.

Memory fragmentation is not as much of a problem on operating systems that support *virtual memory*. A virtual memory system maps discontiguous blocks of physical memory known as *pages* into a *virtual address space*, in which the pages appear to the application to be contiguous. Stale pages can be swapped to the hard disk when physical memory is in short supply and reloaded from disk when they are needed. For a detailed discussion of how virtual memory works, see http://lyle.smu.edu/~kocan/7343/fall05/slides/chapter08.ppt. Most embedded systems cannot afford to implement a virtual memory system. While some modern consoles do technically support it, most console game engines still do not make use of virtual memory due to the inherent performance overhead.

### 5.2.2.1. Avoiding Fragmentation with Stack and Pool Allocators

The detrimental effects of memory fragmentation can be avoided by using stack and/or pool allocators.

- A stack allocator is impervious to fragmentation because allocations are always contiguous, and blocks must be freed in an order opposite to that in which they were allocated. This is illustrated in Figure 5.4.

- A pool allocator is also free from fragmentation problems. Pools *do* become fragmented, but the fragmentation never causes premature out-of-memory conditions as it does in a general-purpose heap. Pool allocation requests can never fail due to a lack of a large enough contiguous free block, because all of the blocks are exactly the same size. This is shown in Figure 5.5.

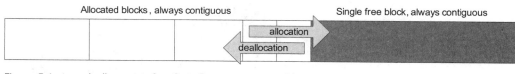

Figure 5.4. A stack allocator is free from fragmentation problems.

Figure 5.5. A pool allocator is not degraded by fragmentation.

### 5.2.2.2. Defragmentation and Relocation

When differently-sized objects are being allocated and freed in a random order, neither a stack-based allocator nor a pool-based allocator can be used. In
such cases, fragmentation can be avoided by periodically *defragmenting* the
heap. Defragmentation involves coalescing all of the free "holes" in the heap
by shifting allocated blocks from higher memory addresses down to lower
addresses (thereby shifting the holes up to higher addresses). One simple algorithm is to search for the first "hole" and then take the allocated block immediately above the hole and shift it down to the start of the hole. This has the
effect of "bubbling up" the hole to a higher memory address. If this process is
repeated, eventually all the allocated blocks will occupy a contiguous region
of memory at the low end of the heap's address space, and all the holes will
have bubbled up into one big hole at the high end of the heap. This is illustrated in Figure 5.6.

The shifting of memory blocks described above is not particularly tricky
to implement. What *is* tricky is accounting for the fact that we're moving *allocated* blocks of memory around. If anyone has a *pointer* into one of these allocated blocks, then moving the block will invalidate the pointer.

The solution to this problem is to patch any and all pointers into a shifted
memory block so that they point to the correct new address after the shift.
This procedure is known as pointer *relocation.* Unfortunately, there is no general-purpose way to *find* all the pointers that point into a particular region

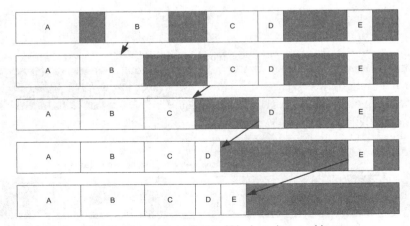

**Figure 5.6.** Defragmentation by shifting allocated blocks to lower addresses.

of memory. So if we are going to support memory defragmentation in our game engine, programmers must either carefully keep track of all the pointers manually so they can be relocated, or pointers must be abandoned in favor of something inherently more amenable to relocation, such as *smart pointers* or *handles*.

A smart pointer is a small class that contains a pointer and acts like a pointer for most intents and purposes. But because a smart pointer is a class, it can be coded to handle memory relocation properly. One approach is to arrange for all smart pointers to add themselves to a global linked list. Whenever a block of memory is shifted within the heap, the linked list of all smart pointers can be scanned, and each pointer that points into the shifted block of memory can be adjusted appropriately.

A handle is usually implemented as an index into a non-relocatable table which itself contains the pointers. When an allocated block is shifted in memory, the handle table can be scanned and all relevant pointers found and updated automatically. Because the handles are just indices into the pointer table, their values never change no matter how the memory blocks are shifted, so the objects that use the handles are never affected by memory relocation.

Another problem with relocation arises when certain memory blocks cannot be relocated. For example, if you are using a third-party library that does not use smart pointers or handles, it's possible that any pointers into its data structures will not be relocatable. The best way around this problem is usually to arrange for the library in question to allocate its memory from a special buffer outside of the relocatable memory area. The other option is to simply accept that some blocks will not be relocatable. If the number and size of the non-relocatable blocks are both small, a relocation system will still perform quite well.

It is interesting to note that all of Naughty Dog's engines have supported defragmentation. Handles are used wherever possible to avoid the need to relocate pointers. However, in some cases raw pointers cannot be avoided. These pointers are carefully tracked and relocated manually whenever a memory block is shifted due to defragmentation. A few of Naughty Dog's game object classes are not relocatable for various reasons. However, as mentioned above, this doesn't pose any practical problems, because the number of such objects is always very small, and their sizes are tiny when compared to the overall size of the relocatable memory area.

### Amortizing Defragmentation Costs

Defragmentation can be a slow operation because it involves copying memory blocks. However, we needn't fully defragment the heap all at once. Instead, the cost can be amortized over many frames. We can allow up to $N$ allocated blocks to be shifted each frame, for some small value of $N$ like 8 or 16. If our game is running at 30 frames per second, then each frame lasts 1/30 of a second (33 ms). So the heap can usually be completely defragmented in less than one second without having any noticeable effect on the game's frame rate. As long as allocations and deallocations aren't happening at a faster rate than the defragmentation shifts, the heap will remain mostly defragmented at all times.

This approach is only valid when the size of each block is relatively small, so that the time required to move a single block does not exceed the time allotted to relocation each frame. If very large blocks need to be relocated, we can often break them up into two or more subblocks, each of which can be relocated independently. This hasn't proved to be a problem in Naughty Dog's engine, because relocation is only used for dynamic game objects, and they are never larger than a few kilobytes—and usually much smaller.

### 5.2.3. Cache Coherency

To understand why memory access patterns affect performance, we need first to understand how modern processors read and write memory. Accessing main system RAM is always a slow operation, often taking thousands of processor cycles to complete. Contrast this with a register access on the CPU itself, which takes on the order of tens of cycles or sometimes even a single cycle. To reduce the average cost of reading and writing to main RAM, modern processors utilize a high-speed memory *cache*.

A cache is a special type of memory that can be read from and written to by the CPU much more quickly than main RAM. The basic idea of memory caching is to load a small chunk of memory into the high-speed cache whenever a given region of main RAM is first read. Such a memory chunk is called a *cache line* and is usually between 8 and 512 bytes, depending on the microprocessor architecture. On subsequent read operations, if the requested data already exists in the cache, it is loaded from the cache directly into the CPU's registers—a much faster operation than reading from main RAM. Only if the required data is not already in the cache does main RAM have to be accessed. This is called a *cache miss*. Whenever a cache miss occurs, the program is forced to wait for the cache line to be refreshed from main RAM.

Similar rules may apply when *writing* data to RAM. The simplest kind of cache is called a *write-through cache*; in such a cache design, all writes to the cache are simply mirrored to main RAM immediately. However, in a *write-back* (or *copy-back*) cache design, data is first written into the cache and the cache line is only flushed out to main RAM under certain circumstances, such as when a dirty cache line needs to be evicted in order to read in a new cache line from main RAM, or when the program explicitly requests a flush to occur.

Obviously cache misses cannot be totally avoided, since data has to move to and from main RAM eventually. However, the trick to high-performance computing is to arrange your data in RAM and code your algorithms in such a way that the minimum number of cache misses occur. We'll see exactly how to accomplish this below.

### 5.2.3.1. Level 1 and Level 2 Caches

When caching techniques were first developed, the cache memory was located on the motherboard, constructed from a faster and more expensive type of memory module than main RAM in order to give it the required boost in speed. However, cache memory was expensive, so the cache size was usually quite small—on the order of 16 kB. As caching techniques evolved, an even faster type of cache memory was developed that was located on the CPU die itself. This gave rise to two distinct types of cache memory: an on-die *level 1* (L1) cache and an on-motherboard *level 2* (L2) cache. More recently, the L2 cache has also migrated onto the CPU die (see Figure 5.7).

The rules for moving data back and forth between main RAM are of course complicated by the presence of a level 2 cache. Now, instead of data hopping from RAM to cache to CPU and back again, it must make two hops—first from main RAM to the L2 cache, and then from L2 cache to L1 cache. We won't go into the specifics of these rules here. (They differ slightly from CPU to CPU anyway.) But suffice it to say that RAM is slower than L2 cache memory, and L2 cache is slower than L1 cache. Hence L2 cache misses are usually more expensive than L1 cache misses, all other things being equal.

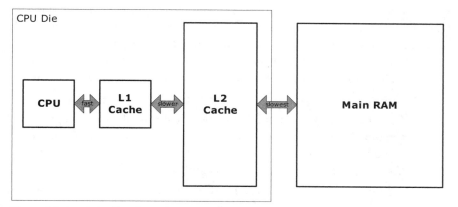

**Figure 5.7.** Level 1 and level 2 caches.

A *load-hit-store* is a particularly bad kind of cache miss, prevalent on the PowerPC architectures found in the Xbox 360 and PLAYSTATION 3, in which the CPU writes data to a memory address and then reads the data back before it has had a chance to make its way through the CPU's instruction pipeline and out into the L1 cache. See http://assemblyrequired.crashworks.org/2008/07/08/load-hit-stores-and-the-__restrict-keyword for more details.

### 5.2.3.2.  Instruction Cache and Data Cache

When writing high-performance code for a game engine or for any other performance-critical system, it is important to realize that both data and code are cached. The instruction cache (I-cache) is used to preload executable machine code before it runs, while the data cache (D-cache) is used to speed up reading and writing of data to main RAM. Most processors separate the two caches physically. Hence it is possible for a program to slow down because of an I-cache miss or because of a D-cache miss.

### 5.2.3.3.  Avoiding Cache Misses

The best way to avoid D-cache misses is to organize your data in *contiguous* blocks that are as *small* as possible and then access them *sequentially*. This yields the minimum number of cache misses. When the data is contiguous (i.e., you don't "jump around" in memory a lot), a single cache miss will load the maximum amount of relevant data in one go. When the data is small, it is more likely to fit into a single cache line (or at least a minimum number of cache lines). And when you access your data sequentially (i.e., you don't "jump around" *within* the contiguous memory block), you achieve the minimum number of cache misses, since the CPU never has to reload a cache line from the same region of RAM.

Avoiding I-cache misses follows the same basic principle as avoiding D-cache misses. However, the implementation requires a different approach. The compiler and linker dictate how your code is laid out in memory, so you might think you have little control over I-cache misses. However, most C/C++ linkers follow some simple rules that you can leverage, once you know what they are:

- The machine code for a single function is almost always contiguous in memory. That is, the linker almost never splits a function up in order to intersperse another function in the middle. (Inline functions are the exception to this rule—more on this topic below.)

- Functions are laid out in memory in the order they appear in the translation unit's source code (.cpp file).

- Therefore, functions in a single translation unit are always contiguous in memory. That is, the linker never splits up a complied translation unit (.obj file) in order to intersperse code from some other translation unit.

So, following the same principles that apply to avoiding D-cache misses, we should follow the rules of thumb listed below.

- Keep high-performance code *as small as possible,* in terms of number of machine language instructions. (The compiler and linker take care of keeping our functions *contiguous* in memory.)
- *Avoid calling functions* from within a performance-critical section of code.
- If you do have to call a function, place it as *close as possible* to the calling function—preferably immediately before or after the calling function and *never* in a different translation unit (because then you completely lose control over its proximity to the calling function).
- Use inline functions judiciously. Inlining a small function can be a big performance boost. However, too much inlining bloats the size of the code, which can cause a performance-critical section of code to no longer fit within the cache. Let's say we write a tight loop that processes a large amount of data—if the entire body of that loop doesn't fit into the cache, then we are signing up for two I-cache misses during every iteration of the loop. In such a situation, it is probably best to rethink the algorithm and/or implementation so that less code is required within critical loops.

## 5.3. Containers

Game programmers employ a wide variety of collection-oriented data structures, also known as *containers* or *collections.* The job of a container is always the same—to house and manage zero or more data elements; however, the details of how they do this varies greatly, and each type of container has its pros and cons. Common container data types include, but are certainly not limited to, the following.

- *Array.* An ordered, contiguous collection of elements accessed by index. The length of the array is usually statically defined at compile time. It may be multidimensional. C and C++ support these natively (e.g., `int a[5]`).
- *Dynamic array.* An array whose length can change dynamically at runtime (e.g., STL's `std::vector`)

- *Linked list.* An ordered collection of elements not stored contiguously in memory but rather linked to one another via pointers (e.g., STL's `std::list`).

- *Stack.* A container that supports the last-in-first-out (LIFO) model for adding and removing elements, also known as push/pop (e.g., `std::stack`).

- *Queue.* A container that supports the first-in-first-out (FIFO) model for adding and removing elements (e.g., `std::queue`).

- *Deque.* A double-ended queue—supports efficient insertion and removal at both ends of the array (e.g., `std::deque`).

- *Priority queue.* A container that permits elements to be added in any order and then removed in an order defined by some property of the elements themselves (i.e., their *priority*). It can be thought of as a list that stays sorted at all times. A priority queue is typically implemented as a binary search tree (e.g., `std::priority_queue`).

- *Tree.* A container in which elements are grouped hierarchically. Each element (node) has zero or one parent and zero or more children. A tree is a special case of a DAG (see below).

- *Binary search tree (BST) .* A tree in which each node has at most two children, with an order property to keep the nodes sorted by some well-defined criteria. There are various kinds of binary search trees, including red-black trees, splay trees, SVL trees, etc.

- *Binary heap.* A binary tree that maintains itself in sorted order, much like a binary search tree, via two rules: the *shape property*, which specifies that the tree must be fully filled and that the last row of the tree is filled from left to right; and the *heap property*, which states that every node is, by some user-defined criterion, "greater than" or "equal to" all of its children.

- *Dictionary.* A table of key-value pairs. A value can be "looked up" efficiently given the corresponding key. A dictionary is also known as a *map* or *hash table,* although technically a hash table is just one possible implementation of a dictionary (e.g., `std::map`, `std::hash_map`).

- *Set.* A container that guarantees that all elements are unique according to some criteria. A set acts like a dictionary with only keys, but no values.

- *Graph.* A collection of nodes connected to one another by unidirectional or bidirectional pathways in an arbitrary pattern.

- *Directed acyclic graph (DAG).* A collection of nodes with unidirectional (i.e., *directed*) interconnections, with no *cycles* (i.e., there is no non-empty path that starts and ends on the same node).

### 5.3.1. Container Operations

Game engines that make use of container classes inevitably make use of various commonplace algorithms as well. Some examples include:

- *Insert.* Add a new element to the container. The new element might be placed at the beginning of the list, or the end, or in some other location; or the container might not have a notion of ordering at all.

- *Remove.* Remove an element from the container; may require a find operation (see below). However if an iterator is available that refers to the desired element, it may be more efficient to remove the element using the iterator.

- *Sequential access (iteration).* Accessing each element of the container in some "natural" predefined order.

- *Random access.* Accessing elements in the container in an arbitrary order.

- *Find.* Search a container for an element that meets a given criterion. There are all sorts of variants on the find operation, including finding in reverse, finding multiple elements, etc. In addition, different types of data structures and different situations call for different algorithms (see http://en.wikipedia.org/wiki/Search_algorithm).

- *Sort.* Sort the contents of a container according to some given criteria. There are many different sorting algorithms, including bubble sort, selection sort, insertion sort, quicksort, and so on. (See http://en.wikipedia.org/wiki/Sorting_algorithm for details.)

### 5.3.2. Iterators

An iterator is a little class that "knows" how to efficiently visit the elements in a particular kind of container. It acts like an array index or pointer—it refers to one element in the container at a time, it can be advanced to the next element, and it provides some sort of mechanism for testing whether or not all elements in the container have been visited. As an example, the first of the following two code snippets iterates over a C-style array using a pointer, while the second iterates over an STL linked list using almost identical syntax.

```
void processArray(int container[], int numElements)
{
    int* pBegin = &container[0];
    int* pEnd = &container[numElements];
```

```
    for (int* p = pBegin; p != pEnd; ++p)
    {
        int element = *p;
        // process element...
    }
}

void processList(std::list<int>& container)
{
    std::list<int>::iterator pBegin = container.begin();
    std::list<int>::iterator pEnd = container.end();
    std::list<inf>::iterator p;

    for (p = pBegin; p != pEnd; ++p)
    {
        int element = *p;
        // process element...
    }
}
```

The key benefits to using an iterator over attempting to access the container's elements directly are:

- Direct access would break the container class' encapsulation. An iterator, on the other hand, is typically a *friend* of the container class, and as such it can iterate efficiently without exposing any implementation details to the outside world. (In fact, most good container classes hide their internal details and cannot be iterated over *without* an iterator.)

- An iterator can simplify the process of iterating. Most iterators act like array indices or pointers, so a simple loop can be written in which the iterator is incremented and compared against a terminating condition— even when the underlying data structure is arbitrarily complex. For example, an iterator can make an in-order depth-first tree traversal look no more complex than a simple array iteration.

### 5.3.2.1. Preincrement versus Postincrement

Notice in the above example that we are using C++'s *preincrement* operator, ++p, rather than the *postincrement* operator, p++. This is a subtle but sometimes important optimization. The preincrement operator returns the value of the operand after the increment has been performed, whereas postincrement returns the previous, unincremented value. Hence preincrement can simply increment the pointer or iterator in place and return a reference to it. Postincrement must cache the old value, then increment the pointer or iterator, and finally return the cached value. This isn't a big deal for pointers or integer indices, except in very tight, highly-optimized loops. But for iterators, postin-crement can be the source of significant performance losses due to the some-times non-trivial cost of constructing and copying iterator objects. (See [31] for a more-detailed discussion of this issue.) Therefore, it's good to get in the habit of *always* using preincrement, unless you absolutely need the semantics of postincrement.

### 5.3.3.  Algorithmic Complexity

The choice of which container type to use for a given application depends upon the performance and memory characteristics of the container being considered. For each container type, we can determine the theoretical perfor-mance of common operations such as insertion, removal, find, and sort.

We usually indicate the amount of time $T$ that an operation is expected to take as a function of the number of elements $n$ in the container:

$$T = f(n).$$

Rather than try to find the exact function $f$, we concern ourselves only with finding the overall *order* of the function. For example, if the actual theoretical function were any of the following,

$$T = 5n^2 + 17,$$

$$T = 102n^2 + 50n + 12,$$

$$T = \tfrac{1}{2}n^2,$$

we would, in all cases, simplify the expression down to its most relevant term—in this case $n^2$. To indicate that we are only stating the *order* of the func-tion, not its exact equation, we use "big-O" notation, and write

$$T = O(n^2).$$

The order of an algorithm can usually be determined via an inspection of the pseudocode. If the algorithm's execution time is not dependent upon the number of elements in the container at all, we say it is $O(1)$ (i.e., it completes in *constant time*). If the algorithm performs a *loop* over the elements in the con-tainer and visits each element once, such as in a linear search of an unsorted list, we say the algorithm is $O(n)$. (Note that this order holds even if the loop might terminate early.) If two loops are nested, each of which potentially visits each node once, then we say the algorithm is $O(n^2)$. If a divide-and-conquer approach is used, as in a *binary search* (where half of the list is eliminated at each step), then we would expect that only $\log_2 n$ elements will actually be vis-ited by the algorithm on average, and hence we refer to it as an $O(\log n)$ operation. If an algorithm executes a subalgorithm $n$ times, and the subalgorithm is $O(\log n)$, then the resulting algorithm would be $O(n \log n)$.

To select an appropriate container class, we should look at the operations that we expect to be most common, then select the container whose performance characteristics for those operations are most favorable. The most common orders you'll encounter are listed here from fastest to slowest: $O(1)$, $O(\log n)$, $O(n)$, $O(n \log n)$, $O(n^2)$, $O(n^k)$ for $k > 2$.

We should also take the memory layout and usage characteristics of our containers into account. For example, an array (e.g., `int a[5]` or `std::vector`) stores its elements *contiguously* in memory and requires *no overhead storage* for anything other than the elements themselves. (Note that a *dynamic* array does require a small fixed overhead.) On the other hand, a linked list (e.g., `std::list`) wraps each element in a "link" data structure that contains a pointer to the next element and possibly also a pointer to the previous element, for a total of up to *eight bytes* of overhead per element. Also, the elements in a linked list need not be contiguous in memory and often aren't. A contiguous block of memory is usually much more cache-friendly than a set of disparate memory blocks. Hence, for high-speed algorithms, arrays are usually better than linked lists in terms of cache performance (unless the nodes of the linked list are themselves allocated from a small, contiguous memory block of memory, which is rare but not entirely unheard of). But a linked list is better for situations in which speed of inserting and removing elements is of prime importance.

### 5.3.4. Building Custom Container Classes

Many game engines provide their own custom implementations of the common container data structures. This practice is especially prevalent in console game engines and games targeted at mobile phone and PDA platforms. The reasons for building these classes yourself include:

- *Total control.* You control the data structure's memory requirements, the algorithms used, when and how memory is allocated, etc.

- *Opportunities for optimization.* You can optimize your data structures and algorithms to take advantage of hardware features specific to the console(s) you are targeting; or fine-tune them for a particular application within your engine.

- *Customizability.* You can provide custom algorithms not prevalent in third-party libraries like STL (for example, searching for the $n$ most-relevant elements in a container, instead of just the single most-relevant).

- *Elimination of external dependencies.* Since you built the software yourself, you are not beholden to any other company or team to maintain it. If problems arise, they can be debugged and fixed immediately, rather than waiting until the next release of the library (which might not be until after you have shipped your game!)

We cannot cover all possible data structures here, but let's look at a few common ways in which game engine programmers tend to tackle containers.

### 5.3.4.1. To Build or Not to Build

We will not discuss the details of how to implement all of these data types and algorithms here—a plethora of books and online resources are available for that purpose. However, we *will* concern ourselves with the question of where to obtain implementations of the types and algorithms that you need. As game engine designers, we have a number of choices:

1. Build the needed data structures manually.
2. Rely on third-party implementations. Some common choices include
   a. the C++ standard template library (STL),
   b. a variant of STL, such as STLport,
   c. the powerful and robust Boost libraries (http://www.boost.org).

Both STL and Boost are attractive, because they provide a rich and powerful set of container classes covering pretty much every type of data structure imaginable. In addition, both of these packages provide a powerful suite of template-based *generic algorithms*—implementations of common algorithms, such as finding an element in a container, which can be applied to virtually any type of data object. However, third-party packages like these may not be appropriate for some kinds of game engines. And even if we decide to use a third-party package, we must select between Boost and the various flavors of STL, or another third-party library. So let's take a moment to investigate some of the pros and cons of each approach.

*STL*

The benefits of the standard template library include:

- STL offers a rich set of features.
- Reasonably robust implementations are available on a wide variety of platforms.
- STL comes "standard" with virtually all C++ compilers.

However, the STL also has numerous drawbacks, including:

- STL has a steep learning curve. The documentation is now quite good, but the header files are cryptic and difficult to understand on most platforms.
- STL is often slower than a data structure that has been crafted specifically for a particular problem.
- STL also almost always eats up more memory than a custom-designed data structure.
- STL does a lot of dynamic memory allocation, and it's sometimes challenging to control its appetite for memory in a way that is suitable for high-performance, memory-limited console games.
- STL's implementation and behavior varies slightly from compiler to compiler, making its use in multiplatform engines more difficult.

As long as the programmer is aware of the pitfalls of STL and uses it judiciously, it can have a place in game engine programming. It is best suited to a game engine that will run on a personal computer platform, because the advanced virtual memory systems on modern PCs make memory allocation cheaper, and the probability of running out of physical RAM is often negligible. On the other hand, STL is not generally well-suited for use on memory-limited consoles that lack advanced CPUs and virtual memory. And code that uses STL may not port easily to other platforms. Here are some rules of thumb that I use:

- First and foremost, be aware of the performance and memory characteristics of the particular STL class you are using.
- Try to avoid heavier-weight STL classes in code that you believe will be a performance bottleneck.
- Prefer STL in situations where memory is not at a premium. For example, embedding a `std::list` inside a game object is OK, but embedding a `std::list` inside every vertex of a 3D mesh is probably not a good idea. Adding every vertex of your 3D mesh to a `std::list` is probably also not OK—the `std::list` class dynamically allocates a small "link" object for every element inserted into it, and that can result in a lot of tiny, fragmented memory allocations.
- If your engine is to be multiplatform, I highly recommend *STLport* (http://www.stlport.org), an implementation of STL that was specifically designed to be portable across a wide range of compilers and target platforms, more efficient, and more feature-rich than the original STL implementations.

The *Medal of Honor: Pacific Assault* engine for the PC made heavy use of STL, and while *MOHPA* did have its share of frame rate problems, the team was able to work around the performance problems caused by STL (primarily by carefully limiting and controlling its use). Ogre3D, the popular object-oriented rendering library that we use for some of the examples in this book, also makes heavy use of STL. Your mileage may vary. Using STL on a game engine project is certainly feasible, but it must be used with utmost care.

*Boost*

The Boost project was started by members of the C++ Standards Committee Library Working Group, but it is now an open-source project with many contributors from across the globe. The aim of the project is to produce libraries that extend and work together with STL, for both commercial and non-commercial use. Many of the Boost libraries have already been included in the C++ Standards Committee's Library Technical Report (TR1), which is a step toward becoming part of a future C++ standard. Here is a brief summary of what Boost brings to the table:

- Boost provides a lot of useful facilities not available in STL.
- In some cases, Boost provides alternatives to work around certain problems with STL's design or implementation.
- Boost does a great job of handling some very complex problems, like smart pointers. (Bear in mind that smart pointers are complex beasts, and they can be performance hogs. Handles are usually preferable; see Section 14.5 for details.)
- The Boost libraries' documentation is usually excellent. Not only does the documentation explain what each library does and how to use it, but in most cases it also provides an excellent in-depth discussion of the design decisions, constraints, and requirements that went into constructing the library. As such, reading the Boost documentation is a great way to learn about the principles of software design.

If you are already using STL, then Boost can serve as an excellent extension and/or alterative to many of STL's features. However, be aware of the following caveats:

- Most of the core Boost classes are templates, so all that one needs in order to use them is the appropriate set of header files. However, some of the Boost libraries build into rather large .lib files and may not be feasible for use in very small-scale game projects.
- While the world-wide Boost community is an excellent support network, the Boost libraries come with no guarantees. If you encounter a

bug, it will ultimately be your team's responsibility to work around it or fix it.

- Backward compatibility may not be supported.
- The Boost libraries are distributed under the Boost Software License. Read the license information (http://www.boost.org/more/license_info. html) carefully to be sure it is right for your engine.

### Loki

There is a rather esoteric branch of C++ programming known as *template meta-programming*. The core idea is to use the compiler to do a lot of the work that would otherwise have to be done at runtime by exploiting the template feature of C++ and in effect "tricking" the compiler into doing things it wasn't originally designed to do. This can lead to some startlingly powerful and useful programming tools.

By far the most well-known and probably most powerful template meta-programming library for C++ is Loki, a library designed and written by Andrei Alexandrescu (whose home page is at http://www.erdani.org). The library can be obtained from SourceForge at http://loki-lib.sourceforge.net.

Loki is extremely powerful; it is a fascinating body of code to study and learn from. However, its two big weaknesses are of a practical nature: (a) its code can be daunting to read and use, much less truly understand, and (b) some of its components are dependent upon exploiting "side-effect" behaviors of the compiler that require careful customization in order to be made to work on new compilers. So Loki can be somewhat tough to use, and it is not as portable as some of its "less-extreme" counterparts. Loki is not for the faint of heart. That said, some of Loki's concepts such as *policy-based programming* can be applied to any C++ project, even if you don't use the Loki library per se. I highly recommend that all software engineers read Andrei's ground-breaking book, *Modern C++ Design* [2], from which the Loki library was born.

### 5.3.4.2. Dynamic Arrays and Chunky Allocation

Fixed-size C-style arrays are used quite a lot in game programming, because they require no memory allocation, are contiguous and hence cache-friendly, and support many common operations such as appending data and searching very efficiently.

When the size of an array cannot be determined a priori, programmers tend to turn either to *linked lists* or *dynamic arrays*. If we wish to maintain the performance and memory characteristics of fixed-length arrays, then the dynamic array is often the data structure of choice.

The easiest way to implement a dynamic array is to allocate an $n$-element buffer initially and then *grow* the list only if an attempt is made to add more than $n$ elements to it. This gives us the favorable characteristics of a fixed-size array but with no upper bound. Growing is implemented by allocating a new larger buffer, copying the data from the original buffer into the new buffer, and then freeing the original buffer. The size of the buffer is increased in some orderly manner, such as adding $n$ to it on each grow, or doubling it on each grow. Most of the implementations I've encountered never shrink the array, only grow it (with the notable exception of clearing the array to zero size, which might or might not free the buffer). Hence the size of the array becomes a sort of "high water mark." The STL `std::vector` class works in this manner.

Of course, if you can establish a high water mark for your data, then you're probably better off just allocating a single buffer of that size when the engine starts up. Growing a dynamic array can be incredibly costly due to reallocation and data copying costs. The impact of these things depends on the sizes of the buffers involved. Growing can also lead to fragmentation when discarded buffers are freed. So, as with all data structures that allocate memory, caution must be exercised when working with dynamic arrays. Dynamic arrays are probably best used during development, when you are as yet unsure of the buffer sizes you'll require. They can always be converted into fixed size arrays once suitable memory budgets have been established.)

### 5.3.4.3. Linked Lists

If contiguous memory is not a primary concern, but the ability to insert and remove elements at random is paramount, then a *linked list* is usually the data structure of choice. Linked lists are quite easy to implement, but they're also quite easy to get wrong if you're not careful. This section provides a few tips and tricks for creating robust linked lists.

#### The Basics of Linked Lists

A linked list is a very simple data structure. Each element in the list has a pointer to the next element, and, in a doubly-linked list, it also has a pointer to the previous element. These two pointers are referred to as *links*. The list as a whole is tracked using a special pair of pointers called the *head* and *tail* pointers. The head pointer points to the first element, while the tail pointer points to the last element.

Inserting a new element into a doubly-linked list involves adjusting the next pointer of the previous element and the previous pointer of the next element to both point at the new element and then setting the new element's next

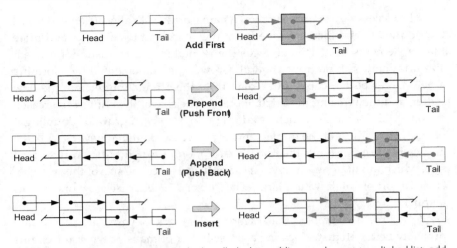

Figure 5.8. The four cases that must be handled when adding an element to a linked list: add first, prepend, append, and insert.

and previous pointers appropriately as well. There are four cases to handle when adding a node to a linked list:

- Adding the first element to a previously-empty list;
- Prepending an element before the current head element;
- Appending an element after the current tail element;
- Inserting an interior element.

These cases are illustrated in Figure 5.8.

Removing an element involves the same kinds of operations in and around the node being removed. Again there are four cases: removing the head element, removing the tail element, removing an interior element, and removing the last element (emptying the list).

### The Link Data Structure

Linked list code isn't particularly tough to write, but it can be error-prone. As such, it's usually a good idea to write a general-purpose linked list facility that can be used to manage lists of any element type. To do this, we need to separate the data structure that contains the links (i.e., the next and previous pointers) from the element data structure. The link data structure is typically a simple `struct` or `class`, often called something like `Link`, `Node`, or `LinkNode`, and templated on the type of element to which it refers. It will usually look something like this.

```
template< typename ELEMENT >
struct Link
{
    Link<ELEMENT>*    m_pPrev;
    Link<ELEMENT>*    m_pNext;
    ELEMENT*          m_pElem;
};
```

### Extrusive Lists

An *extrusive list* is a linked list in which the Link data structures are entirely separate from the element data structures. Each Link contains a pointer to the element, as shown in the example. Whenever an element is to be inserted into a linked list, a link is allocated for it, and the pointers to the element and the next and previous links are set up appropriately. When an element is removed from a linked list, its link can be freed.

The benefit of the extrusive design is that an element can reside in multiple linked lists simultaneously—all we need is one link per list. The down side is that the Link objects must be dynamically allocated. Often a pool allocator (see Section 5.2.1.2) is used to allocate links, because they are always exactly the same size (viz., 12 bytes on a machine with 32-bit pointers). A pool allocator is an excellent choice due to its speed and its freedom from fragmentation problems.

### Intrusive Lists

An *intrusive list* is a linked list in which the Link data structure is embedded in the target element itself. The big benefit of this approach is that we no longer need to dynamically allocate the links—we get a link "for free" whenever we allocate an element. For example, we might have:

```
class SomeElement
{
    Link<SomeElement>    m_link;

    // other members...
};
```

We can also derive our element class from class Link. Using inheritance like this is virtually identical to embedding a Link as the first member of the class, but it has the additional benefit of allowing a pointer to a link (Link<SomeElement>*) to be down-cast into a pointer to the element itself (SomeElement*). This means we can eliminate the back-pointer to the element that would otherwise have to be embedded within the Link. Here's how such a design might be implemented in C++.

```
template< typename ELEMENT >
struct Link
{
    Link<ELEMENT>*   m_pPrev;
    Link<ELEMENT>*   m_pNext;
    // No ELEMENT* pointer required, thanks to
    // inheritance.
};

class SomeElement : public Link<SomeElement>
{
    // other members...
};
```

The big pitfall of the intrusive linked list design is that it prevents an element from residing in more than one linked list at a time (because each element has one and only one link). We can allow an element to be a member of $N$ concurrent lists by providing it with $N$ embedded link instances (in which case we cannot use the inheritance method). However, the number $N$ must be fixed a priori, so this approach is still not quite as flexible as the extrusive design.

The choice between intrusive and extrusive linked lists depends on the application and the constraints under which you are operating. If dynamic memory allocation must be avoided at all costs, then an intrusive list is probably best. If you can afford the overhead of pool allocation, then an extrusive design may be preferable. Sometimes only one of the two approaches will be feasible. For example, if we wish to store instances of a class defined by a third-party library in a linked list and are unable or unwilling to modify that library's source code, then an extrusive list is the only option.

### Head and Tail Pointers: Circular Lists

To fully implement a linked list, we need to provide a head and a tail pointer. The simplest approach is to embed these pointers in their own data structure, perhaps called LinkedList, as follows.

```
template< typename ELEMENT >
class LinkedList
{
    Link<ELEMENT>*   m_pTail;
    Link<ELEMENT>*   m_pHead;

    // member functions for manipulating the list...
};
```

You may have noticed that there isn't much difference between a LinkedList and a Link—they both contain a pair of pointers to Link. As it

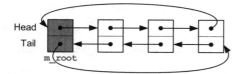
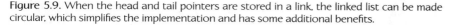

**Figure 5.9.** When the head and tail pointers are stored in a link, the linked list can be made circular, which simplifies the implementation and has some additional benefits.

turns out, there are some distinct benefits to using an instance of class `Link` to manage the head and tail of the list, like this:

```
template< typename ELEMENT >
class LinkedList
{
    Link<ELEMENT> m_root;        // contains head and tail

    // member functions for manipulating the list...
};
```

The embedded `m_root` member is a `Link`, no different from any other `Link` in the list (except that its `m_pElement` member will always be `NULL`). This allows us to make the linked list *circular* as shown in Figure 5.9. In other words, the `m_pNext` pointer of the last "real" node in the list points to `m_root`, as does the `m_pPrev` pointer of the first "real" node in the list.

This design is preferable to the one involving two "loose" pointers for the head and tail, because it simplifies the logic for inserting and removing elements. To see why this is the case, consider the code that would be required to remove an element from a linked list when "loose" head and tail pointers are being used.

```
void LinkedList::remove(Link<ELEMENT>& link)
{
    if (link.m_pNext)
        link.m_pNext->m_pPrev = link.m_pPrev;
    else
        // Removing last element in the list.
        m_pTail = link.m_pPrev;

    if (link.m_pPrev)
        link.m_pPrev->m_pNext = link.m_pNext;
    else
        // Removing first element in the list.
        m_pHead = link.m_pNext;
```

```
                    link.m_pPrev = link.m_pNext = NULL;
}
```

The code is a bit simpler when we use the m_root design:

```
void LinkedList::remove(Link<ELEMENT>& link)
{
    // The link must currently be a member of the list.

    ASSERT(link.m_pNext != NULL);
    ASSERT(link.m_pPrev != NULL);

    link.m_pNext->m_pPrev = link.m_pPrev;
    link.m_pPrev->m_pNext = link.m_pNext;

    // Do this to indicate the link is no longer in any
    // list.
    link.m_pPrev = link.m_pNext = NULL;
}
```

The example code shown above highlights an additional benefit of the circularly linked list approach: A link's m_pPrev and m_pNext pointers are *never null*, unless the link is not a member of any list (i.e., the link is unused/inactive). This gives us a simple test for list membership.

Contrast this with the "loose" head/tail pointer design. In that case, the m_pPrev pointer of the first element in the list is always null, as is the m_pNext pointer of the last element. And if there is only one element in the list, that link's next and previous pointers will *both* be null. This makes it impossible to know whether or not a given Link is a member of a list or not.

### Singly-Linked Lists

A *singly-linked list* is one in which the elements have a next pointer, but no previous pointer. (The list as a whole might have both a head and a tail pointer, or it might have only a head pointer.) Such a design is obviously a memory saver, but the cost of this approach becomes evident when inserting or removing an element from the list. We have no m_pPrev pointer, so we need to traverse the list from the head in order to find the previous element, so that *its* m_pNext pointer can be updated appropriately. Therefore, removal is an $O(1)$ operation for a doubly-linked list, but it's an $O(n)$ operation for a singly-linked list.

This inherent insertion and removal cost is often prohibitive, so most linked lists are doubly linked. However, if you know for certain that you will only ever add and remove elements from the head of the list (as when implementing a stack), or if you always add to the head and remove from the tail (as with a queue—and your list has both a head and a tail pointer), then you can get away with a singly-linked list and save yourself some memory.

#### 5.3.4.4. Dictionaries and Hash Tables

A dictionary is a table of key-value pairs. A value in the dictionary can be looked up quickly, given its key. The keys and values can be of any data type. This kind of data structure is usually implemented either as a binary search tree or as a hash table.

In a binary tree implementation, the key-value pairs are stored in the nodes of the binary tree, and the tree is maintained in key-sorted order. Looking up a value by key involves performing an $O(\log n)$ binary search.

In a hash table implementation, the values are stored in a fixed-size table, where each slot in the table represents one or more keys. To insert a key-value pair into a hash table, the key is first converted into integer form via a process known as *hashing* (if it is not already an integer). Then an *index* into the hash table is calculated by taking the hashed key *modulo* the size of the table. Finally, the key-value pair is stored in the slot corresponding to that index. Recall that the *modulo* operator (% in C/C++) finds the remainder of dividing the integer key by the table size. So if the hash table has five slots, then a key of 3 would be stored at index 3 (3 % 5 == 3), while a key of 6 would be stored at index 1 (6 % 5 == 1). Finding a key-value pair is an $O(1)$ operation in the absence of collisions.

*Collisions: Open and Closed Hash Tables*

Sometimes two or more keys end up occupying the same slot in the hash table. This is known as a *collision*. There are two basic ways to *resolve* a collision, giving rise to two different kinds of hash tables:

- *Open.* In an open hash table (see Figure 5.10), collisions are resolved by simply storing more than one key-value pair at each index, usually in the form of a linked list. This approach is easy to implement and imposes no upper bound on the number of key-value pairs that can be stored. However, it does require memory to be allocated dynamically whenever a new key-value pair is added to the table.

- *Closed.* In a closed hash table (see Figure 5.11), collisions are resolved via a process of *probing* until a vacant slot is found. ("Probing" means applying a well-defined algorithm to search for a free slot.) This approach is a bit more difficult to implement, and it imposes an upper limit on the number of key-value pairs that can reside in the table (because each slot can hold only one key-value pair). But the main benefit of this kind of hash table is that it uses up a fixed amount of memory and requires no dynamic memory allocation. Therefore it is often a good choice in a console engine.

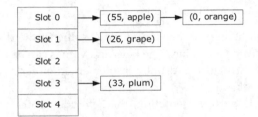

Figure 5.10. An open hash table.

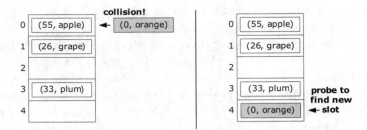

Figure 5.11. A closed hash table.

*Hashing*

Hashing is the process of turning a key of some arbitrary data type into an integer, which can be used modulo the table size as an index into the table. Mathematically, given a key $k$, we want to generate an integer hash value $h$ using the hash function $H$, and then find the index $i$ into the table as follows:

$$h = H(k),$$

$$i = h \bmod N,$$

where $N$ is the number of slots in the table, and the symbol mod represents the *modulo* operation, i.e., finding the *remainder* of the quotient $h/N$.

If the keys are unique integers, the hash function can be the identity function, $H(k) = k$. If the keys are unique 32-bit floating-point numbers, a hash function might simply re-interpret the bit pattern of the 32-bit float as if it were a 32-bit integer.

```
U32 hashFloat(float f)
{
    union
    {
        float asFloat;
```

```
    U32     asU32;
  } u;

  u.asFloat = f;
  return u.asU32;
}
```

If the key is a string, we can employ a *string hashing function,* which combines the ASCII or UTF codes of all the characters in the string into a single 32-bit integer value.

The *quality* of the hashing function $H(k)$ is crucial to the efficiency of the hash table. A "good" hashing function is one that distributes the set of all valid keys evenly across the table, thereby minimizing the likelihood of collisions. A hash function must also be reasonably quick to calculate and *deterministic* in the sense that it must produce the exact same output every time it is called with an indentical input.

Strings are probably the most prevalent type of key you'll encounter, so it's particularly helpful to know a "good" string hashing function. Here are a few reasonably good ones:

- LOOKUP3 by Bob Jenkins (http://burtleburtle.net/bob/c/lookup3.c).
- Cyclic redundancy check functions, such as CRC-32 (http://en.wikipedia. org/wiki/Cyclic_redundancy_check).
- Message-digest algorithm 5 (MD5), a cryptographic hash which yields excellent results but is quite expensive to calculate (http://en.wikipedia. org/wiki/MD5).
- A number of other excellent alternatives can be found in an article by Paul Hsieh available at http://www.azillionmonkeys.com/qed/hash. html.

### Implementing a Closed Hash Table

In a closed hash table, the key-value pairs are stored directly in the table, rather than in a linked list at each table entry. This approach allows the programmer to define a priori the exact amount of memory that will be used by the hash table. A problem arises when we encounter a *collision*—two keys that end up wanting to be stored in the same slot in the table. To address this, we use a process known as *probing.*

The simplest approach is *linear probing.* Imagining that our hashing function has yielded a table index of $i$, but that slot is already occupied, we simply try slots $(i + 1)$, $(i + 2)$, and so on until an empty slot is found (wrapping around to the start of the table when $i = N$). Another variation on linear probing is to alternate searching forwards and backwards, $(i + 1)$, $(i - 1)$, $(i + 2)$, $(i - 2)$, and so on, making sure to modulo the resulting indices into the valid range of the table.

Linear probing tends to cause key-value pairs to "clump up." To avoid these clusters, we can use an algorithm known as *quadratic probing*. We start at the occupied table index $i$ and use the sequence of probes $i_j = (i \pm j^2)$ for $j = 1, 2, 3, \ldots$. In other words, we try $(i + 1^2)$, $(i - 1^2)$, $(i + 2^2)$, $(i - 2^2)$, and so on, remembering to always modulo the resulting index into the valid range of the table.

When using closed hashing, it is a good idea to make your table size a *prime number*. Using a prime table size in conjunction with quadratic probing tends to yield the best coverage of the available table slots with minimal clustering. See http://www.cs.utk.edu/~eijkhout/594-LaTeX/handouts/hashing-slides.pdf for a good discussion of why prime hash table sizes are preferable.

## 5.4. Strings

Strings are ubiquitous in almost every software project, and game engines are no exception. On the surface, the string may seem like a simple, fundamental data type. But when you start using strings in your projects, you will quickly discover a wide range of design issues and constraints, all of which must be carefully accounted for.

### 5.4.1. The Problem with Strings

The most fundamental question is how strings should be stored and managed in your program. In C and C++, strings aren't even an atomic type—they are implemented as *arrays of characters*. The variable length of strings means we either have to hard-code limitations on the sizes of our strings, or we need to dynamically allocate our string buffers. C++ programmers often prefer to use a *string class,* rather than deal directly with character arrays. But then, which string class should we use? STL provides a reasonably good string class, but if you've decided not to use STL you might be stuck writing your own.

Another big string-related problem is that of *localization*—the process of adapting your software for release in other languages. This is also known as *internationalization,* or I18N for short. Any string that you display to the user in English must be translated into whatever languages you plan to support. (Strings that are used internally to the program but are never displayed to the user are exempt from localization, of course.) This not only involves making sure that you can represent all the character glyphs of all the languages you plan to support (via an appropriate set of fonts), but it also means ensuring that your game can handle different text orientations. For example, Chinese text is oriented vertically instead of horizontally, and some languages like Hebrew read right-to-left. Your game also needs to gracefully deal with the possibility that a translated string will be either much longer, or much shorter, than its English counterpart.

Finally, it's important to realize that strings are used internally within a game engine for things like resource file names and object ids. For example, when a game designer lays out a level, it's highly convenient to permit him or her to identify the objects in the level using meaningful names, like "Player-Camera," "enemy-tank-01," or "explosionTrigger."

How our engine deals with these internal strings often has pervasive ramifications on the performance of the game. This is because strings are inherently expensive to work with at runtime. Comparing or copying ints or floats can be accomplished via simple machine language instructions. On the other hand, comparing strings requires an $O(n)$ scan of the character arrays using a function like strcmp() (where $n$ is the length of the string). Copying a string requires an $O(n)$ memory copy, not to mention the possibility of having to dynamically allocate the memory for the copy. During one project I worked on, we profiled our game's performance only to discover that strcmp() and strcpy() were the top two most expensive functions! By eliminating unnecessary string operations and using some of the techniques outlined in this section, we were able to all but eliminate these functions from our profile, and increase the game's frame rate significantly. (I've heard similar stories from developers at a number of different studios.)

## 5.4.2. String Classes

String classes can make working with strings much more convenient for the programmer. However, a string class can have hidden costs that are difficult to see until the game is profiled. For example, passing a string to a function using a C-style character array is fast because the address of the first character is typically passed in a hardware register. On the other hand, passing a string object might incur the overhead of one or more copy constructors, if the function is not declared or used properly. Copying strings might involve dynamic memory allocation, causing what looks like an innocuous function call to end up costing literally thousands of machine cycles.

For this reason, in game programming I generally like to avoid string classes. However, if you feel a strong urge to use a string class, make sure you pick or implement one that has acceptable runtime performance characteristics—and be sure all programmers that use it are aware of its costs. Know your string class: Does it treat all string buffers as read-only? Does it utilize the *copy on write* optimization? (See http://en.wikipedia.org/wiki/Copy-on-write.) As a rule of thumb, always pass string objects by reference, never by value (as the latter often incurs string-copying costs). Profile your code early and often to ensure that your string class isn't becoming a major source of lost frame rate!

One situation in which a specialized string class does seem justifiable to me is when storing and managing file system paths. Here, a hypothetical `Path` class could add significant value over a raw C-style character array. For example, it might provide functions for extracting the filename, file extension or directory from the path. It might hide operating system differences by automatically converting Windows-style backslashes to UNIX-style forward slashes or some other operating system's path separator. Writing a `Path` class that provides this kind of functionality in a cross-platform way could be highly valuable within a game engine context. (See Section 6.1.1.4 for more details on this topic.)

## 5.4.3. Unique Identifiers

The *objects* in any virtual game world need to be uniquely identified in some way. For example, in Pac Man we might encounter game objects named "pac_man," "blinky," "pinky," "inky," and "clyde." Unique object identifiers allow game designers to keep track of the myriad objects that make up their game worlds and also permit those objects to be found and operated on at runtime by the engine. In addition, the *assets* from which our game objects are constructed—meshes, materials, textures, audio clips, animations, and so on—all need unique identifiers as well.

Strings seem like a natural choice for such identifiers. Assets are often stored in individual files on disk, so they can usually be identified uniquely by their file paths, which of course are strings. And game objects are created by game designers, so it is natural for them to assign their objects understandable string names, rather than have to remember integer object indices, or 64- or 128-bit globally unique identifiers (GUIDs). However, the speed with which *comparisons* between unique identifiers can be made is of paramount importance in a game, so `strcmp()` simply doesn't cut it. We need a way to have our cake and eat it too—a way to get all the descriptiveness and flexibility of a string, but with the speed of an integer.

### 5.4.3.1.   Hashed String Ids

One good solution is to *hash* our strings. As we've seen, a hash function maps a string onto a semi-unique integer. String hash codes can be compared just like any other integers, so comparisons are fast. If we store the actual strings in a hash table, then the original string can always be recovered from the hash code. This is useful for debugging purposes and to permit hashed strings to be displayed on-screen or in log files. Game programmers sometimes use the term *string id* to refer to such a hashed string. The Unreal engine uses the term *name* instead (implemented by class `FName`).

As with any hashing system, *collisions* are a possibility (i.e., two different strings might end up with the same hash code). However, with a suitable hash function, we can all but guarantee that collisions will not occur for all reasonable input strings we might use in our game. After all, a 32-bit hash code represents more than four billion possible values. So if our hash function does a good job of distributing strings evenly throughout this very large range, we are unlikely to collide. At Naughty Dog, we used a variant of the CRC-32 algorithm to hash our strings, and we didn't encounter a single collision in over two years of development on *Uncharted: Drake's Fortune*.

### 5.4.3.2. Some Implementation Ideas

Conceptually, it's easy enough to run a hash function on your strings in order to generate string ids. Practically speaking, however, it's important to consider *when* the hash will be calculated. Most game engines that use string ids do the hashing at runtime. At Naughty Dog, we permit runtime hashing of strings, but we also preprocess our source code using a simple utility that searches for macros of the form `SID` (*any-string*) and translates each one directly into the appropriate hashed integer value. This permits string ids to be used anywhere that an integer manifest constant can be used, including the constant `case` labels of a `switch` statement. (The result of a function call that generates a string id at runtime is not a constant, so it cannot be used as a `case` label.)

The process of generating a string id from a string is sometimes called *interning* the string, because in addition to hashing it, the string is typically also added to a global string table. This allows the original string to be recovered from the hash code later. You may also want your tools to be capable of hashing strings into string ids. That way, when the tool generates data for consumption by your engine, the strings will already have been hashed.

The main problem with interning a string is that it is a slow operation. The hashing function must be run on the string, which can be an expensive proposition, especially when a large number of strings are being interned. In addition, memory must be allocated for the string, and it must be copied into the lookup table. As a result (if you are not generating string ids at compile-time), it is usually best to intern each string only once and save off the result for later use. For example, it would be preferable to write code like

this because the latter implementation causes the strings to be unnecessarily
re-interned every time the function f() is called.

```
static StringId   sid_foo = internString("foo");
static StringId   sid_bar = internString("bar");

// ...

void f(StringId id)
{
    if (id == sid_foo)
    {
        // handle case of id == "foo"
    }

    else if (id == sid_bar)
    {
        // handle case of id == "bar"
    }

}
```

This approach is much less efficient.

```
void f(StringId id)
{
    if (id == internString("foo"))
    {
        // handle case of id == "foo"
    }

    else if (id == internString("bar"))
    {
        // handle case of id == "bar"
    }

}
```

Here's one possible implementation of internString().

*stringid.h*

```
typedef U32 StringId;

extern StringId internString(const char* str);
```

*stringid.cpp*

```
static HashTable<StringId, const char*> gStringIdTable;
```

```
StringId internString(const char* str)
{
    StringId sid = hashCrc32(str);

    HashTable<StringId, const char*>::iterator it
        = gStringIdTable.find(sid);

    if (it == gStringTable.end())
    {
        // This string has not yet been added to the
        // table. Add it, being sure to copy it in case
        // the original was dynamically allocated and
        // might later be freed.
        gStringTable[sid] = strdup(str);
    }

    return sid;
}
```

Another idea employed by the Unreal Engine is to wrap the string id and a pointer to the corresponding C-style character array in a tiny class. In the Unreal Engine, this class is called FName.

*Using Debug Memory for Strings*

When using string ids, the strings themselves are only kept around for human consumption. When you ship your game, you almost certainly won't need the strings—the game itself should only ever use the ids. As such, it's a good idea to store your string table in a region of memory that won't exist in the retail game. For example, a PS3 development kit has 256 MB of retail memory, plus an additional 256 MB of "debug" memory that is not available on a retail unit. If we store our strings in debug memory, we needn't worry about their impact on the memory footprint of the final shipping game. (We just need to be careful never to write production code that depends on the strings being available!)

## 5.4.4. Localization

Localization of a game (or any software project) is a big undertaking. It is a task which is best handled by planning for it from day one and accounting for it at every step of development. However, this is not done as often as we all would like. Here are some tips that should help you plan your game engine project for localization. For an in-depth treatment of software localization, see [29].

### 5.4.4.1. Unicode

The problem for most English-speaking software developers is that they are trained from birth (or thereabouts!) to think of strings as arrays of 8-bit ASCII character codes (i.e., characters following the ANSI standard). ANSI strings work great for a language with a simple alphabet, like English. But they just don't cut it for languages with complex alphabets containing a great many more characters, sometimes totally different glyphs than English's 26 letters. To address the limitations of the ANSI standard, the Unicode character set system was devised.

Please set down this book right now and read the article entitled, "The Absolute Minimum Every Software Developer Absolutely, Positively Must Know About Unicode and Character Sets (No Excuses!)" by Joel Spolsky. You can find it here: http://www.joelonsoftware.com/articles/Unicode.html. (Once you've done that, please pick up the book again!)

As Joel describes in his article, Unicode is not a single standard but actually a family of related standards. You will need to select the specific standard that best suits your needs. The two most common choices I've seen used in game engines are UTF-8 and UTF-16.

#### UTF-8

In UTF-8, the character codes are 8 bits each, but certain characters occupy more than one byte. Hence the number of bytes occupied by a UTF-8 character string is not necessarily the length of the string in characters. This is known as a *multibyte character set* (MBCS), because each character may take one or more bytes of storage.

One of the big benefits of the UTF-8 encoding is that it is backwards-compatible with the ANSI encoding. This works because the first character of a multibyte character sequence always has its most significant bit set (i.e., lies between 128 and 255, inclusive). Since the standard ANSI character codes are all less than 128, a plain old ANSI string is a valid and unambiguous UTF-8 string as well.

#### UTF-16

The UTF-16 standard employs a simpler, albeit more expensive, approach. Each character takes up exactly 16 bits (whether it needs all of those bits or not). As a result, dividing the number of bytes occupied by the string by two yields the number of characters. This is known as a wide character set (WCS), because each character is 16 bits wide instead of the 8 bits used by "regular" ANSI `char`s.

*Unicode under Windows*

Under Microsoft Windows, the data type `wchar_t` is used to represent a single "wide" UTF-16 character (WCS), while the `char` type is used both for ANSI strings and for multibyte UTF-16 strings (MBCS). What's more, Windows permits you to write code that is *character set independent*. To accomplish this, a data type known as `TCHAR` is provided. The data type `TCHAR` is a `typedef` to `char` when building your application in ANSI mode and is a `typedef` to `wchar_t` when building your application in UTF-16 (WCS) mode. (For consistency, the type `WCHAR` is also provided as a synonym for `wchar_t`.)

Throughout the Windows API, a prefix or suffix of "w," "wcs," or "W" indicates wide (UTF-16) characters; a prefix or suffix of "t," "tcs," or "T" indicates the current character type (which might be ANSI or might be UTF-16, depending on how your application was built); and no prefix or suffix indicates plain old ANSI. STL uses a similar convention—for example, `std::string` is STL's ANSI string class, while `std::wstring` is its wide character equivalent.

Pretty much every standard C library function that deals with strings has equivalent WCS and MBCS versions under Windows. Unfortunately, the API calls don't use the terms UTF-8 and UTF-16, and the names of the functions aren't always 100% consistent. This all leads to some confusion among programmers who aren't in the know. (But *you* aren't one of those programmers!) Table 5.1 lists some examples.

Windows also provides functions for translating between ANSI character strings, multibyte UTF-8 strings, and wide UTF-16 strings. For example, `wcstombs()` converts a wide UTF-16 string into a multibyte UTF-8 string.

Complete documentation for these functions can be found on Microsoft's MSDN web site. Here's a link to the documentation for `strcmp()` and its ilk, from which you can quite easily navigate to the other related string-manipulation functions using the tree view on the left-hand side of the page, or via the search bar: http://msdn2.microsoft.com/en-us/library/kk6xf663(VS.80).aspx.

| ANSI | WCS | MBCS |
|---|---|---|
| `strcmp()` | `wcscmp()` | `_mbscmp()` |
| `strcpy()` | `wcscpy()` | `_mbscpy()` |
| `strlen()` | `wcslen()` | `_mbstrlen()` |

Table 5.1. Variants of some common standard C library string functions for use with ANSI, wide and multibyte character sets.

*Unicode on Consoles*

The Xbox 360 software development kit (XDK) uses WCS strings pretty much exclusively, for all strings—even for internal strings like file paths. This is certainly one valid approach to the localization problem, and it makes for very consistent string handling throughout the XDK. However, the UTF-16 encoding is a bit wasteful on memory, so different game engines may employ different conventions. At Naughty Dog, we use 8-bit `char` strings throughout our engine, and we handle foreign languages via a UTF-8 encoding. The choice of encoding is not important, as long as you select one as early in the project as possible and stick with it consistently.

### 5.4.4.2.  Other Localization Concerns

Even once you have adapted your software to use Unicode characters, there are still a host of other localization problems to contend with. For one thing, strings aren't the only place where localization issues arise. Audio clips including recorded voices must be translated. Textures may have English words painted into them that require translation. Many symbols have different meanings in different cultures. Even something as innocuous as a no-smoking sign might be misinterpreted in another culture. In addition, some markets draw the boundaries between the various game-rating levels differently. For example, in Japan a Teen-rated game is not permitted to show blood of any kind, whereas in North America small red blood spatters are considered acceptable.

For strings, there are other details to worry about as well. You will need to manage a database of all human-readable strings in your game, so that they can all be reliably translated. The software must display the proper language given the user's installation settings. The formatting of the strings may be totally different in different languages—for example, Chinese is written vertically, and Hebrew reads right-to-left. The lengths of the strings will vary greatly from language to language. You'll also need to decide whether to ship a single DVD or Blu-ray disc that contains all languages or ship different discs for particular territories.

The most crucial components in your localization system will be the central database of human-readable strings and an in-game system for looking up those strings by id. For example, let's say you want a heads-up display that lists the score of each player with "Player 1 Score:" and "Player 2 Score:" labels and that also displays the text "Player 1 Wins" or "Player 2 Wins" at the end of a round. These four strings would be stored in the localization database under unique ids that are understandable to you, the developer of the game. So our database might use the ids "p1score," "p2score," "p1wins," and "p2wins," respectively. Once our game's strings have been translated into

| Id | English | French |
|---------|----------------|-----------------------|
| p1score | "Player 1 Score" | "Grade Joueur 1" |
| p2score | "Player 2 Score" | "Grade Joueur 2" |
| p1wins | "Player 1 wins!" | "Joueur un gagne!" |
| p2wins | "Player 2 wins!" | "Joueur deux gagne!" |

Table 5.2. Example of a string database used for localization.

French, our database would look something like the simple example shown in Table 5.2. Additional columns can be added for each new language your game supports.

The exact format of this database is up to you. It might be as simple as a Microsoft Excel worksheet that can be saved as a comma-separated values (CSV) file and parsed by the game engine or as complex as a full-fledged Oracle database. The specifics of the string database are largely unimportant to the game engine, as long as it can read in the string ids and the corresponding Unicode strings for whatever language(s) your game supports. (However, the specifics of the database may be *very* important from a practical point of view, depending upon the organizational structure of your game studio. A small studio with in-house translators can probably get away with an Excel spreadsheet located on a network drive. But a large studio with branch offices in Britain, Europe, South America, and Japan would probably find some kind of distributed database a great deal more amenable.)

At runtime, you'll need to provide a simple function that returns the Unicode string in the "current" language, given the unique id of that string. The function might be declared like this:

```
wchar_t getLocalizedString(const char* id);
```

and it might be used like this:

```
void drawScoreHud(const Vector3& score1Pos,
                  const Vector3& score2Pos)
{
    renderer.displayTextOrtho(
        getLocalizedString("p1score"),
        score1Pos);
    renderer.displayTextOrtho(
        getLocalizedString("p2score"),
        score2Pos);
    // ...
}
```

Of course, you'll need some way to set the "current" language globally. This might be done via a configuration setting which is fixed during the installation of the game. Or you might allow users to change the current language on the fly via an in-game menu. Either way, the setting is not difficult to implement; it can be as simple as a global integer variable specifying the index of the column in the string table from which to read (e.g., column one might be English, column two French, column three Spanish, and so on).

Once you have this infrastructure in place, your programmers must remember to *never display a raw string to the user*. They must always use the id of a string in the database and call the look-up function in order to retrieve the string in question.

## 5.5.  Engine Configuration

Game engines are complex beasts, and they invariably end up having a large number of configurable options. Some of these options are exposed to the player via one or more options menus in-game. For example, a game might expose options related to graphics quality, the volume of music and sound effects, or controller configuration. Other options are created for the benefit of the game development team only and are either hidden or stripped out of the game completely before it ships. For example, the player character's maximum walk speed might be exposed as an option so that it can be fine-tuned during development, but it might be changed to a hard-coded value prior to ship.

### 5.5.1.  Loading and Saving Options

A configurable option can be implemented trivially as a global variable or a member variable of a singleton class. However, configurable options are not particularly useful unless their values can be configured, stored on a hard disk, memory card, or other storage medium and later retrieved by the game. There are a number of simple ways to load and save configuration options:

- *Text configuration files.* By far the most common method of saving and loading configuration options is by placing them into one or more text files. The format of these files varies widely from engine to engine, but it is usually very simple. For example, Windows INI files (which are used by the Ogre3D renderer) consist of flat lists of key-value pairs grouped into logical sections.

  ```
  [SomeSection]
  Key1=Value1
  Key2=Value2
  ```

```
[AnotherSection]
Key3=Value3
Key4=Value4
Key5=Value5
```

The XML format is another common choice for configurable game options files.

- *Compressed binary files.* Most modern consoles have hard disk drives in them, but older consoles could not afford this luxury. As a result, all game consoles since the Super Nintendo Entertainment System (SNES) have come equipped with proprietary removable memory cards that permit both reading and writing of data. Game options are sometimes stored on these cards, along with saved games. Compressed binary files are the format of choice on a memory card, because the storage space available on these cards is often very limited.

- *The Windows registry.* The Microsoft Windows operating system provides a global options database known as the registry. It is stored as a tree, where the interior nodes (known as *registry keys*) act like file folders, and the leaf nodes store the individual options as key-value pairs. Any application, game or otherwise, can reserve an entire subtree (i.e., a registry key) for its exclusive use, and then store any set of options within it. The Windows registry acts like a carefully-organized collection of INI files, and in fact it was introduced into Windows as a replacement for the ever-growing network of INI files used by both the operating system and Windows applications.

- *Command line options.* The command line can be scanned for option settings. The engine might provide a mechanism for controlling any option in the game via the command line, or it might expose only a small subset of the game's options here.

- *Environment variables.* On personal computers running Windows, Linux, or MacOS, environment variables are sometimes used to store configuration options as well.

- *Online user profiles.* With the advent of online gaming communities like Xbox Live, each user can create a profile and use it to save achievements, purchased and unlockable game features, game options, and other information. The data is stored on a central server and can be accessed by the player wherever an Internet connection is available.

## 5.5.2. Per-User Options

Most game engines differentiate between global options and per-user options. This is necessary because most games allow each player to configure the game to his or her liking. It is also a useful concept during development of the game, because it allows each programmer, artist, and designer to customize his or her work environment without affecting other team members.

Obviously care must be taken to store per-user options in such a way that each player "sees" only his or her options and not the options of other players on the same computer or console. In a console game, the user is typically allowed to save his or her progress, along with per-user options such as controller preferences, in "slots" on a memory card or hard disk. These slots are usually implemented as files on the media in question.

On a Windows machine, each user has a folder under *C:\Documents and Settings* containing information such as the user's desktop, his or her My Documents folder, his or her Internet browsing history and temporary files, and so on. A hidden subfolder named *Application Data* is used to store per-user information on a per-application basis; each application creates a folder under *Application Data* and can use it to store whatever per-user information it requires.

Windows games sometimes store per-user configuration data in the registry. The registry is arranged as a tree, and one of the top-level children of the root node, called `HKEY_CURRENT_USER`, stores settings for whichever user happens to be logged on. Every user has his or her own subtree in the registry (stored under the top-level subtree `HKEY_USERS`), and `HKEY_CURRENT_USER` is really just an alias to the current user's subtree. So games and other applications can manage per-user configuration options by simply reading and writing them to keys under the `HKEY_CURRENT_USER` subtree.

### 5.5.3. Configuration Management in Some Real Engines

In this section, we'll take a brief look at how some real game engines manage their configuration options.

#### 5.5.3.1. Example: Quake's CVARs

The Quake family of engines uses a configuration management system known as *console variables,* or CVARs for short. A CVAR is just a floating-point or string global variable whose value can be inspected and modified from within Quake's in-game console. The values of some CVARs can be saved to disk and later reloaded by the engine.

At runtime, CVARs are stored in a global linked list. Each CVAR is a dynamically-allocated instance of `struct cvar_t`, which contains the variable's name, its value as a string or float, a set of flag bits, and a pointer to the next CVAR in the linked list of all CVARs. CVARs are accessed by calling `Cvar_Get()`, which creates the variable if it doesn't already exist and modified by calling `Cvar_Set()`. One of the bit flags, `CVAR_ARCHIVE`, controls whether or not the CVAR will be saved into a configuration file called *config.cfg*. If this flag is set, the value of the CVAR will persist across multiple runs of the game.

### 5.5.3.2. Example: Ogre3D

The Ogre3D rendering engine uses a collection of text files in Windows INI format for its configuration options. By default, the options are stored in three files, each of which is located in the same folder as the executable program:

- *plugins.cfg* contains options specifying which optional engine plug-ins are enabled and where to find them on disk.
- *resources.cfg* contains a *search path* specifying where game assets (a.k.a. media, a.k.a. resources) can be found.
- *ogre.cfg* contains a rich set of options specifying which renderer (DirectX or OpenGL) to use and the preferred video mode, screen size, etc.

Out of the box, Ogre provides no mechanism for storing per-user configuration options. However, the Ogre source code is freely available, so it would be quite easy to change it to search for its configuration files in the user's *C:\ Documents and Settings* folder instead of in the folder containing the executable. The `Ogre::ConfigFile` class makes it easy to write code that reads and writes brand new configuration files, as well.

### 5.5.3.3. Example: *Uncharted: Drake's Fortune*

Naughty Dog's *Uncharted* engine makes use of a number of configuration mechanisms.

#### In-Game Menu Settings

The *Uncharted* engine supports a powerful in-game menu system, allowing developers to control global configuration options and invoke commands. The data types of the configurable options must be relatively simple (primarily Boolean, integer, and floating-point variables), but this limitation did not prevent the developers of *Uncharted* from creating literally hundreds of useful menu-driven options.

Each configuration option is implemented as a global variable. When the menu option that controls an option is created, the address of the global variable is provided, and the menu item directly controls its value. As an example, the following function creates a submenu item containing some options for *Uncharted*'s rail vehicles (the vehicles used in the "Out of the Frying Pan" jeep chase level). It defines menu items controlling three global variables: two Booleans and one floating-point value. The items are collected onto a menu,

and a special item is returned that will bring up the menu when selected.
Presumably the code calling this function would add this item to the parent
menu that it is building.

```cpp
DMENU::ItemSubmenu * CreateRailVehicleMenu()
{
    extern bool g_railVehicleDebugDraw2D;
    extern bool g_railVehicleDebugDrawCameraGoals;
    extern float g_railVehicleFlameProbability;

    DMENU::Menu * pMenu = new DMENU::Menu(
        "RailVehicle");

    pMenu->PushBackItem(
        new DMENU::ItemBool("Draw 2D Spring Graphs",
            DMENU::ToggleBool,
            &g_railVehicleDebugDraw2D));

    pMenu->PushBackItem(
        new DMENU::ItemBool("Draw Goals (Untracked)",
            DMENU::ToggleBool,
            &g_railVehicleDebugDrawCameraGoals));

    DMENU::ItemFloat * pItemFloat;
    pItemFloat = new DMENU::ItemFloat(
        "FlameProbability",
        DMENU::EditFloat, 5, "%5.2f",
        &g_railVehicleFlameProbability);

    pItemFloat->SetRangeAndStep(0.0f, 1.0f, 0.1f, 0.01f);
    pMenu->PushBackItem(pItemFloat);

    DMENU::ItemSubmenu * pSubmenuItem;
    pSubmenuItem = new DMENU::ItemSubmenu(
        "RailVehicle...", pMenu);

    return pSubmenuItem;
}
```

The value of any option can be saved by simply marking it with the circle
button on the PS3 joypad when the corresponding menu item is selected. The
menu settings are saved in an INI-style text file, allowing the saved global variables to retain the values across multiple runs of the game. The ability to control which options are saved on a *per-menu-item basis* is highly useful, because
any option which is not saved will take on its programmer-specified default
value. If a programmer changes a default, all users will "see" the new value,
unless of course a user has saved a custom value for that particular option.

*Command Line Arguments*

The *Uncharted* engine scans the command line for a predefined set of special options. The name of the level to load can be specified, along with a number of other commonly-used arguments.

*Scheme Data Definitions*

The vast majority of engine and game configuration information in *Uncharted* is specified using a Lisp-like language called Scheme. Using a proprietary data compiler, data structures defined in the Scheme language are transformed into binary files that can be loaded by the engine. The data compiler also spits out header files containing C `struct` declarations for every data type defined in Scheme. These header files allow the engine to properly interpret the data contained in the loaded binary files. The binary files can even be recompiled and reloaded on the fly, allowing developers to alter the data in Scheme and see the effects of their changes immediately (as long as data members are not added or removed, as that would require a recompile of the engine).

The following example illustrates the creation of a data structure specifying the properties of an animation. It then exports three unique animations to the game. You may have never read Scheme code before, but for this relatively simple example it should be pretty self-explanatory. One oddity you'll notice is that hyphens are permitted within Scheme symbols, so `simple-animation` is a single symbol (unlike in C/C++ where `simple-animation` would be the subtraction of two variables, `simple` and `animation`).

*simple-animation.scm*

```
;; Define a new data type called simple-animation.
(deftype simple-animation ()
    (
        (name              string)
        (speed             float    :default 1.0)
        (fade-in-seconds   float    :default 0.25)
        (fade-out-seconds  float    :default 0.25)
    )
)

;; Now define three instances of this data structure...
(define-export anim-walk
    (new simple-animation
        :name "walk"
        :speed 1.0
    )
)
```

```
(define-export anim-walk-fast
   (new simple-animation
      :name "walk"
      :speed 2.0
   )
)

(define-export anim-jump
   (new simple-animation
      :name "jump"
      :fade-in-seconds 0.1
      :fade-out-seconds 0.1
   )
)
```

This Scheme code would generate the following C/C++ header file:

*simple-animation.h*

```
// WARNING: This file was automatically generated from
// Scheme. Do not hand-edit.

struct SimpleAnimation
{
   const char*   m_name;
   float         m_speed;
   float         m_fadeInSeconds;
   float         m_fadeOutSeconds;
};
```

In-game, the data can be read by calling the LookupSymbol() function, which is templated on the data type returned, as follows:

```
#include "simple-animation.h"

void someFunction()
{

   SimpleAnimation* pWalkAnim
      = LookupSymbol<SimpleAnimation*>("anim-walk");

   SimpleAnimation* pFastWalkAnim
      = LookupSymbol<SimpleAnimation*>(
         "anim-walk-fast");

   SimpleAnimation* pJumpAnim
      = LookupSymbol<SimpleAnimation*>("anim-jump");

   // use the data here...
}
```

This system gives the programmers a great deal of flexibility in defining all sorts of configuration data—from simple Boolean, floating-point, and string options all the way to complex, nested, interconnected data structures. It is used to specify detailed animation trees, physics parameters, player mechanics, and so on.

# 6
# Resources and the File System

Games are by nature multimedia experiences. A game engine therefore needs to be capable of loading and managing a wide variety of different kinds of media—texture bitmaps, 3D mesh data, animations, audio clips, collision and physics data, game world layouts, and the list goes on. Moreover, because memory is usually scarce, a game engine needs to ensure that only one copy of each media file is loaded into memory at any given time. For example, if five meshes share the same texture, then we would like to have only one copy of that texture in memory, not five. Most game engines employ some kind of *resource manager* (a.k.a. *asset manager*, a.k.a. *media manager*) to load and manage the myriad resources that make up a modern 3D game.

Every resource manager makes heavy use of the file system. On a personal computer, the file system is exposed to the programmer via a library of operating system calls. However, game engines often "wrap" the native file system API in an engine-specific API, for two primary reasons. First, the engine might be cross-platform, in which case the game engine's file system API can shield the rest of the software from differences between different target hardware platforms. Second, the operating system's file system API might not provide all the tools needed by a game engine. For example, many engines support file *streaming* (i.e., the ability to load data "on the fly" while the game is running), yet most operating systems don't provide a streaming file system API out of the box. Console game engines also need to provide access to a variety of removable and non-removable media, from memory sticks to optional hard drives to a DVD-ROM or Blu-ray fixed disk to network file systems (e.g., Xbox Live or the PlayStation Network, PSN). The differences between various kinds of media can likewise be "hidden" behind a game engine's file system API.

In this chapter, we'll first explore the kinds of file system APIs found in modern 3D game engines. Then we'll see how a typical resource manager works.

## 6.1.  File System

A game engine's file system API typically addresses the following areas of functionality:

- manipulating file names and paths,
- opening, closing, reading and writing individual files,
- scanning the contents of a directory,
- handling asynchronous file I/O requests (for streaming).

We'll take a brief look at each of these in the following sections.

### 6.1.1.  File Names and Paths

A *path* is a string describing the location of a file or directory within a file system hierarchy. Each operating system uses a slightly different path format, but paths have essentially the same structure on every operating system. A path generally takes the following form:

> volume/directory1/ directory2/.../directoryN/file-name

> or

> volume/directory1/directory2/.../directory(N – 1)/directoryN

In other words, a path generally consists of an optional *volume specifier* followed by a sequence of *path components* separated by a reserved path separator character such as the forward or backward slash (/ or \). Each component names a directory along the route from the root directory to the file or directory in question. If the path specifies the location of a file, the last component in the path is the file name; otherwise it names the target directory. The root directory is usually indicated by a path consisting of the optional volume specifier followed by a single path separator character (e.g., / on UNIX, or C:\ on Windows).

### 6.1.1.1. Differences Across Operating Systems

Each operating system introduces slight variations on this general path structure. Here are some of the key differences between Microsoft DOS, Microsoft Windows, the UNIX family of operating systems, and Apple Macintosh OS:

- UNIX uses a forward slash (/) as its path component separator, while DOS and older versions of Windows used a backslash (\) as the path separator. Recent versions of Windows allow either forward or backward slashes to be used to separate path components, although some applications still fail to accept forward slashes.

- Mac OS 8 and 9 use the colon (:) as the path separator character. Mac OS X is based on UNIX, so it supports UNIX's forward slash notation.

- UNIX and its variants don't support volumes as separate directory hierarchies. The entire file system is contained within a single monolithic hierarchy, and local disk drives, network drives, and other resources are *mounted* so that they appear to be subtrees within the main hierarchy. As a result, UNIX paths never have a volume specifier.

- On Microsoft Windows, volumes can be specified in two ways. A local disk drive is specified using a single letter followed by a colon (e.g., the ubiquitous `c:`). A remote network share can either be mounted so that it looks like a local disk, or it can be referenced via a volume specifier consisting of two backslashes followed by the remote computer name and the name of a shared directory or resource on that machine (e.g., `\\some-computer\some-share`). This double backslash notation is an example of the Universal Naming Convention (UNC).

- Under DOS and early versions of Windows, a file name could be up to eight characters in length, with a three-character *extension* which was separated from the main file name by a dot. The extension described the file's type, for example `.txt` for a text file or `.exe` for an executable file. In recent Windows implementations, file names can contain any number of dots (as they can under UNIX), but the characters after the final dot are still interpreted as the file's extension by many applications including the Windows Explorer.

- Each operating system disallows certain characters in the names of files and directories. For example, a colon cannot appear anywhere in a Windows or DOS path except as part of a drive letter volume specifier. Some operating systems permit a subset of these reserved characters to appear in a path as long as the path is quoted in its entirety or the offending character is *escaped* by preceding it with a backslash or some other reserved *escape character*. For example, file and directory names may contain spaces under Windows, but such a path must be surrounded by double quotes in certain contexts.

- Both UNIX and Windows have the concept of a *current working directory* or CWD (also known as the *present working directory* or PWD). The CWD can be set from a command shell via the cd (*change directory*) command on both operating systems, and it can be queried by typing cd with no arguments under Windows or by executing the pwd command on UNIX. Under UNIX there is only one CWD. Under Windows, each volume has its own private CWD.

- Operating systems that support multiple volumes, like Windows, also have the concept of a *current working volume*. From a Windows command shell, the current volume can be set by entering its drive letter and a colon followed by the Enter key (e.g., C:<Enter>).

- Consoles often also employ a set of predefined path prefixes to represent multiple volumes. For example, PLAYSTATION 3 uses the prefix /dev_bdvd/ to refer to the Bluray disk drive, while /dev_hdd$x$/ refers to one or more hard disks (where $x$ is the index of the device). On a PS3 development kit, /app_home/ maps to a user-defined path on whatever host machine is being used for development. During development, the game usually reads its assets from /app_home/ rather than from the Bluray or the hard disk.

### 6.1.1.2.  Absolute and Relative Paths

All paths are specified relative to some location within the file system. When a path is specified relative to the root directory, we call it an *absolute path*. When it is relative to some *other* directory in the file system hierarchy, we call it a *relative path*.

Under both UNIX and Windows, absolute paths start with a path separator character (/ or \), while relative paths have no leading path separator. On Windows, both absolute and relative paths may have an optional volume specifier—if the volume is omitted, then the path is assumed to refer to the current working volume.

The following paths are all absolute:

*Windows*

- C:\Windows\System32
- D:\ (root directory on the D: volume)
- \ (root directory on the current working volume)

- `\game\assets\animation\walk.anim` (current working volume)
- `\\joe-dell\Shared_Files\Images\foo.jpg` (network path)

*UNIX*

- `/usr/local/bin/grep`
- `/game/src/audio/effects.cpp`
- `/` (root directory)

The following paths are all relative:

*Windows*

- `System32` (relative to CWD `\Windows` on the current volume)
- `X:animation\walk.anim` (relative to CWD `\game\assets` on the `X:` volume)

*UNIX*

- `bin/grep` (relative to CWD `/usr/local`)
- `src/audio/effects.cpp` (relative to CWD `/game`)

### 6.1.1.3.   Search Paths

The term *path* should not be confused with the term *search path*. A *path* is a string representing the location of a single file or directory within the file system hierarchy. A *search path* is a string containing a list of paths, each separated by a special character such as a colon or semicolon, which is searched when looking for a file. For example, when you run any program from a command prompt, the operating system finds the executable file by searching each directory on the search path contained in the shell's `PATH` environment variable.

Some game engines also use search paths to locate resource files. For example, the Ogre3D rendering engine uses a resource search path contained in a text file named `resources.cfg`. The file provides a simple list of directories and Zip archives that should be searched in order when trying to find an asset. That said, searching for assets at runtime is a time-consuming proposition. Usually there's no reason our assets' paths cannot be known a priori. Presuming this is the case, we can avoid having to search for assets at all—which is clearly a superior approach.

### 6.1.1.4.   Path APIs

Clearly paths are much more complex than simple strings. There are many things a programmer may need to do when dealing with paths, such as isolating the directory, filename and extension, canonicalizing a path, converting back and forth between absolute and relative paths, and so on. It can be extremely helpful to have a feature-rich API to help with these tasks.

Microsoft Windows provides an API for this purpose. It is implemented by the dynamic link library `shlwapi.dll`, and exposed via the header file `shlwapi.h`. Complete documentation for this API is provided on the Microsoft Developer's Network (MSDN) at the following URL: http://msdn2. microsoft.com/en-us/library/bb773559(VS.85).aspx.

Of course, the `shlwapi` API is only available on Win32 platforms. Sony provides a similar API for use on the PLAYSTATION 3. But when writing a cross-platform game engine, we cannot use platform-specific APIs directly. A game engine may not need all of the functions provided by an API like `shlwapi` anyway. For these reasons, game engines often implement a stripped-down path-handling API that meets the engine's particular needs and works on every operating system targeted by the engine. Such an API can be implemented as a thin wrapper around the native API on each platform or it can be written from scratch.

### 6.1.2.  Basic File I/O

The standard C library provides two APIs for opening, reading, and writing the contents of files—one buffered and the other unbuffered. Every file I/O API requires data blocks known as *buffers* to serve as the source or destination of the bytes passing between the program and the file on disk. We say a file I/O API is *buffered* when the API manages the necessary input and output data buffers for you. With an unbuffered API, it is the responsibility of the programmer using the API to allocate and manage the data buffers. The standard C library's buffered file I/O routines are sometimes referred to as the *stream I/O* API, because they provide an abstraction which makes disk files look like streams of bytes.

The standard C library functions for buffered and un-buffered file I/O are listed in Table 6.1.

The standard C library I/O functions are well-documented, so we will not repeat detailed documentation for them here. For more information, please refer to http://msdn2.microsoft.com/en-us/library/c565h7xx(VS.71).aspx for Microsoft's implementation of the buffered (stream I/O) API, and to http://msdn2.microsoft.com/en-us/library/40bbyw78(VS.71).aspx for Microsoft's implementation of the unbuffered (low-level I/O) API.

On UNIX and its variants, the standard C library's unbuffered I/O routes are native operating system calls. However, on Microsoft Windows these routines are merely wrappers around an even lower-level API. The Win32 function `CreateFile()` creates or opens a file for writing or reading, `ReadFile()`

| Operation | Buffered API | Unbuffered API |
|---|---|---|
| Open a file | `fopen()` | `open()` |
| Close a file | `fclose()` | `close()` |
| Read from a file | `fread()` | `read()` |
| Write to a file | `fwrite()` | `write()` |
| Seek to an offset | `fseek()` | `seek()` |
| Return current offset | `ftell()` | `tell()` |
| Read a single line | `fgets()` | n/a |
| Write a single line | `fputs()` | n/a |
| Read formatted string | `fscanf()` | n/a |
| Write formatted string | `fprintf()` | n/a |
| Query file status | `fstat()` | `stat()` |

Table 6.1. Buffered and unbuffered file operations in the standard C library.

and `WriteFile()` read and write data, respectively, and `CloseFile()` closes an open file handle. The advantage to using low-level system calls as opposed to standard C library functions is that they expose all of the details of the native file system. For example, you can query and control the security attributes of files when using the Windows native API—something you cannot do with the standard C library.

Some game teams find it useful to manage their own buffers. For example, the *Red Alert 3* team at Electronic Arts observed that writing data into log files was causing significant performance degradation. They changed the logging system so that it accumulated its output into a memory buffer, writing the buffer out to disk only when it was filled. Then they moved the buffer dump routine out into a separate thread to avoid stalling the main game loop.

### 6.1.2.1. To Wrap or Not To Wrap

A game engine can be written to use the standard C library's file I/O functions or the operating system's native API. However, many game engines *wrap* the file I/O API in a library of custom I/O functions. There are at least three advantages to wrapping the operating system's I/O API. First, the engine programmers can guarantee identical behavior across all target platforms, even when native libraries are inconsistent or buggy on a particular platform. Second, the API can be simplified down to only those functions actually required by the engine, which keeps maintenance efforts to a minimum. Third, extended functionality can be provided. For example, the engine's custom wrapper API might be capable of dealing files on a hard disk, a DVD-ROM or Blu-ray disk on a console, files on a network (e.g., remote files managed by Xbox Live or PSN), and also with files on memory sticks or other kinds of removable media.

### 6.1.2.2.   Synchronous File I/O

Both of the standard C library's file I/O libraries are *synchronous,* meaning that the program making the I/O request must wait until the data has been completely transferred to or from the media device before continuing. The following code snippet demonstrates how the entire contents of a file might be read into an in-memory buffer using the synchronous I/O function fread(). Notice how the function syncReadFile() does not return until all the data has been read into the buffer provided.

```
bool syncReadFile(const char* filePath,
    U8* buffer, size_t bufferSize, size_t& rBytesRead)
{
    FILE* handle = fopen(filePath, "rb");
    if (handle)
    {
        // BLOCK here until all data has been read.
        size_t bytesRead = fread(buffer, 1, bufferSize,
            handle);

        int err = ferror(handle); // get error if any

        fclose(handle);

        if (0 == err)
        {
            rBytesRead = bytesRead;
            return true;
        }
    }
    return false;
}

void main(int argc, const char* argv[])
{
    U8 testBuffer[512];
    size_t bytesRead = 0;

    if (syncReadFile("C:\\testfile.bin",
        testBuffer, sizeof(testBuffer), bytesRead))
    {
        printf("success: read %u bytes\n", bytesRead);
        // Contents of buffer can be used here...
    }
}
```

### 6.1.3.  Asynchronous File I/O

*Streaming* refers to the act of loading data in the background while the main program continues to run. Many games provide the player with a seamless, load-screen-free playing experience by streaming data for upcoming levels from the DVD-ROM, Blu-ray disk, or hard drive while the game is being played. Audio and texture data are probably the most commonly streamed types of data, but any type of data can be streamed, including geometry, level layouts, and animation clips.

In order to support streaming, we must utilize an *asynchronous* file I/O library, i.e., one which permits the program to continue to run while its I/O requests are being satisfied. Some operating systems provide an asynchronous file I/O library out of the box. For example, the Windows Common Language Runtime (CLR, the virtual machine upon which languages like Visual BASIC, C#, managed C++ and J# are implemented) provides functions like `System.IO.BeginRead()` and `System.IO.BeginWrite()`. An asynchronous API known as `fios` is available for the PLAYSTATION 3. If an asynchronous file I/O library is not available for your target platform, it is possible to write one yourself. And even if you don't have to write it from scratch, it's probably a good idea to wrap the system API for portability.

The following code snippet demonstrates how the entire contents of a file might be read into an in-memory buffer using an asynchronous read operation. Notice that the `asyncReadFile()` function returns immediately—the data is not present in the buffer until our callback function `asyncReadComplete()` has been called by the I/O library.

```
AsyncRequestHandle g_hRequest; // handle to async I/O
                               // request
U8 g_asyncBuffer[512];         // input buffer

static void asyncReadComplete(AsyncRequestHandle
    hRequest);

void main(int argc, const char* argv[])
{

    // NOTE: This call to asyncOpen() might itself be an
    // asynchronous call, but we'll ignore that detail
    // here and just assume it's a blocking function.
    AsyncFileHandle hFile = asyncOpen(
        "C:\\testfile.bin");

    if (hFile)
    {
```

```
        // This function requests an I/O read, then
        // returns immediately (non-blocking).
        g_hRequest = asyncReadFile(
            hFile,                    // file handle
            g_asyncBuffer,            // input buffer
            sizeof(g_asyncBuffer),    // size of buffer
            asyncReadComplete);       // callback function
    }

    // Now go on our merry way...
    // (This loop simulates doing real work while we wait
    // for the I/O read to complete.)
    for (;;)
    {
        OutputDebugString("zzz...\n");
        Sleep(50);
    }
}

// This function will be called when the data has been read.
static void asyncReadComplete(
    AsyncRequestHandle hRequest)
{
    if (hRequest == g_hRequest
        && asyncWasSuccessful(hRequest))
    {
        // The data is now present in g_asyncBuffer[] and
        // can be used. Query for the number of bytes
        // actually read:
        size_t bytes = asyncGetBytesReadOrWritten(
            hRequest);

        char msg[256];
        sprintf(msg, "async success, read %u bytes\n",
            bytes);
        OutputDebugString(msg);
    }
}
```

Most asynchronous I/O libraries permit the main program to wait for an I/O operation to complete some time after the request was made. This can be useful in situations where only a limited amount of work can be done before the results of a pending I/O request are needed. This is illustrated in the following code snippet.

```
U8 g_asyncBuffer[512];              // input buffer

void main(int argc, const char* argv[])
{
```

```
AsyncRequestHandle hRequest = ASYNC_INVALID_HANDLE;

AsyncFileHandle hFile = asyncOpen(
    "C:\\testfile.bin");

if (hFile)
{
    // This function requests an I/O read, then
    // returns immediately (non-blocking).
    hRequest = asyncReadFile(
        hFile,                      // file handle
        g_asyncBuffer,              // input buffer
        sizeof(g_asyncBuffer),      // size of buffer
        NULL);                      // no callback
}

// Now do some limited amount of work...
for (int i = 0; i < 10; ++i)
{
    OutputDebugString("zzz...\n");
    Sleep(50);
}

// We can't do anything further until we have that
// data, so wait for it here.
asyncWait(hRequest);

if (asyncWasSuccessful(hRequest))
{
    // The data is now present in g_asyncBuffer[] and
    // can be used. Query for the number of bytes
    // actually read:

    size_t bytes = asyncGetBytesReadOrWritten(
        hRequest);

    char msg[256];
    sprintf(msg, "async success, read %u bytes\n",
        bytes);
    OutputDebugString(msg);
}
}
```

Some asynchronous I/O libraries allow the programmer to ask for an estimate of how long a particular asynchronous operation will take to complete. Some APIs also allow you to set *deadlines* on a request (effectively prioritizes the request relative to other pending requests), and to specify what happens when a request misses its deadline (e.g., cancel the request, notify the program and keep trying, etc.)

### 6.1.3.1.    Priorities

It's important to remember that file I/O is a real-time system, subject to deadlines just like the rest of the game. Therefore, asynchronous I/O operations often have varying priorities. For example, if we are streaming audio from the hard disk or Bluray and playing it on the fly, loading the next buffer-full of audio data is clearly higher priority than, say, loading a texture or a chunk of a game level. Asynchronous I/O systems must be capable of suspending lower-priority requests, so that higher-priority I/O requests have a chance to complete within their deadlines.

### 6.1.3.2.    How Asynchronous File I/O Works

Asynchronous file I/O works by handling I/O requests in a separate thread. The main thread calls functions that simply place requests on a queue and then return immediately. Meanwhile, the I/O thread picks up requests from the queue and handles them sequentially using blocking I/O routines like `read()` or `fread()`. When a request is completed, a callback provided by the main thread is called, thereby notifying it that the operation is done. If the main thread chooses to wait for an I/O request to complete, this is handled via a *semaphore*. (Each request has an associated semaphore, and the main thread can put itself to sleep waiting for that semaphore to be signaled by the I/O thread upon completion of the request.)

Virtually *any* synchronous operation you can imagine can be transformed into an asynchronous operation by moving the code into a separate thread—or by running it on a physically separate processor, such as on one of the six synergistic processing units (SPUs) on the PLAYSTATION 3. See Section 7.6 for more details.

## 6.2.   The Resource Manager

Every game is constructed from a wide variety of *resources* (sometimes called *assets* or *media*). Examples include meshes, materials, textures, shader programs, animations, audio clips, level layouts, collision primitives, physics parameters, and the list goes on. A game's resources must be managed, both in terms of the offline tools used to create them, and in terms of loading, unloading, and manipulating them at runtime. Therefore every game engine has a *resource manager* of some kind.

Every resource manager is comprised of two distinct but integrated components. One component manages the chain of off-line tools used to create the assets and transform them into their engine-ready form. The other component manages the resources at runtime, ensuring that they are loaded into memory in advance of being needed by the game and making sure they are unloaded from memory when no longer needed.

In some engines, the resource manager is a cleanly-designed, unified, centralized subsystem that manages all types of resources used by the game. In other engines, the resource manager doesn't exist as a single subsystem per se, but is rather spread across a disparate collection of subsystems, perhaps written by different individuals at various times over the engine's long and sometimes colorful history. But no matter how it is implemented, a resource manager invariably takes on certain responsibilities and solves a well-understood set of problems. In this section, we'll explore the functionality and some of the implementation details of a typical game engine resource manager.

## 6.2.1. Off-Line Resource Management and the Tool Chain

### 6.2.1.1. Revision Control for Assets

On a small game project, the game's assets can be managed by keeping loose files sitting around on a shared network drive with an ad hoc directory structure. This approach is not feasible for a modern commercial 3D game, comprised of a massive number and variety of assets. For such a project, the team requires a more formalized way to track and manage its assets.

Some game teams use a source code revision control system to manage their resources. Art source files (Maya scenes, Photoshop .PSD files, Illustrator files, etc.) are checked in to Perforce or a similar package by the artists. This approach works reasonably well, although some game teams build custom asset management tools to help flatten the learning curve for their artists. Such tools may be simple wrappers around a commercial revision control system, or they might be entirely custom.

*Dealing with Data Size*

One of the biggest problems in the revision control of art assets is the sheer amount of data. Whereas C++ and script source code files are small, relative to their impact on the project, art files tend to be much, much larger. Because many source control systems work by copying files from the central repository down to the user's local machine, the sheer size of the asset files can render these packages almost entirely useless.

I've seen a number of different solutions to this problem employed at various studios. Some studios turn to commercial revision control systems like Alienbrain that have been specifically designed to handle very large data sizes. Some teams simply "take their lumps" and allow their revision control tool to copy assets locally. This can work, as long as your disks are big enough and your network bandwidth sufficient, but it can also be inefficient and slow the team down. Some teams build elaborate systems on top of their revision control tool to ensure that a particular end-user only gets local copies of the files he or she actually needs. In this model, the user either has no access to the rest of the repository or can access it on a shared network drive when needed.

At Naughty Dog we use a proprietary tool that makes use of UNIX symbolic links to virtually eliminate data copying, while permitting each user to have a complete local view of the asset repository. As long as a file is not checked out for editing, it is a symlink to a master file on a shared network drive. Symbolic links occupy very little space on the local disk, because it is nothing more than a directory entry. When the user checks out a file for editing, the symlink is removed, and a local copy of the file replaces it. When the user is done editing and checks the file in, the local copy becomes the new master copy, its revision history is updated in a master database, and the local file turns back into a symlink. This systems works very well, but it requires the team to build their own revision control system from scratch; I am unaware of any commercial tool that works like this. Also, symbolic links are a UNIX feature—such a tool could probably be built with Windows junctions (the Windows equivalent of a symbolic link), but I haven't seen anyone try it as yet.

### 6.2.1.2. The Resource Database

As we'll explore in depth in the next section, most assets are not used in their original format by the game engine. They need to pass through some kind of asset conditioning pipeline, whose job it is to convert the assets into the binary format needed by the engine. For every resource that passes through the asset conditioning pipeline, there is some amount of *metadata* that describes *how* that resource should be processed. When compressing a texture bitmap, we need to know what *type* of compression best suits that particular image. When exporting an animation, we need to know what range of frames in Maya should be exported. When exporting character meshes out of a Maya scene containing multiple characters, we need to know which mesh corresponds to which character in the game.

To manage all of this metadata, we need some kind of database. If we are making a very small game, this database might be housed in the brains of the developers themselves. I can hear them now: "Remember: the player's animations need to have the 'flip X' flag set, but the other characters must *not* have it set… or… rats… is it the other way around?"

Clearly for any game of respectable size, we simply cannot rely on the memories of our developers in this manner. For one thing, the sheer volume of assets becomes overwhelming quite quickly. Processing individual resource files by hand is also far too time-consuming to be practical on a full-fledged commercial game production. Therefore, every professional game team has some kind of semi-automated resource pipeline, and the data that drives the pipeline is stored in some kind of *resource database.*

The resource database takes on vastly different forms in different game engines. In one engine, the metadata describing how a resource should be built might be embedded into the source assets themselves (e.g., it might be stored as so-called blind data within a Maya file). In another engine, each source resource file might be accompanied by a small text file that describes how it should be processed. Still other engines encode their resource building metadata in a set of XML files, perhaps wrapped in some kind of custom graphical user interface. Some engines employ a true relational database, such as Microsoft Access, MySQL, or conceivably even a heavy-weight database like Oracle.

Whatever its form, a resource database must provide the following basic functionality:

- The ability to deal with multiple *types* of resources, ideally (but certainly not necessarily) in a somewhat consistent manner.
- The ability to create new resources.
- The ability to delete resources.
- The ability to inspect and modify existing resources.
- The ability to move a resource's source file(s) from one location to another on-disk. (This is very helpful because artists and game designers often need to rearrange assets to reflect changing project goals, re-thinking of game designs, feature additions and cuts, etc.)
- The ability of a resource to cross-reference other resources (e.g., the material used by a mesh, or the collection of animations needed by level 17). These cross-references typically drive both the resource building process and the loading process at runtime.
- The ability to maintain *referential integrity* of all cross-references within the database and to do so in the face of all common operations such as deleting or moving resources around.
- The ability to maintain a revision history, complete with a log of who made each change and why.
- It is also very helpful if the resource database supports searching or querying in various ways. For example, a developer might want to

know in which levels a particular animation is used or which textures are referenced by a set of materials. Or they might simply be trying to find a resource whose name momentarily escapes them.

It should be pretty obvious from looking at the above list that creating a reliable and robust resource database is no small task. When designed well and implemented properly, the resource database can quite literally make the difference between a team that ships a hit game and a team that spins its wheels for 18 months before being forced by management to abandon the project (or worse). I know this to be true, because I've personally experienced both.

### 6.2.1.3.   Some Successful Resource Database Designs

Every game team will have different requirements and make different decisions when designing their resource database. However, for what it's worth, here are some designs that have worked well in my own experience:

*Unreal Engine 3*

Unreal's resource database is managed by their über-tool, UnrealEd. UnrealEd is responsible for literally everything, from resource metadata management to asset creation to level layout and more. UnrealEd has its drawbacks, but its single biggest benefit is that UnrealEd is a part of the game engine itself. This permits assets to be created and then immediately viewed in their full glory, exactly as they will appear in-game. The game can even be run from within UnrealEd, in order to visualize the assets in their natural surroundings and see if and how they work in-game.

Another big benefit of UnrealEd is what I would call *one-stop shopping*. UnrealEd's Generic Browser (depicted in Figure 6.1) allows a developer to access literally every resource that is consumed by the engine. Having a single, unified, and reasonably-consistent interface for creating and managing all types of resources is a big win. This is especially true considering that the resource data in most other game engines is fragmented across countless inconsistent and often cryptic tools. Just being able to *find* any resource easily in UnrealEd is a big plus.

Unreal can be less error-prone than many other engines, because assets must be explicitly imported into Unreal's resource database. This allows resources to be checked for validity very early in the production process. In most game engines, any old data can be thrown into the resource database, and you only know whether or not that data is valid when it is eventually built—or sometimes not until it is actually loaded into the game at runtime. But with Unreal, assets can be validated as soon as they are imported into

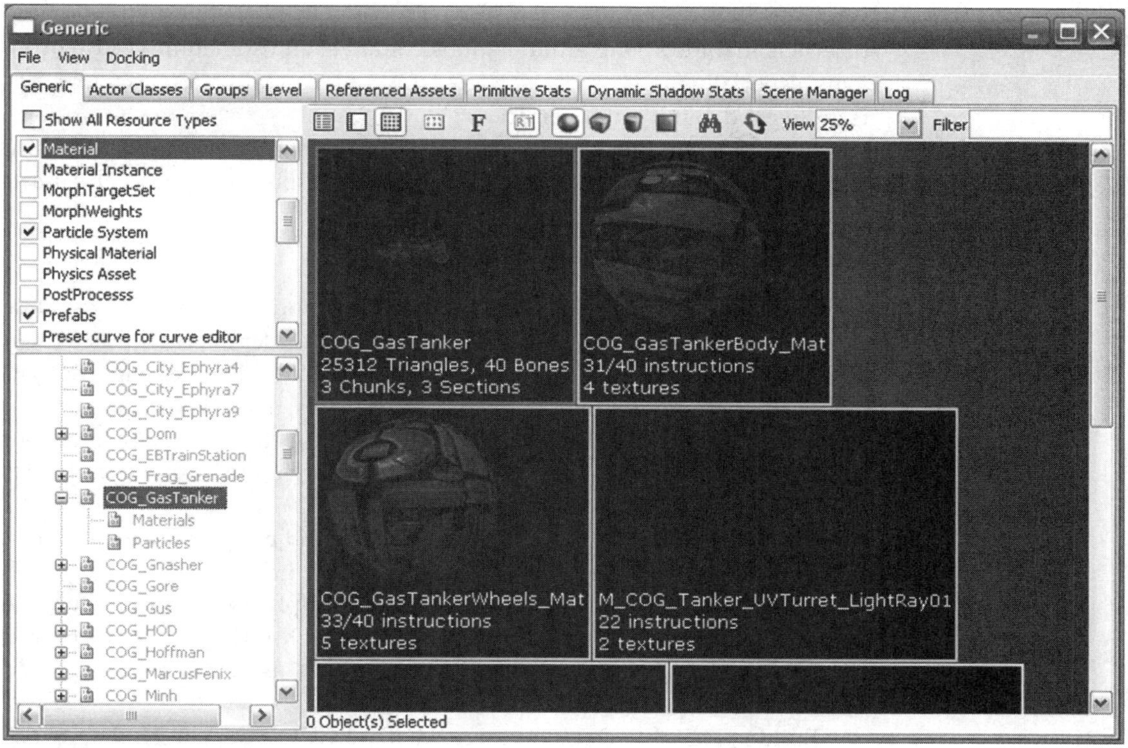

Figure 6.1. UnrealEd's Generic Browser.

UnrealEd. This means that the person who created the asset gets immediate feedback as to whether his or her asset is configured properly.

Of course, Unreal's approach has some serious drawbacks. For one thing, all resource data is stored in a small number of large package files. These files are binary, so they are not easily merged by a revision control package like CVS, Subversion, or Perforce. This presents some major problems when more than one user wants to modify resources that reside in a single package. Even if the users are trying to modify *different* resources, only one user can lock the package at a time, so the other has to wait. The severity of this problem can be reduced by dividing resources into relatively small, granular packages, but it cannot practically be eliminated.

Referential integrity is quite good in UnrealEd, but there are still some problems. When a resource is renamed or moved around, all references to it are maintained automatically using a dummy object that remaps the old resource to its new name/location. The problem with these dummy remapping objects is that they hang around and accumulate and sometimes cause problems, especially if a resource is deleted. Overall, Unreal's referential integrity is quite good, but it is not perfect.

Despite its problems, UnrealEd is by far the most user-friendly, well-integrated, and streamlined asset creation toolkit, resource database, and asset-conditioning pipeline that I have ever worked with.

### Naughty Dog's Uncharted: Drake's Fortune Engine

For *Uncharted: Drake's Fortune* (UDF), Naughty Dog stored its resource metadata in a MySQL database. A custom graphical user interface was written to manage the contents of the database. This tool allowed artists, game designers, and programmers alike to create new resources, delete existing resources, and inspect and modify resources as well. This GUI was a crucial component of the system, because it allowed users to avoid having to learn the intricacies of interacting with a relational database via SQL.

The original MySQL database used on *UDF* did not provide a useful history of the changes made to the database, nor did it provide a good way to roll back "bad" changes. It also did not support multiple users editing the same resource, and it was difficult to administer. Naughty Dog has since moved away from MySQL in favor of an XML file-based asset database, managed under Perforce.

Builder, Naughty Dog's resource database GUI, is depicted in Figure 6.2. The window is broken into two main sections: a tree view showing all resources in the game on the left and a properties window on the right, allowing the resource(s) that are selected in the tree view to be viewed and edited. The resource tree contains folders for organizational purposes, so that the artists and game designers can organize their resources in any way they see fit. Various types of resources can be created and managed within any folder, including actors and levels, and the various subresources that comprise them (primarily meshes, skeletons, and animations). Animations can also be grouped into pseudo-folders known as bundles. This allows large groups of animations to be created and then managed as a unit, and prevents a lot of wasted time dragging individual animations around in the tree view.

The asset conditioning pipeline on *UDF* consists of a set of resource exporters, compilers, and linkers that are run from the command line. The engine is capable of dealing with a wide variety of different kinds of data objects, but these are packaged into one of two types of resource files: actors and levels. An actor can contain skeletons, meshes, materials, textures, and/or animations. A level contains static background meshes, materials and textures, and also level-layout information. To build an actor, one simply types ba *name-of-actor*

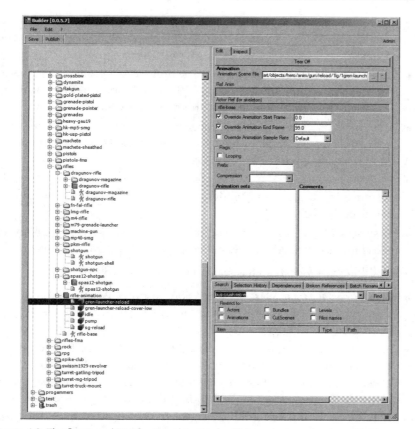

Figure 6.2. The front-end GUI for Naughty Dog's off-line resource database, Builder.

on the command line; to build a level, one types bl *name-of-level*. These command-line tools query the database to determine exactly *how* to build the actor or level in question. This includes information on how to export the assets from DCC tools like Maya, Photoshop etc., how to process the data, and how to package it into binary .pak files that can be loaded by the game engine. This is much simpler than in many engines, where resources have to be *exported manually* by the artists—a time-consuming, tedious, and error-prone task.

The benefits of the resource pipeline design used by Naughty Dog include:

- *Granular resources*. Resources can be manipulated in terms of logical entities in the game—meshes, materials, skeletons, and animations. These resource types are granular enough that the team almost never has conflicts in which two users want to edit the same resource simultaneously.

- *The necessary features (and no more).* The Builder tool provides a powerful set of features that meet the needs of the team, but Naughty Dog didn't waste any resources creating features they didn't need.

- *Obvious mapping to source files.* A user can very quickly determine which source assets (native DCC files, like Maya .ma files or photoshop .psd files) make up a particular resource.

- *Easy to change how DCC data is exported and processed.* Just click on the resource in question and twiddle its processing properties within the resource database GUI.

- *Easy to build assets.* Just type ba or bl followed by the resource name on the command line. The dependency system takes care of the rest.

Of course, the *UDF* tool chain has some drawbacks as well, including:

- *Lack of visualization tools.* The only way to preview an asset is to load it into the game or the model/animation viewer (which is really just a special mode of the game itself).

- *The tools aren't fully integrated.* Naughty Dog uses one tool to lay out levels, another to manage the majority of resources in the resource database, and a third to set up materials and shaders (this is not part of the resource database front-end). Building the assets is done on the command line. It might be a bit more convenient if all of these functions were to be integrated into a single tool. However, Naughty Dog has no plans to do this, because the benefit would probably not outweigh the costs involved.

### Ogre's Resource Manager System

Ogre3D is a rendering engine, not a full-fledged game engine. That said, Ogre does boast a reasonably complete and very well-designed runtime resource manager. A simple, consistent interface is used to load virtually any kind of resource. And the system has been designed with extensibility in mind. Any programmer can quite easily implement a resource manager for a brand new kind of asset and integrate it easily into Ogre's resource framework.

One of the drawbacks of Ogre's resource manager is that it is a runtime-only solution. Ogre lacks any kind of off-line resource database. Ogre does provide some exporters which are capable of converting a Maya file into a mesh that can be used by Ogre (complete with materials, shaders, a skeleton and optional animations). However, the exporter must be run manually from within Maya itself. Worse, all of the metadata describing how a particular Maya file should be exported and processed must be entered by the user doing the export.

In summary, Ogre's runtime resource manager is powerful and well-designed. But Ogre would benefit a great deal from an equally powerful and modern resource database and asset conditioning pipeline on the tools side.

### Microsoft's XNA

XNA is a game development toolkit by Microsoft, targeted at the PC and Xbox 360 platforms. XNA's resource management system is unique, in that it leverages the project management and build systems of the Visual Studio IDE to manage and build the assets in the game as well. XNA's game development tool, Game Studio Express, is just a plug-in to Visual Studio Express. You can read more about Game Studio Express at http://msdn.microsoft.com/en-us/library/bb203894.aspx.

### 6.2.1.4. The Asset Conditioning Pipeline

In Section 1.7, we learned that resource data is typically created using advanced digital content creation (DCC) tools like Maya, Z-Brush, Photoshop, or Houdini. However, the data formats used by these tools are usually not suitable for direct consumption by a game engine. So the majority of resource data is passed through an *asset conditioning pipeline* (ACP) on its way to the game engine. The ACP is sometimes referred to as the *resource conditioning pipeline* (RCP), or simply the *tool chain*.

Every resource pipeline starts with a collection of *source assets* in native DCC formats (e.g., Maya .ma or .mb files, Photoshop .psd files, etc.) These assets are typically passed through three processing stages on their way to the game engine:

1.  *Exporters.* We need some way of getting the data out of the DCC's native format and into a format that we can manipulate. This is usually accomplished by writing a custom plug-in for the DCC in question. It is the plug-in's job to export the data into some kind of intermediate file format that can be passed to later stages in the pipeline. Most DCC applications provide a reasonably convenient mechanism for doing this. Maya actually provides three: a C++ SDK, a scripting language called MEL, and most recently a Python interface as well.

    In cases where a DCC application provides no customization hooks, we can always save the data in one of the DCC tool's native formats. With any luck, one of these will be an open format, a reasonably-intuitive text format, or some other format that we can reverse engineer. Presuming this is the case, we can pass the file directly to the next stage of the pipe-line.

2. *Resource compilers.* We often have to "massage" the raw data exported from a DCC application in various ways in order to make it game-ready. For example, we might need to rearrange a mesh's triangles into strips, or compress a texture bitmap, or calculate the arc lengths of the segments of a Catmull-Rom spline. Not all types of resources need to be compiled—some might be game-ready immediately upon being exported.

3. *Resource linkers.* Multiple resource files sometimes need to be combined into a single useful package prior to being loaded by the game engine. This mimics the process of linking together the object files of a compiled C++ program into an executable file, and so this process is sometimes called *resource linking.* For example, when building a complex compos-ite resource like a 3D model, we might need to combine the data from multiple exported mesh files, multiple material files, a skeleton file, and multiple animation files into a single resource. Not all types of resources need to be linked—some assets are game-ready after the export or com-pile steps.

### Resource Dependencies and Build Rules

Much like compiling the source files in a C or C++ project and then linking them into an executable, the asset conditioning pipeline processes source as-sets (in the form of Maya geometry and animation files, Photoshop PSD files, raw audio clips, text files, etc.), converts them into game-ready form, and then links them together into a cohesive whole for use by the engine. And just like the source files in a computer program, game assets often have interdepen-dencies. (For example, a mesh refers to one or more materials, which in turn refer to various textures.) These interdependencies typically have an impact on the order in which assets must be processed by the pipeline. (For example, we might need to build a character's skeleton before we can process any of that character's animations.) In addition, the dependencies between assets tell us which assets need to be rebuilt when a particular source asset changes.

Build dependencies revolve not only around changes to the assets them-selves, but also around changes to data formats. If the format of the files used to store triangle meshes changes, for instance, all meshes in the entire game may need to be reexported and/or rebuilt. Some game engines employ data formats that are robust to version changes. For example, an asset may contain a version number, and the game engine may include code that "knows" how to load and make use of legacy assets. The downside of such a policy is that asset files and engine code tend to become bulky. When data format changes are relatively rare, it may be better to just bite the bullet and reprocess all the files when format changes do occur.

Every asset conditioning pipeline requires a set of rules that describe the interdependencies between the assets, and some kind of build tool that can use this information to ensure that the proper assets are built, in the proper order, when a source asset is modified. Some game teams roll their own build system. Others use an established tool, such as make. Whatever solution is selected, teams should treat their build dependency system with utmost care. If you don't, changes to sources assets may not trigger the proper assets to be rebuilt. The result can be inconsistent game assets, which may lead to visual anomalies or even engine crashes. In my personal experience, I've witnessed countness hours wasted in tracking down problems that could have been avoided had the asset interdependencies been properly specified and the build system implemented to use them reliably.

## 6.2.2. Runtime Resource Management

Let us turn our attention now to how the assets in our resource database are loaded, managed, and unloaded within the engine at runtime.

### 6.2.2.1. Responsibilities of the Runtime Resource Manager

A game engine's runtime resource manager takes on a wide range of responsibilities, all related to its primary mandate of loading resources into memory:

- Ensures that only *one copy* of each unique resource exists in memory at any given time.
- Manages the *lifetime* of each resource loads needed resources and unloads resources that are no longer needed.
- Handles loading of *composite resources*. A composite resource is a resource comprised of other resources. For example, a *3D model* is a composite resource that consists of a mesh, one or more materials, one or more textures, and optionally a skeleton and multiple skeletal animations.
- Maintains *referential integrity*. This includes *internal* referential integrity (cross-references within a single resource) and *external* referential integrity (cross-references between resources). For example, a model refers to its mesh and skeleton; a mesh refers to its materials, which in turn refer to texture resources; animations refer to a skeleton, which ultimately ties them to one or more models. When loading a composite resource, the resource manager must ensure that all necessary subresources are loaded, and it must patch in all of the cross-references properly.
- Manages the *memory usage* of loaded resources and ensures that resources are stored in the appropriate place(s) in memory.

- Permits *custom processing* to be performed on a resource after it has been loaded, on a per-resource-type basis. This process is sometimes known as *logging in* or *load-initializing* the resource.

- Usually (but not always) provides a single *unified interface* through which a wide variety of resource types can be managed. Ideally a resource manager is also easily extensible, so that it can handle new types of resources as they are needed by the game development team.

- Handles *streaming* (i.e., asynchronous resource loading), if the engine supports this feature.

### 6.2.2.2. Resource File and Directory Organization

In some game engines (typically PC engines), each individual resource is managed in a separate "loose" file on-disk. These files are typically contained within a tree of directories whose internal organization is designed primarily for the convenience of the people creating the assets; the engine typically doesn't care where resource files are located within the resource tree. Here's a typical resource directory tree for a hypothetical game called *Space Evaders:*

| | |
|---|---|
| `SpaceEvaders` | Root directory for entire game. |
| `Resources` | Root of all resources. |
| `Characters` | Non-player character models and animations. |
| `Pirate` | Models and animations for pirates. |
| `Marine` | Models and animations for marines. |
| `. . .` | |
| `Player` | Player character models and animations. |
| `Weapons` | Models and animations for weapons. |
| `Pistol` | Models and animations for the pistol. |
| `Rifle` | Models and animations for the rifle. |
| `BFG` | Models and animations for the big... uh... gun. |
| `. . .` | |
| `Levels` | Background geometry and level layouts. |
| `Level1` | First level's resources. |
| `Level2` | Second level's resources. |
| `. . .` | |
| `Objects` | Miscellaneous 3D objects. |
| `Crate` | The ubiquitous breakable crate. |
| `Barrel` | The ubiquitous exploding barrel. |

Other engines package multiple resources together in a single file, such as a ZIP archive, or some other composite file (perhaps of a proprietary format).

The primary benefit of this approach is improved load times. When loading data from files, the three biggest costs are *seek times* (i.e., moving the read head to the correct place on the physical media), the time required to open each individual file, and the time to read the data from the file into memory. Of these, the seek times and file-open times can be non-trivial on many operating systems. When a single large file is used, all of these costs are minimized. A single file can be organized sequentially on the disk, reducing seek times to a minimum. And with only one file to open, the cost of opening individual resource files is eliminated.

The Ogre3D rendering engine's resource manager permits resources to exist as loose files on disk, or as virtual files within a large ZIP archive. The primary benefits of the ZIP format are the following:

1. *It is an open format.* The `zlib` and `zziplib` libraries used to read and write ZIP archives are freely available. The zlib SDK is totally free (see http://www.zlib.net), while the zziplib SDK falls under the Lesser Gnu Public License (LGPL) (see http://zziplib.sourceforge.net).

2. *The virtual files within a ZIP archive "remember" their relative paths.* This means that a ZIP archive "looks like" a raw file system for most intents and purposes. The Ogre resource manager identifies all resources uniquely via strings that appear to be file system paths. However, these paths sometimes identify virtual files within a ZIP archive instead of loose files on disk, and a game programmer needn't be aware of the difference in most situations.

3. *ZIP archives may be compressed.* This reduces the amount of disk space occupied by resources. But, more importantly, it again speeds up load times, as less data need be loaded into memory from the fixed disk. This is especially helpful when reading data from a DVD-ROM or Blu-ray disk, as the data transfer rates of these devices are much slower than a hard disk drive. Hence the cost of decompressing the data after it has been loaded into memory is often more than offset by the time saved in loading less data from the device.

4. *ZIP archives are modular.* Resources can be grouped together into a ZIP file and managed as a unit. One particularly elegant application of this idea is in product localization. All of the assets that need to be localized (such as audio clips containing dialogue and textures that contain words or region-specific symbols) can be placed in a single ZIP file, and then different versions of this ZIP file can be generated, one for each language or region. To run the game for a particular region, the engine simply loads the corresponding version of the ZIP archive.

Unreal Engine 3 takes a similar approach, with a few important differences. In Unreal, all resources must be contained within large composite files known as *packages* (a.k.a. "pak files"). No loose disk files are permitted. The format of a package file is proprietary. The Unreal Engine's game editor, UnrealEd, allows developers to create and manage packages and the resources they contain.

### 6.2.2.3. Resource File Formats

Each type of resource file potentially has a different format. For example, a mesh file is always stored in a different format than that of a texture bitmap. Some kinds of assets are stored in standardized, open formats. For example, textures are typically stored as Targa files (TGA), Portable Network Graphics files (PNG), Tagged Image File Format files (TIFF), Joint Photographic Experts Group files (JPEG), or Windows Bitmap files (BMP)—or in a standardized compressed format such as DirectX's S3 Texture Compression family of formats (S3TC, also known as DXT$n$ or DXTC). Likewise, 3D mesh data is often exported out of a modeling tool like Maya or Lightwave into a standardized format such as OBJ or COLLADA for consumption by the game engine.

Sometimes a single file format can be used to house many different types of assets. For example, the *Granny* SDK by Rad Game Tools (http://www.radgametools.com) implements a flexible open file format that can be used to store 3D mesh data, skeletal hierarchies, and skeletal animation data. (In fact the Granny file format can be easily repurposed to store virtually any kind of data imaginable.)

Many game engine programmers roll their own file formats for various reasons. This might be necessary if no standardized format provides all of the information needed by the engine. Also, many game engines endeavor to do as much off-line processing as possible in order to minimize the amount of time needed to load and process resource data at runtime. If the data needs to conform to a particular layout in memory, for example, a raw binary format might be chosen so that the data can be laid out by an off-line tool (rather than attempting to format it at runtime after the resource has been loaded).

### 6.2.2.4. Resource GUIDs

Every resource in a game must have some kind of *globally unique identifier* (GUID). The most common choice of GUID is the resource's file system path (stored either as a string or a 32-bit hash). This kind of GUID is intuitive, because it clearly maps each resource to a physical file on-disk. And it's guaranteed to be unique across the entire game, because the operating system already guarantees that no two files will have the same path.

However, a file system path is by no means the only choice for a resource GUID. Some engines use a less-intuitive type of GUID, such as a 128-bit hash code, perhaps assigned by a tool that guarantees uniqueness. In other engines, using a file system path as a resource identifier is infeasible. For example, Unreal Engine 3 stores many resources in a single large file known as a *package*, so the path to the package file does not uniquely identify any one resource. To overcome this problem, an Unreal package file is organized into a folder hierarchy containing individual resources. Unreal gives each individual resource within a package a unique name which looks much like a file system path. So in Unreal, a resource GUID is formed by concatenating the (unique) name of the package file with the in-package path of the resource in question. For example, the *Gears of War* resource GUID `Locust_Boomer.PhysicalMaterials.LocustBoomerLeather` identifies a material called `LocustBoomerLeather` within the `PhysicalMaterials` folder of the `Locust_Boomer` package file.

### 6.2.2.5. The Resource Registry

In order to ensure that only one copy of each unique resource is loaded into memory at any given time, most resource managers maintain some kind of *registry* of loaded resources. The simplest implementation is a *dictionary*—i.e., a collection of *key-value pairs*. The keys contain the unique ids of the resources, while the values are typically pointers to the resources in memory.

Whenever a resource is loaded into memory, an entry for it is added to the resource registry dictionary, using its GUID as the key. Whenever a resource is unloaded, its registry entry is removed. When a resource is requested by the game, the resource manager looks up the resource by its GUID within the resource registry. If the resource can be found, a pointer to it is simply returned. If the resource cannot be found, it can either be loaded automatically or a failure code can be returned.

At first blush, it might seem most intuitive to automatically load a requested resource if it cannot be found in the resource registry. And in fact, some game engines do this. However, there are some serious problems with this approach. Loading a resource is a slow operation, because it involves locating and opening a file on disk, reading a potentially large amount of data into memory (from a potentially slow device like a DVD-ROM drive), and also possibly performing post-load initialization of the resource data once it has been loaded. If the request comes during active gameplay, the time it takes to load the resource might cause a very noticeable hitch in the game's frame rate, or even a multi-second freeze. For this reason, engines tend to take one of two alternative approaches:

1. Resource loading might be disallowed completely during active game-play. In this model, all of the resources for a game level are loaded *en masse* just prior to gameplay, usually while the player watches a loading screen or progress bar of some kind.

2. Resource loading might be done *asynchronously* (i.e., the data might be *streamed*). In this model, while the player is engaged in level A, the resources for level B are being loaded in the background. This approach is preferable because it provides the player with a load-screen-free play experience. However, it is considerably more difficult to implement.

### 6.2.2.6. Resource Lifetime

The *lifetime* of a resource is defined as the time period between when it is first loaded into memory and when its memory is reclaimed for other purposes. One of the resource manager's jobs is to manage resource lifetimes—either automatically, or by providing the necessary API functions to the game, so it can manage resource lifetimes manually.

Each resource has its own lifetime requirements:

- Some resources must be loaded when the game first starts up and must stay resident in memory for the entire duration of the game. That is, their lifetimes are effectively infinite. These are sometimes called *load-and-stay-resident* (LSR) resources. Typical examples include the player character's mesh, materials, textures and core animations, textures and fonts used on the heads-up display (HUD), and the resources for all of the standard-issue weapons used throughout the game. Any resource that is visible or audible to the player throughout the entire game (and cannot be loaded on the fly when needed) should be treated as an LSR resource.

- Other resources have a lifetime that matches that of a particular game level. These resources must be in memory by the time the level is first seen by the player and can be dumped once the player has permanently left the level.

- Some resources might have a lifetime that is shorter than the duration of the level in which they are found. For example, the animations and audio clips that make up an *in-game cut-scene* (a mini-movie that advances the story or provides the player with important information) might be loaded in advance of the player seeing the cut-scene and then dumped once the cut-scene has played.

- Some resources like background music, ambient sound effects, or full-screen movies are streamed "live" as they play. The lifetime of this kind of resource is difficult to define, because each byte only persists in memory for a tiny fraction of a second, but the entire piece of music sounds like it lasts for a long period of time. Such assets are typically loaded in chunks of a size that matches the underlying hardware's requirements. For example, a music track might be read in 4 kB chunks, because that might be the buffer size used by the low-level sound system. Only two chunks are ever present in memory at any given moment—the chunk that is currently playing and the chunk immediately following it that is being loaded into memory.

The question of when to load a resource is usually answered quite easily, based on knowledge of when the asset is first seen by the player. However, the question of when to unload a resource and reclaim its memory is not so easily answered. The problem is that many resources are shared across multiple levels. We don't want to unload a resource when level A is done, only to immediately reload it because level B needs the same resource.

One solution to this problem is to reference-count the resources. Whenever a new game level needs to be loaded, the list of all resources used by that level is traversed, and the reference count for each resource is incremented by one (but they are not loaded yet). Next, we traverse the resources of any unneeded levels and decrement their reference counts by one; any resource whose reference count drops to zero is unloaded. Finally, we run through the list of all resources whose reference count just went from zero to one and load those assets into memory.

For example, imagine that level 1 uses resources A, B, and C, and that level 2 uses resources B, C, D, and E. (B and C are shared between both levels.) Table 6.2 shows the reference counts of these five resources as the player plays through levels 1 and 2. In this table, reference counts are shown in boldface type to indicate that the corresponding resource actually exists in memory, while a grey background indicates that the resource is not in memory. A reference count in parentheses indicates that the corresponding resource data is being loaded or unloaded.

### 6.2.2.7. Memory Management for Resources

Resource management is closely related to memory management, because we must inevitably decide *where* the resources should end up in memory once they have been loaded. The destination of every resource is not always the same. For one thing, certain types of resources must reside in video RAM. Typical examples include textures, vertex buffers, index buffers, and shader

| Event | A | B | C | D | E |
|---|---|---|---|---|---|
| Initial state | 0 | 0 | 0 | 0 | 0 |
| Level 1 counts incremented | 1 | 1 | 1 | 0 | 0 |
| Level 1 loads | (1) | (1) | (1) | 0 | 0 |
| Level 1 plays | 1 | 1 | 1 | 0 | 0 |
| Level 2 counts incremented | 1 | 2 | 2 | 1 | 1 |
| Level 1 counts decremented | 0 | 1 | 1 | 1 | 1 |
| Level 1 unloads, level 2 loads | (0) | 1 | 1 | (1) | (1) |
| Level 2 plays | 0 | 1 | 1 | 1 | 1 |

Table 6.2. Resource usage as two levels load and unload.

code. Most other resources can reside in main RAM, but different kinds of resources might need to reside within different address ranges. For example, a resource that is loaded and stays resident for the entire game (LSR resources) might be loaded into one region of memory, while resources that are loaded and unloaded frequently might go somewhere else.

The design of a game engine's memory allocation subsystem is usually closely tied to that of its resource manager. Sometimes we will design the resource manager to take best advantage of the types of memory allocators we have available; or vice-versa, we may design our memory allocators to suit the needs of the resource manager.

As we saw in Section 5.2.1.4, one of the primary problems facing any resource management system is the need to avoid fragmenting memory as resources are loaded and unloaded. We'll discuss a few of the more-common solutions to this problem below.

### Heap-Based Resource Allocation

One approach is to simply ignore memory fragmentation issues and use a general-purpose heap allocator to allocate your resources (like the one implemented by `malloc()` in C, or the global `new` operator in C++). This works best if your game is only intended to run on personal computers, on operating systems that support advanced virtual memory allocation. On such a system, physical memory will become fragmented, but the operating system's ability to map non-contiguous pages of physical RAM into a contiguous virtual memory space helps to mitigate some of the effects of fragmentation.

If your game is running on a console with limited physical RAM and only a rudimentary virtual memory manager (or none whatsoever), then fragmentation will become a problem. In this case, one alternative is to defragment your memory periodically. We saw how to do this in Section 5.2.2.2.

*Stack-Based Resource Allocation*

A stack allocator does not suffer from fragmentation problems, because memory is allocated contiguously and freed in an order opposite to that in which it was allocated. A stack allocator can be used to load resources if the following two conditions are met:

- The game is linear and level-centric (i.e., the player watches a loading screen, then plays a level, then watches another loading screen, then plays another level).

- Each level fits into memory in its entirety.

Presuming that these requirements are satisfied, we can use a stack allocator to load resources as follows: When the game first starts up, the load-and-stay-resident (LSR) resources are allocated first. The top of the stack is then marked, so that we can free back to this position later. To load a level, we simply allocate its resources on the top of the stack. When the level is complete, we can simply set the stack top back to the marker we took earlier, thereby freeing all of the level's resources in one fell swoop without disturbing the LSR resources. This process can be repeated for any number of levels, without ever fragmenting memory. Figure 6.3 illustrates how this is accomplished.

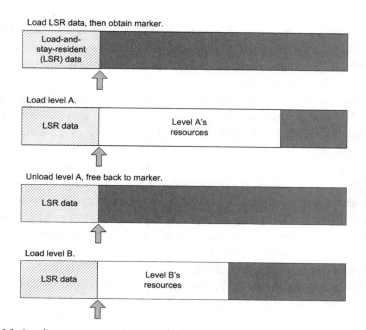

**Figure 6.3.** Loading resources using a stack allocator.

A double-ended stack allocator can be used to augment this approach. Two stacks are defined within a single large memory block. One grows up from the bottom of the memory area, while the other grows down from the top. As long as the two stacks never overlap, the stacks can trade memory resources back and forth naturally—something that wouldn't be possible if each stack resided in its own fixed-size block.

On *Hydro Thunder*, Midway used a double-ended stack allocator. The lower stack was used for persistent data loads, while the upper was used for temporary allocations that were freed every frame. Another way a double-ended stack allocator can be used is to ping-pong level loads. Such an approach was used at Bionic Games Inc. for one of their projects. The basic idea is to load a compressed version of level B into the upper stack, while the currently-active level A resides (in uncompressed form) in the lower stack. To switch from level A to level B, we simply free level A's resources (by clearing the lower stack) and then decompress level B from the upper stack into the lower stack. Decompression is generally much faster than loading data from disk, so this approach effectively eliminates the load time that would otherwise be experienced by the player beween levels.

### Pool-Based Resource Allocation

Another resource allocation technique that is common in game engines that support streaming is to load resource data in equally-sized chunks. Because the chunks are all the same size, they can be allocated using a *pool allocator* (see Section 5.2.1.2). When resources are later unloaded, the chunks can be freed without causing fragmentation.

Of course, a chunk-based allocation approach requires that all resource data be laid out in a manner that permits division into equally-sized chunks. We cannot simply load an arbitrary resource file in chunks, because the file might contain a contiguous data structure like an array or a very large `struct` that is larger than a single chunk. For example, if the chunks that contain an array are not arranged sequentially in RAM, the continuity of the array will be lost, and array indexing will cease to function properly. This means that all resource data must be designed with "chunkiness" in mind. Large contiguous data structures must be avoided in favor of data structures that are either small enough to fit within a single chunk or do not require contiguous RAM to function properly (e.g., linked lists).

Each chunk in the pool is typically associated with a particular game level. (One simple way to do this is to give each level a linked list of its chunks.) This allows the engine to manage the lifetimes of each chunk appropriately, even when multiple levels with different life spans are in memory concur-

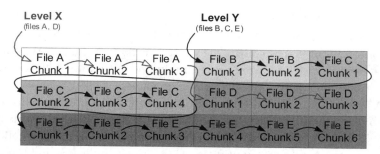

Figure 6.4. Chunky allocation of resources for levels A and B.

rently. For example, when level A is loaded, it might allocate and make use of
$N$ chunks. Later, level B might allocate an additional $M$ chunks. When level
A is eventually unloaded, its $N$ chunks are returned to the free pool. If level
B is still active, its $M$ chunks need to remain in memory. By associating each
chunk with a specific level, the lifetimes of the chunks can be managed easily
and efficiently. This is illustrated in Figure 6.4.

One big trade-off inherent in a "chunky" resource allocation scheme is
wasted space. Unless a resource file's size is an exact multiple of the chunk
size, the last chunk in a file will not be fully utilized (see Figure 6.5). Choosing a smaller chunk size can help to mitigate this problem, but the smaller the
chunks, the more onerous the restrictions on the layout of the resource data.
(As an extreme example, if a chunk size of one byte were selected, then no
data structure could be larger than a single byte—clearly an untenable situation.) A typical chunk size is on the order of a few kilobytes. For example
at Naughty Dog, we use a chunky resource allocator as part of our resource
streaming system, and our chunks are 512 kB in size. You may also want to
consider selecting a chunk size that is a multiple of the operating system's I/O
buffer size to maximize efficiency when loading individual chunks.

Figure 6.5. The last chunk of a resource file is often not fully utilized.

### Resource Chunk Allocators

One way to limit the effects of wasted chunk memory is to set up a special memory allocator that can utilize the unused portions of chunks. As far as I'm aware, there is no standardized name for this kind of allocator, but we will call it a *resource chunk allocator* for lack of a better name.

A resource chunk allocator is not particularly difficult to implement. We need only maintain a linked list of all chunks that contain unused memory, along with the locations and sizes of each free block. We can then allocate from these free blocks in any way we see fit. For example, we might manage the linked list of free blocks using a general-purpose heap allocator. Or we might map a small stack allocator onto each free block; whenever a request for memory comes in, we could then scan the free blocks for one whose stack has enough free RAM, and then use that stack to satisfy the request.

Unfortunately, there's a rather grotesque-looking fly in our ointment here. If we allocate memory in the unused regions of our resource chunks, what happens when those chunks are freed? We cannot free part of a chunk—it's an all or nothing proposition. So any memory we allocate within an unused portion of a resource chunk will magically disappear when that resource is unloaded.

A simple solution to this problem is to only use our free-chunk allocator for memory requests whose lifetimes match the lifetime of the level with which a particular chunk is associated. In other words, we should only allocate memory out of level A's chunks for data that is associated exclusively with level A and only allocate from B's chunks memory that is used exclusively by level B. This requires our resource chunk allocator to manage each level's chunks separately. And it requires the users of the chunk allocator to specify which level they are allocating for, so that the correct linked list of free blocks can be used to satisfy the request.

Thankfully, most game engines need to allocate memory dynamically when loading resources, over and above the memory required for the resource files themselves. So a resource chunk allocator can be a fruitful way to reclaim chunk memory that would otherwise have been wasted.

### Sectioned Resource Files

Another useful idea that is related to "chunky" resource files is the concept of *file sections*. A typical resource file might contain between one and four sections, each of which is divided into one or more chunks for the purposes of pool allocation as described above. One section might contain data that is destined for main RAM, while another section might contain video RAM data. Another section could contain temporary data that is needed during the loading process but is discarded once the resource has been completely loaded. Yet another section might contain debugging information. This debug data could be loaded when running the game in debug mode, but not loaded at all in the final production build of the game. The Granny SDK's file system (http://www.radgametools.com) is an excellent example of how to implement file sectioning in a simple and flexible manner.

### 6.2.2.8. Composite Resources and Referential Integrity

Usually a game's resource database consists of multiple *resource files*, each file containing one or more *data objects*. These data objects can refer to and depend upon one another in arbitrary ways. For example, a mesh data structure might contain a reference to its material, which in turn contains a list of references to textures. Usually cross-references imply dependency (i.e., if resource A refers to resource B, then both A and B must be in memory in order for the resources to be functional in the game.) In general, a game's resource database can be represented by a *directed graph* of interdependent data objects.

Cross-references between data objects can be *internal* (a reference between two objects within a single file) or *external* (a reference to an object in a different file). This distinction is important because internal and external cross-references are often implemented differently. When visualizing a game's resource database, we can draw dotted lines surrounding individual resource files to make the internal/external distinction clear—any edge of the graph that crosses a dotted line file boundary is an external reference, while edges that do not cross file boundaries are internal. This is illustrated in Fiure 6.6.

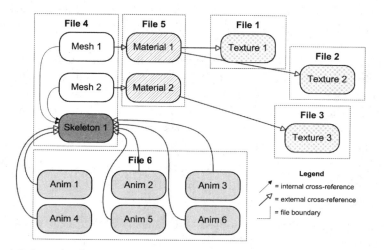

**Figure 6.6.** Example of a resource database dependency graph.

We sometimes use the term *composite resource* to describe a self-sufficient cluster of interdependent resources. For example, a *model* is a composite resource consisting of one or more *triangle meshes,* an optional *skeleton,* and an optional collection of *animations.* Each mesh is mapped with a *material,* and each material refers to one or more *textures.* To fully load a composite resource like a 3D model into memory, all of its dependent resources must be loaded as well.

### 6.2.2.9.  Handling Cross-References between Resources

One of the more-challenging aspects of implementing a resource manager is managing the cross-references between resource objects and guaranteeing that referential integrity is maintained. To understand how a resource manager accomplishes this, let's look at how cross-references are represented in memory, and how they are represented on-disk.

In C++, a cross-reference between two data objects is usually implemented via a *pointer* or a *reference.* For example, a mesh might contain the data member `Material* m_pMaterial` (a pointer) or `Material& m_material` (a reference) in order to refer to its material. However, pointers are just memory addresses—they lose their meaning when taken out of the context of the running application. In fact, memory addresses can and do change even between subsequent runs of the same application. Clearly when storing data to a disk file, we cannot use pointers to describe inter-object dependencies.

### GUIDs As Cross-References

One good approach is to store each cross-reference as a string or hash code containing the unique id of the referenced object. This implies that every resource object that might be cross-referenced must have a *globally unique identifier* or *GUID.*

To make this kind of cross-reference work, the runtime resource manager maintains a global resource look-up table. Whenever a resource object is loaded into memory, a pointer to that object is stored in the table with its GUID as the look-up key. After all resource objects have been loaded into memory and their entries added to the table, we can make a pass over all of the objects and convert all of their cross-references into pointers, by looking up the address of each cross-referenced object in the global resource look-up table via that object's GUID.

### Pointer Fix-Up Tables

Another approach that is often used when storing data objects into a binary file is to convert the *pointers* into *file offsets.* Consider a group of C structs or C++ objects that cross-reference each other via pointers. To store this group

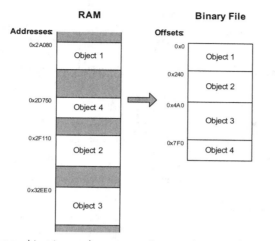

Figure 6.7. In-memory object images become contiguous when saved into a binary file.

of objects into a binary file, we need to visit each object once (and only once) in an arbitrary order and write each object's memory image into the file sequentially. This has the effect of serializing the objects into a *contiguous* image within the file, even when their memory images are not contiguous in RAM. This is shown in Figure 6.7.

Because the objects' memory images are now contiguous within the file, we can determine the *offset* of each object's image relative to the beginning of the file. During the process of writing the binary file image, we locate every pointer within every data object, convert each pointer into an offset, and store those offsets into the file in place of the pointers. We can simply overwrite the pointers with their offsets, because the offsets never require more bits to store than the original pointers. In effect, an *offset* is the binary file equivalent of a *pointer* in memory. (Do be aware of the differences between your development platform and your target platform. If you write out a memory image on a 64-bit Windows machine, its pointers will all be 64 bits wide and the resulting file won't be compatible with a 32-bit console.)

Of course, we'll need to convert the offsets back into pointers when the file is loaded into memory some time later. Such conversions are known as *pointer fix-ups*. When the file's binary image is loaded, the objects contained in the image retain their contiguous layout. So it is trivial to convert an offset into a pointer. We merely add the offset to the address of the file image as a whole. This is demonstrated by the code snippet below, and illustrated in Figure 6.8.

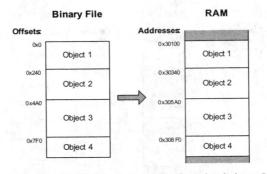

**Figure 6.8.** Contiguous resource file image, after it has been loaded into RAM.

```
U8* ConvertOffsetToPointer(U32 objectOffset,
                            U8* pAddressOfFileImage)
{
    U8* pObject = pAddressOfFileImage + objectOffset;
    return pObject;
}
```

The problem we encounter when trying to convert pointers into offsets, and vice-versa, is how to *find* all of the pointers that require conversion. This problem is usually solved at the time the binary file is written. The code that writes out the images of the data objects has knowledge of the data types and classes being written, so it has knowledge of the locations of all the pointers

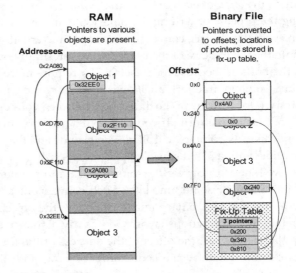

**Figure 6.9.** A pointer fix-up table.

within each object. The locations of the pointers are stored into a simple table known as a *pointer fix-up table*. This table is written into the binary file along with the binary images of all the objects. Later, when the file is loaded into RAM again, the table can be consulted in order to find and fix up every pointer. The table itself is just a list of offsets within the file—each offset represents a single pointer that requires fixing up. This is illustrated in Figure 6.9.

*Storing C++ Objects as Binary Images: Constructors*

One important step that is easy to overlook when loading C++ objects from a binary file is to ensure that the objects' constructors are called. For example, if we load a binary image containing three objects—an instance of class A, an instance of class B, and an instance of class C—then we must make sure that the correct constructor is called on each of these three objects.

There are two common solutions to this problem. First, you can simply decide not to support C++ objects in your binary files at all. In other words, restrict yourself to plain old data structures (PODS)—i.e., C structs and C++ structs and classes that contain *no virtual functions* and *trivial do-nothing constructors* (See http://en.wikipedia.org/wiki/Plain_Old_Data_Structures for a more complete discussion of PODS.)

Second, you can save off a table containing the offsets of all non-PODS objects in your binary image along with some indication of which class each object is an instance of. Then, once the binary image has been loaded, you can iterate through this table, visit each object, and call the appropriate constructor using *placement new* syntax (i.e., calling the constructor on a preallocated block of memory). For example, given the offset to an object within the binary image, we might write:

```
void* pObject = ConvertOffsetToPointer(objectOffset);
::new(pObject) ClassName; // placement-new syntax
```

where *ClassName* is the class of which the object is an instance.

*Handling External References*

The two approaches described above work very well when applied to resources in which all of the cross-references are *internal*—i.e., they only reference objects within a single resource file. In this simple case, you can load the binary image into memory and then apply the pointer fix-ups to resolve all the cross-references. But when cross-references reach out into other resource files, a slightly augmented approach is required.

To successfully represent an *external* cross-reference, we must specify not only the offset or GUID of the data object in question, but also the path to the resource file in which the referenced object resides.

The key to loading a multi-file composite resource is to load *all* of the interdependent files first. This can be done by loading one resource file and then scanning through its table of cross-references and loading any externally-referenced files that have not already been loaded. As we load each data object into RAM, we can add the object's address to the master look-up table. Once all of the interdependent files have been loaded and all of the objects are present in RAM, we can make a final pass to fix up all of the pointers using the master look-up table to convert GUIDs or file offsets into real addresses.

### 6.2.2.10. Post-Load Initialization

Ideally, each and every resource would be completely prepared by our off-line tools, so that it is ready for use the moment it has been loaded into memory. Practically speaking, this is not always possible. Many types of resources require at least some "massaging" after having been loaded, in order to prepare them for use by the engine. In this book, I will use the term *post-load initialization* to refer to any processing of resource data after it has been loaded. Other engines may use different terminology. (For example, at Naughty Dog we call this *logging in* a resource.) Most resource managers also support some kind of tear-down step prior to a resource's memory being freed. (At Naughty Dog, we call this *logging out* a resource.)

Post-load initialization generally comes in one of two varieties:

- In some cases, post-load initialization is an unavoidable step. For example, the vertices and indices that describe a 3D mesh are loaded into main RAM, but they almost always need to be transferred into video RAM. This can only be accomplished at runtime, by creating a Direct X vertex buffer or index buffer, locking it, copying or reading the data into the buffer, and then unlocking it.

- In other cases, the processing done during post-load initialization is avoidable (i.e., could be moved into the tools), but is done for convenience or expedience. For example, a programmer might want to add the calculation of accurate arc lengths to our engine's spline library. Rather than spend the time to modify the tools to generate the arc length data, the programmer might simply calculate it at runtime during post-load initialization. Later, when the calculations are perfected, this code can be moved into the tools, thereby avoiding the cost of doing the calculations at runtime.

Clearly, each type of resource has its own unique requirements for post-load initialization and tear-down. So resource managers typically permit these two steps to be configurable on a per-resource-type basis. In a non-object-oriented language like C, we can envision a look-up table that maps each type of resource to a pair of function pointers, one for post-load initialization and one for tear-down. In an object-oriented language like C++, life is even easier — we can make use of polymorphism to permit each class to handle post-load initialization and tear-down in a unique way.

In C++, post-load initialization could be implemented as a special constructor, and tear-down could be done in the class' destructor. However, there are some problems with using constructors and destructors for this purpose. (For example, constructors cannot be virtual in C++, so it would be difficult for a derived class to modify or augment the post-load initialization of its base class.) Many developers prefer to defer post-load initialization and tear-down to plain old virtual functions. For example, we might choose to use a pair of virtual functions named something sensible like Init() and Destroy().

Post-load initialization is closely related to a resource's memory allocation strategy, because new data is often generated by the initialization routine. In some cases, the data generated by the post-load initialization step *augments* the data loaded from the file. (For example, if we are calculating the arc lengths of the segments of a Catmull-Rom spline curve after it has been loaded, we would probably want to allocate some additional memory in which to store the results.) In other cases, the data generated during post-load initialization *replaces* the loaded data. (For example, we might allow mesh data in an older out-of-date format to be loaded and then automatically converted into the latest format for backwards compatibility reasons.) In this case, the loaded data may need to be discarded, either partially or in its entirety, after the post-load step has generated the new data.

The *Hydro Thunder* engine had a simple but powerful way of handling this. It would permit resources to be loaded in one of two ways: (a) directly into its final resting place in memory, or (b) into a temporary area of memory. In the latter case, the post-load initialization routine was responsible for copying the finalized data into its ultimate destination; the temporary copy of the resource would be discarded after post-load initialization was complete. This was very useful for loading resource files that contained both relevant and irrelevant data. The relevant data would be copied into its final destination in memory, while the irrelevant data would be discarded. For example, mesh data in an out-of-date format could be loaded into temporary memory and then converted into the latest format by the post-load initialization routine, without having to waste any memory keeping the old-format data kicking around.

# 7
# The Game Loop and
# Real-Time Simulation

Games are real-time, dynamic, interactive computer simulations. As such, *time* plays an incredibly important role in any electronic game. There are many different kinds of time to deal with in a game engine—real time, game time, the local timeline of an animation, the actual CPU cycles spent within a particular function, and the list goes on. Every engine system might define and manipulate time differently. We must have a solid understanding of all the ways time can be used in a game. In this chapter, we'll take a look at how real-time, dynamic simulation software works and explore the common ways in which time plays a role in such a simulation.

## 7.1. The Rendering Loop

In a graphical user interface (GUI), of the sort found on a Windows PC or a Macintosh, the majority of the screen's contents are static. Only a small part of any one window is actively changing appearance at any given moment. Because of this, graphical user interfaces have traditionally been drawn on-screen via a technique known as *rectangle invalidation*, in which only the small portions of the screen whose contents have actually changed are re-drawn. Older 2D video games used similar techniques to minimize the number of pixels that needed to be drawn.

Real-time 3D computer graphics are implemented in an entirely different way. As the camera moves about in a 3D scene, the *entire contents* of the screen or window change continually, so the concept of invalid rectangles no longer applies. Instead, an illusion of motion and interactivity is produced in much the same way that a movie produces it—by presenting the viewer with a series of still images in rapid succession.

Obviously, producing a rapid succession of still images on-screen requires a loop. In a real-time rendering application, this is sometimes known as the *render loop*. At its simplest, a rendering loop is structured as follows:

```
while (!quit)
{

    // Update the camera transform based on interactive
    // inputs or by following a predefined path.
    updateCamera();

    // Update positions, orientations and any other
    // relevant visual state of any dynamic elements
    // in the scene.
    updateSceneElements();

    // Render a still frame into an off-screen frame
    // buffer known as the "back buffer".
    renderScene();

    // Swap the back buffer with the front buffer, making
    // the most-recently-rendered image visible
    // on-screen. (Or, in windowed mode, copy (blit) the
    // back buffer's contents to the front buffer.
    swapBuffers();
}
```

## 7.2.   The Game Loop

A game is composed of many interacting subsystems, including device I/O, rendering, animation, collision detection and resolution, optional rigid body dynamics simulation, multiplayer networking, audio, and the list goes on. Most game engine subsystems require periodic *servicing* while the game is running. However, the *rate* at which these subsystems need to be serviced varies from subsystem to subsystem. Animation typically needs to be updated at a rate of 30 or 60 Hz, in synchronization with the rendering subsystem. However, a dynamics simulation may actually require more frequent updates (e.g., 120 Hz). Higher-level systems, like AI, might only need to be serviced once or twice per second, and they needn't necessarily be synchronized with the rendering loop at all.

There are a number of ways to implement the periodic updating of our game engine subsystems. We'll explore some of the possible architectures in a moment. But for the time being, let's stick with the simplest way to update our engine's subsystems—using a single loop to update everything. Such a loop is often called the *game loop*, because it is the master loop that services every subsystem in the engine.

## 7.2.1. A Simple Example: Pong

Pong is a well-known genre of table tennis video games that got its start in 1958, in the form of an analog computer game called *Tennis for Two*, created by William A. Higinbotham at the Brookhaven National Laboratory and displayed on an oscilloscope. The genre is best known by its later incarnations on digital computers—the Magnavox Oddysey game *Table Tennis* and the Atari arcade game *Pong*.

In pong, a ball bounces back and forth between two movable vertical paddles and two fixed horizontal walls. The human players control the positions of the paddles via control wheels. (Modern re-implementations allow control via a joystick, the keyboard, or some other human interface device.) If the ball passes by a paddle without striking it, the other team wins the point and the ball is reset for a new round of play.

The following pseudocode demonstrates what the game loop of a pong game might look like at its core:

```
void main() // Pong
{
    initGame();

    while (true) // game loop
    {
        readHumanInterfaceDevices();

        if (quitButtonPressed())
        {
            break; // exit the game loop
        }

        movePaddles();

        moveBall();
```

```
        collideAndBounceBall();

        if (ballImpactedSide(LEFT_PLAYER))
        {
            incremenentScore(RIGHT_PLAYER);
            resetBall();
        }

        else if (ballImpactedSide(RIGHT_PLAYER))
        {
            incrementScore(LEFT_PLAYER);
            resetBall();
        }

        renderPlayfield();
    }
}
```

Clearly this example is somewhat contrived. The original pong games were certainly not implemented by redrawing the entire screen at a rate of 30 frames per second. Back then, CPUs were so slow that they could barely muster the power to draw two lines for the paddles and a box for the ball in real time. Specialized 2D sprite hardware was often used to draw moving objects on-screen. However, we're only interested in the concepts here, not the implementation details of the original Pong.

As you can see, when the game first runs, it calls initGame() to do whatever set-up might be required by the graphics system, human I/O devices, audio system, etc. Then the main game loop is entered. The statement while (true) tells us that the loop will continue forever, unless interrupted internally. The first thing we do inside the loop is to read the human interface device(s). We check to see whether either human player pressed the "quit" button—if so, we exit the game via a break statement. Next, the positions of the paddles are adjusted slightly upward or downward in movePaddles(), based on the current deflection of the control wheels, joysticks, or other I/O devices. The function moveBall() adds the ball's current velocity vector to its position in order to find its new position next frame. In collideAndBounce-Ball(), this position is then checked for collisions against both the fixed horizontal walls and the paddles. If collisions are detected, the ball's position is recalculated to account for any bounce. We also note whether the ball impacted either the left or right edge of the screen. This means that it missed one of the paddles, in which case we increment the other player's score and reset the ball for the next round. Finally, renderPlayfield() draws the entire contents of the screen.

## 7.3.  Game Loop Architectural Styles

Game loops can be implemented in a number of different ways—but at their core, they usually boil down to one or more simple loops, with various embellishments. We'll explore a few of the more common architectures below.

### 7.3.1.  Windows Message Pumps

On a Windows platform, games need to service messages from the Windows operating system in addition to servicing the various subsystems in the game engine itself. Windows games therefore contain a chunk of code known as a *message pump*. The basic idea is to service Windows messages whenever they arrive and to service the game engine only when no Windows messages are pending. A message pump typically looks something like this:

```
while (true)
{
    // Service any and all pending Windows messages.

    MSG msg;

    while (PeekMessage(&msg, NULL, 0, 0) > 0)
    {
        TranslateMessage(&msg);

        DispatchMessage(&msg);
    }

    // No more Windows messages to process - run one
    // iteration of our "real" game loop.

    RunOneIterationOfGameLoop();

}
```

One of the side-effects of implementing the game loop like this is that Windows messages take precedence over rendering and simulating the game. As a result, the game will temporarily freeze whenever you resize or drag the game's window around on the desktop.

### 7.3.2.  Callback-Driven Frameworks

Most game engine subsystems and third-party game middleware packages are structured as *libraries*. A library is a suite of functions and/or classes that can be called in any way the application programmer sees fit. Libraries provide maximum flexibility to the programmer. But libraries are sometimes difficult to use, because the programmer must understand how to properly use the functions and classes they provide.

In contrast, some game engines and game middleware packages are structured as *frameworks*. A framework is a partially-constructed application—the programmer completes the application by providing custom implementations of missing functionality within the framework (or overriding its default behavior). But he or she has little or no control over the overall flow of control within the application, because it is controlled by the framework.

In a framework-based rendering engine or game engine, the main game loop has been written for us, but it is largely empty. The game programmer can write callback functions in order to "fill in" the missing details. The Ogre3D rendering engine is an example of a library that has been wrapped in a framework. At the lowest level, Ogre provides functions that can be called directly by a game engine programmer. However, Ogre also provides a framework that encapsulates knowledge of how to use the low-level Ogre library effectively. If the programmer chooses to use the Ogre framework, he or she derives a class from `Ogre::FrameListener` and overrides two virtual functions: `frameStarted()` and `frameEnded()`. As you might guess, these functions are called before and after the main 3D scene has been rendered by Ogre, respectively. The Ogre framework's implementation of its internal game loop looks something like the following pseudocode. (See `Ogre::Root::renderOneFrame()` in *OgreRoot.cpp* for the actual source code.)

```
while (true)
{
    for (each frameListener)
    {
        frameListener.frameStarted();
    }

    renderCurrentScene();

    for (each frameListener)
    {
        frameListener.frameEnded();
    }

    finalizeSceneAndSwapBuffers();
}
```

A particular game's frame listener implementation might look something like this.

```cpp
class GameFrameListener : public Ogre::FrameListener
{
public:
    virtual void frameStarted(const FrameEvent& event)
    {
        // Do things that must happen before the 3D scene
        // is rendered (i.e., service all game engine
        // subsystems).
        pollJoypad(event);
        updatePlayerControls(event);
        updateDynamicsSimulation(event);
        resolveCollisions(event);
        updateCamera(event);
        // etc.
    }

    virtual void frameEnded(const FrameEvent& event)
    {
        // Do things that must happen after the 3D scene
        // has been rendered.
        drawHud(event);

        // etc.
    }
};
```

### 7.3.3. Event-Based Updating

In games, an *event* is any interesting change in the state of the game or its environment. Some examples include: the human player pressing a button on the joypad, an explosion going off, an enemy character spotting the player, and the list goes on. Most game engines have an *event system*, which permits various engine subsystems to register interest in particular kinds of events and to respond to those events when they occur (see Section 14.7 for details). A game's event system is usually very similar to the event/messaging system underlying virtually all graphical user interfaces (for example, Microsoft Windows' window messages, the event handling system in Java's AWT, or the services provided by C#'s `delegate` and `event` keywords).

Some game engines leverage their event system in order to implement the periodic servicing of some or all of their subsystems. For this to work, the event system must permit events to be posted into the future—that is, to be queued for later delivery. A game engine can then implement periodic updating by simply posting an event. In the event handler, the code can perform whatever periodic servicing is required. It can then post a new event 1/30 or 1/60 of a second into the future, thus continuing the periodic servicing for as long as it is required.

## 7.4. Abstract Timelines

In game programming, it can be extremely useful to think in terms of *abstract timelines*. A timeline is a continuous, one-dimensional axis whose origin ($t = 0$) can lie at any arbitrary location relative to other timelines in the system. A timeline can be implemented via a simple clock variable that stores absolute time values in either integer or floating-point format.

### 7.4.1. Real Time

We can think of times measured directly via the CPU's high-resolution timer register (see Section 7.5.3) as lying on what we'll call the *real timeline*. The origin of this timeline is defined to coincide with the moment the CPU was last powered on or reset. It measures times in units of CPU cycles (or some multiple thereof), although these time values can be easily converted into units of seconds by multiplying them by the frequency of the high-resolution timer on the current CPU.

### 7.4.2. Game Time

We needn't limit ourselves to working with the real timeline exclusively. We can define as many other timeline(s) as we need, in order to solve the problems at hand. For example, we can define a *game timeline* that is technically independent of real time. Under normal circumstances, game time coincides with real time. If we wish to pause the game, we can simply stop updating the game timeline temporarily. If we want our game to go into slow-motion, we can update the game clock more slowly than the real-time clock. All sorts of effects can be achieved by scaling and warping one timeline relative to another.

Pausing or slowing down the game clock is also a highly useful debugging tool. To track down a visual anomaly, a developer can pause game time in order to freeze the action. Meanwhile, the rendering engine and debug fly-through camera can continue to run, as long as they are governed by a different clock (either the *real-time clock*, or a separate *camera clock*). This allows the developer to fly the camera around the game world to inspect it from any angle desired. We can even support single-stepping the game clock, by advancing the game clock by one target frame interval (e.g., 1/30 of a second) each time a "single-step" button is pressed on the joypad or keyboard while the game is in a paused state.

When using the approach described above, it's important to realize that the game loop is still running when the game is paused—only the game clock has stopped. Single-stepping the game by adding 1/30 of a second to a paused game clock is not the same thing as setting a break point in your main loop, and then hitting the F5 key repeatedly to run one iteration of the loop at a time. Both kinds of single-stepping can be useful for tracking down different kinds of problems. We just need to keep the differences between these approaches in mind.

### 7.4.3. Local and Global Timelines

We can envision all sorts of other timelines. For example, an animation clip or audio clip might have a *local timeline*, with its origin ($t = 0$) defined to coincide with the start of the clip. The local timeline measures how time progressed when the clip was originally authored or recorded. When the clip is played back in-game, we needn't play it at the original rate. We might want to speed up an animation, or slow down an audio sample. We can even play an animation backwards by running its local clock in reverse.

Any one of these effects can be visualized as a *mapping* between the local timeline and a global timeline, such as real time or game time. To play an animation clip back at its originally-authored speed, we simply map the start of the animation's local timeline ($t = 0$) onto the desired start time ($\tau = \tau_{start}$) along the global timeline. This is shown in Figure 7.1.

To play an animation clip back at half speed, we can imagine scaling the local timeline to twice its original size prior to mapping it onto the global timeline. To accomplish this, we simply keep track of a time scale factor or playback rate $R$, in addition to the clip's global start time $\tau_{start}$. This is illustrated in Figure 7.2. A clip can even be played in reverse, by using a negative time scale ($R < 0$) as shown in Figure 7.3.

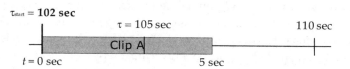

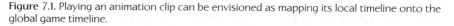

**Figure 7.1.** Playing an animation clip can be envisioned as mapping its local timeline onto the global game timeline.

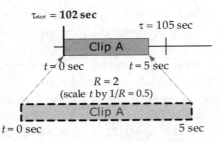

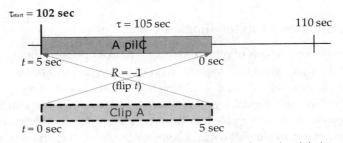

**Figure 7.2.** Animation play-back speed can be controlled by simply scaling the local time line prior to mapping it onto the global time line.

**Figure 7.3.** Playing an animation in reverse is like mapping the clip to the global time line with a time scale of $R = -1$.

## 7.5. Measuring and Dealing with Time

In this section, we'll investigate some of the subtle and not-so-subtle distinctions between different kinds of timelines and clocks and see how they are implemented in real game engines.

### 7.5.1. Frame Rate and Time Deltas

The *frame rate* of a real-time game describes how rapidly the sequence of still 3D frames is presented to the viewer. The unit of *Hertz* (Hz), defined as the number of cycles per second, can be used to describe the rate of any periodic process. In games and film, frame rate is typically measured in *frames per second* (FPS), which is the same thing as Hertz for all intents and purposes. Films traditionally run at 24 FPS. Games in North America and Japan are typically rendered at 30 or 60 FPS, because this is the natural refresh rate of the NTSC color television standard used in these regions. In Europe and most of the rest of the world, games update at 50 FPS, because this is the natural refresh rate of a PAL or SECAM color television signal.

The amount of time that elapses between frames is known as the *frame time*, *time delta*, or *delta time*. This last term is commonplace because the duration between frames is often represented mathematically by the symbol $\Delta t$. (Technically speaking, $\Delta t$ should really be called the *frame period*, since it is the inverse of the *frame frequency*: $T = 1/f$. But game programmers hardly ever use the term "period" in this context.) If a game is being rendered at exactly 30 FPS, then its delta time is 1/30 of a second, or 33.3 ms (milliseconds). At 60 FPS, the delta time is half as big, 1/60 of a second or 16.6 ms. To really know how much time has elapsed during one iteration of the game loop, we need to measure it. We'll see how this is done below.

We should note here that milliseconds are a common unit of time measurement in games. For example, we might say that animation is taking 4 ms, which implies that it occupies about 12% of the entire frame ($4 / 33.3 \approx 0.12$). Other common units include seconds and machine cycles. We'll discuss time units and clock variables in more depth below.

## 7.5.2. From Frame Rate to Speed

Let's imagine that we want to make a spaceship fly through our game world at a constant speed of 40 meters per second (or in a 2D game, we might specify this as 40 *pixels* per second!) One simple way to accomplish this is to multiply the ship's speed $v$ (measured in meters per second) by the duration of one frame $\Delta t$ (measured in seconds), yielding a change in position $\Delta x = v \, \Delta t$ (which is measured in *meters per frame*). This position delta can then be added to the ship's current position $x_1$, in order to find its position next frame: $x_2 = x_1 + \Delta x = x_1 + v \, \Delta t$.

This is actually a simple form of *numerical integration* known as the *explicit Euler* method (see Section 12.4.4). It works well as long as the speeds of our objects are roughly constant. To handle variable speeds, we need to resort to somewhat more-complex integration methods. But all numerical integration techniques make use of the elapsed frame time $\Delta t$ in one way or another. So it is safe to say that the *perceived speeds* of the objects in a game are dependent upon the frame duration, $\Delta t$. Hence a central problem in game programming is to determine a suitable value for $\Delta t$. In the sections that follow, we'll discuss various ways of doing this.

### 7.5.2.1. Old-School CPU-Dependent Games

In many early video games, no attempt was made to measure how much real time had elapsed during the game loop. The programmers would essentially ignore $\Delta t$ altogether and instead specify the speeds of objects directly in terms of meters (or pixels, or some other distance unit) per *frame*. In other words, they were, perhaps unwittingly, specifying object speeds in terms of $\Delta x = v \, \Delta t$, instead of in terms of $v$.

The net effect of this simplistic approach was that the perceived speeds of the objects in these games were entirely dependent upon the frame rate that the game was actually achieving on a particular piece of hardware. If this kind of game were to be run on a computer with a faster CPU than the machine for which it was originally written, the game would appear to be running in fast forward. For this reason, I'll call these games *CPU-dependent games*.

Some older PCs provided a "Turbo" button to support these kinds of games. When the Turbo button was pressed, the PC would run at its fastest speed, but CPU-dependent games would run in fast forward. When the Turbo button was not pressed, the PC would mimic the processor speed of an older generation of PCs, allowing CPU-dependent games written for those PCs to run properly.

### 7.5.2.2. Updating Based on Elapsed Time

To make our games CPU-independent, we must measure $\Delta t$ in some way, rather than simply ignoring it. Doing this is quite straightforward. We simply read the value of the CPU's high resolution timer twice—once at the beginning of the frame and once at the end. Then we subtract, producing an accurate measure of $\Delta t$ for the frame that has just passed. This delta is then made available to all engine subsystems that need it, either by passing it to every function that we call from within the game loop or by storing it in a global variable or encapsulating it within a singleton class of some kind. (We'll describe the CPU's high resolution timer in more detail Section 7.5.3.)

The approach outlined above is used by many game engines. In fact, I am tempted to go out on a limb and say that *most* game engines use it. However, there is one big problem with this technique: We are using the measured value of $\Delta t$ taken during frame $k$ as an estimate of the duration of the *upcoming* frame ($k + 1$). This isn't necessarily very accurate. (As they say in investing, "past performance is not a guarantee of future results.") Something might happen next frame that causes it to take much more time (or much less) than the current frame. We call such an event a *frame-rate spike*.

Using last frame's delta as an estimate of the upcoming frame can have some very real detrimental effects. For example, if we're not careful it can put the game into a "viscious cycle" of poor frame times. Let's assume that our physics simulation is most stable when updated once every 33.3 ms (i.e., at 30 Hz). If we get one bad frame, taking say 57 ms, then we might make the mistake of stepping the physics system *twice* on the next frame, presumably to "cover" the 57 ms that has passed. Those two steps take roughly twice as long to complete as a regular step, causing the *next* frame to be at least as bad as this one was, and possibly worse. This only serves to exacerbate and prolong the problem.

### 7.5.2.3. Using a Running Average

It is true that game loops tend to have at least some frame-to-frame coherency. If the camera is pointed down a hallway containing lots of expensive-to-draw objects on one frame, there's a good chance it will still be pointed down that hallway on the next. Therefore, one reasonable approach is to average the frame-time measurements over a small number of frames and use that as the next frame's estimate of $\Delta t$. This allows the game to adapt to varying frame rate, while softening the effects of momentary performance spikes. The longer the averaging interval, the less responsive the game will be to varying frame rate, but spikes will have less of an impact as well.

### 7.5.2.4. Governing the Frame Rate

We can avoid the inaccuracy of using last frame's $\Delta t$ as an estimate of this frame's duration altogether, by flipping the problem on its head. Rather than trying to *guess* at what next frame's duration will be, we can instead attempt to *guarantee* that every frame's duration will be exactly 33.3 ms (or 16.6 ms if we're running at 60 FPS). To do this, we measure the duration of the current frame as before. If the measured duration is less than the ideal frame time, we simply put the main thread to sleep until the target frame time has elapsed. If the measured duration is more than the ideal frame time, we must "take our lumps" and wait for one more whole frame time to elapse. This is called *frame-rate governing*.

Clearly this approach only works when your game's frame rate is reasonably close to your target frame rate on average. If your game is ping-ponging between 30 FPS and 15 FPS due to frequent "slow" frames, then the game's quality can degrade significantly. As such, it's still a good idea to design all engine systems so that they are capable of dealing with arbitrary frame durations. During development, you can leave the engine in "variable frame rate" mode, and everything will work as expected. Later on, when the game is getting closer to achieving its target frame rate consistently, we can switch on frame-rate governing and start to reap its benefits.

Keeping the frame rate consistent can be important for a number of reasons. Some engine systems, such as the numerical integrators used in a physics simulation, operate best when updated at a constant rate. A consistent frame rate also looks better, and as we'll see in the next section, it can be used to avoid the *tearing* that can occur when the video buffer is updated at a rate that doesn't match the refresh rate of the monitor.

In addition, when elapsed frame times are consistent, features like *record and play back* become a lot more reliable. As its name implies, the record and play back feature allows a player's gameplay experience to be recorded and later played back in exactly the same way. This can be a fun game feature, and it's also a valuable testing and debugging tool. For example, difficult-to-find bugs can be reproduced by simply playing back a recorded game that demonstrates the bug.

To implement record and play back, we make note of every relevant event that occurs during gameplay, saving each one in a list along with an accurate time stamp. The list of events can then be replayed with exactly the same timing, using the same initial conditions, and an identical initial random seed. In theory, doing this should produce a gameplay experience that is indistinguishable from the original playthrough. However, if the frame rate isn't consistent, things may not happen in exactly the same order. This can cause "drift," and pretty soon your AI characters are flanking when they should have fallen back.

### 7.5.2.5. The Vertical Blanking Interval

A visual anomaly known as *tearing* occurs when the back buffer is swapped with the front buffer while the electron gun in the CRT monitor is only part way through its scan. When tearing occurs, the top portion of the screen shows the old image, while the bottom portion shows the new one. To avoid tearing, many rendering engines wait for the vertical blanking interval of the monitor (the time during which the electron gun is being reset to the top-left corner of the screen) before swapping buffers.

Waiting for the v-blank interval is another form of *frame-rate governing*. It effectively clamps the frame rate of the main game loop to a multiple of the screen's refresh rate. For example, on an NTSC monitor that refreshes at a rate of 60 Hz, the game's real update rate is effectively quantized to a multiple of 1/60 of a second. If more than 1/60 of a second elapses between frames, we must wait until the next v-blank interval, which means waiting 2/60 of a second (30 FPS). If we miss two v-blanks, then we must wait a total of 3/60 of a second (20 FPS), and so on. Also, be careful not to make assumptions about the frame rate of your game, even when it is synchronized to the v-blank interval; remember that the PAL and SECAM standards are based around an update rate of 50 Hz, not 60 Hz.

### 7.5.3. Measuring Real Time with a High-Resolution Timer

We've talked a lot about measuring the amount of real "wall clock" time that elapses during each frame. In this section, we'll investigate how such timing measurements are made in detail.

Most operating systems provide a function for querying the system time, such as the standard C library function `time()`. However, such functions are not suitable for measuring elapsed times in a real-time game, because they do not provide sufficient resolution. For example, `time()` returns an integer representing the number of *seconds* since midnight, January 1, 1970, so its resolution is one second—far too coarse, considering that a frame takes only tens of milliseconds to execute.

All modern CPUs contain a *high-resolution timer*, which is usually implemented as a hardware register that counts the number of CPU cycles (or some multiple thereof) that have elapsed since the last time the processor was powered on or reset. This is the timer that we should use when measuring elapsed time in a game, because its resolution is usually on the order of the duration of a few CPU cycles. For example, on a 3 GHz Pentium processor, the high-resolution timer increments once per CPU cycle, or 3 billion times per second. Hence the resolution of the high-res timer is $1 / 3$ billion $= 3.33 \times 10^{-10}$ seconds $= 0.333$ ns (one-third of a nanosecond). This is more than enough resolution for all of our time-measurement needs in a game.

Different microprocessors and different operating systems provide different ways to query the high-resolution timer. On a Pentium, a special instruction called `rdtsc` (read time-stamp counter) can be used, although the Win32 API wraps this facility in a pair of functions: `QueryPerformanceCounter()` reads the 64-bit counter register and `QueryPerformanceFrequency()` returns the number of counter increments per second for the current CPU. On a PowerPC architecture, such as the chips found in the Xbox 360 and PLAYSTATION 3, the instruction `mftb` (move from time base register) can be used to read the two 32-bit time base registers, while on other PowerPC architectures, the instruction `mfspr` (move from special-purpose register) is used instead.

A CPU's high-resolution timer register is 64 bits wide on most processors, to ensure that it won't wrap too often. The largest possible value of a 64-bit unsigned integer is 0xFFFFFFFFFFFFFFFF $\approx 1.8 \times 10^{19}$ clock ticks. So, on a 3 GHz Pentium processor that updates its high-res timer once per CPU cycle, the register's value will wrap back to zero once every 195 years or so—definitely not a situation we need to lose too much sleep over. In contrast, a 32-bit integer clock will wrap after only about 1.4 seconds at 3 GHz.

### 7.5.3.1.   High-Resolution Clock Drift

Be aware that even timing measurements taken via a high-resolution timer can be inaccurate in certain circumstances. For example, on some multicore processors, the high-resolution timers are independent on each core, and they can (and do) drift apart. If you try to compare absolute timer readings taken on different cores to one another, you might end up with some strange results—even negative time deltas. Be sure to keep an eye out for these kinds of problems.

## 7.5.4.   Time Units and Clock Variables

Whenever we measure or specify time durations in a game, we have two choices to make:

1. What *time units* should be used? Do we want to store our times in seconds, or milliseconds, or machine cycles… or in some other unit?

2. What *data type* should be used to store time measurements? Should we employ a 64-bit integer, or a 32-bit integer, or a 32-bit floating point variable?

The answers to these questions depend on the intended purpose of a given measurement. This gives rise to two more questions: How much precision do we need? And what range of magnitudes do we expect to be able to represent?

### 7.5.4.1.   64-Bit Integer Clocks

We've already seen that a 64-bit unsigned integer clock, measured in machine cycles, supports both an extremely high precision (a single cycle is 0.333 ns in duration on a 3 GHz CPU) and a broad range of magnitudes (a 64-bit clock wraps once roughly every 195 years at 3 GHz). So this is the most flexible time representation, presuming you can afford 64 bits worth of storage.

### 7.5.4.2.   32-Bit Integer Clocks

When measuring relatively short durations with high precision, we can turn to a 32-bit integer clock, measured in machine cycles. For eample, to profile the performance of a block of code, we might do something like this:

```
// Grab a time snapshot.
U64 tBegin = readHiResTimer();

// This is the block of code whose performance we wish
// to measure.
doSomething();
doSomethingElse();
nowReallyDoSomething();
```

```
// Measure the duration.
U64 tEnd = readHiResTimer();
U32 dtCycles = static_cast<U32>(tEnd - tBegin);

// Now use or cache the value of dtCycles...
```

Notice that we still store the raw time measurements in 64-bit integer variables. Only the time delta dt is stored in a 32-bit variable. This circumvents potential problems with wrapping at the 32-bit boundary. For example, if tBegin == 0x12345678FFFFFFB7 and tEnd == 0x1234567900000039, then we would measure a negative time delta if we were to truncate the individual time measurements to 32 bits each prior to subtracting them.

### 7.5.4.3. 32-Bit Floating-Point Clocks

Another common approach is to store relatively small time deltas in floating-point format, measured in units of seconds. To do this, we simply multiply a duration measured in CPU cycles by the CPU's clock frequency, which is in cycles per second. For example:

```
// Start off assuming an ideal frame time (30 FPS).
F32 dtSeconds = 1.0f / 30.0f;

// Prime the pump by reading the current time.
U64 tBegin = readHiResTimer();

while (true) // main game loop
{
    runOneIterationOfGameLoop(dtSeconds);

    // Read the current time again, and calculate the
    // delta.
    U64 tEnd = readHiResTimer();
    dtSeconds = (F32)(tEnd - tBegin)
                * (F32)getHiResTimerFrequency();

    // Use tEnd as the new tBegin for next frame.
    tBegin = tEnd;
}
```

Notice once again that we must be careful to subtract the two 64-bit time measurements *before* converting them into floating point format. This ensures that we don't store too large a magnitude into a 32-bit floating point variable.

### 7.5.4.4. Limitations of Floating Point Clocks

Recall that in a 32-bit IEEE float, the 23 bits of the mantissa are dynamically distributed between the whole and fractional parts of the value, by way of the exponent (see Section 3.2.1.4). Small magnitudes require only a few bits, leaving plenty of bits of precision for the fraction. But once the magnitude of our clock grows too large, its whole part eats up more bits, leaving fewer bits for the fraction. Eventually, even the least-significant bits of the whole part become implicit zeros. This means that we must be cautious when storing *long durations* in a floating-point clock variable. If we keep track of the amount of time that has elapsed since the game was started, a floating-point clock will eventually become inaccurate to the point of being unusable.

Floating-point clocks are usually only used to store relatively short time deltas, measuring at most a few minutes, and more often just a single frame or less. If an absolute-valued floating-point clock is used in a game, you will need to reset the clock to zero periodically, to avoid accumulation of large magnitudes.

### 7.5.4.5.   Other Time Units

Some game engines allow timing values to be specified in a game-defined unit that is fine-grained enough to permit a 32-bit integer format to be used, precise enough to be useful for a wide range of applications within the engine, and yet large enough that the 32-bit clock won't wrap too often. One common choice is a 1/300 second time unit. This works well because (a) it is fine-grained enough for many purposes, (b) it only wraps once every 165.7 days, and (c) it is an even multiple of both NTSC and PAL refresh rates. A 60 FPS frame would be 5 such units in duration, while a 50 FPS frame would be 6 units in duration.

Obviously a 1/300 second time unit is not precise enough to handle subtle effects, like time-scaling an animation. (If we tried to slow a 30 FPS animation down to less than 1/10 of its regular speed, we'd be out of precision!) So for many purposes, it's still best to use floating-point time units, or machine cycles. But a 1/300 second time unit can be used effectively for things like specifying how much time should elapse between the shots of an automatic weapon, or how long an AI-controlled character should wait before starting his patrol, or the amount of time the player can survive when standing in a pool of acid.

## 7.5.5.   Dealing with Break Points

When your game hits a break point, its loop stops running and the debugger takes over. However, the CPU continues to run, and the real-time clock continues to accrue cycles. A large amount of wall clock time can pass while you are inspecting your code at a break point. When you allow the program to continue, this can lead to a measured frame time many seconds, or even minutes or hours in duration!

Clearly if we allow such a huge delta-time to be passed to the subsystems in our engine, bad things will happen. If we are lucky, the game might continue to function properly after lurching forward many seconds in a single frame. Worse, the game might just crash.

A simple approach can be used to get around this problem. In the main game loop, if we ever measure a frame time in excess of some predefined upper limit (e.g., 1/10 of a second), we can assume that we have just resumed execution after a break point, and we set the delta time artificially to 1/30 or 1/60 of a second (or whatever the target frame rate is). In effect, the game becomes frame-locked for one frame, in order to avoid a massive spike in the measured frame duration.

```
// Start off assuming the ideal dt (30 FPS).
F32 dt = 1.0f / 30.0f;

// Prime the pump by reading the current time.
U64 tBegin = readHiResTimer();

while (true) // main game loop
{

    updateSubsystemA(dt);
    updateSubsystemB(dt);
    // ...
    renderScene();
    swapBuffers();

    // Read the current time again, and calculate an
    // estimate of next frame's delta time.
    U64 tEnd = readHiResTimer();
    dt = (F32)(tEnd - tBegin) / (F32)
            getHiResTimerFrequency();

    // If dt is too large, we must have resumed from a
    // break point -- frame-lock to the target rate this
    // frame.
    if (dt > 1.0f/10.0f)
    {
        dt = 1.0f/30.0f;
    }

    // Use tEnd as the new tBegin for next frame.
    tBegin = tEnd;
}
```

## 7.5.6.　A Simple Clock Class

Some game engines encapsulate their clock variables in a class. An engine might have a few instances of this class—one to represent real "wall clock" time, another to represent "game time" (which can be paused, slowed down or sped up relative to real time), another to track time for full-motion videos, and so on. A clock class is reasonably straightforward to implement. I'll present a simple implementation below, making note of a few common tips, tricks, and pitfalls in the process.

A clock class typically contains a variable that tracks the absolute time that has elapsed since the clock was created. As described above, it's important to select a suitable data type and time unit for this variable. In the following example, we'll store absolute times in the same way the CPU does—with a 64-bit unsigned integer, measured in machine cycles. There are other possible implementations, of course, but this is probably the simplest.

A clock class can support some nifty features, like time-scaling. This can be implemented by simply multiplying the measured time delta by an arbitrary scale factor prior to adding it to the clock's running total. We can also pause time by simply skipping its update while the clock is paused. Single-stepping a clock can be implemented by adding a fixed time interval to a paused clock in response to a button press on the joypad or keyboard. All of this is demonstrated by the example `Clock` class shown below.

```
class Clock
{
    U64        m_timeCycles;
    F32        m_timeScale;
    bool       m_isPaused;

    static F32     s_cyclesPerSecond;

    static inline U64 secondsToCycles(F32 timeSeconds)
    {
        return (U64)(timeSeconds * s_cyclesPerSecond);
    }

    // WARNING: Dangerous -- only use to convert small
    // durations into seconds.
    static inline F32 cyclesToSeconds(U64 timeCycles)
    {
        return (F32)timeCycles / s_cyclesPerSecond;
    }
```

```cpp
public:
    // Call this when the game first starts up.
    static void init()
    {
        s_cyclesPerSecond
            = (F32)readHiResTimerFrequency();
    }

    // Construct a clock.
    explicit Clock(F32 startTimeSeconds = 0.0f) :
        m_timeCycles(secondsToCycles(startTimeSeconds)),
        m_timeScale(1.0f), // default to unscaled
        m_isPaused(false)  // default to running
    {
    }

    // Return the current time in cycles. NOTE that we do
    // not return absolute time measurements in floating
    // point seconds, because a 32-bit float doesn't have
    // enough precision. See calcDeltaSeconds().
    U64 getTimeCycles() const
    {
        return m_timeCycles;
    }

    // Determine the difference between this clock's
    // absolute time and that of another clock, in
    // seconds. We only return time deltas as floating
    // point seconds, due to the precision limitations of
    // a 32-bit float.
    F32 calcDeltaSeconds(const Clock& other)
    {
        U64 dt = m_timeCycles - other.m_timeCycles;
        return cyclesToSeconds(dt);
    }

    // This function should be called once per frame,
    // with the real measured frame time delta in seconds.
    void update(F32 dtRealSeconds)
    {
        if (!m_isPaused)
        {
            U64 dtScaledCycles
                = secondsToCycles(
                    dtRealSeconds * m_timeScale);

            m_timeCycles += dtScaledCycles;
        }
    }
```

```
void setPaused(bool isPaused)
{
    m_isPaused = isPaused;
}

bool isPaused() const
{
    return m_isPaused;
}

void setTimeScale(F32 scale)
{
    m_timeScale = scale;
}

F32 getTimeScale() const
{
    return m_timeScale;
}

void singleStep()
{
    if (m_isPaused)
    {
        // Add one ideal frame interval; don't forget
        // to scale it by our current time scale!
        U64 dtScaledCycles = secondsToCycles(
            (1.0f/30.0f) * m_timeScale);

        m_timeCycles += dtScaledCycles;
    }
}
};
```

## 7.6.   Multiprocessor Game Loops

Now that we've investigated basic single-threaded game loops and learned some of the ways in which time is commonly measured and manipulated in a game engine, let's turn our attention to some more complex kinds of game loops. In this section, we'll explore how game loops have evolved to take advantage of modern multiprocessor hardware. In the following section, we'll see how networked multiplayer games typically structure their game loops.

In 2004, microprocessor manufacturers industry-wide encountered a problem with heat dissipation that prevented them from producing faster

CPUs. Moore's Law, which predicts an approximate doubling in transistor counts every 18 to 24 months, still holds true. But in 2004, its assumed correlation with doubling processor speeds was shown to be no longer valid. As a result, microprocessor manufacturers shifted their focus toward multicore CPUs. (For more information on this trend, see Microsoft's "The Manycore Shift Whitepaper," available at http://www.microsoftpost.com/ microsoft-download/the-manycore-shift-white-paper, and "Multicore Eroding Moore's Law" by Dean Dauger, available at http://www.macresearch. org/multicore_eroding_moores_law.) The net effect on the software industry was a major shift toward parallel processing techniques. As a result, modern game engines running on multicore systems like the Xbox 360 and the PLAYSTATION 3 can no longer rely on a single main game loop to service their subsystems.

The shift from single core to multicore has been painful. Multithreaded program design is a lot harder than single-threaded programming. Most game companies took on the transformation gradually, by selecting a handful of engine subsystems for parallelization, and leaving the rest under the control of the old, single-threaded main loop. By 2008, most game studios had completed the transformation for the most part and have embraced parallelism to varying degrees within their engines.

We don't have room here for a full treatise on parallel programming architectures and techniques. (Refer to [20] for an in-depth discussion of this topic.) However, we will take a brief look at some of the most common ways in which game engines leverage multicore hardware. There are many different software architectures possible—but the goal of all of these architectures is to maximize hardware utilization (i.e., to attempt to minimize the amount of time during which any particular hardware thread, core or CPU is idle).

## 7.6.1. Multiprocessor Game Console Architectures

The Xbox 360 and the PLAYSTATION 3 are both multiprocessor consoles. In order to have a meaningful discussion of parallel software architectures, let's take a brief look at how these two consoles are structured internally.

### 7.6.1.1. Xbox 360

The Xbox 360 consists of three identical PowerPC processor cores. Each core has a dedicated L1 instruction cache and L1 data cache, and the three cores share a single L2 cache. The three cores and the GPU share a unified 512 MB pool of RAM, which can be used for executable code, application data, textures, video RAM—you name it. The Xbox 360 architecture is described in

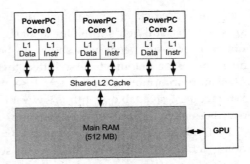

Figure 7.4. A simplified view of the Xbox 360 hardware architecture.

a great deal more depth in the PowerPoint presentation entitled "Xbox 360 System Architecture," by Jeff Andrews and Nick Baker of the Xbox Semiconductor Technology Group, available at http://www.hotchips.org/archives/ hc17/3_Tue/HC17.S8/HC17.S8T4.pdf. However, the preceding extremely brief overview should suffice for our purposes. Figure 7.4 shows the Xbox 360's architecture in highly simplified form.

### 7.6.1.2.    PLAYSTATION 3

The PLAYSTATION 3 hardware makes use of the Cell Broadband Engine (CBE) architecture (see Figure 7.5), developed jointly by Sony, Toshiba, and IBM. The PS3 takes a radically different approach to the one employed by the Xbox 360. Instead of three identical processors, it contains a number of different types of processors, each designed for specific tasks. And instead of a unified memory architecture, the PS3 divides its RAM into a number of blocks, each of which is designed for efficient use by certain processing units in the system. The architecture is described in detail at http://www.blachford.info/ computer/Cell/Cell1_v2.html, but the following overview and the diagram shown in Figure 7.5 should suffice for our purposes.

The PS3's main CPU is called the Power Processing Unit (PPU). It is a PowerPC processor, much like the ones found in the Xbox 360. In addition to this central processor, the PS3 has six coprocessors known as Synergistic Processing Units (SPUs). These coprocessors are based around the PowerPC instruction set, but they have been streamlined for maximum performance.

The GPU on the PS3 has a dedicated 256 MB of video RAM. The PPU has access to 256 MB of system RAM. In addition, each SPU has a dedicated high-speed 256 kB RAM area called its *local store* (LS). Local store memory performs about as efficiently as an L1 cache, making the SPUs blindingly fast.

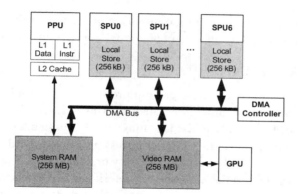

Figure 7.5. Simplified view of the PS3's cell broadband architecture.

The SPUs never read directly from main RAM. Instead, a direct memory access (DMA) controller allows blocks of data to be copied back and forth between system RAM and the SPUs' local stores. These data transfers happen in parallel, so both the PPU and SPUs can be doing useful calculations while they wait for data to arrive.

## 7.6.2. SIMD

As we saw in Section 4.7, most modern CPUs (including the Xbox 360's three PowerPC processors, and the PS3's PPU and SPUs) provide a class of instructions known as *single instruction, multiple data* (SIMD). Such instructions can perform a particular operation on more than one piece of data simultaneously, and as such they represent a fine-grained form of hardware parallelism. CPUs provide a number of different SIMD instruction variants, but by far the most commonly-used in games are instructions that operate on four 32-bit floating-point values in parallel, because they allow 3D vector and matrix math to be performed four times more quickly than with their *single instruction, single data* (SISD) counterparts.

Retrofitting existing 3D math code to leverage SIMD instructions can be tricky, although the task is much easier if a well-encapsulated 3D math library was used in the original code. For example, if a dot product is calculated in long hand everywhere (e.g., `float d = a.x * b.x + a.y * b.y + a.z * b.z;`), then a very large amount of code will need to be re-written. However, if dot products are calculated by calling a function (e.g., `float d = Dot(a, b);`), and if vectors are treated largely as black boxes throughout the code base, then retrofitting for SIMD can be accomplished by modifying the

3D math library, without having to modify much if any of the calling code
(except perhaps to ensure alignment of vector data to 16-byte boundaries).

### 7.6.3. Fork and Join

Another way to utilize multicore or multiprocessor hardware is to adapt divide-and-conquer algorithms for parallelism. This is often called the *fork/join*
approach. The basic idea is to divide a unit of work into smaller subunits, dis-
tribute these workloads onto multiple processing cores or hardware threads
(fork), and then merge the results once all workloads have been completed
(join). When applied to the game loop, the fork/join architecture results in a
main loop that looks very similar to its single-threaded counterpart, but with
some of the major phases of the update loop being parallelized. This architecture is illustrated in Figure 7.6.

Let's take a look at a concrete example. Blending animations using linear
interpolation (LERP) is an operation that can be done on each joint independently of all other joints within a skeleton (see Section 11.5.2.2). We'll assume
that we want to blend pairs of skeletal poses for five characters, each of which
has 100 joints, meaning that we need to process 500 pairs of joint poses.

To parallelize this task, we can divide the work into $N$ batches, each containing roughly $500/N$ joint-pose pairs, where $N$ is selected based on the avail-

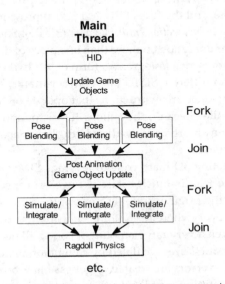

Figure 7.6. Fork and join used to parallelize selected CPU-intensive phases of the game loop.

able processing resources. (On the Xbox 360, $N$ should probably be 3 or 6, because the console has three cores with two hardware threads each. On a PS3, $N$ might range anywhere from 1 to 6, depending on how many SPUs are available.) We then "fork" (i.e., create) $N$ threads, requesting each one to work on a different group of pose pairs. The main thread can either continue doing some useful but work that is independent of the animation blending task, or it can go to sleep, waiting on a semaphore that will tell it when all of the worker threads have completed their tasks. Finally, we "join" the individual resultant joint poses into a cohesive whole—in this case, by calculating the final global pose of each of our five skeletons. (The global pose calculation needs access to the local poses of all the joints in each skeleton, so it doesn't parallelize well within a single skeleton. However, we could imagine forking again to calculate the global pose, this time with each thread working on one or more whole skeletons.)

You can find sample code illustrating how to fork and join worker threads using Win32 system calls at http://msdn.microsoft.com/en-us/library/ms682516(VS.85).aspx.

## 7.6.4.  One Thread per Subsystem

Yet another approach to multitasking is to assign particular engine subsystems to run in separate threads. A master thread controls and synchronizes the operations of these secondary subsystem threads and also continues to handle the lion's share of the game's high-level logic (the main game loop). On a hardware platform with multiple physical CPUs or hardware threads, this design allows these threaded engine subsystems to execute in parallel. This design is well suited to any engine subsystem that performs a relatively isolated function repeatedly, such as a rendering engine, physics simulation, animation pipeline, or audio engine. The architecture is depicted in Figure 7.7.

Threaded architectures are usually supported by some kind of thread library on the target hardware system. On a personal computer running Windows, the Win32 thread API is usually used. On a UNIX-based system, a library like *pthreads* might be the best choice. On the PLAYSTATION 3, a library known as SPURS permits workloads to be run on the six synergistic processing units (SPUs). SPURS provides two primary ways to run code on the SPUs—the *task model* and the *job model*. The task model can be used to segregate engine subsystems into coarse-grained independent units of execution that act very much like threads. We'll discuss the SPURS job model in the next section.

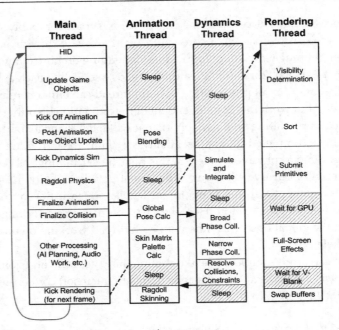

**Figure 7.7.** One thread per major engine subsystem.

## 7.6.5. Jobs

One problem with the multithreaded approach is that each thread represents a relatively coarse-grained chunk of work (e.g., all animation tasks are in one thread, all collision and physics tasks in another). This can place restrictions on how the various processors in the system can be utilized. If one of the subsystem threads has not completed its work, the progress of other threads, including that of the main game loop, may be blocked.

Another way to take advantage of parallel hardware architecture is to divide up the work that is done by the game engine into multiple small, relatively independent *jobs*. A job is best thought of as a pairing between a chunk of data and a bit of code that operates on that data. When a job is ready to be run, it is placed on a queue, to be picked up and worked on by the next available processing unit. This approach is supported on the PLAYSTATION 3 via the SPURS *job model*. The main game loop runs on the PPU, and the six SPUs are used as job processors. Each job's code and data are sent to an SPU's local store via a DMA transfer. The SPU processes the job, and then it DMAs its results back to main RAM.

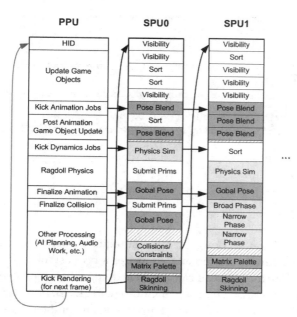

**Figure** 7.8. In a job architecture, work is broken down into fine-grained chunks that can be picked up by any available processor. This can help maximize processor utilization, while providing the main game loop with improved flexibility.

As shown in Figure 7.8, the fact that jobs are relatively fine-grained and independent of one another helps to maximize processor utilization. It can also reduce or eliminate some of the restrictions placed on the main thread in the one-thread-per-subsystem design. This architecture also scales up or down naturally to hardware with any number of processing units (something the one-thread-per-subsystem architecture does not do particularly well).

## 7.6.6. Asynchronous Program Design

When writing or retrofitting a game engine to take advantage of multitasking hardware, programmers must be careful to design their code in an asynchronous manner. This means that the results of an operation will usually not be available immediately after requesting it, as they would be in a synchronous design. For example, a game might request that a ray be cast into the world, in order to determine whether the player has line-of-sight to an enemy character. In a synchronous design, the ray cast would be done immediately in response to the request, and when the ray casting function returned, the results would be available, as shown below.

```
while (true) // main game loop
{
    // ...

    // Cast a ray to see if the player has line of sight
    // to the enemy.
    RayCastResult r = castRay(playerPos, enemyPos);

    // Now process the results...
    if (r.hitSomething() && isEnemy(r.getHitObject()))
    {
        // Player can see the enemy.
        // ...
    }

    // ...
}
```

In an asynchronous design, a ray cast request would be made by calling a function that simply sets up and enqueues a ray cast job, and then returns immediately. The main thread can continue doing other unrelated work while the job is being processed by another CPU or core. Later, once the job has been completed, the main thread can pick up the results of the ray cast query and process them:

```
while (true) // main game loop
{
    // ...

    // Cast a ray to see if the player has line of sight
    // to the enemy.
    RayCastResult r;
    requestRayCast(playerPos, enemyPos, &r);

    // Do other unrelated work while we wait for the
    // other CPU to perform the ray cast for us.

    // ...

    // OK, we can't do any more useful work. Wait for the
    // results of our ray cast job. If the job is
    // complete, this function will return immediately.
    // Otherwise, the main thread will idle until they
    // are ready...
    waitForRayCastResults(&r);

    // Process results...
    if (r.hitSomething() && isEnemy(r.getHitObject()))
    {
        // Player can see the enemy.
        // ...
    }
```

```
    // ...
}
```

In many instances, asynchronous code can kick off a request on one frame, and pick up the results on the next. In this case, you may see code that looks like this:

```
RayCastResult r;
bool rayJobPending = false;

while (true) // main game loop
{

    // ...

    // Wait for the results of last frame's ray cast job.
    if (rayJobPending)
    {
        waitForRayCastResults(&r);

        // Process results...
        if (r.hitSomething() && isEnemy(r.getHitObject()))
        {
            // Player can see the enemy.
            // ...
        }
    }

    // Cast a new ray for next frame.
    rayJobPending = true;
    requestRayCast(playerPos, enemyPos, &r);

    // Do other work...

    // ...
}
```

## 7.7.  Networked Multiplayer Game Loops

The game loop of a networked multiplayer game is particularly interesting, so we'll have a brief look at how such loops are structured. We don't have room here to go into the all of the details of how multiplayer games work. (Refer to [3] for an excellent in-depth discussion of the topic.) However, we'll provide a brief overview of the two most-common multiplayer architectures here, and then look at how these architectures affect the structure of the game loop.

## 7.7.1. Client-Server

In the *client-server* model, the vast majority of the game's logic runs on a single server machine. Hence the server's code closely resembles that of a non-networked single-player game. Multiple client machines can connect to the server in order to take part in the online game. The client is basically a "dumb" rendering engine that also reads human interface devices and controls the local player character, but otherwise simply renders whatever the server tells it to render. Great pains are taken in the client code to ensure that the inputs of the local human player are immediately translated into the actions of the player's character on-screen. This avoids what would otherwise be an extremely annoying sense of delayed reaction on the part of the player character. But other than this so-called *player prediction* code, the client is usually not much more than a rendering and audio engine, combined with some networking code.

The server may be running on a dedicated machine, in which case we say it is running in *dedicated server* mode. However, the client and server needn't be on separate machines, and in fact it is quite typical for one of the client machines to also be running the server. In fact, in many client-server multiplayer games, the single-player game mode is really just a degenerate multiplayer game, in which there is only one client, and both the client and server are running on the same machine. This is known as *client-on-top-of-server* mode.

The game loop of a client-server multiplayer game can be implemented in a number of different ways. Since the client and server are conceptually separate entities, they could be implemented as entirely separate processes (i.e., separate applications). They could also be implemented as two separate threads of execution, within a single process. However, both of these approaches require quite a lot of overhead to permit the client and server to communicate locally, when being run in client-on-top-of-server mode. As a result, a lot of multiplayer games run both client and server in a single thread, serviced by a single game loop.

It's important to realize that the client and server code can be updated at different rates. For example, in *Quake,* the server runs at 20 FPS (50 ms per frame), while the client typically runs at 60 FPS (16.6 ms per frame). This is implemented by running the main game loop at the faster of the two rates (60 FPS) and then servicing the server code once roughly every three frames. In reality, the amount of time that has elapsed since the last server update is tracked, and when it reaches or exceeds 50 ms, a server frame is run and the timer is reset. Such a game loop might look something like this:

```
F32 dtReal = 1.0f/30.0f; // the real frame delta time
F32 dtServer = 0.0f;      // the server's delta time
```

```
U64 tBegin = readHiResTimer();

while (true) // main game loop
{
    // Run the server at 50 ms intervals.
    dtServer += dtReal;

    if (dtServer >= 0.05f) // 50 ms
    {
        runServerFrame(0.05f);
        dtServer -= 0.05f;  // reset for next update
    }

    // Run the client at maximum frame rate.
    runClientFrame(dtReal);

    // Read the current time, and calculate an estimate
    // of next frame's real delta time.
    U64 tEnd = readHiResTimer();
    dtReal   = (F32)(tEnd - tBegin)
             / (F32)getHiResTimerFrequency();

    // Use tEnd as the new tBegin for next frame.
    tBegin = tEnd;
}
```

### 7.7.2. Peer-to-Peer

In the *peer-to-peer* multiplayer architecture, every machine in the online game acts somewhat like a server, and somewhat like a client. One and only one machine has authority over each dynamic object in the game. So each machine acts like a server for those objects over which it has authority. For all other objects in the game world, the machine acts like a client, rendering the objects in whatever state is provided to it by that object's remote authority.

The structure of a peer-to-peer multiplayer game loop is much simpler than a client-server game loop, in that at the top-most level, it looks very much like a single-player game loop. However, the internal details of the code can be a bit more confusing. In a client-server model, it is usually quite clear which code is running on the server and which code is client-side. But in a peer-to-peer architecture, much of the code needs to be set up to handle two possible cases: one in which the local machine has authority over the state of an object in the game, and one in which the object is just a dumb proxy for a remote authoritative representation. These two modes of operation are often implemented by having two kinds of game objects—a full-fledged "real" game object, over which the local machine has authority and a "proxy" version that contains a minimal subset of the state of the remote object.

Peer-to-peer architectures are made even more complex because authority over an object sometimes needs to migrate from machine to machine. For example, if one computer drops out of the game, all of the objects over which it had authority must be picked up by the other machines in the game. Likewise, when a new machine joins the game, it should ideally take over authority of some game objects from other machines, in order to balance the load. The details are beyond the scope of this book. The key point here is that multiplayer architectures can have profound effects on the structure of a game's main loop.

### 7.7.3. Case Study: *Quake II*

The following is an excerpt from the *Quake II* game loop. The source code for *Quake*, *Quake II*, and *Quake 3 Arena* is available on Id Software's website, http://www.idsoftware.com. As you can see, all of the elements we've discussed are present, including the Windows message pump (in the Win32 version of the game), calculation of the real frame delta time, fixed-time and time-scaled modes of operation, and servicing of both server-side and client-side engine systems.

```
int WINAPI WinMain (HINSTANCE hInstance,
                    HINSTANCE hPrevInstance,
                    LPSTR lpCmdLine, int nCmdShow)
{
    MSG         msg;
    int         time, oldtime, newtime;
    char        *cddir;

    ParseCommandLine (lpCmdLine);

    Qcommon_Init (argc, argv);
    oldtime = Sys_Milliseconds ();

    /* main window message loop */
    while (1)
    {
        // Windows message pump.
        while (PeekMessage (&msg, NULL, 0, 0,
            PM_NOREMOVE))
        {
            if (!GetMessage (&msg, NULL, 0, 0))
                Com_Quit ();
            sys_msg_time = msg.time;
```

```
            TranslateMessage (&msg);
            DispatchMessage (&msg);
        }

        // Measure real delta time in milliseconds.
        do
        {
            newtime = Sys_Milliseconds ();
            time = newtime - oldtime;
        } while (time < 1);

        // Run a frame of the game.
        Qcommon_Frame (time);

        oldtime = newtime;
    }

    // never gets here
    return TRUE;
}

void Qcommon_Frame (int msec)
{
    char    *s;
    int     time_before, time_between, time_after;

    // [some details omitted...]

    // Handle fixed-time mode and time scaling.
    if (fixedtime->value)
        msec = fixedtime->value;
    else if (timescale->value)
    {
        msec *= timescale->value;
        if (msec < 1)
            msec = 1;
    }

    // Service the in-game console.
    do
    {
        s = Sys_ConsoleInput ();
        if (s)
            Cbuf_AddText (va("%s\n",s));
    } while (s);
    Cbuf_Execute ();
```

```
                    // Run a server frame.
                    SV_Frame (msec);

                    // Run a client frame.
                    CL_Frame (msec);

                    // [some details omitted...]
                }
```

# 8

# Human Interface
# Devices (HID)

Games are interactive computer simulations, so the human player(s) need some way of providing inputs to the game. All sorts of *human interface devices* (HID) exist for gaming, including joysticks, joypads, keyboards and mice, track balls, the Wii remote, and specialized input devices like steering wheels, fishing rods, dance pads, and even electric guitars. In this chapter, we'll investigate how game engines typically read, process, and utilize the inputs from human interface devices. We'll also have a look at how outputs from these devices provide feedback to the human player.

## 8.1. Types of Human Interface Devices

A wide range of human interface devices are available for gaming purposes. Consoles like the Xbox 360 and PS3 come equipped with joypad controllers, as shown in Figure 8.1. Nintendo's Wii console is well known for its unique and innovative WiiMote controller, shown in Figure 8.2. PC games are generally either controlled via a keyboard and the mouse, or via a joypad. (Microsoft designed the Xbox 360 joypad so that it can be used both on the Xbox 360 and on Windows/DirectX PC platforms.) As shown in Figure 8.3, arcade machines have one or more built-in controllers, such as a joystick and various buttons, or a track ball, a steering wheel, etc. An arcade machine's input device is usually

**Figure 8.1.** Standard joypads for the Xbox 360 and PLAYSTATION 3 consoles.

**Figure 8.2.** The innovative WiiMote for the Nintendo Wii.

**Figure 8.3.** Various custom input devices for the arcade game *Mortal Kombat II* by Midway.

**Figure 8.4.** Many specialized input devices are available for use with consoles.

**Figure 8.5.** Steering wheel adapter for the Nintendo Wii.

somewhat customized to the game in question, although input hardware is often re-used among arcade machines produced by the same manufacturer.

On console platforms, specialized input devices and adapters are usually available, in addition to the "standard" input device such as the joypad. For example, guitar and drum devices are available for the *Guitar Hero* series of games, steering wheels can be purchased for driving games, and games like *Dance Dance Revolution* use a special dance pad device. Some of these devices are shown in Figure 8.4.

The Nintendo WiiMote is one of the most flexible input devices on the market today. As such, it is often adapted to new purposes, rather than re-placed with an entirely new device. For example, *Mario Kart Wii* comes with a pastic steering wheel adapter into which the WiiMote can be inserted (see Figure 8.5).

## 8.2. Interfacing with a HID

All human interface devices provide input to the game software, and some also allow the software to provide feedback to the human player via various kinds of outputs as well. Game software reads and writes HID inputs and outputs in various ways, depending on the specific design of the device in question.

### 8.2.1. Polling

Some simple devices, like game pads and old-school joysticks, are read by *polling* the hardware periodically (usually once per iteration of the main game loop). This means explicitly querying the state of the device, either by read-ing hardware registers directly, reading a memory-mapped I/O port, or via a higher-level software interface (which, in turn, reads the appropriate registers or memory-mapped I/O ports). Likewise, outputs might be sent to the HID by writing to special registers or memory-mapped I/O addresses, or via a higher-level API that does our dirty work for us.

Microsoft's XInput API, for use with Xbox 360 game pads on both the Xbox 360 and Windows PC platforms, is a good example of a simple polling mechanism. Every frame, the game calls the function `XInputGetState()`. This function communicates with the hardware and/or drivers, reads the data in the appropriate way, and packages it all up for convenient use by the software. It returns a pointer to an `XINPUT_STATE` struct, which in turn contains an embedded instance of a struct called `XINPUT_GAMEPAD`. This struct contains the current states of all of the controls (buttons, thumb sticks, and triggers) on the device.

### 8.2.2.  Interrupts

Some HIDs only send data to the game engine when the state of the controller changes in some way. For example, a mouse spends a lot of its time just sitting still on the mouse pad. There's no reason to send a continuous stream of data between the mouse and the computer when the mouse isn't moving—we need only transmit information when it moves, or a button is pressed or released.

This kind of device usually communicates with the host computer via *hardware interrupts*. An interrupt is an electronic signal generated by the hardware, which causes the CPU to temporarily suspend execution of the main program and run a small chunk of code called an *interrupt service routine* (ISR). Interrupts are used for all sorts of things, but in the case of a HID, the ISR code will probably read the state of the device, store it off for later processing, and then relinquish the CPU back to the main program. The game engine can pick up the data the next time it is convenient to do so.

### 8.2.3.  Wireless Devices

The inputs and outputs of a Bluetooth device, like the WiiMote, the DualShock 3 and the Xbox 360 wireless controller, cannot be read and written by simply accessing registers or memory-mapped I/O ports. Instead, the software must "talk" to the device via the Bluetooth protocol. The software can request the HID to send input data (such as the states of its buttons) back to the host, or it can send output data (such as rumble settings or a stream of audio data) to the device. This communication is often handled by a thread separate from the game engine's main loop, or at least encapsulated behind a relatively simple interface that can be called from the main loop. So from the point of view of the game programmer, the state of a Bluetooth device can be made to look pretty much indistinguishable from a traditional polled device.

# 8.3.  Types of Inputs

Although human interface devices for games vary widely in terms of form factor and layout, most of the inputs they provide fall into one of a small number of categories. We'll investigate each category in depth below.

## 8.3.1.  Digital Buttons

Almost every HID has at least a few *digital buttons*. These are buttons that can only be in one of two states: *pressed* and *not pressed*. Game programmers often refer to a pressed button as being *down* and a non-pressed button as being *up*.

Electrical engineers speak of a circuit containing a switch as being *closed* (meaning electricity is flowing through the circuit) or *open* (no electricity is flowing—the circuit has infinite *resistance*). Whether *closed* corresponds to *pressed* or *not pressed* depends on the hardware. If the switch is *normally open*, then when it is not pressed (up), the circuit is *open*, and when it is pressed (down), the circuit is *closed*. If the switch is *normally closed*, the reverse is true— the act of pressing the button opens the circuit.

In software, the state of a digital button (pressed or not pressed) is usually represented by a single bit. It's common for 0 to represent not pressed (up) and 1 to represent pressed (down). But again, depending on the nature of the circuitry, and the decisions made by the programmers who wrote the device driver, the sense of these values might be reversed.

It is quite common for the states of all of the buttons on a device to be packed into a single unsigned integer value. For example, in Microsoft's XInput API, the state of the Xbox 360 joypad is returned in a struct called XINPUT_GAMEPAD, shown below.

```
typedef struct _XINPUT_GAMEPAD {
    WORD   wButtons;
    BYTE   bLeftTrigger;
    BYTE   bRightTrigger;

    SHORT sThumbLX;

    SHORT sThumbLY;

    SHORT sThumbRX;
    SHORT sThumbRY;
} XINPUT_GAMEPAD;
```

This struct contains a 16-bit unsigned integer (WORD) variable named wButtons that holds the state of all buttons. The following masks define which physical button corresponds to each bit in the word. (Note that bits 10 and 11 are unused.)

```
#define XINPUT_GAMEPAD_DPAD_UP              0x0001 // bit 0

#define XINPUT_GAMEPAD_DPAD_DOWN            0x0002 // bit 1

#define XINPUT_GAMEPAD_DPAD_LEFT            0x0004 // bit 2

#define XINPUT_GAMEPAD_DPAD_RIGHT           0x0008 // bit 3

#define XINPUT_GAMEPAD_START                0x0010 // bit 4

#define XINPUT_GAMEPAD_BACK                 0x0020 // bit 5

#define XINPUT_GAMEPAD_LEFT_THUMB           0x0040 // bit 6

#define XINPUT_GAMEPAD_RIGHT_THUMB          0x0080 // bit 7

#define XINPUT_GAMEPAD_LEFT_SHOULDER        0x0100 // bit 8

#define XINPUT_GAMEPAD_RIGHT_SHOULDER       0x0200 // bit 9

#define XINPUT_GAMEPAD_A                    0x1000 // bit 12

#define XINPUT_GAMEPAD_B                    0x2000 // bit 13

#define XINPUT_GAMEPAD_X                    0x4000 // bit 14

#define XINPUT_GAMEPAD_Y                    0x8000 // bit 15
```

An individual button's state can be read by masking the wButtons word with the appropriate bit mask via C/C++'s bitwise AND operator (&) and then checking if the result is non-zero. For example, to determine if the A button is pressed (down), we would write:

```
bool IsButtonADown(const XINPUT_GAMEPAD& pad)
{
    // Mask off all bits but bit 12 (the A button).
    return ((pad.wButtons & XINPUT_GAMEPAD_A) != 0);
}
```

### 8.3.2. Analog Axes and Buttons

An *analog input* is one that can take on a range of values (rather than just 0 or 1). These kinds of inputs are often used to represent the degree to which a trigger is pressed, or the two-dimensional position of a joystick (which is represented using two analog inputs, one for the *x*-axis and one for the *y*-axis,

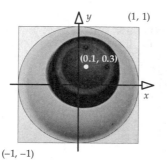

**Figure 8.6.** Two analog inputs can be used to represent the *x* and *y* deflection of a joystick.

as shown in Figure 8.6). Because of this common usage, analog inputs are sometimes called *analog axes*, or just *axes*.

On some devices, certain buttons are analog as well, meaning that the game can actually detect how hard the player is pressing on them. However, the signals produced by analog buttons are usually too noisy to be particularly usable. I have yet to see a game that uses analog button inputs effectively (although some may very well exist!)

Strictly speaking, analog inputs are not really analog by the time they make it to the game engine. An analog input signal is usually *digitized*, meaning it is quantized and represented using an integer in software. For example, an analog input might range from –32,768 to 32,767 if represented by a 16-bit signed integer. Sometimes analog inputs are converted to floating-point—the values might range from –1 to 1, for instance. But as we know from Section 3.2.1.3, floating-point numbers are really just quantized digital values as well.

Reviewing the definition of XINPUT_GAMEPAD (repeated below), we can see that Microsoft chose to represent the deflections of the left and right thumb sticks on the Xbox 360 gamepad using 16-bit signed integers (sThumbLX and sThumbLY for the left stick and sThumbRX and sThumbRY for the right). Hence, these values range from –32,768 (left or down) to 32,767 (right or up). However, to represent the positions of the left and right shoulder triggers, Microsoft chose to use 8-bit unsigned integers (bLeftTrigger and bRight-Trigger respectively). These input values range from 0 (not pressed) to 255 (fully pressed). Different game machines use different digital representations for their analog axes.

```
typedef struct _XINPUT_GAMEPAD {
    WORD   wButtons;
```

```
                    // 8-bit unsigned
             BYTE    bLeftTrigger;
             BYTE    bRightTrigger;

                    // 16-bit signed
             SHORT   sThumbLX;
             SHORT   sThumbLY;

             SHORT   sThumbRX;
             SHORT   sThumbRY;
         } XINPUT_GAMEPAD;
```

### 8.3.3. Relative Axes

The position of an analog button, trigger, joystick, or thumb stick is *absolute*, meaning that there is a clear understanding of where zero lies. However, the inputs of some devices are *relative*. For these devices, there is no clear location at which the input value should be zero. Instead, a zero input indicates that the position of the device has not changed, while non-zero values represent a delta from the last time the input value was read. Examples include mice, mouse wheels, and track balls.

### 8.3.4. Accelerometers

The PLAYSTATION 3's Sixaxis and DualShock 3 joypads, and the Nintendo WiiMote, all contain acceleration sensors (accelerometers). These devices can detect acceleration along the three principle axes ($x$, $y$, and $z$), as shown in Figure 8.7. These are *relative* analog inputs, much like a mouse's two-dimensional axes. When the controller is not accelerating these inputs are zero, but when the controller is accelerating, they measure the acceleration up to $\pm 3$ g along each axis, quantized into three signed 8-bit integers, one for each of $x$, $y$, and $z$.

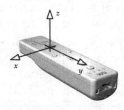

Figure 8.7. Accelerometer axes for the WiiMote.

### 8.3.5.  3D Orientation with the WiiMote or Sixaxis

Some Wii and PS3 games make use of the three accelerometers in the WiiMote or Sixaxis joypad to estimate the orientation of the controller in the player's hand. For example, in *Super Mario Galaxy*, Mario hops onto a large ball and rolls it around with his feet. To control Mario in this mode, the WiiMote is held with the IR sensor facing the ceiling. Tilting the WiiMote left, right, forward, or back causes the ball to accelerate in the corresponding direction.

A trio of accelerometers can be used to detect the orientation of the WiiMote or Sixaxis joypad, because of the fact that we are playing these games on the surface of the Earth where there is a constant downward acceleration due to gravity of 1g ($\approx 9.8$ m/s$^2$). If the controller is held perfectly level, with the IR sensor pointing toward your TV set, the vertical ($z$) acceleration should be approximately $-1$ g.

If the controller is held upright, with the IR sensor pointing toward the ceiling, we would expect to see a 0 g acceleration on the $z$ sensor, and +1 g on the $y$ sensor (because it is now experiencing the full gravitational effect). Holding the WiiMote at a 45-degree angle should produce roughly $\sin(45°) = \cos(45°) = 0.707$ g on both the $y$ and $z$ inputs. Once we've calibrated the accelerometer inputs to find the zero points along each axis, we can calculate pitch, yaw, and roll easily, using inverse sine and cosine operations.

Two caveats here: First, if the person holding the WiiMote is not holding it still, the accelerometer inputs will include this acceleration in their values, invalidating our math. Second, the $z$-axis of the accelerometer has been calibrated to account for gravity, but the other two axes have not. This means that the $z$-axis has less precision available for detecting orientation. Many Wii games request that the user hold the WiiMote in a non-standard orientation, such as with the buttons facing the player's chest, or with the IR sensor pointing toward the ceiling. This maximizes the precision of the orientation reading, by placing the $x$- or $y$-accelerometer axis in line with gravity, instead of the gravity-calibrated $z$- axis. For more information on this topic, see http://druid.caughq.org/presentations/turbo/Wiimote-Hacking.pdf and http://www.wiili.org/index.php/Motion_analysis.

## 8.3.6. Cameras

The WiiMote has a unique feature not found on any other standard console HID—an infrared (IR) sensor. This sensor is essentially a low-resolution camera that records a two-dimension infrared image of whatever the WiiMote is pointed at. The Wii comes with a "sensor bar" that sits on top of your television set and contains two infrared light emitting diodes (LEDs). In the image recorded by the IR camera, these LEDs appear as two bright dots on an otherwise dark background. Image processing software in the WiiMote analyzes the image and isolates the location and size of the two dots. (Actually, it can detect and transmit the locations and sizes of up to four dots.) This position

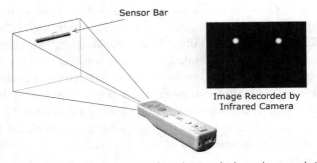

Sensor Bar

Image Recorded by
Infrared Camera

**Figure 8.8.** The Wii sensor bar houses two infrared LEDs which produce two bright spots on the image recorded by the WiiMote's IR camera.

and size information can be read by the console via a Bluetooth wireless connection.

The position and orientation of the line segment formed by the two dots can be used to determine the pitch, yaw, and roll of the WiiMote (as long as it is being pointed toward the sensor bar). By looking at the separation between the dots, software can also determine how close or far away the WiiMote is from the TV. Some software also makes use of the sizes of the dots. This is illustrated in Figure 8.8.

Another popular camera device is Sony's EyeToy for the PlayStation line of consoles, shown in Figure 8.9. This device is basically a high quality color camera, which can be used for a wide range of applications. It can be used for simple video conferencing, like any web cam. It could also conceivably be used much like the WiiMote's IR camera, for position, orientation, and depth sensing. The gamut of possibilities for these kinds of advanced input devices has only begun to be tapped by the gaming community.

**Figure 8.9.** Sony's Eye-Toy for the PlayStation3.

## 8.4.  Types of Outputs

Human interface devices are primarily used to transmit inputs from the player to the game software. However, some HIDs can also provide feedback to the human player via various kinds of outputs.

### 8.4.1.  Rumble

Game pads like the PlayStation's DualShock line of controllers and the Xbox and Xbox 360 controllers have a *rumble* feature. This allows the controller to vibrate in the player's hands, simulating the turbulence or impacts that the character in the game world might be experiencing. Vibrations are usually produced by one or more motors, each of which rotates a slightly unbalanced weight at various speeds. The game can turn these motors on and off, and control their speeds to produce different tactile effects in the player's hands.

### 8.4.2. Force-Feedback

Force feedback is a technique in which an actuator on the HID is driven by a motor in order to slightly resist the motion the human operator is trying to impart to it. It is common in arcade driving games, where the steering wheel resists the player's attempt to turn it, simulating difficult driving conditions or tight turns. As with rumble, the game software can typically turn the motor(s) on and off, and can also control the strength and direction of the forces applied to the actuator.

### 8.4.3. Audio

Audio is usually a stand-alone engine system. However, some HIDs provide outputs that can be utilized by the audio system. For example, the WiiMote contains a small, low-quality speaker. The Xbox 360 controller has a headset jack and can be used just like any USB audio device for both output (speakers) and input (microphone). One common use of USB headsets is for multiplayer games, in which human players can communicate with one another via a voice over IP (VOIP) connection.

### 8.4.4. Other Inputs and Outputs

Human interface devices may of course support many other kinds of inputs and outputs. On some older consoles like the Sega Dreamcast, the memory card slots were located on the game pad. The Xbox 360 game pad, the Sixaxis and DualShock 3, and the WiiMote all have four LEDs which can be illuminated by game software if desired. And of course specialized devices like musical instruments, dance pads, etc. have their own particular kinds of inputs and outputs.

Innovation is actively taking place in the field of human interfaces. Some of the most interesting areas today are gestural interfaces and thought-controlled devices. We can certainly expect more innovation from console and HID manufacturers in years to come.

## 8.5.   Game Engine HID Systems

Most game engines don't use "raw" HID inputs directly. The data is usually massaged in various ways to ensure that the inputs coming from the HID translate into smooth, pleasing, intuitive behaviors in-game. In addition, most engines introduce at least one additional level of indirection between the HID and the game in order to abstract HID inputs in various ways. For example, a button-mapping table might be used to translate raw button inputs into logical game actions, so that human players can re-assign the buttons' functions as they see fit. In this section, we'll outline the typical requirements of a game engine HID system and then explore each one in some depth.

## 8.5.1. Typical Requirements

A game engine's HID system usually provides some or all of the following features:

- dead zones,
- analog signal filtering,
- event detection (e.g., button up, button down),
- detection of button *sequences* and multibutton combinations (known as *chords*),
- gesture detection,
- management of multiple HIDs for multiple players,
- multiplatform HID support,
- controller input re-mapping,
- context-sensitive inputs,
- the ability to temporarily disable certain inputs.

## 8.5.2. Dead Zone

A joystick, thumb stick, shoulder trigger, or any other analog axis produces input values that range between a predefined minimum and maximum value, which we'll call $I_{min}$ and $I_{max}$. When the control is not being touched, we would expect it to produce a steady and clear "undisturbed" value, which we'll call $I_0$. The undisturbed value is usually numerically equal to zero, and it either lies half-way between $I_{min}$ and $I_{max}$ for a centered, two-way control like a joystick axis, or it coincides with $I_{min}$ for a one-way control like a trigger.

Unfortunately, because HIDs are analog devices by nature, the voltage produced by the device is noisy, and the actual inputs we observe may fluctuate slightly around $I_0$. The most common solution to this problem is to introduce a small *dead zone* around $I_0$. The dead zone might be defined as $[I_0 - \delta, I_0 + \delta]$ for a joy stick, or $[I_0, I_0 + \delta]$ for a trigger. Any input values that are within the dead zone are simply clamped to $I_0$. The dead zone must be wide enough to account for the noisiest inputs generated by an undisturbed control, but small enough not to interfere with the player's sense of the HID's responsiveness.

### 8.5.3.  Analog Signal Filtering

Signal noise is a problem even when the controls are not within their dead zones. This noise can sometimes cause the in-game behaviors controlled by the HID to appear jerky or unnatural. For this reason, many games *filter* the raw inputs coming from the HID. A noise signal is usually of a high-frequency, relative to the signal produced by the human player. Therefore, one solution is to pass the raw input data through a simple *low-pass filter*, prior to it being used by the game.

A discrete first-order low-pass filter can be implemented by combining the current unfiltered input value with last frame's filtered input. If we denote the sequence of unfiltered inputs by the time-varying function $u(t)$ and the filtered inputs by $f(t)$, where $t$ denotes time, then we can write

$$f(t) = (1-a)f(t-\Delta t) + au(t), \tag{8.1}$$

where the parameter $a$ is determined by the frame duration $\Delta t$ and a filtering constant $RC$ (which is just the product of the resistance and the capacitance in a traditional analog RC low-pass filter circuit):

$$a = \frac{\Delta t}{RC + \Delta t}. \tag{8.2}$$

This can be implemented trivially in C or C++ as follows, where it is assumed the calling code will keep track of last frame's filtered input for use on the subsequent frame. For more information, see http://en.wikipedia.org/wiki/Low-pass_filter.

```
F32 lowPassFilter(F32 unfilteredInput,
                  F32 lastFramesFilteredInput,
                  F32 rc, F32 dt)
{

    F32 a = dt / (rc + dt);

    return (1 - a) * lastFramesFilteredInput
           + a * unfilteredInput;
}
```

Another way to filter HID input data is to calculate a simple moving average. For example, if we wish to average the input data over a 3/30 second (3 frame) interval, we simply store the raw input values in a 3-element circular buffer. The filtered input value is then the sum of the values in this array at any moment, divided by 3. There are a few minor details to account for when implementing such a filter. For example, we need to properly handle the first two frames of input, during which the 3-element array has not yet been filled with valid data. However, the implementation is not particularly complicated. The code below shows one way to properly implement an *N*-element moving average.

```cpp
template< typename TYPE, int SIZE >
class MovingAverage
{
    TYPE        m_samples[SIZE];
    TYPE        m_sum;
    U32         m_curSample;
    U32         m_sampleCount;

public:
    MovingAverage() :
        m_sum(static_cast<TYPE>(0)),
        m_curSample(0),
        m_sampleCount(0)
    {
    }

    void addSample(TYPE data)
    {
        if (m_sampleCount == SIZE)
        {
            m_sum -= m_samples[m_curSample];
        }
        else
        {
            ++m_sampleCount;
        }

        m_samples[m_curSample] = data;
        m_sum += data;
        ++m_curSample;
        if (m_curSample >= SIZE)
        {

            m_curSample = 0;
        }
    }

    F32 getCurrentAverage() const
    {
```

```
            if (m_sampleCount != 0)
            {
                return static_cast<F32>(m_sum)
                    / static_cast<F32>(m_sampleCount);
            }
            return 0.0f;
        }
    };
```

## 8.5.4. Detecting Input Events

The low-level HID interface typically provides the game with the current states of the device's various inputs. However, games are often interested in detecting *events*, such as changes in state, rather than just inspecting the current state each frame. The most common HID events are probably button down (pressed) and button up (released), but of course we can detect other kinds of events as well.

### 8.5.4.1. Button Up and Button Down

Let's assume for the moment that our buttons' input bits are 0 when not pressed and 1 when pressed. The easiest way to detect a change in button state is to keep track of the buttons' state bits as observed last frame and compare them to the state bits observed this frame. If they differ, we know an event occurred. The current state of each button tells us whether the event is a button-up or a button-down.

We can use simple bit-wise operators to detect button-down and button-up events. Given a 32-bit word `buttonStates`, containing the current state bits of up to 32 buttons, we want to generate two new 32-bit words: one for button-down events which we'll call `buttonDowns` and one for button-up events which we'll call `buttonUps`. In both cases, the bit corresponding to each button will be 0 if the event has not occurred this frame and 1 if it has. To implement this, we also need last frame's button states, `prevButtonStates`.

The exclusive OR (XOR) operator produces a 0 if its two inputs are identical and a 1 if they differ. So if we apply the XOR operator to the previous and current button state words, we'll get 1's only for buttons whose states have changed between last frame and this frame. To determine whether the event is a button-up or a button-down, we need to look at the current state of each button. Any button whose state has changed that is currently down generates a button-down event, and vice-versa for button-up events. The following code applies these ideas in order to generate our two button event words:

```
class ButtonState
{

    U32 m_buttonStates;       // current frame's button
                              // states
    U32 m_prevButtonStates;   // previous frame's states

    U32 m_buttonDowns;        // 1 = button pressed this
                              // frame
    U32 m_buttonUps;          // 1 = button released this
                              // frame

    void DetectButtonUpDownEvents()
    {
        // Assuming that m_buttonStates and
        // m_prevButtonStates are valid, generate
        // m_buttonDowns and m_buttonUps.

        // First determine which bits have changed via
        // XOR.
        U32 buttonChanges = m_buttonStates
                          ^ m_prevButtonStates;

        // Now use AND to mask off only the bits that are
        // DOWN.
        m_buttonDowns = buttonChanges & m_buttonStates;

        // Use AND-NOT to mask off only the bits that are
        // UP.
        m_buttonUps = buttonChanges & (~m_buttonStates);
    }

    // ...
};
```

### 8.5.4.2. Chords

A *chord* is a group of buttons that, when pressed at the same time, produce a unique behavior in the game. Here are a few examples:

- *Super Mario Galaxy*'s start-up screen requires you to press the A and B buttons on the WiiMote together in order to start a new game.

- Pressing the 1 and 2 buttons on the WiiMote at the same time put it into Bluetooth discovery mode (no matter what game you're playing).

- The "grapple" move in many fighting games is triggered by a two-button combination.

- For development purposes, holding down both the left and right triggers on the DualShock 3 in *Uncharted: Drake's Fortune* allows the player character to fly anywhere in the game world, with collisions turned off. (Sorry, this doesn't work in the shipping game!) Many games have a cheat like this to make development easier. (It may or may not be triggered by a chord, of course.) It is called *no-clip mode* in the Quake engine, because the character's collision volume is not *clipped* to the valid playable area of the world. Other engines use different terminology.

Detecting chords is quite simple in principle: We merely watch the states of two or more buttons and only perform the requested operation when *all* of them are down.

There are some subtleties to account for, however. For one thing, if the chord includes a button or buttons that have other purposes in the game, we must take care not to perform *both* the actions of the individual buttons and the action of chord when it is pressed. This is usually done by including a check that the other buttons in the chord are *not* down when detecting the individual button-presses.

Another fly in the ointment is that humans aren't perfect, and they often press one or more of the buttons in the chord slightly earlier than the rest. So our chord-detection code must be robust to the possibility that we'll observe one or more individual buttons on frame $i$ and the rest of the chord on frame $i + 1$ (or even multiple frames later). There are a number of ways to handle this:

- You can design your button inputs such that a chord always does the actions of the individual buttons *plus* some additional action. For example, if pressing L1 fires the primary weapon and L2 lobs a grenade, perhaps the L1 + L2 chord could fire the primary weapon, lob a grenade, *and* send out an energy wave that doubles the damage done by these weapons. That way, whether or not the individual buttons are detected before the chord or not, the behavior will be identical from the point of view of the player.

- You can introduce a delay between when an individual button-down event is seen and when it "counts" as a valid game event. During the delay period (say 2 or 3 frames), if a chord is detected, then it takes precedence over the individual button-down events. This gives the human player some leeway in performing the chord.

- You can detect the chord when the buttons are pressed, but wait to trigger the effect until the buttons are released again.

- You can begin the single-button move immediately and allow it to be preempted by the chord move.

### 8.5.4.3. Sequences and Gesture Detection

The idea of introducing a delay between when a button actually goes down and when it really "counts" as down is a special case of *gesture detection*. A gesture is a sequence of actions performed via a HID by the human player over a period of time. For example, in a fighting game or brawler, we might want to detect a *sequence* of button presses, such as A-B-A. We can extend this idea to non-button inputs as well. For example, A-B-A-Left-Right-Left, where the latter three actions are side-to-side motions of one of the thumb sticks on the game pad. Usually a sequence or gesture is only considered to be valid if it is performed within some maximum time-frame. So a rapid A-B-A within a quarter of a second might "count," but a slow A-B-A performed over a second or two might not.

Gesture detection is generally implemented by keeping a brief history of the HID actions performed by the player. When the first component of the gesture is detected, it is stored in the history buffer, along with a time stamp indicating when it occurred. As each subsequent component is detected, the time between it and the previous component is checked. If it is within the allowable time window, it too is added to the history buffer. If the entire sequence is completed within the allotted time (i.e., the history buffer is filled), an event is generated telling the rest of the game engine that the gesture has occurred. However, if any non-valid intervening inputs are detected, or if any component of the gesture occurs outside of its valid time window, the entire history buffer is reset, and the player must start the gesture over again.

Let's look at three concrete examples, so we can really understand how this works.

### Rapid Button Tapping

Many games require the user to tap a button rapidly in order to perform an action. The frequency of the button presses may or may not translate into some quantity in the game, such as the speed with which the player character runs or performs some other action. The frequency is usually also used to define the validity of the gesture—if the frequency drops below some minimum value, the gesture is no longer considered valid.

We can detect the frequency of a button press by simply keeping track of the last time we saw a button-down event for the button in question. We'll call this $T_{last}$. The frequency $f$ is then just the inverse of the time interval between presses ($\Delta T = T_{cur} - T_{last}$ and $f = 1/\Delta T$). Every time we detect a new button-down event, we calculate a new frequency $f$. To implement a minimum valid frequency, we simply check $f$ against the minimum frequency $f_{min}$ (or we can just check $\Delta T$ against the maximum period $\Delta T_{max} = 1/f_{min}$ directly). If this threshold is satisified, we update the value of $T_{last}$, and the gesture is considered to be on-going. If the threshold is not satisfied, we simply don't update $T_{last}$. The gesture will be considered invalid until a new pair of rapid-enough button-down events occurs. This is illustrated by the following pseudocode:

```
class ButtonTapDetector
{
    U32     m_buttonMask;  // which button to observe (bit
                           // mask)
    F32     m_dtMax;       // max allowed time between
                           // presses
    F32     m_tLast;       // last button-down event, in
                           // seconds

public:
    // Construct an object that detects rapid tapping of
    // the given button (identified by an index).
    ButtonTapDetector(U32 buttonId, F32 dtMax) :
        m_buttonMask(1U << buttonId),
        m_dtMax(dtMax),
        m_tLast(CurrentTime() - dtMax) // start out
                                       // invalid
    {
    }

    // Call this at any time to query whether or not the
    // gesture is currently being performed.
    void IsGestureValid() const
    {
        F32 t = CurrentTime();
        F32 dt = t - m_tLast;
        return (dt < m_dtMax);
    }

    // Call this once per frame.
    void Update()
    {

        if (ButtonsJustWentDown(m_buttonMask))
        {
            m_tLast = CurrentTime();
        }
    }
};
```

In the above code excerpt, we assume that each button is identified by a unique id. The id is really just an index, ranging from 0 to $N-1$ (where $N$ is the number of buttons on the HID in question). We convert the button id to a bit mask by shifting an unsigned 1 bit to the left by an amount equaling the button's index (`1U << buttonId`). The function `ButtonsJustWentDown()` returns a non-zero value if *any one* of the buttons specified by the given bit mask just went down this frame. Here, we're only checking for a single button-down event, but we can and will use this same function later to check for multiple simultaneous button-down events.

### Multibutton Sequence

Let's say we want to detect the sequence A-B-A, performed within at most one second. We can detect this button sequence as follows: We maintain a variable that tracks which button in the sequence we're currently looking for. If we define the sequence with an array of button ids (e.g., aButtons[3] = {A, B, A}), then our variable is just an index $i$ into this array. It starts out initialized to the first button in the sequence, $i = 0$. We also maintain a start time for the entire sequence, $T_{start}$, much as we did in the rapid button-pressing example.

The logic goes like this: Whenever we see a button-down event that matches the button we're currently looking for, we check its time stamp against the start time of the entire sequence, $T_{start}$. If it occurred within the valid time window, we advance the current button to the next button in the sequence; for the first button in the sequence only ($i = 0$), we also update $T_{start}$. If we see a button-down event that doesn't match the next button in the sequence, or if the time delta has grown too large, we reset the button index $i$ back to the beginning of the sequence and set $T_{start}$ to some invalid value (such as 0). This is illustrated by the code below.

```
class ButtonSequenceDetector
{
    U32*    m_aButtonIds;    // sequence of buttons to watch for
    U32     m_buttonCount;   // number of buttons in sequence
    F32     m_dtMax;         // max time for entire sequence
    U32     m_iButton;       // next button to watch for in seq.
    F32     m_tStart;        // start time of sequence, in
                             // seconds

public:
    // Construct an object that detects the given button
    // sequence. When the sequence is successfully
    // detected, the given event is broadcast, so the
    // rest of the game can respond in an appropriate way.
    ButtonSequenceDetector(U32* aButtonIds,
                    U32 buttonCount,
                    F32 dtMax,
                    EventId eventIdToSend)  :
        m_aButtonIds(aButtonIds),
        m_buttonCount(buttonCount),
```

```
            m_dtMax(dtMax),
            m_eventId(eventIdToSend), // event to send when
                                      // complete
            m_iButton(0),             // start of sequence
            m_tStart(0)               // initial value
                                      // irrelevant
    {
    }

    // Call this once per frame.
    void Update()
    {
        ASSERT(m_iButton < m_buttonCount);

        // Determine which button we're expecting next, as
        // a bit mask (shift a 1 up to the correct bit
        // index).
        U32 buttonMask = (1U << m_aButtonId[m_iButton]);

        // If any button OTHER than the expected button
        // just went down, invalidate the sequence. (Use
        // the bitwise NOT operator to check for all other
        // buttons.)
        if (ButtonsJustWentDown(~buttonMask))
        {

            m_iButton = 0; // reset
        }

        // Otherwise, if the expected button just went
        // down, check dt and update our state appropriately.
        else if (ButtonsJustWentDown(buttonMask))
        {
            if (m_iButton == 0)
            {
                // This is the first button in the
                // sequence.
                m_tStart = CurrentTime();
                ++m_iButton; // advance to next button
            }

            else
            {
                F32 dt = CurrentTime() - m_tStart;

                if (dt < m_dtMax)
                {
                    // Sequence is still valid.
```

```
                                      ++m_iButton; // advance to next button

                                      // Is the sequence complete?
                                      if (m_iButton == m_buttonCount)
                                      {
                                          BroadcastEvent(m_eventId);
                                          m_iButton = 0; // reset
                                      }
                                  }

                                  else
                                  {
                                      // Sorry, not fast enough.
                                      m_iButton = 0; // reset
                                  }

                              }
                          }

                      }
                  };
```

*Thumb Stick Rotation*

As an example of a more-complex gesture, let's see how we might detect when
the player is rotating the left thumb stick in a clockwise circle. We can detect
this quite easily by dividing the two-dimensional range of possible stick positions into quadrants, as shown in Figure 8.10. In a clockwise rotation, the
stick passes through the upper-left quadrant, then the upper-right, then the
lower-right, and finally the lower-left. We can treat each of these cases like a
button press and detect a full rotation with a slightly modified version of the
sequence detection code shown above. We'll leave this one as an exercise for
the reader. Try it!

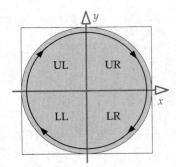

**Figure 8.10.** Detecting circular rotations of the stick by dividing the 2D range of stick inputs
into quadrants.

## 8.5.5. Managing Multiple HIDs for Multiple Players

Most game machines allow two or more HIDs to be attached for multiplayer games. The engine must keep track of which devices are currently attached and route each one's inputs to the appropriate player in the game. This implies that we need some way of mapping controllers to players. This might be as simple as a one-to-one mapping between controller index and player index, or it might be something more sophisticated, such as assigning controllers to players at the time the user hits the Start button.

Even in a single-player game with only one HID, the engine needs to be robust to various exceptional conditions, such as the controller being accidentally unplugged or running out of batteries. When a controller's connection is lost, most games pause gameplay, display a message, and wait for the controller to be reconnected. Some multiplayer games suspend or temporarily remove the avatar corresponding to a removed controller, but allow the other players to continue playing the game; the removed/suspended avatar might reactivate when the controller is reconnected.

On systems with battery-operated HIDs, the game or the operating system is responsible for detecting low-battery conditions. In response, the player is usually warned in some way, for example via an unobtrusive on-screen message and/or a sound effect.

## 8.5.6. Cross-Platform HID Systems

Many game engines are cross-platform. One way to handle HID inputs and outputs in such an engine would be to sprinkle conditional compilation directives all over the code, wherever interactions with the HID take place, as shown below. This is clearly not an ideal solution, but it does work.

```
#if TARGET_XBOX360
    if (ButtonsJustWentDown(XB360_BUTTONMASK_A))
#elif TARGET_PS3
    if (ButtonsJustWentDown(PS3_BUTTONMASK_TRIANGLE))
#elif TARGET_WII
    if (ButtonsJustWentDown(WII_BUTTONMASK_A))
#endif
{
    // do something...
}
```

A better solution is to provide some kind of hardware abstraction layer, thereby insulating the game code from hardware-specific details.

If we're lucky, we can abstract most of the differences beween the HIDs on the different platforms by a judicious choice of abstract button and axis ids. For example, if our game is to ship on Xbox 360 and PS3, the layout of the controls (buttons, axes and triggers) on these two joypads are almost identical. The controls have different ids on each platform, but we can come up with generic control ids that cover both types of joypad quite easily. For example:

```
enum AbstractControlIndex
{
    // Start and back buttons
    AINDEX_START,              // Xbox 360 Start, PS3 Start
    AINDEX_BACK_PAUSE,         // Xbox 360 Back, PS3 Pause

    // Left D-pad
    AINDEX_LPAD_DOWN,
    AINDEX_LPAD_UP,
    AINDEX_LPAD_LEFT,
    AINDEX_LPAD_RIGHT,

    // Right "pad" of four buttons
    AINDEX_RPAD_DOWN,          // Xbox 360 A, PS3 X
    AINDEX_RPAD_UP,            // Xbox 360 Y, PS3 Triangle
    AINDEX_RPAD_LEFT,          // Xbox 360 X, PS3 Square
    AINDEX_RPAD_RIGHT,         // Xbox 360 B, PS3 Circle

    // Left and right thumb stick buttons
    AINDEX_LSTICK_BUTTON,      // Xbox 360 LThumb, PS3 L3,
                               // Xbox white
    AINDEX_RSTICK_BUTTON,      // Xbox 360 RThumb, PS3 R3,
                               // Xbox black

    // Left and right shoulder buttons
    AINDEX_LSHOULDER,          // Xbox 360 L shoulder, PS3 L1
    AINDEX_RSHOULDER,          // Xbox 360 R shoulder, PS3 R1

    // Left thumb stick axes
    AINDEX_LSTICK_X,
    AINDEX_LSTICK_Y,

    // Right thumb stick axes
    AINDEX_RSTICK_X,
    AINDEX_RSTICK_Y,

    // Left and right trigger axes
    AINDEX_LTRIGGER,           // Xbox 360 -Z, PS3 L2
    AINDEX_RTRIGGER,           // Xbox 360 +Z, PS3 R2
};
```

Our abstraction layer can translate between the raw control ids on the current target hardware into our abstract control indices. For example, whenever we read the state of the buttons into a 32-bit word, we can perform a bit-swizzling operation that rearranges the bits into the proper order to correspond to our abstract indices. Analog inputs can likewise be shuffled around into the proper order.

In performing the mapping between physical and abstract controls, we'll sometimes need to get a bit clever. For example, on the Xbox, the left and right triggers act as a single axis, producing negative values when the left trigger is pressed, zero when neither is trigger is pressed, and positive values when the right trigger is pressed. To match the behavior of the PlayStation's DualShock controller, we might want to separate this axis into two distinct axes on the Xbox, scaling the values appropriately so the range of valid values is the same on all platforms.

This is certainly not the only way to handle HID I/O in a multiplatform engine. We might want to take a more functional approach, for example, by naming our abstract controls according to their function in the game, rather than their physical locations on the joypad. We might introduce higher-level functions that detect abstract gestures, with custom detection code on each platform, or we might just bite the bullet and write platform-specific versions of all of the game code that requires HID I/O. The possibilities are numerous, but virtually all cross-platform game engines insulate the game from hardware details in *some* manner.

## 8.5.7. Input Re-Mapping

Many games allow the player some degree of choice with regard to the functionality of the various controls on the physical HID. A common option is the sense of the vertical axis of the right thumb stick for camera control in a console game. Some folks like to push forward on the stick to angle the camera up, while others like an inverted control scheme, where pulling back on the stick angles the camera up (much like an airplane control stick). Other games allow the player to select between two or more predefined button mappings. Some PC games allow the user full control over the functions of individual keys on the keyboard, the mouse buttons, and the mouse wheel, plus a choice between various control schemes for the two mouse axes.

To implement this, we turn to a favorite saying of an old professor of mine, Professor Jay Black of the University of Waterloo, "Every problem in computer science can be solved with a level of indirection." We assign each function in the game a unique id and then provide a simple table which maps each physical or abstract control index to a logical function in the game. Whenever the game wishes to determine whether a particular logical game function should be activated, it looks up the corresponding abstract or physical control id in the table and then reads the state of that control. To change the mapping, we can either swap out the entire table wholesale, or we can allow the user to edit individual entries in the table.

We're glossing over a few details here. For one thing, different controls produce different kinds of inputs. Analog axes may produce values ranging from −32,768 to 32,767, or from 0 to 255, or some other range. The states of all the digital buttons on a HID are usually packed into a single machine word. Therefore, we must be careful to only permit control mappings that make sense. We cannot use a button as the control for a logical game function that requires an axis, for example. One way around this problem is to normalize all of the inputs. For example, we could re-scale the inputs from all analog axes and buttons into the range [0, 1]. This isn't quite as helpful as you might at first think, because some axes are inherently bidirectional (like a joy stick) while others are unidirectional (like a trigger). But if we group our controls into a few classes, we can normalize the inputs within those classes, and permit remapping only within compatible classes. A reasonable set of classes for a standard console joypad and their normalized input values might be:

- *Digital buttons.* States are packed into a 32-bit word, one bit per button.
- *Unidirectional absolute axes (e.g., triggers, analog buttons).* Produce floating-point input values in the range [0, 1].
- *Bidirectional absolute axes (e.g., joy sticks).* Produce floating-point input values in the range [−1, 1].
- *Relative axes (e.g., mouse axes, wheels, track balls).* Produce floating-point input values in the range [−1, 1], where ±1 represents the maximum relative offset possible within a single game frame (i.e., during a period of 1/30 or 1/60 of a second).

### 8.5.8. Context-Sensitive Controls

In many games, a single physical control can have different functions, depending on context. A simple example is the ubiquitous "use" button. If pressed while standing in front of a door, the "use" button might cause the character to open the door. If it is pressed while standing near an object, it might cause the player character to pick up the object, and so on. Another common example is a modal control scheme. When the player is walking around, the controls are used to navigate and control the camera. When the player is riding a vehicle, the controls are used to steer the vehicle, and the camera controls might be different as well.

Context-sensitive controls are reasonably straightforward to implement via a state machine. Depending on what state we're in, a particular HID control may have a different purpose. The tricky part is deciding what state to be in. For example, when the context-sensitive "use" button is pressed, the player might be standing at a point equidistant between a weapon and a health pack, facing the center point between them. Which object do we use in this case? Some games implement a priority system to break ties like this. Perhaps the weapon has a higher weight than the health pack, so it would "win" in this example. Implementing context-sensitive controls isn't rocket science, but it invariably requires lots of trial-and-error to get it feeling and behaving just right. Plan on lots of iteration and focus testing!

Another related concept is that of *control ownership*. Certain controls on the HID might be "owned" by different parts of the game. For example, some inputs are for player control, some for camera control, and still others are for use by the game's wrapper and menu system (pausing the game, etc.) Some game engines introduce the concept of a logical device, which is composed of only a subset of the inputs on the physical device. One logical device might be used for player control, while another is used by the camera system, and another by the menu system.

### 8.5.9. Disabling Inputs

In most games, it is sometimes necessary to disallow the player from controlling his or her character. For example, when the player character is involved in an in-game cinematic, we might want to disable all player controls temporarily; or when the player is walking through a narrow doorway, we might want to temporarily disable free camera rotation.

One rather heavy-handed approach is to use a bit mask to disable individual controls on the input device itself. Whenever the control is read, the disable mask is checked, and if the corresponding bit is set, a neutral or zero value is returned instead of the actual value read from the device. We must be particularly cautious when disabling controls, however. If we forget to reset the disable mask, the game can get itself into a state where the player looses all control forever, and must restart the game. It's important to check our logic carefully, and it's also a good idea to put in some fail-safe mechanisms to ensure that the disable mask is cleared at certain key times, such as whenever the player dies and re-spawns.

Disabling a HID input masks it for all possible clients, which can be overly limiting. A better approach is probably to put the logic for disabling specific player actions or camera behaviors directly into the player or camera code itself. That way, if the camera decides to ignore the deflection of the right thumb stick, for example, other game engine systems still have the freedom to read the state of that stick for other purposes.

## 8.6. Human Interface Devices in Practice

Correct and smooth handling of human interface devices is an important part of any good game. Conceptually speaking, HIDs may seem quite straightforward. However, there can be quite a few "gotchas" to deal with, including variations between different physical input devices, proper implementation of low-pass filtering, bug-free handling of control scheme mappings, achieving just the right "feel" in your joypad rumble, limitations imposed by console manufacturers via their technical requirements checklists (TRCs), and the list goes on. A game team should expect to devote a non-trivial amount of time and engineering bandwidth to a careful and complete implementation of the human interface device system. This is extremely important because the HID system forms the underpinnings of your game's most precious resource—its player mechanics.

9

# Tools for Debugging
# and Development

Developing game software is a complex, intricate, math-intensive, and error-prone business. So it should be no surprise that virtually every professional game team builds a suite of tools for themselves, in order to make the game development process easier and less error-prone. In this chapter, we'll take a look at the development and debugging tools most often found in professional-grade game engines.

## 9.1. Logging and Tracing

Remember when you wrote your first program in BASIC or Pascal? (OK, maybe you don't. If you're significantly younger than me—and there's a pretty good chance of that—you probably wrote your first program in Java, or maybe Python or Lua.) In any case, you probably remember how you debugged your programs back then. You know, back when you thought a *debugger* was one of those glowing blue insect zapper things? You probably used *print statements* to dump out the internal state of your program. C/C++ programmers call this *printf debugging* (after the standard C library function, `printf()`).

It turns out that *printf debugging* is still a perfectly valid thing to do—even *if* you know that a debugger isn't a device for frying hapless insects at night. Especially in real-time programming, it can be difficult to trace certain kinds of bugs using breakpoints and watch windows. Some bugs are timing-dependent; they only happen when the program is running at full speed. Other bugs are caused by a complex sequence of events too long and intricate to trace manually one-by-one. In these situations, the most powerful debugging tool is often a sequence of print statements.

Every game platform has some kind of console or teletype (TTY) output device. Here are some examples:

- In a console application written in C/C++, running under Linux or Win32, you can produce output in the console by printing to `stdout` or `stderr` via `printf()`, `fprintf()`, or STL's `iostream` interface.
- Unfortunately, `printf()` and `iostream` don't work if your game is built as a windowed application under Win32, because there's no console in which to display the output. However, if you're running under the Visual Studio debugger, it provides a debug console to which you can print via the Win32 function `OutputDebugString()`.
- On the PLAYSTATION 3, an application known as the Target Manager runs on your PC and allows you to launch programs on the console. The Target Manager includes a set of TTY output windows to which messages can be printed by the game engine.

So printing out information for debugging purposes is almost always as easy as adding calls to `printf()` throughout your code. However, most game engines go a bit farther than this. In the following sections, we'll investigate the kinds of printing facilities most game engines provide.

## 9.1.1.    Formatted Output with OutputDebugString()

The Win32 function `OutputDebugString()` is great for printing debugging information to Visual Studio's Debug Output window. However, unlike `printf()`, `OutputDebugString()` does not support *formatted* output—it can only print raw strings in the form of `char` arrays. For this reason, most Windows game engines wrap `OutputDebugString()` in a custom function, like this:

```
#include <stdio.h>        // for va_list et al

#ifndef WIN32_LEAN_AND_MEAN
#define WIN32_LEAN_AND_MEAN 1
#endif
#include <windows.h>    // for OutputDebugString()

int VDebugPrintF(const char* format, va_list argList)
{
    const U32 MAX_CHARS = 1023;
    static char s_buffer[MAX_CHARS + 1];
```

```
    int charsWritten
        = vsnprintf(s_buffer, MAX_CHARS, format, argList);
    s_buffer[MAX_CHARS] = '\0'; // be sure to
                                    // NIL-terminate

    // Now that we have a formatted string, call the
    // Win32 API.
    OutputDebugString(s_buffer);

    return charsWritten;
}

int DebugPrintF(const char* format, ...)
{
    va_list argList;
    va_start(argList, format);

    int charsWritten = VDebugPrintF(format, argList);

    va_end(argList);

    return charsWritten;
}
```

Notice that two functions are implemented: `DebugPrintF()` takes a variable-length argument list (specified via the ellipsis, ...), while `VDebugPrintF()` takes a `va_list` argument. This is done so that programmers can build additional printing functions in terms of `VDebugPrintF()`. (It's impossible to pass ellipses from one function to another, but it *is* possible to pass `va_lists` around.)

## 9.1.2.  Verbosity

Once you've gone to the trouble of adding a bunch of print statements to your code in strategically chosen locations, it's nice to be able to leave them there, in case they're needed again later. To permit this, most engines provide some kind of mechanism for controlling the level of *verbosity* via the command-line, or dynamically at runtime. When the verbosity level is at its minimum value (usually zero), only critical error messages are printed. When the verbosity is higher, more of the print statements embedded in the code start to contribute to the output.

The simplest way to implement this is to store the current verbosity level in a global integer variable, perhaps called `g_verbosity`. We then provide a `VerboseDebugPrintF()` function whose first argument is the verbosity level at or above which the message will be printed. This function could be implemented as follows:

```
int g_verbosity = 0;

void VerboseDebugPrintF(int verbosity,
    const char* format, ...)
{
    // Only print when the global verbosity level is
    // high enough.
    if (g_verbosity >= verbosity)
    {
        va_list argList;
        va_start(argList, format);

        VDebugPrintF(format, argList);

        va_end(argList);
    }
}
```

### 9.1.3.  Channels

It's also extremely useful to be able to categorize your debug output into *channels*. One channel might contain messages from the animation system, while another might be used to print messages from the physics system, for example.

On some platforms, like the PLAYSTATION 3, debug output can be directed to one of 14 distinct TTY windows. In addition, messages are mirrored to a special TTY window that contains the output from all of the other 14 windows. This makes it very easy for a developer to focus in on only the messages he or she wants to see. When working on an animation problem, one can simply flip to the animation TTY and ignore all the other output. When working on a general problem of unknown origin, the "all" TTY can be consulted for clues.

Other platforms like Windows provide only a single debug output console. However, even on these systems it can be helpful to divide your output into channels. The output from each channel might be assigned a different color. You might also implement *filters*, which can be turned on and off at runtime, and restrict output to only a specified channel or set of channels. In this model, if a developer is debugging an animation-related problem, for example, he or she can simply filter out all of the channels except the animation channel.

A channel-based debug output system can be implemented quite easily by adding an additional channel argument to our debug printing function. Channels might be numbered, or better, assigned symbolic values via a C/C++ enum declaration. Or channels might be named using a string or hashed string id. The printing function can simply consult the list of active channels and only print the message if the specified channel is among them.

If you don't have more than 32 or 64 channels, it can be helpful to identify the channels via a 32- or 64-bit mask. This makes implementing a channel filter as easy as specifying a single integer. When a bit in the mask is 1, the corresponding channel is active; when the bit is 0, the channel is muted.

### 9.1.4. Mirroring Output to a File

It's a good idea to mirror all debug output to one or more log files (e.g., one file per channel). This permits problems to be diagnosed after the fact. Ideally the log file(s) should contain *all* of the debug output, independent of the current verbosity level and active channels mask. This allows *unexpected* problems to be caught and tracked down by simply inspecting the most-recent log files.

You may want to consider *flushing* your log file(s) after every call to your debug output function to ensure that if the game crashes the log file(s) won't be missing the last buffer-full of output. The last data printed is usually the most crucial to determine the cause of a crash, so we want to be sure that the log file always contains the most up-to-date output. Of course, flushing the output buffer can be expensive. So you should only flush buffers after every debug output call if either (a) you are not doing a lot of logging, or (b) you discover that it is truly necessary on your particular platform. If flushing is deemed to be necessary, you can always provide an engine configuration option to turn it on and off.

### 9.1.5. Crash Reports

Some game engines produce special text output and/or log files when the game crashes. In most operating systems, a top-level exception handler can be installed that will catch most crashes. In this function, you could print out all sorts of useful information. You could even consider emailing the crash report to the entire programming team. This can be incredibly enlightening for the programmers: When they see just how often the art and design teams are crashing, they may discover a renewed sense of urgency in their debugging tasks!

Here are just a few examples of the kinds of information you can include in a crash report:

- Current level(s) being played at the time of the crash.
- World-space location of the player character when the crash occurred.
- Animation/action state of the player when the game crashed.

- Gameplay script(s) that were running at the time of the crash. (This can be especially helpful if the script is the cause of the crash!)

- Stack trace. Most operating systems provide a mechanism for walking the call stack (although they are nonstandard and highly platform specific). With such a facility, you can print out the symbolic names of all non-inline functions on the stack at the time the crash occurred.

- State of all memory allocators in the engine (amount of memory free, degree of fragmentation, etc.). This kind of data can be helpful when bugs are caused by low-memory conditions, for example.

- Any other information you think might be relevant when tracking down the cause of a crash.

## 9.2.  Debug Drawing Facilities

Modern interactive games are driven almost entirely by math. We use math to position and orient objects in the game world, move them around, test for collisions, cast rays to determine lines of sight, and of course use matrix multiplication to transform objects from object space to world space and eventually into screen space for rendering. Almost all modern games are three-dimensional, but even in a two-dimensional game it can be very difficult to mentally visualize the results of all these mathematical calculations. For this reason, most good game engines provide an API for drawing colored lines, simple shapes, and 3D text. We call this a *debug drawing* facility, because the lines, shapes, and text that are drawn with it are intended for visualization during development and debugging and are removed prior to shipping the game.

A *debug drawing* API can save you huge amounts of time. For example, if you are trying to figure out why your projectiles are not hitting the enemy characters, which is easier? Deciphering a bunch of numbers in the debugger? Or drawing a line showing the trajectory of the projectile in three dimensions within your game? With a debug drawing API, logical and mathematical errors become immediately obvious. One might say that a picture is worth 1,000 minutes of debugging.

Here are some examples of debug drawing in action within Naughty Dog's *Uncharted: Drake's Fortune* engine. The following screen shots were all taken within our *play-test* level, one of many special levels we use for testing out new features and debugging problems in the game.

- Figure 9.1 shows how a single line can help developers understand whether a target is within the line of sight of an enemy character. You'll

**Figure 9.1.** Visualizing the line of sight from an NPC to the player.

also notice some debug text rendered just above the head of the enemy, in this case showing weapon ranges, a damage multiplier, the distance to the target, and the character's percentage chance of striking the target. Being able to print out arbitrary information in three-dimensional space is an incredibly useful feature.

- Figure 9.2 shows how a wireframe sphere can be used to visualize the dynamically expanding blast radius of an explosion.

- Figure 9.3 shows how spheres can be used to visualize the radii used by Drake when searching for ledges to hang from in the game. A red line shows the ledge he is currently hanging from. Notice that in this diagram, white text is displayed in the upper left-hand corner of the screen. In the *Uncharted: Drake's Fortune* engine, we have the ability to display text in two-dimensional screen space, as well as in full 3D. This can be useful when you want the text to be displayed independently of the current camera angle.

- Figure 9.4 shows an AI character that has been placed in a special debugging mode. In this mode, the character's brain is effectively turned

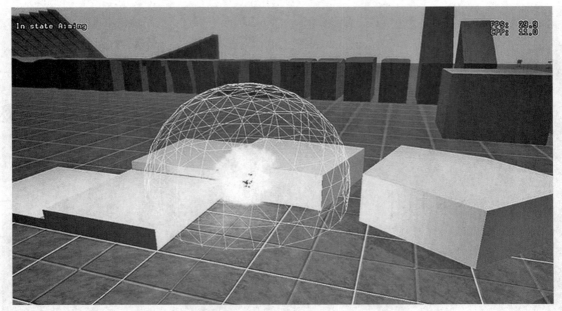

**Figure 9.2.** Visualizing the expanding blast sphere of an explosion.

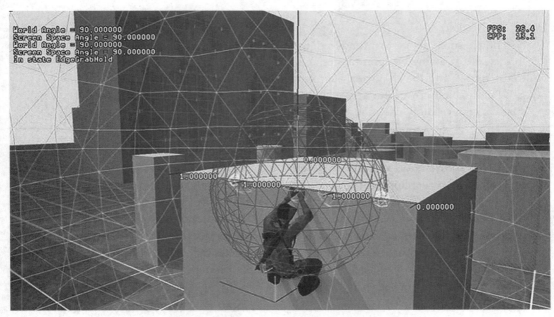

**Figure 9.3.** Spheres and vectors used in Drake's ledge hang and shimmy system.

**Figure 9.4.** Manually controlling an NPC's actions for debugging purposes.

off, and the developer is given full control over the character's movements and actions via a simple heads-up menu. The developer can paint target points in the game world by simply aiming the camera and can then instruct the character to walk, run, or sprint to the specified points. The user can also tell the character to enter or leave nearby cover, fire its weapon, and so on.

## 9.2.1. Debug Drawing API

A debug drawing API generally needs to satisfy the following requirements:

- The API should be simple and easy to use.
- It should support a useful set of primitives, including (but not limited to):
  - lines,
  - spheres,
  - points (usually represented as small crosses or spheres, because a single pixel is very difficult to see),

- □ coordinate axes (typically the $x$-axis is drawn in red, $y$ in green and $z$ in blue),
- □ bounding boxes, and
- □ formatted text.

- It should provide a good deal of flexibility in controlling how primitives are drawn, including:
  - □ color,
  - □ line width,
  - □ sphere radii,
  - □ the size of points, lengths of coordinate axes, and dimensions of other "canned" primitives.

- It should be possible to draw primitives in world space (full 3D, using the game camera's perspective projection matrix) or in screen space (either using an orthographic projection, or possibly a perspective projection). World-space primitives are useful for annotating objects in the 3D scene. Screen-space primitives are helpful for displaying debugging information in the form of a heads-up display that is independent of camera position or orientation.

- It should be possible to draw primitives with or without *depth testing* enabled.
  - □ When depth testing is enabled, the primitives will be occluded by real objects in your scene. This makes their depth easy to visualize, but it also means that the primitives may sometimes be difficult to see or totally hidden by the geometry of your scene.
  - □ With depth testing disabled, the primitives will "hover" over the real objects in the scene. This makes it harder to gauge their real depth, but it also ensures that no primitive is ever hidden from view.

- It should be possible to make calls to the drawing API from anywhere in your code. Most rendering engines require that geometry be submitted for rendering during a specific phase of the game loop, usually at the end of each frame. So this requirement implies that the system must queue up all incoming debug drawing requests, so that they may be submitted at the proper time later on.

- Ideally, every debug primitive should have a *lifetime* associated with it. The lifetime controls how long the primitive will remain on-screen after having been requested. If the code that is drawing the primitive is called every frame, the lifetime can be one frame—the primitive will remain on-screen because it will be refreshed every frame. However, if the code that draws the primitive is called rarely or intermittently (e.g., a function that calculates the initial velocity of a projectile), then you do not want the primitive to flicker on-screen for just one frame and then disappear. In such situations the programmer should be able to give his or her debug primitives a longer lifetime, on the order of a few seconds.

- It's also important that the debug drawing system be capable of handling a large number of debug primitives efficiently. When you're drawing debug information for 1,000 game objects, the number of primitives can really add up, and you don't want your game to be unusable when debug drawing is turned on.

The debug drawing API in Naughty Dog's *Uncharted: Drake's Fortune* engine looks something like this:

```
class DebugDrawManager
{
public:

    // Adds a line segment to the debug drawing queue.
    void AddLine(    const Point& fromPosition,
                     const Point& toPosition,
                     Color color,
                     float lineWidth = 1.0f,
                     float duration = 0.0f,
                     bool depthEnabled = true);

    // Adds an axis-aligned cross (3 lines converging at
    // a point) to the debug drawing queue.
    void AddCross(   const Point& position,
                     Color color,
                     float size,
                     float duration = 0.0f,
                     bool depthEnabled = true);

    // Adds a wireframe sphere to the debug drawing queue.
    void AddSphere(  const Point& centerPosition,
                     float radius,
                     Color color,
                     float duration = 0.0f,
                     bool depthEnabled = true);

    // Adds a circle to the debug drawing queue.
    void AddCircle(  const Point& centerPosition,
                     const Vector& planeNormal,
                     float radius,
                     Color color,
                     float duration = 0.0f,
                     bool depthEnabled = true);
```

```cpp
    // Adds a set of coordinate axes depicting the
    // position and orientation of the given
    // transformation to the debug drawing queue.
    void AddAxes(    const Transform& xfm,
                     Color color,
                     float size,
                     float duration = 0.0f,
                     bool depthEnabled = true);

    // Adds a wireframe triangle to the debug drawing
    // queue.
    void AddTriangle(    const Point& vertex0,
                         const Point& vertex1,
                         const Point& vertex2,
                         Color color,
                         float lineWidth = 1.0f,
                         float duration = 0.0f,
                         bool depthEnabled = true);

    // Adds an axis-aligned bounding box to the debug
    // queue.
    void AddAABB(const Point& minCoords,
                 const Point& maxCoords,
                 Color color,
                 float lineWidth = 1.0f,
                 float duration = 0.0f,
                 bool depthEnabled = true);

    // Adds an oriented bounding box to the debug queue.
    void AddOBB(    const Mat44& centerTransform,
                    const Vector& scaleXYZ,
                    Color color,
                    float lineWidth = 1.0f,

                    float duration = 0.0f,
                    bool depthEnabled = true);

    // Adds a text string to the debug drawing queue.
    void AddString(    const Point& pos,
                       const char* text,
                       Color color,
                       float duration = 0.0f,
                       bool depthEnabled = true);
};

// This global debug drawing manager is configured for
// drawing in full 3D with a perspective projection.
extern DebugDrawManager g_debugDrawMgr;
```

```
// This global debug drawing manager draws its
// primitives in 2D screen space. The (x,y) coordinates
// of a point specify a 2D location on-screen, and the
// z coordinate contains a special code that indicates
// whether the (x,y) coordinates are measured in absolute
// pixels or in normalized coordinates that range from
// 0.0 to 1.0. (The latter mode allows drawing to be
// independent of the actual resolution of  the screen.)
extern DebugDrawManager g_debugDrawMgr2D;
```

Here's an example of this API being used within game code:

```
void Vehicle::Update()
{

    // Do some calculations...

    // Debug-draw my velocity vector.
    Point start = GetWorldSpacePosition();
    Point end = start + GetVelocity();
    g_debugDrawMgr.AddLine(start, end, kColorRed);

    // Do some other calculations...

    // Debug-draw my name and number of passengers.
    {
        char buffer[128];
        sprintf(buffer, "Vehicle %s: %d passengers",
            GetName(), GetNumPassengers());
        g_debugDrawMgr.AddString(GetWorldSpacePosition(),
            buffer, kColorWhite, 0.0f, false);
    }

}
```

You'll notice that the names of the drawing functions use the verb "add" rather than "draw." This is because the debug primitives are typically not drawn immediately when the drawing function is called. Instead, they are added to a list of visual elements that will be drawn at a later time. Most high-speed 3D rendering engines require that all visual elements be maintained in a *scene* data structure so that they can be drawn efficiently, usually at the end of the game loop. We'll learn a lot more about how rendering engines work in Chapter 10.

## 9.3. In-Game Menus

Every game engine has a large number of configuration options and features. In fact, each major subsystem, including rendering, animation, collision,

**Figure 9.5.** Main development menu in *Uncharted*.

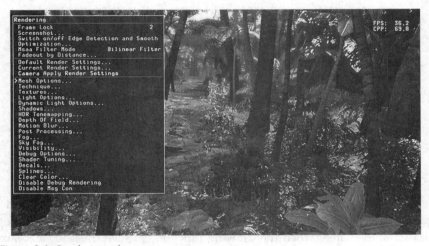

**Figure 9.6.** Rendering submenu.

physics, audio, networking, player mechanics, AI, and so on, exposes its own specialized configuration options. It is highly useful to programmers, artists, and game designers alike to be able to configure these options while the game is running, without having to change the source code, recompile and relink the game executable, and then rerun the game. This can greatly reduce the amount of time the game development team spends on debugging problems and setting up new levels or game mechanics.

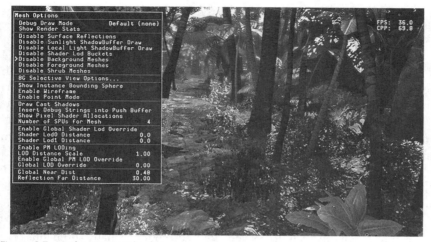

Figure 9.7. Mesh options subsubmenu.

Figure 9.8. Background meshes turned off.

One simple and convenient way to permit this kind of thing is to provide a system of *in-game menus*. Items on an in-game menu can do any number of things, including (but certainly not limited to):

- toggling global Boolean settings,
- adjusting global integer and floating-point values,
- calling arbitrary functions, which can perform literally any task within the engine,

- bringing up submenus, allowing the menu system to be organized hierarchically for easy navigation.

An in-game menu should be easy and convenient to bring up, perhaps via a simple button-press on the joypad. (Of course, you'll want to choose a button combination that doesn't occur during normal gameplay.) Bringing up the menus usually pauses the game. This allows the developer to play the game until the moment just before a problem occurs, then pause the game by bringing up the menus, adjust engine settings in order to visualize the problem more clearly, and then un-pause the game to inspect the problem in depth.

Let's take a brief look at how the menu system works in the *Uncharted: Drake's Fortune* engine, by Naughty Dog. Figure 9.5 shows the top-level menu. It contains submenus for each major subsystem in the engine. In Figure 9.6, we've drilled down one level into the *Rendering…* submenu. Since the rendering engine is a highly complex system, its menu contains many submenus controlling various aspects of rendering. To control the way in which 3D meshes are rendered, we drill down further into the *Mesh Options…* submenu, shown in Figure 9.7. On this menu, we can turn off rendering of all static background meshes, leaving only the dynamic foreground meshes visible. This is shown in Figure 9.8.

## 9.4. In-Game Console

Some engines provide an in-game console, either in lieu of or in addition to an in-game menu system. An in-game console provides a command-line interface to the game engine's features, much as a DOS *command prompt* provides users with access to various features of the Windows operating system, or a csh, tcsh, ksh or bash *shell prompt* provides users with access to the features of UNIX-like operating systems. Much like a menu system, the game engine console can provide commands allowing a developer to view and manipulate global engine settings, as well as running arbitrary commands.

A console is somewhat less convenient than a menu system, especially for those who aren't very fast typists. However, a console can be much more powerful than a menu. Some in-game consoles provide only a rudimentary set of hard-coded commands, making them about as flexible as a menu system. But others provide a rich interface to virtually every feature of the engine. A screen shot of the in-game console in Quake 4 is shown in Figure 9.9.

Some game engines provide a powerful scripting language that can be used by programmers and game designers to extend the functionality of the engine, or even build entirely new games. If the in-game console "speaks"

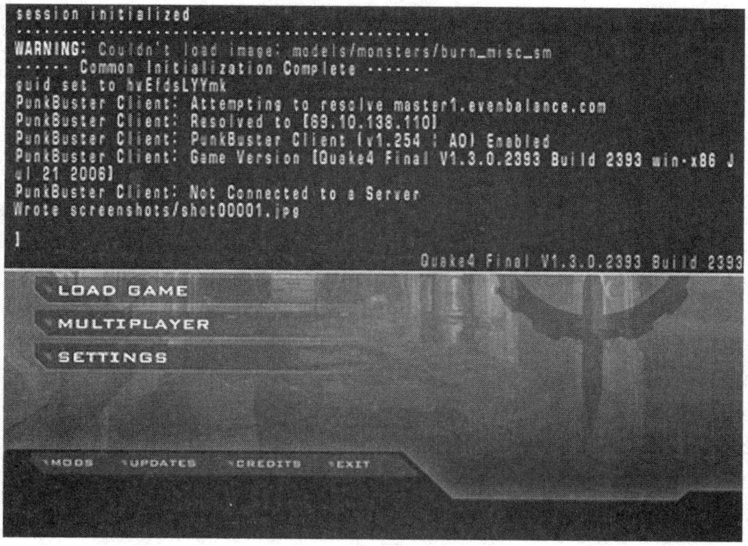

**Figure 9.9.** The in-game console in *Quake 4*, overlaid on top of the main game menu.

this same scripting language, then anything you can do in script can also be done interactively via the console. We'll explore scripting languages in depth in Section 14.8.

## 9.5.   Debug Cameras and Pausing the Game

An in-game menu or console system is best accompanied by two other crucial features: (a) the ability to detach the camera from the player character and fly it around the game world in order to scrutinize any aspect of the scene, and (b) the ability to pause, un-pause and single-step the game (see Section 7.5.6). When the game is paused, it is important to still be able to control the camera. To support this, we can simply keep the rendering engine and camera controls running, even when the game's logical clock is paused.

Slow motion mode is another incredibly useful feature for scrutinizing animations, particle effects, physics and collision behaviors, AI behaviors, and the list goes on. This feature is easy to implement. Presuming we've taken care to update all gameplay elements using a clock that is distinct from the real-time clock, we can put the game into slo-mo by simply updating the gameplay clock at a rate that is slower than usual. This approach can also be used to implement a fast-motion mode, which can be useful for moving rapidly through time-consuming portions of gameplay in order to get to an area of interest.

## 9.6. Cheats

When developing or debugging a game, it's important to allow the user to break the rules of the game in the name of expediency. Such features are aptly named *cheats*. For example, many engines allow you to "pick up" the player character and fly him or her around in the game world, with collisions disabled so he or she can pass through all obstacles. This can be incredibly helpful for testing out gameplay. Rather than taking the time to actually play the game in an attempt to get the player character into some desirable location, you can simply pick him up, fly him over to where you want him to be, and then drop him back into his regular gameplay mode.

Other useful cheats include, but are certainly not limited to:

- *Invincible player.* As a developer, you often don't want to be bothered having to defend yourself from enemy characters, or worrying about falling from too high a height, as you test out a feature or track down a bug.
- *Give player weapon.* It's often useful to be able to give the player any weapon in the game for testing purposes.
- *Infinite ammo.* When you're trying to kill bad guys to test out the weapon system or AI hit reactions, you don't want to be scrounging for clips!
- *Select player mesh.* If the player character has more than one "costume," it can be useful to be able to select any of them for testing purposes.

Obviously this list could go on for pages. The sky's the limit—you can add whatever cheats you need in order to develop or debug the game. You might even want to expose some of your favorite cheats to the players of the final shipping game. Players can usually activate cheats by entering unpublished *cheat codes* on the joypad or keyboard, and/or by accomplishing certain objectives in the game.

## 9.7. Screen Shots and Movie Capture

Another extremely useful facility is the ability to capture screen shots and write them to disk in a suitable image format such as Windows Bitmap files

(.bmp) or Targa (.tga). The details of how to capture a screen shot vary from platform to platform, but they typically involve making a call to the graphics API that allows the contents of the frame buffer to be transferred from video RAM to main RAM, where it can be scanned and converted into the image file format of your choice. The image files are typically written to a predefined folder on disk and named using a date and time stamp to guarantee unique file names.

You may want to provide your users with various options controlling how screen shots are to be captured. Some common examples include:

- Whether or not to include debug lines and text in the screen shot.

- Whether or not to include heads-up display (HUD) elements in the screen shot.

- The resolution at which to capture. Some engines allow high resolution screen shots to be captured, perhaps by modifying the projection matrix so that separate screen shots can be taken of the four quadrants of the screen at normal resolution and then combined into the final high-res image.

- Simple camera animations. For example, you could allow the user to mark the starting and ending positions and orientations of the camera. A sequence of screen shots could then be taken while gradually interpolating the camera from the start location to the ending location.

Some engines also provide a full-fledged movie capture mode. Such a system captures a sequence of screen shots at the target frame rate of the game, which are typically processed offline to generate a movie file in a suitable format such as AVI or MP4.

Capturing a screen shot is usually a relatively slow operation, due in part to the time required to transfer the frame buffer data from video RAM to main RAM (an operation for which the graphics hardware is usually not optimized), and in larger part to the time required to write image files to disk. If you want to capture movies in real time (or at least *close* to real time), you'll almost certainly need to store the captured images to a buffer in main RAM, only writing them out to disk when the buffer has been filled (during which the game will typically be frozen).

## 9.8.  In-Game Profiling

Games are real-time systems, so achieving and maintaining a high frame rate (usually 30 FPS or 60 FPS) is important. Therefore, part of any game programmer's job is ensuring that his or her code runs efficiently and within budget. As we saw when we discussed the 80-20 and 90-10 rules in Chapter 2, a large percentage of your code probably doesn't need to be optimized. The only way to know *which* bits require optimization is to *measure your game's performance.* We discussed various third-party profiling tools in Chapter 2. However, these tools have various limitations and may not be available at all on a console. For

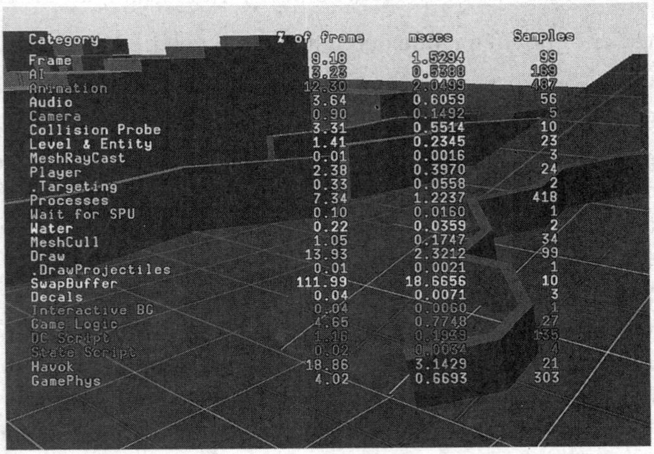

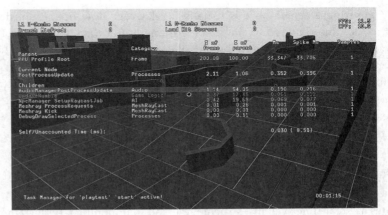

**Figure 9.10.** The profile category display in the *Uncharted 2: Among Theives* engine shows coarse timing figures for various top-level engine systems.

**Figure 9.11.** The *Uncharted 2* engine also provides a profile hierarchy display that allows the user to drill down into particular function calls in inspect their costs.

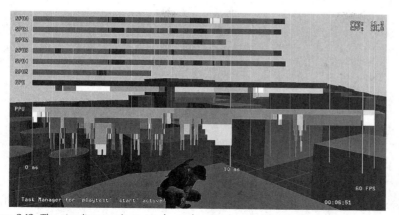

**Figure 9.12.** The timeline mode in *Uncharted 2* shows exactly when various operations are performed across a single frame on the PS3's SPUs, GPU and PPU.

this reason, and/or for convenience, many game engines provide an in-game profiling tool of some sort.

Typically an in-game profiler permits the programmer to annotate blocks of code which should be timed and give them human-readable names. The profiler measures the execution time of each annotated block via the CPU's hi-res timer, and stores the results in memory. A heads-up display is provided which shows up-to-date execution times for each code block (examples are shown in Figure 9.10, Figure 9.11, and Figure 9.12). The display often provides the data in various forms, including raw numbers of cycles, execution times in micro-seconds, and percentages relative to the execution time of the entire frame.

## 9.8.1. Hierarchical Profiling

Computer programs written in an imperative language are inherently *hierarchical*—a function calls other functions, which in turn call still more functions. For example, let's imagine that function a() calls functions b() and c(), and function b() in turn calls functions d(), e() and f(). The pseudocode for this is shown below.

```
void a()
{
    b();
    c();
}
```

```
void b()
{
    d();
    e();
    f();
}

void c() { ... }

void d() { ... }

void e() { ... }

void f() { ... }
```

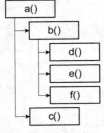

Figure 9.13. A hypothetical function call hierarchy.

Assuming function a() is called directly from main(), this function call hierarchy is shown in Figure 9.13.

When debugging a program, the *call stack* shows only a snapshot of this tree. Specifically, it shows us the path from whichever function in the hierarchy is *currently executing* all the way to the root function in the tree. In C/C++, the root function is usually main() or WinMain(), although technically this function is called by a start-up function that is part of the standard C runtime library (CRT), so that function is the true root of the hierarchy. If we set a breakpoint in function e(), for example, the call stack would look something like this:

```
e()                          ← The currently-executing function.
b()
a()
main()
_crt_startup()               ← Root of the call hierarchy.
```

This call stack is depicted in Figure 9.14 as a pathway from function e() to the root of the function call tree.

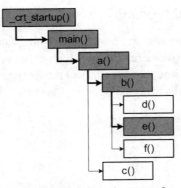

Figure 9.14. Call stack resulting from setting a break point in function e().

### 9.8.1.1. Measuring Execution Times Hierarchically

If we measure the execution time of a single function, the time we measure includes the execution time of any the child functions called and all of their grandchildren, great grandchildren, and so on as well. To properly interpret any profiling data we might collect, we must be sure to take the function call hierarchy into account.

Many commercial profilers can *automatically* instrument every single function in your program. This permits them to measure both the *inclusive* and *exclusive* execution times of every function that is called during a profiling session. As the name implies, inclusive times measure the execution time of the function including all of its children, while exclusive times measure only the time spent in the function itself. (The exclusive time of a function can be calculated by subtracting the inclusive times of all its immediate children from the inclusive time of the function in question.) In addition, some profilers record how many times each function is called. This is an important piece of information to have when optimizing a program, because it allows you to differentiate between functions that eat up a lot of time internally and functions that eat up time because they are called a very large number of times.

In contrast, in-game profiling tools are not so sophisticated and usually rely on *manual* instrumentation of the code. If our game engine's main loop is structured simply enough, we may be able to obtain valid data at a coarse level without thinking much about the function call hierarchy. For example, a typical game loop might look roughly like this:

```
while (!quitGame)
{
    PollJoypad();
    UpdateGameObjects();
    UpdateAllAnimations();
    PostProcessJoints();
    DetectCollisions();
    RunPhysics();
    GenerateFinalAnimationPoses();
    UpdateCameras();
    RenderScene();
    UpdateAudio();
}
```

We could profile this game at a very coarse level by measuring the execution times of each major phase of the game loop:

```
while (!quitGame)
{
```

```
        {
            PROFILE("Poll Joypad");
            PollJoypad();
        }
        {
            PROFILE("Game Object Update");
            UpdateGameObjects();
        }
        {
            PROFILE("Animation");
            UpdateAllAnimations();
        }
        {
            PROFILE("Joint Post-Processing");
            PostProcessJoints();
        }
        {
            PROFILE("Collision");
            DetectCollisions();
        }
        {
            PROFILE("Physics");
            RunPhysics();
        }
        {
            PROFILE("Animation Finaling");
            GenerateFinalAnimationPoses();
        }
        {
            PROFILE("Cameras");
            UpdateCameras();
        }
        {
            PROFILE("Rendering");
            RenderScene();
        }
        {
            PROFILE("Audio");
            UpdateAudio();
        }
    }
```

The PROFILE() macro shown above would probably be implemented as a
class whose constructor starts the timer and whose destructor stops the timer
and records the execution time under the given name. Thus it only times the
code within its containing block, by nature of the way C++ automatically constructs and destroys objects as they go in and out of scope.

```
struct AutoProfile
{
    AutoProfile(const char* name)
    {
        m_name = name;
        m_startTime = QueryPerformanceCounter();
    }

    ~AutoProfile()
    {
        __int64 endTime = QueryPerformanceCounter();
        __int64 elapsedTime = endTime - m_startTime;
        g_profileManager.storeSample(m_name, elapsedTime);
    }


    const char*    m_name;
    __int64        m_startTime;
};

#define PROFILE(name) AutoProfile p(name)
```

The problem with this simplistic approach is that it breaks down when used within deeper levels of function call nesting. For example, if we embed additional PROFILE() annotations within the RenderScene() function, we need to understand the function call hierarchy in order to properly interpret those measurements.

One solution to this problem is to allow the programmer who is annotating the code to indicate the hierarchical interrelationships between profiling samples. For example, any PROFILE(...) samples taken within the RenderScene() function could be declared to be children of the PROFILE("Rendering") sample. These relationships are usually set up separately from the annotations themselves, by predeclaring all of the sample bins. For example, we might set up the in-game profiler during engine initialization as follows:

```
// This code declares various profile sample "bins",
// listing the name of the bin and the name of its
// parent bin, if any.
ProfilerDeclareSampleBin("Rendering", NULL);
    ProfilerDeclareSampleBin("Visibility", "Rendering");
    ProfilerDeclareSampleBin("ShaderSetUp", "Rendering");
        ProfilerDeclareSampleBin("Materials", "Shaders");
    ProfilerDeclareSampleBin("SubmitGeo", "Rendering");
ProfilerDeclareSampleBin("Audio", NULL);

    ...
```

This approach still has its problems. Specifically, it works well when every function in the call hierarchy has only one parent, but it breaks down when we try to profile a function that is called by more than one parent function. The reason for this should be pretty obvious. We're statically declaring our sample bins *as if* every function can only appear once in the function call hierarchy, but actually the same function can reappear many times in the tree, each time with a different parent. The result can be misleading data, because a function's time will be included in one of the parent bins, but really should be distributed across all of its parents' bins. Most game engines don't make an attempt to remedy this problem, since they are primarily interested in profiling coarse-grained functions that are only called from one specific location in the function call hierarchy. But this limitation is something to be aware of when profiling your code with a simple in-engine profile of the sort found in most game engines.

We would also like to account for how many *times* a given function is called. In the example above, we know that each of the functions we profiled are called exactly once per frame. But other functions, deeper in the function call hierarchy, may be called more than once per frame. If we measure function x() to take 2 ms to execute, it's important to know whether it takes 2 ms to execute on its own, or whether it executes in 2 μs but was called 1000 times during the frame. Keeping track of the number of times a function is called per frame is quite simple—the profiling system can simply increment a counter each time a sample is received and reset the counters at the start of each frame.

## 9.8.2. Exporting to Excel

Some game engines permit the data captured by the in-game profiler to be dumped to a text file for subsequent analysis. I find that a comma-separated values (CSV) format is best, because such files can be loaded easily into a Microsoft Excel spreadsheet, where the data can be manipulated and analyzed in myriad ways. I wrote such an exporter for the *Medal of Honor: Pacific Assault* engine. The columns corresponded to the various annotated blocks, and each row represented the profiling sample taken during one frame of the game's execution. The first column contained frame numbers and the second actual game time measured in seconds. This allowed the team to graph how the performance statistics varied over time and to determine how long each frame actually took to execute. By adding some simple formulae to the exported spreadsheet, we could calculate frame rates, execution time percentages, and so on.

# 9.9.   In-Game Memory Stats and Leak Detection

In addition to runtime performance (i.e., frame rate), most game engines are also constrained by the amount of memory available on the target hardware. PC games are least affected by such constraints, because modern PCs have sophisticated virtual memory managers. But even PC games are constrained by the memory limitations of their so-called "min spec" machine—the least-powerful machine on which the game is guaranteed to run, as promised by the publisher and stated on the game's packaging.

For this reason, most game engines implement custom memory-tracking tools. These tools allow the developers to see how much memory is being used by each engine subsystem and whether or not any memory is leaking (i.e., memory is allocated but never freed). It's important to have this information, so that you can make informed decisions when trying to cut back the memory usage of your game so that it will fit onto the console or type of PC you are targeting.

Keeping track of how much memory a game actually uses can be a surprisingly tricky job. You'd think you could simply wrap `malloc()`/`free()` or `new`/`delete` in a pair of functions or macros that keep track of the amount of memory that is allocated and freed. However, it's never that simple for a few reasons:

1.  *You often can't control the allocation behavior of other people's code.* Unless you write the operating system, drivers, and the game engine entirely from scratch, there's a good chance you're going to end up linking your game with at least some third-party libraries. Most good libraries provide *memory allocation hooks*, so that you can replace their allocators with your own. But some do not. It's often difficult to keep track of the memory allocated by each and every third-party library you use in your game engine—but it usually *can* be done if you're thorough and selective in your choice of third-party libraries.

2.  *Memory comes in different flavors.* For example, a PC has two kinds of RAM: main RAM and video RAM (the memory residing on your graphics card, which is used primarily for geometry and texture data). Even if you manage to track all of the memory allocations and deallocations occurring within main RAM, it can be well neigh impossible to track video RAM usage. This is because graphics APIs like DirectX actually hide the details of how video RAM is being allocated and used from the developer. On a console, life is a bit easier, only because you often end up having to write a video RAM manager yourself. This is more difficult

than using DirectX, but at least you have complete knowledge of what's going on.

3. *Allocators come in different flavors.* Many games make use of specialized allocators for various purposes. For example, the *Uncharted: Drake's Fortune* engine has a *global heap* for general-purpose allocations, a special heap for managing the memory created by *game objects* as they spawn into the game world and are destroyed, a *level-loading heap* for data that is *streamed* into memory during gameplay, a stack allocator for *single-frame allocations* (the stack is cleared automatically every frame), an allocator for *video RAM,* and a *debug memory heap* used only for allocations that will not be needed in the final shipping game. Each of these allocators grabs a large hunk of memory when the game starts up and then manages that memory block itself. If we were to track all the calls to new and delete, we'd see one new for each of these six allocators and that's all. To get any useful information, we really need to track all of the allocations *within* each of these allocators' memory blocks.

Most professional game teams expend a significant amount of effort on creating in-engine memory-tracking tools that provide accurate and detailed information. The resulting tools usually provide their output in a variety of forms. For example, the engine might produce a detailed dump of all memory allocations made by the game during a specific period of time. The data might include high water marks for each memory allocator or each game system, indicating the maximum amount of physical RAM required by each. Some engines also provide heads-up displays of memory usage while the game is

```
-[ Retail Memory ]-
OS Memory              :   43.00 /   43.00 MB
Code And Static Data   :            30.25 MB
PRXs                   :             3.63 MB
Global Memory          :   56.63 /   58.00 MB
IO Memory              :  119.75 /  120.00 MB
Spurs + Threads        :             1.09 MB
Available Memory       :            30.04 MB
                          ----------------
                  Total:           286.00 MB

-[ Debug Memory ]-
Extra OS Memory        :   62.00 /   62.00 MB
Code/Data Overflow Mem :    0.00 /   10.00 MB
IO Debug Memory        :   52.14 /   75.00 MB
Physics Overflow Mem   :    0.00 /    3.00 MB
Debug Memory           :   23.57 /   89.00 MB
                          ----------------
                  Total:           241.00 MB
```

Figure 9.15. Tabular memory statistics from the *Uncharted 2: Among Thieves* engine.

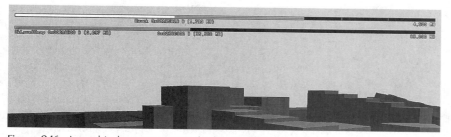

**Figure 9.16.** A graphical memory usage display, also from *Uncharted 2*.

running. This data might be tabular, as shown in Figure 9.15, or graphical as shown in Figure 9.16.

In addition, when low-memory or out-of-memory conditions arise, a good engine will provide this information in as helpful a way as possible. When PC games are developed, the game team usually works on high-powered PCs with more RAM than the min-spec machine being targeted. Likewise, console games are developed on special *development kits* which have more memory than a retail console. So in both cases, the game can continue to run even when it technically has run out of memory (i.e., would no longer fit on a retail console or min-spec PC). When this kind of out-of-memory condition arises, the game engine can display a message saying something like, "Out of memory — this level will not run on a retail system."

There are lots of other ways in which a game engine's memory tracking system can aid developers in pinpointing problems as early and as conveniently as possible. Here are just a few examples:

- If a model fails to load, a bright red text string could be displayed in 3D hovering in the game world where that object would have been.

- If a texture fails to load, the object could be drawn with an ugly pink texture that is very obviously not part of the final game.

- If an animation fails to load, the character could assume a special (possibly humorous) pose that indicates a missing animation, and the name of the missing asset could hover over the character's head.

The key to providing good memory analysis tools is (a) to provide accurate information, (b) to present the data in a way that is convenient and that makes problems obvious, and (c) to provide contextual information to aid the team in tracking down the root cause of problems when they occur.

# Part III
# Graphics and Motion

# 10
# The Rendering Engine

When most people think about computer and video games, the first thing that comes to mind is the stunning three-dimensional graphics. Real-time 3D rendering is an exceptionally broad and profound topic, so there's simply no way to cover all of the details in a single chapter. Thankfully there are a great many excellent books and other resources available on this topic. In fact, real-time 3D graphics is perhaps one of the best covered of all the technologies that make up a game engine. The goal of this chapter, then, is to provide you with a broad understanding of real-time rendering technology and to serve as a jumping-off point for further learning. After you've read through these pages, you should find that reading other books on 3D graphics seems like a journey through familiar territory. You might even be able to impress your friends at parties (… or alienate them…)

We'll begin by laying a solid foundation in the concepts, theory, and mathematics that underlie any real-time 3D rendering engine. Next, we'll have a look at the software and hardware pipelines used to turn this theoretical framework into reality. We'll discuss some of the most common optimization techniques and see how they drive the structure of the tools pipeline and the runtime rendering API in most engines. We'll end with a survey of some of the advanced rendering techniques and lighting models in use by game engines today. Throughout this chapter, I'll point you to some of my favorite books and other resources that should help you to gain an even deeper understanding of the topics we'll cover here.

## 10.1. Foundations of Depth-Buffered Triangle Rasterization

When you boil it down to its essence, rendering a three-dimensional scene involves the following basic steps:

- A *virtual scene* is described, usually in terms of 3D surfaces represented in some mathematical form.
- A *virtual camera* is positioned and oriented to produce the desired view of the scene. Typically the camera is modeled as an idealized focal point, with an imaging surface hovering some small distance in front of it, composed of *virtual light sensors* corresponding to the picture elements (*pixels*) of the target display device.
- Various *light sources* are defined. These sources provide all the light rays that will interact with and reflect off the objects in the environment and eventually find their way onto the image-sensing surface of the virtual camera.
- The *visual properties* of the surfaces in the scene are described. This defines how light should interact with each surface.
- For each pixel within the imaging rectangle, the rendering engine calculates the color and intensity of the light ray(s) converging on the virtual camera's focal point through that pixel. This is known as *solving the rendering equation* (also called the *shading equation*).

This high-level rendering process is depicted in Figure 10.1.

Many different technologies can be used to perform the basic rendering steps described above. The primary goal is usually *photorealism*, although some games aim for a more stylized look (e.g., cartoon, charcoal sketch, watercolor, and so on). As such, rendering engineers and artists usually attempt to describe the properties of their scenes as realistically as possible and to use light transport models that match physical reality as closely as possible. Within this context, the gamut of rendering technologies ranges from techniques designed for real-time performance at the expense of visual fidelity, to those designed for photorealism but which are not intended to operate in real time.

Real-time rendering engines perform the steps listed above repeatedly, displaying rendered images at a rate of 30, 50, or 60 frames per second to

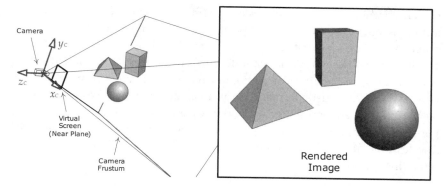

**Figure 10.1.** The high-level rendering approach used by virtually all 3D computer graphics technologies.

provide the illusion of motion. This means a real-time rendering engine has at most 33.3 ms to generate each image (to achieve a frame rate of 30 FPS). Usually much less time is available, because bandwidth is also consumed by other engine systems like animation, AI, collision detection, physics simulation, audio, player mechanics, and other gameplay logic. Considering that film rendering engines often take anywhere from many minutes to many hours to render a single frame, the quality of real-time computer graphics these days is truly astounding.

### 10.1.1. Describing a Scene

A real-world scene is composed of objects. Some objects are solid, like a brick, and some are amorphous, like a cloud of smoke, but every object occupies a volume of 3D space. An object might be *opaque* (in which case light cannot pass through its volume), *transparent* (in which case light passes through it without being scattered, so that we can see a reasonably clear image of whatever is behind the object), or *translucent* (meaning that light can pass through the object but is scattered in all directions in the process, yielding only a blur of colors that hint at the objects behind it).

Opaque objects can be rendered by considering only their *surfaces*. We don't need to know what's inside an opaque object in order to render it, because light cannot penetrate its surface. When rendering a transparent or translucent object, we really should model how light is reflected, refracted, scattered, and absorbed as it passes through the object's volume. This requires knowledge of the interior structure and properties of the object. However, most game engines don't go to all that trouble. They just render the surfaces of transparent and translucent objects in almost the same way opaque objects are rendered. A simple numeric opacity measure known as *alpha* is used to describe how opaque or transparent a surface is. This approach can lead to various visual anomalies (for example, surface features on the far side of the object may be rendered incorrectly), but the approximation can be made to look reasonably realistic in many cases. Even amorphous objects like clouds of smoke are often represented using particle effects, which are typically composed of large numbers of semi-transparent rectangular cards. Therefore, it's safe to say that most game rendering engines are primarily concerned with rendering *surfaces*.

### 10.1.1.1. Representations Used by High-End Rendering Packages

Theoretically, a surface is a two-dimensional sheet comprised of an infinite number of points in three-dimensional space. However, such a description is clearly not practical. In order for a computer to process and render arbitrary surfaces, we need a compact way to represent them numerically.

Some surfaces can be described exactly in analytical form, using a *parametric surface equation*. For example, a sphere centered at the origin can be represented by the equation $x^2 + y^2 + z^2 = r^2$. However, parametric equations aren't particularly useful for modeling arbitrary shapes.

In the film industry, surfaces are often represented by a collection of rectangular *patches* each formed from a two-dimensional spline defined by a small number of control points. Various kinds of splines are used, including Bézier surfaces (e.g., bicubic patches, which are third-order Béziers—see http://en.wikipedia.org/wiki/Bezier_surface for more information), nonuniform rational B-splines (NURBS—see http://en.wikipedia.org/wiki/Nurbs), Bézier triangles, and *N*-patches (also known as *normal patches*—see http://www.gamasutra.com/features/20020715/mollerhaines_01.htm for more details). Modeling with patches is a bit like covering a statue with little rectangles of cloth or paper maché.

High-end film rendering engines like Pixar's RenderMan use *subdivision surfaces* to define geometric shapes. Each surface is represented by a mesh of control polygons (much like a spline), but the polygons can be subdivided into smaller and smaller polygons using the Catmull-Clark algorithm. This subdivision typically proceeds until the individual polygons are smaller than a single pixel in size. The biggest benefit of this approach is that no matter how close the camera gets to the surface, it can always be subdivided further so that its silhouette edges won't look faceted. To learn more about subdivision surfaces, check out the following great article on Gamasutra: http://www.gamasutra.com/features/20000411/sharp_pfv.htm.

### 10.1.1.2. Triangle Meshes

Game developers have traditionally modeled their surfaces using triangle meshes. Triangles serve as a piece-wise linear approximation to a surface, much as a chain of connected line segments acts as a piece-wise approximation to a function or curve (see Figure 10.2).

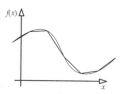

Figure 10.2. A mesh of triangles is a linear approximation to a surface, just as a series of connected line segments can serve as a linear approximation to a function or curve.

Triangles are the polygon of choice for real-time rendering because they have the following desirable properties:

- *The triangle is the simplest type of polygon.* Any fewer than three vertices, and we wouldn't have a surface at all.

- *A triangle is always planar.* Any polygon with four or more vertices need not have this property, because while the first three vertices define a plane, the fourth vertex might lie above or below that plane.

- *Triangles remain triangles under most kinds of transformations, including affine transforms and perspective projections.* At worst, a triangle viewed edge-on will degenerate into a line segment. At every other orientation, it remains triangular.

- *Virtually all commercial graphics-acceleration hardware is designed around triangle rasterization.* Starting with the earliest 3D graphics accelerators for the PC, rendering hardware has been designed almost exclusively around triangle rasterization. This decision can be traced all the way back to the first software rasterizers used in the earliest 3D games like *Castle Wolfenstein 3D* and *Doom*. Like it or not, triangle-based technologies are entrenched in our industry and probably will be for years to come.

#### Tessellation

The term *tessellation* describes a process of dividing a surface up into a collection of discrete polygons (which are usually either quadrilaterals, also known as *quads*, or triangles). *Triangulation* is tessellation of a surface into triangles.

One problem with the kind of triangle mesh used in games is that its level of tessellation is fixed by the artist when he or she creates it. Fixed tessellation

Figure 10.3. Fixed tessellation can cause an object's silhouette edges to look blocky, especially when the object is close to the camera.

can cause an object's *silhouette edges* to look blocky, as shown in Figure 10.3; this is especially noticeable when the object is close to the camera.

Ideally, we'd like a solution that can arbitrarily increase tessellation as an object gets closer to the virtual camera. In other words, we'd like to have a uniform triangle-to-pixel density, no matter how close or far away the object is. Subdivision surfaces can achieve this ideal—surfaces can be tessellated based on distance from the camera, so that every triangle is less than one pixel in size.

Game developers often attempt to approximate this ideal of uniform triangle-to-pixel density by creating a chain of alternate versions of each triangle mesh, each known as a *level of detail* (LOD). The first LOD, often called LOD 0, represents the highest level of tessellation; it is used when the object is very close to the camera. Subsequent LODs are tessellated at lower and lower resolutions (see Figure 10.4). As the object moves farther away from the camera, the engine switches from LOD 0 to LOD 1 to LOD 2, and so on. This allows the rendering engine to spend the majority of its time transforming and lighting the vertices of the objects that are closest to the camera (and therefore occupy the largest number of pixels on-screen).

Some game engines apply *dynamic tessellation* techniques to expansive meshes like water or terrain. In this technique, the mesh is usually represented by a height field defined on some kind of regular grid pattern. The region of the mesh that is closest to the camera is tessellated to the full resolution of the grid. Regions that are farther away from the camera are tessellated using fewer and fewer grid points.

*Progressive meshes* are another technique for dynamic tessellation and LODing. With this technique, a single high-resolution mesh is created for display when the object is very close to the camera. (This is essentially the LOD 0

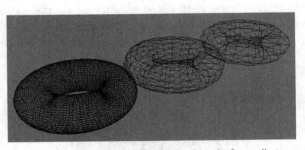

Figure 10.4. A chain of LOD meshes, each with a fixed level of tessellation, can be used to approximate uniform triangle-to-pixel density. The leftmost torus is constructed from 5000 triangles, the center torus from 450 triangles, and the rightmost torus from 200 triangles.

mesh.) This mesh is automatically detessellated as the object gets farther away by collapsing certain edges. In effect, this process automatically generates a semi-continuous chain of LODs. See http://research.microsoft.com/en-us/um/people/hoppe/pm.pdf for a detailed discussion of progressive mesh technology.

### 10.1.1.3. Constructing a Triangle Mesh

Now that we understand what triangle meshes are and why they're used, let's take a brief look at how they're constructed.

*Winding Order*

A triangle is defined by the position vectors of its three vertices, which we can denote $\mathbf{p}_1$, $\mathbf{p}_2$, and $\mathbf{p}_3$. The edges of a triangle can be found by simply subtracting the position vectors of adjacent vertices. For example,

$$\mathbf{e}_{12} = \mathbf{p}_2 - \mathbf{p}_1,$$
$$\mathbf{e}_{13} = \mathbf{p}_3 - \mathbf{p}_1,$$
$$\mathbf{e}_{23} = \mathbf{p}_3 - \mathbf{p}_2.$$

The normalized cross product of any two edges defines a unit *face normal* $\mathbf{N}$:

$$\mathbf{N} = \frac{\mathbf{e}_{12} \times \mathbf{e}_{13}}{|\mathbf{e}_{12} \times \mathbf{e}_{13}|}.$$

These derivations are illustrated in Figure 10.5. To know the *direction* of the face normal (i.e., the sense of the edge cross product), we need to define which side of the triangle should be considered the front (i.e., the outside surface of an object) and which should be the back (i.e., its inside surface). This can be defined easily by specifying a *winding order*—clockwise (CW) or counterclockwise (CCW).

Most low-level graphics APIs give us a way to *cull* back-facing triangles based on winding order. For example, if we set the cull mode parameter in Di-

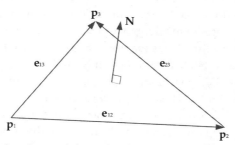

Figure 10.5. Deriving the edges and plane of a triangle from its vertices.

rect3D (`D3DRS_CULL`) to `D3DCULLMODE_CW`, then any triangle whose vertices wind in a clockwise fashion in screen space will be treated as a back-facing triangle and will not be drawn.

Back face culling is important because we generally don't want to waste time drawing triangles that aren't going to be visible anyway. Also, rendering the back faces of transparent objects can actually cause visual anomalies. The choice of winding order is an arbitrary one, but of course it must be consistent across all assets in the entire game. Inconsistent winding order is a common error among junior 3D modelers.

### Triangle Lists

The easiest way to define a mesh is simply to list the vertices in groups of three, each triple corresponding to a single triangle. This data structure is known as a *triangle list*; it is illustrated in Figure 10.6.

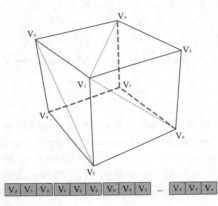

Figure 10.6. A triangle list.

### Indexed Triangle Lists

You probably noticed that many of the vertices in the triangle list shown in Figure 10.6 were duplicated, often multiple times. As we'll see in Section 10.1.2.1, we often store quite a lot of metadata with each vertex, so repeating this data in a triangle list wastes memory. It also wastes GPU bandwidth, because a duplicated vertex will be transformed and lit multiple times.

For these reasons, most rendering engines make use of a more efficient data structure known as an *indexed triangle list*. The basic idea is to list the vertices once with no duplication and then to use light-weight vertex *indices* (usually occupying only 16 bits each) to define the triples of vertices that constitute the triangles. The vertices are stored in an array known as a *vertex*

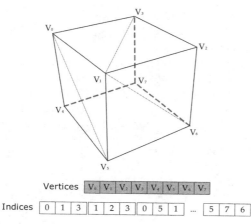

Figure 10.7. An indexed triangle list.

*buffer* (DirectX) or *vertex array* (OpenGL). The indices are stored in a separate buffer known as an *index buffer* or *index array*. This technique is shown in Figure 10.7.

### Strips and Fans

Specialized mesh data structures known as *triangle strips* and *triangle fans* are sometimes used for game rendering. Both of these data structures eliminate the need for an index buffer, while still reducing vertex duplication to some degree. They accomplish this by predefining the order in which vertices must appear and how they are combined to form triangles.

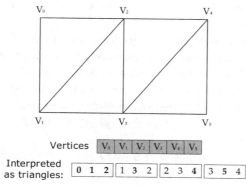

Figure 10.8. A triangle strip.

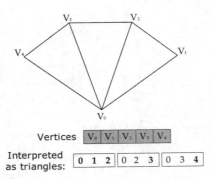

Figure 10.9. A triangle fan.

In a strip, the first three vertices define the first triangle. Each subsequent vertex forms an entirely new triangle, along with its previous two neighbors. To keep the winding order of a triangle strip consistent, the previous two neighbor vertices swap places after each new triangle. A triangle strip is shown in Figure 10.8.

In a fan, the first three vertices define the first triangle and each subsequent vertex defines a new triangle with the previous vertex and the first vertex in the fan. This is illustrated in Figure 10.9.

*Vertex Cache Optimization*

When a GPU processes an indexed triangle list, each triangle can refer to any vertex within the vertex buffer. The vertices must be processed in the order they appear within the triangles, because the integrity of each triangle must be maintained for the rasterization stage. As vertices are processed by the vertex shader, they are cached for reuse. If a subsequent primitive refers to a vertex that already resides in the cache, its processed attributes are used instead of reprocessing the vertex.

Strips and fans are used in part because they can potentially save memory (no index buffer required) and in part because they tend to improve the cache coherency of the memory accesses made by the GPU to video RAM. Even better, we can use an *indexed strip* or *indexed fan* to virtually eliminate vertex duplication (which can often save more memory than eliminating the index buffer), while still reaping the cache coherency benefits of the strip or fan vertex ordering.

Indexed triangle lists can also be cache-optimized without restricting ourselves to strip or fan vertex ordering. A *vertex cache optimizer* is an offline geometry processing tool that attempts to list the triangles in an order that optimizes vertex reuse within the cache. It generally takes into account factors such as the size of the vertex cache(s) present on a particular type of GPU and the algorithms used by the GPU to decide when to cache vertices and when to discard them. For example, the vertex cache optimizer included in Sony's *Edge* geometry processing library can achieve rendering throughput that is up to 4% better than what is possible with triangle stripping.

### 10.1.1.4. Model Space

The position vectors of a triangle mesh's vertices are usually specified relative to a convenient local coordinate system called *model space, local space,* or *object space.* The origin of model space is usually either in the center of the object or at some other convenient location, like on the floor between the feet of a character or on the ground at the horizontal centroid of the wheels of a vehicle.

As we learned in Section 4.3.9.1, the sense of the model space axes is arbitrary, but the axes typically align with the natural "front," "left" or "right," and "up" directions on the model. For a little mathematical rigor, we can define three unit vectors $\mathbf{F}$, $\mathbf{L}$ (or $\mathbf{R}$), and $\mathbf{U}$ and map them as desired onto the unit basis vectors $\mathbf{i}$, $\mathbf{j}$, and $\mathbf{k}$ (and hence to the $x$-, $y$-, and $z$-axes, respectively) in model space. For example, a common mapping is $\mathbf{L} = \mathbf{i}$, $\mathbf{U} = \mathbf{j}$, and $\mathbf{F} = \mathbf{k}$. The mapping is completely arbitrary, but it's important to be consistent for all models across the entire engine. Figure 10.10 shows one possible mapping of the model space axes for an aircraft model.

Figure 10.10. One possible mapping of the model space axes.

### 10.1.1.5. World Space and Mesh Instancing

Many individual meshes are composed into a complete scene by positioning and orienting them within a common coordinate system known as *world space.* Any one mesh might appear many times in a scene—examples include a street lined with identical lamp posts, a faceless mob of soldiers, or a swarm of spiders attacking the player. We call each such object a *mesh instance.*

A mesh instance contains a reference to its shared mesh data and also includes a transformation matrix that converts the mesh's vertices from model space to world space, within the context of that particular instance. This matrix is called the *model-to-world* matrix, or sometimes just the *world matrix*. Using the notation from Section 4.3.10.2, this matrix can be written as follows:

$$\mathbf{M}_{M \to W} = \begin{bmatrix} (\mathbf{RS})_{M \to W} & \mathbf{0} \\ \mathbf{t}_M & 1 \end{bmatrix},$$

where the upper $3 \times 3$ matrix $(\mathbf{RS})_{M \to W}$ rotates and scales model-space vertices into world space, and $\mathbf{t}_M$ is the translation of the model space axes expressed in world space. If we have the unit model space basis vectors $\mathbf{i}_M$, $\mathbf{j}_M$, and $\mathbf{k}_M$, expressed in world space coordinates, this matrix can also be written as follows:

$$\mathbf{M}_{M \to W} = \begin{bmatrix} \mathbf{i}_M & 0 \\ \mathbf{j}_M & 0 \\ \mathbf{k}_M & 0 \\ \mathbf{t}_M & 1 \end{bmatrix}.$$

Given a vertex expressed in model-space coordinates, the rendering engine calculates its world-space equivalent as follows:

$$\mathbf{v}_W = \mathbf{v}_M \mathbf{M}_{M \to W}.$$

We can think of the matrix $\mathbf{M}_{M \to W}$ as a description of the position and orientation of the model space axes themselves, expressed in world space coordinates. Or we can think of it as a matrix that transforms vertices from model space to world space.

When rendering a mesh, the model-to-world matrix is also applied to the surface normals of the mesh (see Section 10.1.2.1). Recall from Section 4.3.11, that in order to transform normal vectors properly, we must multiply them by the inverse transpose of the model-to-world matrix. If our matrix does not contain any scale or shear, we can transform our normal vectors correctly by simply setting their $w$ components to zero prior to multiplication by the model-to-world matrix, as described in Section 4.3.6.1.

Some meshes like buildings, terrain, and other background elements are entirely static and unique. The vertices of these meshes are often expressed in world space, so their model-to-world matrices are identity and can be ignored.

## 10.1.2. Describing the Visual Properties of a Surface

In order to properly render and light a surface, we need a description of its *visual properties*. Surface properties include geometric information, such as the direction of the surface normal at various points on the surface. They also encompass a description of how light should interact with the surface. This includes diffuse color, shininess/reflectivity, roughness or texture, degree of opacity or transparency, index of refraction, and other optical properties. Surface properties might also include a specification of how the surface should change over time (e.g., how an animated character's skin should track the joints of its skeleton or how the surface of a body of water should move).

The key to rendering photorealistic images is properly accounting for light's behavior as it interacts with the objects in the scene. Hence rendering engineers need to have a good understanding of how light works, how it is transported through an environment, and how the virtual camera "senses" it and translates it into the colors stored in the pixels on-screen.

### 10.1.2.1. Introduction to Light and Color

Light is electromagnetic radiation; it acts like both a wave and a particle in different situations. The color of light is determined by its *intensity I* and its *wavelength* $\lambda$ (or its frequency $f$, where $f = 1/\lambda$). The visible gamut ranges from a wavelength of 740 nm (or a frequency of 430 THz) to a wavelength of 380 nm (750 THz). A beam of light may contain a single pure wavelength (i.e., the colors of the rainbow, also known as the *spectral colors*), or it may contain a mixture of various wavelengths. We can draw a graph showing how much of each frequency a given beam of light contains, called a *spectral plot*. White light contains a little bit of all wavelengths, so its spectral plot would look roughly like a box extending across the entire visible band. Pure green light contains only one wavelength, so its spectral plot would look like a single infinitesimally narrow spike at about 570 THz.

### Light-Object Interactions

Light can have many complex interactions with matter. Its behavior is governed in part by the *medium* through which it is traveling and in part by the shape and properties of the *interfaces* between different types of media (air-solid, air-water, water-glass, etc.). Technically speaking, a surface is really just an interface between two different types of media.

Despite all of its complexity, light can really only do four things:

- It can be *absorbed*;
- It can be *reflected*;
- It can be *transmitted* through an object, usually being *refracted* (bent) in the process;
- It can be *diffracted* when passing through very narrow openings.

Most photorealistic rendering engines account for the first three of these behaviors; diffraction is not usually taken into account because its effects are rarely noticeable in most scenes.

Only certain wavelengths may be absorbed by a surface, while others are reflected. This is what gives rise to our perception of the color of an object. For example, when white light falls on a red object, all wavelengths except red are absorbed, hence the object appears red. The same perceptual effect is achieved when red light is cast onto a white object—our eyes don't know the difference.

Reflections can be *diffuse*, meaning that an incoming ray is scattered equally in all directions. Reflections can also be *specular*, meaning that an incident light ray will reflect directly or be spread only into a narrow cone. Reflections can also be *anisotropic*, meaning that the way in which light reflects from a surface changes depending on the angle at which the surface is viewed.

When light is transmitted through a volume, it can be *scattered* (as is the case for translucent objects), partially *absorbed* (as with colored glass), or *refracted* (as happens when light travels through a prism). The refraction angles can be different for different wavelengths, leading to spectral spreading. This is why we see rainbows when light passes through raindrops and glass prisms. Light can also enter a semi-solid surface, bounce around, and then exit the surface at a different point from the one at which it entered the surface. We call this *subsurface scattering*, and it is one of the effects that gives skin, wax, and marble their characteristic warm appearance.

*Color Spaces and Color Models*

A *color model* is a three-dimensional coordinate system that measures colors. A *color space* is a specific standard for how numerical colors in a particular color model should be mapped onto the colors perceived by human beings in the real world. Color models are typically three-dimensional because of the three types of color sensors (cones) in our eyes, which are sensitive to different wavelengths of light.

The most commonly used color model in computer graphics is the RGB model. In this model, color space is represented by a unit cube, with the relative intensities of red, green, and blue light measured along its axes. The red, green, and blue components are called *color channels*. In the canonical RGB color model, each channel ranges from zero to one. So the color (0, 0, 0) represents black, while (1, 1, 1) represents white.

When colors are stored in a bitmapped image, various color formats can be employed. A color format is defined in part by the number of *bits per pixel* it occupies and, more specifically, the number of bits used to represent each color channel. The RGB888 format uses eight bits per channel, for a total of

24 bits per pixel. In this format, each channel ranges from 0 to 255 rather than from zero to one. RGB565 uses five bits for red and blue and six for green, for a total of 16 bits per pixel. A paletted format might use eight bits per pixel to store indices into a 256-element color palette, each entry of which might be stored in RGB888 or some other suitable format.

A number of other color models are also used in 3D rendering. We'll see how the log-LUV color model is used for *high dynamic range* (HDR) lighting in Section 10.3.1.5.

### Opacity and the Alpha Channel

A fourth channel called *alpha* is often tacked on to RGB color vectors. As mentioned in Section 10.1.1, alpha measures the opacity of an object. When stored in an image pixel, alpha represents the opacity of the pixel.

RGB color formats can be extended to include an alpha channel, in which case they are referred to as RGBA or ARGB color formats. For example, RGBA8888 is a 32 bit-per-pixel format with eight bits each for red, green, blue, and alpha. RGBA5551 is a 16 bit-per-pixel format with one-bit alpha; in this format, colors can either be fully opaque or fully transparent.

### 10.1.2.2. Vertex Attributes

The simplest way to describe the visual properties of a surface is to specify them at discrete points on the surface. The vertices of a mesh are a convenient place to store surface properties, in which case they are called *vertex attributes*.

A typical triangle mesh includes some or all of the following attributes at each vertex. As rendering engineers, we are of course free to define any additional attributes that may be required in order to achieve a desired visual effect on-screen.

- *Position vector* ($\mathbf{p}_i = [\, p_{ix} \ p_{iy} \ p_{iz} \,]$). This is the 3D position of the $i$th vertex in the mesh. It is usually specified in a coordinate space local to the object, known as *model space*.

- *Vertex normal* ($\mathbf{n}_i = [\, n_{ix} \ n_{iy} \ n_{iz} \,]$). This vector defines the unit surface normal at the position of vertex $i$. It is used in per-vertex dynamic lighting calculations.

- *Vertex tangent* ($\mathbf{t}_i = [\, t_{ix} \ t_{iy} \ t_{iz} \,]$) and *bitangent* ($\mathbf{b}_i = [\, b_{ix} \ b_{iy} \ b_{iz} \,]$). These two unit vectors lie perpendicular to one another and to the vertex normal $\mathbf{n}_i$. Together, the three vectors $\mathbf{n}_i$, $\mathbf{t}_i$, and $\mathbf{b}_i$ define a set of coordinate axes known as *tangent space*. This space is used for various per-pixel lighting calculations, such as normal mapping and environment mapping. (The bitangent $\mathbf{b}_i$ is sometimes confusingly called the *binormal*, even though it is *not* normal to the surface.)

- *Diffuse color* ($\mathbf{d}_i = [\ d_{Ri}\ \ d_{Gi}\ \ d_{Bi}\ \ d_{Ai}\ ]$). This four-element vector describes the diffuse color of the surface, expressed in the RGB color space. It typically also includes a specification of the opacity or *alpha* (A) of the surface at the position of the vertex. This color may be calculated off-line (static lighting) or at runtime (dynamic lighting).

- *Specular color* ($\mathbf{s}_i = [\ s_{Ri}\ s_{Gi}\ s_{Bi}\ s_{Ai}\ ]$). This quantity describes the color of the specular highlight that should appear when light reflects directly from a shiny surface onto the virtual camera's imaging plane.

- *Texture coordinates* ($\mathbf{u}_{ij} = [\ u_{ij}\ \ v_{ij}\ ]$). Texture coordinates allow a two- (or sometimes three-) dimensional bitmap to be "shrink wrapped" onto the surface of a mesh—a process known as *texture mapping*. A texture coordinate ($u, v$) describes the location of a particular vertex within the two-dimensional normalized coordinate space of the texture. A triangle can be mapped with more than one texture; hence it can have more than one set of texture coordinates. We've denoted the distinct sets of texture coordinates via the subscript *j* above.

- *Skinning weights* ($k_{ij}, w_{ij}$). In skeletal animation, the vertices of a mesh are attached to individual joints in an articulated skeleton. In this case, each vertex must specify to which joint it is attached via an index, $k$. A vertex can be influenced by multiple joints, in which case the final vertex position becomes a *weighted average* of these influences. Thus, the weight of each joint's influence is denoted by a weighting factor $w$. In general, a vertex $i$ can have multiple joint influences $j$, each denoted by the pair of numbers $[\ k_{ij}\ \ w_{ij}\ ]$.

### 10.1.2.3. Vertex Formats

Vertex attributes are typically stored within a data structure such as a C `struct` or a C++ class. The layout of such a data structure is known as a *vertex format*. Different meshes require different combinations of attributes and hence need different vertex formats. The following are some examples of common vertex formats:

```
// Simplest possible vertex - position only (useful for
// shadow volume extrusion, silhouette edge detection
// for cartoon rendering, z prepass, etc.)

struct Vertex1P
{
    Vector3        m_p;        // position
};
```

```
// A typical vertex format with position, vertex normal
// and one set of texture coordinates.

struct Vertex1P1N1UV
{
    Vector3    m_p;         // position
    Vector3    m_n;         // vertex normal
    F32        m_uv[2];     // (u, v) texture coordinate
};


// A skinned vertex with position, diffuse and specular
// colors and four weighted joint influences.

struct Vertex1P1D1S2UV4J
{
    Vector3    m_p;         // position
    Color4     m_d;         // diffuse color and translucency
    Color4     m_S;         // specular color
    F32        m_uv0[2];    // first set of tex coords
    F32        m_uv1[2];    // second set of tex coords
    U8         m_k[4];      // four joint indices, and...
    F32        m_w[3];      // three joint weights, for
                            // skinning
                            // (fourth calc'd from other
                            // three)
};
```

Clearly the number of possible permutations of vertex attributes—and hence the number of distinct vertex formats—can grow to be extremely large. (In fact the number of formats is theoretically unbounded, if one were to permit any number of texture coordinates and/or joint weights.) Management of all these vertex formats is a common source of headaches for any graphics programmer.

Some steps can be taken to reduce the number of vertex formats that an engine has to support. In practical graphics applications, many of the theoretically possible vertex formats are simply not useful, or they cannot be handled by the graphics hardware or the game's shaders. Some game teams also limit themselves to a subset of the useful/feasible vertex formats in order to keep things more manageable. For example, they might only allow zero, two, or four joint weights per vertex, or they might decide to support no more than two sets of texture coordinates per vertex. Modern GPUs are capable of extracting a subset of attributes from a vertex data structure, so game teams can also choose to use a single "überformat" for all meshes and let the hardware select the relevant attributes based on the requirements of the shader.

### 10.1.2.4. Attribute Interpolation

The attributes at a triangle's vertices are just a coarse, discretized approximation to the visual properties of the surface as a whole. When rendering a triangle, what really matters are the visual properties at the interior points of the triangle as "seen" through each pixel on-screen. In other words, we need to know the values of the attributes on a *per-pixel* basis, not a per-vertex basis.

One simple way to determine the per-pixel values of a mesh's surface attributes is to *linearly interpolate* the per-vertex attribute data. When applied to vertex colors, attribute interpolation is known as *Gouraud shading*. An example of Gouraud shading applied to a triangle is shown in Figure 10.11, and its effects on a simple triangle mesh are illustrated in Figure 10.12. Interpolation is routinely applied to other kinds of vertex attribute information as well, such as vertex normals, texture coordinates, and depth.

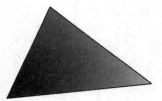

**Figure 10.11.** A Gouraud-shaded triangle with different shades of gray at the vertices.

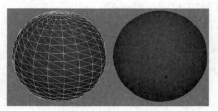

**Figure 10.12.** Gouraud shading can make faceted objects appear to be smooth.

### *Vertex Normals and Smoothing*

As we'll see in Section 10.1.3, *lighting* is the process of calculating the color of an object at various points on its surface, based on the visual properties of the surface and the properties of the light impinging upon it. The simplest way to light a mesh is to calculate the color of the surface on a *per-vertex* basis. In other words, we use the properties of the surface and the incoming light to calculate the diffuse color of each vertex ($\mathbf{d}_i$). These vertex colors are then interpolated across the triangles of the mesh via Gouraud shading.

In order to determine how a ray of light will reflect from a point on a surface, most lighting models make use of a vector that is *normal* to the surface at the point of the light ray's impact. Since we're performing lighting calculations on a per-vertex basis, we can use the vertex normal $\mathbf{n}_i$ for this purpose. Therefore, the directions of a mesh's vertex normals can have a significant impact on the final appearance of a mesh.

As an example, consider a tall, thin, four-sided box. If we want the box to appear to be sharp-edged, we can specify the vertex normals to be perpendicular to the faces of the box. As we light each triangle, we will encounter the same normal vector at all three vertices, so the resulting lighting will appear flat, and it will abruptly change at the corners of the box just as the vertex normals do.

We can also make the same box mesh look a bit like a smooth cylinder by specifying vertex normals that point radially outward from the box's center line. In this case, the vertices of each triangle will have different vertex normals, causing us to calculate different colors at each vertex. Gouraud shading will smoothly interpolate these vertex colors, resulting in lighting that appears to vary smoothly across the surface. This effect is illustrated in Figure 10.13.

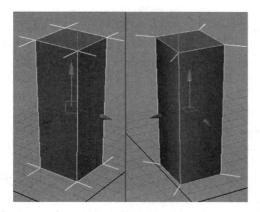

**Figure 10.13.** The directions of a mesh's vertex normals can have a profound effect on the colors calculated during per-vertex lighting calculations.

### 10.1.2.5. Textures

When triangles are relatively large, specifying surface properties on a per-vertex basis can be too coarse-grained. Linear attribute interpolation isn't always what we want, and it can lead to undesirable visual anomalies.

As an example, consider the problem of rendering the bright *specular highlight* that can occur when light shines on a glossy object. If the mesh is

**Figure 10.14.** Linear interpolation of vertex attributes does not always yield an adequate description of the visual properties of a surface, especially when tessellation is low.

highly tessellated, per-vertex lighting combined with Gouraud shading can yield reasonably good results. However, when the triangles are too large, the errors that arise from linearly interpolating the specular highlight can become jarringly obvious, as shown in Figure 10.14.

To overcome the limitations of per-vertex surface attributes, rendering engineers use bitmapped images known as *texture maps*. A texture often contains color information and is usually projected onto the triangles of a mesh. In this case, it acts a bit like those silly fake tattoos we used to apply to our arms when we were kids. But a texture can contain other kinds of visual surface properties as well as colors. And a texture needn't be projected onto a mesh—for example, a texture might be used as a stand-alone data table. The individual picture elements of a texture are called *texels* to differentiate them from the pixels on the screen.

The dimensions of a texture bitmap are constrained to be powers of two on some graphics hardware. Typical texture dimensions include 256 × 256, 512 × 512, 1024 × 1024, and 2048 × 2048, although textures can be any size on most hardware, provided the texture fits into video memory. Some graphics hardware imposes additional restrictions, such as requiring textures to be square, or lifts some restrictions, such as not constraining texture dimensions to be powers of two.

### Types of Textures

The most common type of texture is known as a *diffuse map*, or *albedo map*. It describes the diffuse surface color at each texel on a surface and acts like a decal or paint job on the surface.

Other types of textures are used in computer graphics as well, including *normal maps* (which store unit normal vectors at each texel, encoded as RGB values), *gloss maps* (which encode how shiny a surface should be at each texel), environment maps (which contain a picture of the surrounding environment for rendering reflections), and many others. See Section 10.3.1 for a discussion of how various types of textures can be used for image-based lighting and other effects.

We can actually use texture maps to store any information that we happen to need in our lighting calculations. For example, a one-dimensional texture could be used to store sampled values of a complex math function, a color-to-color mapping table, or any other kind of look-up table (LUT).

### Texture Coordinates

Let's consider how to project a two-dimensional texture onto a mesh. To do this, we define a two-dimensional coordinate system known as *texture space*. A texture coordinate is usually represented by a normalized pair of numbers denoted $(u, v)$. These coordinates always range from $(0, 0)$ at the bottom left corner of the texture to $(1, 1)$ at the top right. Using normalized coordinates like this allows the same coordinate system to be used regardless of the dimensions of the texture.

To map a triangle onto a 2D texture, we simply specify a pair of texture coordinates $(u_i, v_i)$ at each vertex $i$. This effectively maps the triangle onto the image plane in texture space. An example of texture mapping is depicted in Figure 10.15.

**Figure 10.15.** An example of texture mapping. The triangles are shown both in three-dimensional space and in texture space.

### Texture Addressing Modes

Texture coordinates are permitted to extend beyond the [0, 1] range. The graphics hardware can handle out-of-range texture coordinates in any one of the following ways. These are known as *texture addressing modes*; which mode is used is under the control of the user.

- *Wrap.* In this mode, the texture is repeated over and over in every direction. All texture coordinates of the form $(ju, kv)$ are equivalent to the coordinate $(u, v)$, where $j$ and $k$ are arbitrary integers.

- *Mirror.* This mode acts like wrap mode, except that the texture is mirrored about the $v$-axis for odd integer multiples of $u$, and about the $u$-axis for odd integer multiples of $v$.

- *Clamp.* In this mode, the colors of the texels around the outer edge of the texture are simply extended when texture coordinates fall outside the normal range.

- *Border color.* In this mode, an arbitrary user-specified color is used for the region outside the [0, 1] texture coordinate range.

These texture addressing modes are depicted in Figure 10.16.

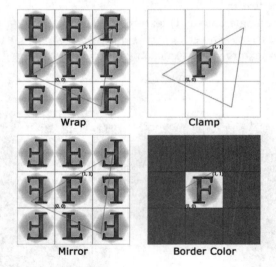

Figure 10.16. Texture addressing modes.

### Texture Formats

Texture bitmaps can be stored on disk in virtually any image format provided your game engine includes the code necessary to read it into memory. Common formats include Targa (.tga), Portable Network Graphics (.png), Windows Bitmap (.bmp), and Tagged Image File Format (.tif). In memory, textures are usually represented as two-dimensional (strided) arrays of pixels using various color formats, including RGB888, RGBA8888, RGB565, RGBA5551, and so on.

Most modern graphics cards and graphics APIs support *compressed textures*. DirectX supports a family of compressed formats known as DXT or S3 Texture Compression (S3TC). We won't cover the details here, but the basic idea is to break the texture into 2 × 2 blocks of pixels and use a small color palette to store the colors for each block. You can read more about S3 compressed texture formats at http://en.wikipedia.org/wiki/S3_Texture_Compression.

Compressed textures have the obvious benefit of using less memory than their uncompressed counterparts. An additional unexpected plus is that they are faster to render with as well. S3 compressed textures achieve this speed-up because of more cache-friendly memory access patterns—4 × 4 blocks of adjacent pixels are stored in a single 64- or 128-bit machine word—and because more of the texture can fit into the cache at once. Compressed textures do suffer from compression artifacts. While the anomalies are usually not noticeable, there are situations in which uncompressed textures must be used.

### Texel Density and Mipmapping

Imagine rendering a full-screen quad (a rectangle composed of two triangles) that has been mapped with a texture whose resolution exactly matches that of the screen. In this case, each texel maps exactly to a single pixel on-screen, and we say that the *texel density* (ratio of texels to pixels) is one. When this same quad is viewed at a distance, its on-screen area becomes smaller. The resolution of the texture hasn't changed, so the quad's texel density is now greater than one (meaning that more than one texel is contributing to each pixel).

Clearly texel density is not a fixed quantity—it changes as a texture-mapped object moves relative to the camera. Texel density affects the memory consumption and the visual quality of a three-dimensional scene. When the texel density is much less than one, the texels become significantly larger than a pixel on-screen, and you can start to see the edges of the texels. This destroys the illusion. When texel density is much greater than one, many texels contribute to a single pixel on-screen. This can cause a *moiré banding pattern*, as shown in Figure 10.17. Worse, a pixel's color can appear to swim and flicker as different texels within the boundaries of the pixel dominate its color depending on subtle changes in camera angle or position. Rendering a distant object with a very high texel density can also be a waste of memory if the player can *never* get close to it. After all, why keep such a high-res texture in memory if no one will ever see all that detail?

Ideally we'd like to maintain a texel density that is close to one at all times, for both nearby and distant objects. This is impossible to achieve exactly, but it can be approximated via a technique called *mipmapping*. For each texture,

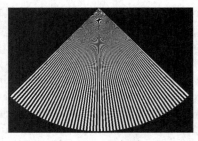

Figure 10.17. A texel density greater than one can lead to a moiré pattern.

we create a sequence of lower-resolution bitmaps, each of which is one-half the width and one-half the height of its predecessor. We call each of these images a *mipmap*, or *mip level*. For example, a 64 × 64 texture would have the following mip levels: 64 × 64, 32 × 32, 16 × 16, 8 × 8, 4 × 4, 2 × 2, and 1 × 1, as shown in Figure 10.18. Once we have mipmapped our textures, the graphics hardware selects the appropriate mip level based on a triangle's distance away from the camera, in an attempt to maintain a texel density that is close to one. For example, if a texture takes up an area of 40 × 40 on-screen, the 64 × 64 mip level might be selected; if that same texture takes up only a 10 × 10 area, the 16 × 16 mip level might be used. As we'll see below, *trilinear filtering* allows the hardware to sample two adjacent mip levels and blend the results. In this case, a 10 × 10 area might be mapped by blending the 16 × 16 and 8 × 8 mip levels together.

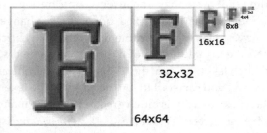

Figure 10.18. Mip levels for a 64×64 texture.

### World Space Texel Density

The term "texel density" can also be used to describe the ratio of texels to world space area on a textured surface. For example, a two meter cube mapped with a 256 × 256 texture would have a texel density of $256^2/2^2 = 16{,}384$. I will call this *world space texel density* to differentiate it from the screen space texel density we've been discussing thus far.

World-space texel density need not be close to one, and in fact the specific value will usually be much greater than one and depends entirely upon your choice of world units. Nonetheless, it is important for objects to be texture mapped with a reasonably consistent world space texel density. For example, we would expect all six sides of a cube to occupy the same texture area. If this were not the case, the texture on one side of the cube would have a lower-resolution appearance than another side, which can be noticeable to the player. Many game studios provide their art teams with guidelines and in-engine texel density visualization tools in an effort to ensure that all objects in the game have a reasonably consistent world space texel density.

*Texture Filtering*

When rendering a pixel of a textured triangle, the graphics hardware samples the texture map by considering where the pixel center falls in texture space. There is usually not a clean one-to-one mapping between texels and pixels, and pixel centers can fall at any place in texture space, including directly on the boundary between two or more texels. Therefore, the graphics hardware usually has to sample more than one texel and blend the resulting colors to arrive at the actual sampled texel color. We call this *texture filtering*.

Most graphics cards support the following kinds of texture filtering:

- *Nearest neighbor.* In this crude approach, the texel whose center is closest to the pixel center is selected. When mipmapping is enabled, the mip level is selected whose resolution is nearest to but greater than the ideal theoretical resolution needed to achieve a screen-space texel density of one.

- *Bilinear.* In this approach, the four texels surrounding the pixel center are sampled, and the resulting color is a weighted average of their colors (where the weights are based on the distances of the texel centers from the pixel center). When mipmapping is enabled, the nearest mip level is selected.

- *Trilinear.* In this approach, bilinear filtering is used on each of the two nearest mip levels (one higher-res than the ideal and the other lower-res), and these results are then linearly interpolated. This eliminates abrupt visual boundaries between mip levels on-screen.

- *Anisotropic.* Both bilinear and trilinear filtering sample $2 \times 2$ square blocks of texels. This is the right thing to do when the textured surface is being viewed head-on, but it's incorrect when the surface is at an oblique angle relative to the virtual screen plane. Anisotropic filtering samples texels within a trapezoidal region corresponding to the view angle, thereby increasing the quality of textured surfaces when viewed at an angle.

### 10.1.2.6. Materials

A *material* is a complete description of the visual properties of a mesh. This includes a specification of the textures that are mapped to its surface and also various higher-level properties, such as which shader programs to use when rendering the mesh, the input parameters to those shaders, and other parameters that control the functionality of the graphics acceleration hardware itself.

While technically part of the surface properties description, vertex attributes are not considered to be part of the material. However, they come along for the ride with the mesh, so a mesh-material pair contains all the information we need to render the object. Mesh-material pairs are sometimes called *render packets*, and the term "geometric primitive" is sometimes extended to encompass mesh-material pairs as well.

A 3D model typically uses more than one material. For example, a model of a human would have separate materials for the hair, skin, eyes, teeth, and various kinds of clothing. For this reason, a mesh is usually divided into *submeshes*, each mapped to a single material. The Ogre3D rendering engine implements this design via its `Ogre::SubMesh` class.

## 10.1.3.  Lighting Basics

Lighting is at the heart of all CG rendering. Without good lighting, an otherwise beautifully modeled scene will look flat and artificial. Likewise, even the

**Figure 10.19.** A variation on the classic "Cornell box" scene illustrating how realistic lighting can make even the simplest scene appear photorealistic.

simplest of scenes can be made to look extremely realistic when it is lit accurately. The classic "Cornell box" scene, shown in Figure 10.19, is an excellent example of this.

The following sequence of screen shots from Naughty Dog's *Uncharted: Drake's Fortune* is another good illustration of the importance of lighting. In Figure 10.20, the scene is rendered without textures. Figure 10.21 shows the same scene with diffuse textures applied. The fully lit scene is shown in Figure 10.22. Notice the marked jump in realism when lighting is applied to the scene.

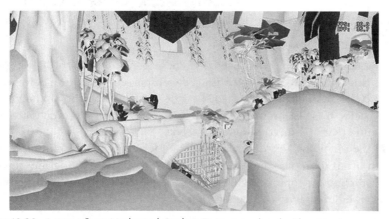

**Figure 10.20.** A scene from *Uncharted: Drake's Fortune* rendered without textures.

**Figure 10.21.** The same *UDF* scene with only diffuse textures applied.

Figure 10.22. The *UDF* scene with full lighting.

The term *shading* is often used as a loose generalization of lighting plus other visual effects. As such, "shading" encompasses procedural deformation of vertices to simulate the motion of a water surface, generation of hair curves or fur shells, tessellation of high-order surfaces, and pretty much any other calculation that's required to render a scene.

In the following sections, we'll lay the foundations of lighting that we'll need in order to understand graphics hardware and the rendering pipeline. We'll return to the topic of lighting in Section 10.3, where we'll survey some advanced lighting and shading techniques.

### 10.1.3.1. Local and Global Illumination Models

Rendering engines use various mathematical models of light-surface and light-volume interactions called *light transport models*. The simplest models only account for *direct lighting* in which light is emitted, bounces off a single object in the scene, and then proceeds directly to the imaging plane of the virtual camera. Such simple models are called *local illumination models*, because only the local effects of light on a single object are considered; objects do not affect one another's appearance in a local lighting model. Not surprisingly, local models were the first to be used in games, and they are still in use today—local lighting can produce surprisingly realistic results in some circumstances.

True photorealism can only be achieved by accounting for *indirect lighting*, where light bounces multiple times off many surfaces before reaching the virtual camera. Lighting models that account for indirect lighting are called *global illumination models*. Some global illumination models are targeted at simulating one specific visual phenomenon, such as producing realistic shadows, modeling reflective surfaces, accounting for interreflection between objects (where the color of one object affects the colors of surrounding objects), and modeling caustic effects (the intense reflections from water or a shiny metal surface). Other global illumination models attempt to provide a holistic account of a wide range of optical phenomena. Ray tracing and radiosity methods are examples of such technologies.

Global illumination is described completely by a mathematical formulation known as the *rendering equation* or *shading equation*. It was introduced in 1986 by J. T. Kajiya as part of a seminal SIGGRAPH paper. In a sense, every rendering technique can be thought of as a full or partial solution to the rendering equation, although they differ in their fundamental approach to solving it and in the assumptions, simplifications, and approximations they make. See http://en.wikipedia.org/wiki/Rendering_equation, [8], [1], and virtually any other text on advanced rendering and lighting for more details on the rendering equation.

### 10.1.3.2. The Phong Lighting Model

The most common local lighting model employed by game rendering engines is the *Phong* reflection model. It models the light reflected from a surface as a sum of three distinct terms:

- The *ambient* term models the overall lighting level of the scene. It is a gross approximation of the amount of indirect bounced light present in the scene. Indirect bounces are what cause regions in shadow not to appear totally black.

- The *diffuse* term accounts for light that is reflected uniformly in all directions from each direct light source. This is a good approximation to the way in which real light bounces off a matte surface, such as a block of wood or a piece of cloth.

- The *specular* term models the bright highlights we sometimes see when viewing a glossy surface. Specular highlights occur when the viewing angle is closely aligned with a path of direct reflection from a light source.

Figure 10.23 shows how the ambient, diffuse, and specular terms add together to produce the final intensity and color of a surface.

To calculate Phong reflection at a specific point on a surface, we require a number of input parameters. The Phong model is normally applied to all three color channels (R, G and B) independently, so all of the color parameters in the following discussion are three-element vectors. The inputs to the Phong model are:

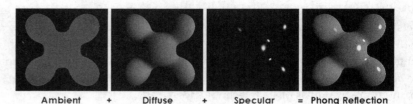

Figure 10.23. Ambient, diffuse and specular terms are summed to calculate Phong reflection.

- the viewing direction vector $\mathbf{V} = [\, V_x \; V_y \; V_z \,]$, which extends from the reflection point to the virtual camera's focal point (i.e., the negation of the camera's world-space "front" vector);
- the ambient light intensity for the three color channels, $\mathbf{A} = [\, A_R \; A_G \; A_B \,]$;
- the surface normal $\mathbf{N} = [\, N_x \; N_y \; N_z \,]$ at the point the light ray impinges on the surface;
- the surface reflectance properties, which are
  □ the ambient reflectivity $k_A$,
  □ the diffuse reflectivity $k_D$,
  □ the specular reflectivity $k_S$,
  □ and a specular "glossiness" exponent $\alpha$;
- and, for each light source $i$,
  □ the light's color and intensity $\mathbf{C}_i = [\, C_{Ri} \; C_{Gi} \; C_{Bi} \,]$,
  □ the direction vector $\mathbf{L}_i$ from the reflection point to the light source.

In the Phong model, the intensity $\mathbf{I}$ of light reflected from a point can be expressed with the following vector equation:

$$\mathbf{I} = k_A \mathbf{A} + \sum_i \left[ k_D (\mathbf{N} \cdot \mathbf{L}_i) + k_S (\mathbf{R}_i \cdot \mathbf{V})^\alpha \right] \mathbf{C}_i,$$

where the sum is taken over all lights $i$ affecting the point in question. This can be broken into three scalar equations, one for each color channel:

$$I_R = k_A A_R + \sum_i \left[ k_D (\mathbf{N} \cdot \mathbf{L}_i) + k_S (\mathbf{R}_i \cdot \mathbf{V})^\alpha \right] C_{Ri},$$

$$I_G = k_A A_G + \sum_i \left[ k_D (\mathbf{N} \cdot \mathbf{L}_i) + k_S (\mathbf{R}_i \cdot \mathbf{V})^\alpha \right] C_{Gi},$$

$$I_B = k_A A_B + \sum_i \left[ k_D (\mathbf{N} \cdot \mathbf{L}_i) + k_S (\mathbf{R}_i \cdot \mathbf{V})^\alpha \right] C_{Bi}.$$

In these equations, the vector $\mathbf{R}_i = [\, R_{xi} \;\; R_{yi} \;\; R_{zi} \,]$ is the *reflection* of the light ray's direction vector $\mathbf{L}_i$ about the surface normal $\mathbf{N}$.

The vector $\mathbf{R}_i$ can be easily calculated via a bit of vector math. Any vector can be expressed as a sum of its tangential and normal components. For example, we can break up the light direction vector $\mathbf{L}$ as follows:

$$\mathbf{L} = \mathbf{L}_T + \mathbf{L}_N.$$

We know that the dot product $(\mathbf{N} \cdot \mathbf{L})$ represents the projection of $\mathbf{L}$ normal to the surface (a scalar quantity). So the normal component $\mathbf{L}_N$ is just the unit normal vector $\mathbf{N}$ scaled by this dot product:

$$\mathbf{L}_N = (\mathbf{N} \cdot \mathbf{L})\mathbf{N}.$$

The reflected vector $\mathbf{R}$ has the same normal component as $\mathbf{L}$ but the *opposite* tangential component $(-\mathbf{L}_T)$. So we can find $\mathbf{R}$ as follows:

$$\begin{aligned} \mathbf{R} &= \mathbf{L}_N - \mathbf{L}_T \\ &= \mathbf{L}_N - (\mathbf{L} - \mathbf{L}_N) \\ &= 2\mathbf{L}_N - \mathbf{L}; \\ \mathbf{R} &= 2(\mathbf{N} \cdot \mathbf{L})\mathbf{N} - \mathbf{L}. \end{aligned}$$

This equation can be used to find all of the $\mathbf{R}_i$ values corresponding to the light directions $\mathbf{L}_i$.

### Blinn-Phong

The *Blinn-Phong* lighting model is a variation on Phong shading that calculates specular reflection in a slightly different way. We define the vector $\mathbf{H}$ to be the vector that lies halfway between the view vector $\mathbf{V}$ and the light direction vector $\mathbf{L}$. The Blinn-Phong specular component is then $(\mathbf{N} \cdot \mathbf{H})^a$, as opposed to Phong's $(\mathbf{R} \cdot \mathbf{V})^\alpha$. The exponent $a$ is slightly different than the Phong exponent $\alpha$, but its value is chosen in order to closely match the equivalent Phong specular term.

The Blinn-Phong model offers increased runtime efficiency at the cost of some accuracy, although it actually matches empirical results more closely than Phong for some kinds of surfaces. The Blinn-Phong model was used almost exclusively in early computer games and was hard-wired into the fixed-function pipelines of early GPUs. See http://en.wikipedia.org/wiki/Blinn%E2%80%93Phong_shading_model for more details.

### BRDF Plots

The three terms in the Phong lighting model are special cases of a general local reflection model known as a *bidirectional reflection distribution function* (BRDF).

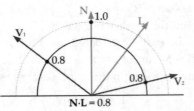

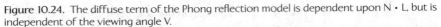

Figure 10.24. The diffuse term of the Phong reflection model is dependent upon N · L, but is independent of the viewing angle V.

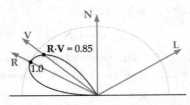

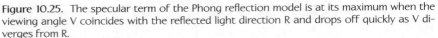

Figure 10.25. The specular term of the Phong reflection model is at its maximum when the viewing angle V coincides with the reflected light direction R and drops off quickly as V diverges from R.

A BRDF calculates the ratio of the outgoing (reflected) radiance along a given viewing direction **V** to the incoming irradiance along the incident ray **L**.

A BRDF can be visualized as a hemispherical plot, where the radial distance from the origin represents the intensity of the light that would be seen if the reflection point were viewed from that direction. The *diffuse* Phong reflection term is $k_D(\mathbf{N} \cdot \mathbf{L})$. This term only accounts for the incoming illumination ray **L**, not the viewing angle **V**. Hence the value of this term is the same for all viewing angles. If we were to plot this term as a function of the viewing angle in three dimensions, it would look like a hemisphere centered on the point at which we are calculating the Phong reflection. This is shown in two dimensions in Figure 10.24.

The specular term of the Phong model is $k_S(\mathbf{R} \cdot \mathbf{V})^\alpha$. This term is dependent on both the illumination direction **L** and the viewing direction **V**. It produces a specular "hot spot" when the viewing angle aligns closely with the reflection **R** of the illumination direction **L** about the surface normal. However, its contribution falls off very quickly as the viewing angle diverges from the reflected illumination direction. This is shown in two dimensions in Figure 10.25.

### 10.1.3.3. Modeling Light Sources

In addition to modeling the light's interactions with surfaces, we need to describe the sources of light in the scene. As with all things in real-time rendering, we approximate real-world light sources using various simplified models.

*Static Lighting*

The fastest lighting calculation is the one you don't do at all. Lighting is therefore performed off-line whenever possible. We can precalculate Phong reflection at the vertices of a mesh and store the results as diffuse vertex color attributes. We can also precalculate lighting on a per pixel basis and store the results in a kind of texture map known as a *light map*. At runtime, the light map texture is projected onto the objects in the scene in order to determine the light's effects on them.

You might wonder why we don't just bake lighting information directly into the diffuse textures in the scene. There are a few reasons for this. For one thing, diffuse texture maps are often tiled and/or repeated throughout a scene, so baking lighting into them wouldn't be practical. Instead, a single light map is usually generated per light source and applied to any objects that fall within that light's area of influence. This approach permits dynamic objects to move past a light source and be properly illuminated by it. It also means that our light maps can be of a different (often lower) resolution than our diffuse texture maps. Finally, a "pure" light map usually compresses better than one that includes diffuse color information.

*Ambient Lights*

An *ambient light* corresponds to the ambient term in the Phong lighting model. This term is independent of the viewing angle and has no specific direction. An ambient light is therefore represented by a single color, corresponding to the **A** color term in the Phong equation (which is scaled by the surface's ambient reflectivity $k_A$ at runtime). The intensity and color of ambient light may vary from region to region within the game world.

*Directional Lights*

A *directional light* models a light source that is effectively an infinite distance away from the surface being illuminated—like the sun. The rays emanating from a directional light are parallel, and the light itself does not have any particular location in the game world. A directional light is therefore modeled as a light color **C** and a direction vector **L**. A directional light is depicted in Figure 10.26.

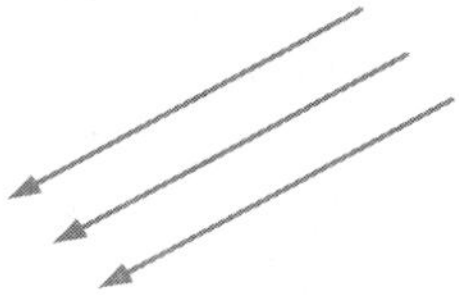

Figure 10.26. Model of a directional light source.

*Point (Omni-Directional) Lights*

A *point light* (*omni-directional* light) has a distinct position in the game world and radiates uniformly in all directions. The intensity of the light is usually considered to fall off with the square of the distance from the light source, and beyond a predefined maximum radius its effects are simply clamped to zero. A point light is modeled as a light position **P**, a source color/intensity **C**,

Figure 10.27. Model of a point light source.

and a maximum radius $r_{max}$. The rendering engine only applies the effects of a point light to those surfaces that fall within is sphere of influence (a significant optimization). Figure 10.27 illustrates a point light.

### Spot Lights

A *spot light* acts like a point light whose rays are restricted to a cone-shaped region, like a flashlight. Usually two cones are specified with an inner and an outer angle. Within the inner cone, the light is considered to be at full intensity. The light intensity falls off as the angle increases from the inner to the outer angle, and beyond the outer cone it is considered to be zero. Within both cones, the light intensity also falls off with radial distance. A spot light is modeled as a position $\mathbf{P}$, a source color $\mathbf{C}$, a central direction vector $\mathbf{L}$, a maximum radius $r_{max}$, and inner and outer cone angles $\theta_{min}$ and $\theta_{max}$. Figure 10.28 illustrates a spot light source.

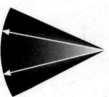

**Figure 10.28.** Model of a spot light source.

### Area Lights

All of the light sources we've discussed thus far radiate from an idealized point, either at infinity or locally. A real light source almost always has a non-zero area—this is what gives rise to the umbra and penumbra in the shadows it casts.

Rather than trying to model area lights explicitly, CG engineers often use various "tricks" to account for their behavior. For example to simulate a penumbra, we might cast multiple shadows and blend the results, or we might blur the edges of a sharp shadow in some manner.

### Emissive Objects

Some surfaces in a scene are themselves light sources. Examples include flashlights, glowing crystal balls, flames from a rocket engine, and so on. Glowing surfaces can be modeled using an *emissive texture map*—a texture whose colors are always at full intensity, independent of the surrounding lighting environment. Such a texture could be used to define a neon sign, a car's headlights, and so on.

Some kinds of emissive objects are rendered by combining multiple techniques. For example, a flashlight might be rendered using an emissive texture for when you're looking head-on into the beam, a colocated spot light that casts light into the scene, a yellow translucent mesh to simulate the light cone, some camera-facing transparent cards to simulate lens flare (or a *bloom* effect if high dynamic range lighting is supported by the engine), and a projected texture to produce the caustic effect that a flashlight has on the surfaces it illuminates. The flashlight in *Luigi's Mansion* is a great example of this kind of effect combination, as shown in Figure 10.29.

**Figure 10.29.** The flashlight in Luigi's Mansion is composed of numerous visual effects, including a cone of translucent geometry for the beam, a dynamic spot light to cast light into the scene, an emissive texture on the lens, and camera-facing cards for the lens flare.

## 10.1.4. The Virtual Camera

In computer graphics, the virtual camera is much simpler than a real camera or the human eye. We treat the camera as an ideal focal point with a rectangular virtual sensing surface called the *imaging rectangle* floating some small distance in front of it. The imaging rectangle consists of a grid of square or rectangular virtual light sensors, each corresponding to a single pixel on-screen. Rendering can be thought of as the process of determining what color and intensity of light would be recorded by each of these virtual sensors.

### 10.1.4.1. View Space

The focal point of the virtual camera is the origin of a 3D coordinate system known as *view space* or *camera space*. The camera usually "looks" down the positive or negative z-axis in view space, with y up and x to the left or right. Typical left- and right-handed view space axes are illustrated in Figure 10.30.

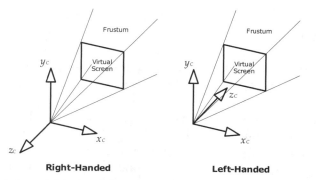

**Figure 10.30.** Left- and right-handed camera space axes.

The camera's position and orientation can be specified using a view-to-world matrix, just as a mesh instance is located in the scene with its model-to-world matrix. If we know the position vector and three unit basis vectors of camera space, expressed in world-space coordinates, the view-to-world matrix can be written as follows, in a manner analogous to that used to construct a model-to-view matrix:

$$\mathbf{M}_{V \to W} = \begin{bmatrix} \mathbf{i}_V & 0 \\ \mathbf{j}_V & 0 \\ \mathbf{k}_V & 0 \\ \hline \mathbf{t}_V & 1 \end{bmatrix}.$$

When rendering a triangle mesh, its vertices are transformed first from model space to world space, and then from world space to view space. To perform this latter transformation, we need the world-to-view matrix, which is the inverse of the view-to-world matrix. This matrix is sometimes called the *view matrix*:

$$\mathbf{M}_{W \to V} = (\mathbf{M}_{V \to W})^{-1} = \mathbf{M}_{\text{view}}.$$

Be careful here. The fact that the camera's matrix is inverted relative to the matrices of the objects in the scene is a common point of confusion and bugs among new game developers.

The world-to-view matrix is often concatenated to the model-to-world matrix prior to rendering a particular mesh instance. This combined matrix is called the *model-view matrix* in OpenGL. We precalculate this matrix so that the rendering engine only needs to do a single matrix multiply when transforming vertices from model into view space:

$$\mathbf{M}_{M \to V} = \mathbf{M}_{M \to W}\, \mathbf{M}_{W \to V} = \mathbf{M}_{\text{model-view}}.$$

### 10.1.4.2. Projections

In order to render a 3D scene onto a 2D image plane, we use a special kind of transformation known as a *projection*. The *perspective* projection is the most common projection in computer graphics, because it mimics the kinds of images produced by a typical camera. With this projection, objects appear smaller the farther away they are from the camera—an effect known as *perspective foreshortening*.

The length-preserving *orthographic* projection is also used by some games, primarily for rendering *plan views* (e.g., front, side, and top) of 3D models or game levels for editing purposes, and for overlaying 2D graphics onto the screen for heads-up displays (HUDs) and the like. Figure 10.31 illustrates how a cube would look when rendered with these two types of projections.

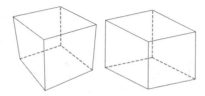

**Figure 10.31.** A cube rendered using a perspective projection (on the left) and an orthographic projection (on the right).

### 10.1.4.3. The View Volume and the Frustum

The region of space that the camera can "see" is known as the view volume. A view volume is defined by six planes. The *near plane* corresponds to the virtual image-sensing surface. The four side planes correspond to the edges of the virtual screen. The *far plane* is used as a rendering optimization to ensure that extremely distant objects are not drawn. It also provides an upper limit for the depths that will be stored in the depth buffer (see Section 10.1.4.8).

When rendering the scene with a *perspective* projection, the shape of the view volume is a truncated pyramid known as a *frustum*. When using an orthographic projection, the view volume is a rectangular prism. Perspective and orthographic view volumes are illustrated in Figure 10.32 and Figure 10.33, respectively.

The six planes of the view volume can be represented compactly using six four-element vectors $(n_{xi}, n_{yi}, n_{zi}, d_i)$, where $\mathbf{n} = (n_x, n_y, n_z)$ is the plane normal and $d$ is its perpendicular distance from the origin. If we prefer the point-normal plane representation, we can also describe the planes with six pairs of vectors $(\mathbf{Q}_i, \mathbf{n}_i)$, where $\mathbf{Q}$ is the arbitrary point on the plane and $\mathbf{n}$ is the plane normal. (In both cases, $i$ is the index of the plane.)

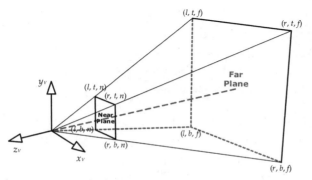

**Figure 10.32.** A perspective view volume (frustum).

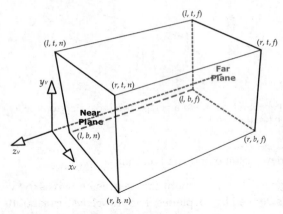

Figure 10.33. An orthographic view volume.

### 10.1.4.4. Projection and Homogeneous Clip Space

Both perspective and orthographic projections transform points in view space into a coordinate space called *homogeneous clip space*. This three-dimensional space is really just a warped version of view space. The purpose of clip space is to convert the camera-space view volume into a canonical view volume that is independent both of the kind of *projection* used to convert the 3D scene into 2D screen space, and of the *resolution* and *aspect ratio* of the screen onto which the scene is going to be rendered.

   In clip space, the canonical view volume is a rectangular prism extending from −1 to +1 along the *x*- and *y*-axes. Along the *z*-axis, the view volume extends either from −1 to +1 (OpenGL) or from 0 to 1 (DirectX). We call this coor-

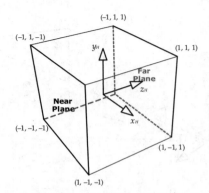

Figure 10.34. The canonical view volume in homogeneous clip space.

dinate system "clip space" because the view volume planes are axis-aligned, making it convenient to *clip* triangles to the view volume in this space (even when a perspective projection is being used). The canonical clip-space view volume for OpenGL is depicted in Figure 10.34. Notice that the z-axis of clip space goes into the screen, with $y$ up and $x$ to the right. In other words, homogeneous clip space is usually *left-handed*.

*Perspective Projection*

An excellent explanation of perspective projection is given in Section 4.5.1 of [28], so we won't repeat it here. Instead, we'll simply present the perspective projection matrix $\mathbf{M}_{V \to H}$ below. (The subscript V→H indicates that this matrix transforms vertices from view space into homogeneous clip space.) If we take view space to be right-handed, then the near plane intersects the z-axis at $z = -n$, and the far plane intersects it at $z = -f$. The virtual screen's left, right, bottom, and top edges lie at $x = l$, $x = r$, $y = b$, and $y = t$ on the near plane, respectively. (Typically the virtual screen is centered on the camera-space z-axis, in which case $l = -r$ and $b = -t$, but this isn't always the case.) Using these definitions, the perspective projection matrix for OpenGL is as follows:

$$\mathbf{M}_{V \to H} = \begin{bmatrix} \left(\dfrac{2n}{r-l}\right) & 0 & 0 & 0 \\[2ex] 0 & \left(\dfrac{2n}{t-b}\right) & 0 & 0 \\[2ex] \left(\dfrac{r+l}{r-l}\right) & \left(\dfrac{t+b}{t-b}\right) & \left(-\dfrac{f+n}{f-n}\right) & -1 \\[2ex] 0 & 0 & \left(-\dfrac{2nf}{f-n}\right) & 0 \end{bmatrix}.$$

DirectX defines the z-axis extents of the clip-space view volume to lie in the range [0, 1] rather thanin the range [−1, 1] as OpenGL does. We can easily adjust the perspective projection matrix to account for DirectX's conventions as follows:

$$(\mathbf{M}_{V \to H})_{\text{DirectX}} = \begin{bmatrix} \left(\dfrac{2n}{r-l}\right) & 0 & 0 & 0 \\[2ex] 0 & \left(\dfrac{2n}{t-b}\right) & 0 & 0 \\[2ex] \left(\dfrac{r+l}{r-l}\right) & \left(\dfrac{t+b}{t-b}\right) & \left(-\dfrac{f}{f-n}\right) & -1 \\[2ex] 0 & 0 & \left(-\dfrac{nf}{f-n}\right) & 0 \end{bmatrix}.$$

*Division by Z*

Perspective projection results in each vertex's $x$- and $y$-coordinates being divided by its $z$-coordinate. This is what produces perspective foreshortening. To understand why this happens, consider multiplying a view-space point $\mathbf{p}_V$ expressed in four-element homogeneous coordinates by the OpenGL perspective projection matrix:

$$\mathbf{p}_H = \mathbf{p}_V \, \mathbf{M}_{V \to H}$$

$$= \begin{bmatrix} p_{Vx} & p_{Vy} & p_{Vz} & 1 \end{bmatrix} \begin{bmatrix} \left(\dfrac{2n}{r-l}\right) & 0 & 0 & 0 \\ 0 & \left(\dfrac{2n}{t-b}\right) & 0 & 0 \\ \left(\dfrac{r+l}{r-l}\right) & \left(\dfrac{t+b}{t-b}\right) & \left(-\dfrac{f+n}{f-n}\right) & -1 \\ 0 & 0 & \left(-\dfrac{2nf}{f-n}\right) & 0 \end{bmatrix}.$$

The result of this multiplication takes the form

$$\mathbf{p}_H = \begin{bmatrix} a & b & c & -p_{Vz} \end{bmatrix}. \tag{10.1}$$

When we convert any homogeneous vector into three dimensional coordinates, the $x$-, $y$-, and $z$-components are divided by the $w$-component:

$$\begin{bmatrix} x & y & z & w \end{bmatrix} \equiv \begin{bmatrix} \dfrac{x}{w} & \dfrac{y}{w} & \dfrac{z}{w} \end{bmatrix}.$$

So, after dividing Equation (10.1) by the homogeneous $w$-component, which is really just the negative view-space $z$-coordinate $-p_{Vz}$, we have:

$$\mathbf{p}_H = \begin{bmatrix} \dfrac{a}{-p_{Vz}} & \dfrac{b}{-p_{Vz}} & \dfrac{c}{-p_{Vz}} \end{bmatrix}$$

$$= \begin{bmatrix} p_{Hx} & p_{Hy} & p_{Hz} \end{bmatrix}.$$

Thus the homogeneous clip space coordinates have been divided by the view-space $z$-coordinate, which is what causes perspective foreshortening.

*Perspective-Correct Vertex Attribute Interpolation*

In Section 10.1.2.4, we learned that vertex attributes are interpolated in order to determine appropriate values for them within the interior of a triangle. Attribute interpolation is performed in *screen space*. We iterate over each pixel of the screen and attempt to determine the value of each attribute at the corresponding location *on the surface of the triangle*. When rendering a scene with a perspective projection, we must do this very carefully so as to account for perspective foreshortening. This is known as *perspective-correct* attribute interpolation.

A derivation of perspective-correct interpolation is beyond our scope, but suffice it to say that we must divide our interpolated attribute values by the corresponding $z$-coordinates (depths) at each vertex. For any pair of vertex attributes $A_1$ and $A_2$, we can write the interpolated attribute at a percentage $t$ of the distance between them as follows:

$$\frac{A}{p_z} = (1-t)\frac{A_1}{p_{z1}} + t\frac{A_2}{p_{z2}} = \text{LERP}\left(\frac{A_1}{p_{z1}}, \frac{A_2}{p_{z2}}, t\right).$$

Refer to [28] for an excellent derivation of the math behind perspective-correct attribute interpolation.

*Orthographic Projection*

An orthographic projection is performed by the following matrix:

$$(\mathbf{M}_{V \to H})_{\text{ortho}} = \begin{bmatrix} \left(\dfrac{2}{r-l}\right) & 0 & 0 & 0 \\ 0 & \left(\dfrac{2}{t-b}\right) & 0 & 0 \\ 0 & 0 & \left(-\dfrac{2}{f-n}\right) & 0 \\ \left(-\dfrac{r+l}{r-l}\right) & \left(-\dfrac{t+b}{t-b}\right) & \left(-\dfrac{f+n}{f-n}\right) & 1 \end{bmatrix}.$$

This is just an everyday scale-and-translate matrix. (The upper-left $3 \times 3$ contains a diagonal nonuniform scaling matrix, and the lower row contains the translation.) Since the view volume is a rectangular prism in both view space and clip space, we need only scale and translate our vertices to convert from one space to the other.

### 10.1.4.5. Screen Space and Aspect Ratios

Screen space is a two-dimensional coordinate system whose axes are measured in terms of screen pixels. The $x$-axis typically points to the right, with the origin at the top-left corner of the screen and $y$ pointing down. (The reason for the inverted $y$-axis is that CRT monitors scan the screen from top to bottom.) The ratio of screen width to screen height is known as the *aspect ratio*. The most common aspect ratios are 4:3 (the aspect ratio of a traditional television screen) and 16:9 (the aspect ratio of a movie screen or HDTV). These aspect ratios are illustrated in Figure 10.35.

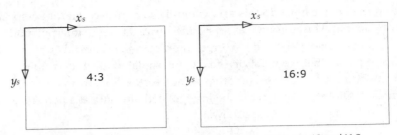

Figure 10.35. The two most prevalent screen space aspect ratios are 4:3 and 16:9.

We can render triangles expressed in homogeneous clip space by simply drawing their $(x, y)$ coordinates and ignoring $z$. But before we do, we scale and shift the clip-space coordinates so that they lie in screen space rather than within the normalized unit square. This scale-and-shift operation is known as *screen mapping*.

### 10.1.4.6. The Frame Buffer

The final rendered image is stored in a bitmapped color buffer known as the *frame buffer*. Pixel colors are usually stored in RGBA8888 format, although other frame buffer formats are supported by most graphics cards as well. Some common formats include RGB565, RGB5551, and one or more paletted modes.

The display hardware (CRT, flat-screen monitor, HDTV, etc.) reads the contents of the frame buffer at a periodic rate of 60 Hz for NTSC televisions used in North America and Japan, or 50 Hz for PAL/SECAM televisions used in Europe and many other places in the world. Rendering engines typically maintain at least two frame buffers. While one is being scanned by the display hardware, the other one can be updated by the rendering engine. This is known as *double buffering*. By swapping or "flipping" the two buffers during the *vertical blanking interval* (the period during which the CRT's electron gun is being reset to the top-left corner of the screen), double buffering ensures that the display hardware always scans the complete frame buffer. This avoids a jarring effect known as *tearing*, in which the upper portion of the screen displays the newly rendered image while the bottom shows the remnants of the previous frame's image.

Some engines make use of three frame buffers—a technique aptly known as *triple buffering*. This is done so that the rendering engine can start work on the next frame, even when the previous frame is still being scanned by the display hardware. For example, the hardware might still be scanning buffer A when the engine finishes drawing buffer B. With triple buffering, it can proceed to render a new frame into buffer C, rather than idling while it waits for the display hardware to finish scanning buffer A.

### Render Targets

Any buffer into which the rendering engine draws graphics is known as a *render target*. As we'll see later in this chapter, rendering engines make use of all sorts of other off-screen render targets, in addition to the frame buffers. These include the depth buffer, the stencil buffer, and various other buffers used for storing intermediate rendering results.

#### 10.1.4.7. Triangle Rasterization and Fragments

To produce an image of a triangle on-screen, we need to fill in the pixels it overlaps. This process is known as rasterization. During rasterization, the triangle's surface is broken into pieces called *fragments*, each one representing a small region of the triangle's surface that corresponds to a single pixel on the screen. (In the case of multisample antialiasing, a fragment corresponds to a *portion* of a pixel—see below.)

A fragment is like a pixel in training. Before it is written into the frame buffer, it must pass a number of tests (described in more depth below). If it fails any of these tests, it will be discarded. Fragments that pass the tests are shaded (i.e., their colors are determined), and the fragment color is either written into the frame buffer or blended with the pixel color that's already there. Figure 10.36 illustrates how a fragment becomes a pixel.

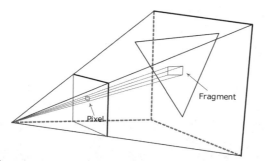

**Figure 10.36.** A fragment is a small region of a triangle corresponding to a pixel on the screen. It passes through the rendering pipeline and is either discarded or its color is written into the frame buffer.

### Antialiasing

When a triangle is rasterized, its edges can look jagged—the familiar "stair step" effect we have all come to know and love (or hate). Technically speaking, aliasing arises because we are using a discrete set of pixels to *sample* an image that is really a smooth, continuous two-dimensional signal. (In the frequency domain, sampling causes a signal to be shifted and copied multiple times along the frequency axis. Aliasing literally means that these copies of the signal overlap and get confused with one another.)

*Antialiasing* is a technique that reduces the visual artifacts caused by aliasing. In effect, antialiasing causes the edges of the triangle to be blended with the surrounding colors in the frame buffer.

There are a number of ways to antialias a 3D rendered image. In *full-screen antialiasing* (FSAA), the image is rendered into a frame buffer that is twice as wide and twice as tall as the actual screen. The resulting image is downsampled to the desired resolution afterwards. FSAA can be expensive because rendering a double-sized frame means filling four times the number of pixels. FSAA frame buffers also consume four times the memory of a regular frame buffer.

Modern graphics hardware can antialias a rendered image without actually rendering a double-size image, via a technique called *multisample antialiasing* (MSAA). The basic idea is to break a triangle down into more than one fragment per pixel. These supersampled fragments are combined into a single pixel at the end of the pipeline. MSAA does not require a double-width frame buffer, and it can handle higher levels of supersampling as well. (4× and 8× supersampling are commonly supported by modern GPUs.)

### 10.1.4.8. Occlusion and the Depth Buffer

When rendering two triangles that overlap each other in screen space, we need some way of ensuring that the triangle that is closer to the camera will appear on top. We could accomplish this by always rendering our triangles in

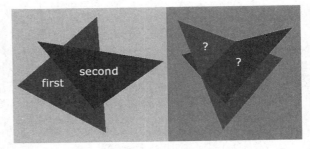

**Figure 10.37.** The painter's algorithm renders triangles in a back-to-front order to produce proper triangle occlusion. However, the algorithm breaks down when triangles intersect one another.

back-to-front order (the so-called painter's algorithm). However, as shown in Figure 10.37, this doesn't work if the triangles are intersecting one another.

To implement triangle occlusion properly, independent of the order in which the triangles are rendered, rendering engines use a technique known as *depth buffering* or *z-buffering*. The depth buffer is a full-screen buffer that typically contains 16- or 24-bit floating-point depth information for each pixel in the frame buffer. Every fragment has a z-coordinate that measures its depth "into" the screen. (The depth of a fragment is found by interpolating the depths of the triangle's vertices.) When a fragment's color is written into the frame buffer, it depth is stored into the corresponding pixel of the depth buffer. When another fragment (from another triangle) is drawn into the same pixel, the engine compares the new fragment's depth to the depth already present in the depth buffer. If the fragment is closer to the camera (i.e., if it has a smaller depth), it overwrites the pixel in the frame buffer. Otherwise the fragment is discarded.

### Z-Fighting and the W-Buffer

When rendering parallel surfaces that are very close to one another, it's important that the rendering engine can distinguish between the depths of the two planes. If our depth buffer had infinite precision, this would never be a problem. Unfortunately, a real depth buffer only has limited precision, so the depth values of two planes can collapse into a single discrete value when the planes are close enough together. When this happens, the more-distant plane's pixels start to "poke through" the nearer plane, resulting in a noisy effect known as *z-fighting*.

To reduce z-fighting to a minimum across the entire scene, we would like to have equal precision whether we're rendering surfaces that are close to the camera or far away. However, with z-buffering this is not the case. The precision of clip-space z-depths ( $p_{Hz}$ ) are not evenly distributed across the entire range from the near plane to the far plane, because of the division by the view-space z-coordinate. Because of the shape of the $1/z$ curve, most of the depth buffer's precision is concentrated near the camera.

The plot of the function $p_{Hz} = 1/p_{Vz}$ shown in Figure 10.38 demonstrates this effect. Near the camera, the distance between two planes in view space $\Delta p_{Vz}$ gets transformed into a reasonably large delta in clip space, $\Delta p_{Hz}$. But far from the camera, this same separation gets transformed into a tiny delta in clip space. The result is z fighting, and it becomes rapidly more prevalent as objects get farther away from the camera.

To circumvent this problem, we would like to store *view-space z-coordinates* ( $p_{Vz}$ ) in the depth buffer instead of clip-space z-coordinates ( $p_{Hz}$ ). View-space z-coordinates vary linearly with the distance from the camera, so

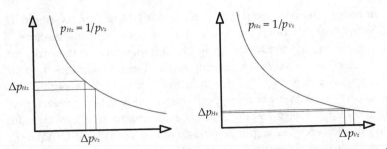

**Figure 10.38.** A plot of the function $1/p_{Vz}$, showing how most of the precision lies close to the camera.

using them as our depth measure achieves uniform precision across the entire depth range. This technique is called *w-buffering*, because the view-space *z*-coordinate conveniently appears in the *w*-component of our homogeneous clip-space coordinates. (Recall from Equation (10.1) that $p_{Hw} = -p_{Vz}$.)

The terminology can be a very confusing here. The *z*- and *w*-buffers store coordinates that are expressed in *clip space*. But in terms of *view-space* coordinates, the *z*-buffer stores $1/z$ (i.e., $1/p_{Vz}$) while the *w*-buffer stores *z* (i.e., $p_{Vz}$)!

We should note here that the *w*-buffering approach is a bit more expensive than its *z*-based counterpart. This is because with *w*-buffering, we cannot linearly interpolate depths directly. Depths must be inverted prior to interpolation and then re-inverted prior to being stored in the *w*-buffer.

## 10.2. The Rendering Pipeline

Now that we've completed our whirlwind tour of the major theoretical and practical underpinnings of triangle rasterization, let's turn our attention to how it is typically implemented. In real-time game rendering engines, the high-level rendering steps described in Section 10.1 are implemented using a software/hardware architecture known as a *pipeline*. A pipeline is just an ordered chain of computational stages, each with a specific purpose, operating on a stream of input data items and producing a stream of output data.

Each stage of a pipeline can typically operate independently of the other stages. Hence, one of the biggest advantages of a pipelined architecture is that it lends itself extremely well to parallelization. While the first stage is chewing on one data element, the second stage can be processing the results previously produced by the first stage, and so on down the chain.

Parallelization can also be achieved within an individual stage of the pipeline. For example, if the computing hardware for a particular stage is du-

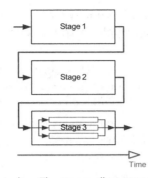

Figure 10.39. A parallelized pipeline. The stages all operate in parallel and some stages are capable of operating on multiple data items simultaneously as well.

plicated $N$ times on the die, $N$ data elements can be processed in parallel by that stage. A parallelized pipeline is shown in Figure 10.39. Ideally the stages operate in parallel (most of the time), and certain stages are capable of operating on multiple data items simultaneously as well.

The *throughput* of a pipeline measures how many data items are processed per second overall. The pipeline's *latency* measures the amount of time it takes for a single data element to make it through the entire pipeline. The latency of an individual stage measures how long that stage takes to process a single item. The slowest stage of a pipeline dictates the throughput of the entire pipeline. It also has an impact on the average latency of the pipeline as a whole. Therefore, when designing a rendering pipeline, we attempt to minimize and balance latency across the entire pipeline and eliminate bottlenecks. In a well-designed pipeline, all the stages operate simultaneously, and no stage is ever idle for very long waiting for another stage to become free.

## 10.2.1. Overview of the Rendering Pipeline

Some graphics texts divide the rendering pipeline into three coarse-grained stages. In this book, we'll extend this pipeline back even further, to encompass the offline tools used to create the scenes that are ultimately rendered by the game engine. The high level stages in our pipeline are:

- *Tools stage (offline).* Geometry and surface properties (materials) are defined.

- *Asset conditioning stage (offline).* The geometry and material data are processed by the asset conditioning pipeline (ACP) into an engine-ready format.

- *Application stage (CPU).* Potentially visible mesh instances are identified and submitted to the graphics hardware along with their materials for rendering.

- *Geometry processing stage (GPU).* Vertices are transformed and lit and projected into homogeneous clip space. Triangles are processed by the optional geometry shader and then clipped to the frustum.

- *Rasterization stage (GPU).* Triangles are converted into fragments that are shaded, passed through various tests (z test, alpha test, stencil test, etc.) and finally blended into the frame buffer.

### 10.2.1.1. How the Rendering Pipeline Transforms Data

It's interesting to note how the format of geometry data changes as it passes through the rendering pipeline. The tools and asset conditioning stages deal with meshes and materials. The application stage deals in terms of mesh instances and submeshes, each of which is associated with a single material. During the geometry stage, each submesh is broken down into individual vertices, which are processed largely in parallel. At the conclusion of this stage, the triangles are reconstructed from the fully transformed and shaded vertices. In the rasterization stage, each triangle is broken into fragments, and these fragments are either discarded, or they are eventually written into the frame buffer as colors. This process is illustrated in Figure 10.40.

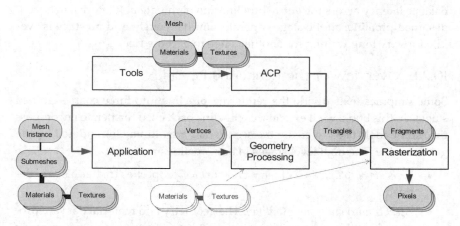

Figure 10.40. The format of geometric data changes radically as it passes through the various stages of the rendering pipeline.

### 10.2.1.2. Implementation of the Pipeline

The first two stages of the rendering pipeline are implemented offline, usually executed by a PC or Linux machine. The application stage is run either by the main CPU of the game console or PC, or by parallel processing units like the PS3's SPUs. The geometry and rasterization stages are usually implemented on the graphics processing unit (GPU). In the following sections, we'll explore some of the details of how each of these stages is implemented.

## 10.2.2. The Tools Stage

In the tools stage, meshes are authored by 3D modelers in a *digital content creation* (DCC) application like Maya, 3ds Max, Lightwave, Softimage/XSI, SketchUp, etc. The models may be defined using any convenient surface description—NURBS, quads, triangles, etc. However, they are invariably tessellated into triangles prior to rendering by the runtime portion of the pipeline.

The vertices of a mesh may also be skinned. This involves associating each vertex with one or more joints in an articulated skeletal structure, along with weights describing each joint's relative influence over the vertex. Skinning information and the skeleton are used by the animation system to drive the movements of a model—see Chapter 11 for more details.

Materials are also defined by the artists during the tools stage. This involves selecting a shader for each material, selecting textures as required by the shader, and specifying the configuration parameters and options of each shader. Textures are mapped onto the surfaces, and other vertex attributes are also defined, often by "painting" them with some kind of intuitive tool within the DCC application.

Materials are usually authored using a commercial or custom in-house material editor. The material editor is sometimes integrated directly into the DCC application as a plug-in, or it may be a stand-alone program. Some material editors are live-linked to the game, so that material authors can see what the materials will look like in the real game. Other editors provide an offline 3D visualization view. Some editors even allow shader programs to be written and debugged by the artist or a shader engineer. NVIDIA's Fx Composer is an example of such a tool; it is depicted in Figure 10.41.

Both FxComposer and Unreal Engine 3 provide powerful graphical shading languages. Such tools allow rapid prototyping of visual effects by connecting various kinds of nodes together with a mouse. These tools generally provide a WYSIWYG display of the resulting material. The shaders created by a graphical language usually need to be hand-optimized by a rendering engineer, because a graphical language invariably trades some runtime per-

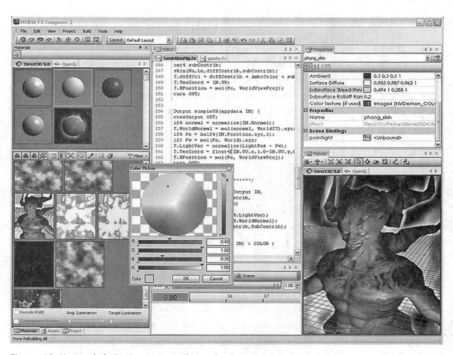

**Figure 10.41.** Nvidia's Fx Composer allows shader programs to be written, previsualized, and debugged easily.

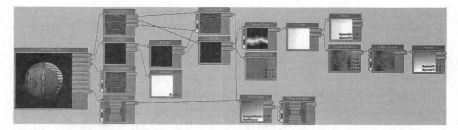

**Figure 10.42.** The Unreal Engine 3 graphical shader language.

formance for its incredible flexibility, generality, and ease of use. The Unreal graphical shader editor is shown in Figure 10.42.

Materials may be stored and managed with the individual meshes. However, this can lead to duplication of data—and effort. In many games, a relatively small number of materials can be used to define a wide range of objects in the game. For example, we might define some standard, reusable materials like wood, rock, metal, plastic, cloth, skin, and so on. There's no reason to duplicate these materials inside every mesh. Instead, many game teams build up a library of materials from which to choose, and the individual meshes refer to the materials in a loosely-coupled manner.

### 10.2.3. The Asset Conditioning Stage

The asset conditioning stage is itself a pipeline, sometimes called the *asset conditioning pipeline* or ACP. As we saw in Section 6.2.1.4, its job is to export, process, and link together multiple types of assets into a cohesive whole. For example, a 3D model is comprised of geometry (vertex and index buffers), materials, textures, and an optional skeleton. The ACP ensures that all of the individual assets referenced by a 3D model are available and ready to be loaded by the engine.

Geometric and material data is extracted from the DCC application and is usually stored in a platform-independent intermediate format. The data is then further processed into one or more platform-specific formats, depending on how many target platforms the engine supports. Ideally the platform-specific assets produced by this stage are ready to load into memory and use with little or no postprocessing at runtime. For example, mesh data targeted for the Xbox 360 might be output as index and vertex buffers that are ready to be uploaded to video RAM; on the PS3, geometry might be produced in compressed data streams that are ready to be DMA'd to the SPUs for decompression. The ACP often takes the needs of the material/shader into account when building assets. For example, a particular shader might require tangent and bitangent vectors as well as a vertex normal; the ACP could generate these vectors automatically.

High-level *scene graph* data structures may also be computed during the asset conditioning stage. For example, static level geometry may be processed in order to build a BSP tree. (As we'll investigate in Section 10.2.7.4, scene graph data structures help the rendering engine to very quickly determine which objects should be rendered, given a particular camera position and orientation.)

Expensive lighting calculations are often done offline as part of the asset conditioning stage. This is called *static lighting*; it may include calculation of light colors at the vertices of a mesh (this is called "baked" vertex lighting), construction of texture maps that encode per-pixel lighting information known as *light maps*, calculation of *precomputed radiance transfer* (PRT) coefficients (usually represented by spherical harmonic functions), and so on.

### 10.2.4. A Brief History of the GPU

In the early days of game development, all rendering was done on the CPU. Games like *Castle Wolfenstein 3D* and *Doom* pushed the limits of what early PCs could do, rendering interactive 3D scenes without any help from specialized graphics hardware (other than a standard VGA card).

As the popularity of these and other PC games took off, graphics hardware was developed to offload work from the CPU. The earliest graphics accelerators, like 3Dfx's Voodoo line of cards, handled only the most expensive stage in the pipeline—the rasterization stage. Subsequent graphics accelerators provided support for the geometry processing stage as well.

At first, graphics hardware provided only a hard-wired but configurable implementation known as the *fixed-function pipeline*. This technology was known as *hardware transformation and lighting*, or *hardware T&L* for short. Later, certain substages of the pipeline were made programmable. Engineers could now write programs called *shaders* to control exactly how the pipeline processed vertices (*vertex shaders*) and fragments (*fragment shaders*, more commonly known as *pixel shaders*). With the introduction of DirectX 10, a third type of shader known as a *geometry shader* was added. It permits rendering engineers to modify, cull, or create entire primitives (triangles, lines, and points).

Graphics hardware has evolved around a specialized type of microprocessor known as the *graphics processing unit* or GPU. A GPU is designed to maximize throughput of the pipeline, which it achieves through massive parallelization. For example, a modern GPU like the GeForce 8800 can process 128 vertices or fragments simultaneously.

Even in its fully programmable form, a GPU is not a general-purpose microprocessor—nor should it be. A GPU achieves its high processing speeds (on the order of teraflops on today's GPUs) by carefully controlling the flow of data through the pipeline. Certain pipeline stages are either entirely fixed in their function, or they are configurable but not programmable. Memory can only be accessed in controlled ways, and specialized data caches are used to minimize unnecessary duplication of computations.

In the following sections, we'll briefly explore the architecture of a modern GPU and see how the runtime portion of the rendering pipeline is typically implemented. We'll speak primarily about current GPU architectures, which are used on personal computers with the latest graphics cards and on console platforms like the Xbox 360 and the PS3. However, not all platforms support all of the features we'll be discussing here. For example, the Wii does not support programmable shaders, and most PC games need to support fallback rendering solutions to support older graphics cards with only limited programmable shader support.

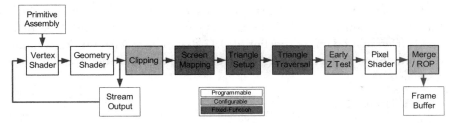

**Figure 10.43.** The geometry processing and rasterization stages of the rendering pipeline, as implemented by a typical GPU. The white stages are programmable, the light grey stages are configurable, and the dark grey boxes are fixed-function.

## 10.2.5. The GPU Pipeline

Virtually all GPUs break the pipeline into the substages described below and depicted in Figure 10.43. Each stage is shaded to indicate whether its functionality is programmable, fixed but configurable, or fixed and non-configurable.

### 10.2.5.1. Vertex Shader

This stage is fully programmable. It is responsible for transformation and shading/lighting of individual vertices. The input to this stage is a single vertex (although in practice many vertices are processed in parallel). Its position and normal are typically expressed in model space or world space. The vertex shader handles transformation from model space to view space via the model-view transform. Perspective projection is also applied, as well as per-vertex lighting and texturing calculations, and skinning for animated characters. The vertex shader can also perform procedural animation by modifying the position of the vertex. Examples of this include foliage that sways in the breeze or an undulating water surface. The output of this stage is a fully transformed and lit vertex, whose position and normal are expressed in homogeneous clip space (see Section 10.1.4.4).

On modern GPUs, the vertex shader has full access to texture data—a capability that used to be available only to the pixel shader. This is particularly useful when textures are used as stand-alone data structures like height maps or look-up tables.

### 10.2.5.2. Geometry Shader

This optional stage is also fully programmable. The geometry shader operates on entire primitives (triangles, lines, and points) in homogeneous clip space. It is capable of culling or modifying input primitives, and it can also generate new primitives. Typical uses include shadow volume extrusion (see

Section 10.3.3.1), rendering the six faces of a cube map (see Section 10.3.1.4), fur fin extrusion around silhouette edges of meshes, creation of particle quads from point data (see Section 10.4.1), dynamic tessellation, fractal subdivision of line segments for lightning effects, cloth simulations, and the list goes on.

### 10.2.5.3. Stream Output

Modern GPUs permit the data that has been processed up to this point in the pipeline to be written back to memory. From there, it can then be looped back to the top of the pipeline for further processing. This feature is called *stream output*.

Stream output permits a number of intriguing visual effects to be achieved without the aid of the CPU. An excellent example is hair rendering. Hair is often represented as a collection of cubic spline curves. It used to be that hair physics simulation would be done on the CPU. The CPU would also tessellate the splines into line segments. Finally the GPU would render the segments.

With stream output, the GPU can do the physics simulation on the control points of the hair splines within the vertex shader. The geometry shader tessellates the splines, and the stream output feature is used to write the tessellated vertex data to memory. The line segments are then piped back into the top of the pipeline so they can be rendered.

### 10.2.5.4. Clipping

The clipping stage chops off those portions of the triangles that straddle the frustum. Clipping is done by identifying vertices that lie outside the frustum and then finding the intersection of the triangle's edges with the planes of the frustum. These intersection points become new vertices that define one or more clipped triangles.

This stage is fixed in function, but it is somewhat configurable. For example, user-defined clipping planes can be added in addition to the frustum planes. This stage can also be configured to cull triangles that lie entirely outside the frustum.

### 10.2.5.5. Screen Mapping

Screen mapping simply scales and shifts the vertices from homogeneous clip space into screen space. This stage is entirely fixed and non-configurable.

### 10.2.5.6. Triangle Setup

During triangle setup, the rasterization hardware is initialized for efficient conversion of the triangle into fragments. This stage is not configurable.

### 10.2.5.7. Triangle Traversal

Each triangle is broken into fragments (i.e., rasterized) by the triangle traversal stage. Usually one fragment is generated for each pixel, although with multisample antialiasing (MSAA), multiple fragments are created per pixel (see Section 10.1.4.7). The triangle traversal stage also interpolates vertex attributes in order to generate per-fragment attributes for processing by the pixel shader. Perspective-correct interpolation is used where appropriate. This stage's functionality is fixed and not configurable.

### 10.2.5.8. Early Z Test

Many graphics cards are capable of checking the depth of the fragment at this point in the pipeline, discarding it if it is being occluded by the pixel already in the frame buffer. This allows the (potentially very expensive) pixel shader stage to be skipped entirely for occluded fragments.

Surprisingly, not all graphics hardware supports depth testing at this stage of the pipeline. In older GPU designs, the z test was done along with alpha testing, after the pixel shader had run. For this reason, this stage is called the *early z test* or *early depth test* stage.

### 10.2.5.9. Pixel Shader

This stage is fully programmable. Its job is to shade (i.e., light and otherwise process) each fragment. The pixel shader can also discard fragments, for example because they are deemed to be entirely transparent. The pixel shader can address one or more texture maps, run per-pixel lighting calculations, and do whatever else is necessary to determine the fragment's color.

The input to this stage is a collection of per-fragment attributes (which have been interpolated from the vertex attributes by the triangle traversal stage). The output is a single color vector describing the desired color of the fragment.

### 10.2.5.10. Merging / Raster Operations Stage

The final stage of the pipeline is known as the *merging stage* or *blending stage,* also known as the *raster operations* stage or ROP in NVIDIA parlance. This stage is not programmable, but it is highly configurable. It is responsible for running various fragment tests including the depth test (see Section 10.1.4.8), alpha test (in which the values of the fragment's and pixel's alpha channels can be used to reject certain fragments), and stencil test (see Section 10.3.3.1).

If the fragment passes all of the tests, its color is blended (merged) with the color that is already present in the frame buffer. The way in which blending occurs is controlled by the *alpha blending function*—a function whose basic structure is hard-wired, but whose operators and parameters can be configured in order to produce a wide variety of blending operations.

Alpha blending is most commonly used to render semi-transparent geometry. In this case, the following blending function is used:

$$\mathbf{C}'_D = A_S \mathbf{C}_S + (1 - A_S)\mathbf{C}_D.$$

The subscripts $S$ and $D$ stand for "source" (the incoming fragment) and "destination" (the pixel in the frame buffer), respectively. Therefore, the color that is written into the frame buffer ($\mathbf{C}'_D$) is a *weighted average* of the existing frame buffer contents ($\mathbf{C}_D$) and the color of the fragment being drawn ($\mathbf{C}_S$). The blend weight ($A_S$) is just the source alpha of the incoming fragment.

For alpha blending to look right, the semi-transparent and translucent surfaces in the scene must be sorted and rendered in back-to-front order, *after* the opaque geometry has been rendered to the frame buffer. This is because after alpha blending has been performed, the depth of the new fragment *overwrites* the depth of the pixel with which it was blended. In other words, the depth buffer ignores transparency (unless depth writes have been turned off, of course). If we are rendering a stack of translucent objects on top of an opaque backdrop, the resulting pixel color should ideally be a blend between the opaque surface's color and the colors of *all* of the translucent surfaces in the stack. If we try to render the stack in any order other than back-to-front, depth test failures will cause some of the translucent fragments to be discarded, resulting in an incomplete blend (and a rather odd-looking image).

Other alpha blending functions can be defined as well, for purposes other than transparency blending. The general blending equation takes the form $\mathbf{C}'_D = (\mathbf{w}_S \otimes \mathbf{C}_S) + (\mathbf{w}_D \otimes \mathbf{C}_D)$, where the weighting factors $\mathbf{w}_S$ and $\mathbf{w}_D$ can be selected by the programmer from a predefined set of values including zero, one, source or destination color, source or destination alpha, and one minus the source or destination color or alpha. The operator $\otimes$ is either a regular scalar-vector multiplication or a component-wise vector-vector multiplication (a Hadamard product—see Section 4.2.4.1) depending on the data types of $\mathbf{w}_S$ and $\mathbf{w}_D$.

## 10.2.6. Programmable Shaders

Now that we have an end-to-end picture of the GPU pipeline in mind, let's take a deeper look at the most interesting part of the pipeline—the programmable shaders. Shader architectures have evolved significantly since their introduction with DirectX 8. Early *shader models* supported only low-level assembly language programming, and the instruction set and register set of the pixel shader differed significantly from those of the vertex shader. DirectX

9 brought with it support for high-level C-like shader languages such as Cg (C for graphics), HLSL (High-Level Shading Language—Microsoft's implementation of the Cg language), and GLSL (OpenGL shading language). With DirectX 10, the geometry shader was introduced, and with it came a unified shader architecture called *shader model 4.0* in DirectX parlance. In the unified shader model, all three types of shaders support roughly the same instruction set and have roughly the same set of capabilities, including the ability to read texture memory.

A shader takes a single element of input data and transforms it into zero or more elements of output data.

- In the case of the vertex shader, the input is a vertex whose position and normal are expressed in model space or world space. The output of the vertex shader is a fully transformed and lit vertex, expressed in homogeneous clip space.

- The input to the geometry shader is a single $n$-vertex primitive—a point ($n = 1$), line segment ($n = 2$), or triangle ($n = 3$)—with up to $n$ additional vertices that act as control points. The output is zero or more primitives, possibly of a different type than the input. For example, the geometry shader could convert points into two-triangle quads, or it could transform triangles into triangles but optionally discard some triangles, and so on.

- The pixel shader's input is a fragment whose attributes have been interpolated from the three vertices of the triangle from which it came. The output of the pixel shader is the color that will be written into the frame buffer (presuming the fragment passes the depth test and other optional tests). The pixel shader is also capable of discarding fragments explicitly, in which case it produces no output.

### 10.2.6.1. Accessing Memory

Because the GPU implements a data processing pipeline, access to RAM is very carefully controlled. A shader program cannot read from or write to memory directly. Instead, its memory accesses are limited to two methods: registers and texture maps.

*Shader Registers*

A shader can access RAM indirectly via *registers*. All GPU registers are in 128-bit SIMD format. Each register is capable of holding four 32-bit floating-point or integer values (represented by the `float4` data type in the Cg language). Such a register can contain a four-element vector in homogeneous coordinates or a color in RGBA format, with each component in 32-bit floating-point format. Matrices can be represented by groups of three or four registers (represented by built-in matrix types like `float4x4` in Cg). A GPU register can also be used to hold a single 32-bit scalar, in which case the value is usually replicated across all four 32-bit fields. Some GPUs can operate on 16-bit fields, known as *halfs*. (Cg provides various built-in types like `half4` and `half4x4` for this purpose.)

Registers come in four flavors, as follows:

- *Input registers.* These registers are the shader's primary source of input data. In a vertex shader, the input registers contain attribute data obtained directly from the vertices. In a pixel shader, the input registers contain interpolated vertex attribute data corresponding to a single fragment. The values of all input registers are set automatically by the GPU prior to invoking the shader.

- *Constant registers.* The values of constant registers are set by the application and can change from primitive to primitive. Their values are constant only from the point of view of the shader program. They provide a secondary form of input to the shader. Typical contents include the model-view matrix, the projection matrix, light parameters, and any other parameters required by the shader that are not available as vertex attributes.

- *Temporary registers.* These registers are for use by the shader program internally and are typically used to store intermediate results of calculations.

- *Output registers.* The contents of these registers are filled in by the shader and serve as its only form of output. In a vertex shader, the output registers contain vertex attributes such as the transformed position and normal vectors in homogeneous clip space, optional vertex colors, texture coordinates, and so on. In a pixel shader, the output register contains the final color of the fragment being shaded.

The application provides the values of the constant registers when it submits primitives for rendering. The GPU automatically copies vertex or fragment attribute data from video RAM into the appropriate input registers prior to calling the shader program, and it also writes the contents of the output registers back into RAM at the conclusion of the program's execution so that the data can be passed to the next stage of the pipeline.

GPUs typically cache output data so that it can be reused without being recalculated. For example, the *post-transform vertex cache* stores the most-recently processed vertices emitted by the vertex shader. If a triangle is encountered that refers to a previously-processed vertex, it will be read from the post-transform vertex cache if possible—the vertex shader need only be called again if the vertex in question has since been ejected from the cache to make room for newly processed vertices.

*Textures*

A shader also has direct read-only access to *texture maps*. Texture data is addressed via texture coordinates, rather than via absolute memory addresses. The GPU's texture samplers automatically *filter* the texture data, blending values between adjacent texels or adjacent mipmap levels as appropriate. Texture filtering can be disabled in order to gain direct access to the values of particular texels. This can be useful when a texture map is used as a data table, for example.

Shaders can only *write* to texture maps in an indirect manner—by rendering the scene to an off-screen frame buffer that is interpreted as a texture map by subsequent rendering passes. This feature is known as *render to texture*.

### 10.2.6.2. Introduction to High-Level Shader Language Syntax

High-level shader languages like Cg and GLSL are modeled after the C programming language. The programmer can declare functions, define a simple `struct`, and perform arithmetic. However, as we said above, a shader program only has access to registers and textures. As such, the `struct` and variable we declare in Cg or GLSL is mapped directly onto registers by the shader compiler. We define these mappings in the following ways:

- *Semantics.* Variables and `struct` members can be suffixed with a colon followed by a keyword known as a *semantic*. The semantic tells the shader compiler to bind the variable or data member to a particular vertex or fragment attribute. For example, in a vertex shader we might declare an input `struct` whose members map to the *position* and *color* attributes of a vertex as follows:

```
struct VtxOut
{

  float4 pos  : POSITION;  // map to the position
                           // attribute
  float4 color : COLOR;  // map to the color attribute
};
```

- *Input versus output.* The compiler determines whether a particular variable or `struct` should map to input or output registers from the context in which it is used. If a variable is passed as an argument to the shader program's main function, it is assumed to be an input; if it is the return value of the main function, it is taken to be an output.

```
VtxOut vshaderMain(VtxIn in) // in maps to input
                                 // registers
{
    VtxOut out;
    // ...
    return out;        // out maps to output registers
}
```

- *Uniform declaration.* To gain access to the data supplied by the application via the constant registers, we can declare a variable with the keyword uniform. For example, the model-view matrix could be passed to
  a vertex shader as follows:

```
VtxOut vshaderMain(VtxIn in,
                    uniform float4x4 modelViewMatrix)
{
    VtxOut out;
    // ...
    return out;
}
```

Arithmetic operations can be performed by invoking C-style operators,
or by calling intrinsic functions as appropriate. For example, to multiply the
input vertex position by the model-view matrix, we could write:

```
VtxOut vshaderMain(VtxIn in,
                    uniform float4x4 modelViewMatrix)
{
    VtxOut out;
    out.pos = mul(modelViewMatrix, in.pos);
    out.color = float4(0, 1, 0, 1); // RGBA green
    return out;
}
```

Data is obtained from textures by calling special intrinsic functions that
read the value of the texels at a specified texture coordinate. A number of variants are available for reading one-, two- and three-dimensional textures in
various formats, with and without filtering. Special texture addressing modes
are also available for accessing cube maps and shadow maps. References to
the texture maps themselves are declared using a special data type known as
a *texture sampler* declaration. For example, the data type sampler2D represents a reference to a typical two-dimensional texture. The following simple
Cg pixel shader applies a diffuse texture to a triangle:

```
struct FragmentOut
{
    float4 color : COLOR;
};
```

```
FragmentOut pshaderMain(float2 uv : TEXCOORD0,
                        uniform sampler2D texture)
{
    FragmentOut out;

    out.color = tex2D(texture, uv);   // look up texel at
                                      // (u,v)
    return out;
}
```

### 10.2.6.3. Effect Files

By itself, a shader program isn't particularly useful. Additional information is required by the GPU pipeline in order to call the shader program with meaningful inputs. For example, we need to specify how the application-specified parameters, like the model-view matrix, light parameters, and so on, map to the uniform variables declared in the shader program. In addition, some visual effects require two or more rendering passes, but a shader program only describes the operations to be applied during a single rendering pass. If we are writing a game for the PC platform, we will need to define "fallback" versions of some of our more-advanced rendering effects, so that they will work even on older graphics cards. To tie our shader program(s) together into a complete visual effect, we turn to a file format known as an *effect file*.

Different rendering engines implement effects in slightly different ways. In Cg, the effect file format is known as *CgFX*. Ogre3D uses a file format very similar to CgFX known as a *material file*. GLSL effects can be described using the COLLADA format, which is based on XML. Despite the differences, effects generally take on the following hierarchical format:

- At global scope, structs, shader programs (implemented as various "main" functions), and global variables (which map to application-specified constant parameters) are defined.

- One or more *techniques* are defined. A technique represents one way to render a particular visual effect. An effect typically provides a primary technique for its highest-quality implementation and possibly a number of fall back techniques for use on lower-powered graphics hardware.

- Within each technique, one or more *passes* are defined. A pass describes how a single full-frame image should be rendered. It typically includes a reference to a vertex, geometry and/or pixel shader program's "main" function, various parameter bindings, and optional render state settings.

### 10.2.6.4. Further Reading

In this section, we've only had a small taste of what high-level shader programming is like—a complete tutorial is beyond our scope here. For a much more-detailed introduction to Cg shader programming, refer to the Cg tutorial available on NVIDIA's website at http://developer.nvidia.com/object/cg_tutorial_home.html.

## 10.2.7. The Application Stage

Now that we understand how the GPU works, we can discuss the pipeline stage that is responsible for driving it—the application stage. This stage has three roles:

1. *Visibility determination.* Only objects that are visible (or at least *potentially* visible) should be submitted to the GPU, lest we waste valuable resources processing triangles that will never be seen.

2. *Submitting geometry to the GPU for rendering.* Submesh-material pairs are sent to the GPU via a rendering call like `DrawIndexedPrimitive()` (DirectX) or `glDrawArrays()` (OpenGL), or via direct construction of the GPU command list. The geometry may be sorted for optimal rendering performance. Geometry might be submitted more than once if the scene needs to be rendered in multiple passes.

3. *Controlling shader parameters and render state.* The uniform parameters passed to the shader via constant registers are configured by the application stage on a per-primitive basis. In addition, the application stage must set all of the configurable parameters of the non-programmable pipeline stages to ensure that each primitive is rendered appropriately.

In the following sections, we'll briefly explore how the application stage performs these tasks.

### 10.2.7.1. Visibility Determination

The cheapest triangles are the ones you never draw. So it's incredibly important to *cull* objects from the scene that do not contribute to the final rendered image prior to submitting them to the GPU. The process of constructing the list of visible mesh instances is known as *visibility determination*.

*Frustum Culling*

In frustum culling, all objects that lie entirely outside the frustum are excluded from our render list. Given a candidate mesh instance, we can determine whether or not it lies inside the frustum by performing some simple tests between the object's *bounding volume* and the six frustum planes. The bounding volume is usually a sphere, because spheres are particularly easy to cull. For each frustum plane, we move the plane inward a distance equal to the radius of the sphere, then we determine on which side of each modified plane the center point of the sphere lies. If the sphere is found to be on the front side of all six modified planes, the sphere is inside the frustum.

A scene graph data structure, described in Section 10.2.7.4, can help optimize frustum culling by allowing us to ignore objects whose bounding spheres are nowhere close to being inside the frustum.

### Occlusion and Potentially Visible Sets

Even when objects lie entirely within the frustum, they may occlude one another. Removing objects from the visible list that are entirely occluded by other objects is called *occlusion culling*. In crowded environments viewed from ground level, there can be a great deal of inter-object occlusion, making occlusion culling extremely important. In less crowded scenes, or when scenes are viewed from above, much less occlusion may be present and the cost of occlusion culling may outweigh its benefits.

Gross occlusion culling of a large-scale environment can be done by precalculating a *potentially visible set* (PVS). For any given camera vantage point, a PVS lists those scene objects that might be visible. A PVS errs on the side of including objects that aren't actually visible, rather than excluding objects that actually would have contributed to the rendered scene.

One way to implement a PVS system is to chop the level up into regions of some kind. Each region can be provided with a list of the other regions that can be seen when the camera is inside it. These PVSs might be manually specified by the artists or game designers. More commonly, an automated offline tool generates the PVS based on user-specified regions. Such a tool usually operates by rendering the scene from various randomly distributed vantage points within a region. Every region's geometry is color coded, so the list of visible regions can be found by scanning the resulting frame buffer and tabulating the region colors that are found. Because automated PVS tools are imperfect, they typically provide the user with a mechanism for tweaking the results, either by manually placing vantage points for testing, or by manually specifying a list of regions that should be explicitly included or excluded from a particular region's PVS.

### Portals

Another way to determine what portions of a scene are visible is to use *portals*. In portal rendering, the game world is divided up into semiclosed regions that are connected to one another via holes, such as windows and doorways. These holes are called portals. They are usually represented by polygons that describe their boundaries.

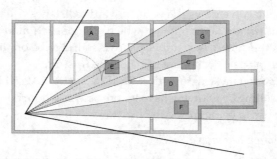

**Figure 10.44.** Portals are used to define frustum-like volumes which are used to cull the contents of neighboring regions. In this example, objects A, B, and D will be culled because they lie outside one of the portals; the other objects will be visible.

To render a scene with portals, we start by rendering the region that contains the camera. Then, for each portal in the region, we extend a frustum-like volume consisting of planes extending from the camera's focal point through each edge of the portal's bounding polygon. The contents of the neighboring region can be culled to this portal volume in exactly the same way geometry is culled against the camera frustum. This ensures that only the visible geometry in the adjacent regions will be rendered. Figure 10.44 provides an illustration of this technique.

*Occlusion Volumes (Antiportals)*

If we flip the portal concept on its head, pyramidal volumes can also be used to describe regions of the scene that *cannot* be seen because they are being occluded by an object. These volumes are known as *occlusion volumes* or *antiportals*. To construct an occlusion volume, we find the silhouette edges of each

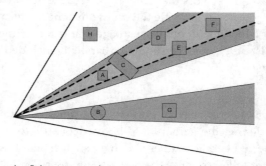

**Figure 10.45.** As a result of the antiportals corresponding to objects A, B, and C, objects D, E, F, and G are culled. Therefore only A, B, C, and H are visible.

occluding object and extend planes outward from the camera's focal point through each of these edges. We test more-distant objects against these occlusion volumes and cull them if they lie entirely within the occlusion region. This is illustrated in Figure 10.45.

Portals are best used when rendering enclosed indoor environments with a relatively small number of windows and doorways between "rooms." In this kind of scene, the portals occupy a relatively small percentage of the total volume of the camera frustum, resulting in a large number of objects outside the portals which can be culled. Antiportals are best applied to large outdoor environments, in which nearby objects often occlude large swaths of the camera frustum. In this case, the antiportals occupy a relatively large percentage of the total camera frustum volume, resulting in large numbers of culled objects.

### 10.2.7.2. Primitive Submission

Once a list of visible geometric primitives has been generated, the individual primitives must be *submitted* to the GPU pipeline for rendering. This can be accomplished by making calls to `DrawIndexedPrimitive()` in DirectX or `glDrawArrays()` in OpenGL.

### Render State

As we learned in Section 10.2.5, the functionality of many of the GPU pipeline's stages is fixed but configurable. And even programmable stages are driven in part by configurable parameters. Some examples of these configurable parameters are listed below (although this is by no means a complete list!)

- world-view matrix;
- light direction vectors;
- texture bindings (i.e., which textures to use for a given material/ shader);
- texture addressing and filtering modes;
- time base for scrolling textures and other animated effects;
- z test (enabled or disabled);
- alpha blending options.

The set of all configurable parameters within the GPU pipeline is known as the *hardware state* or *render state*. It is the application stage's responsibility to ensure that the hardware state is configured properly and completely for each submitted primitive. Ideally these state settings are described completely by the material associated with each submesh. So the application stage's job boils down to iterating through the list of visible mesh instances, iterating over each submesh-material pair, setting the render state based on the material's specifications, and then calling the low level primitive submission functions (`Draw-IndexedPrimitive()`, `glDrawArrays()` or similar).

### State Leaks

If we forget to set some aspect of the render state between submitted primitives, the settings used on the previous primitive will "leak" over onto the new primitive. A *render state leak* might manifest itself as an object with the wrong texture or an incorrect lighting effect, for example. Clearly it's important that the application stage never allow state leaks to occur.

### The GPU Command List

The application stage actually communicates with the GPU via a command list. These commands interleave render state settings with references to the geometry that should be drawn. For example, to render objects A and B with material 1, followed by objects C, D, and E using material 2, the command list might look like this:

- Set render state for material 1 (multiple commands, one per render state setting).
- Submit primitive A.
- Submit primitive B.
- Set render state for material 2 (multiple commands).
- Submit primitive C.
- Submit primitive D.
- Submit primitive E.

Under the hood, API functions like `DrawIndexedPrimitive()` actually just construct and submit GPU command lists. The cost of these API calls can themselves be too high for some applications. To maximize performance, some game engines build GPU command lists manually or by calling a low-level rendering API like the PS3's libgcm library.

### 10.2.7.3. Geometry Sorting

Render state settings are global—they apply to the entire GPU as a whole. So in order to change render state settings, the entire GPU pipeline must be flushed before the new settings can be applied. This can cause massive performance degradation if not managed carefully.

Clearly we'd like to change render settings as infrequently as possible. The best way to accomplish this is to sort our geometry by material. That way, we can install material A's settings, render all geometry associated with material A, and then move on to material B.

Unfortunately, sorting geometry by material can have a detrimental effect on rendering performance because it increases *overdraw*—a situation in which the same pixel is filled multiple times by multiple overlapping triangles. Certainly some overdraw is necessary and desirable, as it is the only way to properly alpha-blend transparent and translucent surfaces into a scene. However, overdraw of *opaque* pixels is always a waste of GPU bandwidth.

The early z test is designed to discard occluded fragments before the expensive pixel shader has a chance to execute. But to take maximum advantage of early z, we need to draw the triangles in front-to-back order. That way, the closest triangles will fill the z-buffer right off the bat, and all of the fragments coming from more-distant triangles behind them can be quickly discarded, with little or no overdraw.

*Z Prepass to the Rescue*

How can we reconcile the need to sort geometry by material with the conflicting need to render opaque geometry in a front-to-back order? The answer lies in a GPU feature known as z *prepass*.

The idea behind z prepass is to render the scene twice: the first time to generate the contents of the z-buffer as efficiently as possible and the second time to populate the frame buffer with full color information (but this time with no overdraw, thanks to the contents of the z-buffer). The GPU provides a special double-speed rendering mode in which the pixel shaders are disabled, and only the z-buffer is updated. Opaque geometry can be rendered in front-to-back order during this phase, to minimize the time required to generate the z-buffer contents. Then the geometry can be resorted into material order and rendered in full color with minimal stage changes for maximum pipeline throughput.

Once the opaque geometry has been rendered, transparent surfaces can be drawn in back-to-front order. Unfortunately, there is no general solution to the material sorting problem for transparent geometry. We must render it in back-to-front order to achieve the proper alpha-blended result. Therefore we must accept the cost of frequent state changes when drawing transparent geometry (unless our particular game's usage of transparent geometry is such that a specific optimization can be implemented).

### 10.2.7.4. Scene Graphs

Modern game worlds can be very large. The majority of the geometry in most scenes does not lie within the camera frustum, so frustum culling all of these

objects explicitly is usually incredibly wasteful. Instead, we would like to de-
vise a data structure that manages all of the geometry in the scene and allows
us to quickly discard large swaths of the world that are nowhere near the camera frustum prior to performing detailed frustum culling. Ideally, this data
structure should also help us to sort the geometry in the scene, either in front-
to-back order for the z prepass or in material order for full-color rendering.

Such a data structure is often called a *scene graph*, in reference to the graph-
like data structures often used by film rendering engines and DCC tools like
Maya. However, a game's scene graph needn't be a graph, and in fact the data
structure of choice is usually some kind of tree. The basic idea behind most
of these data structures is to partition three-dimensional space in a way that
makes it easy to discard regions that do not intersect the frustum, without
having to frustum cull all of the individual objects within them. Examples
include quadtrees and octress, BSP trees, *kd*-trees, and spatial hashing techniques.

*Quadtrees and Octrees*

A *quadtree* divides space into quadrants recursively. Each level of recursion
is represented by a node in the quadtree with four children, one for each
quadrant. The quadrants are typically separated by vertically oriented, axis-aligned planes, so that the quadrants are square or rectangular. However,
some quadtrees subdivide space using arbitrarily-shaped regions.

Quadtrees can be used to store and organize virtually any kind of spa-
tially-distributed data. In the context of rendering engines, quadtrees are often used to store renderable primitives such as mesh instances, subregions of
terrain geometry, or individual triangles of a large static mesh, for the purposes of efficient frustum culling. The renderable primitives are stored at the

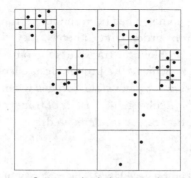

Figure 10.46. A top-down view of a space divided recursively into quadrants for storage in a
quadtree, based on the criterion of one point per region.

leaves of the tree, and we usually aim to achieve a roughly uniform number of primitives within each leaf region. This can be achieved by deciding whether to continue or terminate the subdivision based on the number of primitives within a region.

To determine which primitives are visible within the camera frustum, we walk the tree from the root to the leaves, checking each region for intersection with the frustum. If a given quadrant does not intersect the frustum, then we know that none of its child regions will do so either, and we can stop traversing that branch of the tree. This allows us to search for potentially visible primitives much more quickly than would be possible with a linear search (usually in $O(\log n)$ time). An example of a quadtree subdivision of space is shown in Figure 10.46.

An *octree* is the three-dimensional equivalent of a quadtree, dividing space into eight subregions at each level of the recursive subdivision. The regions of an octree are often cubes or rectangular prisms but can be arbitrarily-shaped three-dimensional regions in general.

### Bounding Sphere Trees

In the same way that a quadtree or octree subdivides space into (usually) rectangular regions, a *bounding sphere tree* divides space into spherical regions hierarchically. The leaves of the tree contain the bounding spheres of the renderable primitives in the scene. We collect these primitives into small logical groups and calculate the net bounding sphere of each group. The groups are themselves collected into larger groups, and this process continues until we have a single group with a bounding sphere that encompasses the entire virtual world. To generate a list of potentially visible primitives, we walk the tree from the root to the leaves, testing each bounding sphere against the frustum, and only recursing down branches that intersect it.

### BSP Trees

A binary space partitioning (BSP) tree divides space in half recursively until the objects within each half-space meet some predefined criteria (much as a quadtree divides space into quadrants). BSP trees have numerous uses, including collision detection and constructive solid geometry, as well as its most well-known application as a method for increasing the performance of frustum culling and geometry sorting for 3D graphics. A *kd*-tree is a generalization of the BSP tree concept to *k* dimensions.

In the context of rendering, a BSP tree divides space with a single plane at each level of the recursion. The dividing planes can be axis-aligned, but more commonly each subdivision corresponds to the plane of a single triangle in the scene. All of the other triangles are then categorized as being either on the front side or the back side of the plane. Any triangles that intersect the dividing plane are themselves divided into three new triangles, so that every triangle lies either entirely in front of or entirely behind the plane, or is coplanar with it. The result is a binary tree with a dividing plane and one or more triangles at each interior node and triangles at the leaves.

A BSP tree can be used for frustum culling in much the same way a quadtree, octree, or bounding sphere tree can. However, when generated with individual triangles as described above, a BSP tree can also be used to sort triangles into a strictly back-to-front or front-to-back order. This was particularly important for early 3D games like *Doom*, which did not have the benefit of a z-buffer and so were forced to use the painter's algorithm (i.e., to render the scene from back to front) to ensure proper inter-triangle occlusion.

Given a camera view point in 3D space, a back-to-front sorting algorithm walks the tree from the root. At each node, we check whether the view point is in front of or behind that node's dividing plane. If the camera is in front of a node's plane, we visit the node's back children first, then draw any triangles that are coplanar with its dividing plane, and finally we visit its front children. Likewise, when the camera's view point is found to be behind a node's dividing plane, we visit the node's front children first, then draw the triangles coplanar with the node's plane, and finally we visit its back children. This traversal scheme ensures that the triangles farthest from the camera will be visited before those that are closer to it, and hence it yields a back-to-front

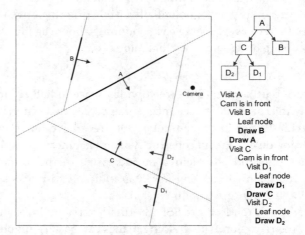

**Figure 10.47.** An example of back-to-front traversal of the triangles in a BSP tree. The triangles are shown edge-on in two dimensions for simplicity, but in a real BSP tree the triangles and dividing planes would be arbitrarily oriented in space.

ordering. Because this algorithm traverses *all* of the triangles in the scene, the order of the traversal is independent of the direction the camera is looking. A secondary frustum culling step would be required in order to traverse only visible triangles. A simple BSP tree is shown in Figure 10.47, along with the tree traversal that would be done for the camera position shown.

Full coverage of BSP tree generation and usage algorithms is beyond our scope here. See http://www.ccs.neu.edu/home/donghui/teaching/slides/geometry/BSP2D.ppt and http://www.gamedev.net/reference/articles/article657.asp for more details on BSP trees.

### 10.2.7.5. Choosing a Scene Graph

Clearly there are many different kinds of scene graphs. Which data structure to select for your game will depend upon the nature of the scenes you expect to be rendering. To make the choice wisely, you must have a clear understanding of what is required—and more importantly what is *not* required—when rendering scenes for your particular game.

For example, if you're implementing a fighting game, in which two characters battle it out in a ring surrounded by a mostly static environment, you may not need much of a scene graph at all. If your game takes place primarily in enclosed indoor environments, a BSP tree or portal system may serve you well. If the action takes place outdoors on relatively flat terrain, and the scene is viewed primarily from above (as might be the case in a real-time strategy game or god game), a simple quad tree might be all that's required to achieve high rendering speeds. On the other hand, if an outdoor scene is viewed primarily from the point of view of someone on the ground, we may need additional culling mechanisms. Densely populated scenes can benefit from an occlusion volume (antiportal) system, because there will be plenty of occluders. On the other hand, if your outdoor scene is very sparse, adding an antiportal system probably won't pay dividends (and might even hurt your frame rate).

Ultimately, your choice of scene graph should be based on hard data obtained by actually measuring the performance of your rendering engine. You may be surprised to learn where all your cycles are actually going! But once you know, you can select scene graph data structures and/or other optimizations to target the specific problems at hand.

## 10.3. Advanced Lighting and Global Illumination

In order to render photorealistic scenes, we need physically accurate global illumination algorithms. A complete coverage of these techniques is beyond our scope. In the following sections, we will briefly outline the most prevalent techniques in use within the game industry today. Our goal here is to provide you with an awareness of these techniques and a jumping off point for further investigation. For an excellent in-depth coverage of this topic, see [8].

### 10.3.1. Image-Based Lighting

A number of advanced lighting and shading techniques make heavy use of image data, usually in the form of two-dimensional texture maps. These are called *image-based lighting* algorithms.

#### 10.3.1.1. Normal Mapping

A *normal map* specifies a surface normal direction vector at each texel. This allows a 3D modeler to provide the rendering engine with a highly detailed description of a surface's shape, without having to tessellate the model to a high degree (as would be required if this same information were to be provided via vertex normals). Using a normal map, a single flat triangle can be made to look as though it were constructed from millions of tiny triangles. An example of normal mapping is shown in Figure 10.48.

The normal vectors are typically encoded in the RGB color channels of the texture, with a suitable bias to overcome the fact that RGB channels are strictly positive while normal vector components can be negative. Sometimes only two coordinates are stored in the texture; the third can be easily calculated at runtime, given the assumption that the surface normals are unit vectors.

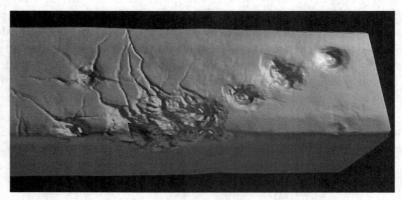

**Figure 10.48.** An example of a normal-mapped surface.

#### 10.3.1.2. Height Maps: Parallax and Relief Mapping

As its name implies, a *height map* encodes the height of the ideal surface above or below the surface of the triangle. Height maps are typically encoded as grayscale images, since we only need a single height value per texel.

**Figure 10.49.** DirectX 9 parallax occlusion mapping. The surface is actually a flat disc; a height map texture is used to define the surface details.

Height maps are often used for *parallax mapping* and *relief mapping*—two techniques that can make a planar surface appear to have rather extreme height variation that properly self-occludes and self-shadows. Figure 10.49 shows an example of parallax occlusion mapping implemented in DirectX 9.

A height map can also be used as a cheap way to generate surface normals. This technique was used in the early days of bump mapping. Nowadays, most game engines store surface normal information explicitly in a normal map, rather than calculating the normals from a height map.

### 10.3.1.3. Specular/Gloss Maps

When light reflects directly off a shiny surface, we call this *specular* reflection. The intensity of a specular reflection depends on the relative angles of the viewer, the light source, and the surface normal. As we saw in Section 10.1.3.2, the specular intensity takes the form $k_S(\mathbf{R} \cdot \mathbf{V})^\alpha$, where $\mathbf{R}$ is the reflection of the light's direction vector about the surface normal, $\mathbf{V}$ is the direction to the viewer, $k_S$ is the overall specular reflectivity of the surface, and $\alpha$ is called the specular power.

Many surfaces aren't uniformly glossy. For example, when a person's face is sweaty and dirty, wet regions appear shiny, while dry or dirty areas appear dull. We can encode high-detail specularity information in a special texture map known as a *specular map*.

If we store the value of $k_S$ in the texels of a specular map, we can control how much specular reflection should be applied at each texel. This kind of specular map is sometimes called a *gloss map*. It is also called a *specular mask*, because zero-valued texels can be used to "mask off" regions of the surface where we do not want specular reflection applied. If we store the value of $\alpha$ in our specular map, we can control the amount of "focus" our specular high-

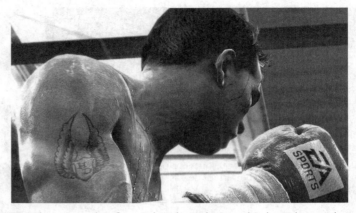

**Figure 10.50.** This screen shot from EA's Fight Night Round 3 shows how a gloss map can be used to control the degree of specular reflection that should be applied to each texel of a surface.

lights will have at each texel. This kind of texture is called a *specular power map*. An example of a gloss map is shown in Figure 10.50.

### 10.3.1.4. Environment Mapping

An environment map looks like a panoramic photograph of the environment taken from the point of view of an object in the scene, covering a full 360 degrees horizontally and either 180 degrees or 360 degrees vertically. An environment map acts like a description of the general lighting environment surrounding an object. It is generally used to inexpensively render reflections.

The two most common formats are *spherical environment maps* and *cubic environment maps*. A spherical map looks like a photograph taken through a fisheye lens, and it is treated as though it were mapped onto the inside of a sphere whose radius is infinite, centered about the object being rendered. The problem with sphere maps is that they are addressed using spherical coordinates. Around the equator, there is plenty of resolution both horizontally and vertically. However, as the vertical (azimuthal) angle approaches vertical, the resolution of the texture along the horizontal (zenith) axis decreases to a single texel. Cube maps were devised to avoid this problem.

A cube map looks like a composite photograph pieced together from photos taken in the six primary directions (up, down, left, right, front, and back). During rendering, a cube map is treated as though it were mapped onto the six inner surfaces of a box at infinity, centered on the object being rendered.

To read the environment map texel corresponding to a point **P** on the surface of an object, we take the ray from the camera to the point **P** and reflect it about the surface normal at **P**. The reflected ray is followed until it intersects the sphere or cube of the environment map. The value of the texel at this intersection point is used when shading the point **P**.

### 10.3.1.5. Three-Dimensional Textures

Modern graphics harware also includes support for three-dimensional textures. A 3D texture can be thought of as a stack of 2D textures. The GPU knows how to address and filter a 3D texture, given a three-dimensional texture coordinate $(u, v, w)$.

Three-dimensional textures can be useful for describing the appearance or volumetric properties of an object. For example, we could render a marble sphere and allow it to be cut by an arbitrary plane. The texture would look continuous and correct across the cut no matter where it was made, because the texture is well-defined and continuous throughout the entire volume of the sphere.

## 10.3.2. High Dynamic Range Lighting

A display device like a television set or CRT monitor can only produce a limited range of intensities. This is why the color channels in the frame buffer are limited to a zero to one range. But in the real world, light intensities can grow arbitrarily large. *High dynamic range* (HDR) lighting attempts to capture this wide range of light intensities.

HDR lighting performs lighting calculations without clamping the resulting intensities arbitrarily. The resulting image is stored in a format that permits intensities to grow beyond one. The net effect is an image in which extreme dark and light regions can be represented without loss of detail within either type of region.

Prior to display on-screen, a process called *tone mapping* is used to shift and scale the image's intensity range into the range supported by the display device. Doing this permits the rendering engine to reproduce many real-world visual effects, like the temporary blindness that occurs when you walk from a dark room into a brightly lit area, or the way light seems to bleed out from behind a brightly back-lit object (an effect known as *bloom*).

One way to represent an HDR image is to store the R, G, and B channels using 32-bit floating point numbers, instead of 8-bit integers. Another alternative is to employ an entirely different color model altogether. The log-LUV color model is a popular choice for HDR lighting. In this model, color is represented as an intensity channel ($L$) and two chromaticity channels ($U$ and $V$). Because the human eye is more sensitive to changes in intensity than it is to changes in chromaticity, the $L$ channel is stored in 16 bits while $U$ and $V$ are given only eight bits each. In addition, $L$ is represented using a logarithmic scale (base two) in order to capture a very wide range of light intensities.

## 10.3.3. Global Illumination

As we noted in Section 10.1.3.1, global illumination refers to a class of lighting algorithms that account for light's interactions with multiple objects in the scene, on its way from the light source to the virtual camera. Global illumination accounts for effects like the shadows that arise when one surface occludes another, reflections, caustics, and the way the color of one object can "bleed" onto the objects around it. In the following sections, we'll take a brief look at some of the most common global illumination techniques. Some of these methods aim to reproduce a single isolated effect, like shadows or reflections. Others like radiosity and ray tracing methods aim to provide a holistic model of global light transport.

### 10.3.3.1. Shadow Rendering

Shadows are created when a surface blocks light's path. The shadows caused by an ideal point light source would be sharp, but in the real world shadows have blurry edges; this is called the penumbra. A penumbra arises because real-world light sources cover some area and so produce light rays that graze the edges of an object at different angles.

The two most prevalent shadow rendering techniques are *shadow volumes* and *shadow maps*. We'll briefly describe each in the sections below. In both techniques, objects in the scene are generally divided into three categories: objects that cast shadows, objects that are to receive shadows, and objects that are entirely excluded from consideration when rendering shadows. Likewise, the lights are tagged to indicate whether or not they should generate shadows. This important optimization limits the number of light-object combinations that need to be processed in order to produce the shadows in a scene.

*Shadow Volumes*

In the shadow volume technique, each shadow caster is viewed from the vantage point of a shadow-generating light source, and the shadow caster's silhouette edges are identified. These edges are extruded in the direction of the light rays emanating from the light source. The result is a new piece of geometry that describes the volume of space in which the light is occluded by the shadow caster in question. This is shown in Figure 10.51.

**Figure 10.51.** A shadow volume generated by extruding the silhouette edges of a shadow casting object as seen from the point of view of the light source.

A shadow volume is used to generate a shadow by making use of a special full-screen buffer known as the stencil buffer. This buffer stores a single integer value corresponding to each pixel of the screen. Rendering can be masked by the values in the stencil buffer—for example, we could configure the GPU to only render fragments whose corresponding stencil values are non-zero. In addition, the GPU can be configured so that rendered geometry updates the values in the stencil buffer in various useful ways.

To render shadows, the scene is first drawn to generate an unshadowed image in the frame buffer, along with an accurate $z$-buffer. The stencil buffer is cleared so that it contains zeros at every pixel. Each shadow volume is then rendered from the point of view of the camera in such a way that front-facing triangles increase the values in the stencil buffer by one, while back-facing triangles decrease them by one. In areas of the screen where the shadow volume does not appear at all, of course the stencil buffer's pixels will be left containing zero. The stencil buffer will also contain zeros where both the front and back faces of the shadow volume are visible, because the front face will increase the stencil value but the back face will decrease it again. In areas where the back face of the shadow volume has been occluded by "real" scene geometry, the stencil value will be one. This tells us which pixels of the screen are in shadow. So we can render shadows in a third pass, by simply darkening those regions of the screen that contain a non-zero stencil buffer value.

*Shadow Maps*

The shadow mapping technique is effectively a per-fragment depth test performed from the point of view of the light instead of from the point of view of the camera. The scene is rendered in two steps: First, a *shadow map* texture is generated by rendering the scene from the point of view of the light source and saving off the contents of the depth buffer. Second, the scene is rendered as usual, and the shadow map is used to determine whether or not each fragment is in shadow. At each fragment in the scene, the shadow map tells us whether or not the light is being occluded by some geometry that is closer to the light source, in just the same way that the $z$-buffer tells us whether a fragment is being occluded by a triangle that is closer to the camera.

A shadow map contains only depth information—each texel records how far away it is from the light source. Shadow maps are therefore typically rendered using the hardware's double-speed $z$-only mode (since all we care about is the depth information). For a point light source, a perspective projection is used when rendering the shadow map; for a directional light source, an orthographic projection is used instead.

To render a scene using a shadow map, we draw the scene as usual from the point of view of the camera. For each vertex of every triangle, we calculate its position in *light space*—i.e., in the same "view space" that was used when generating the shadow map in the first place. These light space coordinates can be interpolated across the triangle, just like any other vertex attribute. This gives us the position of each fragment *in light space*. To determine whether a given fragment is in shadow or not, we convert the fragment's light-space ($x$, $y$)-coordinates into texture coordinates ($u$, $v$) within the shadow map. We then compare the fragment's light-space $z$-coordinate with the depth stored at the corresponding texel in the shadow depth map. If the fragment's light-space $z$ is farther away from the light than the texel in the shadow map, then it must be occluded by some other piece of geometry that is closer to the light source—hence it is in shadow. Likewise, if the fragment's light-space $z$ is closer to the light source than the texel in the shadow map, then it is not occluded and is not in shadow. Based on this information, the fragment's color can be adjusted accordingly. The shadow mapping process is illustrated in Figure 10.52.

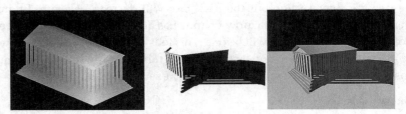

**Figure 10.52.** The far left image is a shadow map—the contents of the z-buffer as rendered from the point of view of a particular light source. The pixels of the center image are black where the light-space depth test failed (fragment in shadow) and white where it succeeded (fragment not in shadow). The far right image shows the final scene rendered with shadows.

### 10.3.3.2. Ambient Occlusion

*Ambient occlusion* is a technique for modeling *contact shadows*—the soft shadows that arise when a scene is illuminated by only ambient light. In effect, ambient occlusion describes how "accessible" each point on a surface is to light in general. For example, the interior of a section of pipe is less accessible to ambient light than its exterior. If the pipe were placed outside on an overcast day, its interior would generally appear darker than its exterior.

Figure 10.53 shows the level of ambient occlusion across an object's surface. Ambient occlusion is measured at a point on a surface by constructing a hemisphere with a very large radius centered on that point and determing what percentage of that hemisphere's area is visible from the point in question. It can be precomputed offline for static objects, because ambient occlusion is independent of view direction and the direction of incident light. It is typically stored in a texture map that records the level of ambient occlusion at each texel across the surface.

**Figure 10.53.** A dragon rendered with ambient occlusion.

### 10.3.3.3. Reflections

Reflections occur when light bounces off a highly specular (shiny) surface producing an image of another portion of the scene in the surface. Reflections can be implemented in a number of ways. Environment maps are used to

**Figure 10.54.** Mirror reflections in *Luigi's Mansion* implemented by rendering the scene to a texture that is subsequently applied to the mirror's surface.

produce general reflections of the surrounding environment on the surfaces of shiny objects. Direct reflections in flat surfaces like mirrors can be produced by reflecting the camera's position about the plane of the reflective surface and then rendering the scene from that reflected point of view into a texture. The texture is then applied to the reflective surface in a second pass.

### 10.3.3.4. Caustics

Caustics are the bright specular highlights arising from intense reflections or refractions from very shiny surfaces like water or polished metal. When the reflective surface moves, as is the case for water, the caustic effects glimmer and "swim" across the surfaces on which they fall. Caustic effects can be produced by projecting a (possibly animated) texture containing semi-random bright highlights onto the affected surfaces. An example of this technique is shown in Figure 10.55.

**Figure 10.55.** Water caustics produced by projecting an animated texture onto the affected surfaces.

### 10.3.3.5. Subsurface Scattering

When light enters a surface at one point, is scattered beneath the surface, and then reemerges at a different point on the surface, we call this *subsurface scattering*. This phenomenon is responsible for the "warm glow" of human skin, wax, and marble statues. Subsurface scattering is described by a more-advanced variant of the BRDF (see Section 10.1.3.2) known as the BSSRDF (*bidirectional surface scattering reflectance distribution function*).

Subsurface scattering can be simulated in a number of ways. Depth-map–based subsurface scattering renders a shadow map (see Section 10.3.3.1), but instead of using it to determine which pixels are in shadow, it is used to measure how far a beam of light would have to travel in order to pass all the way

**Figure 10.56.** On the left, a dragon rendered without subsurface scattering (i.e., using a BRDF lighting model). On the right, the same dragon rendered with subsurface scattering (i.e., using a BSSRDF model). Images rendered by Rui Wang at the University of Virginia.

through the occluding object. The shadowed side of the object is then given an artificial diffuse lighting term whose intensity is inversely proportional to the distance the light had to travel in order to emerge on the opposite side of the object. This causes objects to appear to be glowing slightly on the side opposite to the light source but only where the object is relatively thin. For more information on subsurface scattering techniques, see http://http.developer. nvidia.com/GPUGems/gpugems_ch16.html.

### 10.3.3.6. Precomputed Radiance Transfer (PRT)

*Precomputed radiance transfer* (PRT) is a relatively new technique that attempts to simulate the effects of radiosity-based rendering methods in real time. It does so by precomputing and storing a complete description of how an incident light ray would interact with a surface (reflect, refract, scatter, etc.) when approaching from every possible direction. At runtime, the response to a particular incident light ray can be looked up and quickly converted into very accurate lighting results.

In general the light's response at a point on the surface is a complex function defined on a hemisphere centered about the point. A compact representation of this function is required to make the PRT technique practical. A common approach is to approximate the function as a linear combination of spherical harmonic basis functions. This is essentially the three-dimensional equivalent of encoding a simple scalar function $f(x)$ as a linear combination of shifted and scaled sine waves.

The details of PRT are far beyond our scope. For more information, see http://web4.cs.ucl.ac.uk/staff/j.kautz/publications/prtSIG02.pdf. PRT lighting techniques are demonstrated in a DirectX sample program available in the DirectX SDK—see http://msdn.microsoft.com/en-us/library/bb147287.aspx for more details.

### 10.3.4. Deferred Rendering

In traditional triangle-rasterization–based rendering, all lighting and shading calculations are performed on the triangle fragments in view space. The problem with this technique is that it is inherently inefficient. For one thing, we potentially do work that we don't need to do. We shade the vertices of triangles, only to discover during the rasterization stage that the entire triangle is being depth-culled by the z test. Early z tests help eliminate unnecessary pixel shader evaluations, but even this isn't perfect. What's more, in order to handle a complex scene with lots of lights, we end up with a proliferation of different versions of our vertex and pixel shaders—versions that handle dif-

**Figure 10.57.** Screenshots from *Killzone 2*, showing some of the typical components of the G-buffer used in deferred rendering. The upper image shows the final rendered image. Below it, clockwise from the upper left, are the albedo (diffuse) color, depth, view-space normal, screen space 2D motion vector (for motion blurring), specular power, and specular intensity.

ferent numbers of lights, different types of lights, different numbers of skinning weights, etc.

*Deferred rendering* is an alternative way to shade a scene that addresses many of these problems. In deferred rendering, the majority of the lighting calculations are done in screen space, not view space. We efficiently render the scene without worrying about lighting. During this phase, we store all the information we're going to need to light the pixels in a "deep" frame buffer known as the *G-buffer*. Once the scene has been fully rendered, we use the information in the G-buffer to perform our lighting and shading calculations. This is usually much more efficient than view-space lighting, avoids the proliferation of shader variants, and permits some very pleasing effects to be rendered relatively easily.

The G-buffer may be physically implemented as a collection of buffers, but conceptually it is a single frame buffer containing a rich set of information about the lighting and surface properties of the objects in the scene at every pixel on the screen. A typical G-buffer might contain the following per-pixel attributes: depth, surface normal in clip space, diffuse color, specular power, even precomputed radiance transfer (PRT) coefficients. The following sequence of screen shots from Guerrilla Games' *Killzone 2* shows some of the typical components of the G-buffer.

An in-depth discussion of deferred rendering is beyond our scope, but the folks at Guerrilla Games have prepared an excellent presentation on the topic, which is available at http://www.guerrilla-games.com/publications/dr_kz2_rsx_dev07.pdf.

## 10.4. Visual Effects and Overlays

The rendering pipeline we've discussed to this point is responsible primarily for rendering three-dimensional solid objects. A number of specialized rendering systems are typically layered on top of this pipeline, responsible for rendering visual elements like particle effects, decals (small geometry overlays that represent bullet holes, cracks, scratches, and other surface details), hair and fur, rain or falling snow, water, and other specialized visual effects. Full-screen post effects may be applied, including vignette (slight blur around the edges of the screen), motion blur, depth of field blurring, artificial/enhanced colorization, and the list goes on. Finally, the game's menu system and heads-up display (HUD) are typically realized by rendering text and other two- or three-dimensional graphics in screen space overlaid on top of the three-dimensional scene.

An in-depth coverage of these engine systems is beyond our scope. In the following sections, we'll provide a brief overview of these rendering systems, and point you in the direction of additional information.

## 10.4.1. Particle Effects

A particle rendering system is concerned with rendering amorphous objects like clouds of smoke, sparks, flame, and so on. These are called *particle effects*. The key features that differentiate a particle effect from other kinds of renderable geometry are as follows:

- It is composed of a very *large number* of *relatively simple* pieces of geometry—most often simple cards called *quads*, composed of two triangles each.

- The geometry is often *camera-facing* (i.e., billboarded), meaning that the engine must take steps to ensure that the face normals of each quad always point directly at the camera's focal point.

- Its materials are almost always *semi-transparent* or *translucent*. As such, particle effects have some stringent *rendering order* constraints that do not apply to the majority of opaque objects in a scene.

- Particles *animate* in a rich variety of ways. Their positions, orientations, sizes (scales), texture coordinates, and many of their shader parameters vary from frame to frame. These changes are defined either by hand-authored animation curves or via procedural methods.

- Particles are typically *spawned and killed* continually. A particle emitter is a logical entity in the world that creates particles at some user-specified rate; particles are killed when they hit a predefined death plane, or

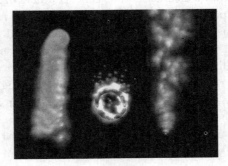

Figure 10.58. Some particle effects.

when they have lived for a user-defined length of time, or as decided by some other user-specified criteria.

Particle effects could be rendered using regular triangle mesh geometry with appropriate shaders. However, because of the unique characteristics listed above, a specialized particle effect animation and rendering system is always used to implement them in a real production game engine. A few example particle effects are shown in Figure 10.58.

Particle system design and implementation is a rich topic that could occupy many chapters all on its own. For more information on particle systems, see [1] Section 10.7, [14] Section 20.5, [9] Section 13.7 and [10] Section 4.1.2.

## 10.4.2. Decals

A *decal* is a relatively small piece of geometry that is overlaid on top of the regular geometry in the scene, allowing the visual appearance of the surface to be modified dynamically. Examples include bullet holes, foot prints, scratches, cracks, etc.

The approach most often used by modern engines is to model a decal as a rectangular area that is to be projected along a ray into the scene. This gives rise to a rectangular prism in 3D space. Whatever surface the prism intersects first becomes the surface of the decal. The triangles of the intersected geometry are extracted and clipped against the four bounding planes of the decal's projected prism. The resulting triangles are texture-mapped with a desired decal texture by generating appropriate texture coordinates for each vertex. These texture-mapped triangles are then rendered over the top of the regular scene, often using parallax mapping to give them the illusion of depth and with a slight *z*-bias (usually implemented by shifting the near plane slightly) so they don't experience *z*-fighting with the geometry on which they are over-

Figure 10.59. Parallax-mapped decals from *Uncharted: Drake's Fortune.*

laid. The result is the appearance of a bullet hole, scratch or other kind of surface modification. Some bullet-hole decals are depicted in Figure 10.59.

For more information on creating and rendering decals, see [7] Section 4.8, and [28] Section 9.2.

### 10.4.3. Environmental Effects

Any game that takes place in a somewhat natural or realistic environment requires some kind of environmental rendering effects. These effects are usually implemented via specialized rendering systems. We'll take a brief look at a few of the more common of these systems in the following sections.

#### 10.4.3.1. Skies

The sky in a game world needs to contain vivid detail, yet technically speaking it lies an extremely long distance away from the camera. Therefore we cannot model it as it really is and must turn instead to various specialized rendering techniques.

One simple approach is to fill the frame buffer with the sky texture prior to rendering any 3D geometry. The sky texture should be rendered at an approximate 1:1 texel-to-pixel ratio, so that the texture is roughly or exactly the resolution of the screen. The sky texture can be rotated and scrolled to correspond to the motions of the camera in-game. During rendering of the sky, we make sure to set the depth of all pixels in the frame buffer to the maximum possible depth value. This ensures that the 3D scene elements will always sort on top of the sky. The arcade hit *Hydro Thunder* rendered its skies in exactly this manner.

For games in which the player can look in any direction, we can use a *sky dome* or *sky box*. The dome or box is rendered with its center always at the camera's current location, so that it appears to lie at infinity, no matter where the camera moves in the game world. As with the sky texture approach, the sky box or dome is rendered before any other 3D geometry, and all of the pixels in the frame buffer are set to the maximum $z$-value when the sky is rendered. This means that the dome or box can actually be tiny, relative to other objects in the scene. Its size is irrelevant, as long as it fills the entire frame buffer when it is drawn. For more information on sky rendering, see [1] Section 10.3 and [38] page 253.

Clouds are often implemented with a specialized rendering and animation system as well. In early games like *Doom* and *Quake*, the clouds were just planes with scrolling semi-transparent cloud textures on them. More-recent cloud techniques include camera-facing cards (billboards), particle-effect based clouds, and volumetric cloud effects.

### 10.4.3.2. Terrain

The goal of a terrain system is to model the surface of the earth and provide a canvas of sorts upon which other static and dynamic elements can be laid out. Terrain is sometimes modeled explicitly in a package like Maya. But if the player can see far into the distance, we usually want some kind of dynamic tessellation or other level of detail (LOD) system. We may also need to limit the amount of data required to represent very large outdoor areas.

*Height field terrain* is one popular choice for modeling large terrain areas. The data size can be kept relatively small because a height field is typically stored in a grayscale texture map. In most height-field–based terrain systems, the horizontal ($y = 0$) plane is tessellated in a regular grid pattern, and the heights of the terrain vertices are determined by sampling the height field texture. The number of triangles per unit area can be varied based on distance from the camera, thereby allowing large-scale features to be seen in the distance, while still permitting a good deal of detail to be represented for nearby terrain. An example of a terrain defined via a height field bitmap is shown in Figure 10.60.

Terrain systems usually provide specialized tools for "painting" the height field itself, carving out terrain features like roads, rivers, and so on. Texture mapping in a terrain system is often a blend between four or more textures. This allows artists to "paint" in grass, dirt, gravel, and other terrain features by simply exposing one of the texture layers. The layers can be cross-blended from one to another to provide smooth textural transitions. Some terrain tools also permit sections of the terrain to be cut out to permit buildings, trenches, and other specialized terrain features to be inserted in the form of regular mesh geometry. Terrain authoring tools are sometimes integrated directly into the game world editor, while in other engines they may be stand-alone tools.

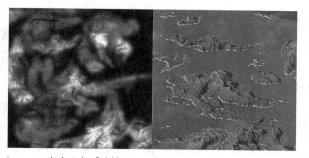

**Figure 10.60.** A grayscale height field bitmap (left) can be used to control the vertical positions of the vertices in a terrain grid mesh (right). In this example, a water plane intersects the terrain mesh to create islands.

Of course, height field terrain is just one of many options for modeling the surface of the Earth in a game. For more information on terrain rendering, see [6] Sections 4.16 through 4.19 and [7] Section 4.2.

### 10.4.3.3. Water

Water renderers are commonplace in games nowadays. There are lots of different possible kinds of water, including oceans, pools, rivers, waterfalls, fountains, jets, puddles, and damp solid surfaces. Each type of water generally requires some specialized rendering technology. Some also require dynamic motion simulations. Large bodies of water may require dynamic tessellation or other LOD methodologies similar to those employed in a terrain system.

Water systems sometimes interact with a game's rigid body dynamics system (flotation, force from water jets, etc.) and with gameplay (slippery surfaces, swimming mechanics, diving mechanics, riding vertical jets of water, and so on). Water effects are often created by combining disparate rendering technologies and subsystems. For example, a waterfall might make use of specialized water shaders, scrolling textures, particle effects for mist at the base, a decal-like overlay for foam, and the list goes on. Today's games offer some pretty amazing water effects, and active research into technologies like real-time fluid dynamics promises to make water simulations even richer and more realistic in the years ahead. For more information on water rendering and simulation techniques, see [1] Sections 9.3, 9.5, and 9.6, [13], and [6] Sections 2.6 and 5.11.

## 10.4.4. Overlays

Most games have heads-up displays, in-game graphical user interfaces, and menu systems. These *overlays* are typically comprised of two- and three-dimensional graphics rendered directly in view space or screen space.

Overlays are generally rendered after the primary scene, with $z$ testing disabled to ensure that they appear on top of the three-dimensional scene. Two-dimensional overlays are typically implemented by rendering quads (triangle pairs) in screen space using an orthographic projection. Three-dimensional overlays may be rendered using an orthographic projection or via the regular perspective projection with the geometry positioned in view space so that it follows the camera around.

### 10.4.4.1. Normalized Screen Coordinates

The coordinates of two-dimensional overlays can be measured in terms of screen pixels. However, if your game is going to be expected to support multiple screen resolutions (which is very common in PC games), it's a far better idea to use *normalized* screen coordinates. Normalized coordinates range from zero to one along *one* of the two axes (but not both—see below), and they can easily be scaled into pixel-based measurements corresponding to an arbitrary screen resolution. This allows us to lay out our overlay elements without worrying about screen resolution at all (and only having to worry a little bit about aspect ratio).

It's easiest to define normalized coordinates so that they range from 0.0 to 1.0 along the *y*-axis. At a 4:3 aspect ratio, this means that the *x*-axis would range from 0.0 to 1.333 (= 4 / 3), while at 16:9 the *x*-axis' range would be from 0.0 to 1.777 (= 16 / 9). It's important *not* to define our coordinates so that they range from zero to one along *both* axes. Doing this would cause square visual elements to have unequal *x* and *y* dimensions—or put another way, a visual element with seemingly square dimensions would not look like a square on-screen! Moreover, our "square" elements would stretch differently at different aspect ratios—definitely not an acceptable state of affairs.

### 10.4.4.2. Relative Screen Coordinates

To really make normalized coordinates work well, it should be possible to specify coordinates in absolute or relative terms. For example, positive coordinates might be interpreted as being relative to the top-left corner of the screen, while negative coordinates are relative to the bottom-right corner. That way, if I want a HUD element to be a certain distance from the right or bottom edges of the screen, I won't have to change its normalized coordinates when the aspect ratio changes. We might want to allow an even richer set of possible alignment choices, such as aligning to the center of the screen or aligning to another visual element.

That said, you'll probably have some overlay elements that simply cannot be laid out using normalized coordinates in such a way that they look right at both the 4:3 and 16:9 aspect ratios. You may want to consider having two distinct layouts, one for each aspect ratio, so you can fine-tune them independently.

### 10.4.4.3. Text and Fonts

A game engine's text/font system is typically implemented as a special kind of two-dimensional (or sometimes three-dimensional) overlay. At its core, a text rendering system needs to be capable of displaying a sequence of character glyphs corresponding to a text string, arranged in various orientations on the screen. A font is often implemented via a texture map containing the various required glyphs. A font description file provides information such as the bounding boxes of each glyph within the texture, and font layout information such as kerning, baseline offsets, and so on.

A good text/font system must account for the differences in character sets and reading directions inherent in various languages. Some text systems also provide various fun features like the ability to animate characters across the screen in various ways, the ability to animate individual characters, and so on. Some game engines even go so far as to implement a subset of the Adobe Flash standard in order to support a rich set of two-dimensional effects in their overlays and text. However, it's important to remember when implementing a game font system that only those features that are *actually required* by the game should be implemented. There's no point in furnishing your engine with an advanced text animation if your game never needs to display animated text!

### 10.4.5. Gamma Correction

CRT monitors tend to have a nonlinear response to luminance values. That is, if a linearly-increasing ramp of R, G, or B values were to be sent to a CRT, the image that would result on-screen would be perceptually nonlinear to the human eye. Visually, the dark regions of the image would look darker than they should. This is illustrated in Figure 10.61.

The gamma response curve of a typical CRT display can be modeled quite simply by the formula

$$V_{\text{out}} = V_{\text{in}}^{\gamma},$$

where $\gamma_{\text{CRT}} > 1$. To correct for this effect, the colors sent to the CRT display are usually passed through an inverse transformation (i.e., using a gamma value $\gamma_{\text{corr}} < 1$). The value of $\gamma_{\text{CRT}}$ for a typical CRT monitor is 2.2, so the correc-

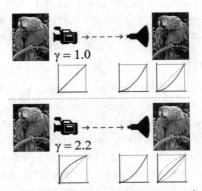

**Figure 10.61.** The effect of a CRT's gamma response on image quality and how the effect can be corrected for. Image courtesy of www.wikipedia.org.

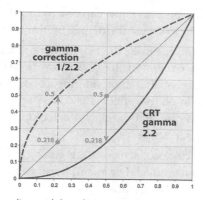

**Figure 10.62.** Gamma encoding and decoding curves. Image courtesy of www.wikipedia.org.

tion value is usually $\gamma_{corr} = 1/2.2 = 0.455$. These gamma encoding and decoding curves are shown in Figure 10.62.

Gamma encoding can be performed by the 3D rendering engine to ensure that the values in the final image are properly gamma-corrected. One problem that is encountered, however, is that the bitmap images used to represent texture maps are often gamma-corrected themselves. A high-quality rendering engine takes this fact into account, by gamma-decoding the textures prior to rendering and then re-encoding the gamma of the final rendered scene so that its colors can be reproduced properly on-screen.

## 10.4.6. Full-Screen Post Effects

Full-screen *post effects* are effects applied to a rendered three-dimensional scene that provide additional realism or a stylized look. These effects are often implemented by passing the entire contents of the screen through a pixel shader that applies the desired effect(s). This can be accomplished by rendering a full-screen quad that has been mapped with a texture containing the unfiltered scene. A few examples of full-screen post effects are given below:

- *Motion blur.* This is typically implemented by rendering a buffer of screen-space velocity vectors and using this vector field to selectively blur the rendered image. Blurring is accomplished by passing a *convolution kernel* over the image (see "Image Smoothing and Sharpening by Discrete Convolution" by Dale A. Schumacher, published in [4], for details).

- *Depth of field blur.* This blur effect can be produced by using the contents of the depth buffer to adjust the degree of blur applied at each pixel.

- *Vignette.* In this filmic effect, the brightness or saturation of the image is reduced at the corners of the screen for dramatic effect. It is sometimes implemented by literally rendering a texture overlay on top of the screen. A variation on this effect is used to produce the classic circular effect used to indicate that the player is looking through a pair of binoculars or a weapon scope.

- *Colorization.* The colors of screen pixels can be altered in arbitrary ways as a post-processing effect. For example, all colors except red could be desaturated to grey to produce a striking effect similar to the famous scene of the little girl in the red coat from *Schindler's List*.

## 10.5. Further Reading

We've covered a lot of material in a very short space in this chapter, but we've only just scratched the surface. No doubt you'll want to explore many of these topics in much greater detail. For an excellent overview of the entire process of creating three-dimensional computer graphics and animation for games and film, I highly recommend [23]. The technology that underlies modern real-time rendering is covered in excellent depth in [1], while [14] is well known as the definitive reference guide to all things related to computer graphics. Other great books on 3D rendering include [42], [9], and [10]. The mathematics of 3D rendering is covered very well in [28]. No graphics programmer's library would be complete without one or more books from the *Graphics Gems* series ([18], [4], [24], [19], and [36]) and/or the *GPU Gems* series ([13], [38], and [35]). Of course, this short reference list is only the beginning—you will undoubtedly encounter a great many more excellent books on rendering and shaders over the course of your career as a game programmer.

# 11
# Animation Systems

The majority of modern 3D games revolve around *characters*—often human or humanoid, sometimes animal or alien. Characters are unique because they need to move in a fluid, organic way. This poses a host of new technical challenges, over and above what is required to simulate and animate rigid objects like vehicles, projectiles, soccer balls, and Tetris pieces. The task of imbuing characters with natural-looking motion is handled by an engine component known as the *character animation system*.

As we'll see, an animation system gives game designers a powerful suite of tools that can be applied to non-characters as well as characters. Any game object that is not 100% rigid can take advantage of the animation system. So whenever you see a vehicle with moving parts, a piece of articulated machinery, trees waving gently in the breeze, or even an exploding building in a game, chances are good that the object makes at least partial use of the game engine's animation system.

## 11.1. Types of Character Animation

Character animation technology has come a long way since *Donkey Kong*. At first, games employed very simple techniques to provide the illusion of life-like movement. As game hardware improved, more-advanced techniques became feasible in real time. Today, game designers have a host of powerful animation methods at their disposal. In this section, we'll take a brief look at the evolution of character animation and outline the three most-common techniques used in modern game engines.

### 11.1.1.  Cel Animation

The precursor to all game animation techniques is known as *traditional anima-tion,* or *hand-drawn animation.* This is the technique used in the earliest animat-ed cartoons. The illusion of motion is produced by displaying a sequence of still pictures known as *frames* in rapid succession. Real-time 3D rendering can be thought of as an electronic form of traditional animation, in that a sequence of still full-screen images is presented to the viewer over and over to produce the illusion of motion.

Cel animation is a specific type of traditional animation. A *cel* is a transpar-ent sheet of plastic on which images can be painted or drawn. An animated sequence of cels can be placed on top of a fixed background painting or draw-ing to produce the illusion of motion without having to redraw the static back-ground over and over.

The electronic equivalent to cel animation is a technology known as *sprite animation.* A sprite is a small bitmap that can be overlaid on top of a full-screen background image without disrupting it, often drawn with the aid of special-ized graphics hardware. Hence, a sprite is to 2D game animation what a cel was to traditional animation. This technique was a staple during the 2D game era. Figure 11.1 shows the famous sequence of sprite bitmaps that were used to produce the illusion of a running humanoid character in almost every Mat-tel Intellivision game ever made. The sequence of frames was designed so that it animates smoothly even when it is repeated indefinitely—this is known as a *looping animation.* This particular animation would be called a *run cycle* in modern parlance, because it makes the character appear to be running. Char-acters typically have a number of looping animation cycles, including various idle cycles, a walk cycle, and a run cycle.

**Figure 11.1.** The sequence of sprite bitmaps used in most Intellivision games.

### 11.1.2.  Rigid Hierarchical Animation

With the advent of 3D graphics, sprite techniques began to lose their appeal. *Doom* made use of a sprite-like animation system: Its monsters were nothing more than camera-facing quads, each of which displayed a sequence of texture bitmaps (known as an *animated texture*) to produce the illusion of motion. And this technique is still used today for low-resolution and/or distant objects—for example crowds in a stadium, or hordes of soldiers fighting a distant battle in the background. But for high-quality foreground characters, 3D graphics brought with it the need for improved character animation methods.

The earliest approach to 3D character animation is a technique known as *rigid hierarchical animation*. In this approach, a character is modeled as a collection of rigid pieces. A typical break-down for a humanoid character might be pelvis, torso, upper arms, lower arms, upper legs, lower legs, hands, feet, and head. The rigid pieces are constrained to one another in a hierarchical fashion, analogous to the manner in which a mammal's bones are connected at the joints. This allows the character to move naturally. For example, when the upper arm is moved, the lower arm and hand will automatically follow it. A typical hierarchy has the pelvis at the root, with the torso and upper legs as its immediate children, and so on as shown below:

```
Pelvis
    Torso
        UpperRightArm
            LowerRightArm
                RightHand
        UpperLeftArm
            UpperLeftArm
                LeftHand
        Head
    UpperRightLeg
        LowerRightLeg
            RightFoot
    UpperLeftLeg
        UpperLeftLeg
            LeftFoot
```

The big problem with the rigid hierarchy technique is that the behavior of the character's body is often not very pleasing due to "cracking" at the joints. This is illustrated in Figure 11.2. Rigid hierarchical animation works well for

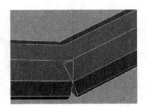

**Figure 11.2.** Cracking at the joints is a big problem in rigid hierarchical animation.

robots and machinery that really is constructed of rigid parts, but it breaks down under scrutiny when applied to "fleshy" characters.

### 11.1.3. Per-Vertex Animation and Morph Targets

Rigid hierarchical animation tends to look unnatural because it is rigid. What we really want is a way to move individual vertices so that triangles can stretch to produce more-natural looking motion.

One way to achieve this is to apply a brute-force technique known as *per-vertex animation*. In this approach, the vertices of the mesh are animated by an artist, and motion data is exported which tells the game engine how to move each vertex at runtime. This technique can produce any mesh deformation imaginable (limited only by the tessellation of the surface). However, it is a data-intensive technique, since time-varying motion information must be stored for each vertex of the mesh. For this reason, it has little application to real-time games.

A variation on this technique known as *morph target animation* is used in some real-time games. In this approach, the vertices of a mesh are moved by an animator to create a relatively small set of fixed, extreme poses. Animations are produced by *blending* between two or more of these fixed poses at runtime. The position of each vertex is calculated using a simple linear interpolation (LERP) between the vertex's positions in each of the extreme poses.

The morph target technique is often used for facial animation, because the human face is an extremely complex piece of anatomy, driven by roughly 50 muscles. Morph target animation gives an animator full control over every vertex of a facial mesh, allowing him or her to produce both subtle and extreme movements that approximate the musculature of the face well. Figure 11.3 shows a set of facial morph targets.

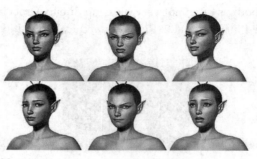

Figure 11.3. A set of facial morph targets for NVIDIA's *Dawn* character.

## 11.1.4.  Skinned Animation

As the capabilities of game hardware improved further, an animation technology known as *skinned animation* was developed. This technique has many
of the benefits of per-vertex and morph target animation—permitting the triangles of an animated mesh to deform. But it also enjoys the much more-
efficient performance and memory usage characteristics of rigid hierarchical
animation. It is capable of producing reasonably realistic approximations to
the movement of skin and clothing.

Skinned animation was first used by games like *Super Mario 64*, and it
is still the most prevalent technique in use today, both by the game industry
and the feature film industry. A host of famous modern game and movie characters, including the dinosaurs from *Jurrasic Park*, Solid Snake (*Metal Gear
Solid 4*), Gollum (*Lord of the Rings*), Nathan Drake (*Uncharted: Drake's Fortune*),
Buzz Lightyear (*Toy Story*), and Marcus Fenix (*Gears of War*) were all animated,
in whole or in part, using skinned animation techniques. The remainder of
this chapter will be devoted primarily to the study of skinned/skeletal animation.

In skinned animation, a *skeleton* is constructed from rigid "bones," just as
in rigid hierarchical animation. However, instead of rendering the rigid pieces
on-screen, they remain hidden. A smooth continuous triangle mesh called a
*skin* is bound to the joints of the skeleton; its vertices track the movements of
the joints. Each vertex of the skin mesh can be weighted to multiple joints, so
the skin can stretch in a natural way as the joints move.

**Figure 11.4.** Eric Browning's Crank the Weasel character, with internal skeletal structure.

In Figure 11.4, we see Crank the Weasel, a game character designed by Eric Browning for Midway Home Entertainment in 2001. Crank's outer skin is composed of a mesh of triangles, just like any other 3D model. However, inside him we can see the rigid bones and joints that make his skin move.

### 11.1.5. Animation Methods as Data Compression Techniques

The most flexible animation system conceivable would give the animator control over literally every infinitesimal point on an object's surface. Of course, animating like this would result in an animation that contains a potentially infinite amount of data! Animating the vertices of a triangle mesh is a simplification of this ideal—in effect, we are *compressing* the amount of information needed to describe an animation by restricting ourselves to moving only the vertices. (Animating a set of control points is the analog of vertex animation for models constructed out of higher-order patches.) Morph targets can be thought of as an additional level of compression, achieved by imposing additional constraints on the system—vertices are constrained to move only along linear paths between a fixed number of predefined vertex positions. Skeletal animation is just another way to compress vertex animation data by imposing constraints. In this case, the motions of a relatively large number of vertices are constrained to follow the motions of a relatively small number of skeletal joints.

When considering the trade-offs between various animation techniques, it can be helpful to think of them as compression methods, analogous in many respects to video compression techniques. We should generally aim to select the animation method that provides the best compression without producing unacceptable visual artifacts. Skeletal animation provides the best compression when the motion of a single joint is magnified into the motions of many vertices. A character's limbs act like rigid bodies for the most part, so they can be moved very efficiently with a skeleton. However, the motion of a face tends to be much more complex, with the motions of individual vertices being more independent. To convincingly animate a face using the skeletal approach, the required number of joints approaches the number of vertices in the mesh, thus diminishing its effectiveness as a compression technique. This is one reason why morph target techniques are often favored over the skeletal approach for facial animation. (Another common reason is that morph targets tend to be a more natural way for animators to work.)

## 11.2. Skeletons

A skeleton is comprised of a *hierarchy* of rigid pieces known as *joints*. In the game industry, we often use the terms "joint" and "bone" interchangeably,

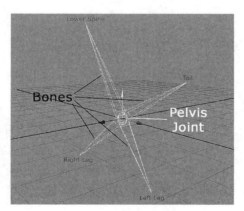

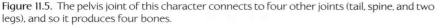

Figure 11.5. The pelvis joint of this character connects to four other joints (tail, spine, and two legs), and so it produces four bones.

but the term *bone* is actually a misnomer. Technically speaking, the joints are the objects that are directly manipulated by the animator, while the bones are simply the empty spaces between the joints. As an example, consider the pelvis joint in the Crank the Weasel character model. It is a single joint, but because it connects to four other joints (the tail, the spine, and the left and right hip joints), this one joint appears to have four bones sticking out of it. This is shown in more detail in Figure 11.5. Game engines don't care a whip about bones—only the joints matter. So whenever you hear the term "bone" being used in the industry, remember that 99% of the time we are actually speaking about joints.

## 11.2.1. The Skeleal Hierarchy

As we've mentioned, the joints in a skeleton form a hierarchy or tree structure. One joint is selected as the root, and all other joints are its children, grandchildren, and so on. A typical joint hierarchy for skinned animation looks almost identical to a typical rigid hierarchy. For example, a humanoid character's joint hierarchy might look something like this:

```
Pelvis
   LowerSpine
      MiddleSpine
         UpperSpine
            RightShoulder
               RightElbow
                  RightHand
                     RightThumb
```

```
                                        RightIndexFinger
                                        RightMiddleFinger
                                        RightRingFinger
                                        RightPinkyFinger
                           LeftShoulder
                              LeftElbow
                                 LeftHand
                                    LeftThumb
                                    LeftIndexFinger
                                    LeftMiddleFinger
                                    LeftRingFinger
                                    LeftPinkyFinger
                        Neck
                           Head
                              LeftEye
                              RightEye
                              various face joints
           RightThigh
              RightKnee
                 RightAnkle
           LeftThigh
              LeftKnee
                 LeftAnkle
```

We usually assign each joint an index from 0 to $N-1$. Because each joint has one and only one parent, the hierarchical structure of a skeleton can be fully described by storing the index of its parent with each joint. The root joint has no parent, so its parent index usually contains an invalid index such as −1.

## 11.2.2.  Representing a Skeleton in Memory

A skeleton is usually represented by a small top-level data structure that contains an array of data structures for the individual joints. The joints are usually listed in an order that ensures a child joint will always appear after its parent in the array. This implies that joint zero is always the root of the skeleton.

*Joint indices* are usually used to refer to joints within animation data structures. For example, a child joint typically refers to its parent joint by specifying its index. Likewise, in a skinned triangle mesh, a vertex refers to the joint or joints to which it is bound by index. This is much more efficient than referring to joints by name, both in terms of the amount of storage required (a joint index can usually be 8 bits wide) and in terms of the amount of time it takes to look up a referenced joint (we can use the joint index to jump immediately to a desired joint in the array).

Each joint data structure typically contains the following information:

- The *name* of the joint, either as a string or a hashed 32-bit string id.

- The *index* of the joint's *parent* within the skeleton.

- The *inverse bind pose transform* of the joint. The bind pose of a joint is the position, orientation, and scale of that joint at the time it was bound to the vertices of the skin mesh. We usually store the *inverse* of this transformation for reasons we'll explore in more depth below.

A typical skeleton data structure might look something like this:

```
struct Joint
{
    Matrix4x3   m_invBindPose;  // inverse bind pose
                                // transform

    const char* m_name;         // human-readable joint
                                // name

    U8          m_iParent;      // parent index or 0xFF
                                // if root
};

struct Skeleton
{
    U32         m_jointCount;   // number of joints
    Joint*      m_aJoint;       // array of joints
};
```

## 11.3. Poses

No matter what technique is used to produce an animation, be it cel-based, rigid hierarchical, or skinned/skeletal, every animation takes place over time. A character is imbued with the illusion of motion by arranging the character's body into a sequence of discrete, still *poses* and then displaying those poses in rapid succession, usually at a rate of 30 or 60 *poses per second*. (Actually, as we'll see in Section 11.4.1.1, we often *interpolate* between adjacent poses rather than displaying a single pose verbatim.) In skeletal animation, the pose of the skeleton directly controls the vertices of the mesh, and posing is the animator's primary tool for breathing life into her characters. So clearly, before we can animate a skeleton, we must first understand how to *pose* it.

A skeleton is posed by rotating, translating, and possibly scaling its joints in arbitrary ways. The *pose* of a joint is defined as the joint's position, orientation, and scale, relative to some frame of reference. A joint pose is usually represented by a 4 × 4 or 4 × 3 matrix, or by an SQT data structure (scale, quaternion rotation and vector translation). The pose of a skeleton is just the set of all of its joints' poses and is normally represented as a simple array of matrices or SQTs.

## 11.3.1.   Bind Pose

Two different poses of the same skeleton are shown in Figure 11.6. The pose on the left is a special pose known as the *bind pose*, also sometimes called the *reference pose* or the *rest pose*. This is the pose of the 3D mesh prior to being bound to the skeleton (hence the name). In other words, it is the pose that the mesh would assume if it were rendered as a regular, unskinned triangle mesh, without any skeleton at all. The bind pose is also called the *T-pose* because the character is usually standing with his feet slightly apart and his arms outstretched in the shape of the letter T. This particular stance is chosen because it keeps the limbs away from the body and each other, making the process of binding the vertices to the joints easier.

**Figure 11.6.** Two different poses of the same skeleton. The pose on the left is the special pose known as *bind pose*.

## 11.3.2.   Local Poses

A joint's pose is most often specified relative to its *parent* joint. A parent-relative pose allows a joint to move naturally. For example, if we rotate the shoulder joint, but leave the parent-relative poses of the elbow, wrist and fingers unchanged, the entire arm will rotate about the shoulder in a rigid manner, as we'd expect. We sometimes use the term *local pose* to describe a parent-relative pose. Local poses are almost always stored in SQT format, for reasons we'll explore when we discuss animation blending.

Graphically, many 3D authoring packages like Maya represent joints as small spheres. However, a joint has a rotation and a scale, not just a translation, so this visualization can be a bit misleading. In fact, a joint actually defines a coordinate space, no different in principle from the other spaces we've encountered (like model space, world space, or view space). So it is best to picture a joint as a set of Cartesian coordinate axes. Maya gives the user the option of displaying a joint's local coordinate axes—this is shown in Figure 11.7.

Mathematically, a joint pose is nothing more than an *affine transformation*. The pose of joint $j$ can be written as the $4 \times 4$ affine transformation matrix $\mathbf{P}_j$, which is comprised of a translation vector $\mathbf{T}_j$, a $3 \times 3$ diagonal scale matrix $\mathbf{S}_j$ and a $3 \times 3$ rotation matrix $\mathbf{R}_j$. The pose of an entire skeleton $\mathbf{P}^{\text{skel}}$ can be written as the set of all poses $\mathbf{P}_j$, where $j$ ranges from 0 to $N - 1$:

$$\mathbf{P}_j = \begin{bmatrix} \mathbf{S}_j \mathbf{R}_j & \mathbf{0} \\ \mathbf{T}_j & 1 \end{bmatrix},$$

$$\mathbf{P}^{\text{skel}} = \left\{ \mathbf{P}_j \right\} \Big|_{j=0}^{N-1}.$$

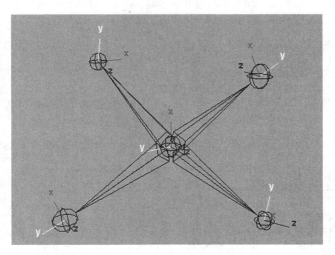

**Figure 11.7.** Every joint in a skeletal hierarchy defines a set of local coordinate space axes, known as joint space.

### 11.3.2.1.  Joint Scale

Some game engines assume that joints will never be scaled, in which case $\mathbf{S}_j$ is simply omitted and assumed to be the identity matrix. Other engines make the assumption that scale will be *uniform* if present, meaning it is the same in all three dimensions. In this case, scale can be represented using a single scalar value $s_j$. Some engines even permit *nonuniform* scale, in which case scale can be compactly represented by the three-element vector $\mathbf{s}_j = [\, s_{jx} \; s_{jy} \; s_{jz} \,]$. The elements of the vector $\mathbf{s}_j$ correspond to the three diagonal elements of the $3 \times 3$ scaling matrix $\mathbf{S}_j$, so it is not really a vector *per se*. Game engines almost never permit shear, so $\mathbf{S}_j$ is almost never represented by a full $3 \times 3$ scale/shear matrix, although it certainly *could* be.

There are a number of benefits to omitting or constraining scale in a pose or animation. Clearly using a lower-dimensional scale representation can save memory. (Uniform scale requires a single floating-point scalar per joint per animation frame, while nonuniform scale requires three floats, and a full $3 \times 3$ scale-shear matrix requires nine.) Restricting our engine to uniform scale has the added benefit of ensuring that the bounding sphere of a joint will never be transformed into an ellipsoid, as it could be when scaled in a nonuniform manner. This greatly simplifies the mathematics of frustum and collision tests in engines that perform such tests on a per-joint basis.

### 11.3.2.2.  Representing a Joint Pose in Memory

As we mentioned above, joint poses are usually stored in SQT format. In C++ such a data structure might look like this, where Q is first to ensure proper alignment and optimal structure packing. (Can you see why?)

```
struct JointPose
{
    Quaternion    m_rot;      // Q
    Vector3       m_trans;    // T
    F32           m_scale;    // S (uniform scale only)
};
```

If nonuniform scale is permitted, we might define a joint pose like this instead:

```
struct JointPose
{
    Quaternion    m_rot;      // Q
    Vector3       m_trans;    // T
    Vector3       m_scale;    // S
    U8            padding[8];
};
```

The local pose of an entire skeleton can be represented as follows, where it is understood that the array `m_aLocalPose` is dynamically allocated to contain just enough occurrences of `JointPose` to match the number of joints in the skeleton.

```
struct SkeletonPose
{
    Skeleton*    m_pSkeleton;   // skeleton + num joints
    JointPose*   m_aLocalPose;  // local joint poses
};
```

### II.3.2.3. The Joint Pose as a Change of Basis

It's important to remember that a *local* joint pose is specified relative to the joint's immediate parent. Any affine transformation can be thought of as transforming points and vectors from one coordinate space to another. So when the joint pose transform $\mathbf{P}_j$ is applied to a point or vector that is expressed in the coordinate system of the joint $j$, the result is that same point or vector expressed in the space of the parent joint.

As we've done in earlier chapters, we'll adopt the convention of using subscripts to denote the direction of a transformation. Since a joint pose takes points and vectors from the *child* joint's space (C) to that of its *parent* joint (P), we can write it $(\mathbf{P}_{C \to P})_j$. Alternatively, we can introduce the function $p(j)$ which returns the parent index of joint $j$, and write the local pose of joint $j$ as $\mathbf{P}_{j \to p(j)}$.

On occasion we will need to transform points and vectors in the opposite direction—from *parent space* into the space of the *child* joint. This transformation is just the inverse of the local joint pose. Mathematically, $\mathbf{P}_{p(j) \to j} = \left( \mathbf{P}_{j \to p(j)} \right)^{-1}$.

## II.3.3. Global Poses

Sometimes it is convenient to express a joint's pose in model space or world space. This is called a *global pose*. Some engines express global poses in matrix form, while others use the SQT format.

Mathematically, the model-space pose of a joint $(j \to M)$ can be found by walking the skeletal hierarchy from the joint in question all the way to the root, multiplying the local poses $(j \to p(j))$ as we go. Consider the hierarchy shown in Figure 11.8. The parent space of the root joint is defined to be model space, so $p(0) \equiv M$. The model-space pose of joint $J_2$ can therefore be written as follows:

$$\mathbf{P}_{2 \to M} = \mathbf{P}_{2 \to 1}\, \mathbf{P}_{1 \to 0}\, \mathbf{P}_{0 \to M}.$$

Likewise, the model-space pose of joint $J_5$ is just

$$\mathbf{P}_{5 \to M} = \mathbf{P}_{5 \to 4}\, \mathbf{P}_{4 \to 3}\, \mathbf{P}_{3 \to 0}\, \mathbf{P}_{0 \to M}.$$

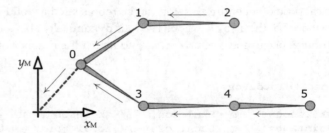

**Figure 11.8.** A global pose can be calculated by walking the hierarchy from the joint in question towards the root and model space origin, concatenating the child-to-parent (local) transforms of each joint as we go.

In general, the global pose (joint-to-model transform) of any joint $j$ can be written as follows:

$$\mathbf{P}_{j \to \mathrm{M}} = \prod_{i=j}^{0} \mathbf{P}_{i \to \mathrm{p}(\,i\,)}, \tag{11.1}$$

where it is implied that $i$ becomes $\mathrm{p}(i)$ (the parent of joint $i$) after each iteration in the product, and $\mathrm{p}(0) \equiv \mathrm{M}$ .

### 11.3.3.1.  Representing a Global Pose in Memory

We can extend our `SkeletonPose` data structure to include the global pose as follows, where again we dynamically allocate the `m_aGlobalPose` array based on the number of joints in the skeleton:

```
struct SkeletonPose
{
    Skeleton*    m_pSkeleton;    // skeleton + num joints
    JointPose*   m_aLocalPose;   // local joint poses
    Matrix44*    m_aGlobalPose;  // global joint poses
};
```

## 11.4.  Clips

In a film, every aspect of each scene is carefully planned out before any animations are created. This includes the movements of every character and prop in the scene, and even the movements of the camera. This means that an entire scene can be animated as one long, contiguous sequence of frames. And characters need not be animated at all whenever they are off-camera.

Game animation is different. A game is an interactive experience, so one cannot predict beforehand how the characters are going to move and behave. The player has full control over his or her character and usually has partial control over the camera as well. Even the decisions of the computer-driven non-player characters are strongly influenced by the unpredictable actions of the human player. As such, game animations are almost never created as long, contiguous sequences of frames. Instead, a game character's movement must be broken down into a large number of fine-grained motions. We call these individual motions *animation clips*, or sometimes just *animations*.

Each clip causes the character to perform a single well-defined action. Some clips are designed to be looped—for example, a walk cycle or run cycle. Others are designed to be played once—for example, throwing an object, or tripping and falling to the ground. Some clips affect the entire body of the character—the character jumping into the air for instance. Other clips affect only a part of the body—perhaps the character waving his right arm. The movements of any one game character are typically broken down into literally thousands of clips.

The only exception to this rule is when game characters are involved in a noninteractive portion of the game, known as an *in-game cinematic* (IGC), *noninteractive sequence* (NIS), or *full-motion video* (FMV). Noninteractive sequences are typically used to communicate story elements that do not lend themselves well to interactive gameplay, and they are created in much the same way computer-generated films are made (although they often make use of in-game assets like character meshes, skeletons, and textures). The terms IGC and NIS typically refer to noninteractive sequences that are rendered in real time by the game engine itself. The term FMV applies to sequences that have been prerendered to an MP4, WMV, or other type of movie file and are played back at runtime by the engine's full-screen movie player.

A variation on this style of animation is a semi-interactive sequence known as a *quick time event* (QTE). In a QTE, the player must hit a button at the right moment during an otherwise noninteractive sequence in order to see the success animation and proceed; otherwise a failure animation is played, and the player must try again, possibly losing a life or suffering some other consequence as a result.

## 11.4.1. The Local Time Line

We can think of every animation clip as having a local time line, usually denoted by the independent variable $t$. At the start of a clip $t = 0$ and at the end $t = T$, where $T$ is the duration of the clip. Each unique value of the variable $t$ is called a *time index*. An example of this is shown in Figure 11.9.

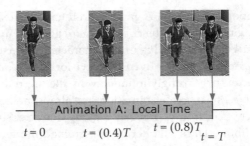

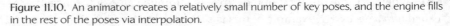

$t = 0$        $t = (0.4)T$      $t = (0.8)T$ $t = T$

**Figure 11.9.** The local time line of an animation showing poses at selected time indices.

### 11.4.1.1. Pose Interpolation and Continuous Time

It's important to realize that the rate at which frames are displayed to the viewer is not necessarily the same as the rate at which poses are created by the animator. In both film and game animation, the animator almost never poses the character every 1/30 or 1/60 of a second. Instead, the animator generates important poses known as *key poses* or *key frames* at specific times within the clip, and the computer calculates the poses in between via linear or curve-based interpolation. This is illustrated in Figure 11.10.

Because of the animation engine's ability to *interpolate* poses (which we'll explore in depth later in this chapter), we can actually sample the pose of the character at *any time* during the clip—not just on integer frame indices. In other words, an animation clip's time line is *continuous*. In computer animation, the time variable $t$ is a *real* (floating-point) number, not an *integer*.

Film animation doesn't take full advantage of the continuous nature of the animation time-line, because its frame rate is locked at exactly 24, 30, or 60 frames per second. In film, the viewer sees the characters' poses at frames

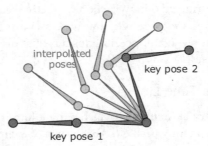

interpolated
poses

key pose 2

key pose 1

**Figure 11.10.** An animator creates a relatively small number of key poses, and the engine fills in the rest of the poses via interpolation.

1, 2, 3, and so on—there's never any need to find a character's pose on frame 3.7, for example. So in film animation, the animator doesn't pay much (if any) attention to how the character looks in between the integral frame indices.

In contrast, a real-time game's frame rate always varies a little, depending on how much load is currently being placed on the CPU and GPU. Also, game animations are sometimes *time-scaled* in order to make the character appear to move faster or slower than originally animated. So in a real-time game, an animation clip is almost *never* sampled on integer frame numbers. In theory, with a time scale of 1.0, a clip should be sampled at frames 1, 2, 3, and so on. But in practice, the player might actually see frames 1.1, 1.9, 3.2, and so on. And if the time scale is 0.5, then the player might actually see frames 1.1, 1.4, 1.9, 2.6, 3.2, and so on. A negative time scale can even be used to play an animation in reverse. So in game animation, time is both *continuous* and *scalable*.

### II.4.1.2.   Time Units

Because an animation's time line is continuous, time is best measured in units of seconds. Time can also be measured in units of *frames*, presuming we define the duration of a frame beforehand. Typical frame durations are 1/30 or 1/60 of a second for game animation. However, it's important not to make the mistake of defining your time variable $t$ as an integer that counts whole frames. No matter which time units are selected, $t$ should be a real (floating-point) quantity, a fixed-point number, or an integer that measures subframe time intervals. The goal is to have sufficient resolution in your time measurements for doing things like "tweening" between frames or scaling an animation's play-back speed.

### II.4.1.3.   Frame versus Sample

Unfortunately, the term *frame* has more than one common meaning in the game industry. This can lead to a great deal of confusion. Sometimes a frame is taken to be a *period of time* that is 1/30 or 1/60 of a second in duration. But in other contexts, the term frame is applied to a *single point in time* (e.g., we might speak of the pose of the character "at frame 42").

I personally prefer to use the term *sample* to refer to a single point in time, and I reserve the word *frame* to describe a time period that is 1/30 or 1/60 of a second in duration. So for example, a one-second animation created at a rate of 30 frames per second would consist of 31 *samples* and would be 30 *frames* in duration, as shown in Figure 11.11. The term "sample" comes from the field of signal processing. A continuous-time signal (i.e., a function $f(t)$) can be converted into a set of discrete data points by sampling that signal at uniformly-spaced time intervals. See http://en.wikipedia.org/wiki/Sampling_%28signal_processing%29 for more information on sampling.

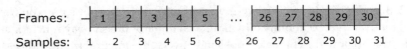

**Figure 11.11.** A one-second animation sampled at 30 frames per second is 30 frames in duration and consists of 31 samples.

### 11.4.1.4. Frames, Samples and Looping Clips

When a clip is designed to be played over and over repeatedly, we say it is a *looped* animation. If we imagine two copies of a 1-second (30-frame/31-sample) clip laid back-to-front, then sample 31 of the first clip will coincide exactly in time with sample 1 of the second clip, as shown in Figure 11.12. For a clip to loop properly, then, we can see that the pose of the character at the end of the clip must exactly match the pose at the beginning. This, in turn, implies that the last sample of a looping clip (in our example, sample 31) is redundant. Many game engines therefore omit the last sample of a looping clip.

This leads us to the following rules governing the number of samples and frames in any animation clip:

- If a clip is *non-looping*, an $N$-frame animation will have $N + 1$ unique samples.
- If a clip is *looping*, then the last sample is redundant, so an $N$-frame animation will have $N$ unique samples.

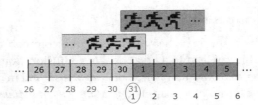

**Figure 11.12.** The last sample of a looping clip coincides in time with its first sample and is, therefore, redundant.

### 11.4.1.5. Normalized Time (Phase)

It is sometimes convenient to employ a normalized time unit $u$, such that $u = 0$ at the start of the animation, and $u = 1$ at the end, no matter what its duration $T$ may be. We sometimes refer to normalized time as the *phase* of the animation clip, because $u$ acts like the phase of a sine wave when the animation is looped. This is illustrated in Figure 11.13.

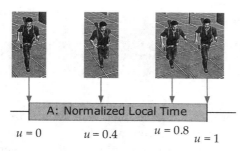

$$u = 0 \qquad u = 0.4 \qquad u = 0.8 \qquad u = 1$$

**Figure 11.13.** An animation clip, showing normalized time units.

Normalized time is useful when synchronizing two or more animation clips that are not necessarily of the same absolute duration. For example, we might want to smoothly cross-fade from a 2-second (60-frame) run cycle into a 3-second (90-frame) walk cycle. To make the cross-fade look good, we want to ensure that the two animations remain synchronized at all times, so that the feet line up properly in both clips. We can accomplish this by simply setting the normalized start time of the walk clip, $u_{walk}$ to match the normalized time index of the run clip, $u_{run}$. We then advance both clips at the same normalized rate, so that they remain in sync. This is quite a bit easier and less error-prone than doing the synchronization using the absolute time indices $t_{walk}$ and $t_{run}$.

## 11.4.2. The Global Time Line

Just as every animation clip has a local time line (whose clock starts at 0 at the beginning of the clip), every character in a game has a global time line (whose clock starts when the character is first spawned into the game world, or perhaps at the start of the level or the entire game). In this book, we'll use the time variable $\tau$ to measure global time, so as not to confuse it with the local time variable $t$.

We can think of *playing* an animation as simply *mapping* that clip's local time line onto the character's global time line. For example, Figure 11.14 illustrates playing animation clip A starting at a global time of $\tau_{start} = 102$ seconds.

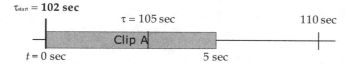

**Figure 11.14.** Playing animation clip A starting at a global time of 102 seconds.

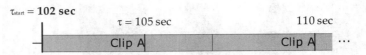

**Figure 11.15.** Playing a looping animation corresponds to laying down multiple back-to-back copies of the clip.

As we saw above, playing a looping animation is like laying down an infinite number of back-to-front copies of the clip onto the global time line. We can also imagine looping an animation a finite number of times, which corresponds to laying down a finite number of copies of the clip. This is illustrated in Figure 11.15.

*Time-scaling* a clip makes it appear to play back more quickly or more slowly than originally animated. To accomplish this, we simply scale the image of the clip when it is laid down onto the global time line. Time-scaling is most naturally expressed as a *playback rate*, which we'll denote $R$. For example, if an animation is to play back at twice the speed ($R = 2$), then we would scale the clip's local time line to one-half ($1/R = 0.5$) of its normal length when mapping it onto the global time line. This is shown in Figure 11.16.

Playing a clip in reverse corresponds to using a time scale of $-1$, as shown in Figure 11.17.

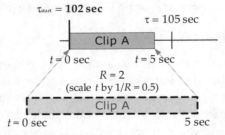

**Figure 11.16.** Playing an animation at twice the speed corresponds to scaling its local time line by a factor of ½.

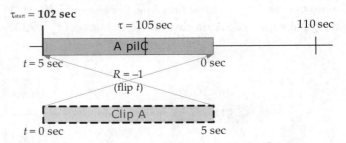

**Figure 11.17.** Playing a clip in reverse corresponds to a time scale of –1.

In order to map an animation clip onto a global time line, we need the following pieces of information about the clip:

- its global start time $\tau_{\text{start}}$,
- its playback rate $R$,
- its duration $T$,
- and the number of times it should loop, which we'll denote $N$.

Given this information, we can map from any global time $\tau$ to the corresponding local time $t$, and vice-versa, using the following two relations:

$$t = R \, (\tau - \tau_{\text{start}}), \qquad\qquad (11.2)$$

$$\tau = \tau_{\text{start}} + \frac{1}{R} t.$$

If the animation doesn't loop ($N = 1$), then we should clamp $t$ into the valid range $[0, T]$ before using it to sample a pose from the clip:

$$t = \text{clamp}\big[R \, (\tau - \tau_{\text{start}})\big] \Big|_0^T.$$

If the animation loops forever ($N = \infty$), then we bring $t$ into the valid range by taking the *remainder* of the result after dividing by the duration $T$. This is accomplished via the *modulo* operator (mod, or % in C/C++), as shown below:

$$t = \big(R \, (\tau - \tau_{\text{start}})\big) \ \text{mod} \ T.$$

If the clip loops a *finite* number of times ($1 < N < \infty$), we must first clamp $t$ into the range $[0, NT]$ and then modulo *that* result by $T$ in order to bring $t$ into a valid range for sampling the clip:

$$t = \big(\text{clamp}\big[R \, (\tau - \tau_{\text{start}})\big] \Big|_0^{NT}\big) \ \text{mod} \ T.$$

Most game engines work directly with local animation time lines and don't use the global time line directly. However, working directly in terms of global times can have some incredibly useful benefits. For one thing, it makes synchronizing animations trivial.

### 11.4.3. Comparison of Local and Global Clocks

The animation system must keep track of the time indices of every animation that is currently playing. To do so, we have two choices:

- *Local clocks.* In this approach, each clip has its own local clock, usually represented by a floating-point time index stored in units of seconds or frames, or in normalized time units (in which case it is often called the *phase* of the animation). At the moment the clip begins to play, the local time index $t$ is usually taken to be zero. To advance the animations forward in time, we advance the local clocks of each clip individually. If a clip has a non-unit playback rate $R$, the amount by which its local clock advances must be scaled by $R$.

- *Global clock.* In this approach, the character has a global clock, usually measured in seconds, and each clip simply records the global time at which it started playing, $\tau_{start}$. The clips' local clocks are *calculated* from this information using Equation (11.2), rather than being stored explicitly.

The local clock approach has the benefit of being simple, and it is the most obvious choice when designing an animation system. However, the global clock approach has some distinct advantages, especially when it comes to synchronizing animations, either within the context of a single character or across multiple characters in a scene.

### 11.4.3.1. Synchronizing Animations with a Local Clock

With a local clock approach, we said that the origin of a clip's local time line ($t = 0$) is usually defined to coincide with the moment at which the clip starts playing. Thus, to synchronize two or more clips, they must be played at exactly the same moment in game time. This seems simple enough, but it can become quite tricky when the commands used to play the animations are coming from disparate engine subsystems.

For example, let's say we want to synchronize the player character's punch animation with a non-player character's corresponding hit reaction animation. The problem is that the player's punch is initiated by the player subsystem in response to detecting that a button was hit on the joy pad. Meanwhile, the NPC's hit reaction animation is played by the artificial intelligence (AI) subsystem. If the AI code runs *before* the player code in the game loop, there will be a one-frame delay between the start of the player's punch and the start of the NPC's reaction. And if the player code runs before the AI code, then the opposite problem occurs when an NPC tries to punch the player. If a message-passing (event) system is used to communicate between the two subsystems, additional delays might be incurred (see Section 14.7 for more details). This problem is illustrated in Figure 11.18.

```
void GameLoop()
{
    while (!quit)
    {
        // preliminary updates...

        UpdateAllNpcs(); // react to punch event
                         // from last frame
```

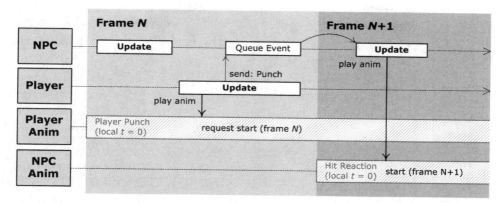

**Figure 11.18.** The order of execution of disparate gameplay systems can introduce animation synchronization problems when local clocks are used.

```
        // more updates...

        UpdatePlayer(); // punch button hit - start punch
                        // anim, and send event to NPC to
                        // react

        // still more updates...
    }
}
```

### 11.4.3.2. Synchronizing Animations with a Global Clock

A global clock approach helps to alleviate many of these synchronization problems, because the origin of the time line ($\tau = 0$) is common across all clips by definition. If two or more animations' global start times are numerically equal, the clips will start in perfect synchronization. If their play back rates are also equal, then they will remain in sync with no drift. It no longer matters *when* the code that plays each animation executes. Even if the AI code that plays the hit reaction ends up running a frame later than the player's punch code, it is still trivial to keep the two clips in sync by simply noting the global start time of the punch and setting the global start time of the reaction animation to match it. This is shown in Figure 11.19.

Of course, we do need to ensure that the two character's global clocks match, but this is trivial to do. We can either adjust the global start times to take account of any differences in the characters' clocks, or we can simply have all characters in the game share a single master clock.

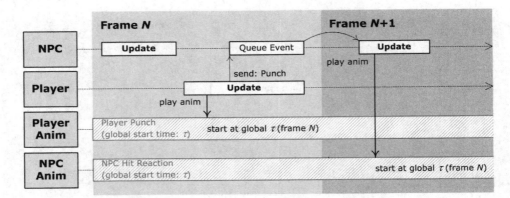

Figure 11.19. A global clock approach can alleviate animation synchronization problems.

### 11.4.4. A Simple Animation Data Format

Typically, animation data is extracted from a Maya scene file by sampling the pose of the skeleton discretely at a rate of 30 or 60 samples per second. A sample comprises a full pose for each joint in the skeleton. The poses are usually stored in SQT format: For each joint $j$, the scale component is either a single floating-point scalar $S_j$, or a three-element vector $\mathbf{S}_j = [\, S_{jx} \; S_{jy} \; S_{jz} \,]$. The rotational component is of course a four-element quaternion $Q_j = [\, Q_{jx} \; Q_{jy} \; Q_{jz} \; Q_{jw} \,]$. And the translational component is a three-element vector $\mathbf{T}_j = [\, T_{jx} \; T_{jy} \; T_{jz} \,]$. We sometimes say that an animation consists of up to 10 *channels* per joint, in reference to the 10 components of $\mathbf{S}_j$, $Q_j$, and $\mathbf{T}_j$. This is illustrated in Figure 11.20.

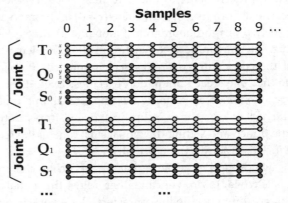

Figure 11.20. An uncompressed animation clip contains 10 channels of floating-point data per sample, per joint.

In C++, an animation clip can be represented in many different ways. Here is one possibility:

```
struct JointPose { ... };  // SQT, defined as above

struct AnimationSample
{
    JointPose*        m_aJointPose; // array of joint
                                    // poses
};

struct AnimationClip
{
    Skeleton*         m_pSkeleton;
    F32               m_framesPerSecond;
    U32               m_frameCount;

    AnimationSample* m_aSamples; // array of samples

    bool              m_isLooping;
};
```

An animation clip is authored for a specific skeleton and generally won't work on any other skeleton. As such, our example AnimationClip data structure contains a reference to its skeleton, m_pSkeleton. (In a real engine, this might be a unique skeleton id rather than a Skeleton* pointer. In this case, the engine would presumably provide a way to quickly and conveniently look up a skeleton by its unique id.)

The number of JointPoses in the m_aJointPose array within each sample is presumed to match the number of joints in the skeleton. The number of samples in the m_aSamples array is dictated by the frame count and by whether or not the clip is intended to loop. For a non-looping animation, the number of samples is (m_frameCount + 1). However, if the animation loops, then the last sample is identical to the first sample and is usually omitted. In this case, the sample count is equal to m_frameCount.

It's important to realize that in a real game engine, animation data isn't actually stored in this simplistic format. As we'll see in Section 11.8, the data is usually *compressed* in various ways to save memory.

### 11.4.4.1. Animation Retargeting

We said above that an animation is typically only compatible with a single skeleton. An exception to this rule can be made for skeletons that are closely related. For example, if a group of skeletons are identical except for a number of optional leaf joints that do not affect the fundamental hierarchy, then an animation authored for one of these skeletons should work on any of them. The only requirement is that the engine be capable of ignoring animation channels for joints that cannot be found in the skeleton being animated.

Other more-advanced techniques exist for retargeting animations authored for one skeleton so that they work on a different skeleton. This is an active area of research, and a full discussion of the topic is beyond the scope of this book. For more information, see for example http://portal.acm.org/citation.cfm?id=1450621 and http://chrishecker.com/Real-time_Motion_Retargeting_to_Highly_Varied_User-Created_Morphologies.

## 11.4.5.  Continuous Channel Functions

The samples of an animation clip are really just definitions of continuous functions over time. You can think of these as 10 scalar-valued functions of time per joint, or as two vector-valued functions and one quaternion-valued function per joint. Theoretically, these *channel functions* are smooth and continuous across the entire clip's local time line, as shown in Figure 11.21 (with the exception of explicitly authored discontinuities like camera cuts). In practice, however, many game engines interpolate *linearly* between the samples, in which case the functions actually used are *piece-wise linear approximations* to the underlying continuous functions. This is depicted in Figure 11.22.

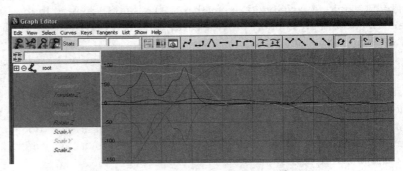

Figure 11.21. The animation samples in a clip define continuous functions over time.

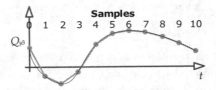

Figure 11.22. Many game engines use a piece-wise linear approximation when interpolating channel functions.

## 11.4.6. Metachannels

Many games permit additional "metachannels" of data to be defined for an animation. These channels can encode game-specific information that doesn't have to do directly with posing the skeleton but which needs to be synchronized with the animation.

It is quite common to define a special channel that contains *event triggers* at various time indices, as shown in Figure 11.23. Whenever the animation's local time index passes one of these triggers, an *event* is sent to the game engine, which can respond as it sees fit. (We'll discuss events in detail in Chapter 14.) One common use of event triggers is to denote at which points during the animation certain sound or particle effects should be played. For example, when the left or right foot touches the ground, a footstep sound and a "cloud of dust" particle effect could be initiated.

Another common practice is to permit special joints, known in Maya as *locators*, to be animated along with the joints of the skeleton itself. Because a joint or locator is just an affine transform, these special joints can be used to encode the position and orientation of virtually any object in the game.

A typical application of animated locators is to specify how the game's camera should be positioned and oriented during an animation. In Maya, a locator is constrained to a camera, and the camera is then animated along with the joints of the character(s) in the scene. The camera's locator is exported and used in-game to move the game's camera around during the animation. The

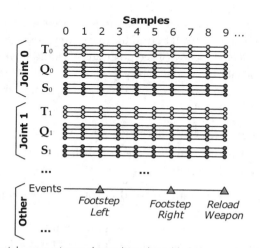

**Figure 11.23.** A special event trigger channel can be added to an animation clip in order to synchronize sound effects, particle effects, and other game events with an animation.

field of view (focal length) of the camera, and possibly other camera attributes, can also be animated by placing the relevant data into one or more additional *floating-point channels*.

Other examples of non-joint animation channels include:

- texture coordinate scrolling,

- texture animation (a special case of texture coordinate scrolling in which frames are arranged linearly within a texture, and the texture is scrolled by one complete frame at each iteration),

- animated material parameters (color, specularity, transparency, etc.),

- animated lighting parameters (radius, cone angle, intensity, color, etc.),

- any other parameters that need to change over time and are in some way synchronized with an animation.

## 11.5.   Skinning and Matrix Palette Generation

We've seen how to pose a skeleton by rotating, translating, and possibly scaling its joints. And we know that any skeletal pose can be represented mathematically as a set of local ( $\mathbf{P}_{j \to p(j)}$ ) or global ( $\mathbf{P}_{j \to M}$ ) joint pose transformations, one for each joint $j$. Next, we will explore the process of attaching the vertices of a 3D mesh to a posed skeleton. This process is known as *skinning*.

### 11.5.1.   Per-Vertex Skinning Information

A skinned mesh is attached to a skeleton by means of its vertices. Each vertex can be *bound* to one or more joints. If bound to a single joint, the vertex tracks that joint's movement exactly. If bound to two or more joints, the vertex's position becomes a *weighted average* of the positions it would have assumed had it been bound to each joint independently.

To skin a mesh to a skeleton, a 3D artist must supply the following additional information at each vertex:

- the *index* or *indices* of the joint(s) to which it is bound,

- for each joint, a *weighting factor* describing how much influence that joint should have on the final vertex position.

The weighting factors are assumed to add to one, as is customary when calculating any weighted average.

Usually a game engine imposes an upper limit on the number of joints to which a single vertex can be bound. A four-joint limit is typical for a number of reasons. First, four 8-bit joint indices can be packed into a 32-bit word, which is convenient. Also, while it's pretty easy to see a difference in quality between a two-, three-, and even a four-joint-per-vertex model, most people cannot see a quality difference as the number of joints per vertex is increased beyond four.

Because the joint weights must sum to one, the last weight can be omitted and often is. (It can be calculated at runtime as $w_3 = 1 - (w_0 + w_1 + w_2)$ .) As such, a typical skinned vertex data structure might look as follows:

```
struct SkinnedVertex
{
    float m_position[3];      // (Px, Py, Pz)

    float m_normal[3];        // (Nx, Ny, Nz)

    float m_u, m_v;           // texture coordinates
                              // (u, v)

    U8     m_jointIndex[4];   // joint indices
    float m_jointWeight[3];   // joint weights, last one
                              // omitted
};
```

## 11.5.2. The Mathematics of Skinning

The vertices of a skinned mesh track the movements of the joint(s) to which they are bound. To make this happen mathematically, we would like to find a matrix that can transform the vertices of the mesh from their original positions (in bind pose) into new positions that correspond to the current pose of the skeleton. We shall call such a matrix a *skinning matrix*.

Like all mesh vertices, the position of a skinned vertex is specified in model space. This is true whether its skeleton is in bind pose, or in any other pose. So the matrix we seek will transform vertices from model space (bind pose) to model space (current pose). Unlike the other transforms we've seen thus far, such as the model-to-world transform or the world-to-view transform, a skinning matrix is *not* a change of basis transform. It morphs vertices into new positions, but the vertices are in model space both before and after the transformation.

### 11.5.2.1. Simple Example: One-Jointed Skeleton

Let us derive the basic equation for a skinning matrix. To keep things simple at first, we'll work with a skeleton consisting of a single joint. We therefore have two coordinate spaces to work with: model space, which we'll denote with the subscript M, and the joint space of our one and only joint, which will be indicated by the subscript J. The joint's coordinate axes start out in bind pose,

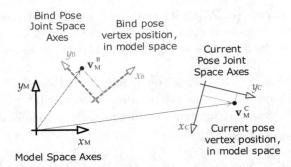

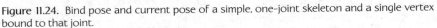

**Figure 11.24.** Bind pose and current pose of a simple, one-joint skeleton and a single vertex bound to that joint.

which we'll denote with the superscript B. At any given moment during an animation, the joint's axes move to a new position and orientation in model space—we'll indicate this *current pose* with the superscript C.

Now consider a single vertex that is skinned to our joint. In bind pose, its model-space position is $\mathbf{v}_M^B$. The skinning process calculates the vertex's new model-space position in the current pose, $\mathbf{v}_M^C$. This is illustrated in Figure 11.24.

The "trick" to finding the skinning matrix for a given joint is to realize that the position of a vertex bound to a joint is *constant* when expressed in *that joint's coordinate space*. So we take the bind-pose position of the vertex in model space, convert it into joint space, move the joint into its current pose, and finally convert the vertex back into model space. The net effect of this round trip from model space to joint space and back again is to "morph" the vertex from bind pose into the current pose.

Referring to the illustration in Figure 11.25, let's assume that the coordinates of the vertex $\mathbf{v}_M^B$ are (4, 6) in model space (when the skeleton is in bind pose). We convert this vertex into its equivalent joint space coordinates $\mathbf{v}_j$, which are roughly (1, 3) as shown in the diagram. Because the vertex is bound to the joint, its joint space coordinates will *always* be (1, 3) no matter how the joint may move. Once we have the joint in the desired current pose, we convert the vertex's coordinates back into model space, which we'll denote with the symbol $\mathbf{v}_M^C$. In our diagram, these coordinates are roughly (18, 2). So the skinning transformation has morphed our vertex from (4, 6) to (18, 2) in model space, due entirely to the motion of the joint from its bind pose to the current pose shown in the diagram.

Looking at the problem mathematically, we can denote the *bind pose* of the joint $j$ in model space by the matrix $\mathbf{B}_{j \to M}$. This matrix transforms a point or

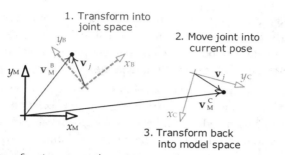

**Figure II.25.** By transforming a vertex's position into joint space, it can be made to "track" the joint's movements.

vector whose coordinates are expressed in joint $j$'s space into an equivalent set of model space coordinates. Now, consider a vertex $\mathbf{v}_M^B$ whose coordinates are expressed in model space with the skeleton in bind pose. To convert these vertex coordinates into the space of joint $j$, we simply multiply it by the *inverse* bind pose matrix, $\mathbf{B}_{M \to j} = (\mathbf{B}_{j \to M})^{-1}$:

$$\mathbf{v}_j = \mathbf{v}_M^B \, \mathbf{B}_{M \to j} = \mathbf{v}_M^B \, (\mathbf{B}_{j \to M})^{-1}. \tag{11.3}$$

Likewise, we can denote the joint's *current pose* (i.e., any pose that is *not* bind pose) by the matrix $\mathbf{C}_{j \to M}$. To convert $\mathbf{v}_j$ from joint space back into model space, we simply multiply it by the current pose matrix as follows:

$$\mathbf{v}_M^C = \mathbf{v}_j \, \mathbf{C}_{j \to M}.$$

If we expand $\mathbf{v}_j$ using Equation (11.3), we obtain an equation that takes our vertex directly from its position in bind pose to its position in the current pose:

$$
\begin{aligned}
\mathbf{v}_M^C &= \mathbf{v}_j \, \mathbf{C}_{j \to M} \\
&= \mathbf{v}_M^B \, (\mathbf{B}_{j \to M})^{-1} \, \mathbf{C}_{j \to M} \\
&= \mathbf{v}_M^B \, \mathbf{K}_j.
\end{aligned}
\tag{11.4}
$$

The combined matrix $\mathbf{K}_j = (\mathbf{B}_{j \to M})^{-1} \mathbf{C}_{j \to M}$ is known as a *skinning matrix*.

### II.5.2.2. Extension to Multijointed Skeletons

In the example above, we considered only a single joint. However, the math we derived above actually applies to any joint in any skeleton imaginable, because we formulated everything in terms of global poses (i.e., joint space to model space transforms). To extend the above formulation to a skeleton containing multiple joints, we therefore need to make only two minor adjustments:

1. We must make sure that our $\mathbf{B}_{j \to M}$ and $\mathbf{C}_{j \to M}$ matrices are calculated properly for the joint in question, using Equation (11.1). $\mathbf{B}_{j \to M}$ and $\mathbf{C}_{j \to M}$ are just the bind pose and current pose equivalents, respectively, of the matrix $\mathbf{P}_{j \to M}$ given in that equation.

2. We must calculate an array of skinning matrices $\mathbf{K}_j$, one for each joint $j$. This array is known as a *matrix palette*. The matrix palette is passed to the rendering engine when rendering a skinned mesh. For each vertex, the renderer looks up the appropriate joint's skinning matrix in the palette and uses it to transform the vertex from bind pose into current pose.

We should note here that the current pose matrix $\mathbf{C}_{j \to M}$ changes every frame as the character assumes different poses over time. However, the inverse bind-pose matrix is constant throughout the entire game, because the bind pose of the skeleton is fixed when the model is created. Therefore, the matrix $(\mathbf{B}_{j \to M})^{-1}$ is generally cached with the skeleton, and needn't be calculated at runtime. Animation engines generally calculate local poses for each joint ($\mathbf{C}_{j \to p(j)}$), then use Equation (11.1) to convert these into global poses ($\mathbf{C}_{j \to M}$), and finally multiply each global pose by the corresponding cached inverse bind pose matrix ($(\mathbf{B}_{j \to M})^{-1}$) in order to generate a skinning matrix ($\mathbf{K}_j$) for each joint.

### 11.5.2.3. Incorporating the Model-to-World Transform

Every vertex must eventually be transformed from model space into world space. Some engines therefore premultiply the palette of skinning matrices by the object's model-to-world transform. This can be a useful optimization, as it saves the rendering engine one matrix multiply per vertex when rendering skinned geometry. (With hundreds of thousands of vertices to process, this savings can really add up!)

To incorporate the model-to-world transform into our skinning matrices, we simply concatenate it to the regular skinning matrix equation, as follows:

$$(\mathbf{K}_j)_W = (\mathbf{B}_{j \to M})^{-1} \mathbf{C}_{j \to M} \mathbf{M}_{M \to W}.$$

Some engines bake the model-to-world transform into the skinning matrices like this, while others don't. The choice is entirely up to the engineering team and is driven by all sorts of factors. For example, one situation in which we would definitely *not* want to do this is when a single animation is being applied to multiple characters simultaneously—a technique known as *animation instancing* that is commonly used for animating large crowds of characters. In this case we need to keep the model-to-world transforms separate so that we can share a single matrix palette across all characters in the crowd.

### 11.5.2.4. Skinning a Vertex to Multiple Joints

When a vertex is skinned to more than one joint, we calculate its final position by assuming it is skinned to each joint individually, calculating a model space position for each joint and then taking a *weighted average* of the resulting positions. The weights are provided by the character rigging artist, and they must always sum to one. (If they do not sum to one, they should be re-normalized by the tools pipeline.)

The general formula for a weighted average of $N$ quantities $a_0$ through $a_{N-1}$, with weights $w_0$ through $w_{N-1}$ and with

$$\sum_{i=0}^{N-1} w_i = 1, \text{ is } \hat{a} = \sum_{i=0}^{N-1} w_i a_i.$$

This works equally well for vector quantities $\mathbf{a}_i$. So, for a vertex skinned to $N$ joints with indices $j_0$ through $j_{N-1}$ and weights $w_0$ through $w_{N-1}$, we can extend Equation (11.4) as follows:

$$\mathbf{v}_M^C = \sum_{i=0}^{N-1} w_{ij} \mathbf{v}_M^B \mathbf{K}_{j_i},$$

where $\mathbf{K}_{j_i}$ is the skinning matrix for the joint $j_i$.

## 11.6.  Animation Blending

The term *animation blending* refers to any technique that allows more than one animation clip to contribute the final pose of the character. To be more precise, blending combines two or more *input poses* to produce an *output pose* for the skeleton.

Blending usually combines two or more poses at a single point in time, and generates an output at that same moment in time. In this context, blending is used to combine two or more animations into a host of new animations, without having to create them manually. For example, by blending an injured walk animation with an uninjured walk, we can generate various intermediate levels of apparent injury for our character while he is walking. As another example, we can blend between an animation in which the character is aiming to the left and one in which he's aiming to the right, in order to make the character aim along any desired angle between the two extremes. Blending can be used to interpolate between extreme facial expressions, body stances, locomotion modes, and so on.

Blending can also be used to find an intermediate pose between two known poses at *different* points in time. This is used when we want to find the pose of a character at a point in time that does not correspond exactly to one of the sampled frames available in the animation data. We can also use temporal animation blending to smoothly transition from one animation to another, by gradually blending from the source animation to the destination over a short period of time.

### 11.6.1.  LERP Blending

Given two skeletal poses $\mathbf{P}_A^{\text{skel}} = \left\{ (\mathbf{P}_A)_j \right\} \big|_{j=0}^{N-1}$ and $\mathbf{P}_B^{\text{skel}} = \left\{ (\mathbf{P}_B)_j \right\} \big|_{j=0}^{N-1}$, we wish to find an intermediate pose $\mathbf{P}_{\text{LERP}}^{\text{skel}}$ between these two extremes. This can be done by performing a *linear interpolation* (LERP) between the local poses of each individual joint in each of the two source poses. This can be written as follows:

$$(\mathbf{P}_{\text{LERP}})_j = \text{LERP}\left[(\mathbf{P}_A)_j, (\mathbf{P}_B)_j, \beta\right]$$
$$= (1-\beta)(\mathbf{P}_A)_j + \beta(\mathbf{P}_B)_j. \tag{11.5}$$

The interpolated pose of the whole skeleton is simply the set of interpolated poses for all of the joints:

$$\mathbf{P}_{\text{LERP}}^{\text{skel}} = \left\{ (\mathbf{P}_{\text{LERP}})_j \right\} \big|_{j=0}^{N-1}. \tag{11.6}$$

In these equations, $\beta$ is called the *blend percentage* or *blend factor*. When $\beta = 0$, the final pose of the skeleton will exactly match $\mathbf{P}_A^{\text{skel}}$; when $\beta = 1$, the final pose will match $\mathbf{P}_B^{\text{skel}}$. When $\beta$ is between zero and one, the final pose is an intermediate between the two extremes. This effect is illustrated in Figure 11.10.

We've glossed over one small detail here: We are linearly interpolating *joint poses*, which means interpolating 4×4 *transformation matrices*. But, as we saw in Chapter 4, interpolating matrices directly is not practical. This is one of the reasons why local poses are usually expressed in SQT format—doing so allows us to apply the LERP operation defined in Section 4.2.5 to each component of the SQT individually. The linear interpolation of the translation component $\mathbf{T}$ of an SQT is just a straightforward vector LERP:

$$(\mathbf{T}_{\text{LERP}})_j = \text{LERP}[(\mathbf{T}_A)_j, (\mathbf{T}_B)_j, \beta]$$
$$= (1-\beta)(\mathbf{T}_A)_j + \beta(\mathbf{T}_B)_j. \tag{11.7}$$

The linear interpolation of the rotation component is a quaternion LERP or SLERP (spherical linear interpolation):

$$(q_{\text{LERP}})_j = \text{LERP}[(q_A)_j, (q_B)_j, \beta]$$
$$= (1-\beta)(q_A)_j + \beta(q_B)_j \tag{11.8a}$$

or

$$(q_{\text{LERP}})_j = \text{SLERP}[(q_A)_j, (q_B)_j, \beta]$$

$$= \frac{\sin((1-\beta)\theta)}{\sin(\theta)}(q_A)_j + \frac{\sin(\beta\theta)}{\sin(\theta)}(q_B)_j. \tag{11.8b}$$

Finally, the linear interpolation of the scale component is either a scalar or vector LERP, depending on the type of scale (uniform or nonuniform) supported by the engine:

$$(\mathbf{s}_{\text{LERP}})_j = \text{LERP}[(\mathbf{s}_A)_j, (\mathbf{s}_B)_j, \beta]$$

$$= (1-\beta)(\mathbf{s}_A)_j + \beta(\mathbf{s}_B)_j \tag{11.9a}$$

or

$$(s_{\text{LERP}})_j = \text{LERP}[(s_A)_j, (s_B)_j, \beta]$$

$$= (1-\beta)(s_A)_j + \beta(s_B)_j. \tag{11.9b}$$

When linearly interpolating between two skeletal poses, the most natural-looking intermediate pose is generally one in which each joint pose is interpolated independently of the others, in the space of that joint's immediate parent. In other words, pose blending is generally performed on *local poses*. If we were to blend global poses directly in model space, the results would tend to look biomechanically implausible.

Because pose blending is done on local poses, the linear interpolation of any one joint's pose is totally independent of the interpolations of the other joints in the skeleton. This means that linear pose interpolation can be performed entirely in parallel on multiprocessor architectures.

## 11.6.2. Applications of LERP Blending

Now that we understand the basics of LERP blending, let's have a look at some typical gaming applications.

### 11.6.2.1. Temporal Interpolation

As we mentioned in Section 11.4.1.1, game animations are almost never sampled exactly on integer frame indices. Because of variable frame rate, the player might actually see frames 0.9, 1.85, and 3.02, rather than frames 1, 2, and 3 as one might expect. In addition, some animation compression techniques involve storing only disparate key frames, spaced at uneven intervals across the clip's local time line. In either case, we need a mechanism for finding intermediate poses between the sampled poses that are actually present in the animation clip.

LERP blending is used to find these intermediate poses. As an example, let's imagine that our animation clip contains evenly-spaced pose samples at times 0, $\Delta t$, $2\Delta t$, $3\Delta t$, and so on. To find a pose at time $t = (2.18)\Delta t$, we simply find the linear interpolation between the poses at times $2\Delta t$ and $3\Delta t$, using a blend percentage of $\beta = 0.18$.

In general, we can find the pose at time $t$ given pose samples at any two times $t_1$ and $t_2$ that bracket $t$, as follows:

$$\mathbf{P}_j(t) = \text{LERP}[\mathbf{P}_j(t_1),\ \mathbf{P}_j(t_2),\ \beta(t)]$$
$$= (1 - \beta(t))\mathbf{P}_j(t_1) + \beta(t)\mathbf{P}_j(t_2), \tag{11.10}$$

where the blend factor $\beta(t)$ is the ratio

$$\beta(t) = \frac{t - t_1}{t_2 - t_1}. \tag{11.11}$$

### 11.6.2.2. Motion Continuity: Cross-Fading

Game characters are animated by piecing together a large number of fine-grained animation clips. If your animators are any good, the character will appear to move in a natural and physically plausible way *within* each individual clip. However, it is notoriously difficult to achieve the same level of quality when transitioning from one clip to the next. The vast majority of the "pops" we see in game animations occur when the character transitions from one clip to the next.

Ideally, we would like the movements of each part of a character's body to be perfectly smooth, even during transitions. In other words, the three-dimensional paths traced out by each joint in the skeleton as it moves should contain no sudden "jumps." We call this *C0 continuity*; it is illustrated in Figure 11.26.

Not only should the paths themselves be continuous, but their first derivatives (velocity curves) should be continuous as well. This is called *C1 continuity* (or continuity of velocity and momentum). The perceived quality and realism of an animated character's movement improves as we move to higher and higher order continuity. For example, we might want to achieve C2 continuity, in which the second derivatives of the motion paths (acceleration curves) are also continuous.

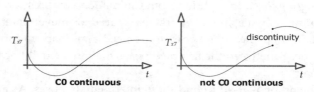

**Figure 11.26.** The channel function on the left has C0 continuity, while the path on the right does not.

Strict mathematical continuity up to C1 or higher is often infeasible to achieve. However, LERP-based animation blending can be applied to achieve a reasonably pleasing form of C0 motion continuity. It usually also does a pretty good job of approximating C1 continuity. When applied to transitions between clips in this manner, LERP blending is sometimes called *cross-fading*. LERP blending can introduce unwanted artifacts, such as the dreaded "sliding feet" problem, so it must be applied judiciously.

To cross-fade between two animations, we overlap the time lines of the two clips by some reasonable amount, and then blend the two clips together. The blend percentage $\beta$ starts at zero at time $t_{start}$, meaning that we see only clip A when the cross-fade begins. We gradually increase $\beta$ until it reaches a value of one at time $t_{end}$. At this point only clip B will be visible, and we can retire clip A altogether. The time interval over which the cross-fade occurs ($\Delta t_{blend} = t_{end} - t_{start}$) is sometimes called the *blend time*.

*Types of Cross-Fades*

There are two common ways to perform a cross-blended transition:

- *Smooth transition.* Clips A and B both play simultaneously as $\beta$ increases from zero to one. For this to work well, the two clips must be looping animations, and their time lines must be synchronized so that the positions of the legs and arms in one clip match up roughly with their positions in the other clip. (If this is not done, the cross-fade will often look totally unnatural.) This technique is illustrated in Figure 11.27.

- *Frozen transition.* The local clock of clip A is stopped at the moment clip B starts playing. Thus the pose of the skeleton from clip A is frozen while clip B gradually takes over the movement. This kind of transitional blend works well when the two clips are unrelated and cannot be

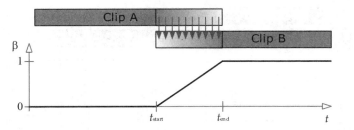

**Figure 11.27.** A smooth transition, in which the local clocks of both clips keep running during the transition.

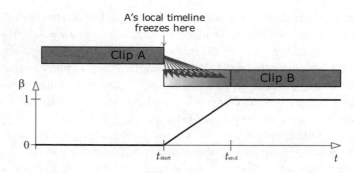

**Figure 11.28.** A frozen transition, in which clip A's local clock is stopped during the transition.

time-synchronized, as they must be when performing a *smooth* transition. This approach is depicted in Figure 11.28.

We can also control how the blend factor $\beta$ varies during the transition. In Figure 11.27 and Figure 11.28, the blend factor varied linearly with time. To achieve an even smoother transition, we could vary $\beta$ according to a cubic function of time, such as a one-dimensional Bézier. When such a curve is applied to a currently-running clip that is being blended out, it is known as an *ease-out curve*; when it is applied to a new clip that is being blended in, it is known as an *ease-in curve*. This is shown in Figure 11.29.

The equation for a Bézier ease-in/ease-out curve is given below. It returns the value of $\beta$ at any time $t$ within the blend interval. $\beta_{start}$ is the blend factor at the start of the blend interval, $t_{start}$, and $\beta_{end}$ is the final blend factor at time $t_{end}$. The parameter $u$ is the *normalized time* between $t_{start}$ and $t_{end}$, and for convenience we'll also define $v = 1 - u$ (the *inverse* normalized time). Note that the Bézier tangents $T_{start}$ and $T_{end}$ are taken to be equal to the corresponding

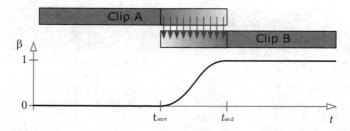

**Figure 11.29.** A smooth transition, with a cubic ease-in/ease-out curve applied to the blend factor.

blend factors $\beta_{start}$ and $\beta_{end}$, because this yields a well-behaved curve for our purposes:

$$\text{let} \quad u = \left( \frac{t - t_{start}}{t_{end} - _{start}} \right)$$

$$\text{and} \quad v = 1 - u :$$

$$\beta(t) = (v^3)\beta_{start} + (3v^2u)T_{start} + (3vu^2)T_{end} + (u^3)\beta_{end}$$

$$= (v^3 + 3v^2u)\beta_{start} + (3vu^2 + u^3)\beta_{end}.$$

### Core Poses

This is an appropriate time to mention that motion continuity can actually be achieved *without* blending if the animator ensures that the last pose in any given clip matches the first pose of the clip that follows it. In practice, animators often decide upon a set of *core poses*—for example, we might have a core pose for standing upright, one for crouching, one for lying prone, and so on. By making sure that the character starts in one of these core poses at the beginning of every clip and returns to a core pose at the end, C0 continuity can be achieved by simply ensuring that the core poses match when animations are spliced together. C1 or higher-order motion continuity can also be achieved by ensuring that the character's movement at the end of one clip smoothly transitions into the motion at the start of the next clip. This is easily achieved by authoring a single smooth animation and then breaking it into two or more clips.

### 11.6.2.3. Directional Locomotion

LERP-based animation blending is often applied to character locomotion. When a real human being walks or runs, he can change the direction in which he is moving in two basic ways: First, he can turn his entire body to change direction, in which case he always faces in the direction he's moving. I'll call

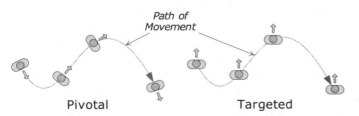

**Figure 11.30.** In pivotal movement, the character faces the direction she is moving and pivots about her vertical axis to turn. In targeted movement, the movement direction need not match the facing direction.

this *pivotal movement*, because the person pivots about his vertical axis when he turns. Second, he can keep facing in one direction, while walking forward, backward, or sideways (known as *strafing* in the gaming world) in order to move in a direction that is independent of his facing direction. I'll call this *targeted movement*, because it is often used in order to keep one's eye—or one's weapon—trained on a target while moving. These two movement styles are illustrated in Figure 11.30.

### Targeted Movement

To implement *targeted movement*, the animator authors three separate looping animation clips—one moving forward, one strafing to the left, and one strafing to the right. I'll call these *directional locomotion clips*. The three directional clips are arranged around the circumference of a semicircle, with forward at 0 degrees, left at 90 degrees and right at –90 degrees. With the character's facing direction fixed at 0 degrees, we find the desired movement direction on the semicircle, select the two adjacent movement animations, and blend them together via LERP-based blending. The blend percentage $\beta$ is determined by how close the angle of movement is to the angles of two adjacent clips. This is illustrated in Figure 11.31.

Note that we did not include backward movement in our blend, for a full circular blend. This is because blending between a sideways strafe and a backward run cannot be made to look natural in general. The problem is that when strafing to the left, the character usually crosses its right foot in front of its left so that the blend into the pure forward run animation looks correct. Likewise, the right strafe is usually authored with the left foot crossing in front of the right. When we try to blend such strafe animations directly into a backward run, one leg will start to pass through the other, which looks extremely awk-

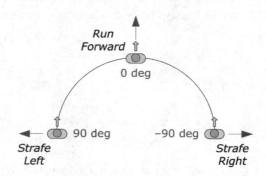

**Figure 11.31.** Targeted movement can be implemented by blending together looping locomotion clips that move in each of the four principal directions.

ward and unnatural. There are a number of ways to solve this problem. One feasible approach is to define two hemispherical blends, one for forward motion and one for backward motion, each with strafe animations that have been crafted to work properly when blended with the corresponding straight run. When passing from one hemisphere to the other, we can play some kind of explicit transition animation so that the character has a chance to adjust its gait and leg crossing appropriately.

*Pivotal Movement*

To implement *pivotal movement*, we can simply play the forward locomotion loop while rotating the entire character about its vertical axis to make it turn. Pivotal movement looks more natural if the character's body doesn't remain bolt upright when it is turning—real humans tend to lean into their turns a little bit. We could try slightly tilting the vertical axis of the character as a whole, but that would cause problems with the inner foot sinking into the ground while the outer foot comes off the ground. A more natural-looking result can be achieved by animating three variations on the basic forward walk or run—one going perfectly straight, one making an extreme left turn, and one making an extreme right turn. We can then LERP-blend between the straight clip and the extreme left turn clip to implement any desired lean angle.

## 11.6.3. Complex LERP Blends

In a real game engine, characters make use of a wide range of complex blends for various purposes. It can be convenient to "prepackage" certain commonly used types of complex blends for ease of use. In the following sections, we'll investigate a few popular types of prepackaged complex blends.

### 11.6.3.1. Generalized One-Dimensional LERP Blending

LERP blending can be easily extended to more than two animation clips, using a technique I call *one-dimensional LERP blending*. We define a new blend parameter $b$ that lies in any linear range desired (e.g., $-1$ to $+1$, or from 0 to 1, or even from 27 to 136). Any number of clips can be positioned at arbitrary points along this range, as shown in Figure 11.32. For any given value of $b$, we select the two clips immediately adjacent to it and blend them together using Equation (11.5). If the two adjacent clips lie at points $b_1$ and $b_2$, then the blend percentage $\beta$ can be determined using a technique analogous to that used in Equation (11.10), as follows:

$$\beta = \frac{b - b_1}{b_2 - b_1}.$$

$$(11.12)$$

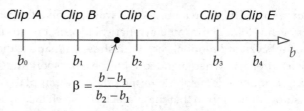

Figure 11.32. A generalized linear blend between $N$ animation clips.

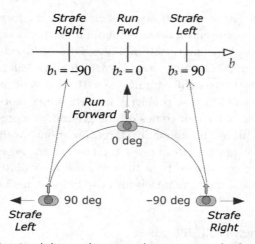

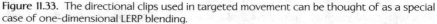

Figure 11.33. The directional clips used in targeted movement can be thought of as a special case of one-dimensional LERP blending.

Targeted movement is just a special case of one-dimensional LERP blending. We simply straighten out the circle on which the directional animation clips were placed and use the movement direction angle $\theta$ as the parameter $b$ (with a range of −90 to 90 degrees). Any number of animation clips can be placed onto this blend range at arbitrary angles. This is shown in Figure 11.33.

### 11.6.3.2. Simple Two-Dimensional LERP Blending

Sometimes we would like to smoothly vary *two* aspects of a character's motion simultaneously. For example, we might want the character to be capable of aiming his weapon vertically and horizontally. Or we might want to allow our character to vary her pace length and the separation of her feet as she moves. We can extend one-dimensional LERP blending to two dimensions in order to achieve these kinds of effects.

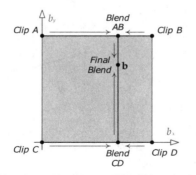

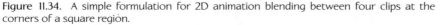

**Figure 11.34.** A simple formulation for 2D animation blending between four clips at the corners of a square region.

If we know that our 2D blend involves only four animation clips, and if those clips are positioned at the four corners of a square region, then we can find a blended pose by performing two 1D blends. Our generalized blend factor $b$ becomes a two-dimensional blend vector $\mathbf{b} = [\, b_x \;\; b_y \,]$. If $\mathbf{b}$ lies within the square region bounded by our four clips, we can find the resulting pose by following these steps:

- Using the horizontal blend factor $b_x$, find two intermediate poses, one between the top two animation clips and one between the bottom two clips. These two poses can be found by performing two simple one-dimensional LERP blends.

- Then, using the vertical blend factor $b_y$, find the final pose by LERP-blending the two intermediate poses together.

This technique is illustrated in Figure 11.34.

### 11.6.3.3. Triangular Two-Dimensional LERP Blending

The simple 2D blending technique we investigated above only works when the animation clips we wish to blend lie at the corners of a square region. How can we blend between an arbitrary number of clips positioned at arbitrary locations in our 2D blend space?

Let's imagine that we have three animation clips that we wish to blend together. Each clip, designated by the index $i$, corresponds to a particular blend coordinate $\mathbf{b}_i = [\, b_{xi} \;\; b_{yi} \,]$ in our two-dimensional blend space, and these three blend coordinates form a triangle in our two-dimensional blend space. Each clip $i$ defines a set of joint poses $\left\{ (\mathbf{P}_{ij}) \right\} \big|_{j=0}^{N-1}$, where $j$ is the joint index and $N$ is the number of joints in the skeleton. We wish to find the interpolated pose

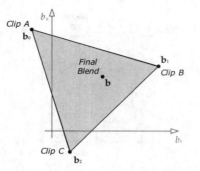

**Figure 11.35.** Two-dimensional animation blending between three animation clips.

of the skeleton corresponding to an arbitrary point **b** within the triangle, as illustrated in Figure 11.35.

But how can we calculate a LERP blend between three animation clips? Thankfully, the answer is simple: the LERP function can actually operate on any number of inputs, because it is really just a *weighted average*. As with any weighted average, the weights must add to one. In the case of a two-input LERP blend, we used the weights $\beta$ and $(1 - \beta)$, which of course add to one. For a three-input LERP, we simply use three weights, $\alpha$, $\beta$, and $\gamma = (1 - \alpha - \beta)$. Then we calculate the LERP as follows:

$$(\mathbf{P}_{\text{LERP}})_j = \alpha(\mathbf{P}_0)_j + \beta(\mathbf{P}_1)_j + (1 - \alpha - \beta)(\mathbf{P}_2)_j. \tag{11.13}$$

Given the two-dimensional blend vector **b**, we find the blend weights $\alpha$, $\beta$, and $\gamma$ by finding the *barycentric coordinates* of the point **b** relative to the triangle formed by the three clips in two-dimensional blend space (http://en.wikipedia.org/wiki/Barycentric_coordinates_%28mathematics%29). In general, the barycentric coordinates of a point **b** within a triangle with vertices $\mathbf{b}_1$, $\mathbf{b}_2$, and $\mathbf{b}_3$ are three scalar values $(\alpha, \beta, \gamma)$ that satisfy the relations

$$\mathbf{b} = \alpha\,\mathbf{b}_0 + \beta\,\mathbf{b}_1 + \gamma\,\mathbf{b}_2 \tag{11.14}$$

and

$$\alpha + \beta + \gamma = 1.$$

These are exactly the weights we seek for our three-clip weighted average. Barycentric coordinates are illustrated in Figure 11.36.

Note that plugging the barycentric coordinate (1, 0, 0) into Equation (11.14) yields $\mathbf{b}_0$, while (0, 1, 0) gives us $\mathbf{b}_1$ and (0, 0, 1) produces $\mathbf{b}_2$. Likewise, plugging these blend weights into Equation (11.13) gives us poses $(\mathbf{P}_0)_j$, $(\mathbf{P}_1)_j$,

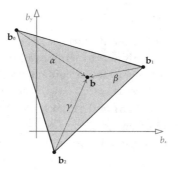

**Figure 11.36.** Various barycentric coordinates within a triangle.

and $(\mathbf{P}_2)_j$, respectively. Furthermore, the barycentric coordinate ($\frac{1}{3}$, $\frac{1}{3}$, $\frac{1}{3}$) lies at the centroid of the triangle and gives us an *equal* blend between the three poses. This is exactly what we'd expect.

### 11.6.3.4. Generalized Two-Dimensional LERP Blending

The barycentric coordinate technique can be extended to an arbitrary number of animation clips positioned at arbitrary locations within the two-dimensional blend space. We won't describe it in its entirety here, but the basic idea is to use a technique known as *Delaunay triangulation* (http://en.wikipedia.org/wiki/Delaunay_triangulation) to find a set of triangles given the positions of the various animation clips $\mathbf{b}_i$. Once the triangles have been determined, we can find the triangle that encloses the desired point $\mathbf{b}$ and then perform a three-clip LERP blend as described above. This is shown in Figure 11.37.

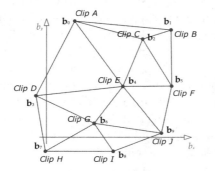

**Figure 11.37.** Delaunay triangulation between an arbitrary number of animation clips positioned at arbitrary locations in two-dimensional blend space.

### 11.6.4.  Partial-Skeleton Blending

A human being can control different parts of his or her body independently. For example, I can wave my right arm while walking and pointing at something with my left arm. One way to implement this kind of movement in a game is via a technique known as *partial-skeleton blending*.

Recall from Equations (11.5) and (11.6) that when doing regular LERP blending, the same blend percentage $\beta$ was used for every joint in the skeleton. Partial-skeleton blending extends this idea by permitting the blend percentage to vary on a per-joint basis. In other words, for each joint $j$, we define a separate blend percentage $\beta_j$. The set of all blend percentages for the entire skeleton $\{\beta_j\}\big|_{j=0}^{N-1}$ is sometimes called a *blend mask* because it can be used to "mask out" certain joints by setting their blend percentages to zero.

As an example, let's say we want our character to wave at someone using his right arm and hand. Moreover, we want him to be able to wave whether he's walking, running, or standing still. To implement this using partial blending, the animator defines three full-body animations: *Walk*, *Run*, and *Stand*. The animator also creates a single waving animation, *Wave*. A blend mask is created in which the blend percentages are zero everywhere except for the right shoulder, elbow, wrist, and finger joints, where they are equal to one:

$$\beta_j = \begin{cases} 1, & j \in \text{right arm}, \\ 0, & \text{otherwise}. \end{cases}$$

When *Walk*, *Run*, or *Stand* is LERP-blended with *Wave* using this blend mask, the result is a character who appears to be walking, running, or standing while waving his right arm.

Partial blending is useful, but it has a tendency to make a character's movement look unnatural. This occurs for two basic reasons:

- An abrupt change in the per-joint blend factors can cause the movements of one part of the body to appear disconnected from the rest of the body. In our example, the blend factors change abruptly at the right shoulder joint. Hence the animation of the upper spine, neck, and head are being driven by one animation, while the right shoulder and arm joints are being entirely driven by a different animation. This can look odd. The problem can be mitigated somewhat by gradually changing the blend factors rather than doing it abruptly. (In our example, we might select a blend percentage of 0.9 at the right shoulder, 0.5 on the upper spine, and 0.2 on the neck and mid-spine.)

- The movements of a real human body are never totally independent. For example, one would expect a person's wave to look more "bouncy" and out of control when he or she is running than when he or she is standing still. Yet with partial blending, the right arm's animation will be identical no matter what the rest of the body is doing. This problem is difficult to overcome using partial blending. Instead, many game developers have recently turned to a more natural-looking technique known as *additive blending*.

## 11.6.5. Additive Blending

Additive blending approaches the problem of combining animations in a totally new way. It introduces a new kind of animation called a *difference clip*, which, as its name implies, represents the difference between two regular animation clips. A difference clip can be added onto a regular animation clip in order to produce interesting variations in the pose and movement of the character. In essence, a difference clip encodes the *changes* that need to be made to one pose in order to transform it into another pose. Difference clips are often called *additive animation clips* in the game industry. We'll stick with the term *difference clip* in this book because it more accurately describes what is going on.

Consider two input clips called the *source clip* (S) and the *reference clip* (R). Conceptually, the difference clip is D = S – R. If a difference clip D is added to its original reference clip, we get back the source clip (S = D + R). We can also generate animations that are partway between R and S by adding a percentage of D to R, in much the same way that LERP blending finds intermediate animations between two extremes. However, the real beauty of the additive blending technique is that once a difference clip has been created, it can be added to other unrelated clips, not just to the original reference clip. We'll call these animations *target clips* and denote them with the symbol T.

As an example, if the reference clip has the character running normally and the source clip has him running in a tired manner, then the difference clip will contain only the changes necessary to make the character look tired while running. If this difference clip is now applied to a clip of the character walking, the resulting animation can make the character look tired while walking. A whole host of interesting and very natural-looking animations can be created by adding a single difference clip onto various "regular" animation clips, or a collection of difference clips can be created, each of which produces a different effect when added to a single target animation.

### 11.6.5.1. Mathematical Formulation

A difference animation D is defined as the difference between some source animation S and some reference animation R. So conceptually, the difference pose (at a single point in time) is D = S − R. Of course, we're dealing with joint poses, not scalar quantities, so we cannot simply subtract the poses. In general, a joint pose is a 4 × 4 affine transformation matrix $\mathbf{P}_{C \to P}$ that transforms points and vectors from the child joint's local space to the space of its parent joint. The matrix equivalent of subtraction is multiplication by the inverse matrix. So given the source pose $\mathbf{S}_j$ and the reference pose $\mathbf{R}_j$ for any joint $j$ in the skeleton, we can define the difference pose $\mathbf{D}_j$ at that joint as follows (for this discussion, we'll drop the C→P or $j$→p($j$) subscript, as it is understood that we are dealing with child-to-parent pose matrices):

$$\mathbf{D}_j = \mathbf{S}_j \mathbf{R}_j^{-1}.$$

"Adding" a difference pose $\mathbf{D}_j$ onto a target pose $\mathbf{T}_j$ yields a new additive pose $\mathbf{A}_j$. This is achieved by simply concatenating the difference transform and the target transform as follows:

$$\mathbf{A}_j = \mathbf{D}_j \mathbf{T}_j = (\mathbf{S}_j \mathbf{R}_j^{-1}) \mathbf{T}_j. \tag{11.15}$$

We can verify that this is correct by looking at what happens when the difference pose is "added" back onto the original reference pose:

$$\mathbf{A}_j = \mathbf{D}_j \mathbf{R}_j$$

$$= \mathbf{S}_j \mathbf{R}_j^{-1} \mathbf{R}_j$$

$$= \mathbf{S}_j.$$

In other words, adding the difference animation D back onto the original reference animation R yields the source animation S, as we'd expect.

### Temporal Interpolation of Difference Clips

As we learned in Section 11.4.1.1, game animations are almost never sampled on integer frame indices. To find a pose at an arbitrary time $t$, we must often *temporally interpolate* between adjacent pose samples at times $t_1$ and $t_2$. Thankfully, difference clips can be temporally interpolated just like their non-additive counterparts. We can simply apply Equations (11.10) and (11.11) directly to our difference clips as if they were ordinary animations.

Note that a difference animation can only be found when the input clips S and R are of the same duration. Otherwise there would be a period of time during which either S or R is undefined, meaning D would be undefined as well.

### Additive Blend Percentage

In games, we often wish to blend in only a percentage of a difference animation to achieve varying degrees of the effect it produces. For example, if a difference clip causes the character to turn his head 80 degrees to the right, blending in 50% of the difference clip should make him turn his head only 40 degrees to the right.

To accomplish this, we turn once again to our old friend LERP. We wish to interpolate between the unaltered target animation and the new animation that would result from a full application of the difference animation. To do this, we extend Equation (11.15) as follows:

$$\mathbf{A}_j = \text{LERP}(\mathbf{T}_j,\ \mathbf{D}_j\mathbf{T}_j,\ \beta)$$
$$= (1-\beta)(\mathbf{T}_j) + \beta(\mathbf{D}_j\mathbf{T}_j). \tag{11.16}$$

As we saw in Chapter 4, we cannot LERP matrices directly. So Equation (11.16) must be broken down into three separate interpolations for S, Q, and T, just as we did in Equations (11.7), (11.8), and (11.9).

### 11.6.5.2. Additive Blending Versus Partial Blending

Additive blending is similar in some ways to partial blending. For example, we can take the difference between a standing clip and a clip of standing while waving the right arm. The result will be almost the same as using a partial blend to make the right arm wave. However, additive blends suffer less from the "disconnected" look of animations combined via partial blending. This is because, with an additive blend, we are not replacing the animation for a subset of joints or interpolating between two potentially unrelated poses. Rather, we are adding movement to the original animation—possibly across the entire skeleton. In effect, a difference animation "knows" how to change a character's pose in order to get him to do something specific, like being tired, aiming his head in a certain direction, or waving his arm. These changes can be applied to a wide variety of animations, and the result often looks very natural.

### 11.6.5.3. Limitations of Additive Blending

Of course, additive animation is not a silver bullet. Because it adds movement to an existing animation, it can have a tendency to over-rotate the joints in the skeleton, especially when multiple difference clips are applied simultaneously. As a simple example, imagine a target animation in which the character's left arm is bent at a 90 degree angle. If we add a difference animation that also rotates the elbow by 90 degrees, then the net effect would be to rotate the arm by 90 + 90 = 180 degrees. This would cause the lower arm to interpenetrate the upper arm—not a comfortable position for most individuals!

Clearly we must be careful when selecting the reference clip and also when choosing the target clips to which to apply it. Here are some simple rules of thumb:

- Keep hip rotations to a minimum in the reference clip.

- The shoulder and elbow joints should usually be in neutral poses in the reference clip to minimize over-rotation of the arms when the difference clip is added to other targets.

- Animators should create a new difference animation for each core pose (e.g., standing upright, crouched down, lying prone, etc.). This allows the animator to account for the way in which a real human would move when in each of these stances.

These rules of thumb can be a helpful starting point, but the only way to really learn how to create and apply difference clips is by trial and error or by apprenticing with animators or engineers who have experience creating and applying difference animations. If your team hasn't used additive blending in the past, expect to spend a significant amount of time learning the art of additive blending.

## 11.6.6. Applications of Additive Blending

### 11.6.6.1. Stance Variation

One particularly striking application of additive blending is *stance variation*. For each desired stance, the animator creates a one-frame difference animation. When one of these single-frame clips is additively blended with a base animation, it causes the entire stance of the character to change drastically while he continues to perform the fundamental action he's supposed to perform. This idea is illustrated in Figure 11.38.

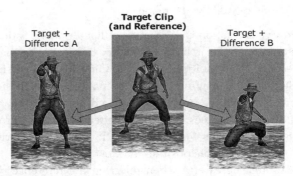

**Figure 11.38.** Two single-frame difference animations A and B can cause a target animation clip to assume two totally different stances. (Character from Naughty Dog's *Uncharted: Drake's Fortune*.)

**Target Clip
(and Reference)**

Target +
Difference A

Target +
Difference B

Target +
Difference C

Figure 11.39. Additive blends can be used to add variation to a repetitive idle animation. Images courtesy of Naughty Dog Inc.

### 11.6.6.2. Locomotion Noise

Real humans don't run exactly the same way with every footfall—there is variation in their movement over time. This is especially true if the person is distracted (for example, by attacking enemies). Additive blending can be used to layer randomness, or reactions to distractions, on top of an otherwise entirely repetitive locomotion cycle. This is illustrated in Figure 11.39.

### 11.6.6.3. Aim and Look-At

Another common use for additive blending is to permit the character to look around or to aim his weapon. To accomplish this, the character is first animated doing some action, such as running, with his head or weapon facing straight ahead. Then the animator changes the direction of the head or the aim of the weapon to the extreme right and saves off a one-frame or multi-frame difference animation. This process is repeated for the extreme left, up, and down directions. These four difference animations can then be additively blended onto the original straight ahead animation clip, causing the character to aim right, left, up, down, or anywhere in between.

The angle of the aim is governed by the additive blend factor of each clip. For example, blending in 100 percent of the right additive causes the character

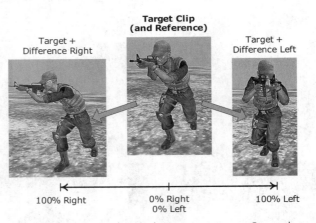

**Figure 11.40.** Additive blending can be used to aim a weapon. Screenshots courtesy of Naughty Dog Inc.

to aim as far right as possible. Blending 50 percent of the left additive causes him to aim at an angle that is one-half of his leftmost aim. We can also combine this with an up or down additive to aim diagonally. This is demonstrated in Figure 11.40.

### 11.6.6.4. Overloading the Time Axis

It's interesting to note that the time axis of an animation clip needn't be used to represent time. For example, a three-frame animation clip could be used to provide three aim poses to the engine—a left aim pose on frame 1, a forward aim pose on frame 2, and a right aim pose on frame 3. To make the character aim to the right, we can simply fix the local clock of the aim animation on frame 3. To perform a 50% blend between aiming forward and aiming right, we can dial in frame 2.5. This is a great example of leveraging existing features of the engine for new purposes.

## 11.7. Post-Processing

Once a skeleton as been posed by one or more animation clips and the results have been blended together using linear interpolation or additive blending, it is often necessary to modify the pose prior to rendering the character. This is called *animation post-processing*. In this section, we'll look at a few of the most common kinds of animation post-processing.

### 11.7.1. Procedural Animations

A *procedural animation* is any animation generated at runtime rather than being driven by data exported from an animation tool such as Maya. Sometimes, hand-animated clips are used to pose the skeleton initially, and then the pose is modified in some way via procedural animation as a post-processing step. A procedural animation can also be used as an input to the system in place of a hand-animated clip.

For example, imagine that a regular animation clip is used to make a vehicle appear to be bouncing up and down on the terrain as it moves. The direction in which the vehicle travels is under player control. We would like to adjust the rotation of the front wheels and steering wheel so that they move convincingly when the vehicle is turning. This can be done by post-processing the pose generated by the animation. Let's assume that the original animation has the front tires pointing straight ahead and the steering wheel in a neutral position. We can use the current angle of turn to create a quaternion about the vertical axis that will deflect the front tires by the desired amount. This quaternion can be multiplied with the front tire joints' Q channel to produce the final pose of the tires. Likewise, we can generate a quaternion about the axis of the steering column and multiply it in to the steering wheel joint's Q channel to deflect it. These adjustments are made to the *local pose*, prior to global pose calculation and matrix palette generation.

As another example, let's say that we wish to make the trees and bushes in our game world sway naturally in the wind and get brushed aside when characters move through them. We can do this by modeling the trees and bushes as skinned meshes with simple skeletons. Procedural animation can be used, in place of or in addition to hand-animated clips, to cause the joints to move in a natural-looking way. We might apply one or more sinusoids to the rotation of various joints to make them sway in the breeze, and when a character moves through a region containing a bush or grass, we can deflect its root joint quaternion radially outward to make it appear to be pushed over by the character.

### 11.7.2. Inverse Kinematics

Let's say we have an animation clip in which a character leans over to pick up an object from the ground. In Maya, the clip looks great, but in our production game level, the ground is not perfectly flat, so sometimes the character's hand misses the object or appears to pass through it. In this case, we would like to adjust the final pose of the skeleton so that the hand lines up exactly with the target object. A technique known as *inverse kinematics* (IK) can be used to make this happen.

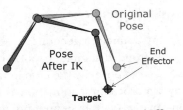

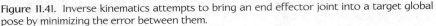

**Figure 11.41.** Inverse kinematics attempts to bring an end effector joint into a target global pose by minimizing the error between them.

A regular animation clip is an example of *forward kinematics* (FK). In forward kinematics, the input is a set of local joint poses, and the output is a global pose and a skinning matrix for each joint. Inverse kinematics goes in the other direction: The input is the desired global pose of a single joint, which is known as the *end effector*. We solve for the *local* poses of other joints in the skeleton that will bring the end effector to the desired location.

Mathematically, IK boils down to an *error minimization* problem. As with most minimization problems, there might be one solution, many, or none at all. This makes intuitive sense: If I try to reach a doorknob that is on the other side of the room, I won't be able to reach it without walking over to it. IK works best when the skeleton starts out in a pose that is reasonably close to the desired target. This helps the algorithm to focus in on the "closest" solution and to do so in a reasonable amount of processing time. Figure 11.41 shows IK in action.

Imagine a two-joint skeleton, each of which can rotate only about a single axis. The rotation of these two joints can be described by a two-dimensional angle vector $\theta = [\, \theta_1 \ \theta_2 \,]$. The set of all possible angles for our two joints forms a two-dimensional space called *configuration space*. Obviously, for more-complex skeletons with more degrees of freedom per joint, configuration space becomes multidimensional, but the concepts described here work equally well no matter how many dimensions we have.

Now imagine plotting a three-dimensional graph, where for each combination of joint rotations (i.e., for each point in our two-dimensional configuration space), we plot the distance from the end effector to the desired target. An example of this kind of plot is shown in Figure 11.42. The "valleys" in this three-dimensional surface represent regions in which the end effector is as close as possible to the target. When the height of the surface is zero, the end effector has reached its target. Inverse kinematics, then, attempts to find minima (low points) on this surface.

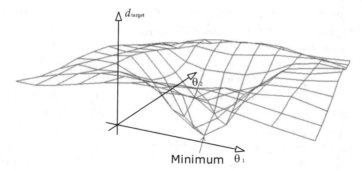

**Figure 11.42.** A three-dimensional plot of the distance from the end effector to the target for each point in two-dimensional configuration space. IK finds the local minimum.

We won't get into the details of solving the IK minimization problem here. You can read more about IK at http://en.wikipedia.org/wiki/Inverse_kinematics and in Jason Weber's article, "Constrained Inverse Kinematics," in [40].

### 11.7.3. Rag Dolls

A character's body goes limp when he dies or becomes unconscious. In such situations, we want the body to react in a physically realistic way with its surroundings. To do this, we can use a *rag doll*. A rag doll is a collection of physically simulated rigid bodies, each one representing a semi-rigid part of the character's body, such as his lower arm or his upper leg. The rigid bodies are constrained to one another at the joints of the character in such a way as to produce natural-looking "lifeless" body movement. The positions and orientations of the rigid bodies are determined by the physics system and are then used to drive the positions and orientations of certain key joints in the character's skeleton. The transfer of data from the physics system to the skeleton is typically done as a post-processing step.

To really understand rag doll physics, we must first have an understanding of how the collision and physics systems work. Rag dolls are covered in more detail in Sections 12.4.8.7 and 12.5.3.8.

## 11.8.  Compression Techniques

Animation data can take up a lot of memory. A single joint pose might be composed of ten floating-point channels (three for translation, four for rotation, and up to three more for scale). Assuming each channel contains a four-byte floating-point value, a one-second clip sampled at 30 samples per second would occupy 4 bytes × 10 channels × 30 samples/second = 1200 bytes per joint per second, or a data rate of about 1.17 kB per joint per second. For a 100-joint skeleton (which is small by today's standards), an uncompressed animation clip would occupy 117 kB per joint per second. If our game contained 1000 seconds of animation (which is on the low side for a modern game), the entire data set would occupy a whopping 114.4 MB. That's probably more than most games can spare, considering that a PLAYSTATION 3 has only 256 MB of main RAM and 256 MB of video RAM. Therefore, game engineers invest a significant amount of effort into compressing animation data in order to permit the maximum richness and variety of movement at the minimum memory cost.

### 11.8.1.  Channel Omission

One simple way to reduce the size of an animation clip is to omit channels that are irrelevant. Many characters do not require nonuniform scaling, so the three scale channels can be reduced to a single uniform scale channel. In some games, the scale channel can actually be omitted altogether for all joints (except possibly the joints in the face). The bones of a humanoid character generally cannot stretch, so translation can often be omitted for all joints except the root, the facial joints, and sometimes the collar bones. Finally, because quaternions are always normalized, we can store only three components per quat (e.g., $x$, $y$, and $z$) and reconstruct the fourth component (e.g., $w$) at runtime.

As a further optimization, channels whose pose does not change over the course of the entire animation can be stored as a single sample at time $t = 0$ plus a single bit indicating that the channel is constant for all other values of $t$.

Channel omission can significantly reduce the size of an animation clip. A 100-joint character with no scale and no translation requires only 303 channels—three channels for the quaternions at each joint, plus three channels for the root joint's translation. Compare this to the 1,000 channels that would be required if all ten channels were included for all 100 joints.

### 11.8.2.  Quantization

Another way to reduce the size of an animation is to reduce the size of each channel. A floating-point value is normally stored in 32-bit IEEE format. This format provides 23 bits of precision in the mantissa and an 8-bit exponent. However, it's often not necessary to retain that kind of precision and range in an animation clip. When storing a quaternion, the channel values are guaranteed to lie in the range [−1, 1]. At a magnitude of 1, the exponent of a 32-bit IEEE float is zero, and 23 bits of precision give us accuracy down to the seventh decimal place. Experience shows that a quaternion can be encoded well with only 16 bits of precision, so we're really wasting 16 bits per channel if we store our quats using 32-bit floats.

Converting a 32-bit IEEE float into an *n*-bit integer representation is called *quantization*. There are actually two components to this operation: *Encoding* is the process of converting the original floating-point value to a quantized integer representation. *Decoding* is the process of recovering an approximation to the original floating-point value from the quantized integer. (We can only recover an *approximation* to the original data—quantization is a *lossy* compression method because it effectively reduces the number of bits of precision used to represent the value.)

To encode a floating-point value as an integer, we first divide the valid range of possible input values into $N$ equally sized *intervals*. We then determine within which interval a particular floating-point value lies and represent that value by the *integer index* of its interval. To decode this quantized value, we simply convert the integer index into floating-point format and shift and scale it back into the original range. $N$ is usually chosen to correspond to the range of possible integer values that can be represented by an *n*-bit integer. For example, if we're encoding a 32-bit floating-point value as a 16-bit integer, the number of intervals would be $N = 2^{16} = 65{,}536$.

Jonathan Blow wrote an excellent article on the topic of floating-point scalar quantization in the *Inner Product* column of Game Developer Magazine, available at http://number-none.com/product/Scalar%20Quantization/index.html. (Jonathan's source code is also available at http://www.gdmag.com/src/jun02.zip.) The article presents two ways to map a floating-point value to an interval during the encoding process: We can either *truncate* the float to the next lowest interval boundary (*T encoding*), or we can *round* the float to the center of the enclosing interval (*R encoding*). Likewise, it describes two approaches to reconstructing the floating-point value from its integer representation: We can either return the value of the *lefthand side* of the interval to which our original value was mapped (*L reconstruction*), or we can return the value of the center of the interval (*C reconstruction*). This gives us four possible encode/decode methods: TL, TC, RL, and RC. Of these, TL and RC are to be avoided because they tend to remove or add energy to the data set, which can often have disastrous effects. TC has the benefit of being the most efficient method in terms of bandwidth, but it suffers from a severe problem—there is no way to represent the value zero exactly. (If you encode `0.0f`, it becomes a small positive value when decoded.) RL is therefore usually the best choice and is the method we'll demonstrate here.

The article only talks about quantizing positive floating-point values, and in the examples, the input range is assumed to be [0, 1] for simplicity. However, we can always shift and scale any floating-point range into the range [0, 1]. For example, the range of quaternion channels is [–1, 1], but we can convert this to the range [0, 1] by adding one and then dividing by two.

The following pair of routines encode and decode an input floating-point value lying in the range [0, 1] into an $n$-bit integer, according to Jonathan Blow's RL method. The quantized value is always returned as a 32-bit unsigned integer (U32), but only the least-significant $n$ bits are actually used, as specified by the nBits argument. For example, if you pass nBits==16, you can safely cast the result to a U16.

```
U32 CompressUnitFloatRL(F32 unitFloat, U32 nBits)
{
    // Determine the number of intervals based on the
    // number of output bits we've been asked to produce.
    U32 nIntervals = 1u << nBits;

    // Scale the input value from the range [0, 1] into
    // the range [0, nIntervals - 1]. We subtract one
    //  interval because we want the largest output value
    //  to fit into nBits bits.

    F32 scaled = unitFloat * (F32)(nIntervals - 1u);

    // Finally, round to the nearest interval center. We
    // do this by adding 0.5f, and then truncating to the
    // next-lowest interval index (by casting to U32).
    U32 rounded = (U32)(scaled * 0.5f);

    // Guard against invalid input values.
    if (rounded > nIntervals - 1u)
        rounded = nIntervals - 1u;
    return rounded;
}


F32 DecompressUnitFloatRL(U32 quantized, U32 nBits)
{
    // Determine the number of intervals based on the
    // number of bits we used when we encoded the value.
    U32 nIntervals = 1u << nBits;

    // Decode by simply converting the U32 to an F32, and
    // scaling by the interval size.
    F32 intervalSize = 1.0f / (F32)(nIntervals - 1u);

    F32 approxUnitFloat = (F32)quantized * intervalSize;
    return approxUnitFloat;
}
```

To handle arbitrary input values in the range [*min, max*], we can use these routines:

```
U32 CompressFloatRL(F32 value, F32 min, F32 max,
                    U32 nBits)
{
    F32 unitFloat = (value - min) / (max - min);
    U32 quantized = CompressUnitFloatRL(unitFloat,
        nBits);
    return quantized;
}

F32 DecompressFloatRL(U32 quantized, F32 min, F32 max,
                      U32 nBits)
{
    F32 unitFloat = DecompressUnitFloatRL(quantized,
        nBits);
    F32 value = min + (unitFloat * (max - min));
    return value;
}
```

Let's return to our original problem of animation channel compression. To compress and decompress a quaternion's four components into 16 bits per channel, we simply call CompressFloatRL() and DecompressFloatRL() with *min* = −1, *max* = 1, and *n* = 16:

```
inline U16 CompressRotationChannel(F32 qx)
{
    return (U16)CompressFloatRL(qx, -1.0f, 1.0f, 16u);
}

inline F32 DecompressRotationChannel(U16 qx)
{
    return DecompressFloatRL((U32)qx, -1.0f, 1.0f, 16u);
}
```

Compression of translation channels is a bit trickier than rotations, because unlike quaternion channels, the range of a translation channel could theoretically be unbounded. Thankfully, the joints of a character don't move very far in practice, so we can decide upon a reasonable range of motion and flag an error if we ever see an animation that contains translations outside the valid range. In-game cinematics are an exception to this rule—when an IGC is animated in world space, the translations of the characters' root joints can grow very large. To address this, we can select the range of valid translations on a per-animation or per-joint basis, depending on the maximum translations actually achieved within each clip. Because the data range might differ

from animation to animation, or from joint to joint, we must store the range
with the compressed clip data. This will add data to each animation, so it may
or may not be worth the trade-off.

```
// We'll use a 2 meter range -- your mileage may vary.
F32 MAX_TRANSLATION = 2.0f;

inline U16 CompressTranslationChannel(F32 vx)
{
    // Clamp to valid range...
    if (value < -MAX_TRANSLATION)
        value = -MAX_TRANSLATION;
    if (value > MAX_TRANSLATION)
        value = MAX_TRANSLATION;

    return (U16)CompressFloatRL(vx,
        -MAX_TRANSLATION, MAX_TRANSLATION, 16);
}

inline F32 DecompressTranslationChannel(U16 vx)
{
    return DecompressFloatRL((U32)vx,
        -MAX_TRANSLATION, MAX_TRANSLATION, 16);
}
```

### 11.8.3.  Sampling Frequency and Key Omission

Animation data tends to be large for three reasons: first, because the pose of
each joint can contain upwards of ten channels of floating-point data; second,
because a skeleton contains a large number of joints (100 or more for a humanoid character); third, because the pose of the character is typically sampled
at a high rate (e.g., 30 frames per second). We've seen some ways to address
the first problem. We can't really reduce the number of joints for our high-
resolution characters, so we're stuck with the second problem. To attack the
third problem, we can do two things:

- *Reduce the sample rate overall.* Some animations look fine when exported
  at 15 samples per second, and doing so cuts the animation data size in
  half.
- *Omit some of the samples.* If a channel's data varies in an approximately
  linear fashion during some interval of time within the clip, we can omit
  all of the samples in this interval except the endpoints. Then, at runtime,
  we can use linear interpolation to recover the dropped samples.

The latter technique is a bit involved, and it requires us to store information about the *time* of each sample. This additional data can erode the savings

we achieved by omitting samples in the first place. However, some game engines have used this technique successfully.

### II.8.4. Curve-Based Compression

One of the most powerful, easiest-to-use, and best thought-out animation APIs I've ever worked with is Granny, by Rad Game Tools. Granny stores animations not as a regularly spaced sequence of pose samples but as a collection of $n$th-order nonuniform, nonrational B-splines, describing the paths of a joint's S, Q, and T channels over time. Using B-splines allows channels with a lot of curvature to be encoded using only a few data points.

Granny exports an animation by sampling the joint poses at regular intervals, much like traditional animation data. For each channel, Granny then fits a set of B-splines to the sampled data set to within a user-specified tolerance. The end result is an animation clip that is usually significantly smaller than its uniformly sampled, linearly interpolated counterpart. This process is illustrated in Figure 11.43.

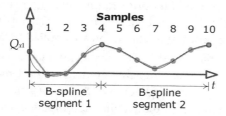

**Figure II.43.** One form of animation compression fits B-splines to the animation channel data.

### II.8.5. Selective Loading and Streaming

The cheapest animation clip is the one that isn't in memory at all. Most games don't need every animation clip to be in memory simultaneously. Some clips apply only to certain classes of character, so they needn't be loaded during levels in which that class of character is never encountered. Other clips apply to one-off moments in the game. These can be loaded or streamed into memory just before being needed and dumped from memory once they have played.

Most games load a core set of animation clips into memory when the game first boots and keep them there for the duration of the game. These include the player character's core move set and animations that apply to objects that reappear over and over throughout the game, such as weapons or power-ups.

All other animations are usually loaded on an as-needed basis. Some game engines load animation clips individually, but many package them together into logical groups that can be loaded and unloaded as a unit.

## 11.9.  Animation System Architecture

Now that we understand the theory that underlies a game's animation system, let's turn our attention to how such a system is structured from a software architecture standpoint. We'll also investigate what kinds of interfaces exist between the animation system and the other systems in a typical game engine.

Most animation systems are comprised of up to three distinct layers:

- *Animation pipeline.* For each animating character and object in the game, the animation pipeline takes one or more animation clips and corresponding blend factors as input, blends them together, and generates a single local skeletal pose as output. It also calculates a global pose for the skeleton, and a palette of skinning matrices for use by the rendering engine. Post-processing hooks are usually provided, which permit the local pose to be modified prior to final global pose and matrix palette generation. This is where inverse kinematics (IK), rag doll physics, and other forms of procedural animation are applied to the skeleton.

- *Action state machine (ASM).* The actions of a game character (standing, walking, running, jumping, etc.) are usually best modeled via a finite state machine, commonly known as the *action state machine* (ASM). The ASM subsystem sits atop the animation pipeline and provides a state-driven animation interface for use by virtually all higher-level game code. It ensures that characters can *transition* smoothly from state to state. In addition, most animation engines permit different parts of the character's body to be doing different, independent actions simultaneously, such as aiming and firing a weapon while running. This can be accomplished by allowing multiple independent state machines to control a single character via *state layers*.

- *Animation controllers.* In many game engines, the behaviors of a player or non-player character are ultimately controlled by a high-level system of *animation controllers*. Each controller is custom-tailored to manage the character's behavior when in a particular mode. There might be one controller handling the character's actions when he is fighting and moving around out in the open ("run-and-gun" mode), one for when he is in cover, one for driving a vehicle, one for climbing a ladder, and so on. These high-level animation controllers allow most if not all of the animation-related code to be encapsulated, allowing top-level player control or AI logic to remain uncluttered by animation micro-management.

Some game engines draw the lines between these layers differently than we do here. Other engines meld two or more of the layers into a single system. However, all animation engines need to perform these tasks in one form or another. In the following sections, we'll explore animation architecture in terms of these three layers, noting in our examples when a particular game engine takes a more or less unified approach.

## 11.10. The Animation Pipeline

The operations performed by the low-level animation engine form a *pipeline* that transforms its inputs (animation clips and blend specifications) into the desired outputs (local and global poses, plus a matrix palette for rendering). The stages of this pipeline are:

1. *Clip decompression and pose extraction.* In this stage, each individual clip's data is decompressed, and a static pose is extracted for the time index in question. The output of this phase is a local skeletal pose for each input clip. This pose might contain information for every joint in the skeleton (a *full-body pose*), for only a subset of joints (a *partial pose*), or it might be a *difference pose* for use in additive blending.

2. *Pose blending.* In this stage, the input poses are combined via full-body LERP blending, partial-skeleton LERP blending, and/or additive blending. The output of this stage is a single local pose for all joints in the skeleton. This stage is of course only executed when blending more than one animation clip together—otherwise the output pose from stage 1 can be used directly.

3. *Global pose generation.* In this stage, the skeletal hierarchy is walked, and local joint poses are concatenated in order to generate a global pose for the skeleton.

4. *Post-processing.* In this optional stage, the local and/or global poses of the skeleton can be modified prior to finalization of the pose. Post-processing is used for inverse kinematics, rag doll physics, and other forms of procedural animation adjustment.

5. *Recalculation of global poses.* Many types of post-processing require global pose information as input but generate local poses as output. After such a post-processing step has run, we must recalculate the global pose

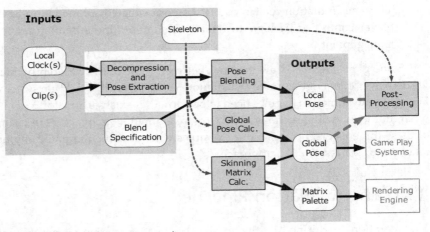

**Figure 11.44.** A typical animation pipeline.

from the modified local pose. Obviously, a post-processing operation that does not require global pose information can be done between stages 2 and 3, thus avoiding the need for global pose recalculation.

6. *Matrix palette generation.* Once the final global pose has been generated, each joint's global pose matrix is multiplied by the corresponding inverse bind pose matrix. The output of this stage is a palette of skinning matrices suitable for input to the rendering engine.

A typical animation pipeline is depicted in Figure 11.44.

## 11.10.1. Data Structures

Every animation pipeline is architected differently, but most operate in terms of data structures that are similar to the ones described in this section.

### 11.10.1.1. Shared Resource Data

As with all game engine systems, a strong distinction must be made between *shared resource data* and *per-instance state information*. Each individual character or object in the game has its own per-instance data structures, but characters or objects of the same type typically share a single set of resource data. This shared data typically includes the following:

- *Skeleton.* The skeleton describes the joint hierarchy and its bind pose.
- *Skinned meshes.* One or more meshes can be skinned to a single skeleton. Each vertex within a skinned mesh contains the indices of one or more

joints within the skeleton, plus weights governing how much influence each joint should have on that vertex's position.

- *Animation clips.* Many hundreds or even thousands of animation clips are created for a character's skeleton. These may be full-body clips, partial-skeleton clips, or difference clips for use in additive blending.

A UML diagram of these data structures is shown in Figure 11.45. Pay particular attention to the *cardinality* and *direction* of the relationships between these classes. The cardinality is shown just beside the tip or tail of the relationship arrow between classes—a one represents a single instance of the class, while an asterisk indicates many instances. For any one type of character, there will be one skeleton, one or more meshes, and one or more animation clips. The skeleton is the central unifying element—the skins are attached to the skeleton but don't have any relationship with the animation clips. Likewise, the clips are targeted at a particular skeleton, but they have no "knowledge" of the skin meshes. Figure 11.46 illustrates these relationships.

Game designers often try to reduce the number of unique skeletons in the game to one, or just a few, because each new skeleton generally requires a whole new set of animation clips. To provide the illusion of many different

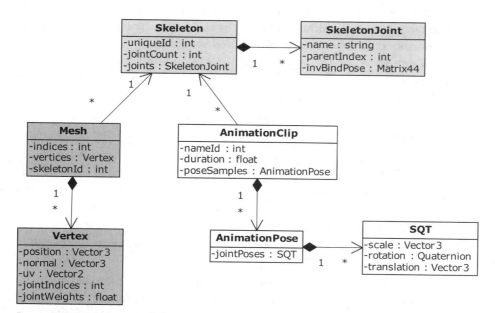

Figure 11.45. UML diagram of shared animation resources.

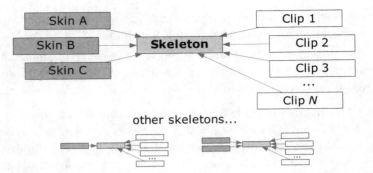

Figure 11.46. Many animation clips and one or more meshes target a single skeleton.

types of characters, it is usually better to create multiple meshes skinned to the same skeleton when possible, so that all of the characters can share a single set of animations.

### 11.10.1.2. Per-Instance Data

In most games, multiple *instances* of each character type can appear on-screen at the same time. Every instance of a particular character type needs its own private data structures, allowing it to keep track of its currently playing animation clip(s), a specification of how the clips are to be blended together (if there's more than one), and its current skeletal pose.

There is no one universally accepted way to represent per-instance animation data. However, virtually every animation engine keeps track of the following pieces of information.

- *Clip state.* For each playing clip, the following information is maintained:
  - □ *Local clock.* A clip's local clock describes the point along its local time line at which its current pose should be extracted. This may be replaced by a global start time in some engines. (A comparison between local and global clocks was provided in Section 11.4.3.)
  - □ *Playback rate.* A clip can be played at an arbitrary rate, denoted $R$ in Section 11.4.2.
- *Blend specification.* The blend specification is a description of which animation clips are currently playing and how these clips are to be blended together. The degree to which each clip contributes to the final pose is

controlled by one or more *blend weights*. There are two primary methods of describing the set of clips that should be blended together: a *flat weighted average* approach and a *tree of blend nodes*. When the tree approach is used, the structure of the blend tree is usually treated as a *shared resource*, while the blend weights are stored as part of the *per-instance* state information.

- *Partial-skeleton joint weights.* If a partial-skeleton blend is to be performed, the degrees to which each joint should contribute to the final pose are specified via a set of *joint weights*. In some animation engines, the joint weights are binary: either a joint contributes or it does not. In other engines, the weights can lie anywhere from zero (no contribution) to one (full contribution).

- *Local pose.* This is typically an array of SQT data structures, one per joint, holding the final pose of the skeleton in parent-relative format. This array might also be reused to store an intermediate pose that serves both as the input to and the output of the post-processing stage of the pipeline.

- *Global pose.* This is an array of SQTs, or $4 \times 4$ or $4 \times 3$ matrices, one per joint, that holds the final pose of the skeleton in model-space or world-space format. The global pose may serve as an input to the post-processing stage.

- *Matrix palette.* This is an array of $4 \times 4$ or $4 \times 3$ matrices, one per joint, containing skinning matrices for input to the rendering engine.

## 11.10.2. The Flat Weighted Average Blend Representation

All but the most rudimentary game engines support animation blending in some form. This means that at any given time, multiple animation clips may be contributing to the final pose of a character's skeleton. One simple way to describe how the currently active clips should be blended together is via a *weighted average*.

In this approach, every animation clip is associated with a blend weight indicating how much it should contribute to the final pose of the character. A flat list of all *active* animation clips (i.e., clips whose blend weights are non-zero) is maintained. To calculate the final pose of the skeleton, we extract a pose at the appropriate time index for each of the $N$ active clips. Then, for each joint of the skeleton, we calculate a simple $N$-point weighted average of the translation vectors, rotation quaternions, and scale factors extracted from the $N$ active animations. This yields the final pose of the skeleton.

The equation for the weighted average of a set of $N$ vectors $\{\mathbf{v}_i\}$ is as follows:

$$\mathbf{v}_{\text{avg}} = \frac{\displaystyle\sum_{i=0}^{N-1} w_i \mathbf{v}_i}{\displaystyle\sum_{i=0}^{N-1} w_i}.$$

If the weights are *normalized*, meaning they sum to one, then this equation can be simplified to the following:

$$\mathbf{v}_{\text{avg}} = \sum_{i=0}^{N-1} w_i \mathbf{v}_i \quad \left( \text{when } \sum_{i=0}^{N-1} w_i = 1 \right).$$

In the case of $N = 2$, if we let $w_1 = \beta$ and $w_0 = (1 - \beta)$, the weighted average reduces to the familiar equation for the linear interpolation (LERP) between two vectors:

$$\mathbf{v}_{\text{LERP}} = \text{LERP}[\mathbf{v}_A, \mathbf{v}_B, \beta]$$

$$= (1 - \beta)\mathbf{v}_A + \beta\mathbf{v}_B.$$

We can apply this same weighted average formulation equally well to quaternions by simply treating them as four-element vectors.

### 11.10.2.1. Example: Ogre3D

The Ogre3D animation system works in exactly this way. An `Ogre::Entity` represents an instance of a 3D mesh (e.g., one particular character walking around in the game world). The `Entity` aggregates an object called an `Ogre::AnimationStateSet`, which in turn maintains a list of `Ogre::AnimationState` objects, one for each active animation. The `Ogre::AnimationState` class is shown in the code snippet below. (A few irrelevant details have been omitted for clarity.)

```
/** Represents the state of an animation clip and the
    weight of its influence on the overall pose of the
    character.
*/
class AnimationState
{

protected:
    String              mAnimationName; // reference to
                                        // clip
    Real                mTimePos;       // local clock
    Real                mWeight;        // blend weight

    bool                mEnabled;       // is this anim
                                        // running?
```

```
    bool                mLoop;              // should the
                                            // anim loop?

public:
    /// Gets the name of the animation.
    const String& getAnimationName() const;

    /// Gets the time position (local clock) for this
    /// anim.
    Real getTimePosition(void) const;

    /// Sets the time position (local clock) for this
    /// anim.
    void setTimePosition(Real timePos);

    /// Gets the weight (influence) of this animation
    Real getWeight(void) const;

    /// Sets the weight (influence) of this animation
    void setWeight(Real weight);

    /// Modifies the time position, adjusting for
    /// animation duration. This method loops if looping
    /// is enabled.
    void addTime(Real offset);

    /// Returns true if the animation has reached the
    /// end of local time line, and is not looping.
    bool hasEnded(void) const;

    /// Returns true if this animation is currently
    /// enabled.
    bool getEnabled(void) const;

    /// Sets whether or not this animation is enabled.
    void setEnabled(bool enabled);

    /// Sets whether or not this animation should loop.
    void setLoop(bool loop) { mLoop = loop; }

    /// Gets whether or not this animation loops.
    bool getLoop(void) const { return mLoop; }

};
```

Each `AnimationState` keeps track of one animation clip's local clock and its blend weight. When calculating the final pose of the skeleton for a particular `Ogre::Entity`, Ogre's animation system simply loops through each active

`AnimationState` in its `AnimationStateSet`. A skeletal pose is extracted from the animation clip corresponding to each state at the time index specified by that state's local clock. For each joint in the skeleton, an *N*-point weighted average is then calculated for the translation vectors, rotation quaternions, and scales, yielding the final skeletal pose.

### Ogre and the Playback Rate

It is interesting to note that Ogre has no concept of a playback rate (*R*). If it did, we would have expected to see a data member like this in the `Ogre::AnimationState` class:

```
Real    mPlaybackRate;
```

Of course, we can still make animations play more slowly or more quickly in Ogre by simply scaling the amount of time we pass to the `addTime()` function, but unfortunately, Ogre does not support animation time scaling out of the box.

### 11.10.2.2. Example: Granny

The Granny animation system, by Rad Game Tools (http://www.radgame-tools.com/granny.html), provides a flat, weighted average animation blending system similar to Ogre's. Granny permits any number of animations to be played on a single character simultaneously. The state of each active animation is maintained in a data structure known as a `granny_control`. Granny calculates a weighted average to determine the final pose, automatically normalizing the weights of all active clips. In this sense, its architecture is virtually identical to that of Ogre's animation system. But where Granny really shines is in its handling of time. Granny uses the global clock approach discussed in Section 11.4.3. It allows each clip to be looped an arbitrary number of times or infinitely. Clips can also be time-scaled; a negative time scale allows an animation to be played in reverse.

## 11.10.3. Blend Trees

For reasons we'll explore below, some animation engines represent their blend specifications not as a flat weighted average but as a tree of blend operations. An animation blend tree is an example of what is known in compiler theory as an *expression tree* or a *syntax tree*. The interior nodes of such a tree are operators, and the leaf nodes serve as the inputs to those operators. (More correctly, the interior nodes represent the *non-terminals* of the grammar, while the leaf nodes represent the *terminals*.) In the following sections, we'll briefly revisit the various kinds of animation blends we learned about in Sections 11.6.3 and 11.6.5 and see how each can be represented by an expression tree.

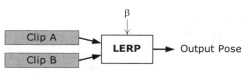

Figure 11.47. A binary LERP blend, represented by a binary expression tree.

### 11.10.3.1. Binary LERP Blend

As we saw in Section 11.6.1, a binary linear interpolation (LERP) blend takes two input poses and blends them together into a single output pose. A blend weight $\beta$ controls the percentage of the second input pose that should appear at the output, while $(1 - \beta)$ specifies the percentage of the first input pose. This can be represented by the binary expression tree shown in Figure 11.47.

### 11.10.3.2. Generalized One-Dimensional LERP Blend

In Section 11.6.3.1, we learned that it can be convenient to define a generalized one-dimensional LERP blend by placing an arbitrary number of clips along a linear scale. A blend factor $b$ specifies the desired blend along this scale. Such a blend can be pictured as an $n$-input operator, as shown in Figure 11.48.

Given a specific value for $b$, such a linear blend can always be transformed into a binary LERP blend. We simply use the two clips immediately adjacent to $b$ as the inputs to the binary blend and calculate the blend weight $\beta$ as specified in Equation (11.12). This is illustrated in Figure 11.48.

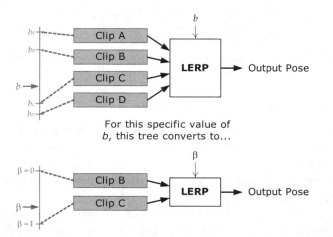

Figure 11.48. A multi-input expression tree can be used to represent a generalized 1D blend. Such a tree can always be transformed into a binary expression tree for any specific value of the blend factor b.

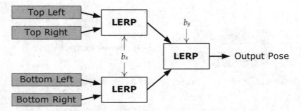

Figure 11.49. A simple 2D LERP blend, implemented as cascaded binary blends.

### 11.10.3.3. Simple Two-Dimensional LERP Blend

In Section 11.6.3.2, we saw how a two-dimensional LERP blend can be realized by simply cascading the results of two binary LERP blends. Given a desired two-dimensional blend point $\mathbf{b} = [\, b_x \ b_y \,]$, Figure 11.49 shows how this kind of blend can be represented in tree form.

### 11.10.3.4. Triangular LERP Blend

Section 11.6.3.3 introduced us to triangular LERP blending, using the barycentric coordinates $\alpha$, $\beta$, and $\gamma = (1 - \alpha - \beta)$ as the blend weights. To represent this kind of blend in tree form, we need a ternary (three-input) expression tree node, as shown in Figure 11.50.

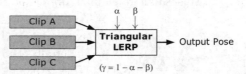

Figure 11.50. A triangular 2D LERP blend, represented as a ternary expression tree.

### 11.10.3.5. Generalized Triangular LERP Blend

In Section 11.6.3.4, we saw that a generalized two-dimensional LERP blend can be specified by placing clips at arbitrary locations on a plane. A desired output pose is specified by a point $\mathbf{b} = [\, b_x \ b_y \,]$ on the plane. This kind of blend can be represented as a tree node with an arbitrary number of inputs, as shown in Figure 11.51.

A generalized triangular LERP blend can always be transformed into a ternary tree by using Delaunay triangulation to identify the triangle that surrounds the point $\mathbf{b}$. The point is then converted into barycentric coordinates $\alpha$, $\beta$, and $\gamma = (1 - \alpha - \beta)$, and these coordinates are used as the blend weights

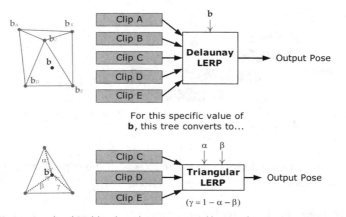

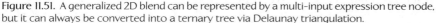

Figure 11.51. A generalized 2D blend can be represented by a multi-input expression tree node, but it can always be converted into a ternary tree via Delaunay triangulation.

of a ternary blend node with the three clips at the vertices of the triangle as its inputs. This is demonstrated in Figure 11.51.

### 11.10.3.6. Additive Blend

Section 11.6.5 described additive blending. This is a binary operation, so it can be represented by a binary tree node, as shown in Figure 11.52. A single blend weight $\beta$ controls the amount of the additive animation that should appear at the output—when $\beta = 0$, the additive clip does not affect the output at all, while when $\beta = 1$, the additive clip has its maximum effect on the output.

Additive blend nodes must be handled carefully, because the inputs are not interchangeable (as they are with most types of blend operators). One of the two inputs is a regular skeletal pose, while the other is a special kind of pose known as a *difference pose* (also known as an *additive pose*). A difference pose may *only* be applied to a regular pose, and the result of an additive blend is another regular pose. This implies that the additive input of a blend node must always be a leaf node, while the regular input may be a leaf or an interior node. If we want to apply more than one additive animation to our character,

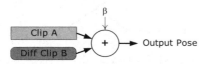

Figure 11.52. An additive blend represented as a binary tree.

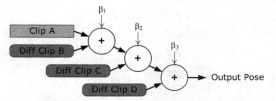

**Figure 11.53.** In order to additively blend more than one difference pose onto a regular "base" pose, a cascaded binary expression tree must be used.

we must use a cascaded binary tree with the additive clips always applied to the additive inputs, as shown in Figure 11.53.

## 11.10.4. Cross-Fading Architectures

As we saw in Section 11.6.2.2, cross-fading between animations is generally accomplished by LERP blending from the previous animation to the next one. Cross-fades can be implemented in one of two ways, depending on whether your animation engine uses the flat weighted average architecture or the expression tree architecture. In this section, we'll take a look at both implementations.

### 11.10.4.1. Cross-Fades with a Flat Weighted Average

In an animation engine that employs the flat weighted average architecture, cross-fades are implemented by adjusting the weights of the clips themselves. Recall that any clip whose weight $w_i = 0$ will not contribute to the current pose of the character, while those whose weights are non-zero are averaged together to generate the final pose. If we wish to transition smoothly from clip A to clip B, we simply ramp up clip B's weight, $w_B$, while simultaneously ramping down clip A's weight, $w_A$. This is illustrated in Figure 11.54.

Cross-fading in a weighted average architecture becomes a bit trickier when we wish to transition from one complex blend to another. As an example, let's say we wish to transition the character from walking to jumping.

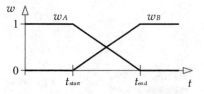

**Figure 11.54.** A simple cross-fade from clip A to clip B, as implemented in a weighted average animation architecture.

Let's assume that the walk movement is produced by a three-way average between clips A, B, and C, and that the jump movement is produced by a two-way average between clips D and E.

We want the character to look like he's smoothly transitioning from walking to jumping, without affecting how the walk or jump animations look individually. So during the transition, we want to ramp down the ABC clips and ramp up the DE clips while keeping the *relative weights* of the ABC and DE clip groups constant. If the cross-fade's blend factor is denoted by $\lambda$, we can meet this requirement by simply setting the weights of *both* clip groups to their desired values and then multiplying the weights of the source group by $(1 - \lambda)$ and the weights of the destination group by $\lambda$.

Let's look at a concrete example to convince ourselves that this will work properly. Imagine that before the transition from ABC to DE, the non-zero weights are as follows: $w_A = 0.2$, $w_B = 0.3$, and $w_C = 0.5$. After the transition, we want the non-zero weights to be $w_D = 0.33$, and $w_E = 0.66$. So, we set the weights as follows:

$$w_A = (1 - \lambda)(0.2), \qquad w_D = \lambda(0.33),$$
$$w_B = (1 - \lambda)(0.3), \qquad w_E = \lambda(0.66). \qquad (11.17)$$
$$w_C = (1 - \lambda)(0.5),$$

From Equations (11.17), you should be able to convince yourself of the following:

1. When $\lambda = 0$, the output pose is the correct blend of clips A, B, and C, with zero contribution from clips D and E.

2. When $\lambda = 1$, the output pose is the correct blend of clips D and E, with no contribution from A, B ,or C.

3. When $0 < \lambda < 1$, the *relative* weights of both the ABC group and the DE group remain correct, although they no longer add to one. (In fact, group ABC's weights add to $(1 - \lambda)$, and group DE's weights add to $\lambda$.)

For this approach to work, the implementation must keep track of the logical groupings between clips (even though, at the lowest level, all of the clips' states are maintained in one big, flat array—for example, the `Ogre::AnimationStateSet` in Ogre). In our example above, the system must "know" that A, B, and C form a group, that D and E form another group, and that we wish to transition from group ABC to group DE. This requires additional meta-data to be maintained, on top of the flat array of clip states.

### 11.10.4.2. Cross-Fades with Expression Trees

Implementing a cross-fade in an expression-tree-based animation engine is a bit more intuitive than it is in a weighted average architecture. Whether we're

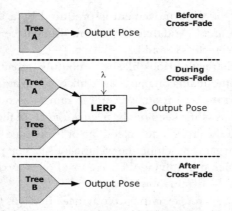

**Figure 11.55.** A cross-fade between two arbitrary blend trees A and B.

transitioning from one clip to another or from one complex blend to another, the approach is always the same: We simply introduce a new, binary LERP node at the root of the blend tree for the duration of the cross-fade.

We'll denote the blend factor of the cross-fade node with the symbol $\lambda$ as before. Its top input is the source tree (which can be a single clip or a complex blend), and its bottom input is the destination tree (again a clip or a complex blend). During the transition, $\lambda$ is ramped from zero to one. Once $\lambda = 1$, the transition is complete, and the cross-fade LERP node and its top input tree can be retired. This leaves its bottom input tree as the root of the overall blend tree, thus completing the transition. This process is illustrated in Figure 11.55.

### 11.10.5. Animation Pipeline Optimization

Optimization is a crucial aspect of any animation pipeline. Some pipelines expose all of their nitty-gritty optimization details, effectively placing the responsibility for proper optimization on the calling code. Others attempt to encapsulate most of the optimization details behind a convenient API, but even in these cases, the API still must be structured in a particular way so as to permit the desired optimizations to be implemented behind the scenes.

Animation pipeline optimizations are usually highly specific to the architecture of the hardware on which the game will run. For example, on modern hardware architectures, memory access patterns can greatly affect the performance of the code. Cache misses and load-hit-store operations must be avoided to ensure maximum speed. But on other hardware, floating-point operations might be the bottleneck, in which case the code might be structured to take maximum advantage of SIMD vector math. Each hardware platform presents a unique set of optimization challenges to the programmer. As a result, some animation pipeline APIs are highly specific to a particular platform. Other pipelines attempt to present an API that can be optimized in different ways on different processors. Let's take a look at a few examples.

### 11.10.5.1. Optimization on the PlayStation 2

The PlayStation 2 has a region of ultra-fast memory known as the *scratch pad*. It also has a fast *direct memory access* (DMA) controller, which is capable of copying data to and from the scratch pad efficiently. Some animation pipelines take advantage of this hardware architecture by arranging for all animation blending to take place within the scratch pad. When two skeletal poses are to be blended, they are DMA'd from main RAM to the scratch pad. The blend is performed, and the result is written into another buffer within the scratch pad. Finally, the resulting pose is DMA'd back into main RAM.

The PS2's DMA controller can move memory around in parallel with the main CPU. So, to maximize throughput, PS2 programmers are always looking for ways to keep the CPU and the DMA controller busy simultaneously. Often the best way to accomplish this is to use a *batch-style* API, where the game queues up requests for animation blends in a big list and then kicks everything off in one go. This permits the animation pipeline to maximize the utilization of both the DMA controller and the CPU, because it can feed a large number of pose requests through the pipeline with no "dead space" between them and even overlap the DMA of one request with the processing of an unrelated request.

### 11.10.5.2. Optimization on the PLAYSTATION 3

As we saw in Section 7.6.1.2, the PLAYSTATION 3 has six specialized processors known as *synergistic processing units* (SPU). The SPUs execute most code much more quickly than the main CPU (known as the *power processing unit* or PPU). Each SPU also has a 256 kB region of ultra-fast *local store* memory for its exclusive use. Like the PS2, the PS3 has a powerful DMA controller capable of moving memory back and forth between main RAM and the SPUs' memories in parallel with computing tasks. If one could write an ideal animation pipeline for the PS3, as much processing as possible would be executed on the SPUs, and neither the PPU nor any SPU would ever be idle waiting for a DMA to complete.

This architecture leads to animation pipeline APIs that look similar in some respects to their PlayStation 2 counterparts, in the sense that animation requests are again batched so that they can be interleaved efficiently. In addition, a PLAYSTATION 3 animation API will usually expose the concept of *animation jobs*, because a *job* is a fundamental unit of execution on the SPUs.

### 11.10.5.3. Optimization on the Xbox and Xbox 360

Rather than having specialized memory regions and a DMA controller to move data from region to region, the Xbox and the Xbox 360 both employ a unified memory architecture. All processors, including the main CPU (or in the case of the 360, the three PowerPC cores), the GPU, and all other hardware systems, tap into a single big block of main RAM.

In theory, the Xbox architecture requires a totally different set of optimizations than would be required on the PlayStation architectures, and so we might expect to see very different animation APIs between these two platforms. However, the Xbox serves as an example of how optimizations for one platform can *sometimes* be beneficial to other platforms as well. As it turns out, both the Xbox and PlayStation platforms incur massive performance degradation in the presence of cache misses and load-hit-store memory access patterns. So, it is beneficial on both systems to keep animation data as localized as possible in physical RAM. An animation pipeline that processes animations in large batches and operates on data within relatively small regions of memory (such as the PS2's scratch pad or PS3's SPU memories) will also perform well on a unified memory architecture like that of the Xbox. Achieving this kind of synergy between platforms is not always possible, and every hardware platform requires its own specific optimizations. However, when such an opportunity does arise, it is wise to take advantage of it.

A good rule of thumb is to optimize your engine for the platform with the most stringent performance restrictions. When your optimized code is ported to other platforms with fewer restrictions, there's a good chance that the optimizations you made will remain beneficial, or at worst will have few adverse affects on performance. Going in the other direction—porting from the least stringent platform to the more stringent ones—almost always results in less-than-optimal performance on the most stringent platform.

## 11.11.   Action State Machines

The low-level pipeline is the equivalent of OpenGL or DirectX for animation—it is very powerful but can be rather inconvenient for direct use by game code. Therefore, it is usually convenient to introduce a layer between the low-level pipeline and the game characters and other clients of the animation system. This layer is usually implemented as a state machine, known as the *action state machine* or the *animation state machine* (ASM).

The ASM sits on top of the animation pipeline, permitting the actions of the characters in a game to be controlled in a straightforward, state-driven manner. The ASM is also responsible for ensuring that transitions from state to state are smooth and natural-looking. Some animation engines permit multiple independent state machines to control different aspects of a character's movement, such as full-body locomotion, upper-body gestures, and facial animations. This can be accomplished by introducing the concept of state layering. In this section, we'll explore how a typical animation state machine is architected.

## 11.11.1. Animation States

Each state in an ASM corresponds to an arbitrarily complex blend of simultaneous animation clips. In a blend tree architecture, each state corresponds to a particular predefined blend tree. In a flat weighted average architecture, a state represents a group of clips with a specific set of relative weights. It is somewhat more convenient and expressive to think in terms of blend trees, so we will do so for the remainder of this discussion. However, everything we describe here can also be implemented using the flat weighted average approach, as long as additive blending or quaternion SLERP operations are not involved.

The blend tree corresponding to a particular animation state can be as simple or as complex as required by the game's design (provided it remains within the memory and performance limitations of the engine). For example, an "idle" state might be comprised of a single full-body animation. A "running" state might correspond to a semicircular blend, with strafing left, running forward, and strafing right at the −90 degrees, 0 degrees, and +90 degrees points, respectively. The blend tree for a "running while shooting" state might include a semicircular directional blend, plus additive or partial-skeleton blend nodes for aiming the character's weapon up, down, left, and right, and additional blends to permit the character to look around with its eyes, head, and shoulders. More additive animations might be included to control the character's overall stance, gait, and foot spacing while locomoting and to provide a degree of "humanness" through random movement variations.

### 11.11.1.1. State and Blend Tree Specifications

Animators, game designers, and programmers usually cooperate to create the animation and control systems for the central characters in a game. These developers need a way to specify the states that make up a character's ASM, to lay out the tree structure of each blend tree, and to select the clips that will serve as their inputs. Although the states and blend trees could be hard-coded, most modern game engines provide a *data-driven* means of defining animation states. The goal of a data-driven approach is permit a user to create new animation states, remove unwanted states, fine-tune existing states, and then see the effects of his or her changes reasonably quickly. In other words, the central goal of a data-driven animation engine is to enable *rapid iteration*.

The means by which the users enter animation state data varies widely. Some game engines employ a simple, bare-bones approach, allowing animation states to be specified in a text file with a simple syntax. Other engines provide a slick, graphical editor that permits animation states to be constructed by dragging atomic components such as clips and blend nodes onto a canvas and linking them together in arbitrary ways. Such editors usually provide a live preview of the character so that the user can see immediately how the character will look in the final game. In my opinion, the specific method chosen has little bearing on the quality of the final game—what matters most is that the user can make changes and see the results of those changes reasonably quickly and easily.

### 11.11.1.2.  Custom Blend Tree Node Types

To build an arbitrarily complex blend tree, we really only require four atomic types of blend nodes: clips, binary LERP blends, binary additive blends, and ternary (triangular) LERP blends. Virtually any blend tree imaginable can be created as compositions of these atomic nodes.

A blend tree built exclusively from atomic nodes can quickly become large and unwieldy. As a result, many game engines permit custom compound node types to be predefined for convenience. The $N$-dimensional linear blend node discussed in Sections 11.6.3.4 and 11.10.3.2 is an example of a compound node. One can imagine myriad complex blend node types, each one addressing a particular problem specific to the particular game being made. A soccer game might define a node that allows the character to dribble the ball. A war game could define a special node that handles aiming and firing a weapon. A brawler could define custom nodes for each fight move the characters can perform. Once we have the ability to define custom node types, the sky's the limit.

### 11.11.1.3.  Example: Naughty Dog's *Uncharted* Engine

The animation engine used in Naughty Dog's *Uncharted: Drake's Fortune* and *Uncharted 2: Among Thieves* employs a simple, text-based approach to specifying animation states. For reasons related to Naughty Dog's rich history with the Lisp language, state specifications in the *Uncharted* engine are written in a customized version of the Scheme programming language (which itself is a Lisp variant). Two basic state types can be used: *simple* and *complex*.

*Simple States*

A *simple* state contains a single animation clip. For example:

```
(define-state simple
    :name "pirate-b-bump-back"
    :clip "pirate-b-bump-back"
    :flags (anim-state-flag no-adjust-to-ground)
)
```

Don't let the Lisp-style syntax throw you. All this block of code does is to define a state named "pirate-b-bump-back" whose animation clip also happens to be named "pirate-b-bump-back." The :flags parameter allows users to specify various Boolean options on the state.

*Complex States*

A *complex* state contains an arbitrary tree of LERP or additive blends. For example, the following state defines a tree that contains a single binary LERP blend node, with two clips ("walk-l-to-r" and "run-l-to-r") as its inputs:

```
(define-state complex

    :name "move-l-to-r"

    :tree
        (anim-node-lerp
            (anim-node-clip "walk-l-to-r")
            (anim-node-clip "run-l-to-r")
        )
)
```

The :tree argument allows the user to specify an arbitrary blend tree, composed of LERP or additive blend nodes and nodes that play individual animation clips.

From this, we can see how the (define-state simple ...) example shown above might really work under the hood—it probably defines a complex blend tree containing a single "clip" node, like this:

```
(define-state complex
    :name "pirate-b-unimog-bump-back"
    :tree (anim-node-clip "pirate-b-unimog-bump-back")
    :flags (anim-state-flag no-adjust-to-ground)
)
```

The following complex state shows how blend nodes can be cascaded into arbitrarily deep blend trees:

```
(define-state complex

    :name "move-b-to-f"
```

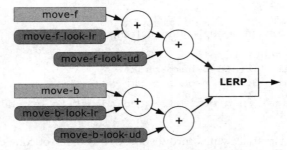

**Figure 11.56.** Blend tree corresponding to the example state "move-b-to-f."

```
:tree
  (anim-node-lerp
    (anim-node-additive
      (anim-node-additive
        (anim-node-clip "move-f")
        (anim-node-clip "move-f-look-lr")
      )

      (anim-node-clip "move-f-look-ud")
    )

    (anim-node-additive
      (anim-node-additive
        (anim-node-clip "move-b")
        (anim-node-clip "move-b-look-lr")
      )

      (anim-node-clip "move-b-look-ud")
    )
  )

)
```

This corresponds to the tree shown in Figure 11.56.

*Custom Tree Syntax*

Thanks to the powerful macro language in Scheme, custom blend trees can also be defined by the user in terms of the basic clip, LERP, and additive blend nodes. This allows us to define multiple states, each of which has a nearly identical tree structure but with different input clips or any number of other variations. For example, the complex blend tree used in the state "move-b-to-f" shown above could be partially defined via a macro as follows:

```
(define-syntax look-tree
  (syntax-rules ()
```

```
((look-tree base-clip look-lr-clip look-ud-clip)

    ;; This means "whenever the compiler sees
    ;; code of the form (look-tree b lr ud),
    ;; replace it with the following code..."

    (anim-node-additive
        (anim-node-additive
            (anim-node-clip base-clip)
            (anim-node-clip look-lr-clip)
        )
        (anim-node-clip look-ud-clip)
    )
  )
 )
)
```

The original "move-b-to-f" state could then be redefined in terms of this macro as follows:

```
(define-state complex

    :name "move-b-to-f"

    :tree
        (anim-node-lerp
            (look-tree "move-f"
                "move-f-look-lr"
                "move-f-look-ud")
            (look-tree "move-b"
                "move-b-look-lr"
                "move-b-look-ud")
        )

)
```

The (look-tree ...) macro can be used to define any number of states that require this same basic tree structure but want different animation clips as inputs. They can also combine their "look trees" in any number of ways.

### Rapid Iteration

Rapid iteration is achieved in *Uncharted* with the help of two important tools. An in-game animation viewer allows a character to be spawned into the game and its animations controlled via an in-game menu. And a simple command-line tool allows animation scripts to be recompiled and reloaded into the running game on the fly. To tweak a character's animations, the user can make changes to the text file containing the animation state specifications, quickly reload the animation states, and immediately see the effects of his or her changes on an animating character in the game.

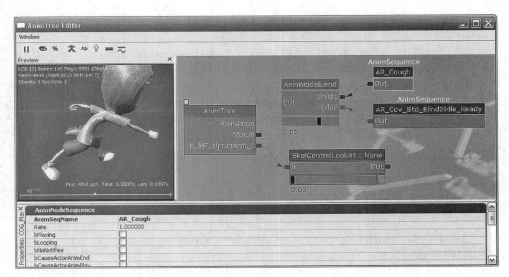

Figure 11.57.  The Unreal Engine 3 graphical animation editor.

### 11.11.1.4.   Example: Unreal Engine 3

Unreal Engine 3 (UE3) provides its users with a graphical interface to the animation system. As shown in Figure 11.57, an animation blend tree in Unreal is comprised of a special root node called an AnimTree. This node takes three kinds of inputs: animations, morphs, and special nodes known as *skel controls*. The animation input can be connected to the root of an arbitrarily complex blend tree (which happens to be drawn with poses flowing from right to left—opposite of the convention we use in this book). The "morph" input allows morph-target-based animations to drive the character; this is most often used for facial animation. The "skel control" inputs allow various kinds of procedural post-processing, such as inverse kinematics (IK), to be performed on the pose generated by the animation and/or morph trees.

*The UE3 Animation Tree*

The Unreal animation tree is essentially a blend tree. Individual animation clips (called *sequences* in Unreal) are represented by nodes of type Anim Sequence. A sequence node has a single output, which may either be connected directly to the "animation" input of the AnimTree node or to other complex node types. Unreal provides a wide selection of blend node types out of the box, including binary blends, four-way two-dimensional blends (known as *blend by aim*), and so on. It also provides various special nodes that are capable of doing things like scaling the playback rate ($R$) of a clip, mirroring the animation (which turns a right-handed motion into a left-handed one, for example), and more.

The UE3 animation tree is also highly customizable. A programmer can create new types of nodes that perform arbitrarily complex operations. So the Unreal developer is not limited to simple binary and ternary LERP blends. At the time this chapter was written, Unreal Engine 3 did not support additive animation blending out of the box, although it's certainly possible for a game team to extend the Unreal engine to support it.

It is interesting to note that Unreal's approach to character animation is not explicitly state-based. Rather than defining multiple states, each with its own local blend tree, the Unreal developer typically builds a single monolithic tree. The character can be put into different "states" by simply turning on or off certain parts of the tree. Some game teams implement a system for replacing portions of the UE3 animation tree dynamically, so that a game's monolithic tree can be broken into more manageable subtrees.

### The UE3 Post-Processing Tree (Skel Controls)

As we have seen, animation post-processing involves procedurally modifying the pose of the skeleton that has been generated by the blend tree. In UE3, skel control nodes are used for this purpose. To use a skel control, the user first creates an input on the `AnimTree` node corresponding to the joint in the skeleton that he or she wishes to control procedurally. Then a suitable skel control node is created, and its output is hooked up to the new input on the `AnimTree` node.

Unreal provides a number of skel controls out of the box, to perform foot IK (which ensures that the feet conform to ground contours), procedural "look-at" (which allows the character to look at arbitrary points in space), other forms of IK, and so on. As with animation nodes, it is quite easy for a programmer to create custom skel control nodes in order to meet the particular needs of the game being developed.

## 11.11.2.  Transitions

To create a high-quality animating character, we must carefully manage the *transitions* between states in the action state machine to ensure that the splices between animations do not have a jarring and unpolished appearance. Most modern animation engines provide a data-driven mechanism for specifying exactly how transitions should be handled. In this section, we'll explore how this mechanism works.

### 11.11.2.1. Kinds of Transitions

There are many different ways to manage the transition between states. If we know that the final pose of the source state exactly matches the first pose of the destination state, we can simply "pop" from one state to another. Otherwise, we can cross-fade from one state to the next. Cross-fading is not always a suitable choice when transitioning from state to state. For example, there is no way that a cross-fade can produce a realistic transition from lying on the ground to standing upright. For this kind of state transition, we need one or more custom animations. This kind of transition is often implemented by introducing special *transitional states* into the state machine. These states are intended for use only when going from one state to another—they are never used as a steady-state node. But because they are full-fledged states, they can be comprised of arbitrarily complex blend trees. This provides maximum flexibility when authoring custom-animated transitions.

### 11.11.2.2. Transition Parameters

When describing a particular transition between two states, we generally need to specify various parameters, controlling exactly how the transition will occur. These include but are not limited to the following.

- *Source and destination states.* To which state(s) does this transition apply?
- *Transition type.* Is the transition immediate, cross-faded, or performed via a transitional state?
- *Duration.* For cross-faded transitions, we need to specify how long the cross-fade should take.
- *Ease-in/ease-out curve type.* In a cross-faded transition, we may wish to specify the type of ease-in/ease-out curve to use to vary the blend factor during the fade.
- *Transition window.* Certain transitions can only be taken when the source animation is within a specified window of its local time line. For example, a transition from a punch animation to an impact reaction might only make sense when the arm is in the second half of its swing. If an attempt to perform the transition is made during the first half of the swing, the transition would be disallowed (or a different transition might be selected instead).

### 11.11.2.3. The Transition Matrix

Specifying transitions between states can be challenging, because the number of possible transitions is usually very large. In a state machine with $n$ states, the worst-case number of possible transitions is $n^2$. We can imagine a two-dimensional square matrix with every possible state listed along both the vertical and horizontal axes. Such a table can be used to specify all of the possible transitions from any state along the vertical axis to any other state along the horizontal axis.

In a real game, this *transition matrix* is usually quite sparse, because not all state-to-state transitions are possible. For example, transitions are usually disallowed from a death state to any other state. Likewise, there is probably no way to go from a driving state to a swimming state (without going through at least one intermediate state that causes the character to jump out of his vehicle!). The number of unique transitions in the table may be significantly less even than the number of valid transitions between states. This is because we can often re-use a single transition specification between many different pairs of states.

### 11.11.2.4. Implementing a Transition Matrix

There are all sorts of ways to implement a transition matrix. We could use a spreadsheet application to tabulate all the transitions in matrix form, or we might permit transitions to be authored in the same text file used to author our action states. If a graphical user interface is provided for state editing, transitions could be added to this GUI as well. In the following sections, we'll take a brief look at a few transition matrix implementations from real game engines.

*Example: Wild-Carded Transitions in Medal of Honor: Pacific Assault*

On *Medal of Honor: Pacific Assault* (*MOHPA*), we used the sparseness of the transition matrix to our advantage by supporting wild-carded transition specifications. For each transition specification, the names of both the source and destination states could contain asterisks (*) as a wild-card character. This allowed us to specify a single default transition from any state to any other state (via the syntax `from="*" to="*"`) and then refine this global default easily for entire categories of states. The refinement could be taken all the way down to custom transitions between specific state pairs when necessary. The *MOHPA* transition matrix looked something like this:

```
<transitions>
  // global default
  <trans from="*" to="*" type=frozen duration=0.2>

  . . .

  // default for any walk to any run
  <trans from="walk*" to="run*" type=smooth
      duration=0.15>
```

```
      ...

      // special handling from any prone to any getting-up
      // action (only valid from 2 sec to 7.5 sec on the
      // local timeline)
      <trans from="*prone" to="*get-up" type=smooth
           duration=0.1
      window-start=2.0 window-end=7.5>

      ...

      // special case between crouched walking and jumping
      <trans from="walk-crouch" to="jump" type=frozen
           duration=0.3>
      ...
   </transitions>
```

*Example: First-Class Transitions in Uncharted*

In some animation engines, high-level game code requests transitions from the current state to a new state by naming the destination state explicitly. The problem with this approach is that the calling code must have intimate knowledge of the names of the states and of which transitions are valid when in a particular state.

In Naughty Dog's *Uncharted* engine, this problem is overcome by turning state transitions from secondary implementation details into first-class entities. Each state provides a list of valid transitions to other states, and each transition is given a unique name. The names of the transitions are standardized in order to make the *effect* of each transition predictable. For example, if a transition is called "walk," then it *always* goes from the current state to a walking state of some kind, no matter what the current state is. Whenever the high-level animation control code wants to transition from state A to state B, it asks for a transition by name (rather than requesting the destination state explicitly). If such a transition can be found and is valid, it is taken; otherwise, the request fails.

The following example state defines four transitions named "reload," "step-left," "step-right," and "fire." The (transition-group ...) line invokes a previously defined group of transitions; it is useful when the same set of transitions is to be used in multiple states. The (transition-end ...) command specifies a transition that is taken upon reaching the end of the state's local time line if no other transition has been taken before then.

```
   (define-state complex
      :name "s_turret-idle"
```

```
:tree (aim-tree (anim-node-clip
                    "turret-aim-all--base")
                "turret-aim-all--left-right"
                "turret-aim-all--up-down")

:transitions (
    (transition "reload" "s_turret-reload"
        (range - -) :fade-time 0.2)

    (transition "step-left" "s_turret-step-left"
        (range - -) :fade-time 0.2)

    (transition "step-right" "s_turret-step-right"
        (range - -) :fade-time 0.2)

    (transition "fire" "s_turret-fire"
        (range - -) :fade-time 0.1)

    (transition-group "combat-gunout-idle^move")

    (transition-end "s_turret-idle")
)
)
```

The beauty of this approach may be difficult to see at first. Its primary purpose is to allow transitions and states to be modified in a data-driven manner, without requiring changes to the C++ source code in many cases. This degree of flexibility is accomplished by shielding the animation control code from knowledge of the structure of the state graph. For example, let's say that we have ten different walking states (normal, scared, crouched, injured, and so on). All of them can transition into a jumping state, but different kinds of walks might require different jump animations (e.g., normal jump, scared jump, jump from crouch, injured jump, etc.). For each of the ten walking states, we define a transition simply called "jump." At first, we can point all of these transitions to a single generic "jump" state, just to get things up and running. Later, we can fine-tune some of these transitions so that they point to custom jump states. We can even introduce transitional states between some of the "walk" states and their corresponding "jump" states. All sorts of changes can be made to the structure of the state graph and the parameters of the transitions without affecting the C++ source code—as long as the *names* of the transitions don't change.

## 11.11.3. State Layers

Most living creatures can do more than one thing at once with their bodies. For example, a human can walk around with her lower body while looking at something with her shoulders, head, and eyes and making a gesture with her hands and arms. The movements of different parts of the body aren't generally in perfect sync—certain parts of the body tend to "lead" the movements of other parts (e.g., the head leads a turn, followed by the shoulders, the hips, and finally the legs). In traditional animation, this well-known technique is known as *anticipation* [44].

This kind of movement seems to be at odds with a state-machine-based approach to animation. After all, we can only be in one state at a time. So how can we get different parts of the body to operate independently? One solution to this problem is to introduce the concept of *state layers*. Each layer can be in only one state at a time, but the layers are temporally independent of one another. The final pose of the skeleton is calculated by evaluating the blend trees on each of the $n$ layers, thus generating $n$ skeletal poses, and then blending these poses together in a predefined manner. This is illustrated in Figure 11.58.

The *Uncharted* engine uses a layered state architecture. The layers form a stack, with the bottom-most layer (called the *base layer*) always producing a full-body skeletal pose and each upper layer blending in a new full-body, partial-skeleton, or additive pose on top of the base pose. Two kinds of layers are supported: LERP and additive. A LERP layer blends its output pose with the pose generated by the layer(s) below it. An additive layer assumes that its output pose is always a difference pose and uses additive blending to combine it with the pose generated by the layer(s) below it. In effect, a layered state ma-

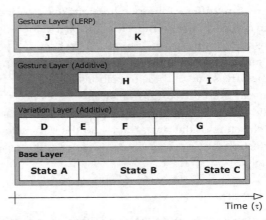
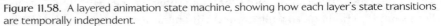

**Figure 11.58.** A layered animation state machine, showing how each layer's state transitions are temporally independent.

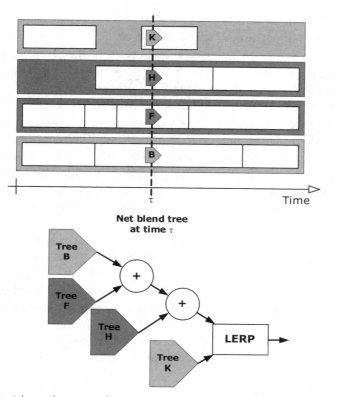

**Figure 11.59.** A layered state machine converts the blend trees from multiple states into a single, unified tree.

chine converts multiple, temporally independent blend trees (one per layer) into a single unified blend tree. This is shown in Figure 11.59.

## 11.11.4.  Control Parameters

From a software engineering perspective, it can be challenging to orchestrate all of the blend weights, playback rates, and other control parameters of a complex animating character. Different blend weights have different effects on the way the character animates. For example, one weight might control the character's movement direction, while others control its movement speed, horizontal and vertical weapon aim, head/eye look direction, and so on. We need some way of exposing all of these blend weights to the code that is responsible for controlling them.

In a flat weighted average architecture, we have a flat list of all the animation clips that could possibly be played on the character. Each clip state has a blend weight, a playback rate, and possibly other control parameters. The code that controls the character must look up individual clip states by name and adjust each one's blend weight appropriately. This makes for a simple interface, but it shifts most of the responsibility for controlling the blend weights to the character control system. For example, to adjust the direction in which a character is running, the character control code must know that the "run" action is comprised of a group of animation clips, named something like "StrafeLeft," "RunForward," "StrafeRight," and "RunBackward." It must look up these clip states by name and manually control all four blend weights in order to achieve a particular angled run animation. Needless to say, controlling animation parameters in such a fine-grained way can be tedious and can lead to difficult-to-understand source code.

In a blend tree, a different set of problems arise. Thanks to the tree structure, the clips are grouped naturally into functional units. Custom tree nodes can encapsulate complex character motions. These are both helpful advantages over the flat weighted average approach. However, the control parameters are buried within the tree. Code that wishes to control the horizontal look-at direction of the head and eyes needs *a priori* knowledge of the structure of the blend tree so that it can find the appropriate nodes in the tree in order to control their parameters.

Different animation engines solve these problems in different ways. Here are some examples:

- *Node search.* Some engines provide a way for higher-level code to *find* blend nodes in the tree. For example, relevant nodes in the tree can be given special names, such as "HorizAim" for the node that controls horizontal weapon aiming. The control code can simply search the tree for a node of a particular name; if one is found, then we know what effect adjusting its blend weight will have.

- *Named variables.* Some engines allow names to be assigned to the individual control parameters. The controlling code can look up a control parameter by name in order to adjust its value.

- *Control structure.* In other engines, a simple data structure, such as an array of floating-point values or a C `struct`, contains all of the control parameters for the entire character. The nodes in the blend tree(s) are connected to particular control parameters, either by being hard-coded to use certain `struct` members or by looking up the parameters by name or index.

Of course, there are many other alternatives as well. Every animation engine tackles this problem in a slightly different way, but the net effect is always roughly the same.

## 11.11.5. Constraints

We've seen how action state machines can be used to specify complex blend trees and how a transition matrix can be used to control how transitions between states should work. Another important aspect of character animation control is to constrain the movement of the characters and/or objects in the scene in various ways. For example, we might want to constrain a weapon so that it always appears to be in the hand of the character who is carrying it. We might wish to constrain two characters so that they line up properly when shaking hands. A character's feet are often constrained so that they line up with the floor, and its hands might be constrained to line up with the rungs on a ladder or the steering wheel of a vehicle. In this section, we'll take a brief look at how these constraints are handled in a typical animation system.

### 11.11.5.1. Attachments

Virtually all modern game engines permit objects to be attached to one another. At its simplest, object-to-object attachment involves constraining the position and/or orientation of a particular joint $J_A$ within the skeleton of object A so that it coincides with a joint $J_B$ in the skeleton of object B. An attachment is usually a parent-child relationship. When the parent's skeleton moves, the child object is adjusted to satisfy the constraint. However, when the child moves, the parent's skeleton is usually not affected. This is illustrated in Figure 11.60.

Sometimes it can be convenient to introduce an *offset* between the parent joint and the child joint. For example, when placing a gun into a character's

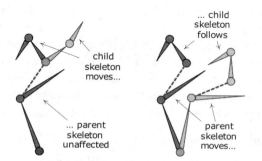

**Figure 11.60.** An attachment, showing how movement of the parent automatically produces movement of the child but not vice-versa.

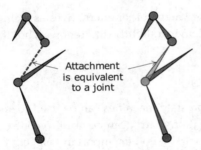

**Figure 11.61.** An attach point acts like an extra joint between the parent and the child.

hand, we could constrain the "Grip" joint of the gun so that it coincides with the "RightWrist" joint of the character. However, this might not produce the correct alignment of the gun with the hand. One solution to this problem is to introduce a special joint into one of the two skeletons. For example, we could add a "RightGun" joint to the character's skeleton, make it a child of the "RightWrist" joint, and position it so that when the "Grip" joint of the gun is constrained to it, the gun looks like it is being held naturally by the character. The problem with this approach, however, is that it increases the number of joints in the skeleton. Each joint has a processing cost associated with animation blending and matrix palette calculation and a memory cost for storing its animation keys. So adding new joints is often not a viable option.

We know that an additional joint added for attachment purposes will not contribute to the pose of the character—it merely introduces an additional transform between the parent and child joint in an attachment. What we really want, then, is a way to mark certain joints so that they can be ignored by the animation blending pipeline but can still be used for attachment purposes. Such special joints are sometimes called *attach points*. They are illustrated in Figure 11.61.

Attach points might be modeled in Maya just like regular joints or locators, although many game engines define attach points in a more convenient manner. For example, they might be specified as part of the action state machine text file or via a custom GUI within the animation authoring tool. This allows the animators to focus only on the joints that affect the look of the character, while the power to control attachments is put conveniently into the hands of the people who need it—the game designers and the engineers.

### 11.11.5.2. Interobject Registration

The interactions between game characters and their environments is growing ever more complex and nuanced with each new title. Hence, it is important to have a system that allows characters and objects to be aligned with one another when animating. Such a system can be used for in-game cinematics and interactive gameplay elements alike.

Imagine that an animator, working in Maya or some other animation tool, sets up a scene involving two characters and a door object. The two characters shake hands, and then one of them opens the door and they both walk through it. The animator can ensure that all three actors in the scene line up perfectly. However, when the animations are exported, they become three separate clips, to be played on three separate objects in the game world. The two characters might have been under AI or player control prior to the start of this animated sequence. How, then, can we ensure that the three objects line up correctly with one another when the three clips are played back in-game?

### Reference Locators

One good solution is to introduce a common reference point into all three animation clips. In Maya, the animator can drop a *locator* (which is just a 3D transform, much like a skeletal joint) into the scene, placing it anywhere that seems convenient. Its location and orientation are actually irrelevant, as we'll see. The locator is tagged in some way to tell the animation export tools that it is to be treated specially.

When the three animation clips are exported, the tools store the position and orientation of the reference locator, expressed in coordinates that are relative to the local object space of each actor, into all three clip's data files. Later, when the three clips are played back in-game, the animation engine can look up the relative position and orientation of the reference locator in all three clips. It can then transform the origins of the three objects in such a way as to make all three reference locators coincide in world space. The reference locator acts much like an *attach point* (Section 11.11.5.1) and, in fact, could be implemented as one. The net effect—all three actors now line up with one another, exactly as they had been aligned in the original Maya scene.

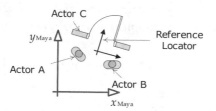

**Figure 11.62.** Original Maya scene containing three actors and a reference locator.

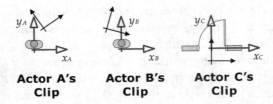

**Figure 11.63.** The reference locator is encoded in each actor's animation file.

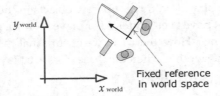

**Figure 11.64.** At runtime, the local-space reference transforms are aligned to a world-space reference locator, causing the actors to line up properly.

Figure 11.62 illustrates how the door and the two characters from the above example might be set up in a Maya scene. As shown in Figure 11.63, the reference locator appears in each exported animation clip (expressed in that actor's local space). In-game, these local-space reference locators are aligned to a fixed world-space locator in order to re-align the actors, as shown in Figure 11.64.

*Finding the World-Space Reference Location*

We've glossed over one important detail here—who decides what the world-space position and orientation of the reference locator should be? Each animation clip provides the reference locator's transform in the coordinate space of *its actor*. But we need some way to define where that reference locator should be in world space.

In our example with the door and the two characters shaking hands, one of the actors is fixed in the world (the door). So one viable solution is to ask the door for the location of the reference locator and then align the two characters to it. The commands to do accomplish this might look similar to the following pseudocode.

```
void playShakingHandsDoorSequence(
    Actor& door,
    Actor& characterA,
    Actor& characterB)
{
```

```
    // Find the world-space transform of the reference
    // locator as specified in the door's animation.
    Transform refLoc = getReferenceLocatorWs(door,
        "shake-hands-door");

    // Play the door's animation in-place. (It's alread
    // in the correct place in the world.)
    playAnimation("shake-hands-door", door);

    // Play the two characters' animations relative to
    // the world-space reference locator obtained from
    // the door.
    playAnimationRelativeToReference
        ("shake-hands-character-a", characterA, refLoc);

    playAnimationRelativeToReference
        ("shake-hands-character-b", characterB, refLoc);
}
```

Another option is to define the world-space transform of the reference locator independently of the three actors in the scene. We could place the reference locator into the world using our world-building tool, for example (see Section 13.3). In this case, the pseudocode above should be changed to look something like this:

```
void playShakingHandsDoorSequence(
    Actor& door,
    Actor& characterA,
    Actor& characterB,
    Actor& refLocatorActor)
{

    // Find the world-space transform of the reference
    // locator by simply querying the transform of an
    // independent actor (presumably placed into the
    // world manually).
    Transform refLoc = getActorTransformWs
        (refLocatorActor);

    // Play all animations relative to the world-space
    // reference locator obtained above.
    playAnimationRelativeToReference("shake-hands-door",
        door, refLoc);

    playAnimationRelativeToReference
        ("shake-hands-character-a", characterA, refLoc);

    playAnimationRelativeToReference
        ("shake-hands-character-b", characterB, refLoc);
}
```

### 11.11.5.3. Grabbing and Hand IK

Even after using an attachment to connect two objects, we sometimes find that the alignment does not look exactly right in-game. For example, a character might be holding a rifle in her right hand, with her left hand supporting the stock. As the character aims the weapon in various directions, we may notice that the left hand no longer aligns properly with the stock at certain aim angles. This kind of joint misalignment is caused by LERP blending. Even if the joints in question are aligned perfectly in clip A and in clip B, LERP blending does not guarantee that those joints will be in alignment when A and B are blended together.

One solution to this problem is to use *inverse kinematics* (IK) to correct the position of the left hand. The basic approach is to determine the desired target position for the joint in question. IK is then applied to a short chain of joints (usually two, three, or four joints), starting with the joint in question and progressing up the hierarchy to its parent, grandparent, and so on. The joint whose position we are trying to correct is known as the *end effector*. The IK solver adjusts the orientations of the end effector's parent joint(s) in order to get the end effector as close as possible to the target.

The API for an IK system usually takes the form of a request to enable or disable IK on a particular chain of joints, plus a specification of the desired target point. The actual IK calculation is usually done internally by the low-level animation pipeline. This allows it to do the calculation at the proper time—namely, after intermediate local and global skeletal poses have been calculated but before the final matrix palette calculation.

Some animation engines allow IK chains to be defined a priori. For example, we might define one IK chain for the left arm, one for the right arm, and two for the two legs. Let's assume for the purposes of this example that a particular IK chain is identified by the name of its end-effector joint. (Other engines might use an index or handle or some other unique identifier, but the concept remains the same.) The function to enable an IK calculation might look something like this:

```
void enableIkChain(
    Actor& actor,
    const char* endEffectorJointName,
    const Vector3& targetLocationWs);
```

and the function to disable an IK chain might look like this:

```
void disableIkChain(
    Actor& actor,
    const char* endEffectorJointName);
```

IK is usually enabled and disabled relatively infrequently, but the world-space target location must be kept up-to-date every frame (if the target is moving). Therefore, the low-level animation pipeline always provides some mechanism for updating an active IK target point. For example, the pipeline might allow us to call `enableIkChain()` multiple times. The first time it is called, the IK chain is enabled, and its target point is set. All subsequent calls simply update the target point.

IK is well-suited to making minor corrections to joint alignment when the joint is already reasonably close to its target. It does not work nearly as well when the error between a joint's desired location and its actual location is large. Note also that most IK algorithms solve only for the *position* of a joint. You may need to write additional code to ensure that the *orientation* of the end effector aligns properly with its target as well. IK is not a cure-all, and it may have significant performance costs. So always use it judiciously.

### 11.11.5.4. Motion Extraction and Foot IK

In games, we usually want the locomotion animations of our characters to look realistic and "grounded." One of the biggest factors contributing to the realism of a locomotion animation is whether or not the feet slide around on the ground. *Foot sliding* can be overcome in a number of ways, the most common of which are *motion extraction* and *foot IK*.

*Motion Extraction*

Let's imagine how we'd animate a character walking forward in a straight line. In Maya (or his or her animation package of choice), the animator makes

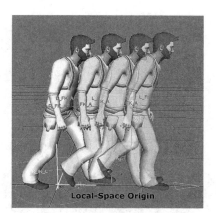

**Figure 11.65.** In the animation authoring package, the character moves forward in space, and its feet appear grounded.

the character take one complete step forward, first with the left foot and then with the right foot. The resulting animation clip is known as a *locomotion cycle*, because it is intended to be looped indefinitely, for as long as the character is walking forward in-game. The animator takes care to ensure that the feet of the character appear grounded and don't slide as it moves. The character moves from its initial location on frame 0 to a new location at the end of the cycle. This is shown in Figure 11.65.

Notice that the local-space origin of the character remains fixed during the entire walk cycle. In effect, the character is "leaving his origin behind him" as he takes his step forward. Now imagine playing this animation as a loop. We would see the character take one complete step forward, and then pop back to where he was on the first frame of the animation. Clearly this won't work in-game.

To make this work, we need to remove the forward motion of the character, so that his local-space origin remains roughly under the center of mass of the character at all times. We could do this by zeroing out the forward translation of the root joint of the character's skeleton. The resulting animation clip would make the character look like he's "moonwalking," as shown in Figure 11.66.

In order to get the feet to appear to "stick" to the ground the way they did in the original Maya scene, we need the character to move forward by just the right amount each frame. We could look at the distance the character moved, divide by the amount of time it took for him to get there, and hence find his average movement speed. But a character's forward

**Figure 11.66.** Walk cycle after zeroing out the root joint's forward motion.

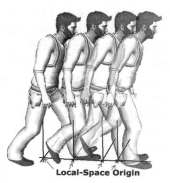

**Local-Space Origin**

**Figure 11.67.** Walk cycle in-game, with extracted root motion data applied to the local-space origin of the character.

speed is not constant when walking. This is especially evident when a character is limping (quick forward motion on the injured leg, followed by slower motion on the "good" leg), but it is true for all natural-looking walk cycles.

Therefore, before we zero out the forward motion of the root joint, we first save the animation data in a special "extracted motion" channel. This data can be used in-game to move the local-space origin of the character forward by the exact amount that the root joint had moved in Maya each frame. The net result is that the character will walk forward exactly as he was authored, but now his local-space origin comes along for the ride, allowing the animation to loop properly. This is shown in Figure 11.67.

If the character moves forward by 4 feet in the animation and the animation takes one second to complete, then we know that the character is moving at an average speed of 4 feet/second. To make the character walk at a different speed, we can simply scale the playback rate of the walk cycle animation. For example, to make the character walk at 2 feet/second, we can simply play the animation at half speed ($R = 0.5$).

*Foot IK*

Motion extraction does a good job of making a character's feet appear grounded when it is moving in a straight line (or, more correctly, when it moves in a path that exactly matches the path animated by the animator). However, a real game character must be turned and moved in ways that don't coincide with the original hand-animated path of motion (e.g., when moving over uneven terrain). This results in additional foot sliding.

One solution to this problem is to use IK to correct for any sliding in the feet. The basic idea is to analyze the animations to determine during which periods of time each foot is fully in contact with the ground. At the moment a foot contacts the ground, we note its world-space location. For all subsequent frames while that foot remains on the ground, we use IK to adjust the pose of the leg so that the foot remains fixed to the proper location. This technique sounds easy enough, but getting it to look and feel right can be very challenging. It requires a lot of iteration and fine-tuning. And some natural human motions—like leading into a turn by increasing your stride—cannot be produced by IK alone.

In addition, there is a big trade-off between the *look* of the animations and the *feel* of the character, particularly for a human-controlled character. It's generally more important for the player character control system to feel responsive and fun than it is for the character's animations to look perfect. The upshot is this: Do not take the task of adding foot IK or motion extraction to your game lightly. Budget time for a lot of trail and error, and be prepared to make trade-offs to ensure that your player character not only looks good but *feels* good as well.

### 11.11.5.5. Other Kinds of Constraints

There are plenty of other possible kinds of constraint systems that can be added to a game animation engine. Some examples include:

- *Look-at.* This is the ability for characters to look at points of interest in the environment. A character might look at a point with only his or her eyes, with eyes and head, or with eyes, head, and a twist of the entire upper body. Look-at constraints are sometimes implemented using IK or procedural joint offsets, although a more natural look can often be achieved via additive blending.

- *Cover registration.* This is the ability for a character to align perfectly with an object that is serving as cover. This is often implemented via the reference locator technique described above.

- *Cover entry and departure.* If a character can take cover, animation blending and custom entry and departure animations must usually be used to get the character into and out of cover.

- *Traversal aids.* The ability for a character to navigate over, under, around, or through obstacles in the environment can add a lot of life to a game. This is often done by providing custom animations and using a reference locator to ensure proper registration with the obstacle being overcome.

# 11.12. Animation Controllers

The animation pipeline provides high-speed animation posing and blending facilities, but its interface is usually too cumbersome to be used directly by gameplay code. The action state machine provides a more convenient interface by allowing complex blend trees to be described, often in a data-driven manner, and then encapsulated within easy-to-understand logical states. Transitions between states can also be defined, again often in a data-driven way, so that gameplay code can be written in a fire-and-forget manner, without having to micromanage every transition. The ASM system may also provide a layering mechanism, allowing the motion of a character to be described by multiple state machines running in parallel. But even given the relatively convenient interface provided by the action state machine, some game teams find it convenient to introduce a third layer of software, aimed at providing higher-level control over how characters animate. As such, it is often implemented as a collection of classes known as *animation controllers*.

Controllers tend to manage behaviors over relatively long periods of time—on the order of a few seconds or more. Each animation controller is typically responsible for one type of gross character behavior, like how to behave when in cover, how to behave when locomoting from one place to another in the game world, or how to drive a vehicle. A controller typically orchestrates all aspects of the character's animation-related behavior. It adjusts blend factors to control movement directions, aiming, and so on, manages state transitions, fades in and out layers, and does whatever else is needed to make the character behave as desired.

One benefit of a controller-based design is that all of the code relating to a particular behavioral category is localized in one place. This design also permits higher-level gameplay systems, like player mechanics or AI, to be written in a much simpler way, because all of the details of micromanaging the animations can be extracted and hidden within the controllers.

The animation controller layer takes many different forms and is highly dependent upon the needs of the game and the software design philosophies of the engineering team. Some teams don't use animation controllers at all. On other teams, the animation controllers may be tightly integrated into the AI and/or player mechanics systems. Still other teams implement a suite of relatively general-purpose controllers that can be shared between the player character and the NPCs. For better or for worse, there is no one standard way to implement animation controllers in the game industry (at least not yet).

# 12
# Collision and Rigid Body Dynamics

In the real world, solid objects are inherently, well... solid. They generally avoid doing impossible things, like passing through one another, all by themselves. But in a virtual game world, objects don't do anything unless we tell them to, and game programmers must make an explicit effort to ensure that objects do not pass through one another. This is the role of one of the central components of any game engine—the *collision detection system*.

A game engine's collision system is often closely integrated with a *physics engine*. Of course, the field of physics is vast, and what most of today's game engines call "physics" is more accurately described as a *rigid body dynamics* simulation. A *rigid body* is an idealized, infinitely hard, non-deformable solid object. The term *dynamics* refers to the process of determining how these rigid bodies *move* and *interact* over time under the influence of *forces*. A rigid body dynamics simulation allows motion to be imparted to objects in the game in a highly interactive and naturally chaotic manner—an effect that is much more difficult to achieve when using canned animation clips to move things about.

A dynamics simulation makes heavy use of the collision detection system in order to properly simulate various physical behaviors of the objects in the simulation, including bouncing off one another, sliding under friction, rolling, and coming to rest. Of course, a collision detection system can be used standalone, without a dynamics simulation—many games do not have a "physics" system at all. But all games that involve objects moving about in two- or three-dimensional space have some form of collision detection.

In this chapter, we'll investigate the architecture of both a typical collision detection system and a typical physics (rigid body dynamics) system. As we investigate the components of these two closely interrelated systems, we'll take a look at the mathematics and the theory that underlie them.

## 12.1.   Do You Want Physics in Your Game?

Nowadays, most game engines have some kind of physical simulation capabilities. Some physical effects, like rag doll deaths, are simply expected by gamers. Other effects, like ropes, cloth, hair, or complex physically driven machinery can add that *je ne sais quoi* that sets a game apart from its competitors. In recent years, some game studios have started experimenting with advanced physical simulations, including approximate real-time fluid mechanics effects and simulations of deformable bodies. But adding physics to a game is not without costs, and before we commit ourselves to implementing an exhaustive list of physics-driven features in our game, we should (at the very least) understand the trade-offs involved.

### 12.1.1.   Things You Can Do with a Physics System

Here are just a few of the things you can do or have with a game physics system.

- Detect collisions between dynamic objects and static world geometry.
- Simulate free rigid bodies under the influence of gravity and other forces.
- Spring-mass systems.
- Destructible buildings and structures.
- Ray and shape casts (to determine line of sight, bullet impacts, etc.).
- Trigger volumes (determine when objects enter, leave, or are inside pre-defined regions in the game world).
- Allow characters to pick up rigid objects.
- Complex machines (cranes, moving platform puzzles, and so on).
- Traps (such as an avalanche of boulders).
- Drivable vehicles with realistic suspensions.
- Rag doll character deaths.
- Powered rag doll: a realistic blend between traditional animation and rag doll physics.

- Dangling props (canteens, necklaces, swords), semi-realistic hair, clothing movements.
- Cloth simulations.
- Water surface simulations and buoyancy.
- Audio propagation.

And the list goes on.

We should note here that in addition to running a physics simulation at runtime in our game, we can also run a simulation as part of an offline pre-processing step in order to generate an animation clip. A number of physics plug-ins are available for animation tools like Maya. This is also the approach taken by the Endorphin package by NaturalMotion Inc. (http://www.naturalmotion.com/endorphin.htm). In this chapter, we'll restrict our discussion to runtime rigid body dynamics simulations, but off-line tools are a powerful option, of which we should always remain aware as we plan our game projects.

## 12.1.2. Is Physics Fun?

The presence of a rigid body dynamics system in a game does not necessarily make the game fun. More often than not, the inherently chaotic behavior of a physics sim can actually detract from the gameplay experience rather than enhancing it. The fun derived from physics depends on many factors, including the quality of the simulation itself, the care with which it has been integrated with other engine systems, the selection of physics-driven gameplay elements versus elements that are controlled in a more direct manner, how the physical elements interact with the goals of the player and the abilities of the player character, and the genre of game being made.

Let's take a look at a few broad game genres and how a rigid body dynamics system might fit into each one.

### 12.1.2.1. Simulations (Sims)

The primary goal of a sim is to accurately reproduce a real-life experience. Examples include the *Flight Simulator*, *Gran Turismo*, and *NASCAR Racing* series of games. Clearly, the realism provided by a rigid body dynamics system fits extremely well into these kinds of games.

### 12.1.2.2. Physics Puzzle Games

The whole idea of a physics puzzle is to let the user play around with dynamically simulated toys. So obviously this kind of game relies almost entirely on physics for its core mechanic. Examples of this genre include *Bridge Builder*,

*The Incredible Machine*, the online game *Fantastic Contraption*, and *Crayon Physics* for the iPhone.

### 12.1.2.3.  Sandbox Games

In a sandbox game, there may be no objectives at all, or there may be a large number of optional objectives. The player's primary objective is usually to "mess around" and explore what the objects in the game world can be made to do. Examples of sandbox games include *Grand Theft Auto*, *Spore*, and *LittleBigPlanet*.

Sandbox games can put a realistic dynamics simulation to good use, especially if much of the fun is derived from playing with realistic (or semi-realistic) interactions between objects in the game world. So in these contexts, physics can be fun in and of itself. However, many games trade realism for an increased fun factor (e.g., larger-than-life explosions, gravity that is stronger or weaker than normal, etc.). So the dynamics simulation may need to be tweaked in various ways to achieve the right "feel."

### 12.1.2.4.  Goal-Based and Story-Driven Games

A goal-based game has rules and specific objectives that the player must accomplish in order to progress; in a story-driven game, telling a story is of paramount importance. Integrating a physics system into these kinds of games can be tricky. We generally give away *control* in exchange for a *realistic simulation*, and this loss of control can inhibit the player's ability to accomplish goals or the game's ability to tell the story.

For example, in a character-based platformer game, we want the player character to move in ways that are fun and easy to control but not necessarily physically realistic. In a war game, we might want a bridge to explode in a realistic way, but we also may want to ensure that the debris doesn't end up blocking the player's only path forward. In these kinds of games, physics is often not necessarily fun, and in fact it can often get in the way of fun when the player's goals are at odds with the physically simulated behaviors of the objects in the game world. Therefore, developers must be careful to apply physics judiciously and take steps to control the behavior of the simulation in various ways to ensure it doesn't get in the way of gameplay.

## 12.1.3.  Impact of Physics on a Game

Adding a physics simulation to a game can have all sorts of impacts on the project and the gameplay. Here are a few examples across various game development disciplines.

### 12.1.3.1. Design Impacts

- *Predictability.* The inherent chaos and variability that sets a physically simulated behavior apart from an animated one is also a source of unpredictability. If something absolutely must happen a certain way every time, it's usually better to animate it than to try to coerce your dynamics simulation into producing the motion reliably.

- *Tuning and control.* The laws of physics (when modeled accurately) are fixed. In a game, we can tweak the value of gravity or the coefficient of restitution of a rigid body, which gives back some degree of control. However, the results of tweaking physics parameters are often indirect and difficult to visualize. It's much harder to tweak a force in order to get a character to move in the desired direction than it is to tweak an animation of a character walking.

- *Emergent behaviors.* Sometimes physics introduces unexpected features into a game—for example, the rocket-launcher jump trick in *Team Fortress Classic*, the high-flying exploding Warthog in *Halo*, and the flying "surfboards" in *PsyOps*.

In general, the game design should usually drive the physics requirements of a game engine—not the other way around.

### 12.1.3.2. Engineering Impacts

- *Tools pipeline.* A good collision/physics pipeline takes time to build and maintain.

- *User interface.* How does the player control the physics objects in the world? Does he or she shoot them? Walk into them? Pick them up? Using a virtual arm, as in *Trespasser*? Using a "gravity gun," as in *Half-Life 2*?

- *Collision detection.* Collision models intended for use within a dynamics simulation may need to be more detailed and more carefully constructed than their non-physics-driven counterparts.

- *AI.* Pathing may not be predictable in the presence of physically simulated objects. The engine may need to handle dynamic cover points that can move or blow up. Can the AI use the physics to its advantage?

- *Animation and character motion.* Animation-driven objects can clip slightly through one another with few or no ill effects, but when driven by a dynamics simulation, objects may bounce off one another in unexpected ways or jitter badly. Collision filtering may need to be applied to permit objects to interpenetrate slightly. Mechanisms may need to be put in place to ensure that objects settle and go to sleep properly.

- *Rag doll physics.* Rag dolls require a lot of fine-tuning and often suffer from instability in the simulation. An animation may drive parts of a character's body into penetration with other collision volumes—when the character turns into a rag doll, these interpenetrations can cause enormous instability. Steps must be taken to avoid this.

- *Graphics.* Physics-driven motion can have an effect on renderable objects' bounding volumes (where they would otherwise be static or more predictable). The presence of destructible buildings and objects can invalidate some kinds of precomputed lighting and shadow methods.

- *Networking and multiplayer.* Physics effects that do not affect gameplay may be simulated exclusively (and independently) on each client machine. However, physics that has an effect on gameplay (such as the trajectory that a grenade follows) must be simulated on the server and accurately replicated on all clients.

- *Record and playback.* The ability to record gameplay and play it back at a later time is very useful as a debugging/testing aid, and it can also serve as a fun game feature. This feature is much more difficult to implement in the presence of simulated dynamics because chaotic behavior (in which the simulation takes a very different path as a result of small changes in initial conditions) and differences in the timing of the physics updates can cause playbacks to fail to match the recorded original.

### 12.1.3.3. Art Impacts

- *Additional tool and workflow complexity.* The need to rig up objects with mass, friction, constraints, and other attributes for consumption by the dynamics simulation makes the art department's job more difficult as well.

- *More-complex content.* We may need multiple visually identical versions of an object with different collision and dynamics configurations for different purposes—for example, a pristine version and a destructible version.

- *Loss of control.* The unpredictability of physics-driven objects can make it difficult to control the artistic composition of a scene.

### 12.1.3.4. Other Impacts

- *Interdisciplinary impacts.* The introduction of a dynamics simulation into your game requires close cooperation between engineering, art, and design.

- *Production impacts.* Physics can add to a project's development costs, technical and organizational complexity, and risk.

Having explored the impacts, most teams today do choose to integrate a rigid body dynamics system into their games. With some careful planning and wise choices along the way, adding physics to your game can be rewarding and fruitful. And as we'll see below, third-party middleware is making physics more accessible than ever.

## 12.2. Collision/Physics Middleware

Writing a collision system and rigid body dynamics simulation is challenging and time-consuming work. The collision/physics system of a game engine can account for a significant percentage of the source code in a typical game engine. That's a lot of code to write and maintain!

Thankfully, a number of robust, high-quality collision/physics engines are now available, either as commercial products or in open-source form. Some of these are listed below. For a discussion of the pros and cons of various physics SDKs, check out the on-line game development forums (e.g., http://www.gamedev.net/community/forums/topic.asp?topic_id=463024).

### 12.2.1. I-Collide, SWIFT, V-Collide, and RAPID

I-Collide is an open-source collision detection library developed by the University of North Carolina at Chapel Hill (UNC). It can detect intersections between *convex* volumes. I-Collide has been replaced by a faster, more feature-rich library called SWIFT. UNC has also developed collision detection libraries that can handle complex non-convex shapes, called V-Collide and RAPID. None of these libraries can be used right out of the box in a game, but they might provide a good basis upon which to build a fully functional game collision detection engine. You can read more about I-Collide, SWIFT, and the other UNC geometry libraries at http://www.cs.unc.edu/~geom/I_COLLIDE/.

### 12.2.2. ODE

ODE stands for "Open Dynamics Engine" (http://www.ode.org). As its name implies, ODE is an open-source collision and rigid body dynamics SDK. Its feature set is similar to a commercial product like Havok. Its benefits include being free (a big plus for small game studios and school projects!) and the availability of full source code (which makes debugging much easier and opens up the possibility of modifying the physics engine to meet the specific needs of a particular game).

### 12.2.3. Bullet

Bullet is an open-source collision detection and physics library used by both the game and film industries. Its collision engine is integrated with its dynamics simulation, but hooks are provided so that the collision system can be used standalone or integrated with other physics engines. It supports *continuous collision detection* (CCD)—also known as *time of impact* (TOI) collision detection—which as we'll see below can be extremely helpful when a simulation includes small, fast-moving objects. The Bullet SDK is available for download at http://code.google.com/p/bullet/, and the Bullet wiki is located at http://www.bulletphysics.com/mediawiki-1.5.8/index.php?title=Main_Page.

### 12.2.4.   TrueAxis

TrueAxis is another collision/physics SDK. It is free for non-commercial use. You can learn more about TrueAxis at http://trueaxis.com.

### 12.2.5.  PhysX

PhysX started out as a library called Novodex, produced and distributed by Ageia as part of their strategy to market their dedicated physics coprocessor. It was bought by NVIDIA and is being retooled so that it can run using NVIDIA's GPUs as a coprocessor. (It can also run entirely on a CPU, without GPU support.) It is available at http://www.nvidia.com/object/nvidia_physx.html. Part of Ageia's and NVIDIA's marketing strategy has been to provide the CPU version of the SDK entirely for free, in order to drive the physics coprocessor market forward. Developers can also pay a fee to obtain full source code and the ability to customize the library as needed. PhysX is available for PC, Xbox 360, PLAYSTATION 3, and Wii.

### 12.2.6.  Havok

Havok is the gold standard in commercial physics SDKs, providing one of the richest feature sets available and boasting excellent performance characteristics on all supported platforms. (It's also the most expensive solution.) Havok is comprised of a core collision/physics engine, plus a number of optional add-on products including a vehicle physics system, a system for modeling destructible environments, and a fully featured animation SDK with direct integration into Havok's rag doll physics system. It runs on PC, Xbox 360, PLAYSTATION 3, and Wii and has been specifically optimized for each of these platforms. You can learn more about Havok at http://www.havok.com.

### 12.2.7. Physics Abstraction Layer (PAL)

The Physics Abstraction Layer (PAL) is an open-source library that allows developers to work with more than one physics SDK on a single project. It provides hooks for PhysX (Novodex), Newton, ODE, OpenTissue, Tokamak, TrueAxis, and a few other SDKs. You can read more about PAL at http://www.adrianboeing.com/pal/index.html.

### 12.2.8. Digital Molecular Matter (DMM)

Pixelux Entertainment S.A., located in Geneva, Switzerland, has produced a unique physics engine that uses finite element methods to simulate the dynamics of deformable and breakable objects, called Digital Molecular Matter (DMM). The engine has both an offline and a runtime component. It was released in 2008 and can be seen in action in LucasArts' *Star Wars: The Force Unleashed*. A discussion of deformable body mechanics is beyond our scope here, but you can read more about DMM at http://www.pixeluxentertainment.com.

## 12.3.  The Collision Detection System

The primary purpose of a game engine's collision detection system is to determine whether any of the objects in the game world have come into *contact*. To answer this question, each logical object is represented by one or more geometric *shapes*. These shapes are usually quite simple, such as spheres, boxes, and capsules. However, more-complex shapes can also be used. The collision system determines whether or not any of the shapes are *intersecting* (i.e., overlapping) at any given moment in time. So a collision detection system is essentially a glorified geometric intersection tester.

Of course, the collision system does more than answer yes/no questions about shape intersection. It also provides relevant information about the nature of each contact. Contact information can be used to prevent unrealistic visual anomalies on-screen, such as objects *interpenetrating* one another. This is generally accomplished by moving all interpenetrating objects apart prior to rendering the next frame. Collisions can provide *support* for an object—one or more contacts that together allow the object to come to rest, in equilibrium with gravity and/or any other forces acting on it. Collisions can also be used for other purposes, such as to cause a missile to explode when it strikes its target or to give the player character a health boost when he passes through a floating health pack. A rigid body dynamics simulation is often the most demanding client of the collision system, using it to mimic physically realistic behaviors like bouncing, rolling, sliding, and coming to rest. But, of course, even games that have no physics system can still make heavy use of a collision detection engine.

In this chapter, we'll go on a brief high-level tour of how collision detection engines work. For an in-depth treatment of this topic, a number of excellent books on real-time collision detection are available, including [12], [41], and [9].

### 12.3.1.  Collidable Entities

If we want a particular logical object in our game to be capable of colliding with other objects, we need to provide it with a *collision representation*, describing the object's shape and its position and orientation in the game world. This is a distinct data structure, separate from the object's *gameplay representation* (the code and data that define its role and behavior in the game) and separate from its *visual representation* (which might be an instance of a triangle mesh, a subdivision surface, a particle effect, or some other visual representation).

From the point of view of detecting intersections, we generally favor shapes that are geometrically and mathematically simple. For example, a rock might be modeled as a sphere for collision purposes; the hood of a car might be represented by a rectangular box; a human body might be approximated by a collection of interconnected *capsules* (pill-shaped volumes). Ideally, we should resort to a more-complex shape only when a simpler representation proves inadequate to achieve the desired behavior in the game. Figure 12.1 shows a few examples of using simple shapes to approximate object volumes for collision detection purposes.

Havok uses the term *collidable* to describe a distinct, rigid object that can take part in collision detection. It represents each collidable with an instance of the C++ class `hkpCollidable`. PhysX calls its rigid objects *actors* and represents them as instances of the class `NxActor`. In both of these libraries, a collidable entity contains two basic pieces of information—a *shape* and a *trans-*

Figure 12.1 Simple geometric shapes are often used to approximate the collision volumes of the objects in a game.

*form*. The shape describes the collidable's geometric form, and the transform describes the shape's position and orientation in the game world. Collidables need transforms for three reasons:

1. Technically speaking, a shape only describes the form of an object (i.e., whether it is a sphere, a box, a capsule, or some other kind of volume). It may also describe the object's size (e.g., the radius of a sphere or the dimensions of a box). But a shape is usually defined with its center at the origin and in some sort of canonical orientation relative to the coordinate axes. To be useful, a shape must therefore be transformed in order to position and orient it appropriately in world space.

2. Many of the objects in a game are dynamic. Moving an arbitrarily complex shape through space could be expensive if we had to move the *features* of the shape (vertices, planes, etc.) individually. But with a transform, any shape can be moved in space inexpensively, no matter how simple or complex the shape's features may be.

3. The information describing some of the more-complex kinds of shapes can take up a non-trivial amount of memory. So it can be beneficial to permit more than one collidable to share a single shape description. For example, in a racing game, the shape information for many of the cars might be identical. In that case, all of the car collidables in the game can share a single car shape.

Any particular object in the game may have no collidable at all (if it doesn't require collision detection services), a single collidable (if the object is a simple rigid body), or multiple collidables (each representing one rigid component of an articulated robot arm, for example).

## 12.3.2. The Collision/Physics World

A collision system typically keeps track of all of its collidable entities via a singleton data structure known as the *collision world*. The collision world is a complete representation of the game world designed explicitly for use by the collision detection system. Havok's collision world is an instance of the class `hkpWorld`. Likewise, the PhysX world is an instance of `NxScene`. ODE uses an instance of class `dSpace` to represent the collision world; it is actually the root of a hierarchy of geometric volumes representing all the collidable shapes in the game.

Maintaining all collision information in a private data structure has a number of advantages over attempting to store collision information with the game objects themselves. For one thing, the collision world need only contain collidables for those game objects that can potentially collide with one another.

This eliminates the need for the collision system to iterate over any irrelevant data structures. This design also permits collision data to be organized in the most efficient manner possible. The collision system can take advantage of cache coherency to maximize performance, for example. The collision world is also an effective encapsulation mechanism, which is generally a plus from the perspectives of understandability, maintainability, testability, and the potential for software reuse.

### 12.3.2.1. The Physics World

If a game has a rigid body dynamics system, it is usually tightly integrated with the collision system. It typically shares its "world" data structure with the collision system, and each rigid body in the simulation is usually associated with a single collidable in the collision system. This design is commonplace among physics engines because of the frequent and detailed collision queries required by the physics system. It's typical for the physics system to actually *drive* the operation of the collision system, instructing it to run collision tests at least once, and sometimes multiple times, per simulation time step. For this reason, the collision world is often called the *collision/physics world* or sometimes just the *physics world*.

Each dynamic rigid body in the physics simulation is usually associated with a single collidable object in the collision system (although not all collidables need be dynamic rigid bodies). For example, in Havok, a rigid body is represented by an instance of the class hkpRigidBody, and each rigid body has a pointer to exactly one hkpCollidable. In PhysX, the concepts of collidable and rigid body are comingled—the NxActor class serves both purposes (although the physical properties of the rigid body are stored separately, in an instance of NxBodyDesc). In both SDKs, it is possible to tell a rigid body that its location and orientation are to be fixed in space, meaning that it will be omitted from the dynamics simulation and will serve as a collidable only.

Despite this tight integration, most physics SDKs do make at least some attempt to separate the collision library from the rigid body dynamics simulation. This permits the collision system to be used as a standalone library (which is important for games that don't need physics but do need to detect collisions). It also means that a game studio could *theoretically* replace a physics SDK's collision system entirely, without having to rewrite the dynamics simulation. (Practically speaking, this may be a bit harder than it sounds!)

## 12.3.3. Shape Concepts

A rich body of mathematical theory underlies the everyday concept of *shape* (see http://en.wikipedia.org/wiki/Shape). For our purposes, we can think of a shape simply as a region of space described by a boundary, with a definite *inside* and *outside*. In two dimensions, a shape has area, and its boundary is defined either by a curved line or by three or more straight edges (in which case it's a *polygon*). In three dimensions, a shape has volume, and its boundary is either a curved surface or is composed of polygons (in which case is it called a *polyhedron*).

It's important to note that some kinds of game objects, like terrain, rivers, or thin walls, might be best represented by *surfaces*. In three-space, a surface is a two-dimensional geometric entity with a *front* and a *back* but no inside or outside. Examples include planes, triangles, subdivision surfaces, and surfaces constructed from a group of connected triangles or other polygons. Most collision SDKs provide support for surface primitives and extend the term *shape* to encompass both closed volumes and open surfaces.

It's commonplace for collision libraries to allow surfaces to be given volume via an optional extrusion parameter. Such a parameter specifies how "thick" a surface should be. Doing this helps reduce the occurrence of missed collisions between small, fast-moving objects and infinitesimally thin surfaces (the so-called "bullet through paper" problem—see Section 12.3.5.7).

### 12.3.3.1. Intersection

We all have an intuitive notion of what an *intersection* is. Technically speaking, the term comes from set theory (http://en.wikipedia.org/wiki/Intersection_(set_theory)). The intersection of two sets is comprised of the subset of members that are common to both sets. In geometrical terms, the intersection between two shapes is just the (infinitely large!) set of all points that lie inside both shapes.

### 12.3.3.2. Contact

In games, we're not usually interested in finding the intersection in the strictest sense, as a set of points. Instead, we want to know simply whether or not two objects are intersecting. In the event of a collision, the collision system will usually provide additional information about the nature of the contact. This information allows us to separate the objects in a physically plausible and efficient way, for example.

Collision systems usually package contact information into a convenient data structure that can be instanced for each contact detected. For example, Havok returns contacts as instances of the class `hkContactPoint`. Contact information often includes a *separating vector*—a vector along which we can slide the objects in order to efficiently move them out of collision. It also typically contains information about which two collidables were in contact, including which individual shapes were intersecting and possibly even which individual features of those shapes were in contact. The system may also return additional information, such as the velocity of the bodies projected onto the separating normal.

### 12.3.3.3. Convexity

One of the most important concepts in the field of collision detection is the distinction between *convex* and *non-convex* (i.e., *concave*) shapes. Technically, a convex shape is defined as one for which no ray originating inside the shape will pass through its surface more than once. A simple way to determine if a shape is convex is to imagine shrink-wrapping it with plastic film—if it's convex, no air pockets will be left under the film. So in two dimensions, circles, rectangles and triangles are all convex, but Pac Man is not. The concept extends equally well to three dimensions.

The property of *convexity* is important because, as we'll see, it's generally simpler and less computationally intensive to detect intersections between convex shapes than concave ones. See http://en.wikipedia.org/wiki/Convex for more information about convex shapes.

## 12.3.4. Collision Primitives

Collision detection systems can usually work with a relatively limited set of shape types. Some collision systems refer to these shapes as *collision primitives* because they are the fundamental building blocks out of which more-complex shapes can be constructed. In this section, we'll take a brief look at some of the most common types of collision primitives.

### 12.3.4.1. Spheres

The simplest three-dimensional volume is a sphere. And as you might expect, spheres are the most efficient kind of collision primitive. A sphere is represented by a center point and a radius. This information can be conveniently packed into a four-element floating-point vector—a format that works particularly well with SIMD math libraries.

### 12.3.4.2. Capsules

A capsule is a pill-shaped volume, composed of a cylinder and two hemispherical end caps. It can be thought of as a *swept sphere*—the shape that is traced out as a sphere moves from point A to point B. (There are, however, some important differences between a static capsule and a sphere that sweeps out a capsule-shaped volume over time, so the two are not identical.) Capsules are often represented by two points and a radius (Figure 12.2). Capsules are more

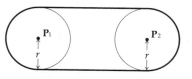

Figure 12.2. A capsule can be represented by two points and a radius.

efficient to intersect than cylinders or boxes, so they are often used to model objects that are roughly cylindrical, such as the limbs of a human body.

### 12.3.4.3. Axis-Aligned Bounding Boxes

An axis-aligned bounding box (AABB) is a rectangular volume (technically known as a *cuboid*) whose faces are parallel to the axes of the coordinate system. Of course, a box that is axis-aligned in one coordinate system will not necessarily be axis-aligned in another. So we can only speak about an AABB in the context of the particular coordinate frame(s) with which it aligns.

An AABB can be conveniently defined by two points: one containing the minimum coordinates of the box along each of the three principal axes and the other containing its maximum coordinates. This is depicted in Figure 12.3.

The primary benefit of axis-aligned boxes is that they can be tested for interpenetration with other axis-aligned boxes in a highly efficient manner. The big limitation of using AABBs is that they must remain axis-aligned at all times if their computational advantages are to be maintained. This means that if an AABB is used to approximate the shape of an object in the game, the AABB will have to be recalculated whenever that object rotates. Even if an object is roughly box-shaped, its AABB may degenerate into a very poor approximation to its shape when the object rotates off-axis. This is shown in Figure 12.4.

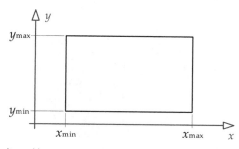

Figure 12.3. An axis-aligned box.

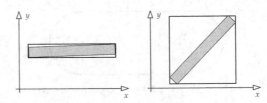

**Figure 12.4.** An AABB is only a good approximation to a box-shaped object when the object's principal axes are roughly aligned with the coorindate system's axes.

### 12.3.4.4. Oriented Bounding Boxes

If we permit an axis-aligned box to rotate relative to its coordinate system, we have what is known as an oriented bounding box (OBB). It is often represented by three half-dimensions (half-width, half-depth, and half-height) and a transformation, which positions the center of the box and defines its orientation relative to the coordinate axes. Oriented boxes are a commonly used collision primitive because they do a better job at fitting arbitrarily oriented objects, yet their representation is still quite simple.

### 12.3.4.5. Discrete Oriented Polytopes (DOP)

A discrete oriented polytope (DOP) is a more-general case of the AABB and OBB. It is a convex polytope that approximates the shape of an object. A DOP can be constructed by taking a number of planes at infinity and sliding them along their normal vectors until they come into contact with the object whose shape is to be approximated. An AABB is a 6-DOP in which the plane normals are taken parallel to the coordinate axes. An OBB is also a 6-DOP in which the plane normals are parallel to the object's natural principal axes. A $k$-DOP is constructed from an arbitrary number of planes $k$. A common method of constructing a DOP is to start with an OBB for the object in question and then bevel the edges and/or corners at 45 degrees with additional planes in an attempt to yield a tighter fit. An example of a $k$-DOP is shown in Figure 12.5.

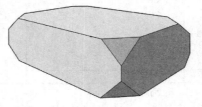

**Figure 12.5.** An OBB that has been beveled on all eight corners is known as a 14-DOP.

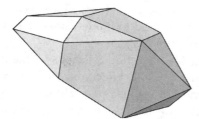

Figure 12.6. An arbitrary convex volume can be represented by a collection of intersecting planes.

### 12.3.4.6. Arbitrary Convex Volumes

Most collision engines permit arbitrary convex volumes to be constructed by a 3D artist in a package like Maya. The artist builds the shape out of polygons (triangles or quads). An off-line tool analyzes the triangles to ensure that they actually do form a convex polyhedron. If the shape passes the convexity test, its triangles are converted into a collection of planes (essentially a $k$-DOP), represented by $k$ plane equations, or $k$ points and $k$ normal vectors. (If it is found to be non-convex, it can still be represented by a polygon soup—described in the next section.) This approach is depicted in Figure 12.6.

Convex volumes are more expensive to intersection-test than the simpler geometric primitives we've discussed thus far. However, as we'll see in Section 12.3.5.5, certain highly efficient intersection-finding algorithms such as GJK are applicable to these shapes because they are convex.

### 12.3.4.7. Poly Soup

Some collision systems also support totally arbitrary, non-convex shapes. These are usually constructed out of triangles or other simple polygons. For

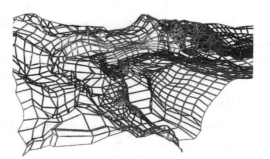

Figure 12.7. A poly soup is often used to model complex static surfaces such as terrain or buildings.

this reason, this type of shape is often called a *polygon soup,* or *poly soup* for short. Poly soups are often used to model complex static geometry, such as terrain and buildings (Figure 12.7).

As you might imagine, detecting collisions with a poly soup is the most expensive kind of collision test. In effect, the collision engine must test every individual triangle, and it must also properly handle spurious intersections with triangle edges that are shared between adjacent triangles. As a result, most games try to limit the use of poly soup shapes to objects that will not take part in the dynamics simulation.

### Does a Poly Soup Have an Inside?

Unlike convex and simple shapes, a poly soup does not necessarily represent a volume—it can represent an open surface as well. Poly soup shapes often don't include enough information to allow the collision system to differentiate between a closed volume and an open surface. This can make it difficult to know in which direction to push an object that is interpenetrating a poly soup in order to bring the two objects out of collision.

Thankfully, this is by no means an intractable problem. Each triangle in a poly soup has a front and a back, as defined by the winding order of its vertices. Therefore, it is possible to carefully construct a poly soup shape so that all of the polygons' vertex winding orders are consistent (i.e. adjacent triangles always "face" in the same direction). This gives the entire poly soup a notion of "front" and "back." If we also store information about whether a given poly soup shape is open or closed (presuming that this fact can be ascertained by off-line tools), then for closed shapes, we can interpret "front" and "back" to mean "outside" and "inside" (or vice-versa, depending on the conventions used when constructing the poly soup).

We can also "fake" an inside and outside for certain kinds of *open* poly soup shapes (i.e., surfaces). For example, if the terrain in our game is represented by an open poly soup, then we can decide arbitrarily that the front of the surface always points away from the Earth. This implies that "front" should always correspond to "outside." Practically speaking, to make this work, we would probably need to customize the collision engine in some way in order to make it aware of our particular choice of conventions.

### 12.3.4.8. Compound Shapes

Some objects that cannot be adequately approximated by a single shape can be approximated well by a *collection* of shapes. For example, a chair might be modeled out of two boxes—one for the back of the chair and one enclosing the seat and all four legs. This is shown in Figure 12.8.

**Figure 12.8.** A chair can be modeled using a pair of interconnected box shapes.

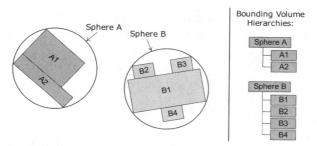

**Figure 12.9.** A collision system need only test the subshapes of a pair of compound shapes when their convex bounding volumes (in this case, Sphere A and Sphere B) are found to be intersecting.

A compound shape can often be a more-efficient alternative to a poly soup for modeling non-convex objects; two or more convex volumes can often out-perform a single poly soup shape. What's more, some collision systems can take advantage of the convex bounding volume of the compound shape as a whole when testing for collisions. In Havok, this is called *midphase* collision detection. As the example in Figure 12.9 shows, the collision system first tests the convex bounding volumes of the two compound shapes. If they do not intersect, the system needn't test the subshapes for collisions at all.

## 12.3.5. Collision Testing and Analytical Geometry

A collision system makes use of *analytical geometry*—mathematical descriptions of three-dimensional volumes and surfaces—in order to detect intersections between shapes computationally. See http://en.wikipedia.org/wiki/Analytic_geometry for more details on this profound and broad area of research. In this section, we'll briefly introduce the concepts behind analytical geometry, show a few common examples, and then discuss the generalized GJK intersection testing algorithm for arbitrary convex polyhedra.

### 12.3.5.1. Point versus Sphere

We can determine whether a point **p** lies within a sphere by simply forming the separation vector **s** between the point and the sphere's center **c** and then checking its length. If it is greater than the radius of the sphere $r$, then the point lies outside the sphere; otherwise, it lies inside:

$$\mathbf{s} = \mathbf{c} - \mathbf{p};$$
$$\text{if } |\mathbf{s}| \leq r, \text{ then } \mathbf{p} \text{ is inside.}$$

### 12.3.5.2. Sphere versus Sphere

Determining if two spheres intersect is almost as simple as testing a point against a sphere. Again, we form a vector **s** connecting the center points of the two spheres. We take its length, and compare it with the sum of the radii of the two spheres. If the length of the separating vector is less than or equal to the sum of the radii, the spheres intersect; otherwise, they do not:

$$\mathbf{s} = \mathbf{c}_1 - \mathbf{c}_2;$$
$$\text{if } |\mathbf{s}| \leq (r_1 + r_2), \text{ then spheres intersect.} \tag{12.1}$$

To avoid the square root operation inherent in calculating the length of vector **s**, we can simply square the entire equation. So Equation (12.1) becomes

$$\mathbf{s} = \mathbf{c}_1 - \mathbf{c}_2;$$
$$|\mathbf{s}|^2 = \mathbf{s} \cdot \mathbf{s};$$
$$\text{if } |\mathbf{s}|^2 \leq (r_1 + r_2)^2, \text{ then spheres intersect.}$$

### 12.3.5.3. The Separating Axis Theorem

Most collision detection systems make heavy use of a theorem known as the *separating axis theorem* (http://en.wikipedia.org/wiki/Separating_axis_theorem). It states that if an axis can be found along which the *projection* of two convex shapes do not overlap, then we can be certain that the two shapes do not intersect at all. If such an axis does not exist *and* the shapes are convex, then we know for certain that they do intersect. (If the shapes are concave, then they may not be interpenetrating despite the lack of a separating axis. This is one reason why we tend to favor convex shapes in collision detection.)

This theorem is easiest to visualize in two dimensions. Intuitively, it says that if a line can be found, such that object A is entirely on one side of the line and object B is entirely on the other side, then objects A and B do not overlap. Such a line is called a *separating line*, and it is always *perpendicular* to the separating axis. So once we've found a separating line, it's a lot easier to convince ourselves that the theory is in fact correct by looking at the projections of our shapes onto the axis that is perpendicular to the separating line.

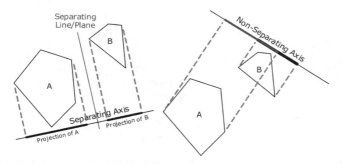

**Figure 12.10.** The projections of two shapes onto a separating axis are always two disjoint line segments. The projections of these same shapes onto a non-separating axis are not necessarily disjoint. If no separating axis exists, the shapes intersect.

The projection of a two-dimensional *convex* shape onto an axis acts like the shadow that the object would leave on a thin wire. It is always a line segment, lying on the axis, that represents the maximum extents of the object in the direction of the axis. We can also think of a projection as a minimum and maximum coordinate along the axis, which we can write as the fully closed interval $[c_{min}, c_{max}]$. As you can see in Figure 12.10, when a separating line exists between two shapes, their projections do not overlap along the separating axis. However, the projections may overlap along other, non-separating axes.

In three dimensions, the separating line becomes a separating plane, but the separating axis is still an axis (i.e., an infinite line). Again, the projection of a three-dimensional *convex* shape onto an axis is a line segment, which we can represent by the fully-closed interval $[c_{min}, c_{max}]$.

Some types of shapes have properties that make the potential separating axes obvious. To detect intersections between two such shapes A and B, we can project the shapes onto each potential separating axis in turn and then check whether or not the two projection intervals, $[c^A_{min}, c^A_{max}]$ and $[c^B_{min}, c^B_{max}]$, are disjoint (i.e., do not overlap). In math terms, the intervals are disjoint if $c^A_{max} < c^B_{min}$ or if $c^B_{max} < c^A_{min}$. If the projection intervals along one of the potential separating axes are disjoint, then we've found a separating axis, and we know the two shapes do not intersect.

One example of this principle in action is the sphere-versus-sphere test. If two spheres do not intersect, then the axis parallel to the line segment joining the spheres' center points will always be a valid separating axis (although other separating axes may exist, depending on how far apart the two spheres are). To visualize this, consider the limit when the two spheres are just about to touch but have not yet come into contact. In that case, the *only* separating

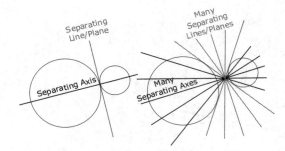

**Figure 12.11.** When two spheres are an infinitesimal distance apart, the only separating axis lies parallel to the line segment formed by the two spheres' center points.

axis is the one parallel to the center-to-center line segment. As the spheres move apart, we can rotate the separating axis more and more in either direction. This is shown in Figure 12.11.

### 12.3.5.4. AABB versus AABB

To determine whether two AABBs are intersecting, we can again apply the separating axis theorem. The fact that the faces of both AABBs are guaranteed to lie parallel to a common set of coordinate axes tells us that if a separating axis exists, it will be one of these three coordinate axes.

So, to test for intersections between two AABBs, which we'll call A and B, we merely inspect the minimum and maximum coordinates of the two boxes along each axis independently. Along the $x$-axis, we have the two intervals $[x_{min}^A, x_{max}^A]$ and $[x_{min}^B, x_{max}^B]$, and we have corresponding intervals for the $y$- and $z$-axes. If the intervals overlap along *all three axes*, then the two AABBs are intersecting—in all other cases, they are not. Examples of intersecting and non-intersecting AABBs are shown in Figure 12.12 (simplified to two dimensions for the purposes of illustration). For an in-depth discussion of AABB collision, see http://www.gamasutra.com/features/20000203/lander_01.htm.

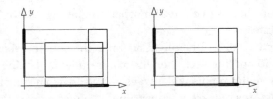

**Figure 12.12.** A two-dimensional example of intersecting and non-intersecting AABBs. Notice that even though the second pair of AABBs are intersecting along the $x$-axis, they are not intersecting along the $y$-axis.

### 12.3.5.5. Detecting Convex Collisions: The GJK Algorithm

A very efficient algorithm exists for detecting intersections between arbitrary convex *polytopes* (i.e. convex polygons in two dimensions or convex polyhedra in three dimensions). It is known as the GJK algorithm, named after its inventors, E. G. Gilbert, D. W. Johnson, and S. S. Keerthi of the University of Michigan. Many papers have been written on the algorithm and its variants, including the original paper (http://ieeexplore.ieee.org/xpl/freeabs_all. jsp?&arnumber=2083), an excellent SIGGRAPH PowerPoint presentation by Christer Ericson (http://realtimecollisiondetection.net/pubs/SIGGRAPH04_ Ericson_the_GJK_algorithm.ppt), and another great PowerPoint presentation by Gino van den Bergen (www.laas.fr/~nic/MOVIE/Workshop/Slides/Gino. vander.Bergen.ppt). However, the easiest-to-understand (and most entertaining) description of the algorithm is probably Casey Muratori's instructional video entitled, "Implementing GJK," available online at http://mollyrocket. com/353. Because these descriptions are so good, I'll just give you a feel for the essence of the algorithm here and then direct you to the Molly Rocket website and the other references cited above for additional details.

The GJK algorithm relies on a geometric operation known as the *Minkowski difference*. This fancy-sounding operation is really quite simple: We take every point that lies within shape B and subtract it pairwise from every point inside shape A. The resulting set of points $\{ (\mathbf{A}_i - \mathbf{B}_j) \}$ is the Minkowski difference.

The useful thing about the Minkowski difference is that, when applied to two convex shapes, it will *contain the origin* if and only if those two shapes intersect. Proof of this statement is a bit beyond our scope, but we can intuit why it is true by remembering that when we say two shapes A and B intersect, we really mean that there are points within A that are *also* within B. During the process of subtracting every point in B from every point in A, we would expect to eventually hit one of those shared points that lies within both shapes. A point minus itself is all zeros, so the Minkowski difference will contain the origin if (and only if) sphere A and sphere B have points in common. This is illustrated in Figure 12.13.

The Minkowski difference of two convex shapes is itself a convex shape. All we care about is the *convex hull* of the Minkowski difference, not all of the interior points. The basic procedure of GJK is to try to find a *tetrahedron* (i.e., a four-sided shape made out of triangles) that lies on the convex hull of the Minkwoski difference and that encloses the origin. If one can be found, then the shapes intersect; if one cannot be found, then they don't.

A tetrahedron is just one case of a geometrical object known as a *simplex*. But don't let that name scare you—a simplex is just a collection of points. A

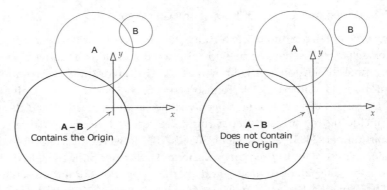

**Figure 12.13.** The Minkowski difference of two intersecting convex shapes contains the origin, but the Minkowski difference of two non-intersecting shapes does not.

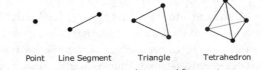

Point     Line Segment     Triangle     Tetrahedron

**Figure 12.14.** Simplexes containing one, two, three, and four points.

single-point simplex is a point, a two-point simplex is a line segment, a three-point simplex is a triangle, and a four-point simplex is a tetrahedron (see Figure 12.14).

GJK is an iterative algorithm that starts with a one-point simplex lying anywhere within the Minkowski difference hull. It then attempts to build higher-order simplexes that might potentially contain the origin. During each iteration of the loop, we take a look at the simplex we currently have and determine in which direction the origin lies relative to it. We then find a *supporting vertex* of the Minkowski difference in that direction—i.e., the vertex of the convex hull that is closest to the origin in the direction we're currently going. We add that new point to the simplex, creating a higher-order simplex (i.e., a point becomes a line segment, a line segment becomes a triangle, and a triangle becomes a tetrahedron). If the addition of this new point causes the simplex to surround the origin, then we're done—we know the two shapes intersect. On the other hand, if we are unable to find a supporting vertex that is closer to the origin than the current simplex, then we know that we can never get there, which implies that the two shapes do *not* intersect. This idea is illustrated in Figure 12.15.

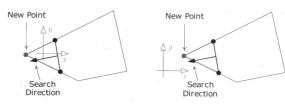
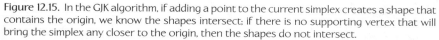

**Figure 12.15.** In the GJK algorithm, if adding a point to the current simplex creates a shape that contains the origin, we know the shapes intersect; if there is no supporting vertex that will bring the simplex any closer to the origin, then the shapes do not intersect.

To truly understand the GJK algorithm, you'll need to check out the papers and video I refernce above. But hopefully this description will whet your appetite for deeper investigation. Or, at the very least, you can impress your friends by dropping the name "GJK" at parties.

### 12.3.5.6. Other Shape-Shape Combinations

We won't cover any of the other shape-shape intersection combinations here, as they are covered well in other texts such as [12], [41], and [9]. The key point to recognize here, however, is that the *number* of shape-shape combinations is very large. In fact, for $N$ shape types, the number of pairwise tests required is $O(N^2)$. Much of the complexity of a collision engine arises because of the sheer number of intersection cases it must handle. This is one reason why the authors of collision engines usually try to limit the number of primitive types—doing so drastically reduces the number of cases the collision detector must handle. (This is also why GJK is popular—it handles collision detection between *all* convex shape types in one fell swoop. The only thing that differs from shape type to shape type is the *support function* used in the algorithm.)

There's also the practical matter of how to implement the code that selects the appropriate collision-testing function given two arbitrary shapes that are to be tested. Many collision engines use a *double dispatch* method (http://en.wikipedia.org/wiki/Double_dispatch). In single dispatch (i.e., virtual functions), the type of a single object is used to determine which concrete implementation of a particular abstract function should be called at runtime. Double dispatch extends the virtual function concept to two object types. It can be implemented via a two-dimensional function look-up table keyed by the types of the two objects being tested. It can also be implemented by arranging for a virtual function based on the type of object A to call a second virtual function based on the type of object B.

Let's take a look at a real-world example. Havok uses objects known as *collision agents* (classes derived from `hkCollisionAgent`) to handle specific intersection test cases. Concrete agent classes include `hkpSphereSphere Agent`, `hkpSphereCapsuleAgent`, `hkpGskConvexConvexAgent`, and so on. The agent types are referenced by what amounts to a two-dimensional dispatch table, managed by the class `hkpCollisionDispatcher`. As you'd expect, the dispatcher's job is to efficiently look up the appropriate agent given a pair of collidables that are to be collision-tested and then call it, passing the two collidables as arguments.

### 12.3.5.7. Detecting Collisions Between Moving Bodies

Thus far, we've considered only static intersection tests between stationary objects. When objects move, this introduces some additional complexity. Motion in games is usually simulated in discrete time steps. So one simple approach is to treat the positions and orientations of each rigid body as stationary at each time step and use static intersection tests on each "snapshot" of the collision world. This technique works as long as objects aren't moving too fast relative to their sizes. In fact, it works so well that many collision/physics engines, including Havok, use this approach by default.

However, this technique breaks down for small, fast-moving objects. Imagine an object that is moving so fast that it covers a distance *larger than its own size* (measured in the direction of travel) between time steps. If we were to overlay two consecutive snapshots of the collision world, we'd notice that there is now a gap between the fast-moving object's images in the two snapshots. If another object happens to lie within this gap, we'll miss the collision with it entirely. This problem, illustrated in Figure 12.16, is known as the "bullet through paper" problem, also known as "tunneling." The following sections describe a number of common ways to overcome this problem.

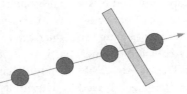

**Figure 12.16.** A small, fast-moving object can leave gaps in its motion path between consecutive snapshots of the collision world, meaning that collisions might be missed entirely.

### Swept Shapes

One way to avoid tunneling is to make use of *swept shapes*. A swept shape is a new shape formed by the motion of a shape from one point to another over time. For example, a swept sphere is a capsule, and a swept triangle is a triangular prism (see Figure 12.17).

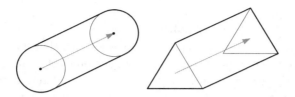

Figure 12.17. A swept sphere is a capsule; a swept triangle is a triangular prism.

Rather than testing static snapshots of the collision world for intersections, we can test the swept shapes formed by moving the shapes from their positions and orientations in the previous snapshot to their positions and orientations in the current snapshot. This approach amounts to *linearly interpolating* the motion of the collidables between snapshots, because we generally sweep the shapes along line segments from snapshot to snapshot.

Of course, linear interpolation may not be a good approximation of the motion of a fast-moving collidable. If the collidable is following a curved path, then theoretically we should sweep its shape along that curved path. Unfortunately, a convex shape that has been swept along a curve is not itself convex, so this can make our collision tests much more complex and computationally intensive.

In addition, if the convex shape we are sweeping is rotating, the resulting swept shape is not necessarily convex, even when it is swept along a line segment. As Figure 12.18 shows, we *can* always form a convex shape by linearly extrapolating the extreme features of the shapes from the previous and current snapshots—but the resulting convex shape is not necessarily an accurate representation of what the shape really would have done over the time step. Put another way, a linear interpolation is not appropriate in general for rotating shapes. So unless our shapes are not permitted to rotate, intersection

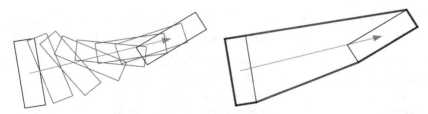

Figure 12.18. A rotating object swept along a line segment does not necessarily generate a convex shape (left). A linear interpolation of the motion does form a convex shape (right), but it can be a fairly inaccurate approximation of what actually happened during the time step.

testing of swept shapes becomes much more complex and computationally intensive than its static snapshot-based counterpart.

Swept shapes can be a useful technique for ensuring that collisions are not missed between static snapshots of the collision world state. However, the results are generally inaccurate when linearly interpolating curved paths or rotating collidables, so more-detailed techniques may be required depending on the needs of the game.

### Continuous Collision Detection (CCD)

Another way to deal with the tunneling problem is to employ a technique known as *continuous collision detection* (CCD). The goal of CCD is to find the earliest *time of impact* (TOI) between two moving objects over a given time interval.

CCD algorithms are generally iterative in nature. For each collidable, we maintain both its position and orientation at the previous time step and its position and orientation at the current time. This information can be used to linearly interpolate the position and rotation independently, yielding an approximation of the collidable's transform at any time between the previous and current time steps. The algorithm then searches for the earliest TOI along the motion path. A number of search algorithms are commonly used, including Brian Mirtich's *conservative advancement* method, performing a ray cast on the Minkowski sum, or considering the minimum TOI of individual feature pairs. Erwin Coumans of Sony Computer Entertainment describes some of these algorithms in http://www.continuousphysics.com/BulletContinuousCollisionDetection.pdf along with his own novel variation on the conservative advancement approach.

## 12.3.6. Performance Optimizations

Collision detection is a CPU-intensive task for two reasons:

1. The calculations required to determine whether two shapes intersect are themselves non-trivial.

2. Most game worlds contain a large number of objects, and the number of intersection tests required grows rapidly as the number of objects increases.

To detect intersections between $n$ objects, the brute-force technique would be to test every possible pair of objects, yielding an $O(n^2)$ algorithm. However, much more efficient algorithms are used in practice. Collision engines typically employ some form of spatial hashing (http://research.microsoft.com/~hoppe/perfecthash.pdf), spatial subdivision, or hierarchical bounding volumes in order to reduce the number of intersection tests that must be performed.

### 12.3.6.1. Temporal Coherency

One common optimization technique is to take advantage of *temporal coherency*, also known as *frame-to-frame coherency*. When collidables are moving at reasonable speeds, their positions and orientations are usually quite similar from time step to time step. We can often avoid recalculating certain kinds of information every frame by caching the results across multiple time steps. For example, in Havok, collision agents (`hkpCollisionAgent`) are usually persistent between frames, allowing them to reuse calculations from previous time steps as long as the motion of the collidables in question hasn't invalidated those calculations.

### 12.3.6.2. Spatial Partitioning

The basic idea of spatial partitioning is to greatly reduce the number of collidables that need to be checked for intersection by dividing space into a number of smaller regions. If we can determine (in an inexpensive manner) that a pair of collidables do not occupy the same region, then we needn't perform more-detailed intersection tests on them.

Various hierarchical partitioning schemes, such as octrees, binary space partitioning (BSP) trees, *k*d-trees, or sphere trees, can be used to subdivide space for the purposes of collision detection optimization. These trees subdivide space in different ways, but they all do so in a hierarchical fashion, starting with a gross subdivision at the root of the tree and further subdividing each region until sufficiently fine-grained regions have been obtained. The tree can then be walked in order to find and test groups of potentially colliding objects for actual intersections. Because the tree partitions space, we know that when we traverse down one branch of the tree, the objects in that branch cannot be colliding with objects in other sibling branches.

### 12.3.6.3. Broad Phase, Midphase, and Narrow Phase

Havok uses a three-tiered approach to prune the set of collidables that need to be tested for collisions during each time step.

- First, gross AABB tests are used to determine which collidables are potentially intersecting. This is known as *broad phase* collision detection.
- Second, the coarse bounding volumes of compound shapes are tested. This is known as *midphase* collision detection. For example, in a compound shape composed of three spheres, the bounding volume might be a fourth, larger sphere that encloses the other spheres. A compound shape may contain other compound shapes, so in general a compound collidable has a bounding volume hierarchy. The midphase traverses this hierarchy in search of subshapes that are potentially intersecting.

- Finally, the collidables' individual primitives are tested for intersection. This is known as *narrow phase* collision detection.

*The Sweep and Prune Algorithm*

In all of the major collision/physics engines (e.g., Havok, ODE, PhysX), broad phase collision detection employs an algorithm known as *sweep and prune* (http://en.wikipedia.org/wiki/Sweep_and_prune). The basic idea is to sort the minimum and maximum dimensions of the collidables' AABBs along the three principal axes, and then check for overlapping AABBs by traversing the sorted lists. Sweep and prune algorithms can make use of frame-to-frame coherency (see Section 12.3.6.1) to reduce an $O(n \log n)$ sort operation to an expected $O(n)$ running time. Frame coherency can also aid in the updating of AABBs when objects rotate.

## 12.3.7. Collision Queries

Another responsibility of the collision detection system is to answer hypothetical questions about the collision volumes in the game world. Examples include the following:

- If a bullet travels from the player's weapon in a given direction, what is the first target it will hit, if any?
- Can a vehicle move from point A to point B without striking anything along the way?
- Find all enemy objects within a given radius of a character.

In general, such operations are known as *collision queries*.

The most common kind of query is a *collision cast*, sometimes just called a *cast*. (The terms *trace* and *probe* are other common synonyms for "cast.") A cast determines what, if anything, a hypothetical object would hit if it were to be placed into the collision world and moved along a ray or line segment. Casts are different from regular collision detection operations because the entity being cast is not really in the collision world—it cannot affect the other objects in the world in any way. This is why we say that a collision cast answers *hypothetical* questions about the collidables in the world.

### 12.3.7.1. Ray Casting

The simplest type of collision cast is a *ray cast*, although this name is actually a bit of a misnomer. What we're really casting is a *directed line segment*—in other words, our casts always have a start point ($\mathbf{p}_0$) and an end point ($\mathbf{p}_1$). (Most collision systems do not support infinite rays, due to the parametric formulation used—see below.) The cast line segment is tested against the collidable objects in the collision world. If it intersects any of them, the contact point or points are returned.

Ray casting systems typically describe the line segment via its start point $\mathbf{p}_0$ and a delta vector $\mathbf{d}$ that, when added to $\mathbf{p}_0$, yields the end point $\mathbf{p}_1$. Any point on this line segment can be found via the following *parametric equation*, where the parameter $t$ is permitted to vary between zero and one:

$$\mathbf{p}(t) = \mathbf{p}_0 + t\mathbf{d}, \quad t \in [0, 1].$$

Clearly, $\mathbf{p}_0 = \mathbf{p}(0)$ and $\mathbf{p}_1 = \mathbf{p}(1)$. In addition, any contact point along the segment can be uniquely described by specifying the value of the parameter $t$ corresponding to the contact. Most ray casting APIs return their contact points as "$t$ values," or they permit a contact point to be converted into its corresponding $t$ by making an additional function call.

Most collision detection systems are capable of returning the *earliest contact*—i.e., the contact point that lies closest to $\mathbf{p}_0$ and corresponds to the smallest value of $t$. Some systems are also capable of returning a complete list of all collidables that were intersected by the ray or line segment. The information returned for each contact typically includes the $t$ value, some kind of unique identifier for the collidable entity that was hit, and possibly other information such as the surface normal at the point of contact or other relevant properties of the shape or surface that was struck. One possible contact point data structure is shown below.

```
struct RayCastContact
{
    F32         m_t;              // the t value for this
                                  // contact

    U32         m_collidableId;   // which collidable did we
                                  // hit?

    Vector      m_normal;         // surface normal at
                                  // contact pt.
    // other information...
};
```

*Applications of Ray Casts*

Ray casts are used heavily in games. For example, we might want to ask the collision system whether character A has a direct line of sight to character B. To determine this, we simply cast a directed line segment from the eyes of character A to the chest of character B. If the ray hits character B, we know that A can "see" B. But if the ray strikes some other object *before* reaching character B, we know that the line of sight is being blocked by that object. Ray casts are used by weapon systems (e.g., to determine bullet hits), player mechanics (e.g., to determine whether or not there is solid ground beneath the character's feet), AI systems (e.g., line of sight checks, targeting, movement queries, etc.), vehicle systems (e.g., to locate and snap the vehicle's tires to the terrain), and so on.

### 12.3.7.2.  Shape Casting

Another common query involves asking the collision system how far an imaginary convex shape would be able to travel along a directed line segment before it hits something solid. This is known as a *sphere cast* when the volume being cast is a sphere, or a *shape cast* in general. (Havok calls them *linear casts*.) As with ray casts, a shape cast is usually described by specifying the start point $\mathbf{p}_0$, the distance to travel $\mathbf{d}$, and of course the type, dimensions, and orientation of the shape we wish to cast.

There are two cases to consider when casting a convex shape.

1. The cast shape is already interpenetrating or contacting at least one other collidable, preventing it from moving away from its starting location.

2. The cast shape is not intersecting with anything else at its starting location, so it is free to move a non-zero distance along its path.

In the first scenario, the collision system typically reports the contact(s) between the cast shape and all of the collidables with which it is initially interpenetrating. These contacts might be *inside* the cast shape or on its *surface*, as shown in Figure 12.19.

In the second case, the shape can move a non-zero distance along the line segment before striking something. Presuming that it hits something, it will usually be a single collidable. However, it is possible for a cast shape to strike more than one collidable simultaneously if its trajectory is just right. And of course, if the impacted collidable is a non-convex poly soup, the cast shape

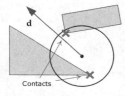

**Figure 12.19.** A cast sphere that starts in penetration will be unable to move, and the possibly many contact points will lie inside the cast shape in general.

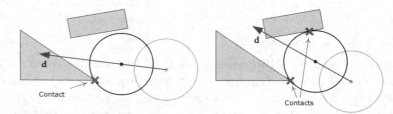

Figure 12.20. If the starting location of a cast shape is not interpenetrating anything, then the shape will move a non-zero distance along its line segment, and its contacts (if any) will always be on its surface.

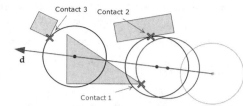

**Figure 12.21.** A shape casting API might return all contacts instead of only the earliest contact.

may end up touching more than one part of the poly soup simultaneously. We can safely say that no matter what kind of convex shape is cast, it is *possible* (albeit unlikely) for the cast to generate multiple contact points. The contacts will always be on the *surface* of the cast shape in this case, never inside it (because we know that the cast shape was not interpenetrating anything when it started its journey). This case is illustrated in Figure 12.20.

As with ray casts, some shape casting APIs report only the *earliest* contact(s) experienced by the cast shape, while others allow the shape to continue along its hypothetical path, returning all the contacts it experiences on its journey. This is illustrated in Figure 12.21.

The contact information returned by a shape cast is necessarily a bit more complex than it is for a ray cast. We cannot simply return one or more $t$ values, because a $t$ value only describes the location of the center point of the shape along its path. It tells us nothing of where, on the surface or interior of the shape, it came into contact with the impacted collidable. As a result, most shape casting APIs return both a $t$ value and the actual contact point, along with other relevant information (such as which collidable was struck, the surface normal at the contact point, etc.).

Unlike ray casting APIs, a shape casting system must always be capable of reporting multiple contacts. This is because even if we only report the contact with the earliest $t$ value, the shape may have touched multiple distinct collidables in the game world, or it may be touching a single non-convex collidable at more than one point. As a result, collision systems usually return an array or list of contact point data structures, each of which might look something like this:

```
struct ShapeCastContact
{
    F32        m_t;                 // the t value for this
                                    // contact

    U32        m_collidableId;  // which collidable did we
                                    // hit?
```

```
    Point       m_contactPoint; // location of actual
                                // contact

    Vector      m_normal;       // surface normal at
                                // contact pt.
    // other information...
};
```

Given a list of contact points, we often want to distinguish between the groups of contact points for each distinct $t$ value. For example, the earliest contact is actually described by the group of contact points that all share the minimum $t$ in the list. It's important to realize that collision systems may or may not return their contact points sorted by $t$. If it does not, it's almost always a good idea to sort the results by $t$ manually. This ensures that if one looks at the first contact point in the list, it will be guaranteed to be among the earliest contact points along the shape's path.

*Applications of Shape Casts*

Shape casts are extremely useful in games. Sphere casts can be used to determine whether the virtual camera is in collision with objects in the game world. Sphere or capsule casts are also commonly used to implement character movement. For example, in order to slide the character forward on uneven terrain, we can cast a sphere or capsule that lies between the character's feet in the direction of motion. We can adjust it up or down via a second cast, to ensure that it remains in contact with the ground. If the sphere hits a very short vertical obstruction, such as a street curb, it can "pop up" over the curb. If the vertical obstruction is too tall, like a wall, the cast sphere can be slid horizontally along the wall. The final resting place of the cast sphere becomes the character's new location next frame.

### 12.3.7.3. Phantoms

Sometimes, games need to determine which collidable objects lie within some specific volume in the game world. For example, we might want the list of all enemies that are within a certain radius of the player character. Havok supports a special kind of collidable object known as a *phantom* for this purpose.

A phantom acts much like a shape cast whose distance vector **d** is zero. At any moment, we can ask the phantom for a list of its contacts with other collidables in the world. It returns this data in essentially the same format that would be returned by a zero-distance shape cast.

However, unlike a shape cast, a phantom is persistent in the collision world. This means that it can take full advantage of the temporal coherency optimizations used by the collision engine when detecting collisions between "real" collidables. In fact, the only difference between a phantom and a regular collidable is that it is "invisible" to all other collidables in the collision world (and it does not take part in the dynamics simulation). This allows it to answer hypothetical questions about what objects it would collide with were it a "real" collidable, but it is guaranteed not to have any effect of the other collidables—including other phantoms—in the collision world.

### 12.3.7.4. Other Types of Queries

Some collision engines support other kinds of queries in addition to casts. For example, Havok supports *closest point* queries, which are used to find the set of points on other collidables that are closest to a given collidable in the collision world.

## 12.3.8. Collision Filtering

It is quite common for game developers to want to enable or disable collisions between certain kinds of objects. For example, most objects are permitted to pass through the surface of a body of water—we might employ a buoyancy simulation to make them float, or they might just sink to the bottom, but in either case we do not want the water's surface to appear solid. Most collision engines allow contacts between collidables to be accepted or rejected based on game-specific critiera. This is known as *collision filtering*.

### 12.3.8.1. Collision Masking and Layers

One common filtering approach is to categorize the objects in the world and then use a look-up table to determine whether certain categories are permitted to collide with one another or not. For example, in Havok, a collidable can be a member of one (and only one) collision layer. The default collision filter in Havok, represented by an instance of the class `hkpGroupFilter`, maintains a 32-bit mask for each layer, each bit of which tells the system whether or not that particular layer can collide with one of the other layers.

### 12.3.8.2. Collision Callbacks

Another filtering technique is to arrange for the collision library to invoke a *callback function* whenever a collision is detected. The callback can inspect the specifics of the collision and make the decision to either allow or reject the collision based on suitable criteria. Havok also supports this kind of filtering. When contact points are first added to the world, the `contactPointAdded()` callback is invoked. If the contact point is later determined to be valid (it may not be if an earlier TOI contact was found), the `contactPointConfirmed()` callback is invoked. The application may reject contact points in these callbacks if desired.

### 12.3.8.3. Game-Specific Collision Materials

Game developers often need to categorize the collidable objects in the game world, in part to control how they collide (as with collision filtering) and in part to control other secondary effects, such as the sound that is made or the particle effect that is generated when one type of object hits another. For example, we might want to differentiate between wood, stone, metal, mud, water, and human flesh.

To accomplish this, many games implement a collision shape categorization mechanism similar in many respects to the *material system* used in the rendering engine. In fact, some game teams use the term *collision material* to describe this categorization. The basic idea is to associate with each collidable surface a set of properties that defines how that particular surface should behave from a physical and collision standpoint. Collision properties can include sound and particle effects, physical properties like coefficient of restitution or friction coefficients, collision filtering information, and whatever other information the game might require.

For simple convex primitives, the collision properties are usually associated with the shape as a whole. For poly soup shapes, the properties might be specified on a per-triangle basis. Because of this latter usage, we usually try to keep the binding between the collision primitive and its collision material as compact as possible. A typical approach is to bind collision primitives to collision materials via an 8-, 16-, or 32-bit integer. This integer indexes into a global array of data structures containing the detailed collision properties themselves.

## 12.4. Rigid Body Dynamics

Many game engines include a *physics system* for the purposes of simulating the motion of the objects in the virtual game world in a somewhat physically realistic way. Technically speaking, game physics engines are typically concerned with a particular field of physics known as *mechanics*. This is the study of how forces affect the behavior of objects. In a game engine, we are particularly concerned with the *dynamics* of objects—how they move over time. Until very recently, game physics systems have been focused almost exclusively on a specific subdiscipline of mechanics known as *classical rigid body dynamics*. This name implies that in a game's physics simulation, two important simplifying assumptions are made:

- *Classical (Newtonian) mechanics.* The objects in the simulation are assumed to obey Newton's laws of motion. The objects are large enough that there are no quantum effects, and their speeds are low enough that there are no relativistic effects.

- *Rigid bodies.* All objects in the simulation are perfectly solid and cannot be deformed. In other words, their shape is constant. This idea meshes well with the assumptions made by the collision detection system. Furthermore, the assumption of rigidity greatly simplifies the mathematics required to simulate the dynamics of solid objects.

Game physics engines are also capable of ensuring that the motions of the rigid bodies in the game world conform to various *constraints*. The most common constraint is that of non-penetration—in other words, objects aren't allowed to pass through one another. Hence the physics system attempts to provide realistic *collision responses* whenever bodies are found to be interpenetrating. This is one of the primary reasons for the tight interconnection between the physics engine and the collision detection system.

Most physics systems also allow game developers to set up other kinds of constraints in order to define realistic interactions between physically simulated rigid bodies. These may include hinges, prismatic joints (sliders), ball joints, wheels, "rag dolls" to emulate unconscious or dead characters, and so on.

The physics system usually shares the collision world data structure, and in fact it usually drives the execution of the collision detection algorithm as part of its time step update routine. There is typically a one-to-one mapping between the rigid bodies in the dynamics simulation and the collidables managed by the collision engine. For example, in Havok, an `hkpRigidBody` object maintains a reference to one and only one `hkpCollidable` (although it is possible to create a collidable that has no rigid body). In PhysX, the two concepts are a bit more tightly integrated—an `NxActor` serves both as a collidable object and as a rigid body for the purposes of the dynamics simulation. These rigid bodies and their corresponding collidables are usually maintained in a singleton data structure known as the *collision/physics world*, or sometimes just the *physics world*.

The rigid bodies in the physics engine are typically distinct from the logical objects that make up the virtual world from a gameplay perspective. The positions and orientations of game objects can be driven by the physics simulation. To accomplish this, we query the physics engine every frame for the transform of each rigid body, and apply it in some way to the transform of the corresponding game object. It's also possible for a game object's motion, as determined by some other engine system (such as the animation system or the character control system) to drive the position and rotation of a rigid body in the physics world. As mentioned in Section 12.3.1, a single logical game object may be represented by one rigid body in the physics world, or by many.

A simple object like a rock, weapon or barrel, might correspond to one rigid body. But an articulated character or a complex machine might be composed of many interconnected rigid pieces.

The remainder of this chapter will be devoted to investigating how game physics engines work. We'll briefly introduce the theory that underlies rigid body dynamics simulations. Then we'll investigate some of the most common features of a game physics system and have a look at how a physics engine might be integrated into a game.

### 12.4.1.  Some Foundations

A great many excellent books, articles, and slide presentations have been written on the topic of classical rigid body dynamics. A solid foundation in analytical mechanics theory can be obtained from [15]. Even more relevant to our discussion are texts like [34], [11], and [25], which have been written specifically about the kind of physics simulations done by games. Other texts, like [1], [9], and [28], include chapters on rigid body dynamics for games. Chris Hecker wrote a series of helpful articles on the topic of game physics for *Game Developer Magazine*; Chris has posted these and a variety of other useful resources at http://chrishecker.com/Rigid_Body_Dynamics. An informative slide presentation on dynamics simulation for games was produced by Russell Smith, the primary author of ODE; it is available at http://www.ode.org/slides/parc/dynamics.pdf.

In this section, I'll summarize the fundamental theoretical concepts that underlie the majority of game physics engines. This will be a whirlwind tour only, and by necessity I'll have to omit some details. Once you've read this chapter, I strongly encourage you to read at least a few of the additional resources cited above.

#### 12.4.1.1.  Units

Most rigid body dynamics simulations operate in the MKS system of units. In this system, distance is measured in meters (abbreviated "m"), mass is measured in kilograms (abbreviated "kg"), and time is measured in seconds (abbreviated "s"). Hence the name MKS.

You could configure your physics system to use other units if you wanted to, but if you do this, you need to make sure everything in the simulation is consistent. For example, constants like the acceleration due to gravity $\mathbf{g}$, which is measured in m/s$^2$ in the MKS system, would have to be re-expressed in whatever unit system you select. Most game teams just stick with MKS to keep life simple.

### 12.4.1.2. Separability of Linear and Angular Dynamics

An *unconstrained* rigid body is one that can translate freely along all three Cartesian axes and that can rotate freely about these three axes as well. We say that such a body has six *degrees of freedom* (DOF).

It is perhaps somewhat surprising that the motion of an unconstrained rigid body can be separated into two independent components:

- *Linear dynamics.* This is a description of the motion of the body when we ignore all rotational effects. (We can use linear dynamics alone to describe the motion of an idealized *point mass*—i.e., a mass that is infinitesimally small and cannot rotate.)

- *Angular dynamics.* This is a description of the rotational motion of the body.

As you can well imagine, this ability to separate the linear and angular components of a rigid body's motion is extremely helpful when analyzing or simulating its behavior. It means that we can calculate a body's linear motion without regard to rotation—as if it were an idealized point mass—and then layer its angular motion on top in order to arrive at a complete description of the body's motion.

### 12.4.1.3. Center of Mass

For the purposes of *linear* dynamics, an unconstrained rigid body acts as though all of its mass were concentrated at a single point known as the *center of mass* (abbreviated CM, or sometimes COM). The center of mass is essentially the balancing point of the body for all possible orientations. In other words, the mass of a rigid body is distributed evenly around its center of mass in all directions.

For a body with uniform density, the center of mass lies at the *centroid* of the body. That is, if we were to divide the body up into $N$ very small pieces, add up the positions of all these pieces as a vector sum, and then divide by the number of pieces, we'd end up with a pretty good approximation to the location of the center of mass. If the body's density is not uniform, the position of each little piece would need to be *weighted* by that piece's mass, meaning that in general the center of mass is really a *weighted average* of the pieces' positions. So we have

$$\mathbf{r}_{CM} = \frac{\sum_{\forall i} m_i\, \mathbf{r}_i}{\sum_{\forall i} m_i} = \frac{\sum_{\forall i} m_i\, \mathbf{r}_i}{m},$$

where the symbol $\mathbf{r}$ represents a *radius vector* or *position vector*—i.e., a vector extending from the world space origin to the point in question. (These sums become integrals in the limit as the sizes and masses of the little pieces approach zero.)

The center of mass always lies inside a convex body, although it may actually lie outside the body if it is concave. (For example, where would the center of mass of the letter "C" lie?)

## 12.4.2. Linear Dynamics

For the purposes of linear dynamics, the position of a rigid body can be fully described by a position vector $\mathbf{r}_{CM}$ that extends from the world space origin to the center of mass of the body, as shown in Figure 12.22. Since we're using the MKS system, position is measured in meters (m). For the remainder of this discussion, we'll drop the CM subscripts, as it is understood that we are describing the motion of the body's center of mass.

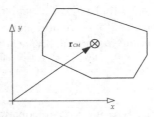

Figure 12.22. For the purposes of linear dynamics, the position of a rigid body can be fully described by the position of its center of mass.

### 12.4.2.1. Linear Velocity and Acceleration

The *linear velocity* of a rigid body defines the speed and direction in which the body's CM is moving. It is a vector quantity, typically measured in meters per second (m/s). Velocity is the first time derivative of position, so we can write

$$\mathbf{v}(t) = \frac{d\mathbf{r}(t)}{dt} = \dot{\mathbf{r}}(t),$$

where the dot over the vector $\mathbf{r}$ denotes taking the derivative with respect to time. Differentiating a vector is the same as differentiating each component independently, so

$$v_x(t) = \frac{dr_x(t)}{dt} = \dot{r}_x(t),$$

and so on for the $y$- and $z$-components.

Linear acceleration is the first derivative of linear velocity with respect to time, or the second derivative of the position of a body's CM versus time. Acceleration is a vector quantity, usually denoted by the symbol $\mathbf{a}$. So we can write

$$\mathbf{a}(t) = \frac{d\mathbf{v}(t)}{dt} = \dot{\mathbf{v}}(t)$$

$$= \frac{d^2\mathbf{r}(t)}{dt^2} = \ddot{\mathbf{r}}(t).$$

#### 12.4.2.2. Force and Momentum

A *force* is defined as anything that causes an object with mass to accelerate or decelerate. A force has both a magnitude and a direction in space, so all forces are represented by vectors. A force is often denoted by the symbol $\mathbf{F}$. When $N$ forces are applied to a rigid body, their net effect on the body's linear motion is found by simply adding up the force vectors:

$$\mathbf{F}_{net} = \sum_{i=1}^{N} \mathbf{F}_i.$$

Newton's famous Second Law states that force is proportional to acceleration and mass:

$$\mathbf{F}(t) = m\,\mathbf{a}(t) = m\,\ddot{\mathbf{r}}(t). \tag{12.2}$$

As Newton's law implies, force is measured in units of kilogram-meters per second squared (kg-m/s²). This unit is also called the Newton.

When we multiply a body's linear velocity by its mass, the result is a quantity known as *linear momentum*. It is customary to denote linear momentum with the symbol $\mathbf{p}$:

$$\mathbf{p}(t) = m\,\mathbf{v}(t).$$

When mass is constant, Equation (12.2) holds true. But if mass is not constant, as would be the case for a rocket whose fuel is being gradually used up and converted into energy, Equation (12.2) is not exactly correct. The proper formulation is actually as follows:

$$\mathbf{F}(t) = \frac{d\mathbf{p}(t)}{dt} = \frac{d(m\,\mathbf{v}(t))}{dt},$$

which of course reduces to the more familiar $\mathbf{F} = m\mathbf{a}$ when the mass is constant and can be brought outside the derivative. Linear momentum is not of much concern to us. However, the concept of momentum will become relevant when we discuss angular dynamics.

### 12.4.3. Solving the Equations of Motion

The central problem in rigid body dynamics is to solve for the motion of the body, given a set of known forces acting on it. For linear dynamics, this means finding $\mathbf{v}(t)$ and $\mathbf{r}(t)$ given knowledge of the net force $\mathbf{F}_{net}(t)$ and possibly other information, such as the position and velocity at some previous time. As we'll see below, this amounts to solving a pair of ordinary differential equations—one to find $\mathbf{v}(t)$ given $\mathbf{a}(t)$ and the other to find $\mathbf{r}(t)$ given $\mathbf{v}(t)$.

### 12.4.3.1.  Force as a Function

A force can be constant, or it can be a function of time as shown above. A force can also be a function of the position of the body, its velocity, or any number of other quantities. So in general, the expression for force should really be written as follows:

$$\mathbf{F}\big(t,\ \mathbf{r}(t),\ \mathbf{v}(t),\ ...\big) = m\,\mathbf{a}(t). \tag{12.3}$$

This can be rewritten in terms of the position vector and its first and second derivatives as follows:

$$\mathbf{F}\big(t,\ \mathbf{r}(t),\ \dot{\mathbf{r}}(t),\ ...\big) = m\,\ddot{\mathbf{r}}(t).$$

For example, the force exerted by a spring is proportional to how far it has been stretched away from its natural resting position. In one dimension, with the spring's resting position at $x = 0$, we can write

$$F\big(t,\ x(t)\big) = -k\,x(t),$$

where $k$ is the *spring constant*, a measure of the spring's stiffness.

As another example, the damping force exerted by a mechanical viscous damper (a so-called dashpot) is proportional to the velocity of the damper's piston. So in one dimension, we can write

$$F\big(t,\ v(t)\big) = -b\,v(t),$$

where $b$ is a *viscous damping coefficient*.

### 12.4.3.2.  Ordinary Differential Equations

In general, an *ordinary differential equation* (ODE) is an equation involving a function of one independent variable and various derivatives of that function. If our independent variable is time and our function is $x(t)$, then an ODE is a relation of the form

$$\frac{d^n x}{dt^n} = f\left(t,\ x(t),\ \frac{dx(t)}{dt},\ \frac{d^2 x(t)}{dt^2},\ ...\ ,\ \frac{d^{n-1}x(t)}{dt^{n-1}}\right).$$

Put another way, the $n$th derivative of $x(t)$ is expressed as a function $f$ whose arguments can be time $(t)$, position $(x(t))$, and any number of derivatives of $x(t)$ as long as those derivatives are of *lower order* than $n$.

As we saw in Equation (12.3), force is a function of time, position, and velocity in general:

$$\ddot{\mathbf{r}}(t) = \frac{1}{m}\mathbf{F}\big(t,\ \mathbf{r}(t),\ \dot{\mathbf{r}}(t)\big). \tag{12.18}$$

This clearly qualifies as an ODE. We wish to solve this ODE in order to find $\mathbf{v}(t)$ and $\mathbf{r}(t)$.

### 12.4.3.3. Analytical Solutions

In some rare situations, the differential equations of motion can be solved *analytically*, meaning that a simple, closed-form function can be found that describes the body's position for *all possible values* of time $t$. A common example is the vertical motion of a projectile under the influence of a constant acceleration due to gravity, $\mathbf{a}(t) = [\ 0,\ g,\ 0\ ]$, where $g = -9.8$ m/s². In this case, the ODE of motion boils down to

$$\ddot{y}(t) = g.$$

Integrating once yields

$$\dot{y}(t) = gt + v_0,$$

where $v_0$ is the vertical velocity at time $t = 0$. Integrating a second time yields the familiar solution

$$y(t) = \tfrac{1}{2}gt^2 + v_0 t + y_0,$$

where $y_0$ is the initial vertical position of the object.

However, analytical solutions are almost never possible in game physics. This is due in part to the fact that closed-form solutions to some differential equations are simply not known. Moreover, a game is an interactive simulation, so we cannot predict how the forces in a game will behave over time. This makes it impossible to find simple, closed-form expressions for the positions and velocities of the objects in the game as functions of time.

## 12.4.4. Numerical Integration

For the reasons cited above, game physics engines turn to a technique known as *numerical integration*. With this technique, we solve our differential equations in a *time-stepped* manner—using the solution from a previous time step to arrive at the solution for the next time step. The duration of the time step is usually taken to be (roughly) constant and is denoted by the symbol $\Delta t$. Given that we know the body's position and velocity at the current time $t_1$ and that the force is known as a function of time, position, and/or velocity, we wish to find the position and velocity at the next time step $t_2 = t_1 + \Delta t$. In other words, given $\mathbf{r}(t_1)$, $\mathbf{v}(t_1)$, and $\mathbf{F}(t, \mathbf{r}, \mathbf{v})$, the problem is to find $\mathbf{r}(t_2)$ and $\mathbf{v}(t_2)$.

### 12.4.4.1. Explicit Euler

One of the simplest numerical solutions to an ODE is known as the *explicit Euler method*. This is the intuitive approach often taken by new game programmers. Let's assume for the moment that we already know the current velocity and that we wish to solve the following ODE to find the body's position on the next frame:

$$\mathbf{v}(t) = \dot{\mathbf{r}}(t). \tag{12.4}$$

Using the explicit Euler method, we simply convert the velocity from meters per second into meters per frame by multiplying by the time delta, and then we add "one frame's worth" of velocity onto the current position in order to find the new position on the next frame. This yields the following approximate solution to the ODE given by Equation (12.4):

$$\mathbf{r}(t_2) = \mathbf{r}(t_1) + \mathbf{v}(t_1)\Delta t. \tag{12.5}$$

We can take an analogous approach to find the body's velocity next frame given the net force acting this frame. Hence, the approximate explicit Euler solution to the ODE

$$\mathbf{a}(t) = \frac{\mathbf{F}_{\text{net}}(t)}{m} = \dot{\mathbf{v}}(t)$$

is as follows:

$$\mathbf{v}(t_2) = \mathbf{v}(t_1) + \frac{\mathbf{F}_{\text{net}}(t_1)}{m}\Delta t. \tag{12.6}$$

*Interpretations of Explicit Euler*

What we're really doing in Equation (12.5) is assuming that the velocity of the body is constant during the time step. Therefore, we can use the *current* velocity to predict the body's position on the *next* frame. The change in position $\Delta \mathbf{r}$ between times $t_1$ and $t_2$ is hence $\Delta \mathbf{r} = \mathbf{v}(t_1)\,\Delta t$. Graphically, if we imagine a plot of the position of the body versus time, we are taking the *slope* of the function at time

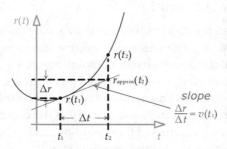

Figure 12.23. In the explicit Euler method, the slope of r(t) at time $t_1$ is used to linearly extrapolate from r($t_1$) to an estimate of the true value of r($t_2$).

$t_1$ (which is just $\mathbf{v}(t_1)$) and extrapolating it linearly to the next time step $t_2$. As we can see in Figure 12.23, linear extrapolation does not necessarily provide us with a particularly good estimate of the true position at the next time step $\mathbf{r}(t_2)$, but it does work reasonably well as long as the velocity is roughly constant.

Figure 12.23 suggests another way to interpret the explicit Euler method — as an approximation of a derivative. By definition, any derivative is the quotient of two infinitesimally small differences (in our case, $d\mathbf{r}/dt$). The explicit Euler method approximates this using the quotient of two *finite* differences. In other words, $d\mathbf{r}$ becomes $\Delta \mathbf{r}$ and $dt$ becomes $\Delta t$. This yields

$$\frac{d\mathbf{r}}{dt} \approx \frac{\Delta \mathbf{r}}{\Delta t};$$
$$\mathbf{v}(t_1) = \frac{\mathbf{r}(t_2) - \mathbf{r}(t_1)}{t_2 - t_1} = \frac{\mathbf{r}(t_2) - \mathbf{r}(t_1)}{\Delta t}.$$

which again simplifies to Equation (12.5). This approximation is really only valid when the velocity is constant over the time step. It is also valid in the limit as $\Delta t$ tends toward zero (at which point it becomes *exactly* right). Obviously, this same analysis can be applied to Equation (12.6) as well.

### 12.4.4.2. Properties of Numerical Methods

We've implied that the explicit Euler method is not particularly accurate. Let's pin this idea down more concretely. A numerical solution to an ordinary differential equation actually has three important and interrelated properties:

- *Convergence.* As the time step $\Delta t$ tends toward zero, does the approximate solution get closer and closer to the real solution?

- *Order.* Given a particular numerical approximation to the solution of an ODE, how "bad" is the error? Errors in numerical ODE solutions are typically proportional to some power of the time step duration $\Delta t$, so they are often written using big "O" notation (e.g., $O(\Delta t^2)$). We say that a particular numerical method is of "order $n$" when its error term is $O(\Delta t^{(n+1)})$.

- *Stability.* Does the numerical solution tend to "settle down" over time? If a numerical method adds energy into the system, object velocities will eventually "explode," and the system will become *unstable*. On the other hand, if a numerical method tends to remove energy from the system, it will have an overall damping effect, and the system will be *stable*.

The concept of order warrants a little more explanation. We usually measure the error of a numerical method by comparing its approximate equation with the infinite Taylor series expansion of the exact solution to the ODE. We then cancel terms by subtracting the two equations. The remaining Taylor terms represent the error inherent in the method. For example, the explicit Euler equation is

$$\mathbf{r}(t_2) = \mathbf{r}(t_1) + \dot{\mathbf{r}}(t_1)\Delta t.$$

The infinite Taylor series expansion of the exact solution is

$$\mathbf{r}(t_2) = \mathbf{r}(t_1) + \dot{\mathbf{r}}(t_1)\Delta t + \tfrac{1}{2}\ddot{\mathbf{r}}(t_1)\Delta t^2 + \tfrac{1}{6}\dddot{\mathbf{r}}(t_1)\Delta t^3 + \dots.$$

Therefore, the error is represented by all of the terms after the $\mathbf{v}\,\Delta t$ term, which is of order $O(\Delta t^2)$ (because this term dwarfs the other higher-order terms):

$$\mathbf{E} = \tfrac{1}{2}\ddot{\mathbf{r}}(t_1)\Delta t^2 + \tfrac{1}{6}\dddot{\mathbf{r}}(t_1)\Delta t^3 + \dots$$
$$= O(\Delta t^2).$$

To make the error of a method explicit, we'll often write its equation with the error term added in big "O" notation at the end. For example, the explicit Euler method's equation is most accurately written as follows:

$$\mathbf{r}(t_2) = \mathbf{r}(t_1) + \dot{\mathbf{r}}(t_1)\Delta t + O(\Delta t^2).$$

We say that the explicit Euler method is an "order one" method because it is accurate up to *and including* the Taylor series term involving $\Delta t$ to the first power. In general, if a method's error term is $O(\Delta t^{(n+1)})$, then it is said to be an "order $n$" method.

### 12.4.4.3. Alternatives to Explicit Euler

The explicit Euler method sees quite a lot of use for simple integration tasks in games, producing the best results when the velocity is nearly constant. However, it is not used in general-purpose dynamics simulations because of its high error and poor stability. There are all sorts of other numerical methods for solving ODEs, including backward Euler (another first-order method), midpoint Euler (a second-order method), and the family of Runge-Kutta methods. (The fourth-order Runge-Kutta, often abbreviated "RK4," is particularly popular.) We won't describe these in any detail here, as you can find voluminous information about them online and in the literature. The Wikipedia page http://en.wikipedia.org/wiki/Numerical_ordinary_differential_equations serves as an excellent jumping-off point for learning these methods.

### 12.4.4.4. Verlet Integration

The numerical ODE method most often used in interactive games these days is probably the Verlet method, so I'll take a moment to describe it in some detail. There are actually two variants of this method: regular Verlet and the so-called *velocity Verlet*. I'll present both methods here, but I'll leave the theory and deep explanations to the myriad papers and Web pages available on the topic. (For a start, check out http://en.wikipedia.org/wiki/Verlet_integration.)

The regular Verlet method is attractive because it achieves a high order (low error), is relatively simple and inexpensive to evaluate, and produces a solution for position directly in terms of acceleration in one step (as opposed to the two steps normally required to go from acceleration to velocity and then from velocity to position). The formula is derived by adding two Taylor series expansions, one going forward in time and one going backward in time:

$$\mathbf{r}(t_1 + \Delta t) = \mathbf{r}(t_1) + \dot{\mathbf{r}}(t_1)\Delta t + \tfrac{1}{2}\ddot{\mathbf{r}}(t_1)\Delta t^2 + \tfrac{1}{6}\dddot{\mathbf{r}}(t_1)\Delta t^3 + O(\Delta t^4);$$

$$\mathbf{r}(t_1 - \Delta t) = \mathbf{r}(t_1) - \dot{\mathbf{r}}(t_1)\Delta t + \tfrac{1}{2}\ddot{\mathbf{r}}(t_1)\Delta t^2 - \tfrac{1}{6}\dddot{\mathbf{r}}(t_1)\Delta t^3 + O(\Delta t^4).$$

Adding these expressions causes the negative terms to cancel with the corresponding positive ones. The result gives us the position at the next time step in terms of the acceleration and the two (known) positions at the current and previous time steps. This is the regular Verlet method:

$$\mathbf{r}(t_1 + \Delta t) = 2\mathbf{r}(t_1) - \mathbf{r}(t_1 - \Delta t) + \mathbf{a}(t_1)\Delta t^2 + O(\Delta t^4).$$

In terms of net force, the Verlet method becomes

$$\mathbf{r}(t_1 + \Delta t) = 2\mathbf{r}(t_1) - \mathbf{r}(t_1 - \Delta t) + \frac{\mathbf{F}_{\text{net}}(t_1)}{m}\Delta t^2 + O(\Delta t^4).$$

The velocity is conspicuously absent from this expression. However, it can be found using the following somewhat inaccurate approximation (among other alternatives):

$$\mathbf{v}(t_1 + \Delta t) = \frac{\mathbf{r}(t_1 + \Delta t) - \mathbf{r}(t_1)}{\Delta t} + O(\Delta t).$$

## 12.4.4.5. Velocity Verlet

The more commonly used *velocity Verlet* method is a four-step process in which the time step is divided into two parts to facilitate the solution. Given that $\mathbf{a}(t_1) = \dfrac{\mathbf{F}(t_1,\ \mathbf{r}(t_1),\ \mathbf{v}(t_1))}{m}$ is known, we do the following:

1. Calculate $\mathbf{r}(t_1 + \Delta t) = \mathbf{r}(t_1) + \mathbf{v}(t_1)\Delta t + \tfrac{1}{2}\mathbf{a}(t_1)\Delta t^2$.

2. Calculate $\mathbf{v}(t_1 + \tfrac{1}{2}\Delta t) = \mathbf{v}(t_1) + \tfrac{1}{2}\mathbf{a}(t_1)\Delta t$.

3. Determine $\mathbf{a}(t_1 + \Delta t) = \mathbf{a}(t_2) = \dfrac{\mathbf{F}(t_2,\ \mathbf{r}(t_2),\ \mathbf{v}(t_2))}{m}$.

4. Calculate $\mathbf{v}(t_1 + \Delta t) = \mathbf{v}(t_1 + \tfrac{1}{2}\Delta t) + \tfrac{1}{2}\mathbf{a}(t_1 + \Delta t)\Delta t$.

Notice in the third step that the force function depends on the position and velocity on the *next* time step, $\mathbf{r}(t_2)$ and $\mathbf{v}(t_2)$. We already calculated $\mathbf{r}(t_2)$ in step 1, so we have all the information we need as long as the force is not velocity-dependent. If it is velocity-dependent, then we must approximate next frame's velocity, perhaps using the explicit Euler method.

### 12.4.5. Angular Dynamics in Two Dimensions

Up until now, we've focused on analyzing the linear motion of a body's center of mass (which acts as if it were a point mass). As I said earlier, an unconstrained rigid body will rotate about its center of mass. This means that we can layer the angular motion of a body on top of the linear motion of its center of mass in order to arrive at a complete description of the body's overall motion. The study of a body's rotational motion in response to applied forces is called *angular dynamics*.

In two dimensions, angular dynamics works almost identically to linear dynamics. For each linear quantity, there's an angular analog, and the mathematics works out quite neatly. So let's investigate two-dimensional angular dynamics first. As we'll see, when we extend the discussion into three dimensions, things get a bit messier, but we'll burn that bridge when we get to it!

#### 12.4.5.1. Orientation and Angular Speed

In two dimensions, every rigid body can be treated as a thin sheet of material. (Some physics texts refer to such a body as a *plane lamina*.) All linear motion occurs in the $xy$-plane, and all rotations occur about the $z$-axis. (Visualize wooden puzzle pieces sliding about on an air hockey table.)

The orientation of a rigid body in 2D is fully described by an angle $\theta$, measured in radians relative to some agreed-upon zero rotation. For example, we might specify that $\theta = 0$ when a race car is facing directly down the positive $x$-axis in world space. This angle is of course a time-varying function, so we denote it $\theta(t)$.

#### 12.4.5.2. Angular Speed and Acceleration

Angular velocity measures the rate at which a body's rotation angle changes over time. In two dimensions, angular velocity is a scalar, more correctly called angular *speed*, since the term "velocity" really only applies to vectors. It is denoted by the scalar function $\omega(t)$ and measured in radians per second (rad/s). Angular speed is the derivative of the orientation angle $\theta(t)$ with respect to time:

$$\text{Angular: } \omega(t) = \frac{d\theta(t)}{dt} = \dot{\theta}(t); \quad \bigg| \quad \text{Linear: } \mathbf{v}(t) = \frac{d\mathbf{r}(t)}{dt} = \dot{\mathbf{r}}(t).$$

And as we'd expect, angular acceleration, denoted $\alpha(t)$ and measured in radians per second squared (rad/s$^2$), is the rate of change of angular speed:

$$\text{Angular:} \quad \alpha(t) = \frac{d\omega(t)}{dt} \qquad \bigg| \qquad \text{Linear:} \quad \mathbf{a}(t) = \frac{d\mathbf{v}(t)}{dt}$$

$$= \dot{\omega}(t) = \ddot{\theta}(t); \qquad \qquad \qquad = \dot{\mathbf{v}}(t) = \ddot{\mathbf{r}}(t).$$

### 12.4.5.3. Moment of Inertia

The rotational equivalent of mass is a quantity known as the *moment of inertia*. Just as mass describes how easy or difficult it is to change the linear velocity of a point mass, the moment of inertia measures how easy or difficult it is to change the angular speed of a rigid body about a particular axis. If a body's mass is concentrated near an axis of rotation, it will be relatively easier to rotate about that axis, and it will hence have a smaller moment of inertia than a body whose mass is spread out away from that axis.

Since we're focusing on two-dimensional angular dynamics right now, the axis of rotation is always $z$, and a body's moment of inertia is a simple scalar value. Moment of inertia is usually denoted by the symbol $I$. We won't get into the details of how to calculate the moment of inertia here. For a full derivation, see [15].

### 12.4.5.4. Torque

Until now, we've assumed that all forces are applied to the center of mass of a rigid body. However, in general, forces can be applied at arbitrary points on a body. If the line of action of a force passes through the body's center of mass, then the force will produce linear motion only, as we've already seen. Otherwise, the force will introduce a rotational force known as a *torque* in addition to the linear motion it normally causes. This is illustrated in Figure 12.24.

We can calculate torque using a cross product. First, we express the location at which the force is applied as a vector $\mathbf{r}$ extending from the body's center of mass to the point of application of the force. (In other words, the vector $\mathbf{r}$ is in *body space*, where the origin of body space is defined to be the center of

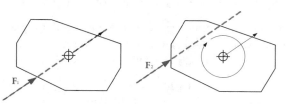

**Figure 12.24.** On the left, a force applied to a body's CM produces purely linear motion. On the right, a force applied off-center will give rise to a torque, producing rotational motion as well as linear motion.

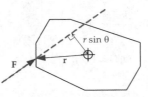

**Figure 12.25.** Torque is calculated by taking the cross product between a force's point of application in body space (i.e., relative to the center of mass) and the force vector. The vectors are shown here in two dimensions for ease of illustration; if it could be drawn, the torque vector would be directed into the page.

mass.) This is illustrated in Figure 12.25. The torque $\mathbf{N}$ caused by a force $\mathbf{F}$ applied at a location $\mathbf{r}$ is

$$\mathbf{N} = \mathbf{r} \times \mathbf{F}. \tag{12.7}$$

Equation (12.7) implies that torque increases as the force is applied farther from the center of mass. This explains why a lever can help us to move a heavy object. It also explains why a force applied directly through the center of mass produces no torque and no rotation—the magnitude of the vector $\mathbf{r}$ is zero in this case.

When two or more forces are applied to a rigid body, the torque vectors produced by each one can be summed, just as we can sum forces. So in general we are interested in the net torque, $\mathbf{N}_{\text{net}}$.

In two dimensions, the vectors $\mathbf{r}$ and $\mathbf{F}$ must both lie in the $xy$-plane, so $\mathbf{N}$ will always be directed along the positive or negative $z$-axis. As such, we'll denote a two-dimensional torque via the scalar $N_z$, which is just the $z$-component of the vector $\mathbf{N}$.

Torque is related to angular acceleration and moment of inertia in much the same way that force is related to linear acceleration and mass:

$$
\text{Angular:} \quad
\begin{aligned}
N_z &= I\alpha(t) \\
&= I\dot{\omega}(t) = I\ddot{\theta}(t);
\end{aligned}
\quad \Bigg| \quad
\text{Linear:} \quad
\begin{aligned}
\mathbf{F} &= m\mathbf{a}(t) \\
&= m\dot{\mathbf{v}}(t) = m\ddot{\mathbf{r}}(t).
\end{aligned}
\tag{12.8}
$$

### 12.4.5.5. Solving the Angular Equations of Motion in Two Dimensions

For the two-dimensional case, we can solve the angular equations of motion using exactly the same numerical integration techniques we applied to the linear dynamics problem. The pair of ODEs that we wish to solve is as follows:

$$
\text{Angular:} \quad
\begin{aligned}
N_{\text{net}}(t) &= I\dot{\omega}(t); \\
\omega(t) &= \dot{\theta}(t);
\end{aligned}
\quad \Bigg| \quad
\text{Linear:} \quad
\begin{aligned}
\mathbf{F}_{\text{net}}(t) &= m\,\dot{\mathbf{v}}(t); \\
\mathbf{v}(t) &= \dot{\mathbf{r}}(t),
\end{aligned}
$$

and their approximate explicit Euler solutions are

Angular:
$$\omega(t_2) = \omega(t_1) + \frac{N_{\text{net}}(t_1)}{I}\Delta t;$$
$$\theta(t_2) = \theta(t_1) + \omega(t_1)\Delta t;$$

Linear:
$$\mathbf{v}(t_2) = \mathbf{v}(t_1) + \frac{\mathbf{F}_{\text{net}}(t_1)}{m}\Delta t;$$
$$\mathbf{r}(t_2) = \mathbf{r}(t_1) + \mathbf{v}(t_1)\Delta t.$$

Of course, we could apply any of the other more-accurate numerical methods as well, such as the velocity Verlet method (I've omitted the linear case here for compactness, but compare this to the steps given in Section 12.4.4.5):

1. Calculate $\theta(t_1 + \Delta t) = \theta(t_1) + \omega(t_1)\Delta t + \frac{1}{2}\alpha(t_1)\Delta t^2$.

2. Calculate $\omega(t_1 + \frac{1}{2}\Delta t) = \omega(t_1) + \frac{1}{2}\alpha(t_1)\Delta t$.

3. Determine $\alpha(t_1 + \Delta t) = \alpha(t_2) = I^{-1}N_{\text{net}}(t_2, \theta(t_2), \omega(t_2))$.

4. Calculate $\omega(t_1 + \Delta t) = \omega(t_1 + \frac{1}{2}\Delta t) + \frac{1}{2}\alpha(t_1 + \Delta t)\Delta t$.

## 12.4.6. Angular Dynamics in Three Dimensions

Angular dynamics in three dimensions is a somewhat more complex topic than its two-dimensional counterpart, although the basic concepts are of course very similar. In the following section, I'll give a very brief overview of how angular dynamics works in 3D, focusing primarily on the things that are typically confusing to someone who is new to the topic. For further information, check out Glenn Fiedler's series of articles on the topic, available at http://gafferongames.wordpress.com/game-physics. Another helpful resource is the paper entitled "An Introduction to Physically Based Modeling" by David Baraff of the Robotics Institute at Carnegie Mellon University, available at http://www-2.cs.cmu.edu/~baraff/sigcourse/notesd1.pdf.

### 12.4.6.1. The Inertia Tensor

A rigid body may have a very different distribution of mass about the three coordinate axes. As such, we should expect a body to have different moments of inertia about different axes. For example, a long thin rod should be relatively easy to make rotate about its long axis because all the mass is concentrated very close to the axis of rotation. Likewise, the rod should be relatively more difficult to make rotate about its short axis because its mass is spread out farther from the axis. This is indeed the case, and it is why a figure skater spins faster when she tucks her limbs in close to her body.

In three dimensions, the rotational mass of a rigid body is represented by a $3 \times 3$ matrix known as its *inertia tensor*. It is usually represented by the symbol $\mathbf{I}$ (as before, we won't describe how to calculate the inertia tensor here; see [15] for details):

$$\mathbf{I} = \begin{bmatrix} I_{xx} & I_{xy} & I_{xz} \\ I_{yx} & I_{yy} & I_{yz} \\ I_{zx} & I_{zy} & I_{zz} \end{bmatrix}.$$

The elements lying along the diagonal of this matrix are the moments of inertia of the body about its three principal axes, $I_{xx}$, $I_{yy}$, and $I_{zz}$. The off-diagonal elements are called *products of inertia*. They are zero when the body is symmetrical about all three principal axes (as would be the case for a rectangular box). When they are non-zero, they tend to produce physically realistic yet somewhat unintuitive motions that the average game player would probably think were "wrong" anyway. Therefore, the inertia tensor is often simplified down to the three-element vector [ $I_{xx}$ $I_{yy}$ $I_{zz}$ ] in game physics engines.

### 12.4.6.2. Orientation in Three Dimensions

In two dimensions, we know that the orientation of a rigid body can be described by a single angle $\theta$, which measures rotation about the z-axis (assuming the motion is taking place in the xy-plane). In three dimensions, a body's orientation could be represented using three Euler angles [ $\theta_x$ $\theta_y$ $\theta_z$ ], each representing the body's rotation about one of the three Cartesian axes. However, as we saw in Chapter 4, Euler angles suffer from gimbal lock problems and can be difficult to work with mathematically. Therefore, the orientation of a body is more often represented using either a $3 \times 3$ matrix **R** or a unit quaternion q. We'll use the quaternion form exclusively in this chapter.

Recall that a quaternion is a four-element vector whose x-, y-, and z-components can be interpreted as a unit vector **u** lying along the axis of rotation, scaled by the sine of the half angle and whose w component is the cosine of the half angle:

$$q = [q_x \quad q_y \quad q_z \quad q_w] = [\mathbf{q} \quad q_w]$$

$$= \left[ \mathbf{u} \sin\left(\tfrac{\theta}{2}\right) \quad \cos\left(\tfrac{\theta}{2}\right) \right].$$

A body's orientation is of course a function of time, so we should write it q(t).

Again, we need to select an arbitrary direction to be our zero rotation. For example, we might say that by default, the front of every object will lie along the positive z-axis in world space, with y up and x to the left. Any non-identity quaternion will serve to rotate the object away from this canonical world space orientation. The choice of the canonical orientation is arbitrary, but of course it's important to be consistent across all assets in the game.

### 12.4.6.3. Angular Velocity and Momentum in Three Dimensions

In three dimensions, angular velocity is a vector quantity, denoted by $\omega(t)$. The angular velocity vector can be visualized as a unit-length vector **u** that defines the axis of rotation, scaled by the two-dimensional angular velocity $\omega_u = \dot{\theta}_u$ of the body about the $u$-axis. Hence,

$$\omega(t) = \omega_u(t)\mathbf{u}(t) = \dot{\theta}_u(t)\mathbf{u}(t).$$

In linear dynamics, we saw that if there are no forces acting on a body, then the linear acceleration is zero, and linear velocity is constant. In two-dimensional angular dynamics, this again holds true: If there are no torques acting on a body in two dimensions, then the angular acceleration $\alpha$ is zero, and the angular speed $\omega$ about the $z$-axis is constant.

Unfortunately, this is *not* the case in three dimensions. It turns out that even when a rigid body is rotating in the absence of all forces, its angular velocity vector $\omega(t)$ may not be constant because the axis of rotation can continually change direction. You can see this effect in action when you try to spin a rectangular object, like a block of wood, in mid-air in front of you. If you throw the block so that it is rotating about its shortest axis, it will spin in a stable way. The orientation of the axis stays roughly constant. The same thing happens if you try to spin the block about its longest axis. But if you try to spin the block around its medium-sized axis, the rotation will be utterly unstable. The axis of rotation itself changes direction wildly as the object spins. This is shown in Figure 12.26.

The fact that the angular velocity vector can change in the absence of torques is another way of saying that angular velocity is not *conserved*. However, a related quantity called the *angular momentum* does remain constant in the absence of forces and hence *is* conserved. Angular momentum is the rotational equivalent of linear momentum:

Angular: $\mathbf{L}(t) = \mathbf{I}\,\omega(t);$  |  Linear: $\mathbf{p}(t) = m\mathbf{v}(t).$

Like the linear case, angular momentum $\mathbf{L}(t)$ is a three-element vector. However, unlike the linear case, rotational mass (the inertia tensor) is not a scalar but rather a $3 \times 3$ matrix. As such, the expression $\mathbf{I}\omega$ is computed via a matrix multiplication:

Figure 12.26. A rectangular object that is spun about its shortest or longest axis has a constant angular velocity vector. However, when spun about its medium-sized axis, the direction of the angular velocity vector changes wildly.

$$\begin{bmatrix} L_x(t) \\ L_y(t) \\ L_z(t) \end{bmatrix} = \begin{bmatrix} I_{xx} & I_{xy} & I_{xz} \\ I_{yx} & I_{yy} & I_{yz} \\ I_{zx} & I_{zy} & I_{zz} \end{bmatrix} \begin{bmatrix} \omega_x(t) \\ \omega_y(t) \\ \omega_z(t) \end{bmatrix}.$$

Because the angular velocity $\boldsymbol{\omega}$ is not conserved, we do not treat it as a primary quantity in our dynamics simulations the way we do the linear velocity $\mathbf{v}$. Instead, we treat angular momentum $\mathbf{L}$ as the primary quantity. The angular velocity is a secondary quantity, determined only after we have determined the value of $\mathbf{L}$ at each time step of the simulation.

### 12.4.6.4. Torque in Three Dimensions

In three dimensions, we still calculate torque as the cross product between the radial position vector of the point of force application and the force vector itself ($\mathbf{N} = \mathbf{r} \times \mathbf{F}$). Equation (12.8) still holds, but we always write it in terms of the angular momentum because angular velocity is not a conserved quantity:

$$\mathbf{N} = \mathbf{I}\boldsymbol{\alpha}(t) = \mathbf{I}\frac{d\boldsymbol{\omega}(t)}{dt} = \frac{d}{dt}(\mathbf{I}\boldsymbol{\omega}(t))$$

$$= \frac{d\mathbf{L}(t)}{dt}.$$

### 12.4.6.5. Solving the Equations of Angular Motion in Three Dimensions

When solving the equations of angular motion in three dimensions, we might be tempted to take exactly the same approach we used for linear motion and two-dimensional angular motion. We might guess that the differential equations of motion should be written

$$\text{A3D(?):} \qquad \begin{aligned} \mathbf{N}_{net}(t) &= \mathbf{I}\dot{\boldsymbol{\omega}}(t); \\ \boldsymbol{\omega}(t) &= \dot{\boldsymbol{\theta}}(t); \end{aligned} \qquad \text{L:} \qquad \begin{aligned} \mathbf{F}_{net}(t) &= m\dot{\mathbf{v}}(t); \\ \mathbf{v}(t) &= \dot{\mathbf{r}}(t), \end{aligned}$$

and using the explicit Euler method, we might guess that the approximate solutions to these ODEs would look something like this:

$$\text{A3D(?):} \qquad \begin{aligned} \boldsymbol{\omega}(t_2) &= \boldsymbol{\omega}(t_1) + \mathbf{I}^{-1}\mathbf{N}_{net}(t_1)\Delta \; ; \\ \boldsymbol{\theta}(t_2) &= \boldsymbol{\theta}(t_1) + \boldsymbol{\omega}(t_1)\Delta t; \end{aligned} \qquad \text{L:} \qquad \begin{aligned} \mathbf{v}(t_2) &= \mathbf{v}(t_1) + \frac{\mathbf{F}_{net}(t_1)}{m}\Delta t; \\ \mathbf{r}(t_2) &= \mathbf{r}(t_1) + \mathbf{v}(t_1)\Delta t. \end{aligned}$$

However, this is *not* actually correct. The differential equations of angular motion differ from their linear and two-dimensional angular counterparts in two important ways:

1. Instead of solving for the angular velocity $\boldsymbol{\omega}$, we solve for the angular momentum $\mathbf{L}$ directly. We then calculate the angular velocity vector as a secondary quantity using $\mathbf{I}$ and $\mathbf{L}$. We do this because angular momentum is conserved, while angular velocity is not.

2. When solving for the orientation given the angular velocity, we have a problem: The angular velocity is a three-element *vector*, while the orientation is a four-element *quaternion*. How can we write an ODE relating a quaternion to a vector? The answer is that we cannot, at least not directly. But what we can do is convert the angular velocity vector into quaternion form and then apply a slightly odd-looking equation that relates the orientation quaternion to the angular velocity quaternion.

It turns out that when we express a rigid body's orientation as a quaternion, the derivative of this quaternion is related to the body's angular velocity vector in the following way. First, we construct an *angular velocity quaternion*. This quaternion contains the three components of the angular velocity vector in $x$, $y$, and $z$, with its $w$-component set to zero:

$$\omega = \begin{bmatrix} \omega_x & \omega_y & \omega_z & 0 \end{bmatrix}$$

Now the differential equation relating the orientation quaternion to the angular velocity quaternion is (for reasons we won't get into here) as follows:

$$\frac{d\mathrm{q}(t)}{dt} = \dot{\mathrm{q}}(t) = \tfrac{1}{2}\omega(t)\,\mathrm{q}(t).$$

It's important to remember here that $\omega(t)$ is the angular velocity *quaternion* as described above and that the product $\omega(t)\mathrm{q}(t)$ is a *quaternion* product (see Section 4.4.2.1 for details).

So, we actually need to write the ODEs of motion as follows (note that I've recast the linear ODEs in terms of linear momentum as well, to underscore the similarities between the two cases):

$$
\text{A3D:} \quad
\begin{aligned}
\mathbf{N}_{\text{net}}(t) &= \dot{\mathbf{L}}(t); \\[4pt]
\boldsymbol{\omega}(t) &= \mathbf{I}^{-1}\mathbf{L}(t); \\[4pt]
\omega(t) &= [\boldsymbol{\omega}(t) \quad 0]; \\[4pt]
\tfrac{1}{2}\omega(t)\mathrm{q}(t) &= \dot{\mathrm{q}}(t);
\end{aligned}
\qquad
\text{L:} \quad
\begin{aligned}
\mathbf{F}_{\text{net}}(t) &= \dot{\mathbf{p}}(t); \\[4pt]
\mathbf{v}(t) &= \frac{\mathbf{p}(t)}{m}; \\[4pt]
\mathbf{v}(t) &= \dot{\mathbf{r}}(t).
\end{aligned}
$$

Using the explicit Euler method, the final approximate solution to the angular ODEs in three dimensions is actually as follows:

$$
\begin{aligned}
\mathbf{L}(t_2) &= \mathbf{L}(t_1) + \mathbf{N}_{\text{net}}(t_1)\Delta t \\
&= \mathbf{L}(t_1) + \Delta t \sum (\mathbf{r}_i \times \mathbf{F}_i(t_1)); && \text{(vectors)} \\[6pt]
\omega(t_2) &= [\mathbf{I}^{-1}\mathbf{L}(t_2) \quad 0]; && \text{(quaternion)} \\[6pt]
\mathrm{q}(t_2) &= \mathrm{q}(t_1) + \tfrac{1}{2}\omega(t_1)\,\mathrm{q}(t_1)\Delta t. && \text{(quaternions)}
\end{aligned}
$$

The orientation quaternion q($t$) should be renormalized periodically to reverse the effects of the inevitable accumulation of floating-point error.

As always, the explicit Euler method is being used here just as an example. In a real engine, we would employ velocity Verlet, RK4, or some other more-stable and more-accurate numerical method.

## 12.4.7. Collision Response

Everything we've discussed so far assumes that our rigid bodies are neither colliding with anything, nor is their motion constrained in any other way. When bodies collide with one another, the dynamics simulation must take steps to ensure that they respond realistically to the collision and that they are never left in a state of interpenetration after the simulation step has been completed. This is known as *collision response*.

### 12.4.7.1. Energy

Before we discuss collision response, we must understand the concept of *energy*. When a force moves a body over a distance, we say that the force does *work*. Work represents a change in energy—that is, a force either adds energy to a system of rigid bodies (e.g., an explosion) or it removes energy from the system (e.g., friction). Energy comes in two forms. The potential energy $V$ of a body is the energy it has simply because of where it is relative to a force field such as a gravitational or a magnetic field. (For example, the higher up a body is above the surface of the Earth, the more gravitational potential energy it has.) The kinetic energy of a body $T$ represents the energy arising from the fact that it is moving relative to other bodies in a system. The total energy $E = V + T$ of an isolated system of bodies is a *conserved* quantity, meaning that it remains constant unless energy is being drained from the system or added from outside the system.

The kinetic energy arising from linear motion can be written

$$T_{\text{linear}} = \tfrac{1}{2}mv^2,$$

or in terms of the linear momentum and velocity vectors:

$$T_{\text{linear}} = \tfrac{1}{2}\mathbf{p} \cdot \mathbf{v}.$$

Analogously, the kinetic energy arising from a body's rotational motion is as follows:

$$T_{\text{angular}} = \tfrac{1}{2}\mathbf{L} \cdot \boldsymbol{\omega}.$$

Energy and its conservation can be extremely useful concepts when solving all sorts of physics problems. We'll see the role that energy plays in the determination of collision responses in the following section.

### 12.4.7.2. Impulsive Collision Response

When two bodies collide in the real world, a complex set of events takes place. The bodies compress slightly and then rebound, changing their velocities and losing energy to sound and heat in the process. Most real-time rigid body dynamics simulations approximate all of these details with a simple model based on an analysis of the momenta and kinetic energies of the colliding objects, called *Newton's law of restitution for instantaneous collisions with no friction*. It makes the following simplifying assumptions about the collision:

- The collision force acts over an infinitesimally short period of time, turning it into what we call an idealized *impulse*. This causes the velocities of the bodies to change *instantaneously* as a result of the collision.

- There is no friction at the point of contact between the objects' surfaces. This is another way of saying that the impulse acting to separate the bodies during the collision is normal to both surfaces—there is no tangential component to the collision impulse. (This is just an idealization of course; we'll get to friction in Section 12.4.7.5.)

- The nature of the complex submolecular interactions between the bodies during the collision can be approximated by a single quantity known as the *coefficient of restitution*, customarily denoted by the symbol $\varepsilon$. This coefficient describes how much energy is lost during the collision. When $\varepsilon = 1$, the collision is perfectly elastic, and no energy is lost. (Picture two billiard balls colliding in mid air.) When $\varepsilon = 0$, the collision is perfectly *inelastic*, also known as perfectly *plastic*, and the kinetic energy of both bodies is lost. The bodies will stick together after the collision, continuing to move in the direction that their mutual center of mass had been moving before the collision. (Picture pieces of putty being slammed together.)

All collision analysis is based around the idea that linear momentum is conserved. So for two bodies 1 and 2, we can write

$$\mathbf{p}_1 + \mathbf{p}_2 = \mathbf{p}'_1 + \mathbf{p}'_2, \qquad \text{or}$$
$$m_1\,\mathbf{v}_1 + m_2\,\mathbf{v}_2 = m_1\,\mathbf{v}'_1 + m_2\,\mathbf{v}'_2,$$

where the primed symbols represent the momenta and velocities after the collision. The kinetic energy of the system is conserved as well, but we must account for the energy lost due to heat and sound by introducing an additional energy loss term $T_{\text{lost}}$:

$$\tfrac{1}{2}m_1\,v_1^2 + \tfrac{1}{2}m_2\,v_2^2 = \tfrac{1}{2}m_1\,v_1'^2 + \tfrac{1}{2}m_2\,v_2'^2 + T_{\text{lost}}.$$

If the collision is perfectly *elastic*, the energy loss $T_{\text{lost}}$ is zero. If it is perfectly *plastic*, the energy loss is equal to the original kinetic energy of the system, the

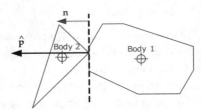

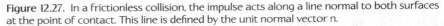

**Figure 12.27.** In a frictionless collision, the impulse acts along a line normal to both surfaces at the point of contact. This line is defined by the unit normal vector n.

primed kinetic energy sum becomes zero, and the bodies stick together after the collision.

To resolve a collision using Newton's law of restitution, we apply an idealized *impulse* to the two bodies. An impulse is like a force that acts over an infinitesimally short period of time and thereby causes an instantaneous change in the velocity of the body to which it is applied. We could denote an impulse with the symbol $\Delta \mathbf{p}$, since it is a change in momentum ($\Delta \mathbf{p} = m\Delta \mathbf{v}$). However, most physics texts use the symbol $\hat{\mathbf{p}}$ (pronounced "p-hat") instead, so we'll do the same.

Because we assume that there is no friction involved in the collision, the impulse vector must be normal to both surfaces at the point of contact. In other words, $\hat{\mathbf{p}} = \hat{p}\mathbf{n}$ , where $\mathbf{n}$ is the unit vector normal to both surfaces. This is illustrated in Figure 12.27. If we assume that the surface normal points toward body 1, then body 1 experiences an impulse of $\hat{\mathbf{p}}$, and body 2 experiences an equal but opposite impulse. Hence, the momenta of the two bodies after the collision can be written in terms of their momenta prior to the collision and the impulse $\hat{\mathbf{p}}$ as follows:

$$\mathbf{p}_1' = \mathbf{p}_1 + \hat{\mathbf{p}}; \qquad \mathbf{p}_2' = \mathbf{p}_2 - \hat{\mathbf{p}};$$

$$m_1\mathbf{v}_1' = m_1\mathbf{v}_1 + \hat{\mathbf{p}}; \qquad m_2\mathbf{v}_2' = m_2\mathbf{v}_2 - \hat{\mathbf{p}};$$

$$\mathbf{v}_1' = \mathbf{v}_1 + \frac{\hat{p}}{m_1}\mathbf{n}; \qquad \mathbf{v}_2' = \mathbf{v}_2 - \frac{\hat{p}}{m_2}\mathbf{n}. \qquad (12.9)$$

The *coefficient of restitution* provides the key relationship between the relative velocities of the bodies before and after the collision. Given that the centers of mass of the bodies have velocities $\mathbf{v}_1$ and $\mathbf{v}_2$ before the collision and $\mathbf{v}_1'$ and $\mathbf{v}_2'$ afterward, the coefficient of restitution $\varepsilon$ is defined as follows:

$$(\mathbf{v}_2' - \mathbf{v}_1') = \varepsilon(\mathbf{v}_2 - \mathbf{v}_1). \qquad (12.10)$$

Solving Equations (12.9) and (12.10) under the temporary assumption that the bodies cannot rotate yields

$$\hat{\mathbf{p}} = \hat{p}\,\mathbf{n} = \frac{(\varepsilon+1)(\mathbf{v}_2 \cdot \mathbf{n} - \mathbf{v}_1 \cdot \mathbf{n})}{\dfrac{1}{m_1} + \dfrac{1}{m_2}}\,\mathbf{n}.$$

Notice that if the coefficient of restitution is one (perfectly elastic collision) and if the mass of body 2 is effectively infinite (as it would be for, say, a concrete driveway), then $(1/m_2) = 0$, $\mathbf{v}_2 = \mathbf{0}$, and this expression reduces to a reflection of the other body's velocity vector about the contact normal, as we'd expect:

$$\hat{\mathbf{p}} = -2m_1(\mathbf{v}_1 \cdot \mathbf{n})\,\mathbf{n};$$

$$\mathbf{v}_1' = \frac{\mathbf{p}_1 + \hat{\mathbf{p}}}{m_1} = \frac{m_1\mathbf{v}_1 - 2m_1(\mathbf{v}_1 \cdot \mathbf{n})\,\mathbf{n}}{m_1}$$

$$= \mathbf{v}_1 - 2(\mathbf{v}_1 \cdot \mathbf{n})\,\mathbf{n}.$$

The solution gets a bit hairier when we take the rotations of the bodies into account. In this case, we need to look at the velocities of the points of contact on the two bodies rather than the velocities of their centers of mass, and we need to calculate the impulse in such a way as to impart a realistic rotational effect as a result of the collision. We won't get into the details here, but Chris Hecker's article, available at http://chrishecker.com/images/e/e7/Gdmphys3.pdf, does an excellent job of describing both the linear and the rotational aspects of collision response. The theory behind collision response is explained more fully in [15].

### 12.4.7.3. Penalty Forces

Another approach to collision response is to introduce imaginary forces called *penalty forces* into the simulation. A penalty force acts like a stiff damped spring attached to the contact points between two bodies that have just interpenetrated. Such a force induces the desired collision response over a short but finite period of time. Using this approach, the spring constant $k$ effectively controls the duration of the interpenetration, and the damping coefficient $b$ acts a bit like the restitution coefficient. When $b = 0$, there is no damping—no energy is lost, and the collision is perfectly elastic. As $b$ increases, the collision becomes more plastic.

Let's take a brief look at some of the pros and cons of the penalty force approach to resolving collisions. On the positive side, penalty forces are easy to implement and understand. They also work well when three or more bodies are interpenetrating each other. This problem is very difficult to solve when resolving collisions one pair at a time. A good example is the Sony PS3 demo in which a huge number of rubber duckies are poured into a bathtub—the simulation was nice and stable despite the very large number of collisions. The penalty force method is a great way to achieve this.

Unfortunately, because penalty forces respond to penetration (i.e., relative position) rather than to relative velocity, the forces may not align with the direction we would intuitively expect, especially during a high-speed collision. A classic example is a car driving head-on into a truck. The car is low while the truck is tall. Using only the penalty force method, it is easy to arrive at a situation in which the penalty force is vertical, rather than horizontal as we would expect given the velocities of the two vehicles. This can cause the truck to pop its nose up into the air while the car drives under it.

In general, the penalty force technique works well for low-speed impacts, but it does not work well at all when objects are moving quickly. It is possible to combine the penalty force method with other collision resolution approaches in order to strike a balance between stability in the presence of large numbers of interpenetrations and responsiveness and more-intuitive behavior at high velocities.

### 12.4.7.4. Using Constraints to Resolve Collisions

As we'll investigate in Section 12.4.8, most physics systems permit various kinds of constraints to be imposed on the motion of the bodies in the simulation. If collisions are treated as constraints that disallow object interpenetration, then they can be resolved by simply running the simulation's general-purpose constraint solver. If the constraint solver is fast and produces high-quality visual results, this can be an effective way to resolve collisions.

### 12.4.7.5. Friction

Friction is a force that arises between two bodies that are in continuous contact, resisting their movement relative to one another. There are a number of types of friction. *Static friction* is the resistance one feels when trying to start a stationary object sliding along a surface. *Dynamic friction* is a resisting force that arises when objects are actually moving relative to one another. *Sliding friction* is a type of dynamic friction that resists movement when an object slides along a surface. *Rolling friction* is a type of static or dynamic friction that acts at the point of contact between a wheel or other round object and the surface it is rolling on. When the surface is very rough, the rolling friction is exactly strong enough to cause the wheel to roll without sliding, and it acts as a form of static friction. If the surface is somewhat smooth, the wheel may slip, and a dynamic form of rolling friction comes into play. *Collision friction* is the friction that acts instantaneously at the point of contact when two bodies collide while moving. (This is the friction force that we ignored when discussing Newton's law of restitution in Section 12.4.7.1.) Various kinds of *constraints*

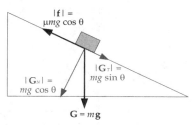

Figure 12.28. The force of friction f is proportional to the normal component of the object's weight. The proportionality constant $\mu$ is called the coefficient of friction.

can have friction as well. For example, a rusted hinge or axle might resist being turned by introducing a friction torque.

Let's look at an example to understand the essence of how friction works. Linear sliding friction is proportional to the component of an object's weight that is acting normal to the surface on which it is sliding. The weight of an object is just the force due to gravity, $\mathbf{G} = m\mathbf{g}$, which is always directed downward. The component of this force normal to an inclined surface that makes an angle $\theta$ with the horizontal is just $G_N = mg \cos \theta$. The friction force $f$ is then

$$f = \mu mg \, \cos\theta,$$

where the constant of proportionality $\mu$ is called the *coefficient of friction*. This force acts tangentially to the surface, in a direction opposite to the attempted or actual motion of the object. This is illustrated in Figure 12.28.

Figure 12.28 also shows the component of the gravitational force acting tangent to the surface, $G_T = mg \sin \theta$. This force tends to make the object accelerate down the plane, but in the presence of sliding friction, it is counteracted by $f$. Hence, the net force tangent to the surface is

$$F_{net} = G_T - f = mg(\sin\theta - \mu \cos\theta).$$

If the angle of inclination is such that the expression in parentheses is zero, the object will slide at a constant speed (if already moving) or be at rest. If the expression is greater than zero, the object will accelerate down the surface. If it is less than zero, the object will decelerate and eventually come to rest.

### 12.4.7.6. Welding

An additional problem arises when an object is sliding across a polygon soup. Recall that a polygon soup is just what its name implies—a soup of essentially unrelated polygons (usually triangles). As an object slides from one triangle of this soup to the next, the collision detection system will generate additional

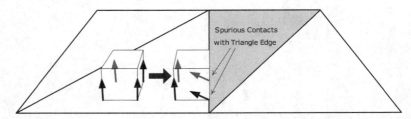

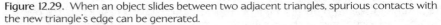

**Figure 12.29.** When an object slides between two adjacent triangles, spurious contacts with the new triangle's edge can be generated.

spurious contacts because it will think that the object is about to hit the edge of the next triangle. This is illustrated in Figure 12.29.

There are a number of solutions to this problem. One is to analyze the set of contacts and discard ones that appear to be spurious, based on various heuristics and possibly some knowledge of the object's contacts on a previous frame (e.g., if we know the object was sliding along a surface and a contact normal arises that is due to the object being near the edge of its current triangle, then discard that contact normal). Versions of Havok prior to 4.5 employed this approach.

Starting with Havok 4.5, a new technique was implemented that essentially annotates the mesh with triangle adjacency information. The collision detection system therefore "knows" which edges are interior edges and can discard spurious collisions reliably and quickly. Havok describes this solution as *welding*, because in effect the edges of the triangles in the poly soup are welded to one another.

### 12.4.7.7. Coming to Rest, Islands, and Sleeping

When energy is removed from a simulated system via friction, damping, or other means, moving objects will eventually come to rest. This seems like a natural consequence of the simulation—something that would just "fall out" of the differential equations of motion. Unfortunately, in a real computerized simulation, coming to rest is never quite that simple. Various factors such as floating-point error, inaccuracies in the calculation of restitution forces, and numerical instability can cause objects to jitter forever rather than coming to rest as they should. For this reason, most physics engines use various heuristic methods to detect when objects are oscillating instead of coming to rest as they should. Additional energy can be removed from the system to ensure that such objects eventually settle down, or they can simply be stopped abruptly once their average velocity drops below a threshold.

When an object really does stop moving (finds itself in a state of equilibrium), there is no reason to continue integrating its equations of motion every frame. To optimize performance, most physics engines allow dynamic objects in the simulation to be *put to sleep*. This excludes them from the simulation temporarily, although sleeping objects are still active from a collision standpoint. If any force or impulse begins acting on a sleeping object, or if the object loses one of the contacts that was holding it in equilibrium, it will be awoken so that its dynamic simulation can be resumed.

### Sleep Criteria

Various criteria can be used to determine whether or not a body qualifies for sleep. It's not always easy to make this determination in a robust manner for all situations. For example, a long pendulum might have very low angular momentum and yet still be moving visibly on-screen.

The most commonly used criteria for equilibrium detection include:

- The body is *supported*. This means it has three or more contact points (or one or more *planar* contacts) that allow it to attain equilibrium with gravity and any other forces that might be affecting it.

- The body's *linear and angular momentum* are below a predefined threshold.

- A *running average* of the linear and angular momentum are below a predefined threshold.

- The total *kinetic energy* of the body ($T = \frac{1}{2}\mathbf{p} \cdot \mathbf{v} + \frac{1}{2}\mathbf{L} \cdot \boldsymbol{\omega}$) is below a predefined threshold. The kinetic energy is usually mass-normalized so that a single threshold can be used for all bodies regardless of their masses.

- The motion of a body that is about to go to sleep might be *progressively damped* so that it comes to a smooth stop rather than stopping abruptly.

### Simulation Islands

Both Havok and PhysX further optimize their performance by automatically grouping objects that either are interacting or have the potential to interact in the near future into sets called *simulation islands*. Each simulation island can be simulated independently of all the other islands—an approach that is highly conducive to cache coherency optimizations and parallel processing.

Havok and PhysX both put entire islands to sleep rather than individual rigid bodies. This approach has its pros and cons. The performance boost is obviously larger when a whole group of interacting objects can be put to sleep. On the other hand, if even one object in an island is awake, the entire island is awake. Overall, it seems that the pros tend to outweigh the cons, so the simulation island design is one we're likely to continue to see in future versions of these SDKs.

## 12.4.8. Constraints

An unconstrained rigid body has six degrees of freedom (DOF): It can translate in three dimensions, and it can rotate about the three Cartesian axes. *Constraints* restrict an object's motion, reducing its degrees of freedom either partially or completely. Constraints can be used to model all sorts of interesting behaviors in a game. Here are a few examples:

- a swinging chandelier (point-to-point constraint);
- a door that can be kicked, slammed, blown of its hinges (hinge constraint);
- a vehicle's wheel assembly (axle constraint with damped springs for suspension);
- a train or a car pulling a trailer (stiff spring/rod constraint);
- a rope or chain (chain of stiff springs or rods);
- a rag doll (specialized constraints that mimic the behavior of various joints in the human skeleton).

In the sections that follow, we'll briefly investigate these and some of the other most common kinds of constraints typically provided by a physics SDK.

### 12.4.8.1. Point-to-Point Constraints

A point-to-point constraint is the simplest type of constraint. It acts like a ball and socket joint—bodies can move in any way they like, as long as a specified point on one body lines up with a specified point on the other body. This is illustrated in Figure 12.30.

### 12.4.8.2. Stiff Springs

A stiff spring constraint is a lot like a point-to-point constraint except that it keeps the two points separated by a specified distance. This kind of constraint

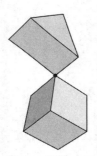

Figure 12.30. A point-to-point constraint requires that a point on body A align with a point on body B.

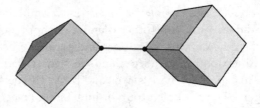

Figure 12.31. A stiff spring constraint requires that a point on body A be separated from a point on body B by a user-specified distance.

acts like an invisible rod between the two constrained points. Figure 12.31 illustrates this constraint.

### 12.4.8.3. Hinge Constraints

A hinge constraint limits rotational motion to only a single degree of freedom, about the hinge's axis. An *unlimited hinge* acts like an axle, allowing the constrained object to complete an unlimited number of full rotations. It's common to define *limited hinges* that can only move through a predefined range of angles about the one allowed axis. For example, a one-way door can only move through a 180 degree arc, because otherwise it would pass through the adjacent wall. Likewise, a two-way door is constrained to move through a ±180 degree arc. Hinge constraints may also be given a degree of friction in the form of a torque that resists rotation about the hinge's axis. A limited hinge constraint is shown in Figure 12.32.

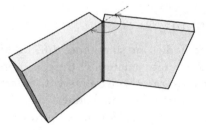

**Figure 12.32.** A limited hinge constraint mimics the behavior of a door.

### 12.4.8.4. Prismatic Constraints

Prismatic constraints act like a piston: A constrained body's motion is restricted to a single translational degree of freedom. A prismatic constraint may or may not permit rotation about the translation axis of the piston. Prismatic constraints can of course be limited or unlimited and may or may not include friction. A prismatic constraint is illustrated in Figure 12.33.

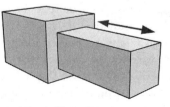

**Figure 12.33.** A prismatic constraint acts like a piston.

### 12.4.8.5. Other Common Constraint Types

Many other types of constraints are possible, of course. Here are just a few examples:

- *Planar.* Objects are constrained to move in a two-dimensional plane.
- *Wheel.* This is typically a hinge constraint with unlimited rotation, coupled with some form of vertical suspension simulated via a spring-damper assembly.
- *Pulley.* In this specialized constraint, an imaginary rope passes through a pulley and is attached to two bodies. The bodies move along the line of the rope via a leverage ratio.

Constraints may be breakable, meaning that after enough force is applied, they automatically come apart. Alternatively, the game can turn the constraint on and off at will, using its own criteria for when the constraint should break.

### 12.4.8.6. Constraint Chains

Long chains of linked bodies are sometimes difficult to simulate in a stable manner because of the iterative nature of the constraint solver. A *constraint chain* is a specialized group of constraints with information that tells the constraint solver how the objects are connected. This allows the solver to deal with the chain in a more stable manner than would otherwise be possible.

### 12.4.8.7. Rag Dolls

A rag doll is a physical simulation of the way a human body might move when it is dead or unconscious and hence entirely limp. Rag dolls are created by linking together a collection of rigid bodies, one for each semi-rigid part of the body. For example, we might have capsules for the feet, calves, thighs, hands, upper and lower arms, and head and possibly a few for the torso to simulate the flexibility of the spine.

The rigid bodies in a rag doll are connected to one another via constraints. Rag doll constraints are specialized to mimic the kinds of motions the joints in a real human body can perform. We usually make use of constraint chains to improve the stability of the simulation.

A rag doll simulation is always tightly integrated with the animation system. As the rag doll moves in the physics world, we extract the positions and rotations of the rigid bodies, and use this information to drive the positions and orientations of certain joints in the animated skeleton. So in effect, a rag doll is really just a form of *procedural animation* that happens to be driven by the physics system. (See Chapter 11 for more details on skeletal animation.)

Of course, implementing a rag doll is not quite as simple as I've made it sound here. For one thing, there's usually not a one-to-one mapping between the rigid bodies in the rag doll and the joints in the animated skeleton—the skeleton usually has more joints than the rag doll has bodies. Therefore, we need a system that can map rigid bodies to joints (i.e., one that "knows" to which joint each rigid body in the rag doll corresponds). There may be additional joints between those that are being driven by the rag doll bodies, so the mapping system must also be capable of determining the correct pose transforms for these intervening joints. This is not an exact science. We must apply artistic judgment and/or some knowledge of human biomechanics in order to achieve a natural-looking rag doll.

### 12.4.8.8. Powered Constraints

Constraints can also be "powered," meaning that an external engine system such as the animation system can indirectly control the translations and orientations of the rigid bodies in the rag doll.

Let's take an elbow joint as an example. An elbow acts pretty much like a limited hinge, with a little less than 180 degrees of free rotation. (Actually, an elbow can also rotate axially, but we'll ignore that for the purposes of this discussion.) To power this constraint, we model the elbow as a *rotational spring*. Such a spring exerts a torque proportional to the spring's angle of deflection away from some predefined rest angle, $N = -k(\theta - \theta_{rest})$. Now imagine changing the rest angle externally, say by ensuring that it always matches the angle of the elbow joint in an animated skeleton. As the rest angle changes, the spring will find itself out of equilibrium, and it will exert a torque that tends

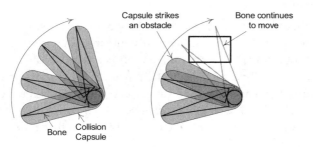

**Figure 12.34.** Left: with a powered rag doll constraint, and in the absence of any additional forces or torques, a rigid body representing the lower arm can be made to exactly track the movements of an animated elbow joint. Right: if an obstacle blocks the motion of the body, it will diverge from that of the animated elbow joint in a realistic way.

to rotate the elbow back into alignment with $\theta_{rest}$. In the absence of any other forces or torques, the rigid bodies will exactly track the motion of the elbow joint in the animated skeleton. But if other forces are introduced (for example, the lower arm comes in contact with an immovable object), then these forces will play into the overall motion of the elbow joint, allowing it to diverge from the animated motion in a realistic manner. As illustrated in Figure 12.34, this provides the illusion of a human who is trying her best to move in a certain way (i.e., the "ideal" motion provided by the animation) but who is sometimes unable to do so due to the limitations of the physical world (e.g., her arm gets caught on something as she tries to swing it forward).

## 12.4.9. Controlling the Motions of Rigid Bodies

Most game designs call for a degree of control over the way rigid bodies move over and above the way they would move naturally under the influence of gravity and in response to collisions with other objects in the scene. For example:

- An air vent applies an upward force to any object that enters its shaft of influence.
- A car is coupled to a trailer and exerts a pulling force on it as it moves.
- A tractor beam exerts a force on an unwitting space craft.
- An anti-gravity device causes objects to hover.
- The flow of a river creates a force field that causes objects floating in the river to move downstream.

And the list goes on. Most physics engines typically provide their users with a number of ways to exert control over the bodies in the simulation. We'll outline the most common of these mechanisms in the following sections.

### 12.4.9.1. Gravity

Gravity is ubiquitous in most games that take place on the surface of the Earth or some other planet (or on a spacecraft with simulated gravity!). Gravity is technically not a force but rather a (roughly) constant acceleration, so it affects all bodies equally regardless of their mass. Because of its ubiquitous and special nature, the magnitude and direction of the gravitational acceleration is specified via a global setting in most SDKs. (If you're writing a space game, you can always set gravity to zero to eliminate it from the simulation.)

### 12.4.9.2. Applying Forces

Any number of forces can be applied to the bodies in a game physics simulation. A force always acts over a finite time interval. (If it acted instantaneously, it would be called an *impulse*—more on that below.) The forces in a game are often dynamic in nature—they often change their directions and/or their magnitudes every frame. So the force-application function in most physics SDKs is designed to be called once per frame for the duration of the force's influence. The signature of such a function usually looks something like this: `applyForce(const Vector& forceInNewtons)`, where the duration of the force is assumed to be $\Delta t$.

### 12.4.9.3. Applying Torques

When a force is applied such that its line of action passes through the center of mass of a body, no torque is generated, and only the body's linear acceleration is affected. If it is applied off-center, it will induce *both* a linear and a rotational acceleration. A *pure torque* can be applied to a body as well by applying two equal and opposite forces to points equidistant from the center of mass. The linear motions induced by such a pair of forces will cancel each other out (since for the purposes of linear dynamics, the forces both act at the center of mass). This leaves only their rotational effects. A pair of torque-inducing forces like this is known as a *couple* (http://en.wikipedia.org/wiki/Couple_(mechanics)). A special function such as `applyTorque(const Vector& torque)` may be provided for this purpose. However, if your physics SDK provides no `applyTorque()` function, you can always write one and have it generate a suitable couple instead.

### 12.4.9.4. Applying Impulses

As we saw in Section 12.4.7.2, an *impulse* is an instantaneous change in velocity (or actually, a change in momentum). Technically speaking, an impulse is a force that acts for an infinitesimal amount of time. However, the shortest possible duration of force application in a time-stepped dynamics simulation is $\Delta t$, which is not short enough to simulate an impulse adequately. As such, most physics SDKs provide a function with a signature such as `applyImpulse(const Vector& impulse)` for the purposes of applying impulses to bodies. Of course, impulses come in two flavors—linear and angular—and a good SDK should provide functions for applying both types.

## 12.4.10. The Collision/Physics Step

Now that we've covered the theory and some of the technical details behind implementing a collision and physics system, let's take a brief look at how these systems actually perform their updates every frame.

Every collision/physics engine performs the following basic tasks during its update step. Different physics SDKs may perform these phases in different orders. That said, the technique I've seen used most often goes something like this:

1. The forces and torques acting on the bodies in the physics world are integrated forward by $\Delta t$ in order to determine their tentative positions and orientations next frame.

2. The collision detection library is called to determine if any new contacts have been generated between any of the objects as a result of their tentative movement. (The bodies normally keep track of their contacts in order to take advantage of temporal coherency. Hence at each step of the simulation, the collision engine need only determine whether any previous contacts have been lost and whether any new contacts have been added.)

3. Collisions are resolved, often by applying impulses or penalty forces or as part of the constraint solving step below. Depending on the SDK, this phase may or may not include continuous collision detection (CCD, otherwise known as time of impact detection or TOI).

4. Constraints are satisfied by the constraint solver.

At the conclusion of step 4, some of the bodies may have moved away from their tentative positions as determined in step 1. This movement may cause additional interpenetrations between objects or cause other previously satisfied constraints to be broken. Therefore, steps 1 through 4 (or sometimes only 2 through 4, depending on how collisions and constraints are resolved) are repeated until either (a) all collisions have been successfully resolved and all constraints are satisfied, or (b) a predefined maximum number of iterations has been exceeded. In the latter case, the solver effectively "gives up," with the hope that things will resolve themselves naturally during subsequent frames of the simulation. This helps to avoid performance spikes by amortizing the cost of collision and constraint resolution over multiple frames. However, it can lead to incorrect-looking behavior if the errors are too large or if the time step is too long or is inconsistent. Penalty forces can be blended into the simulation in order to gradually resolve these problems over time.

### 12.4.10.1. The Constraint Solver

A constraint solver is essentially an iterative algorithm that attempts to satisfy a large number of constraints simultaneously by *minimizing the error* between the actual positions and rotations of the bodies in the physics world and their ideal positions and rotations as defined by the constraints. As such, constraint solvers are essentially iterative error minimization algorithms.

Let's take a look first at how a constraint solver works in the trivial case of a single pair of bodies connected by a single constraint. During each step of the physics simulation, the numerical integrator will find new tentative transforms for the two bodies. The constraint solver then evaluates their relative positions and calculates the error between the positions and orientations of their shared axis of rotation. If any error is detected, the solver moves the bodies in such a way as to minimize or eliminate it. Since there are no other bodies in the system, the second iteration of the step should discover no new contacts, and the constraint solver will find that the one hinge constraint is now satisfied. Hence the loop can exit without further iterations.

When more than one constraint must be satisfied simultaneously, more iterations may be required. During each iteration, the numerical integrator will sometimes tend to move the bodies out of alignment with their constraints, while the constraint solver tends to put them back into alignment. With luck, and a carefully designed approach to minimizing error in the constraint solver, this feedback loop should eventually settle into a valid solution. However, the solution may not always be exact. This is why, in games with physics engines, you sometimes witness seemingly impossible behaviors, like chains that stretch (opening up little gaps between the links), objects that interpenetrate briefly, or hinges that momentarily move beyond their allowable ranges. The goal of the constraint solver is to minimize error—it's not always possible to eliminate it completely.

### 12.4.10.2. Variations between Engines

The description given above is of course an over-simplification of what really goes on in a physics/collision engine every frame. The way in which the various phases of computation are performed, and their order relative to one another, may vary from physics SDK to physics SDK. For example, some kinds of constraints are modeled as forces and torques that are taken care of by the numerical integration step rather than being resolved by the constraint solver. Collision may be run before the integration step rather than after. Collisions may be resolved in any number of different ways. Our goal here is merely to give you a taste of how these systems work. For a detailed understanding of how any one SDK operates, you'll want to read its documentation and probably also inspect its source code (presuming the relevant bits are available for you to read!). The curious and industrious reader can get a good start by downloading and experimenting with ODE and/or PhysX, as these two SDKs are available for free. You can also learn a great deal from ODE's wiki, which is available at http://opende.sourceforge.net/wiki/index. php/Main_Page.

## 12.5. Integrating a Physics Engine into Your Game

Obviously, a collision/physics engine is of little use by itself—it must be integrated into your game engine. In this section, we'll discuss the most common interface points between the collision/physics engine and the rest of the game code.

### 12.5.1. The Linkage between Game Objects and Rigid Bodies

The rigid bodies and collidables in the collision/physics world are nothing more than abstract mathematical descriptions. In order for them to be useful in the context of a game, we need to link them in some way to their visual representations on-screen. Usually, we don't draw the rigid bodies directly (except for debugging purposes). Instead, the rigid bodies are used to describe the shape, size, and physical behavior of the logical objects that make up the virtual game world. We'll discuss game objects in depth in Chapter 14, but for the time being, we'll rely on our intuitive notion of what a game object is—a logical entity in the game world, such as a character, a vehicle, a weapon, a floating power-up, and so on. So the linkage between a rigid body in the physics world and its visual representation on-screen is usually indirect, with the logical game object serving as the hub that links the two together. This is illustrated in Figure 12.35.

In general, a game object is represented in the collision/physics world by zero or more rigid bodies. The following list describes three possible scenarios:

- *Zero rigid bodies*. Game objects without any rigid bodies in the physics world act as though they are not solid, because they have no collision representation at all. Decorative objects with which the player or

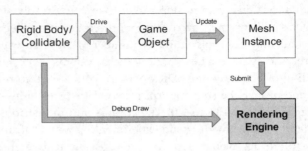

**Figure 12.35.** Rigid bodies are linked to their visual representations by way of game objects. An optional direct rendering path is usually provided so that the locations of the rigid bodies can be visualized for debugging purposes.

non-player characters cannot interact, such as birds flying overhead or portions of the game world that can be seen but never reached, might have no collision. This scenario can also apply to objects whose collision detection is handled manually (without the help of the collision/physics engine) for some reason.

- *One rigid body.* Most simple game objects need only be represented by a single rigid body. In this case, the shape of the rigid body's collidable is chosen to closely approximate the shape of the game object's visual representation, and the rigid body's position and orientation exactly match the position and orientation of the game object itself.

- *Multiple rigid bodies.* Some complex game objects are represented by multiple rigid bodies in the collision/physics world. Examples include characters, machinery, vehicles, or any object that is composed of multiple solid pieces. Such game objects usually make use of a skeleton (i.e., a hierarchy of affine transforms) to track the locations of their component pieces (although other means are certainly possible as well). The rigid bodies are usually linked to the joints of the skeleton in such a way that the position and orientation of each rigid body corresponds to the position and orientation of one of the joints. The joints in the skeleton might be driven by an animation, in which case the associated rigid bodies simply come along for the ride. Alternatively, the physics system might drive the locations of rigid bodies and hence indirectly control the locations of the joints. The mapping from joints to rigid bodies may or may not be one-to-one—some joints might be controlled entirely by animation, while others are linked to rigid bodies.

The linkage between game objects and rigid bodies must be managed by the engine, of course. Typically, each game object will manage its own rigid bodies, creating and destroying them when necessary, adding and removing them from the physics world as needed, and maintaining the connection between each rigid body's location and the location of the game object and/or one of its joints. For complex game objects consisting of multiple rigid bodies, a wrapper class of some kind may be used to manage them. This insulates the game objects from the nitty-gritty details of managing a collection of rigid bodies and allows different kinds of game objects to manage their rigid bodies in a consistent way.

### 12.5.1.1. Physics-Driven Bodies

If our game has a rigid body dynamics system, then presumably we want the motions of at least some of the objects in the game to be driven entirely by the simulation. Such game objects are called *physics-driven* objects. Bits of debris, exploding buildings, rocks rolling down a hillside, empty magazines and shell casings—these are all examples of physics-driven objects.

A physics-driven rigid body is linked to its game object by stepping the simulation and then querying the physics system for the body's position and orientation. This transform is then applied either to the game object as a whole or to a joint or some other data structure within the game object.

### Example: Building a Safe with a Detachable Door

When physics-driven rigid bodies are linked to the joints of a skeleton, the bodies are often *constrained* to produce a desired kind of motion. As an example, let's look at how a safe with a detachable door might be modeled.

Visually, let's assume that the safe consists of a single triangle mesh with two submeshes, one for the housing and one for the door. A two-joint skeleton is used to control the motions of these two pieces. The root joint is bound to the housing of the safe, while the child joint is bound to the door in such a way that rotating the door joint causes the door submesh to swing open and shut in a suitable way.

The collision geometry for the safe is broken into two independent pieces as well, one for the housing and one for the door. These two pieces are used to create two totally separate rigid bodies in the collision/physics world. The rigid body for the safe's housing is attached to the root joint in the skeleton, and the door's rigid body is linked to the door joint. A hinge constraint is then added to the physics world to ensure that the door body swings properly relative to the housing when the dynamics of the two rigid bodies are simulated. The motions of the two rigid bodies representing the housing and the door are used to update the transforms of the two joints in the skeleton. Once the skeleton's matrix palette has been generated by the animation system, the rendering engine will end up drawing the housing and door submeshes in the locations of the rigid bodies within the physics world.

If the door needs to be blown off at some point, the constraint can be broken, and impulses can be applied to the rigid bodies to send them flying. Visibly, it will appear to the human player that the door and the housing have become separate objects. But in reality, it's still a single game object and a single triangle mesh with two joints and two rigid bodies.

### 12.5.1.2. Game-Driven Bodies

In most games, certain objects in the game world need to be moved about in a non-physical way. The motions of such objects might be determined by an animation or by following a spline path, or they might be under the control of the human player. We often want these objects to participate in collision detection—to be capable of pushing the physics-driven objects out of their way, for example—but we do not want the physics system to interfere with their motion in any way. To accommodate such objects, most physics SDKs provide a special type of rigid body known as a *game-driven body*. (Havok calls these "key framed" bodies.)

Game-driven bodies do not experience the effects of gravity. They are also considered to be infinitely massive by the physics system (usually denoted by a mass of zero, since this is an invalid mass for a physics-driven body). The assumption of infinite mass ensures that forces and collision impulses within the simulation can never change the velocity of a game-driven body.

To move a game-driven body around in the physics world, we cannot simply set its position and orientation every frame to match the location of the corresponding game object. Doing so would introduce discontinuities that would be very difficult for the physical simulation to resolve. (For example, a physics-driven body might find itself suddenly interpenetrating a game-driven body, but it would have no information about the game-driven body's momentum with which to resolve the collision.) As such, game-driven bodies are usually moved using impulses—instantaneous changes in velocity that, when integrated forward in time, will position the bodies in the desired places at the end of the time step. Most physics SDKs provide a convenience function that will calculate the linear and angular impulses required in order to achieve a desired position and orientation on the next frame. When moving a game-driven body, we do have to be careful to zero out its velocity when it is supposed to stop. Otherwise, the body will continue forever along its last non-zero trajectory.

### Example: Animated Safe Door

Let's continue our example of the safe with a detachable door. Imagine that we want a character to walk up to the safe, dial the combination, open the door, deposit some money, and close and lock the door again. Later, we want a different character to get the money in a rather less-civilized manner—by blowing the door off the safe. To do this, the safe would be modeled with an additional submesh for the dial and an additional joint that allows the dial to be rotated. No rigid body is required for the dial, however, unless of course we want it to fly off when the door explodes.

During the animated sequence of the person opening and closing the safe, its rigid bodies can be put into game-driven mode. The animation now drives the joints, which in turn drive the rigid bodies. Later, when the door is to be blown off, we can switch the rigid bodies into physics-driven mode, break the hinge constraint, apply the impulse, and watch the door fly.

As you've probably already noticed, the hinge constraint is not actually needed in this particular example. It would only be required if the door is to be left open at some point and we want to see the door swinging naturally in response to the safe being moved or the door being bumped.

### 12.5.1.3.  Fixed Bodies

Most game worlds are composed of both static geometry and dynamic objects. To model the static components of the game world, most physics SDKs provide a special kind of rigid body known as a *fixed body*. Fixed bodies act a bit like game-driven bodies, but they do not take part in the dynamics simulation at all. They are, in effect, collision-only bodies. This optimization can give a big performance boost to most games, especially those whose worlds contain only a small number of dynamic objects moving around within a large static world.

### 12.5.1.4.  Havok's Motion Type

In Havok, all types of rigid body are represented by instances of the class `hkp RigidBody`. Each instance contains a field that specifies its *motion type*. The motion type tells the system whether the body is fixed, game-driven (what Havok calls "key framed"), or physics-driven (what Havok calls "dynamic"). If a rigid body is created with the fixed motion type, its type can never be changed. Otherwise, the motion type of a body can be changed dynamically at runtime. This feature can be incredibly useful. For example, an object that is in a character's hand would be game-driven. But as soon as the character drops or throws the object, it would be changed to physics-driven so the dynamics simulation can take over its motion. This is easily accomplished in Havok by simply changing the motion type at the moment of release.

The motion type also doubles as a way to give Havok some hints about the inertia tensor of a dynamic body. As such, the "dynamic" motion type is broken into subcategories such as "dynamic with sphere inertia," "dynamic with box inertia," and so on. Using the body's motion type, Havok can decide to apply various optimizations based on assumptions about the internal structure of the inertia tensor.

## 12.5.2.  Updating the Simulation

The physics simulation must of course be updated periodically, usually once per frame. This does not merely involve stepping the simulation (numerically integrating, resolving collisions, and applying constraints). The linkages between the game objects and their rigid bodies must be maintained as well. If the game needs to apply any forces or impulses to any of the rigid bodies, this must also be done every frame. The following steps are required to completely update the physics simulation:

- *Update game-driven rigid bodies.* The transforms of all game-driven rigid bodies in the physics world are updated so that they match the transforms of their counterparts (game objects or joints) in the game world.

- *Update phantoms.* A phantom shape acts like a game-driven collidable with no corresponding rigid body. It is used to perform certain kinds of collision queries. The locations of all phantoms are updated prior to the physics step, so that they will be in the right places when collision detection is run.

- *Update forces, apply impulses, and adjust constraints.* Any forces being applied by the game are updated. Any impulses caused by game events that occurred this frame are applied. Constraints are adjusted if necessary. (For example, a breakable hinge might be checked to determine if it has been broken; if so, the physics engine is instructed to remove the constraint.)

- *Step the simulation.* We saw in Section 12.4.10 that the collision and physics engines must both be updated periodically. This involves *numerically integrating* the equations of motion to find the physical state of all bodies on the next frame, running the *collision detection* algorithm to add and remove contacts from all rigid bodies in the physics world, *resolving collisions*, and *applying constraints*. Depending on the SDK, these update phases may be hidden behind a single atomic `step()` function, or it may be possible to run them individually.

- *Update physics-driven game objects.* The transforms of all physics-driven objects are extracted from the physics world, and the transforms of the corresponding game objects or joints are updated to match.

- *Query phantoms.* The contacts of each phantom shape are read after the physics step and used to make decisions.

- *Perform collision cast queries.* Ray casts and shape casts are kicked off, either synchronously or asynchronously. When the results of these queries become available, they are used by various engine systems to make decisions.

These tasks are usually performed in the order shown above, with the exception of ray and shape casts, which can theoretically be done at any time during the game loop. Clearly it makes sense to update game-driven bodies and apply forces and impulses prior to the step, so that the effects will be "seen" by the simulation. Likewise, physics-driven game objects should always be updated after the step, to ensure that we're using the most up-to-date body transforms. Rendering typically happens after everything else in the game loop. This ensures that we are rendering a consistent view of the game world at a particular instant in time.

### 12.5.2.1. Timing Collision Queries

In order to query the collision system for up-to-date information, we need to run our collision queries (ray and shape casts) after the physics step has run during the frame. However, the physics step is usually run toward the end of the frame, after the game logic has made most of its decisions and the new locations of any game-driven physics bodies have been determined. When then should collision queries be run?

This question does not have an easy answer. We have a number of options, and most games end up using some or all of them:

- *Base decisions on last frame's state.* In many cases, decisions can be made correctly based on last frame's collision information. For example, we might want to know whether or not the player was standing on something last frame, in order to decide whether or not he should start falling this frame. In this case, we can safely run our collision queries prior to the physics step.

- *Accept a one-frame lag.* Even if we really want to know what is happening *this frame*, we may be able to tolerate a one-frame lag in our collision query results. This is usually only true if the objects in question aren't moving too fast. For example, we might move one object forward in time and then want to know whether or not that object is now in the player's line of sight. A one-frame-off error in this kind of query may not be noticeable to the player. If this is the case, we can run the collision query prior to the physics step (returning collision information from the previous frame) and then use these results as if they were an *approximation* to the collision state at the end of the current frame.

- *Run the query after the physics step.* Another approach is to run certain queries after the physics step. This is feasible when the decisions being made based on the results of the query can be deferred until late in the frame. For example, a rendering effect that depends on the results of a collision query could be implemented this way.

### 12.5.2.2. Single-Threaded Updating

A very simple single-threaded game loop might look something like this:

```
F32 dt = 1.0f/30.0f;

for (;;) // main game loop
{
    g_hidManager->poll();
```

```
    g_gameObjectManager->preAnimationUpdate(dt);

    g_animationEngine->updateAnimations(dt);

    g_gameObjectManager->postAnimationUpdate(dt);

    g_physicsWorld->step(dt);

    g_animationEngine->updateRagDolls(dt);
    g_gameObjectManager->postPhysicsUpdate(dt);
    g_animationEngine->finalize();

    g_effectManager->update(dt);
    g_audioEngine->udate(dt);
    // etc.

    g_renderManager->render();

    dt = calcDeltaTime();
}
```

In this example, our game objects are updated in three phases: once before animation runs (during which they can queue up new animations, for example), once after the animation system has calculated final local poses and a tentative global pose (but before the final global pose and matrix palette has been generated), and once after the physics system has been stepped.

- The locations of all game-driven rigid bodies are generally updated in preAnimationUpdate() or postAnimationUpdate(). Each game-driven body's transform is set to match the location of either the game object that owns it or a joint in the owner's skeleton.
- The location of each physics-driven rigid body is generally read in postPhysicsUpdate() and used to update the location of either the game object or one of the joints in its skeleton.

One important concern is the frequency with which you are stepping the physics simulation. Most numerical integrators, collision detection algorithms, and constraint solvers operate best when the time between steps ($\Delta t$) is constant. It's usually a good idea to step your physics/collision SDK with an ideal 1/30 second or 1/60 second time delta and then govern the frame rate of your overall game loop.

### 12.5.2.3. Multithreaded Updating

Things get a bit more complicated when a physics engine is integrated into a multiprocessor or multithreaded game engine. In Section 7.6, we saw that there are many possible ways to structure the game loop to take advantage of multiprocessor hardware. Let's take a brief look at some of the physics-specific issues that arise when applying these techniques.

*Running Physics in a Separate Thread*

One option is to run the physics/collision engine in a dedicated thread. As you might guess, this kind of design can lead to race conditions. If a game object doesn't update its game-driven rigid bodies in time, the physics thread might end up using out-of-date locations in the simulation. Likewise, if the simulation isn't quite done by the time we want to update our physics-driven objects, the game objects might end up using out-of-date locations as well.

This problem can be solved by arranging for the physics and main threads to wait for one another—a process known as *thread synchronization*. This is done via mutexes, semaphores, or critical sections. Thread synchronization is usually a relatively expensive operation, so we generally aim to reduce the number of synchronization points between threads. In the case of the physics engine, we need two synchronization points at minimum—one that allows the physics simulation to begin each frame (after all game-driven rigid bodies have been updated) and one that notifies the main thread when the simulation is complete (thereby allowing physics-driven bodies to be queried).

As part of a strategy to reduce synchronization points, communication between threads is usually done via a command queue. The main thread locks a critical section, writes some commands into the queue, and then quickly releases it. The physics thread picks up the next batch of commands whenever it gets the chance, again locking the critical section to ensure that the main thread isn't overwriting the queue during the read.

In the presence of collision queries, things get even more complicated. To manage access to the collision/physics world by multiple threads, physics engines like Havok allow the world to be locked and unlocked separately for reading and for writing. This allows collision queries to be performed at any time during the game loop (during which the world is locked for read) except while the physics world is being updated (during which it is locked for write).

*Fork and Join*

The nice thing about a fork and join architecture for physics is that it essentially eliminates all inter-thread synchronization issues. The main thread runs as usual until the physics system needs to be stepped. Then we fork the step off into separate threads (ideally one per processing core or hardware thread) in order to execute it as quickly as possible. When all threads have completed their work, the results can be collated, and the main thread can continue as in the single-threaded case. Of course, for this to work, the physics system must be designed to support fork and join. Most physics SDKs, including Havok and PhysX, make use of collision islands—groups of rigid bodies that can be simulated independently of one another. This design lends itself well to a fork and join architecture, as the islands can be dynamically distributed among the available threads.

### Jobs

A job model can be particularly useful for physics processing if the physics SDK allows the individual phases of its update step (integration, collision detection, constraint solving, CCD, etc.) to be run independently. This allows us to kick off each phase whenever it is most convenient and perform useful unrelated work in the main thread while we wait for the physics engine to do its thing.

Jobs are even more useful when doing collision queries (ray and shape casts). This is because while a game engine typically only needs to step the physics simulation once per frame, collision queries may be required at many different points during the game loop. If lightweight jobs are used to run queries, we can simply kick off jobs whenever we need them. On the other hand, if collision queries can only be run at certain times during the frame (because they are being executed by a fork or a dedicated thread), this makes the job of the game programmer more difficult. He or she needs to collect all the collision queries in a queue and then execute them as a batch the next time queries are run during the frame. These two approaches are compared in Figure 12.36.

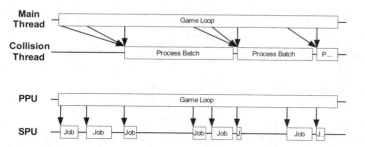

**Figure 12.36.** Collision queries are often batched, to be run at a few well-chosen points during the game loop. However, with a job model, queries can be kicked off at any time, without the need to batch them.

## 12.5.3. Example Uses of Collision and Physics in a Game

To make our discussion of collision and physics more concrete, let's take a high-level look at a few common examples of how collision and/or physics simulations are commonly used in real games.

### 12.5.3.1. Simple Rigid Body Game Objects

Many games include simple physically simulated objects like weapons, rocks that can be picked up and thrown, empty magazines, furniture, objects on shelves that can be shot, and so on. Such objects might be implemented by creating a custom game object class and giving it a reference to a rigid body in the physics world (e.g., `hkRigidBody` if we're using Havok). Or we might create an add-on component class that handles simple rigid body collision and physics, allowing this feature to be added to virtually any type of game object in the engine.

Simple physics objects usually change their motion type at runtime. They are game-driven when being held in a character's hand and physics-driven when in free fall after having been dropped.

Imagine that a simple physics object is to be placed on a table or shelf, to be knocked off at some point by being struck by a bullet or other object. What motion type should it be given initially? Should we make it physics-driven and let the simulation put it to sleep until it is struck? Or should we keep it game-driven when at rest and change it to physics-driven when hit? This depends largely on the game design. If we require tight control over when the object is allowed to be knocked down, then we might go the game-driven route; otherwise, physics-driven may suffice.

### 12.5.3.2. Bullet Traces

Whether or not you approve of game violence, the fact remains that bullets and projectiles of one form or another are a big part of most games. Let's look at how these are typically implemented.

Sometimes bullets are implemented using ray casts. On the frame that the weapon is fired, we shoot off a ray cast, determine what object was hit, and immediately impart the impact to the affected object.

Unfortunately, the ray cast approach does not account for the travel time of the projectile. It also does not account for the slight downward trajectory caused by the influence of gravity. If these details are important to the game, we can model our projectiles using real rigid bodies that move through the collision/physics world over time. This is especially useful for slower-moving projectiles, like thrown objects or rockets.

There are plenty of issues to consider and deal with when implementing bullets and projectiles. Here are a few of the most common ones:

- Does the ray come from the camera focal point or from the tip of the gun in the player character's hands? This is especially problematic in a third-person shooter, where the ray coming out of the player's gun usually does not align with the ray coming from the camera focal point through the reticle in the center of the screen. This can lead to situations in which the reticle appears to be on top of a target yet the third-person character is clearly behind an obstacle and would not be able to shoot that target from his point of view. Various "tricks" must usually be employed to ensure that the player feels like he or she is shooting what he or she is aiming at while maintaining plausible visuals on the screen.

- Mismatches between collision geometry and visible geometry can lead to situations in which the player can see the target through a small crack or just over the edge of some other object and yet the collision geometry is solid and hence the bullet cannot reach the target. (This is usually only a problem for the player character.) One solution to this problem is to use a render query instead of a collision query to determine if the ray actually hit the target. For example, during one of the rendering passes, we could generate a texture in which each pixel stores the unique identifier of the game object to which it corresponds. We can then query this texture to determine whether or not an enemy character or other suitable target is beneath the weapon's reticle.

- AI characters may need to "lead" their shots if projectiles take a finite amount of time to reach their targets.

- When bullets hit their targets, we may want to trigger a sound or a particle effect, lay down a decal, or perform other tasks.

### 12.5.3.3. Grenades

Grenades in games are sometimes implemented as free-moving physics objects. However, this leads to a significant loss of control. Some control can be regained by imposing various artificial forces or impulses on the grenade. For example, we could apply an extreme air drag once the grenade bounces for the first time, in an attempt to limit the distance it can bounce away from its target.

Some game teams actually go so far as to manage the grenade's motion entirely manually. The arc of a grenade's trajectory can be calculated beforehand, using a series of ray casts to determine what target it would hit if released. The trajectory can even be shown to the player via some kind of on-screen display. When the grenade is thrown, the game moves it along its arc and can then carefully control the bounce so that it never goes too far away from its target, while still looking natural.

### 12.5.3.4. Explosions

In a game, an explosion typically has a few components: some kind of visual effect like a fireball and smoke, audio effects to mimic the sound of the explosion and its impacts with objects in the world, and a growing damage radius that affects any objects in its wake.

When an object finds itself in the radius of an explosion, its health is typically reduced, and we often also want to impart some motion to mimic the effect of the shock wave. This might be done via an animation. (For example, the reaction of character to an explosion might best be done this way.) We might also wish to allow the impact reaction to be driven entirely by the dynamics simulation. We can accomplish this by having the explosion apply impulses to any suitable objects within its radius. It's pretty easy to calculate direction of these impulses—they are typically radial, calculated by normalizing the vector from the center of the explosion to the center of the impacted object and then scaling this vector by the magnitude of the explosion (and perhaps falling off as the distance from the epicenter increases).

Explosions may interact with other engine systems as well. For example, we might want to impart a "force" to the animated foliage system, causing grass, plants and trees to momentarily bend as a result of the explosion's shock wave.

### 12.5.3.5. Destructible Objects

Destructible objects are commonplace in many games. These objects are peculiar because they start out in an undamaged state in which they must appear to be a single cohesive object, and yet they must be capable of breaking into many separate pieces. We may want the pieces to break off one by one, allowing the object to be "whittled down" gradually, or we may only require a single catastrophic explosion.

Deformable body simulations like DMM can handle destruction naturally. However, we can also implement breakable objects using rigid body dynamics. This is typically done by dividing a model into a number of breakable pieces and assigning a separate rigid body to each one. For reasons of performance optimization and/or visual quality, we might decide to use special "undamaged" versions of the visual and collision geometry, each of which is constructed as a single solid piece. This model can be swapped out for the damaged version when the object needs to start breaking apart. In other cases, we may want to model the object as separate pieces at all times. This might be appropriate if the object is a stack of bricks or a pile of pots and pans, for example.

To model a multi-piece object, we could simply stack a bunch of rigid bodies and let physics simulation take care of it. This can be made to work in good-quality physics engines (although it's not always trivial to get right). However, we may want some Hollywood-style effects that cannot be achieved with a simple stack of rigid bodies.

For example, we may want to define the structure of the object. Some pieces might be *indestructible*, like the base of a wall or the chassis of a car. Others might be *non-structural*—they just fall off when hit by bullets or other objects. Still other pieces might be *structural*—if they are hit, not only do they fall, but they also impart forces to other pieces lying on top of them. Some pieces could be *explosive*—when they are hit, they create secondary explosions or propagate damage throughout the structure. We may want some pieces to act as valid *cover* points for characters but not others. This implies that our breakable object system may have some connections to the cover system.

We might also want our breakable objects to have a notion of health. Damage might build up until eventually the whole thing collapses, or each piece might have a health, requiring multiples shots or impacts before it is allowed to break. Constraints might also be employed to allow broken pieces to hang off the object rather than coming away from it completely.

We may also want our structures to take time to collapse completely. For example, if a long bridge is hit by an explosion at one end, the collapse should slowly propagate from one end to the other so that the bridge looks massive. This is another example of a feature the physics system won't give you for free—it would just wake up all rigid bodies in the simulation island simultaneously. These kinds of effects can be implemented through judicious use of the game-driven motion type.

### 12.5.3.6. Character Mechanics

For a game like bowling, pinball, or *Marble Madness*, the "main character" is a ball that rolls around in an imaginary game world. For this kind of game, we could very well model the ball as a free-moving rigid body in the physics simulation and control its movements by applying forces and impulses to it during gameplay.

In character-based games, however, we usually don't take this kind of approach. The movement of a humanoid or animal character is usually far too complex to be controlled adequately with forces and impulses. Instead, we usually model characters as a set of game-driven capsule-shaped rigid bodies, each one linked to a joint in the character's animated skeleton. These bodies are primarily used for bullet hit detection or to generate secondary effects such as when a character's arm bumps an object off a table. Because these bodies are game-driven, they won't avoid interpenetrations with immovable objects in the physics world, so it is up to the animator to ensure that the character's movements appear believable.

To move the character around in the game world, most games use sphere or capsule casts to probe in the direction of desired motion. Collisions are resolved manually. This allows us to do cool stuff like:

- having the character slide along walls when he runs into them at an oblique angle;

- allowing the character to "pop up" over low curbs rather than getting stuck;

- preventing the character from entering a "falling" state when he walks off a low curb;

- preventing the character from walking up slopes that are too steep (most games have a cut-off angle after which the character will slide back rather than being able to walk up the slope);

- adjusting animations to accommodate collisions.

As an example of this last point, if the character is running directly into a wall at a roughly 90 degree angle, we can let the character "moonwalk" into the wall forever, or we can slow down his animation. We can also do something even more slick, like playing an animation in which the character sticks out his hand and touches the wall and then idles sensibly until the movement direction changes.

Havok provides a character controller system that handles many of these things. In Havok's system, illustrated in Figure 12.37, a character is modeled as a capsule phantom that is moved each frame to find a potential new location. A collision contact manifold (i.e., a collection of contact planes, cleaned up to eliminate noise) is maintained for the character. This manifold can be

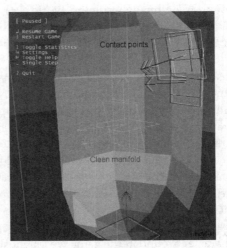

**Figure 12.37.** Havok's character controller models a character as a capsule-shaped phantom. The phantom maintains a noise-reduced collision manifold (a collection of contact planes) that can be used by the game to make movement decisions.

analyzed each frame in order to determine how best to move the character, adjust animations, and so on.

### 12.5.3.7. Camera Collision

In many games, the camera follows the player's character or vehicle around in the game world, and it can often by rotated or controlled in limited ways by the person playing the game. It's important in such games to never permit the camera to interpenetrate geometry in the scene, as this would break the illusion of realism. The camera system is therefore another important client of the collision engine in many games.

The basic idea behind most camera collision systems is to surround the virtual camera with one or more sphere phantoms or sphere cast queries that can detect when it is getting close to colliding with something. The system can respond by adjusting the camera's position and/or orientation in some way to avoid the potential collision before the camera actually passes through the object in question.

This sounds simple enough, but it is actually an incredibly tricky problem requiring a great deal of trial and error to get right. To give you a feel for how much effort can be involved, many game teams have a dedicated engineer working on the camera system for the entire duration of the project. We can't possibly cover camera collision detection and resolution in any depth here, but the following list should give you a sense of some of the most pertinent issues to be aware of:

- Zooming the camera in to avoid collisions works well in a wide variety of situations. In a third-person game, you can zoom all the way in to a first-person view without causing too much trouble (other than making sure the camera doesn't interpenetrate the character's head in the process).

- It's usually a bad idea to drastically change the horizontal angle of the camera in response to collisions, as this tends to mess with camera-relative player controls. However, some degree of horizontal adjustment can work well, depending on what the player is expected to be doing at the time. If she is aiming at a target, she'll be angry with you if you throw off her aim to bring the camera out of collision. But if she's just locomoting through the world, the change in camera orientation may feel entirely natural.

- You can adjust the vertical angle of the camera to some degree, but it's important not to do too much of this or the player will lose track of the horizon and end up looking down onto the top of the player character's head!

- Some games allow the camera to move along an arc lying in a vertical plane, perhaps described by a spline. This permits a single HID control such as the vertical deflection of the left thumb stick to control both the zoom and the vertical angle of the camera in an intuitive way. (The camera in *Uncharted: Drake's Fortune* works this way.) When the camera comes into collision with objects in the world, it can be automatically moved along this same arc to avoid the collision, the arc might be compressed horizontally, or any number of other approaches might be taken.

- It's important to consider not only what's behind and beside the camera but what is in front of it as well. For example, what should happen if a pillar or another character comes between the camera and the player character? In some games, the offending object becomes translucent; in others, the camera zooms in or swings around to avoid the collision. This may or may not feel good to the person playing the game! How you handle these kinds of situations can make or break the perceived quality of your game.

- You may want the camera to react to collisions differently in different situations. For example, when the main character is not engaged in a battle, it might be acceptable to swing the camera horizontally to avoid collisions. But when the player is trying to fire at targets, both horizontal and vertical camera swings will throw off his or her aim, so zoom may be the only option.

Even after taking account of these and many other problematic situations, your camera may not look or feel right! Always budget plenty of time for trial and error when implementing a camera collision system.

### 12.5.3.8. Rag Doll Integration

In Section 12.4.8.7, we learned how special types of constraints can be used to link a collection of rigid bodies together to mimic the behavior of a limp (dead or unconscious) human body. In this section, we'll investigate a few of the issues that arise when integrating rag doll physics into your game.

As we saw in Section 12.5.3.6, the gross movements of a conscious character are usually determined by performing shape casts or moving a phantom shape around in the game world. The detailed movements of the character's body are typically driven by animations. Game-driven rigid bodies are sometimes attached to the limbs for the purposes of weapons targeting or to allow the character to knock over other objects in the world.

When a character becomes unconscious, the rag doll system kicks in. The character's limbs are modeled as capsule-shaped rigid bodies connected via constraints and linked to joints in the character's animated skeleton. The physics system simulates the motions of these bodies, and we update the skeletal joints to match, thereby allowing physics to move the character's body.

The set of rigid bodies used for rag doll physics might not be the same ones affixed to the character's limbs when it was alive. This is because the two collision models have very different requirements. When the character is alive, its rigid bodies are game-driven, so we don't care if they interpenetrate. And in fact, we usually want them to overlap, so there aren't any holes through which an enemy character might shoot. But when the character turns into a rag doll, it's important that the rigid bodies do not interpenetrate, as this would cause the collision resolution system to impart large impulses that would tend to make the limbs explode outward! For these reasons, it's actually quite common for characters to have entirely different collision/physics representations depending on whether they're conscious or unconscious.

Another issue is how to transition from the conscious state to the unconscious state. A simple LERP animation blend between animation-generated and physics-generated poses usually doesn't work very well, because the physics pose very quickly diverges from the animation pose. (A blend between two totally unrelated poses usually doesn't look natural.) As such, we may want to use powered constraints during the transition (see Section 12.4.8.8).

Characters often interpenetrate background geometry when they are conscious (i.e., when their rigid bodies are game-driven). This means that the rigid bodies might be inside another solid object when the character transitions to rag doll (physics-driven) mode. This can give rise to huge impulses that cause rather wild-looking rag doll behavior in-game. To avoid these problems, it is best to author death animations carefully, so that the character's limbs are kept out of collision as best as possible. It's also important to detect collisions via phantoms or collision callbacks during the game-driven mode so that you can drop the character into rag doll mode the moment any part of his body touches something solid.

Even when these steps are taken, rag dolls have a tendency to get stuck inside other objects. Single-sided collision can be an incredibly important feature when trying to make rag dolls look good. If a limb is partly embedded in a wall, it will tend to be pushed out of the wall rather than staying stuck inside it. However, even single-sided collision doesn't solve all problems. For example, when the character is moving quickly or if the transition to rag doll isn't executed properly, one rigid body in the rag doll can end up on the far side of a thin wall. This causes the character to hang in mid air rather than falling properly to the ground.

Another rag doll feature that is in vogue these days is the ability for unconscious characters to regain consciousness and get back up. To implement this, we need a way to search for a suitable "stand up" animation. We want to find an animation whose pose on frame zero most closely matches the rag doll's pose after it has come to rest (which is totally unpredictable in general). This can be done by matching the poses of only a few key joints, like the upper thighs and the upper arms. Another approach is to manually guide the rag doll into a pose suitable for getting up by the time it comes to rest, using powered constraints.

As a final note, we should mention that setting up a rag doll's constraints can be a tricky business. We generally want the limbs to move freely but without doing anything biomechanically impossible. This is one reason specialized types of constraints are often used when constructing rag dolls. Nonetheless, you shouldn't assume that your rag dolls will look great without some effort. High-quality physics engines like Havok provide a rich set of content creation tools that allow an artist to set up constraints within a DCC package like Maya and then test them in real time to see how they might look in-game.

All in all, getting rag doll physics to *work* in your game isn't particularly difficult, but getting it to look *good* can take a lot of work! As with many things in game programming, it's a good idea to budget plenty of time for trial and error, especially when it's your first time working with rag dolls.

## 12.6. A Look Ahead: Advanced Physics Features

A rigid body dynamics simulation with constraints can cover an amazing range of physics-driven effects in a game. However, such a system clearly has its limitations. Recent research and development is seeking to expand physics engines beyond constrained rigid bodies. Here are just a few examples:

- *Deformable bodies.* As hardware capabilities improve and more-efficient algorithms are developed, physics engines are beginning to provide support for deformable bodies. DMM is an excellent example of such an engine.

- *Cloth.* Cloth can be modeled as a sheet of point masses, connected by stiff springs. However, cloth is notoriously difficult to get right, as many difficulties arise with respect to collision between cloth and other objects, numerical stability of the simulation, etc.

- *Hair.* Hair can be modeled by a large number of small physically simulated filments, or a simpler approach can be used to make a character's hair move as if it were a rope or deformable body. This is an active area of research, and the quality of hair in games continues to improve.

- *Water surface simulations and buoyancy.* Games have been doing water surface simulations and buoyancy for some time now. This can be done via a special-case system (not part of the physics engine per se), or it can be modeled via forces within the physics simulation. Organic movement of the water surface is often a rendering effect only and does not affect the physics simulation at all. From the point of view of physics, the water surface is often modeled as a plane. For large displacements in the water surface, the entire plane might be moved. However, some game teams and researchers are pushing the limits of these simulations, allowing for dynamic water surfaces, waves that crest, realistic current simulations, and more.

- *General fluid dynamics simulations.* Right now, fluid dynamics falls into the realm of specialized simulation libraries. However, this is an active area of research, and it may well eventually find its way into mainstream physics engines.

# Part IV
# Gameplay

# 13
# Introduction to Gameplay Systems

Up until now, everything we've talked about in this book has focused on technology. We've learned that a game engine is a complex, layered software system built on top of the hardware, drivers, and operating system of the target machine. We've seen how low-level engine systems provide services that are required by the rest of the engine; how human interface devices such as joypads, keyboards, mice, and other devices can allow a human player to provide inputs to the engine; how the rendering engine produces 3D images on-screen; how the collision system detects and resolves interpenetrations between shapes; how the physics simulation causes objects to move in physically realistic ways; how the animation system allows characters and objects to move naturally. But despite the wide range of powerful features provided by these components, if we were to put them all together, we *still* wouldn't have a game!

A game is defined not by its technology but by its *gameplay*. Gameplay can be defined as the overall experience of playing a game. The term *game mechanics* pins down this idea a bit more concretely—it is usually defined as the set of *rules* that govern the interactions between the various entities in the game. It also defines the *objectives* of the player(s), *criteria* for success and failure, the player character's *abilities*, the number and types of *non-player entities* that exist within the game's virtual world, and the *overall flow* of the gaming experience as a whole. In many games, these elements are intertwined with a compelling story and a rich cast of characters. However, story and characters are definitely not a necessary part of every video game, as evidenced by wildly successful puzzle games like *Tetris*. In their paper, "A Survey of 'Game' Portability" (http://www.dcs.shef.ac.uk/intranet/research/resmes/CS0705.pdf), Ahmed BinSubaih, Steve Maddock, and Daniela Romano of the University of Sheffield refer to the collection of software systems used to implement gameplay as a game's *G-factor*. In the next three chapters, we'll explore the crucial tools and engine systems that define and manage the *game mechanics* (a.k.a. *gameplay*, a.k.a. *G-factor*) of a game.

## 13.1.   Anatomy of a Game World

Gameplay designs vary widely from genre to genre and from game to game. That said, most 3D games, and a good number of 2D games as well, conform more or less to a few basic structural patterns. We'll discuss these patterns in the following sections, but please keep in mind that there are bound to be games out there that do not fit neatly into this mold.

### 13.1.1.   World Elements

Most video games take place in a two- or three-dimensional virtual *game world*. This world is typically comprised of numerous discrete elements. Generally, these elements fall into two categories: static elements and dynamic elements. Static elements include terrain, buildings, roads, bridges, and pretty much anything that doesn't move or interact with gameplay in an active way. Dynamic elements include characters, vehicles, weaponry, floating power-ups and health packs, collectible objects, particle emitters, dynamic lights, invisible regions used to detect important events in the game, splines that define the paths of objects, and so on. This breakdown of the game world is illustrated in Figure 13.1.

Gameplay is generally concentrated within the dynamic elements of a game. Clearly, the layout of the static background plays a crucial role in how the game plays out. For example, a cover-based shooter wouldn't be very much fun if it were played in a big, empty, rectangular room. However, the software systems that implement gameplay are primarily concerned with updating the locations, orientations, and internal states of the dynamic elements, since they are the elements that change over time. The term *game state* refers to the current state of all dynamic game world elements, taken as a whole.

The ratio of dynamic to static elements also varies from game to game. Most 3D games consist of a relatively small number of dynamic elements mov-

**Figure 13.1.** A typical game world is comprised of both static and dynamic elements.

ing about within a relatively large static background area. Other games, like the arcade classic *Asteroids* or the Xbox 360 retro hit *Geometry Wars*, have no static elements to speak of (other than a black screen). The dynamic elements of a game are usually more expensive than the static elements in terms of CPU resources, so most 3D games are constrained to a limited number of dynamic elements. However, the higher the ratio of dynamic to static elements, the more "alive" the game world can seem to the player. As gaming hardware becomes more and more powerful, games are achieving higher and higher dynamic-to-static ratios.

It's important to note that the distinction between the dynamic and static elements in a game world is often a bit blurry. For example, in the arcade game *Hydro Thunder*, the waterfalls were dynamic, in the sense that their textures animated, they had dynamic mist effects at their bases, and they could be placed into the game world and positioned by a game designer independently of the terrain and water surface. However, from an engineering standpoint, waterfalls were treated as static elements because they did not interact with the boats in the race in any way (other than to obscure the player's view of hidden boost power-ups and secret passageways). Different game engines draw different lines between static and dynamic elements, and some don't draw a distinction at all (i.e., everything is potentially a dynamic element).

The distinction between static and dynamic serves primarily as an optimization tool—we can do less work when we know that the state of an object isn't going to change. For example, the vertices of a static triangle mesh can be specified in world space, thereby saving the per-vertex matrix multiplication normally required to transform from model space to world space during rendering. Lighting can be precomputed, in the form of static vertex lighting, light maps, shadow maps, static ambient occlusion information, or precomputed radiance transfer (PRT) spherical harmonics coefficients. Virtually any computation that must be done at runtime for a dynamic world element is a good candidate for precomputation or omission when applied to a static element.

Games with destructible environments are an example of how the line between the static and dynamic elements in a game world can blur. For instance, we might define three versions of every static element—an undamaged version, a damaged version, and a fully destroyed version. These background elements act like static world elements most of the time, but they can be swapped dynamically during an explosion to produce the illusion of becoming damaged. In reality, static and dynamic world elements are just two extremes along a gamut of possible optimizations. Where we draw the line between the two categories (if we draw one at all) shifts as our optimization methodologies change and adapt to the needs of the game design.

### 13.1.1.1. Static Geometry

The geometry of a static world element is often defined in a tool like Maya. It might be one giant triangle mesh, or it might be broken up into discrete pieces. The static portions of the scene are sometimes built out of *instanced geometry*. Instancing is a memory conservation technique in which a relatively small number of unique triangle meshes are rendered multiple times throughout the game world, at different locations and orientations, in order to provide the illusion of variety. For example, a 3D modeler might create five different kinds of short wall sections and then piece them together in random combinations in order to construct miles of unique-looking walls.

Static visual elements and collision data might also be constructed from *brush geometry*. This kind of geometry originated with the Quake family of engines. A *brush* describes a shape as a collection of convex volumes, each bounded by a set of planes. Brush geometry is fast and easy to create and integrates well into a BSP-tree-based rendering engine. Brushes can be really useful for rapidly blocking out the contents of a game world. This allows gameplay to be tested early, when it is cheap to do so. If the layout proves its worth, the art team can either texture map and fine-tune the brush geometry or replace it with more-detailed custom mesh assets. On the other hand, if the level requires redesign, the brush geometry can be easily revised without creating a lot of rework for the art team.

## 13.1.2.  World Chunks

When a game takes place in a very large virtual world, it is typically divided into discrete playable regions, which we'll call *world chunks*. Chunks are also known as *levels*, *maps*, *stages*, or *areas*. The player can usually see only one, or at most a handful, of chunks at any given moment while playing the game, and he or she progresses from chunk to chunk as the game unfolds.

Originally, the concept of "levels" was invented as a mechanism to provide greater variety of gameplay within the memory limitations of early gam-

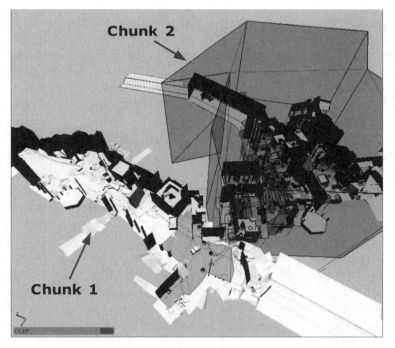

Figure 13.2. Many game worlds are divided into chunks for various reasons, including memory limitations, the need to control the flow of the game through the world, and as a division-of-labor mechanism during development.

ing hardware. Only one level could exist in memory at a time, but the player could progress from level to level for a much richer overall experience. Since then, game designs have branched out in many directions, and linear level-based games are much less common today. Some games are essentially still linear, but the delineations between world chunks are usually not as obvious to the player as they once were. Other games use a star topology, in which the player starts in a central hub area and can access other areas at random from the hub (perhaps only after they have been unlocked). Others use a graph-like topology, where areas are connected to one another in arbitrary ways. Still others provide the illusion of a vast, open world.

Despite the richness of modern game designs, all but the smallest of game worlds are still divided into chunks of some kind. This is done for a number of reasons. First of all, memory limitations are still an important constraint (and will be until game machines with infinite memory hit the market!). World chunks are also a convenient mechanism for controlling the overall flow of the game. Chunks can serve as a division-of-labor mechanism as well; each chunk can be constructed and managed by a relatively small group of designers and artists. World chunks are illustrated in Figure 13.2.

### 13.1.3.  High-Level Game Flow

A game's *high-level flow* defines a sequence, tree, or graph of player *objectives*. Objectives are sometimes called *tasks*, *stages*, *levels* (a term that can also apply to world chunks), or *waves* (if the game is primarily about defeating hordes of attacking enemies). The high-level flow also provides the definition of success for each objective (e.g., clear all the enemies and get the key) and the penalty for failure (e.g., go back to the start of the current area, possibly losing a "life" in the process). In a story-driven game, this flow might also include various in-game movies that serve to advance the player's understanding of the story as it unfolds. These sequences are sometimes called *cut-scenes*, *in-game cinematics* (IGC), or *noninteractive sequences* (NIS). When they are rendered offline and played back as a full-screen movie, such sequences are usually called *full-motion videos* (FMV).

Early games mapped the objectives of the player one-to-one to particular world chunks (hence the dual meaning of the term "level"). For example, in *Donkey Kong*, each new level presents Mario with a new objective (namely to reach the top of the structure and progress to the next level). However, this one-to-one mapping between world chunks and objectives is less popular in modern game design. Each objective is associated with one or more world chunks, but the coupling between chunks and objectives remains deliberately loose. This kind of design offers the flexibility to alter game objectives and

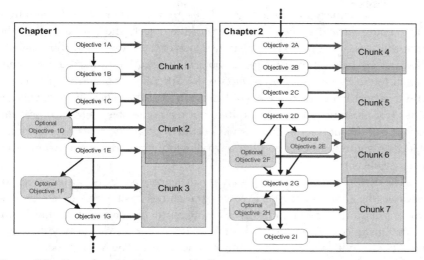

**Figure 13.3.** Gameplay objectives are typically arranged in a sequence, tree, or graph, and each one maps to one or more game world chunks.

world subdivision independently, which is extremely helpful from a logistic and practical standpoint when developing a game. Many games group their objectives into coarser sections of gameplay, often called *chapters* or *acts*. A typical gameplay architecture is shown in Figure 13.3.

## 13.2. Implementing Dynamic Elements: Game Objects

The dynamic elements of a game are usually designed in an object-oriented fashion. This approach is intuitive and natural and maps well to the game designer's notion of how the world is constructed. He or she can visualize characters, vehicles, floating health packs, exploding barrels, and myriad other dynamic objects moving about in the game. So it is only natural to want to be able to create and manipulate these elements in the game world editor. Likewise, programmers usually find it natural to implement dynamic elements as largely autonomous agents at runtime. In this book, we'll use the term *game object* (GO) to refer to virtually any dynamic element within a game world. However, this terminology is by no means standard within the industry. Game objects are commonly referred to as *entities*, *actors*, or *agents*, and the list of terms goes on.

As is customary in object-oriented design, a game object is essentially a collection of *attributes* (the current state of the object) and *behaviors* (how the state changes over time and in response to events). Game objects are usually classified by *type*. Different types of objects have different attribute schemas and different behaviors. All *instances* of a particular type share the same attribute schema and the same set of behaviors, but the *values* of the attributes differ from instance to instance. (Note that if a game object's *behavior* is data-driven, say through script code or via a set of data-driven rules governing the object's responses to events, then behavior too can vary on an instance-by-instance basis.)

The distinction between a *type* and an *instance* of a type is a crucial one. For example, the game of *Pac-Man* involves four game object types: ghosts, pellets, power pills, and Pac-Man. However, at any moment in time, there may be up to four instances of the type "ghost," 50–100 instances of the type "pellet," four "power pill" instances, and one instance of the "Pac-Man" type.

Most object-oriented systems provide some mechanism for the *inheritance* of attributes, behavior, or both. Inheritance encourages code and design reuse. The specifics of how inheritance works varies widely from game to game, but most game engines support it in some form.

## 13.2.1. Game Object Models

In computer science, the term *object model* has two related but distinct meanings. It can refer to the set of features provided by a particular programming language or formal design language. For example, we might speak of the *C++ object model* or the *OMT object model*. It can also refer to a specific object-oriented programming interface (i.e., a collection of classes, methods, and interrelationships designed to solve a particular problem). One example of this latter usage is the *Microsoft Excel object model*, which allows external programs to control Excel in various ways. (See http://en.wikipedia.org/wiki/Object_model for further discussion of the term *object model*.)

In this book, we will use the term *game object model* to describe the facilities provided by a game engine in order to permit the dynamic entities in the virtual game world to be modeled and simulated. In this sense, the term *game object model* has aspects of *both* of the definitions given above:

- A game's object model is a specific object-oriented programming interface intended to solve the particular problem of simulating the specific set of entities that make up a particular game.

- Additionally, a game's object model often extends the programming language in which the engine was written. If the game is implemented in a non-object-oriented language like C, object-oriented facilities can be added by the programmers. And even if the game is written in an object-oriented language like C++, advanced features like reflection, persistence, and network replication are often added. A game object model sometimes melds the features of multiple languages. For example, a game engine might combine a compiled programming language such as C or C++ with a scripting language like Python, Lua, or Pawn and provide a unified object model that can be accessed from either language.

## 13.2.2. Tool-Side Design versus Runtime Design

The object model presented to the designers via the world editor (discussed below) needn't be the same object model used to implement the game at runtime.

- The tool-side game object model might be implemented at runtime using a language with no native object-oriented features at all, like C.

- A single GO type on the tool side might be implemented as a collection of classes at runtime (rather than as a single class as one might at first expect).

- Each tool-side GO might be nothing more than a unique id at runtime, with all of its state data stored in tables or collections of loosely coupled objects.

Therefore, a game really has two distinct but closely interrelated object models:

- The *tool-side object model* is defined by the set of *game object types* seen by the designers within the world editor.

- The *runtime object model* is defined by whatever set of language constructs and software systems the programmers have used to implement the tool-side object model at runtime. The runtime object model might be identical to the tool-side model or map directly to it, or it might be entirely different than the tool-side model under the hood.

In some game engines, the line between the tool-side and runtime designs is blurred or non-existent. In others, it is very well delineated. In some engines, the implementation is actually shared between the tools and the runtime. In others, the runtime implementation looks almost totally alien relative to the tool-side view of things. Some aspects of the implementation almost always creep up into the tool-side design, and game designers must be cognizant of the performance and memory consumption impacts of the game worlds they construct and the gameplay rules and object behaviors they design. That said, virtually all game engines have some form of tool-side object model and a corresponding runtime implementation of that object model.

## 13.3. Data-Driven Game Engines

In the early days of game development, games were largely hard-coded by programmers. Tools, if any, were primitive. This worked because the amount of content in a typical game was miniscule, and the bar wasn't particularly high, thanks in part to the primitive graphics and sound of which early game hardware was capable.

Today, games are orders of magnitude more complex, and the quality bar is so high that game content is often compared to the computer-generated effects in Hollywood blockbusters. Game teams have grown much larger, but the amount of game content is growing faster than team size. In the most recent generation, defined by the Wii, the Xbox 360, and the PLAYSTATION 3, game teams routinely speak of the need to produce ten times the content, with teams that are at most 25% larger than in the previous generation. This trend means that a game team must be capable of producing very large amounts of content in an extremely efficient manner.

Engineering resources are often a production bottleneck because high-quality engineering talent is limited and expensive and because engineers tend to produce content much more slowly than artists and game designers (due to the complexities inherent in computer programming). Most teams now believe that it's a good idea to put at least some of the power to create content directly into the hands of the folks responsible for producing that content—namely the designers and the artists. When the behavior of a game can be controlled, in whole or in part, by *data* provided by artists and designers rather than exclusively by *software* produced by programmers, we say the engine is *data-driven*.

Data-driven architectures can improve team efficiency by fully leveraging all staff members to their fullest potential and by taking some of the heat off the engineering team. It can also lead to improved *iteration times*. Whether a developer wants to make a slight tweak to the game's content or completely revise an entire level, a data-driven design allows the developer to see the effects of the changes quickly, ideally with little or no help from an engineer. This saves valuable time and can permit the team to polish their game to a very high level of quality.

That being said, it's important to realize that data-driven features often come at a heavy cost. Tools must be provided to allow game designers and artists to define game content in a data-driven manner. The runtime code must be changed to handle the wide range of possible inputs in a robust way. Tools must also be provided in-game to allow artists and designers to preview their work and troubleshoot problems. All of this software requires significant time and effort to write, test, and maintain.

Sadly, many teams make a mad rush into data-driven architectures without stopping to study the impacts of their efforts on their particular game design and the specific needs of their team members. In their haste, such teams often dramatically overshoot the mark, producing overly complex tools and engine systems that are difficult to use, bug-ridden, and virtually impossible to adapt to the changing requirements of the project. Ironically, in their efforts to realize the benefits of a data-driven design, a team can easily end up with significantly lower productivity than the old-fashioned hard-coded methods.

Every game engine should have some data-driven components, but a game team must exercise extreme care when selecting which aspects of the engine to data-drive. It's crucial to weigh the costs of creating a data-driven or rapid iteration feature against the amount of time the feature is expected to save the team over the course of the project. It's also incredibly important to keep the KISS mantra ("keep it simple, stupid") in mind when designing and implementing data-driven tools and engine systems. To paraphrase Albert Einstein, everything in a game engine should be made as simple as possible, but no simpler.

## 13.4. The Game World Editor

We've already discussed data-driven asset-creation tools, such as Maya, Photoshop, Havok content tools, and so on. These tools generate individual assets for consumption by the rendering engine, animation system, audio system, physics system, and so on. The analog to these tools in the gameplay space is the *game world editor*—a tool (or a suite of tools) that permits game world chunks to be defined and populated with static and dynamic elements.

All commercial game engines have some kind of world editor tool. A well-known tool called *Radiant* is used to create maps for the *Quake* and *Doom* family of engines. A screen shot of Radiant is shown in Figure 13.4. Valve's *Source* engine, the engine that drives *Half-Life 2*, *The Orange Box* and *Team Fortress 2*, provides an editor called *Hammer* (previously distributed under the names *Worldcraft* and *The Forge*). Figure 13.5 shows a screen shot of Hammer.

The game world editor generally permits the initial states of game objects (i.e., the values of their attributes) to be specified. Most game world editors also give their users some sort of ability to control the *behaviors* of the dynamic objects in the game world. This control might be via data-driven configuration

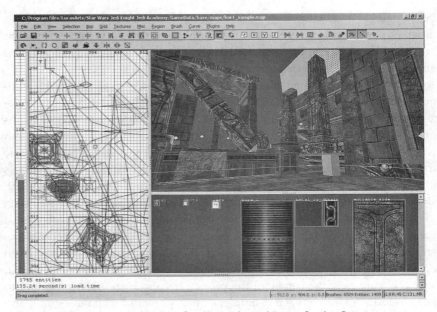

Figure 13.4. The Radiant world editor for the Quake and Doom family of engines.

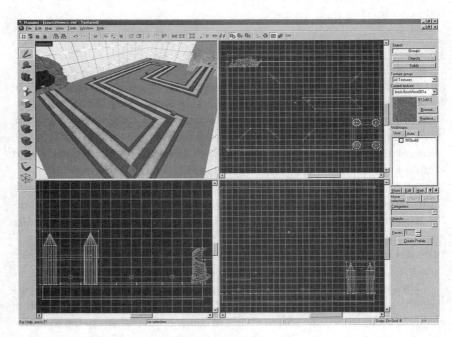

Figure 13.5. Valve's Hammer editor for the Source engine.

parameters (e.g., object A should start in an invisible state, object B should immediately attack the player when spawned, object C is flammable, etc.), or behavioral control might be via a scripting language, thereby shifting the game designers' tasks into the realm of programming. Some world editors even allow entirely new types of game objects to be defined, with little or no programmer intervention.

## 13.4.1. Typical Features of a Game World Editor

The design and layout of game world editors varies widely, but most editors provide a reasonably standard set of features. These include, but are certainly not limited to, the following.

### 13.4.1.1. World Chunk Creation and Management

The unit of world creation is usually a chunk (also known as a level or map— see Section 13.1.2). The game world editor typically allows new chunks to be created and existing chunks to be renamed, broken up, combined, or destroyed. Each chunk can be linked to one or more static meshes and/or other static data elements such as AI navigation maps, descriptions of ledges that can be grabbed by the player, cover point definitions, and so on. In some engines, a chunk is defined by a single background mesh and cannot exist without one. In other engines, a chunk may have an independent existence, perhaps defined by a bounding volume (e.g., AABB, OBB, or arbitrary polygonal region), and can be populated by zero or more meshes and/or brush geometry (see Section 1.7.3.1).

Some world editors provide dedicated tools for authoring terrain, water, and other specialized static elements. In other engines, these elements might be authored using standard DCC applications but tagged in some way to indicate to the asset conditioning pipeline and/or the runtime engine that they are special. (For example, in *Uncharted: Drake's Fortune*, the water was authored as a regular triangle mesh, but it was mapped with a special material that indicated that it was to be treated as water.) Sometimes, special world elements are created and edited in a separate, standalone tool. For example, the height field terrain in *Medal of Honor: Pacific Assault* was authored using a customized version of a tool obtained from another team within Electronic Arts because this was more expedient than trying to integrate a terrain editor into Radiant, the world editor being used on the project at the time.

### 13.4.1.2. Game World Visualization

It's important for the user of a game world editor to be able to visualize the contents of the game world. As such, virtually all game world editors provide a three-dimensional perspective view of the world and/or a two-dimensional orthographic projection. It's common to see the view pane divided into four sections, three for top, side, and front orthographic elevations and one for the 3D perspective view.

Some editors provide these world views via a custom rendering engine integrated directly into the tool. Other editors are themselves integrated into a 3D geometry editor like Maya or 3ds Max, so they can simply leverage the tool's viewports. Still other editors are designed to communicate with the actual game engine and use it to render the 3D perspective view. Some editors are even integrated into the engine itself.

### 13.4.1.3. Navigation

Clearly, a world editor wouldn't be of much use if the user weren't able to move around within the game world. In an orthographic view, it's important to be able to scroll and zoom in and out. In a 3D view, various camera control schemes are used. It may be possible to focus on an individual object and rotate around it. It may also be possible to switch into a "fly through" mode where the camera rotates about its own focal point and can be moved forward, backward, up, and down and panned left and right.

Some editors provide a host of convenience features for navigation. These include the ability to select an object and focus in on it with a single key press, the ability to save various relevant camera locations and then jump between them, various camera movement speed modes for coarse navigation and fine camera control, a Web-browser-like navigation history that can be used to jump around the game world, and so on.

### 13.4.1.4. Selection

A game world editor is primarily designed to allow the user to populate a game world with static and dynamic elements. As such, it's important for the user to be able to select individual elements for editing. Some editors only allow a single object to be selected at a time, while more-advanced editors permit multiobject selections. Objects might be selected via a rubber-band box in the orthographic view or by ray-cast style picking in the 3D view. Many editors also display a list of all world elements in a scrolling list or tree view so that objects can be found and selected by name. Some world editors also allow selections to be named and saved for later retrieval.

Game worlds are often quite densely populated. As such, it can sometimes be difficult to select a desired object because other objects are in the way. This problem can be overcome in a number of ways. When using a ray cast to select objects in 3D, the editor might allow the user to cycle through all of the objects that the ray is currently intersecting rather than always selecting the nearest one. Many editors allow the currently selected object(s) to be temporarily hidden from view. That way, if you don't get the object you want the first time, you can always hide it and try again. As we'll see in the next section, layers can also be an effective way to reduce clutter and improve the user's ability to select objects successfully.

### 13.4.1.5. Layers

Some editors also allow objects to be grouped into predefined or user-defined *layers*. This can be an incredibly useful feature, allowing the contents of the game world to be organized sensibly. Entire layers can be hidden or shown to reduce clutter on-screen. Layers might be color-coded for easy identification. Layers can be an important part of a division-of-labor strategy, as well. For example, when the lighting team is working on a world chunk, they can hide all of the elements in the scene that are not relevant to lighting.

What's more, if the game world editor is capable of loading and saving layers individually, conflicts can be avoided when multiple people are working on a single world chunk at the same time. For example, all of the lights might be stored in one layer, all of the background geometry in another, and all AI characters in a third. Since each layer is totally independent, the lighting, background, and NPC teams can all work simultaneously on the same world chunk.

### 13.4.1.6. Property Grid

The static and dynamic elements that populate a game world chunk typically have various properties (also known as attributes) that can be edited by the user. Properties might be simple key-value pairs and be limited to simple atomic data types like Booleans, integers, floating-point numbers, and strings. In some editors, more-complex properties are supported, including arrays of data and nested compound data structures.

Most world editors display the attributes of the currently selected object(s) in a scrollable property grid view. An example of a property grid is shown in Figure 13.6. The grid allows the user to see the current values of each attribute and edit the values by typing, using check boxes or drop-down combo boxes, dragging spinner controls up and down, and so on.

*Editing Multiobject Selections*

In editors that support multiobject selection, the property grid may support multiobject editing as well. This advanced feature displays an amalgam of the attributes of all objects in the selection. If a particular attribute has the same value across all objects in the selection, the value is shown as-is, and editing

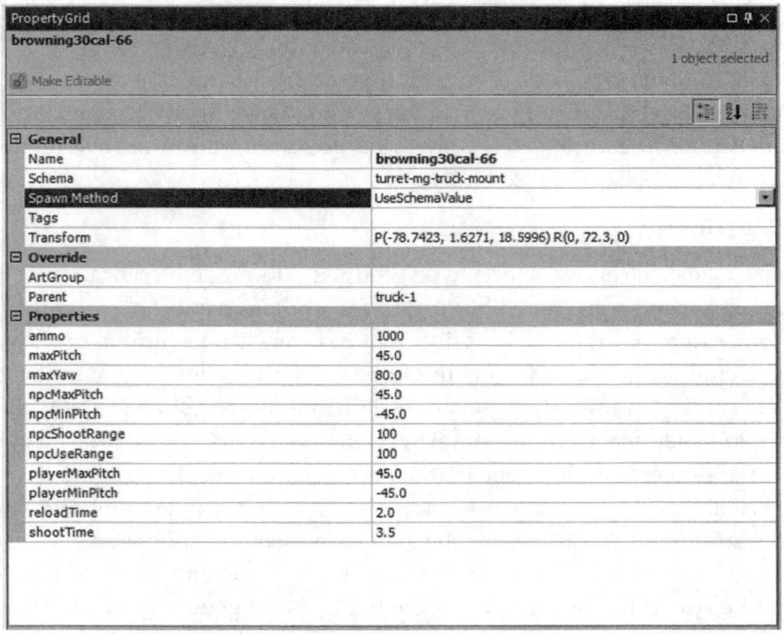

Figure 13.6. A typical property grid.

the value in the grid causes the property value to be updated in all selected objects. If the attribute's value differs from object to object within the selection, the property grid typically shows no value at all. In this case, if a new value is typed into the field in the grid, it will overwrite the values in all selected objects, bringing them all into agreement. Another problem arises when the selection contains a heterogeneous collection of objects (i.e., objects whose types differ). Each type of object can potentially have a different set of attributes, so the property grid must only display those attributes that are common to all object types in the selection. This can still be useful, however, because game object types often inherit from a common base type. For example, most objects have a position and orientation. In a heterogeneous selection, the user can still edit these shared attributes even though more-specific attributes are temporarily hidden from view.

*Free-Form Properties*

Normally, the set of properties associated with an object, and the data types of those properties, are defined on a per-object-type basis. For example, a renderable object has a position, orientation, scale, and mesh, while a light has position, orientation, color, intensity, and light type. Some editors also allow additional "free-form" properties to be defined by the user on a per-instance basis. These properties are usually implemented as a flat list of key-value pairs. The user is free to choose the name (key) of each free-form property, along with its data type and its value. This can be incredibly useful for prototyping new gameplay features or implementing one-off scenarios.

### 13.4.1.7. Object Placement and Alignment Aids

Some object properties are treated in a special way by the world editor. Typically the position, orientation, and scale of an object can be controlled via special handles in the orthographic and perspective viewports, just like in Maya or Max. In addition, asset linkages often need to be handled in a special way. For example, if we change the mesh associated with an object in the world, the editor should display this mesh in the orthographic and 3D perspective viewports. As such, the game world editor must have special knowledge of these properties—it cannot treat them generically, as it can most object properties.

Many world editors provide a host of object placement and alignment aids in addition to the basic translation, rotation, and scale tools. Many of these features borrow heavily from the feature sets of commercial graphics and 3D modeling tools like Photoshop, Maya, Visio, and others. Examples include snap to grid, snap to terrain, align to object, and many more.

### 13.4.1.8. Special Object Types

Just as some object properties must be handled in a special way by the world editor, certain types of objects also require special handling. Examples include:

- *Lights.* The world editor usually uses special icons to represent lights, since they have no mesh. The editor may attempt to display the light's approximate effect on the geometry in the scene as well, so that designers can move lights around in real time and get a reasonably good feel for how the scene will ultimately look.

- *Particle emitters.* Visualization of particle effects can also be problematic in editors that are built on a standalone rendering engine. In this case, particle emitters might be displayed using icons only, or some attempt might be made to emulate the particle effect in the editor. Of course, this is not a problem if the editor is in-game or can communicate with the running game for live tweaking.

- *Regions.* A region is a volume of space that is used by the game to detect relevant events such as objects entering or leaving the volume or to demark areas for various purposes. Some game engines restrict regions to being modeled as spheres or oriented boxes, while others may permit arbitrary convex polygonal shapes when viewed from above, with strictly horizontal sides. Still others might allow regions to be constructed out of more-complex geometry, such as $k$-DOPs (see Section 12.3.4.5). If regions are always spherical then the designers might be able to make do with a "Radius" property in the property grid, but to define or modify the extents of an arbitrarily shaped region, a special-case editing tool is almost certainly required.

- *Splines.* A spline is a three-dimensional curve defined by a set of control points and possibly tangent vectors at the points, depending on the type of mathematical curve used. Catmull-Rom splines are commonly used because they are fully defined by a set of control points (without tangents) and the curve always passes through all of the control points. But no matter what type of splines are supported, the world editor typically needs to provide the ability to display the splines in its viewports, and the user must be able to select and manipulate individual control points. Some world editors actually support two selection modes—a "coarse" mode for selecting objects in the scene and a "fine" mode for selecting the individual components of a selected object, such as the control points of a spline or the vertices of a region.

### 13.4.1.9. Saving and Loading World Chunks

Of course, no world editor would be complete if it were unable to load and save world chunks. The granularity with which world chunks can be loaded and saved differs widely from engine to engine. Some engines store each world chunk in a single file, while others allow individual layers to be loaded and saved independently. Data formats also vary across engines. Some use custom binary formats, others text formats like XML. Each design has its pros and cons, but every editor provides the ability to load and save world chunks in some form—and every game engine is capable of loading world chunks so that they can be played at runtime.

### 13.4.1.10. Rapid Iteration

A good game world editor usually supports some degree of dynamic tweaking for rapid iteration. Some editors run within the game itself, allowing the user to see the effects of his or her changes immediately. Others provide a live connection from the editor to the running game. Still other world editors operate entirely off-line, either as a standalone tool or as a plug-in to a DCC application like Lightwave or Maya. These tools sometimes permit modified data to be reloaded dynamically into the running game. The specific mechanism isn't important—all that matters is that users have a reasonably short *round-trip iteration time* (i.e., the time between making a change to the game world and seeing the effects of that change in-game). It's important to realize that iterations don't have to be instantaneous. Iteration times should be commensurate with the scope and frequency of the changes being made. For example, we might expect tweaking a character's maximum health to be a very fast operation, but when making major changes to the lighting environment for an entire world chunk, a much longer iteration time might be acceptable.

### 13.4.2. Integrated Asset Management Tools

In some engines, the game world editor is integrated with other aspects of game asset database management, such as defining mesh and material properties, defining animations, blend trees, animation state machines, setting up collision and physical properties of objects, managing texture resources, and so on. (See Section 6.2.1.2 for a discussion of the game asset database.)

Perhaps the best-known example of this design in action is *UnrealEd*, the editor used to create content for games built on the Unreal Engine. UnrealEd is integrated directly into the game engine, so any changes made in the editor are made directly to the dynamic elements in the running game. This makes rapid iteration very easy to achieve. But UnrealEd is much more than a game world editor—it is actually a complete content-creation package. It manages

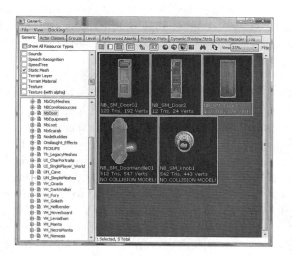

**Figure 13.7.** UnrealEd's Generic Browser provides access to the entire game asset database.

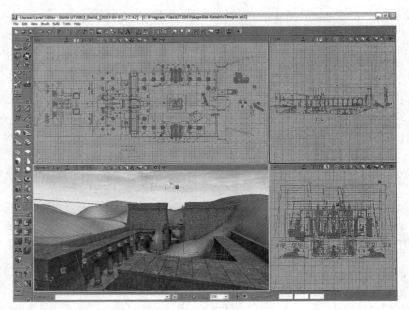

**Figure 13.8.** UnrealEd also provides a world editor.

the entire database of game assets, from animations to audio clips to triangle meshes to textures to materials and shaders and much more. UnrealEd provides its user with a unified, real-time, WYSIWYG view into the entire asset database, making it a powerful enabler of any rapid, efficient game development process. A few screen shots from UnrealEd are shown in Figure 13.7 and Figure 13.8.

### 13.4.2.1. Data Processing Costs

In Section 6.2.1, we learned that the asset conditioning pipeline (ACP) converts game assets from their various source formats into the formats required by the game engine. This is typically a two-step process. First, the asset is exported from the DCC application to a platform-independent intermediate format that only contains the data that is relevant to the game. Second, the asset is processed into a format that is optimized for a specific platform. On a project targeting multiple gaming platforms, a single platform-independent asset gives rise to multiple platform-specific assets during this second phase.

One of the key differences between tools pipelines is the point at which this second platform-specific optimization step is performed. UnrealEd performs it when assets are first imported into the editor. This approach pays off in rapid iteration time when iterating on level design. However, it can make the cost of changing source assets like meshes, animations, audio assets, and so on more painful. Other engines like the Source engine and the *Quake* engine pay the asset optimization cost when baking out the level prior to running the game. *Halo* gives the user the option to change raw assets at any time; they are converted into optimized form when they are first loaded into the engine, and the results are cached to prevent the optimization step from being performed needlessly every time the game is run.

# 14
# Runtime Gameplay Foundation Systems

## 14.1. Components of the Gameplay Foundation System

Most game engines provide a suite of runtime software components that together provide a framework upon which a game's unique rules, objectives, and dynamic world elements can be constructed. There is no standard name for these components within the game industry, but we will refer to them collectively as the engine's *gameplay foundation system*. If a line can reasonably be drawn between the game engine and the game itself, then these systems lie just beneath this line. In theory, one can construct gameplay foundation systems that are for the most part game-agnostic. However, in practice, these systems almost always contain genre- or game-specific details. In fact, the line between the engine and the game can probably be best visualized as one big blur—a gradient that arcs across these components as it links the engine to the game. In some game engines, one might even go so far as to consider the gameplay foundation systems as lying entirely *above* the engine-game line. The differences between game engines are most acute when it comes to the design and implementation of their gameplay components. That said, there are a surprising number of common patterns across engines, and those commonalities will be the topic of our discussions here.

Every game engine approaches the problem of gameplay software design a bit differently. However, most engines provide the following major subsystems in some form:

- *Runtime game object model.* This is an implementation of the abstract game object model advertised to the game designers via the world editor.

- *Level management and streaming.* This system loads and unloads the contents of the virtual worlds in which gameplay takes place. In many engines, level data is streamed into memory during gameplay, thus providing the illusion of a large seamless world (when in fact it is broken into discrete chunks).

- *Real-time object model updating.* In order to permit the game objects in the world to behave autonomously, each object must be updated periodically. This is where all of the disparate systems in a game engine truly come together into a cohesive whole.

- *Messaging and event handling.* Most game objects need to communicate with one another. This is usually done via an abstract messaging system. Inter-object messages often signal changes in the state of the game world called *events*. So the messaging system is referred to as the *event system* in many studios.

- *Scripting.* Programming high-level game logic in a language like C or C++ can be cumbersome. To improve productivity, allow rapid iteration, and put more power into the hands of the non-programmers on the team, a scripting language is often integrated into the game engine. This language might be text-based, like Python or Lua, or it might be a graphical language, like Unreal's Kismet.

- *Objectives and game flow management.* This subsystem manages the player's objectives and the overall flow of the game. This is usually described by a sequence, tree, or graph of player objectives. Objectives are often grouped into chapters, especially if the game is highly story-driven as many modern games are. The game flow management system manages the overall flow of the game, tracks the player's accomplishment of objectives, and gates the player from one area of the game world to the next as the objectives are accomplished. Some designers refer to this as the "spine" of the game.

Of these major systems, the runtime object model is probably the most complex. It typically provides most, if not all, of the following features:

- *Spawning and destroying game objects dynamically.* The dynamic elements in a game world often need to come and go during gameplay. Health packs disappear once they have been picked up, explosions appear and then dissipate, and enemy reinforcements mysteriously come from around a corner just when you think you've cleared the level. Many game engines provide a system for managing the memory and other resources associated with dynamically spawned game objects. Other engines simply disallow dynamic creation or destruction of game objects altogether.

- *Linkage to low-level engine systems.* Every game object has some kind of linkage to one or more underlying engine systems. Most game objects are visually represented by renderable triangle meshes. Some have particle effects. Many generate sounds. Some animate. Many have collision, and some are dynamically simulated by the physics engine. One of the primary responsibilities of the gameplay foundation system is to ensure that every game object has access to the services of the engine systems upon which it depends.

- *Real-time simulation of object behaviors.* At its core, a game engine is a real-time dynamic computer simulation of an agent-based model. This is just a fancy way of saying that the game engine needs to update the states of all the game objects dynamically over time. The objects may need to be updated in a very particular order, dictated in part by dependencies between the objects, in part by their dependencies on various engine subsystems, and in part because of the interdependencies between those engine subsystems themselves.

- *Ability to define new game object types.* Every game's requirements change and evolve as the game is developed. It's important that the game object model be flexible enough to permit new object types to be added easily and exposed to the world editor. In an ideal world, it should be possible to define a new type of object in an entirely data-driven manner. However, in many engines, the services of a programmer are required in order to add new game object types.

- *Unique object ids.* Typical game worlds contain hundreds or even thousands of individual game objects of various types. At runtime, it's important to be able to identify or search for a particular object. This means each object needs some kind of unique identifier. A human-readable name is the most convenient kind of id, but we must be wary of the performance costs of using strings at runtime. Integer ids are the most efficient choice, but they are very difficult for human game developers to work with. Arguably the best solution is to use hashed string ids (see Section 5.4.3.1) as our object identifiers, as they are as efficient as integers but can be converted back into string form for ease of reading.

- *Game object queries.* The gameplay foundation system must provide some means of finding objects within the game world. We might want to find a specific object by its unique id, or all the objects of a particular type, or we might want to perform advanced queries based on arbitrary criteria (e.g., find all enemies within a 20 meter radius of the player character).

- *Game object references.* Once we've found the objects, we need some mechanism for holding *references* to them, either briefly within a single function or for much longer periods of time. An object reference might be as simple as a pointer to a C++ class instance, or it might be something more sophisticated, like a handle or a reference-counted smart pointer.

- *Finite state machine support.* Many types of game objects are best modeled as finite state machines. Some game engines provide the ability for a game object to exist in one of many possible states, each with its own attributes and behavioral characteristics.

- *Network replication.* In a networked multiplayer game, multiple game machines are connected together via a LAN or the Internet. The state of a particular game object is usually owned and managed by one machine. However, that object's state must also be *replicated* (communicated) to the other machines involved in the multiplayer game so that all players have a consistent view of the object.

- *Saving and loading games / object persistence.* Many game engines allow the current states of the game objects in the world to be saved to disk and later reloaded. This might be done to support a "save anywhere" save-game system or as a way of implementing network replication, or it might simply be the primary means of loading game world chunks that were authored in the world editor tool. Object persistence usually requires certain language features, such as *runtime type identification* (RTTI), *reflection*, and *abstract construction*. RTTI and reflection provide software with a means of determining an object's *type*, and what *attributes* and *methods* its class provides, dynamically at runtime. Abstract construction allows instances of a class to be created without having to hard-code the name of the class—a very useful feature when serializing an object instance into memory from disk. If RTTI, reflection, and abstract construction are not natively supported in your language of choice, these features can be added manually.

We'll spend the remainder of this chapter delving into each of these subsystems in depth.

## 14.2.  Runtime Object Model Architectures

In the world editor, the game designer is presented with an abstract game object model, which defines the various types of dynamic elements that can exist in the game, how they behave, and what kinds of attributes they have. At runtime, the gameplay foundation system must provide a concrete implementation of this object model. This is by far the largest component of any gameplay foundation system.

The runtime object model implementation may or may not bear any resemblance to the abstract tool-side object model. For example, it might not be implemented in an object-oriented programming language at all, or it might use a collection of interconnected class instances to represent a single abstract game object. Whatever its design, the runtime object model must provide a faithful reproduction of the object types, attributes, and behaviors advertised by the world editor.

The runtime object model is the in-game manifestation of the abstract tool-side object model presented to the designers in the world editor. Designs vary widely, but most game engines follow one of two basic architectural styles:

- *Object-centric.* In this style, each tool-side game object is represented at runtime by a single class instance or a small collection of interconnected instances. Each object has a set of *attributes* and *behaviors* that are encapsulated within the class (or classes) of which the object is an instance. The game world is just a collection of game objects.

- *Property-centric.* In this style, each tool-side game object is represented only by a unique id (implemented as an integer, hashed string id, or string). The *properties* of each game object are distributed across many data tables, one per property type, and keyed by object id (rather than being centralized within a single class instance or collection of interconnected instances). The properties themselves are often implemented as instances of hard-coded classes. The *behavior* of a game object is implicitly defined by the collection of properties from which it is composed. For example, if an object has the "Health" property, then it can be damaged, lose health, and eventually die. If an object has the "MeshInstance" property, then it can be rendered in 3D as an instance of a triangle mesh.

There are distinct advantages and disadvantages to each of these architectural styles. We'll investigate each one in some detail and note where one style has significant potential benefits over the other as they arise.

## 14.2.1.  Object-Centric Architectures

In an *object-centric* game world object architecture, each logical game object is implemented as an instance of a class, or possibly a collection of interconnected class instances. Under this broad umbrella, many different designs are possible. We'll investigate a few of the most common designs in the following sections.

### 14.2.1.1.  A Simple Object-Based Model in C: *Hydro Thunder*

Game object models needn't be implemented in an object-oriented language like C++ at all. For example, the arcade hit *Hydro Thunder*, by Midway Home Entertainment in San Diego, was written entirely in C. *Hydro* employed a very simple game object model consisting of only a few object types:

- boats (player- and AI-controlled),
- floating blue and red boost icons,
- ambient animated objects (animals on the side of the track, etc.),
- the water surface,
- ramps,
- waterfalls,
- particle effects,
- race track sectors (two-dimensional polygonal regions connected to one another and together defining the watery region in which boats could race),
- static geometry (terrain, foliage, buildings along the sides of the track, etc.),
- two-dimensional heads-up display (HUD) elements.

A few screen shots of *Hydro Thunder* are shown in Figure 14.1. Notice the hovering boost icons in both screen shots and the shark swimming by in the left image (an example of an ambient animated object).

 *Hydro* had a C `struct` named `World_t` that stored and managed the contents of a game world (i.e., a single race track). The world contained pointers to arrays of various kinds of game objects. The static geometry was a single mesh instance. The water surface, waterfalls, and particle effects were each represented by custom data structures. The boats, boost icons, and other dynamic objects in the game were represented by instances of a general-purpose `struct` called `WorldOb_t` (i.e., a world object). This was *Hydro*'s equivalent of a *game object* as we've defined it in this chapter.

 The `WorldOb_t` data structure contained data members encoding the position and orientation of the object, the 3D mesh used to render it, a set of colli-

**Figure 14.1.** Screen shots from the arcade smash *Hydro Thunder*, developed by Midway Home Entertainment in San Diego.

sion spheres, simple animation state information (*Hydro* only supported rigid hierarchical animation), physical properties like velocity, mass, and buoyancy, and other data common to all of the dynamic objects in the game. In addition, each `WorldOb_t` contained three pointers: a `void*` "user data" pointer, a pointer to a custom "update" function, and a pointer to a custom "draw" function. So while *Hydro Thunder* was not object-oriented in the strictest sense, the *Hydro* engine did extend its non-object-oriented language (C) to support rudimentary implementations of two important OOP features: *inheritance* and *polymorphism*. The user data pointer permitted each type of game object to maintain custom state information specific to its type while inheriting the features common to all world objects. For example, the *Banshee* boat had a different booster mechanism than the *Rad Hazard*, and each booster mechanism required different state information to manage its deployment and stowing animations. The two function pointers acted like *virtual functions*, allowing world objects to have polymorphic behaviors (via their "update" functions) and polymorphic visual appearances (via their "draw" functions).

```
struct WorldOb_s
{
    Orient_t  m_transform;      /* position/rotation */

    Mesh3d*   m_pMesh;          /* 3D mesh */

    /* ... */
    void*     m_pUserData;      /* custom state */

    void      (*m_pUpdate)();   /* polymorphic update */
    void      (*m_pDraw)();     /* polymorphic draw */
```

```
};
typedef struct WorldOb_s WorldOb_t;
```

### 14.2.1.2. Monolithic Class Hierarchies

It's natural to want to classify game object types taxonomically. This tends to lead game programmers toward an object-oriented language that supports inheritance. A class hierarchy is the most intuitive and straightforward way to represent a collection of interrelated game object types. So it is not surprising that the majority of commercial game engines employ a class hierarchy based technique.

Figure 14.2 shows a simple class hierarchy that could be used to implement the game *Pac-Man*. This hierarchy is rooted (as many are) at a common class called `GameObject`, which might provide some facilities needed by all object types, such as RTTI or serialization. The `MovableObject` class represents any object that has a position and orientation. `RenderableObject` gives the object an ability to be rendered (in the case of traditional *Pac-Man*, via a sprite, or in the case of a modern 3D *Pac-Man* game, perhaps via a triangle mesh). From `RenderableObject` are derived classes for the ghosts, Pac-Man, pellets, and power pills that make up the game. This is just a hypothetical example, but it illustrates the basic ideas that underlie most game object class hierarchies—namely that common, generic functionality tends to exist at the root of the hierarchy, while classes toward the leaves of the hierarchy tend to add increasingly specific functionality.

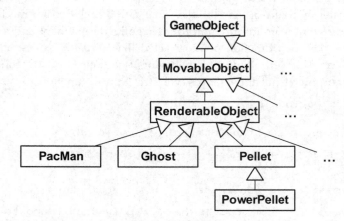

**Figure 14.2.** A hypothetical class hierarchy for the game Pac-Man.

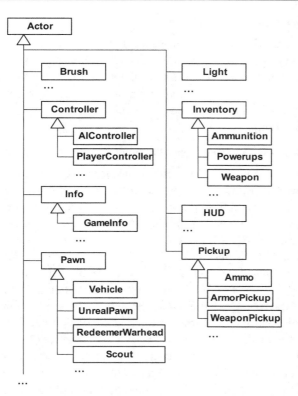

Figure 14.3. An excerpt from the game object class hierarchy from *Unreal Tournament 2004*.

A game object class hierarchy usually begins small and simple, and in that form, it can be a powerful and intuitive way to describe a collection of game object types. However, as class hierarchies grow, they have a tendency to deepen and widen simultaneously, leading to what I call a *monolithic class hierarchy*. This kind of hierarchy arises when virtually all classes in the game object model inherit from a single, common base class. The Unreal Engine's game object model is a classic example, as Figure 14.3 illustrates.

### 14.2.1.3. Problems with Deep, Wide Hierarchies

Monolithic class hierarchies tend to cause problems for the game development team for a wide range of reasons. The deeper and wider a class hierarchy grows, the more extreme these problems can become. In the following sections, we'll explore some of the most common problems caused by wide, deep class hierarchies.

*Understanding, Maintaining, and Modifying Classes*

The deeper a class lies within a class hierarchy, the harder it is to understand, maintain, and modify. This is because to understand a class, you really need to understand all of its parent classes as well. For example, modifying the behavior of an innocuous-looking virtual function in a derived class could violate the assumptions made by any one of the many base classes, leading to subtle, difficult-to-find bugs.

*Inability to Describe Multidimensional Taxonomies*

A hierarchy inherently classifies objects according to a particular system of criteria known as a *taxonomy*. For example, *biological taxonomy* (also known as *alpha taxonomy*) classifies all living things according to genetic similarities, using a tree with eight levels: domain, kingdom, phylum, class, order, family, genus, and species. At each level of the tree, a different criterion is used to divide the myriad life forms on our planet into more and more refined groups.

One of the biggest problems with any hierarchy is that it can only classify objects along a single "axis"—according to one particular set of criteria—at each level of the tree. Once the criteria have been chosen for a particular hierarchy, it becomes difficult or impossible to classify along an entirely different set of "axes." For example, biological taxonomy classifies objects according to genetic traits, but it says nothing about the colors of the organisms. In order to classify organisms by color, we'd need an entirely different tree structure.

In object-oriented programming, this limitation of hierarchical classification often manifests itself in the form of wide, deep, and confusing class hierarchies. When one analyzes a real game's class hierarchy, one often finds that its structure attempts to meld a number of different classification criteria into a single class tree. In other cases, concessions are made in the class hierarchy to accommodate a new type of object whose characteristics were not anticipated when the hierarchy was first designed. For example, imagine the seem-

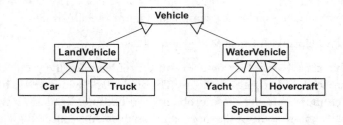

**Figure 14.4.** A seemingly logical class hierarchy describing various kinds of vehicles.

ingly logical class hierarchy describing different types of vehicles, depicted in Figure 14.4.

What happens when the game designers announce to the programmers that they now want the game to include an *amphibious* vehicle? Such a vehicle does not fit into the existing taxonomic system. This may cause the programmers to panic or, more likely, to "hack" their class hierarchy in various ugly and error-prone ways.

*Multiple Inheritance: The Deadly Diamond*

One solution to the amphibious vehicle problem is to utilize C++'s multiple inheritance (MI) features, as shown in Figure 14.5. At first glance, this seems like a good solution. However, multiple inheritance in C++ poses a number of practical problems. For example, multiple inheritance can lead to an object that contains multiple copies of its base class's members—a condition known as the "deadly diamond" or "diamond of death." (See Section 3.1.1.3 for more details.)

The difficulties in building an MI class hierarchy that works and that is understandable and maintainable usually outweigh the benefits. As a result, most game studios prohibit or severely limit the use of multiple inheritance in their class hierarchies.

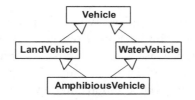

**Figure 14.5.** A diamond-shaped class hierarchy for amphibious vehicles.

*Mix-In Classes*

Some teams do permit a limited form of MI, in which a class may have any number of parent classes but only *one* grandparent. In other words, a class may inherit from one and only one class in the main inheritance hierarchy, but it may also inherit from any number of *mix-in classes* (stand-alone classes with no base class). This permits common functionality to be factored out into a mix-in class and then spot-patched into the main hierarchy wherever it is needed. This is shown in Figure 14.6. However, as we'll see below, it's usually better to *compose* or *aggregate* such classes than to *inherit* from them.

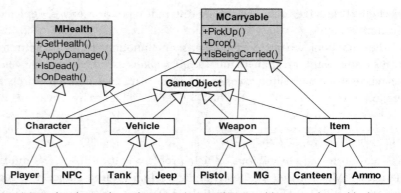

**Figure 14.6.** A class hierarchy with mix-in classes. The MHealth mix-in class adds the notion of health and the ability to be killed to any class that inherits it. The MCarryable mix-in class allows an object that inherits it to be carried by a Character.

*The Bubble-Up Effect*

When a monolithic class hierarchy is first designed, the root class(es) are usually very simple, each one exposing only a minimal feature set. However, as more and more functionality is added to the game, the desire to *share code* between two or more *unrelated* classes begins to cause features to "bubble up" the hierarchy.

For example, we might start out with a design in which only wooden crates can float in water. However, once our game designers see those cool floating crates, they begin to ask for other kinds of floating objects, like characters, bits of paper, vehicles, and so on. Because "floating versus non-floating" was not one of the original classification criteria when the hierarchy was designed, the programmers quickly discover the need to add flotation to classes that are totally unrelated within the class hierarchy. Multiple inheritance is frowned upon, so the programmers decide to move the flotation code up the hierarchy, into a base class that is common to all objects that need to float. The fact that some of the classes that derive from this common base class *cannot float* is seen as less of a problem than duplicating the flotation code across multiple classes. (A Boolean member variable called something like m_bCanFloat might even be added to make the distinction clear.) The ultimate result is that flotation eventually becomes a feature of the root object in the class hierarchy (along with pretty much every other feature in the game).

The Actor class in Unreal is a classic example of this "bubble-up effect." It contains data members and code for managing rendering, animation, physics, world interaction, audio effects, network replication for multiplayer games, object creation and destruction, actor iteration (i.e., the ability to iterate over all actors meeting a certain criteria and perform some operation on them), and message broadcasting. Encapsulating the functionality of various engine subsystems is difficult when features are permitted to "bubble up" to the root-most classes in a monolithic class hierarchy.

### 14.2.1.4. Using Composition to Simplify the Hierarchy

Perhaps the most prevalent cause of monolithic class hierarchies is over-use of the "is-a" relationship in object-oriented design. For example, in a game's GUI, a programmer might decide to derive the class `Window` from a class called `Rectangle`, using the logic that GUI windows are always rectangular. However, a window *is not a* rectangle—it *has a* rectangle, which defines its boundary. So a more workable solution to this particular design problem is to embed an instance of the `Rectangle` class inside the `Window` class, or to give the `Window` a pointer or reference to a `Rectangle`.

In object-oriented design, the "has-a" relationship is known as *composition*. In composition, a class A either contains an *instance* of class B directly, or contains a *pointer* or *reference* to an instance of B. Strictly speaking, in order for the term "composition" to be applicable, class A must *own* class B. This means that when an instance of class A is created, it automatically creates an instance of class B as well; when that instance of A is destroyed, its instance of B is destroyed, too. We can also link classes to one another via a pointer or reference *without* having one of the classes manage the other's lifetime. In that case, the technique is usually called *aggregation*.

#### Converting Is-A to Has-A

Converting "is-a" relationships into "has-a" relationships can be a useful technique for reducing the width, depth, and complexity of a game's class hierarchy. To illustrate, let's take a look at the hypothetical monolithic hierarchy shown in Figure 14.7. The root `GameObject` class provides some basic functionality required by all game objects (e.g., RTTI, reflection, persistence via serialization, network replication, etc.). The `MovableObject` class represents any game object that has a *transform* (i.e., a position, orientation, and optional scale). `RenderableObject` adds the ability to be rendered on-screen. (Not all game objects need to be rendered—for example, an invisible `TriggerRegion` class could be derived directly from `MovableObject`.) The `Collidable Object` class provides collision information to its instances. The `Animating Object` class grants to its instances the ability to be animated via a skeletal joint hierarchy. Finally, the `PhysicalObject` gives its instances the ability to be physically simulated (e.g., a rigid body falling under the influence of gravity and bouncing around in the game world).

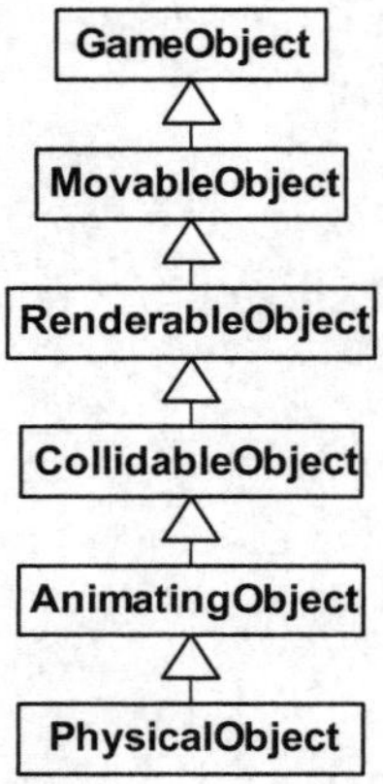

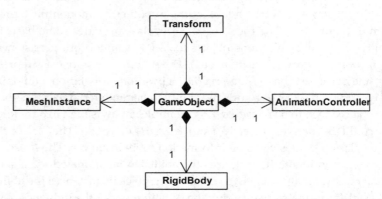

**GameObject**

△

**MovableObject**

△

**RenderableObject**

△

**CollidableObject**

△

**AnimatingObject**

△

**PhysicalObject**

Figure 14.7. A hypothetical game object class hierarchy using only inheritance to associate the classes.

One big problem with this class hierarchy is that it limits our design choices when creating new types of game objects. If we want to define an object type that is physically simulated, we are forced to derive its class from `PhysicalObject` even though it may not require skeletal animation. If we want a game object class with collision, it must inherit from `Collidable` even though it may be invisible and hence not require the services of `Renderable`.

A second problem with the hierarchy shown in Figure 14.7 is that it is difficult to extend the functionality of the existing classes. For example, let's imagine we want to support morph target animation, so we derive two new classes from `AnimatingObject` called `SkeletalObject` and `MorphTarget Object`. If we wanted both of these new classes to have the ability to be physically simulated, we'd be forced to re-factor `PhysicalObject` into two nearly-identical classes, one derived from `SkeletalObject` and one from `Morph TargetObject`, or turn to multiple inheritance.

One solution to these problems is to isolate the various features of a `GameObject` into independent classes, each of which provides a single, well-defined service. Such classes are sometimes called *components* or *service objects*. A componentized design allows us to select only those features we need for each type of game object we create. In addition, it permits each feature to be maintained, extended, or re-factored without affecting the others. The individual components are also easier to understand, and easier to test, because they are decoupled from one another. Some component classes correspond directly to a single engine subsystem, such as rendering, animation, collision, physics, audio, etc. This allows these subsystems to remain distinct and well-

Figure 14.8. Our hypothetical game object class hierarchy, re-factored to favor class composition over inheritance.

encapsulated when they are integrated together for use by a particular game object.

Figure 14.8 shows how our class hierarchy might look after re-factoring it into components. In this revised design, the `GameObject` class acts like a hub, containing pointers to each of the optional components we've defined. The `MeshInstance` component is our replacement for the `Renderable Object` class—it represents an instance of a triangle mesh and encapsulates the knowledge of how to render it. Likewise, the `AnimationController` component replaces `AnimatingObject`, exposing skeletal animation services to the `GameObject`. Class `Transform` replaces `MovableObject` by maintaining the position, orientation, and scale of the object. The `RigidBody` class represents the collision geometry of a game object and provides its `GameObject` with an interface into the low-level collision and physics systems, replacing `CollidableObject` and `PhysicsObject`.

*Component Creation and Ownership*

In this kind of design, it is typical for the "hub" class to *own* its components, meaning that it manages their *lifetimes*. But how should a `GameObject` "know" which components to create? There are numerous ways to solve this problem, but one of the simplest is provide the root `GameObject` class with pointers to all possible components. Each unique type of game object is defined as a derived class of `GameObject`. In the `GameObject` constructor, all of the component pointers are initially set to `NULL`. Each derived class's constructor is then free to create whatever components it may need. For convenience, the default `GameObject` destructor can clean up all of the components automatically. In this design, the hierarchy of classes derived from `GameObject` serves as the primary taxonomy for the kinds of objects we want in our game, and the component classes serve as optional add-on features.

One possible implementation of the component creation and destruction logic for this kind of hierarchy is shown below. However, it's important to realize that this code is just an example—implementation details vary widely, even between engines that employ essentially the same kind of class hierarchy design.

```
class GameObject
{
protected:

    // My transform (position, rotation, scale).
    Transform           m_transform;

    // Standard components:
    MeshInstance*       m_pMeshInst;
```

```cpp
    AnimationController*    m_pAnimController;

    RigidBody*              m_pRigidBody;
public:

    GameObject()
    {
        // Assume no components by default. Derived
        // classes will override.
        m_pMeshInst = NULL;

        m_pAnimController = NULL;

        m_pRigidBody = NULL;
    }

    ~GameObject()
    {
        // Automatically delete any components created by
        // derived classes.
        delete m_pMeshInst;

        delete m_pAnimController;

        delete m_pRigidBody;
    }

    // ...
};

class Vehicle : public GameObject
{
protected:
    // Add some more components specific to Vehicles...
    Chassis*  m_pChassis;
    Engine*   m_pEngine;

    // ...

public:

    Vehicle()
    {
        // Construct standard GameObject components.
        m_pMeshInst = new MeshInstance;

        m_pRigidBody = new RigidBody;

        // NOTE: We'll assume the animation controller
        // must be provided with a reference to the mesh
        // instance so that it can provide it with a
        // matrix palette.
        m_pAnimController
            = new AnimationController(*m_pMeshInst);
```

```
        // Construct vehicle-specific components.
        m_pChassis = new Chassis(*this,
                        *m_pAnimController);
        m_pEngine = new Engine(*this);

    }

    ~Vehicle()
    {
        // Only need to destroy vehicle-specific
        // components, as GameObject cleans up the
        // standard components for us.
        delete m_pChassis;

        delete m_pEngine;
    }
};
```

### 14.2.1.5. Generic Components

Another more-flexible (but also trickier to implement) alternative is to provide the root game object class with a generic linked list of components. The components in such a design usually all derive from a common base class—this allows us to iterate over the linked list and perform polymorphic operations, such as asking each component what type it is or passing an event to each component in turn for possible handling. This design allows the root game object class to be largely oblivious to the component types that are available and thereby permits new types of components to be created without modifying the game object class in many cases. It also allows a particular game object to contain an arbitrary number of instances of each type of component. (The

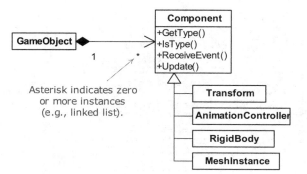

**Figure 14.9.** A linked list of components can provide flexibility by allowing the hub game object to be unaware of the details of any particular component.

hard-coded design permitted only a fixed number, determined by how many pointers to each component existed within the game object class.)

This kind of design is illustrated in Figure 14.9. It is trickier to implement than a hard-coded component model because the game object code must be written in a totally generic way. The component classes can likewise make no assumptions about what other components might or might not exist within the context of a particular game object. The choice between hard-coding the component pointers or using a generic linked list of components is not an easy one to make. Neither design is clearly superior—they each have their pros and cons, and different game teams take different approaches.

### 14.2.1.6. Pure Component Models

What would happen if we were to take the componentization concept to its extreme? We would move literally *all* of the functionality out of our root `GameObject` class into various component classes. At this point, the game object class would quite literally be a behavior-less container, with a unique id and a bunch of pointers to its components, but otherwise containing no logic of its own. So why not eliminate the class entirely? One way to do this is to give each component a copy of the game object's unique id. The components are now linked together into a logical grouping by id. Given a way to quickly look up any component by id, we would no longer need the `GameObject` "hub" class at all. I will use the term *pure component model* to describe this kind of architecture. It is illustrated in Figure 14.10.

A pure component model is not quite as simple as it first sounds, and it is not without its share of problems. For one thing, we still need some way of defining the various concrete types of game objects our game needs and then arranging for the correct component classes to be instantiated whenever

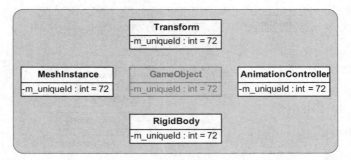

**Figure 14.10.** In a pure component model, a logical game object is comprised of many components, but the components are linked together only indirectly, by sharing a unique id.

an instance of the type is created. Our `GameObject` hierarchy used to handle construction of components for us. Instead, we might use a factory pattern, in which we define factory classes, one per game object type, with a virtual construction function that is overridden to create the proper components for each game object type. Or we might turn to a data-driven model, where the game object types are defined in a text file that can be parsed by the engine and consulted whenever a type is instantiated.

Another issue with a components-only design is inter-component communication. Our central `GameObject` acted as a "hub," marshalling communications between the various components. In pure component architectures, we need an efficient way for the components making up a single game object to talk to one another. This could be done by having each component look up the other components using the game object's unique id. However, we probably want a much more efficient mechanism—for example the components could be prewired into a circular linked list.

In the same sense, sending messages from one game object to another is difficult in a pure componentized model. We can no longer communicate with the `GameObject` instance, so we either need to know a priori with which component we wish to communicate, or we must multicast to all components that make up the game object in question. Neither option is ideal.

Pure component models can and have been made to work on real game projects. These kinds of models have their pros and cons, but again, they are not clearly better than any of the alternative designs. Unless you're part of a research and development effort, you should probably choose the architecture with which you are most comfortable and confident, and which best fits the needs of the particular game you are building.

## 14.2.2. Property-Centric Architectures

Programmers who work frequently in an object-oriented programming language tend to think naturally in terms of objects that contain attributes (data members) and behaviors (methods, member functions). This is the *object-centric view*:

- Object1
  - □ Position = (0, 3, 15)
  - □ Orientation = (0, 43, 0)
- Object2
  - □ Position = (−12, 0, 8)
  - □ Health = 15

- Object3
  - □ Orientation = (0, –87, 10)

However, it is possible to think primarily in terms of the attributes, rather than the objects. We define the set of all properties that a game object might have. Then for each property, we build a table containing the values of that property corresponding to each game object that has it. The property values are keyed by the objects' unique ids. This is what we will call the *property-centric view*:

- Position
  - □ Object1 = (0, 3, 15)
  - □ Object2 = (–12, 0, 8)
- Orientation
  - □ Object1 = (0, 43, 0)
  - □ Object3 = (0, –87, 10)
- Health
  - □ Object2 = 15

Property-centric object models have been used very successfully on many commercial games, including *Deus Ex 2* and the *Thief* series of games. See Section 14.2.2.5 for more details on exactly how these projects designed their object systems.

A property-centric design is more akin to a relational database than an object model. Each attribute acts like a column in a database table (or a stand-alone table), with the game objects' unique id as the *primary key*. Of course, in object-oriented design, an object is defined not only by its *attributes*, but also by its *behavior*. If all we have are tables of properties, then where do we implement the behavior? The answer to this question varies somewhat from engine to engine, but most often the behaviors are implemented in one or both of the following places:

- in the properties themselves, and/or
- via script code.

Let's explore each of these ideas further.

### 14.2.2.1. Implementing Behavior via Property Classes

Each type of property can be implemented as a *property class*. Properties can be as simple as a single Boolean or floating-point value or as complex as a renderable triangle mesh or an AI "brain." Each property class can provide behaviors via its hard-coded methods (member functions). The overall behavior of a particular game object is determined by the aggregation of the behaviors of all its properties.

For example, if a game object contains an instance of the `Health` property, it can be damaged and eventually destroyed or killed. The `Health` object can respond to any attacks made on the game object by decrementing the object's health level appropriately. A property object can also communicate with other property objects within the same game object to produce cooperative behaviors. For example, when the `Health` property detects and responds to an attack, it could possibly send a message to the `AnimatedSkeleton` property, thereby allowing the game object to play a suitable hit reaction animation. Similarly, when the `Health` property detects that the game object is about to die or be destroyed, it can talk to the `RigidBodyDynamics` property to activate a physics-driven explosion or a "rag doll" dead body simulation.

### 14.2.2.2. Implementing Behavior via Script

Another option is to store the property values as raw data in one or more database-like tables and use script code to implement a game object's behaviors. Every game object could have a special property called something like `ScriptId`, which, if present, specifies the block of script code (script function, or script object if the scripting language is itself object-oriented) that will manage the object's behavior. Script code could also be used to allow a game object to respond to events that occur within the game world. See Section 14.7 for more details on event systems and Section 14.8 for a discussion of game scripting languages.

In some property-centric engines, a core set of hard-coded property classes are provided by the engineers, but a facility is provided allowing game designers and programmers to implement new property types entirely in script. This approach was used successfully on the *Dungeon Siege* project, for example.

### 14.2.2.3. Properties versus Components

It's important to note that many of the authors cited in Section 14.2.2.5 use the term "component" to refer to what I call a "property object" here. In Section 14.2.1.4, I used the term "component" to refer to a subobject in an object-centric design, which isn't quite the same as a property object.

However, property objects are very closely related to components in many ways. In both designs, a single logical game object is made up of multiple subobjects. The main distinction lies in the roles of the subobjects. In a property-centric design, each subobject defines a particular attribute of the game object itself (e.g., health, visual representation, inventory, a particular magic power, etc.), whereas in a component-based (object-centric) design, the subobjects often represent linkages to particular low-level engine subsystems (renderer, animation, collision and dynamics, etc.) This distinction is so subtle as to be virtually irrelevant in many cases. You can call your design a *pure component model* (Section 14.2.1.6) or a *property-centric design* as you see fit, but at the end of the day, you'll have essentially the same result—a logical game object that is comprised of, and derives its behavior from, a collection of subobjects.

### 14.2.2.4. Pros and Cons of Property-Centric Designs

There are a number of potential benefits to an attribute-centric approach. It tends to be more memory efficient, because we need only store attribute data that is actually in use (i.e., there are never game objects with unused data members). It is also easier to construct such a model in a data-driven manner—designers can define new attributes easily, without recompiling the game, because there are no game object class definitions to be changed. Programmers need only get involved when entirely new types of properties need to be added (presuming the property cannot be added via script).

A property-centric design can also be more cache-friendly than an object-centric model, because data of the same type is stored *contiguously* in memory. This is a commonplace optimization technique on modern gaming hardware, where the cost of accessing memory is far higher than the cost of executing instructions and performing calculations. (For example, on the PLAYSTA-TION 3, the cost of a single cache miss is equivalent to the cost of executing literally thousands of CPU instructions.) By storing data contiguously in RAM, we can reduce or eliminate cache misses, because when we access one element of a data array, a large number of its neighboring elements are loaded into the same cache line. This approach to data design is sometimes called the *struct of arrays* technique, in contrast to the more-traditional *array of structs* approach. The differences between these two memory layouts are illustrated by the code snippet below. (Note that we wouldn't really implement a game object model in exactly this way—this example is meant only to illustrate the way in which a property-centric design tends to produce many contiguous arrays of like-typed data, rather than a single array of complex objects.)

```
static const U32 MAX_GAME_OBJECTS = 1024;

// Traditional array-of-structs approach.
struct GameObject
{
    U32          m_uniqueId;
    Vector       m_pos;
    Quaternion   m_rot;
    float        m_health;
    // ...
};
GameObject g_aAllGameObjects[MAX_GAME_OBJECTS];
```

```
// Cache-friendlier struct-of-arrays approach.
struct AllGameObjects
{
    U32         m_aUniqueId[MAX_GAME_OBJECTS];
    Vector      m_aPos[MAX_GAME_OBJECTS];
    Quaternion  m_aRot[MAX_GAME_OBJECTS];
    float       m_aHealth[MAX_GAME_OBJECTS];
    // ...
};
AllGameObjects g_allGameObjects;
```

Attribute-centric models have their share of problems as well. For example, when a game object is just a grab bag of properties, it becomes much more difficult to enforce relationships between those properties. It can be hard to implement a desired large-scale behavior merely by cobbling together the fine-grained behaviors of a group of property objects. It's also much trickier to debug such systems, as the programmer cannot slap a game object into the watch window in the debugger in order to inspect all of its properties at once.

### 14.2.2.5. Further Reading

A number of interesting PowerPoint presentations on the topic of property-centric architectures have been given by prominent engineers in the game industry at various game development conferences. You should be able to access them by visiting the following URLs:

- Rob Fermier, "Creating a Data Driven Engine," Game Developer's Conference, 2002. http://www.gamasutra.com/features/gdcarchive/2002/rob_fermier.ppt.

- Scott Bilas, "A Data-Driven Game Object System," Game Developer's Conference, 2002. http://www.drizzle.com/~scottb/gdc/game-objects.ppt.

- Alex Duran, "Building Object Systems: Features, Tradeoffs, and Pitfalls," Game Developer's Conference, 2003. http://www.gamasutra.com/features/gdcarchive/2003/Duran_Alex.ppt.

- Jeremy Chatelaine, "Enabling Data Driven Tuning via Existing Tools," Game Developer's Conference, 2003. http://www.gamasutra.com/features/gdcarchive/2003/Chatelaine_Jeremy.ppt.

- Doug Church, "Object Systems," presented at a game development conference in Seoul, Korea, 2003; conference organized by Chris Hecker, Casey Muratori, Jon Blow, and Doug Church. http://chrishecker.com/images/6/6f/ObjSys.ppt.

## 14.3. World Chunk Data Formats

As we've seen, a world chunk generally contains both *static* and *dynamic* world elements. The static geometry might be represented by one big triangle mesh, or it might be comprised of many smaller meshes. Each mesh might be *instanced* multiple times—for example, a single door mesh might be re-used for all of the doorways in the chunk. The static data usually includes collision information stored as a triangle soup, a collection of convex shapes, and/ or other simpler geometric shapes like planes, boxes, capsules, or spheres. Other static elements include volumetric *regions* that can be used to detect events or delineate areas within the game world, an AI *navigation mesh*, a set of line segments delineating *edges* within the background geometry that can be grabbed by the player character, and so on. We won't get into the details of these data formats here, because we've already discussed most of them in previous chapters.

The dynamic portion of the world chunk contains some kind of representation of the game objects within that chunk. A game object is defined by its *attributes* and its *behaviors*, and an object's behaviors are determined either directly or indirectly by its *type*. In an object-centric design, the object's type directly determines which class(es) to instantiate in order to represent the object at runtime. In a property-centric design, a game object's behavior is determined by the amalgamation of the behaviors of its properties, but the type still determines which properties the object should have (or one might say that an object's properties define its type). So, for each game object, a world chunk data file generally contains:

- *The initial values of the object's attributes.* The world chunk defines the state of each game object as it should exist when first spawned into the game world. An object's attribute data can be stored in a number of different formats. We'll explore a few popular formats below.

- *Some kind of specification of the object's type.* In an object-centric engine, this might be a string, a hashed string id, or some other unique type id. In a property-centric design, the type might be stored explicitly, or it might be defined implicitly by the collection of properties/attributes of which the object is comprised.

### 14.3.1. Binary Object Images

One way to store a collection of game objects into a disk file is to write a binary image of each object into the file, exactly as it looks in memory at runtime. This makes spawning game objects trivial. Once the game world chunk has been loaded into memory, we have ready-made images of all our objects, so we simply let them fly.

Well, not quite. Storing binary images of "live" C++ class instances is problematic for a number of reasons, including the need to handle pointers and virtual tables in a special way, and the possibility of having to endian-swap the data within each class instance. (These techniques are described in detail in Section 6.2.2.9.) Moreover, binary object images are inflexible and not robust to making changes. Gameplay is one of the most dynamic and unstable aspects of any game project, so it is wise to select a data format that supports rapid development and is robust to frequent changes. As such, the binary object image format is not usually a good choice for storing game object data (although this format can be suitable for more stable data structures, like mesh data or collision geometry).

## 14.3.2. Serialized Game Object Descriptions

*Serialization* is another means of storing a representation of a game object's internal state to a disk file. This approach tends to be more portable and simpler to implement than the binary object image technique. To serialize an object out to disk, the object is asked to produce a stream of data that contains enough detail to permit the original object to be reconstructed later. When an object is serialized back into memory from disk, an instance of the appropriate class is created, and then the stream of attribute data is read in order to initialize the new object's internal state. If the original serialized data stream was complete, the new object should be identical to the original for all intents and purposes.

Serialization is supported natively by some programming languages. For example, C# and Java both provide standardized mechanisms for serializing object instances to and from an XML text format. The C++ language unfortunately does not provide a standardized serialization facility. However, many C++ serialization systems have been successfully built, both inside and outside the game industry. We won't get into all the details of how to write a C++ object serialization system here, but we'll describe the data format and a few of the main systems that need to be written in order to get serialization to work in C++.

Serialization data isn't a binary image of the object. Instead, it is usually stored in a more-convenient and more-portable format. XML is a popular format for object serialization because it is well-supported and standardized, it is somewhat human-readable, and it has excellent support for hierarchical data structures, which arise frequently when serializing collections of interrelated game objects. Unfortunately, XML is notoriously slow to parse, which can increase world chunk load times. For this reason, some game engines use a proprietary binary format that is faster to parse and more compact than XML text.

The mechanics of serializing an object to and from disk are usually implemented in one of two basic ways:

- We can introduce a pair of virtual functions called something like `SerializeOut()` and `SerializeIn()` in our base class and arrange for each derived class to provide custom implementations of them that "know" how to serialize the attributes of that particular class.

- We can implement a *reflection* system for our C++ classes. We can then write a generic system that can automatically serialize any C++ object for which reflection information is available.

*Reflection* is a term used by the C# language, among others. In a nutshell, reflection data is a runtime description of the contents of a class. It stores information about the name of the class, what data members it contains, the types of each data member, and the offset of each member within the object's memory image, and it also contains information about all of the class's member functions. Given reflection information for an arbitrary C++ class, we could quite easily write a general-purpose object serialization system.

The tricky part of a C++ reflection system is generating the reflection data for all of the relevant classes. This can be done by encapsulating a class's data members in `#define` macros that extract relevant reflection information by providing a virtual function that can be overridden by each derived class in order to return appropriate reflection data for that class, by hand-coding a reflection data structure for each class, or via some other inventive approach.

In addition to attribute information, the serialization data stream invariably includes the name or unique id of each object's *class* or *type*. The class id is used to instantiate the appropriate class when the object is serialized into memory from disk. A class id can be stored as a string, a hashed string id, or some other kind of unique id.

Unfortunately, C++ provides no way to instantiate a class given only its name as a string or id. The class name must be known at compile time, and so it must be hard-coded by a programmer (e.g., `new ConcreteClass`). To work around this limitation of the language, C++ object serialization systems invariably include a *class factory* of some kind. A factory can be implemented in any number of ways, but the simplest approach is to create a data table that maps each class name/id to some kind of function or functor object that has been hard-coded to instantiate that particular class. Given a class name or id, we simply look up the corresponding function or functor in the table and call it to instantiate the class.

### 14.3.3. Spawners and Type Schemas

Both binary object images and serialization formats have an Achilles heel. They are both defined by the runtime implementation of the game object types they store, and hence they both require the world editor to contain intimate knowledge of the game engine's runtime implementation. For example, in order for the world editor to write out a binary image of a heterogeneous collection of game objects, it must either link directly with the runtime game engine code, or it must be painstakingly hand-coded to produce blocks of bytes that exactly match the data layout of the game objects at runtime. Serialization data is less-tightly coupled to the game object's implementation, but again, the world editor either needs to link with runtime game object code in order to gain access to the classes' `SerializeIn()` and `SerializeOut()` functions, or it needs access to the classes' reflection information in some way.

The coupling between the game world editor and the runtime engine code can be broken by abstracting the descriptions of our game objects in an implementation-independent way. For each game object in a world chunk data file, we store a little block of data, often called a *spawner*. A spawner is a lightweight, data-only representation of a game object that can be used to instantiate and initialize that game object at runtime. It contains the id of the game object's tool-side *type*. It also contains a table of simple key-value pairs that describe the initial attributes of the game object. These attributes often include a model-to-world transform, since most game objects have a distinct position, orientation, and scale in world space. When the game object is spawned, the appropriate class or classes are instantiated, as determined by the spawner's type. These runtime objects can then consult the dictionary of key-value pairs in order to initialize their data members appropriately.

A spawner can be configured to spawn its game object immediately upon being loaded, or it can lie dormant until asked to spawn at some later time during the game. Spawners can be implemented as first-class objects, so they can have a convenient functional interface and can store useful meta-data in addition to object attributes. A spawner can even be used for purposes other than spawning game objects. For example, in *Uncharted: Drake's Fortune*, designers used spawners to define important points or coordinate axes in the game world. These were called *position spawners* or *locator spawners*. Locators have many uses in a game, such as:

- defining points of interest for an AI character,
- defining a set of coordinate axes relative to which a set of animations can be played in perfect synchronization,

- defining the location at which a particle effect or audio effect should originate,
- defining waypoints along a race track,
- and the list goes on.

### 14.3.3.1. Object Type Schemas

A game object's attributes and behaviors are defined by its type. In a game world editor that employs a spawner-based design, a game object type can be represented by a data-driven *schema* that defines the collection of attributes that should be visible to the user when creating or editing an object of that type. At runtime, the tool-side object type can be mapped in either a hard-coded or data-driven way to a class or collection of classes that must be instantiated in order to spawn a game object of the given type.

Type schemas can be stored in a simple text file for consumption by the world editor and for inspection and editing by its users. For example, a schema file might look something like this:

```
enum LightType
{
    Ambient, Directional, Point, Spot
}

type Light
{
    String          UniqueId;
    LightType       Type;

    Vector          Pos;
    Quaternion      Rot;

    Float           Intensity : min(0.0), max(1.0);

    ColorARGB       DiffuseColor;

    ColorARGB       SpecularColor;
    ...
}

type Vehicle
{
    String          UniqueId;
    Vector          Pos;
    Quaternion      Rot;

    MeshReference   Mesh;

    Int             NumWheels : min(2), max(4);
```

```
     Float               TurnRadius;

     Float               TopSpeed : min(0.0);
     ...
  }

  ...
```

The above example brings a few important details to light. You'll notice that the *data types* of each attribute are defined, in addition to their names. These can be simple types like strings, integers, and floating-point values, or they can be specialized types like vectors, quaternions, ARGB colors, or references to special asset types like meshes, collision data, and so on. In this example, we've even provided a mechanism for defining enumerated types, like `LightType`. Another subtle point is that the object type schema provides additional information to the world editor, such as what type of GUI element to use when editing the attribute. Sometimes an attribute's GUI requirements are implied by its data type—strings are generally edited with a text field, Booleans via a check box, vectors via three text fields for the *x-*, *y-*, and *z-*coordinates or perhaps via a specialized GUI element designed for manipulating vectors in 3D. The schema can also specify meta-information for use by the GUI, such as minimum and maximum allowable values for integer and floating-point attributes, lists of available choices for drop-down combo boxes, and so on.

Some game engines permit object type schemas to be inherited, much like classes. For example, every game object needs to know its *type* and must have a *unique id* so that it can be distinguished from all the other game objects at runtime. These attributes could be specified in a top-level schema, from which all other schemas are derived.

### 14.3.3.2. Default Attribute Values

As you can well imagine, the number of attributes in a typical game object schema can grow quite large. This translates into a lot of data that must be specified by the game designer for each instance of each game object type he or she places into the game world. It can be extremely helpful to define *default values* in the schema for many of the attributes. This permits game designers to place "vanilla" instances of a game object type with little effort but still permits him or her to fine-tune the attribute values on specific instances as needed.

One inherent problem with default values arises when the default value of a particular attribute changes. For example, our game designers might have originally wanted Orcs to have 20 hit points. After many months of production, it might be decided that Orcs should have a more powerful 30 hit points by default. Any new Orcs placed into a game world will now have 30 hit points unless otherwise specified. But what about all the Orcs that were placed into game world chunks prior to the change? Do we need to find all of these previously-created Orcs and manually change their hit points to 30?

Ideally, we'd like to design our spawner system so that changes in default values automatically propagate to all preexisting instances that have not had their default values overridden explicitly. One easy way to implement this feature is to simply omit key-value pairs for attributes whose value does not differ from the default value. Whenever an attribute is missing from the spawner, the appropriate default can be used. (This presumes that the game engine has access to the object type schema file, so that it can read in the attributes' default values.) In our example, most of the preexisting Orc spawners would have had no HitPoints key-value pair at all (unless of course one of the spawner's hit points had been changed from the default value manually). So when the default value changes from 20 to 30, these Orcs will automatically use the new value.

Some engines allow default values to be overridden in derived object types. For example, the schema for a type called Vehicle might define a default TopSpeed of 80 miles per hour. A derived Motorcycle type schema could override this TopSpeed to be 100 miles per hour.

### 14.3.3.3. Some Beneifts of Spawners and Type Schemas

The key benefits of separating the spawner from the implementation of the game object are *simplicity*, *flexibility*, and *robustness*. From a data management point of view, it is much simpler to deal with a table of key-value pairs than it is to manage a binary object image with pointer fix-ups or a custom serialized object format. The key-value pairs approach also makes the data format extremely flexible and robust to changes. If a game object encounters key-value pairs that it is not expecting to see, it can simply ignore them. Likewise, if the game object is unable to find a key-value pair that it needs, it has the option of using a default value instead. This makes a key-value pair data format extremely robust to changes made by both the designers and the programmers.

Spawners also simplify the design and implementation of the game world editor, because it only needs to know how to manage lists of key-value pairs and object type schemas. It doesn't need to share code with the runtime game engine in any way, and it is only very loosely coupled to the engine's implementation details.

Spawners and archetypes give game designers and programmers a great deal of flexibility and power. Designers can define new game object type schemas within the world editor with little or no programmer intervention. The programmer can implement the runtime implementation of these new object types whenever his or her schedule allows it. The programmer does not need to immediately provide an implementation of each new object type as it is added in order to avoid breaking the game. New object data can exist safely in the world chunk files with or without a runtime implementation, and runtime implementations can exist with or without corresponding data in the world chunk file.

## 14.4. Loading and Streaming Game Worlds

To bridge the gap between the off-line world editor and our runtime game object model, we need a way to load world chunks into memory and unload them when they are no longer needed. The game world loading system has two main responsibilities: to manage the file I/O necessary to load game world chunks and other needed assets from disk into memory and to manage the allocation and deallocation of memory for these resources. The engine also needs to manage the *spawning* and *destruction* of game objects as they come and go in the game, both in terms of allocating and deallocating memory for the objects and ensuring that the proper classes are instantiated for each game object. In the following sections, we'll investigate how game worlds are loaded and also have a look at how object spawning systems typically work.

### 14.4.1. Simple Level Loading

The most straightforward game world loading approach, and the one used by all of the earliest games, is to allow one and only one game world chunk (a.k.a. level) to be loaded at a time. When the game is first started, and between pairs of levels, the player sees a static or simply animated two-dimensional loading screen while he or she waits for the level to load.

Memory management in this kind of design is quite straightforward. As we mentioned in Section 6.2.2.7, a stack-based allocator is very well-suited to a one-level-at-a-time world loading design. When the game first runs, any resource data that is required across all game levels is loaded at the bottom of the stack. I will call this *load-and-stay-resident* (LSR) data. The location of the stack pointer is recorded after the LSR data has been fully loaded. Each game world chunk, along with its associated mesh, texture, audio, animation, and other resource data, is loaded on top of the LSR data on the stack. When the level has been completed by the player, all of its memory can be

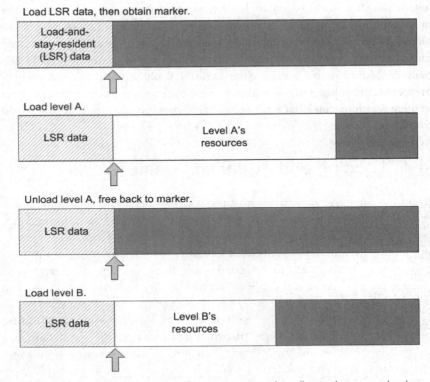

**Figure 14.11.** A stack-based memory allocator is extremely well-suited to a one-level-at-a-time world loading system.

freed by simply resetting the stack pointer to the top of the LSR data block. At this point, a new level can be loaded in its place. This is illustrated in Figure 14.11.

While this design is very simple, it has a number of drawbacks. For one thing, the player only sees the game world in discrete chunks—there is no way to implement a vast, contiguous, seamless world using this technique. Another problem is that during the time the level's resource data is being loaded, there is no game world in memory. So the player is forced to watch a two-dimensional loading screen of some sort.

## 14.4.2. Toward Seamless Loading: Air Locks

The best way to avoid boring level-loading screens is to permit the player to continue playing the game while the next world chunk and its associated resource data are being loaded. One simple approach would be to divide the memory that we've set aside for game world assets into two equally sized blocks. We could load level A into one memory block, allow the player to start playing level A, and then load level B into the other block using a streaming file I/O library (i.e., the loading code would run in a separate thread). The big problem with this technique is that it cuts the size of each level in half relative to what would be possible with a one-level-at-a-time approach.

We can achieve a similar effect by dividing the game world memory into two unequally-sized blocks—a large block that can contain a "full" game world chunk and a small block that is only large enough to contain a tiny world chunk. The small chunk is sometimes known as an "air lock."

When the game starts, a "full" chunk and an "air lock" chunk are loaded. The player progresses through the full chunk and into the air lock, at which point some kind of gate or other impediment ensures that the player can neither see the previous full world area nor return to it. The full chunk can then be un-loaded, and a new full-sized world chunk can be loaded. During the load, the player is kept busy doing some task within the air lock. The task might be as simple as walking from one end of a hallway to the other, or it could be something more engaging, like solving a puzzle or fighting some enemies.

Asynchronous file I/O is what enables the full world chunk to be loaded while the player is simultaneously playing in the air lock region. See Section 6.1.3 for more details. It's important to note that an air lock system does *not* free us from displaying a loading screen whenever a new game is started, because during the initial load there is no game world in memory in which to play. However, once the player is in the game world, he or she needn't see a loading screen ever again, thanks to air locks and asynchronous data loading.

*Halo* for the Xbox used a technique similar to this. The large world areas were invariably connected by smaller, more confined areas. As you play *Halo*, watch for confined areas that prevent you from back-tracking—you'll find one roughly every 5-10 minutes of gameplay. *Jak 2* for the PlayStation 2 used the air lock technique as well. The game world was structured as a hub area (the main city) with a number of off-shoot areas, each of which was connected to the hub via a small, confined air lock region.

## 14.4.3. Game World Streaming

Many game designs call for the player to feel like he or she is playing in a huge, contiguous, seamless world. Ideally, the player should not be confined to small air lock regions periodically—it would be best if the world simply unfolded in front of the player as naturally and believably as possible.

Modern game engines support this kind of seamless world by using a technique known as *streaming*. World streaming can be accomplished in various ways. The main goals are always (a) to load data while the player is engaged in regular gameplay tasks and (b) to manage the memory in such a way as to eliminate *fragmentation* while permitting data to be loaded and unloaded as needed as the player progresses through the game world.

Recent consoles and PCs have a lot more memory than their predecessors, so it is now possible to keep multiple world chunks in memory simultaneously. We could imagine dividing our memory space into, say, three equally sized buffers. At first, we load world chunks A, B, and C into these three buffers and allow the player to start playing through chunk A. When he or she enters chunk B and is far enough along that chunk A can no longer be seen, we can unload chunk A and start loading a new chunk D into the first buffer. When B can no longer be seen, it can be dumped and chunk E loaded. This recycling of buffers can continue until the player has reached the end of the contiguous game world.

The problem with a coarse-grained approach to world streaming is that it places onerous restrictions on the size of a world chunk. All chunks in the entire game must be roughly the same size—large enough to fill up the majority of one of our three memory buffers but never any larger.

One way around this problem is to employ a much finer-grained subdivision of memory. Rather than streaming relatively large chunks of the world, we can divide every game asset, from game world chunks to foreground meshes to textures to animation banks, into equally-sized blocks of data. We can then use a chunky, pool-based memory allocation system like the one described in Section 6.2.2.7 to load and unload resource data as needed without having to worry about memory fragmentation. This is the technique employed by the *Uncharted: Drake's Fortune* engine.

### 14.4.3.1.  Determining Which Resources to Load

One question that arises when using a fine-grained chunky memory allocator for world streaming is how the engine will know what resources to load at any given moment during gameplay. In *Uncharted: Drake's Fortune* (UDF), we used a relatively simple system of *level load regions* to control the loading and unloading of assets.

*UDF* is set in two geographically distinct, contiguous game worlds—the jungle and the island. Each of these worlds exists in a single, consistent world space, but they are divided up into numerous geographically adjacent chunks. A simple convex volume known as a *region* encompasses each of the chunks; the regions overlap each other somewhat. Each region contains a list

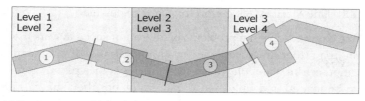

**Figure 14.12.** A game world divided into chunks. Level load regions, each with a requested chunk list, are arranged in such a way as to guarantee that the player never sees a chunk pop in or out of view.

of the world chunks that should be in memory when the player is in that region.

At any given moment, the player is within one or more of these regions. To determine the set of world chunks that should be in memory, we simply take the *union* of the chunk lists from each of the regions enclosing the Nathan Drake character. The level loading system periodically checks this master chunk list and compares it against the set of world chunks that are currently in memory. If a chunk disappears from the master list, it is unloaded, thereby freeing up all of the allocation blocks it occupied. If a new chunk appears in the list, it is loaded into any free allocation blocks that can be found. The level load regions and world chunks are designed in such a way as to ensure that the player never sees a chunk disappear when it is unloaded and that there's enough time between the moment at which a chunk starts loading and the moment its contents are first seen by the player to permit the chunk to be fully streamed into memory. This technique is illustrated in Figure 14.12.

## 14.4.4. Memory Management for Object Spawning

Once a game world has been loaded into memory, we need to manage the process of *spawning* the dynamic game objects in the world. Most game engines have some kind of game object spawning system that manages the instantiation of the class or classes that make up each game object and handles destruction of game objects when they are no longer needed. One of the central jobs of any object spawning system is to manage the dynamic allocation of memory for newly spawned game objects. Dynamic allocation can be slow, so steps must be taken to ensure allocations are as efficient as possible. And because game objects come in a wide variety of sizes, dynamically allocating them can cause memory to become fragmented, leading to premature out-of-memory conditions. There are a number of different approaches to game object memory management. We'll explore a few common ones in the following sections.

### 14.4.4.1. Off-Line Memory Allocation for Object Spawning

Some game engines solve the problems of allocation speed and memory fragmentation in a rather draconian way, by simply disallowing dynamic memory allocation during gameplay altogether. Such engines permit game world chunks to be loaded and unloaded dynamically, but they spawn in all dynamic game objects immediately upon loading a chunk. Thereafter, no game objects can be created or destroyed. You can think of this technique as obeying a "law of conservation of game objects." No game objects are created or destroyed once a world chunk has been loaded.

This technique avoids memory fragmentation because the memory requirements of all the game objects in a world chunk are (a) known a priori and (b) bounded. This means that the memory for the game objects can be allocated off-line by the world editor and included as part of the world chunk data itself. All game objects are therefore allocated out of the same memory used to load the game world and its resources, and they are no more prone to fragmentation than any other loaded resource data. This approach also has the benefit of making the game's memory usage patterns highly predictable. There's no chance that a large group of game objects is going to spawn into the world unexpectedly, and cause the game to run out of memory.

On the downside, this approach can be quite limiting for game designers. Dynamic object spawning can be simulated by allocating a game object in the world editor but instructing it to be invisible and dormant when the world is first loaded. Later, the object can "spawn" by simply activating itself and making itself visible. But the game designers have to predict the total number of game objects of each type that they'll need when the game world is first created in the world editor. If they want to provide the player with an infinite supply of health packs, weapons, enemies, or some other kind of game object, they either need to work out a way to recycle their game objects, or they're out of luck.

### 14.4.4.2. Dynamic Memory Management for Object Spawning

Game designers would probably prefer to work with a game engine that supports true dynamic object spawning. Although this is more difficult to implement than a static game object spawning approach, it can be implemented in a number of different ways.

Again, the primary problem is memory fragmentation. Because different types of game objects (and sometimes even different instances of the same type of object) occupy different amounts of memory, we cannot use our favorite fragmentation-free allocator—the pool allocator. And because game objects are generally destroyed in a different order than that in which they were spawned, we cannot use a stack-based allocator either. Our only choice appears to be a fragmentation-prone heap allocator. Thankfully, there are many ways to deal with the fragmentation problem. We'll investigate a few common ones in the following sections.

### One Memory Pool per Object Type

If the individual instances of each game object type are guaranteed to all occupy the same amount of memory, we could consider using a separate memory pool for each object type. Actually, we only need one pool per *unique game object size,* so object types of the same size can share a single pool.

Doing this allows us to completely avoid memory fragmentation, but one limitation of this approach is that we need to maintain lots of separate pools. We also need to make educated guesses about how many of each type of object we'll need. If a pool has too many elements, we end up wasting memory; if it has too few, we won't be able to satisfy all of the spawn requests at runtime, and game objects will fail to spawn. That said, many commercial game engines do successfully employ this kind of memory management technique.

### Small Memory Allocators

We can transform the idea of one pool per game object type into something more workable by allowing a game object to be allocated out of a pool whose elements are larger than the object itself. This can reduce the number of unique memory pools we need significantly, at the cost of some potentially wasted memory in each pool.

For example, we might create a set of pool allocators, each one with elements that are twice as large as those of its predecessor—perhaps 8, 16, 32, 64, 128, 256, and 512 bytes. We can also use a sequence of element sizes that conforms to some other suitable pattern or base the list of sizes on allocation statistics collected from the running game.

Whenever we try to allocate a game object, we search for the smallest pool whose elements are larger than or equal to the size of the object we're allocating. We accept that for some objects, we'll be wasting space. In return, we alleviate all of our memory fragmentation problems—a reasonably fair trade. If we ever encounter a memory allocation request that is larger than our largest pool, we can always turn it over to the general-purpose heap allocator, knowing that fragmentation of large memory blocks is not nearly as problematic as fragmentation involving tiny blocks.

This type of allocator is sometimes called a *small memory allocator.* It can eliminate fragmentation (for allocations that fit into one of the pools). It can also speed up memory allocations significantly for small chunks of data, because a pool allocation involves two pointer manipulations to remove the element from the linked list of free elements—a much less-expensive operation than a general-purpose heap allocation.

### Memory Relocation

Another way to eliminate fragmentation is to attack the problem directly. This approach is known as *memory relocation*. It involves shifting allocated memory blocks down into adjacent free holes to remove fragmentation. Moving the memory is easy, but because we are moving "live" allocated objects, we need to be very careful about fixing up any pointers into the memory blocks we move. See Section 5.2.2.2 for more details.

## 14.4.5. Saved Games

Many games allow the player to save his or her progress, quit the game, and then load up the game at a later time in exactly the state he or she left it. A saved game system is similar to the world chunk loading system in that it is capable of loading the state of the game world from a disk file or memory card. But the requirements of this system differ somewhat from those of a world loading system, so the two are usually distinct (or overlap only partially).

To understand the differences between the requirements of these two systems, let's briefly compare world chunks to saved game files. World chunks specify the initial conditions of all dynamic objects in the world, but they also contain a full description of all static world elements. Much of the static information, such as background meshes and collision data, tends to take up a lot of disk space. As such, world chunks are sometimes comprised of multiple disk files, and the total amount of data associated with a world chunk is usually large.

A saved game file must also store the current state information of the game objects in the world. However, it does not need to store a duplicate copy of any information that can be determined by reading the world chunk data. For example, there's no need to save out the static geometry in a saved game file. A saved game need not store every detail of every object's state either. Some objects that have no impact on gameplay can be omitted altogether. For the other game objects, we may only need to store partial state information. As long as the player can't tell the difference between the state of the game world before and after it has been saved and reloaded (or if the differences are irrelevant to the player), then we have a successful saved game system. As such, saved game files tend to be much smaller than world chunk files and may place more of an emphasis on data compression and omission. Small file sizes are especially important when numerous saved game files must fit onto the tiny memory cards that were used on older consoles. But even today, with consoles that are equipped with large hard drives, it's still a good idea to keep the size of a saved game file as small as possible.

### 14.4.5.1. Check Points

One approach to save games is to limit saves to specific points in the game, known as *check points*. The benefit of this approach is that most of the knowledge about the state of the game is saved in the current world chunk(s) in the vicinity of each check point. This data is always exactly the same, no matter which player is playing the game, so it needn't be stored in the saved game. As a result, saved game files based on check points can be extremely small. We might need to store only the name of the last check point reached, plus perhaps some information about the current state of the player character, such as the player's health, number of lives remaining, what items he has in his inventory, which weapon(s) he has, and how much ammo each one contains. Some games based on check points don't even store this information—they start the player off in a known state at each check point. Of course, the downside of a game based on check points is the possibility of user frustration, especially if check points are few and far between.

### 14.4.5.2. Save Anywhere

Some games support a feature known as *save anywhere*. As the name implies, such games permit the state of the game to be saved at literally any point during play. To implement this feature, the size of the saved game data file must increase significantly. The current locations and internal states of every game object whose state is relevant to gameplay must be saved and then restored when the game is loaded again later.

In a save anywhere design, a saved game data file contains basically the same information as a world chunk, minus the world's static components. It is possible to utilize the same data format for both systems, although there may be factors that make this infeasible. For example, the world chunk data format might be designed for flexibility, but the saved game format might be compressed to minimize the size of each saved game.

As we've mentioned, one way to reduce the amount of data that needs to be stored in a saved game file is to omit certain irrelevant game objects and to omit some irrelevant details of others. For example, we needn't remember the exact time index within every animation that is currently playing or the exact momentums and velocities of every physically simulated rigid body. We can rely on the imperfect memories of human gamers and save only a rough approximation to the game's state.

# 14.5.  Object References and World Queries

Every game object generally requires some kind of unique id so that it can be distinguished from the other objects in the game, found at runtime, serve as a target of inter-object communication, and so on. Unique object ids are equally helpful on the tool side, as they can be used to identify and find game objects within the world editor.

At runtime, we invariably need various ways to find game objects. We might want to find an object by its unique id, by its type, or by a set of arbitrary criteria. We often need to perform proximity-based queries, for example finding all enemy aliens within a 10 meter radius of the player character.

Once a game object has been found via a query, we need some way to refer to it. In a language like C or C++, object references might be implemented as pointers, or we might use something more sophisticated, like handles or smart pointers. The lifetime of an object reference can vary widely, from the scope of a single function call to a period of many minutes.

In the following sections, we'll first investigate various ways to implement object references. Then we'll explore the kinds of queries we often require when implementing gameplay and how those queries might be implemented.

## 14.5.1.  Pointers

In C or C++, the most straightforward way to implement an object reference is via a pointer (or a reference in C++). Pointers are powerful and are just about as simple and intuitive as you can get. However, pointers suffer from a number of problems:

- *Orphaned objects.* Ideally, every object should have an *owner*—another object that is responsible for managing its lifetime—creating it and then deleting it when it is no longer needed. But pointers don't give the programmer any help in enforcing this rule. The result can be an *orphaned* object—an object that still occupies memory but is no longer needed or referenced by any other object in the system.
- *Stale pointers.* If an object is deleted, ideally we should null-out any and all pointers to that object. If we forget to do so, however, we end up with a stale pointer—a pointer to a block of memory that used to be occupied by a valid object but is now free memory. If anyone tries to read or write data through a stale pointer, the result can be a crash or incorrect program behavior. Stale pointers can be difficult to track down because they may continue to work for some time after the object has deleted. Only much later, when a new object is allocated on top of the stale memory block, does the data actually change and cause a crash.

- *Invalid pointers.* A programmer is free to store any address in a pointer, including a totally invalid address. A common problem is dereferencing a null pointer. These problems can be guarded against by using assertion macros to check that pointers are never null prior to dereferencing them. Even worse, if a piece of data is misinterpreted as a pointer, dereferencing it can cause the program to read or write an essentially random memory address. This usually results in a crash or other major problem that can be very tough to debug.

Many game engines make heavy use of pointers, because they are by far the fastest, most efficient, and easiest-to-work-with way to implement object references. However, experienced programmers are always wary of pointers, and some game teams turn to more sophisticated kinds of object references, either out of a desire to use safer programming practices or out of necessity. For example, if a game engine relocates allocated data blocks at runtime to eliminate memory fragmentation (see Section 5.2.2.2), simple pointers cannot be used. We either need to use a type of object reference that is robust to memory relocation, or we need to manually fix up any pointers into every relocated memory block at the time it is moved.

## 14.5.2. Smart Pointers

A *smart pointer* is a small object that acts like a pointer for most intents and purposes but avoids most of the problems inherent with native C/C++ pointers. At its simplest, a smart pointer contains a native pointer as a data member and provides a set of overloaded operators that make it act like a pointer in most ways. Pointers can be dereferenced, so the * and -> operators are overloaded to return the address as expected. Pointers can undergo arithmetic operations, so the +, -, ++, and -- operators are also overloaded appropriately.

Because a smart pointer is an object, it can contain additional meta-data and/or take additional steps not possible with a regular pointer. For example, a smart pointer might contain information that allows it to recognize when the object to which it points has been deleted and start returning a NULL address if so.

Smart pointers can also help with object lifetime management by cooperating with one another to determine the number of references to a particular object. This is called *reference counting*. When the number of smart pointers that reference a particular object drops to zero, we know that the object is no longer needed, so it can be automatically deleted. This can free the programmer from having to worry about object ownership and orphaned objects.

Smart pointers have their share of problems. For one thing, they are relatively easy to implement, but they are extremely tough to get right. There are a great many cases to handle, and the std::auto_ptr class provided by the standard C++ library is widely recognized to be inadequate in many situations. The Boost C++ template library provides six different varieties of smart pointers:

- `scoped_ptr`. A pointer to a single object with one owner.
- `scoped_array`. A pointer to an array of objects with one owner.
- `shared_ptr`. A pointer to an object whose lifetime is shared by multiple owners.
- `shared_array`. A pointer to an array of objects whose lifetimes are shared by multiple owners.
- `weak_ptr`. A pointer that does not own or automatically destroy the object it references (whose lifetime is assumed to be managed by a `shared_ptr`).
- `intrusive_ptr`. A pointer that implements reference counting by assuming that the pointed-to object will maintain the reference count itself. Intrusive pointers are useful because they are the same size as a native C++ pointer (because no reference-counting apparatus is required) and because they can be constructed directly from native pointers.

Properly implementing a smart pointer class can be a daunting task. Have a glance at the Boost smart pointer documentation (http://www.boost.org/doc/libs/1_36_0/libs/smart_ptr/smart_ptr.htm) to see what I mean. All sorts of issues come up, including:

- type safety of smart pointers,
- the ability for a smart pointer to be used with an incomplete type,
- correct smart pointer behavior when an exception occurs,
- runtime costs, which can be high.

I have worked on a project that attempted to implement its own smart pointers, and we were fixing all sorts of nasty bugs with them up until the very end of the project. My personal recommendation is to stay away from smart pointers, or if you must use them, use a mature implementation such as Boost's rather than trying to roll your own.

## 14.5.3. Handles

A *handle* acts like a smart pointer in many ways, but it is simpler to implement and tends to be less prone to problems. A handle is basically an integer index into a global *handle table*. The handle table, in turn, contains pointers to the objects to which the handles refer. To create a handle, we simply search the handle table for the address of the object in question and store its index in the handle. To dereference a handle, the calling code simply indexes the appropri-

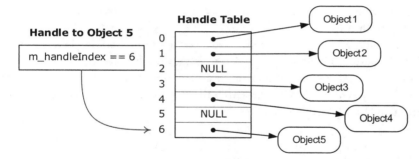

**Figure 14.13.** A handle table contains raw object pointers. A handle is simply an index into this table.

ate slot in the handle table and dereferences the pointer it finds there. This is illustrated in Figure 14.13.

Because of the simple level of indirection afforded by the handle table, handles are much safer and more flexible than raw pointers. If an object is deleted, it can simply null out its entry in the handle table. This causes all existing handles to the object to be immediately and automatically converted to null references. Handles also support memory relocation. When an object is relocated in memory, its address can be found in the handle table and up-dated appropriately. Again, all existing handles to the object are automatically updated as a result.

A handle can be implemented as a raw integer. However, the handle table index is usually wrapped in a simple class so that a convenient interface for creating and dereferencing the handle can be provided.

Handles are prone to the possibility of referencing a stale object. For ex-ample, let's say we create a handle to object A, which occupies slot 17 in the handle table. Later, object A is deleted, and slot 17 is nulled out. Later still, a new object B is created, and it just happens to occupy slot 17 in the handle table. If there are still any handles to object A lying around when object B is created, they will suddenly start referring to object B (instead of null). This is almost certainly not desirable behavior.

One simple solution to the stale object problem is to include a unique object id in each handle. That way, when a handle to object A is created, it con-tains not only slot index 17, but the object id "A." When object B takes A's place in the handle table, any left-over handles to A will agree on the handle index but disagree on the object id. This allows stale object A handles to continue to return null when dereferenced rather than returning a pointer to object B unexpectedly.

The following code snippet shows how a simple handle class might be implemented. Notice that we've also included the handle index in the Game Object class itself—this allows us to create new handles to a GameObject very quickly without having to search the handle table for its address to determine its handle table index.

```cpp
// Within the GameObject class, we store a unique id,
// and also the object's handle index, for efficient
// creation of new handles.
class GameObject
{

private:
    // ...
    GameObjectId m_uniqueId;        // object's unique id
    U32          m_handleIndex;     // speedier handle
                                    // creation

    friend class GameObjectHandle;  // access to id and
                                    // index
    // ...

public:
    GameObject() // constructor
    {
        // The unique id might come from the world editor,
        // or it might be assigned dynamically at runtime.
        m_uniqueId = AssignUniqueObjectId();

        // The handle index is assigned by finding the
        // first free slot in the handle table.
        m_handleIndex = FindFreeSlotInHandleTable();

        // ...
    }

    // ...
};

// This constant defines the size of the handle table,
// and hence the maximum number of game objects that can
// exist at any one time.
static const U32 MAX_GAME_OBJECTS = ...;

// This is the global handle table -- a simple array of
// pointers to GameObjects.
static GameObject* g_apGameObject[MAX_GAME_OBJECTS];
```

```
// This is our simple game object handle class.
class GameObjectHandle
{
private:
    U32 m_handleIndex;        // index into the handle
                              // table
    GameObjectId m_uniqueId;  // unique id avoids stale
                              // handles

public:
    explicit GameObjectHandle(GameObject& object) :
        m_handleIndex(object.m_handleIndex),
        m_uniqueId(object.m_uniqueId)
    {
    }

    // This function dereferences the handle.
    GameObject* ToObject() const
    {
        GameObject* pObject
            = g_apGameObject[m_handleIndex];
        if (pObject != NULL
        &&  pObject->m_uniqueId == m_uniqueId)
        {
            return pObject;
        }
        return NULL;
    }
};
```

This example is functional but incomplete. We might want to implement copy semantics, provide additional constructor variants, and so on. The entries in the global handle table might contain additional information, not just a raw pointer to each game object. And of course, a fixed-size handle table implementation like this one isn't the only possible design; handle systems vary somewhat from engine to engine.

We should note that one fortunate side benefit of a global handle table is that it gives us a ready-made list of all active game objects in the system. The global handle table can be used to quickly and efficiently iterate over all game objects in the world, for example. It can also make implementing other kinds of queries easier in some cases.

## 14.5.4. Game Object Queries

Every game engine provides at least a few ways to find game objects at runtime. We'll call these searches *game object queries*. The simplest type of query is to find a particular game object by its unique id. However, a real game engine makes many other types of game object queries. Here are just a few examples of the kinds of queries a game developer might want to make:

- Find all enemy characters with line of sight to the player.
- Iterate over all game objects of a certain type.
- Find all destructible game objects with more than 80% health.
- Transmit damage to all game objects within the blast radius of an explosion.
- Iterate over all objects in the path of a bullet or other projectile, in nearest-to-farthest order.

This list could go on for many pages, and of course its contents are highly dependent upon the design of the particular game being made.

For maximum flexibility in performing game object queries, we could imagine a general-purpose game object database, complete with the ability to formulate arbitrary queries using arbitrary search criteria. Ideally, our game object database would perform all of these queries extremely efficiently and rapidly, making maximum use of whatever hardware and software resources are available.

In reality, such an ideal combination of flexibility and blinding speed is generally not possible. Instead, game teams usually determine which types of queries are most likely to be needed during development of the game, and specialized data structures are implemented to accelerate those particular types of queries. As new queries become necessary, the engineers either leverage preexisting data structures to implement them, or they invent new ones if sufficient speed cannot be obtained. Here are a few examples of specialized data structures that can accelerate specific types of game object queries:

- *Finding game objects by unique id.* Pointers or handles to the game objects could be stored in a hash table or binary search tree keyed by unique id.
- *Iterating over all objects that meet a particular criterion.* The game objects could be presorted into linked lists based on various criteria (presuming the criteria are known a priori). For example, we might construct a list of all game objects of a particular type, maintain a list of all objects within a particular radius of the player, etc.
- *Finding all objects in the path of a projectile or with line of sight to some target point.* The collision system is usually leveraged to perform these kinds of game object queries. Most collision systems provide ultra-fast ray casts, and some also provide the ability to cast other shapes such as spheres or arbitrary convex volumes into the world to determine what they hit.

- *Finding all objects within a given region or radius.* We might consider storing our game objects in some kind of spatial hash data structure. This could be as simple as a horizontal grid placed over the entire game world or something more sophisticated, such as a quadtree, octtree, kd-tree, or other data structure that encodes spatial proximity.

## 14.6. Updating Game Objects in Real Time

Every game engine, from the simplest to the most complex, requires some means of updating the internal state of every game object over time. The *state* of a game object can be defined as the values of all its *attributes* (sometimes called its *properties,* and called *data members* in the C++ language). For example, the state of the ball in *Pong* is described by its $(x, y)$ position on the screen and its velocity (speed and direction of travel). Because games are dynamic, time-based simulations, a game object's state describes its configuration at *one specific instant in time.* In other words, a game object's notion of time is *discrete* rather than *continuous.* (However, as we'll see, it's helpful to think of the objects' states as changing continuously and then being sampled discretely by the engine, because it helps you to avoid some common pitfalls.)

In the following discussions, we'll use the symbol $S_i(t)$ to denote the state of object $i$ at an arbitrary time $t$. The use of vector notation here is not strictly mathematically correct, but it reminds us that a game object's state acts like a heterogeneous $n$-dimensional vector, containing all sorts of information of various data types. We should note that this usage of the term "state" is not the same as the states in a *finite state machine.* A game object may very well be implemented in terms of one—or many—finite state machines, but in that case, a specification of the current state of each FSM would merely be a part of the game object's overall state vector $S(t)$.

Most low-level engine subsystems (rendering, animation, collision, physics, audio, and so on) require periodic updating, and the game object system is no exception. As we saw in Chapter 7, updating is usually done via a single master loop called the *game loop* (or possibly via multiple game loops, each running in a separate thread). Virtually all game engines update game object states as part of their main game loop—in other words, they treat the game object model as just another engine subsystem that requires periodic servicing.

Game object updating can therefore be thought of as the process of determining the state of each object at the current time $S_i(t)$ given its state at a previous time $S_i(t - \Delta t)$. Once all object states have been updated, the current time $t$ becomes the new previous time $(t - \Delta t)$, and this process repeats for as long as the game is running. Usually, one or more *clocks* are maintained by the engine—one that tracks real time exactly and possibly others that may or may not correspond to real time. These clocks provide the engine with the absolute time $t$ and/or with the change in time $\Delta t$ from iteration to iteration of the game loop. The clock that drives the updating of game object states is usually permitted to diverge from real time. This allows the behaviors of the game objects to be paused, slowed down, sped up, or even run in reverse—whatever is required in order to suit the needs of the game design. These features are also invaluable for debugging and development of the game.

As we mentioned in Chapter 1, a game object updating system is an example of what is known as a *dynamic, real-time, agent-based computer simulation* in computer science. Game object updating systems also exhibit some aspects of *discrete event simulations* (see Section 14.7 for more details on events). These are well-researched areas of computer science, and they have many applications outside the field of interactive entertainment. Games are one of the more-complex kinds of agent-based simulation—as we'll see, updating game object states over time in a dynamic, interactive virtual environment can be surprisingly difficult to get right. Game programmers can learn a lot about game object updating by studying the wider field of agent-based and discrete event simulations. And researchers in those fields can probably learn a thing or two from game engine design as well!

As with all high-level game engine systems, every engine takes a slightly (or sometimes radically) different approach. However, as before, most game teams encounter a common set of problems, and certain design patterns tend to crop up again and again in virtually every engine. In this section, we'll investigate these common problems and some common solutions to them. Please bear in mind that game engines may exist that employ very different solutions to the ones described here, and some game designs face unique problems that we can't possibly cover here.

## 14.6.1. A Simple Approach (That Doesn't Work)

The simplest way to update the states of a collection of game objects is to iterate over the collection and call a virtual function, named something like `Update()`, on each object in turn. This is typically done once during each iteration of the main game loop (i.e., once per *frame*). Game object classes can provide custom implementations of the `Update()` function in order to perform whatever tasks are required to advance the state of that type of object to the next discrete time index. The time delta from the previous frame can be passed to the update function so that objects can take proper account of the passage of time. At its simplest, then, our `Update()` function's signature might look something like this:

```
virtual void Update(float dt);
```

For the purposes of the following discussions, we'll assume that our engine employs a monolithic object hierarchy, in which each game object is represented by a single instance of a single class. However, we can easily extend the ideas here to virtually any object-centric design. For example, to update a component-based object model, we could call `Update()` on every component that makes up each game object, or we could call `Update()` on the "hub" object and let it update its associated components as it sees fit. We can also extend these ideas to property-centric designs, by calling some sort of `Update()` function on each property instance every frame.

They say that the devil is in the details, so let's investigate two important details here. First, how should we maintain the collection of all game objects? And second, what kinds of things should the `Update()` function be responsible for doing?

### 14.6.1.1. Maintaining a Collection of Active Game Objects

The collection of active game objects is often maintained by a singleton manager class, perhaps named something like `GameWorld` or `GameObject Manager`. The collection of game objects generally needs to be dynamic, because game objects are spawned and destroyed as the game is played. Hence a *linked list* of pointers, smart pointers, or handles to game objects is one simple and effective approach. (Some game engines disallow dynamic spawning and destroying of game objects; such engines can use a statically-sized *array* of game object pointers, smart pointers, or handles rather than a linked list.) As we'll see below, most engines use more-complex data structures to keep track of their game objects rather than just a simple, flat linked list. But for the time being, we can visualize the data structure as a linked list for simplicity.

### 14.6.1.2. Responsibilities of the Update() Function

A game object's `Update()` function is primarily responsible for determining the state of that game object at the current discrete time index $S_i(t)$ given its previous state $S_i(t - \Delta t)$. Doing this may involve applying a rigid body dynamics simulation to the object, sampling a preauthored animation, reacting to events that have occurred during the current time step, and so on.

Most game objects interact with one or more engine subsystems. They may need to animate, be rendered, emit particle effects, play audio, collide with other objects and static geometry, and so on. Each of these systems has an internal state that must also be updated over time, usually once or a few times per frame. It might seem reasonable and intuitive to simply update all of these subsystems directly from within the game object's `Update()` function. For example, consider the following hypothetical update function for a `Tank` object:

```
virtual void Tank::Update(float dt)
{

    // Update the state of the tank itself.
    MoveTank(dt);

    DeflectTurret(dt);

    FireIfNecessary();

    // Now update low-level engine subsystems on behalf
    // of this tank. (NOT a good idea... see below!)
    m_pAnimationComponent->Update(dt);

    m_pCollisionComponent->Update(dt);

    m_pPhysicsComponent->Update(dt);

    m_pAudioComponent->Update(dt);
    m_pRenderingComponent->draw();
}
```

Given that our `Update()` functions are structured like this, the game loop could be driven almost entirely by the updating of the game objects, like this:

```
while (true)
{
    PollJoypad();

    float dt = g_gameClock.CalculateDeltaTime();

    for (each gameObject)
    {
        // This hypothetical Update() function updates
        // all engine subsystems!
        gameObject.Update(dt);
    }

    g_renderingEngine.SwapBuffers();
}
```

However attractive the simple approach to object updating shown above may seem, it is usually not viable in a commercial-grade game engine. In the following sections, we'll explore some of the problems with this simplistic approach and investigate common ways in which each problem can be solved.

## 14.6.2. Performance Constraints and Batched Updates

Most low-level engine systems have extremely stringent performance constraints. They operate on a large quantity of data, and they must do a large
number of calculations every frame as quickly as possible. As a result, most
engine systems benefit from *batched updating*. For example, it is usually far
more efficient to update a large number of animations in one batch than it is
to update each object's animation interleaved with other unrelated operations,
such as collision detection, physical simulation, and rendering.

In most commercial game engines, each engine subsystem is updated directly or indirectly by the main game loop rather than being updated on a
per-game object basis from within each object's Update() function. If a game
object requires the services of a particular engine subsystem, it asks that subsystem to allocate some subsystem-specific state information on its behalf. For
example, a game object that wishes to be rendered via a triangle mesh might
request the rendering subsystem to allocate a *mesh instance* for its use. (A mesh
instance represents a single instance of a triangle mesh—it keeps track of the
position, orientation, and scale of the instance in world space whether or not
it is visible, per-instance material data, and any other per-instance information
that may be relevant.) The rendering engine maintains a collection of mesh instances internally. It can manage the mesh instances however it sees fit in order
to maximize its own runtime performance. The game object controls *how* it is
rendered by manipulating the properties of the mesh instance object, but the
game object does not control the rendering of the mesh instance directly. Instead, after all game objects have had a chance to update themselves, the rendering engine draws all visible mesh instances in one efficient batch update.

With batched updating, a particular game object's Update() function,
such as that of our hypothetical tank object, might look more like this:

```
virtual void Tank::Update(float dt)
{
    // Update the state of the tank itself.
    MoveTank(dt);

    DeflectTurret(dt);

    FireIfNecessary();

    // Control the properties of my various engine
    // subsystem components, but do NOT update
    // them here...
    if (justExploded)
    {
        m_pAnimationComponent->PlayAnimation("explode");
    }
}
```

```
            if (isVisible)
            {
                m_pCollisionComponent->Activate();
                m_pRenderingComponent->Show();
            }
            else
            {
                m_pCollisionComponent->Deactivate();

                m_pRenderingComponent->Hide();
            }
            // etc.
    }
```

The game loop then ends up looking more like this:

```
    while (true)
    {
        PollJoypad();

        float dt = g_gameClock.CalculateDeltaTime();

        for (each gameObject)
        {
            gameObject.Update(dt);
        }

        g_animationEngine.Update(dt);

        g_physicsEngine.Simulate(dt);

        g_collisionEngine.DetectAndResolveCollisions(dt);

        g_audioEngine.Update(dt);

        g_renderingEngine.RenderFrameAndSwapBuffers();
    }
```

Batched updating provides many performance benefits, including but not limited to:

- *Maximal cache coherency.* Batched updating allows an engine subsystem to achieve maximum cache coherency because its per-object data is maintained internally and can be arranged in a single, contiguous region of RAM.

- *Minimal duplication of computations.* Global calculations can be done once and reused for many game objects rather than being redone for each object.

- *Reduced reallocation of resources.* Engine subsystems often need to allocate and manage memory and/or other resources during their updates. If the update of a particular subsystem is interleaved with those of other engine subsystems, these resources must be freed and reallocated for each game object that is processed. But if the updates are batched, the resources can be allocated once per frame and reused for all objects in the batch.

- *Efficient pipelining.* Many engine subsystems perform a virtually identical set of calculations on each and every object in the game world. When updates are batched, new optimizations become possible, and specialized hardware resources can be leveraged. For example, the PLAYSTATION 3 provides a battery of high-speed microprocessors known as SPUs, each of which has its own private high-speed memory area. When processing a batch of animations, the pose of one character can be calculated while we simultaneously DMA the data for the next character into SPU memory. This kind of parallelism cannot be achieved when processing each object in isolation.

Performance benefits aren't the only reason to favor a batch updating approach. Some engine subsystems simply don't work at all when updated on a per-object basis. For example, if we are trying to resolve collisions within a system of multiple dynamic rigid bodies, a satisfactory solution cannot be found in general by considering each object in isolation. The interpenetrations between these objects must be resolved as a group, either via an iterative approach or by solving a linear system.

## 14.6.3. Object and Subsystem Interdependencies

Even if we didn't care about performance, a simplistic per-object updating approach breaks down when game objects *depend* on one another. For example, a human character might be holding a cat in her arms. In order to calculate the world-space pose of the cat's skeleton, we first need to calculate the world-space pose of the human. This implies that the *order* in which objects are updated is important to the proper functioning of the game.

Another related problem arises when engine *subsystems* depend on one another. For example, a rag doll physics simulation must be updated in concert with the animation engine. Typically, the animation system produces an intermediate, local-space skeletal pose. These joint transforms are converted to world space and applied to a system of connected rigid bodies that approximate the skeleton within the physics system. The rigid bodies are simulated forward in time by the physics system, and then the final resting places of the joints are applied back to their corresponding joints in the skeleton. Finally, the animation system calculates the final world-space pose and skinning matrix palette. So once again, the updating of the animation and physics systems must occur in a particular order in order to produce correct results. These kinds of inter-subsystem dependencies are commonplace in game engine design.

### 14.6.3.1. Phased Updates

To account for inter-subsystem dependencies, we can explicitly code our engine subsystem updates in the proper order within the main game loop. For example, to handle the interplay between the animation system and rag doll physics, we might write something like this:

```
while (true) // main game loop
{
    // ...

    g_animationEngine.CalculateIntermediatePoses(dt);

    g_ragdollSystem.ApplySkeletonsToRagDolls();

    g_physicsEngine.Simulate(dt); // runs ragdolls too

    g_collisionEngine.DetectAndResolveCollisions(dt);

    g_ragdollSystem.ApplyRagDollsToSkeletons();

    g_animationEngine.FinalizePoseAndMatrixPalette();

    // ...
}
```

We must be careful to update the states of our game objects at the right time during the game loop. This is often not as simple as calling a single Update() function per game object per frame. Game objects may depend upon the intermediate results of calculations performed by various engine subsystems. For example, a game object might request that animations be played prior to the animation system running its update. However, that same object may also want to procedurally adjust the intermediate pose generated by the animation system prior to that pose being used by the rag doll physics system and/or the final pose and matrix palette being generated. This implies that the object must be updated twice, once before the animation calculates its intermediate poses and once afterward.

Many game engines allow game objects to update at multiple points during the frame. For example, an engine might update game objects three times—once before animation blending, once after animation blending but prior to final pose generation, and once after final pose generation. This can be accomplished by providing each game object class with three virtual functions that act as "hooks." In such a system, the game loop ends up looking something like this:

```
while (true) // main game loop
{
    // ...

    for (each gameObject)
    {
        gameObject.PreAnimUpdate(dt);
    }

    g_animationEngine.CalculateIntermediatePoses(dt);


    for (each gameObject)
    {
        gameObject.PostAnimUpdate(dt);
    }

    g_ragdollSystem.ApplySkeletonsToRagDolls();

    g_physicsEngine.Simulate(dt); // runs ragdolls too

    g_collisionEngine.DetectAndResolveCollisions(dt);

    g_ragdollSystem.ApplyRagDollsToSkeletons();

    g_animationEngine.FinalizePoseAndMatrixPalette();

    for (each gameObject)
    {
        gameObject.FinalUpdate(dt);
    }

    // ...
}
```

We can provide our game objects with as many update phases as we see fit. But we must be careful, because iterating over all game objects and calling a virtual function on each one can be expensive. Also, not all game objects require all update phases—iterating over objects that don't require a particular phase is a pure waste of CPU bandwidth. One way to minimize the cost of iteration is to maintain multiple linked lists of game objects—one for each update phase. If a particular object wants to be included in one of the update phases, it adds itself to the corresponding linked list. This avoids having to iterate over objects that are not interested in a particular update phase.

### 14.6.3.2. Bucketed Updates

In the presence of *inter-object* dependencies, the phased updates technique described above must be adjusted a little. This is because inter-object dependencies can lead to conflicting rules governing the order of updating. For example, let's imagine that object B is being held by object A. Further, let's assume that we can only update object B after A has been *fully* updated, including the calculation of its final world-space pose and matrix palette. This conflicts with the need to batch animation updates of all game objects together in order to allow the animation system to achieve maximum throughput.

Inter-object dependencies can be visualized as a forest of dependency trees. The game objects with no parents (no dependencies on any other object) represent the roots of the forest. An object that depends directly on one of these root objects resides in the first tier of children in one of the trees in the forest. An object that depends on a first-tier child becomes a second-tier child, and so on. This is illustrated in Figure 14.14.

One solution to the problem of conflicting update order requirements is to collect objects into independent groups, which we'll call *buckets* here for lack of a better name. The first bucket consists of all root objects in the forest. The second bucket is comprised of all first-tier children. The third bucket contains all second-tier children, and so on. For each bucket, we run a complete update of the game objects and the engine systems, complete with all update

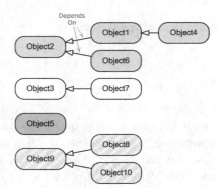

**Figure 14.14.** Inter-object update order dependencies can be viewed as a forest of dependency trees.

phases. Then we repeat the entire process for each bucket until there are no more buckets.

In theory, the depths of the trees in our dependency forest are unbounded. However, in practice, they are usually quite shallow. For example, we might have characters holding weapons, and those characters might or might not be riding on a moving platform or a vehicle. To implement this, we only need three tiers in our dependency forest, and hence only three buckets: one for platforms/vehicles, one for characters, and one for the weapons in the characters' hands. Many game engines explicitly limit the depth of their dependency forest so that they can use a fixed number of buckets (presuming they use a bucketed approach at all—there are of course many other ways to architect a game loop).

Here's what a bucketed, phased, batched update loop might look like:

```
void UpdateBucket(Bucket bucket)
{
    // ...

    for (each gameObject in bucket)
    {
        gameObject.PreAnimUpdate(dt);
    }

    g_animationEngine.CalculateIntermediatePoses
        (bucket, dt);

    for (each gameObject in bucket)
    {
        gameObject.PostAnimUpdate(dt);
    }

    g_ragdollSystem.ApplySkeletonsToRagDolls(bucket);

    g_physicsEngine.Simulate(bucket, dt); // runs
                                          // ragdolls too

    g_collisionEngine.DetectAndResolveCollisions
        (bucket, dt);

    g_ragdollSystem.ApplyRagDollsToSkeletons(bucket);

    g_animationEngine.FinalizePoseAndMatrixPalette
        (bucket);

    for (each gameObject in bucket)
    {
        gameObject.FinalUpdate(dt);
    }
```

```
        // ...
    }

    void RunGameLoop()
    {
        while (true)
        {
            // ...

            UpdateBucket(g_bucketVehiclesAndPlatforms);

            UpdateBucket(g_bucketCharacters);

            UpdateBucket(g_bucketAttachedObjects);

            // ...

            g_renderingEngine.RenderSceneAndSwapBuffers();
        }
    }
```

In practice, things might a bit more complex than this. For example, some engine subsystems like the physics engine might not support the concept of buckets, perhaps because they are third-party SDKs or because they cannot be practically updated in a bucketed manner. However, this bucketed update is essentially what we used at Naughty Dog to implement *Uncharted: Drake's Fortune* and are using again for our upcoming title, *Uncharted 2: Among Thieves*. So it's a method that has proven to be practical and reasonably efficient.

### 14.6.3.3. Object State Inconsistencies and One-Frame-Off Lag

Let's revisit game object updating, but this time thinking in terms of each object's local notion of time. We said in Section 14.6 that the state of game object $i$ at time $t$ can be denoted by a state vector $\mathbf{S}_i(t)$. When we update a game object, we are converting its previous state vector $\mathbf{S}_i(t_1)$ into a new current state vector $\mathbf{S}_i(t_2)$ (where $t_2 = t_1 + \Delta t$).

In theory, the states of all game objects are updated from time $t_1$ to time $t_2$ instantaneously and in parallel, as depicted in Figure 14.15. However, in practice, we can only update the objects one by one—we must loop over each game object and call some kind of update function on each one in turn. If we were to stop the program half-way through this update loop, half of our game objects' states would have been updated to $\mathbf{S}_i(t_2)$, while the remaining half would still be in their previous states, $\mathbf{S}_i(t_1)$. This implies that if we were to ask two of our game objects what the current time is during the update loop, they may or may not agree! What's more, depending on where exactly we interrupt the update loop, the objects may all be in a partially updated

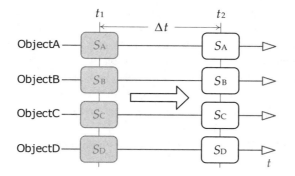

**Figure 14.15.** In theory, the states of all game objects are updated instantaneously and in parallel during each iteration of the game loop.

state. For example, animation pose blending may have been run, but physics and collision resolution may not yet have been applied. This leads us to the following rule:

> The states of all game objects are consistent *before* and *after* the update loop, but they may be inconsistent *during* it.

This is illustrated in Figure 14.16.

The inconsistency of game object states during the update loop is a major source of confusion and bugs, even among professionals within the game industry. The problem rears its head most often when game objects query one

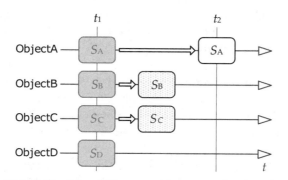

**Figure 14.16.** In practice, the states of the game objects are updated one by one. This means that at some arbitrary moment during the update loop, some objects will think the current time is $t_2$ while others think it is still $t_1$. Some objects may be only partially updated, so their states will be internally inconsistent. In effect, the state of such an object lies at a point *between $t_1$ and $t_2$.*

another for state information during the update loop (which implies that there is a dependency between them). For example, if object B looks at the velocity of object A in order to determine its own velocity at time $t$, then the programmer must be clear about whether he or she wants to read the *previous* state of object A, $S_A(t_1)$, or the *new* state, $S_A(t_2)$. If the new state is needed but object A has not yet been updated, then we have an update order problem that can lead to a class of bugs known as *one-frame-off lags*. In this type of bug, the state of one object lags one frame behind the states of its peers, which manifests itself on-screen as a lack of synchronization between game objects.

### 14.6.3.4. Object State Caching

As described above, one solution to this problem is to group the game objects into buckets (Section 14.6.3.2). One problem with a simple bucketed update approach is that it imposes somewhat arbitrary limitations on the way in which game objects are permitted to query one another for state information. If a game object A wants the *updated* state vector $S_B(t_2)$ of another object B, then object B must reside in a *previously updated* bucket. Likewise, if object A wants the *previous* state vector $S_B(t_1)$ of object B, then object B must reside in a *yet-to-be-updated* bucket. Object A should never ask for the state vector of an object within its own bucket, because as we stated in the rule above, those state vectors may be only partially updated.

One way to improve consistency is to arrange for each game object to *cache* its previous state vector $S_i(t_1)$ while it is calculating its new state vector $S_i(t_2)$ rather than *overwriting* it in-place during its update. This has two immediate benefits. First, it allows any object to safely query the previous state vector of any other object without regard to update order. Second, it guarantees that a totally consistent state vector ($S_i(t_1)$) will always be available, even during the update of the new state vector. To my knowledge there is no standard terminology for this technique, so I'll call it *state caching* for lack of a better name.

Another benefit of state caching is that we can linearly interpolate between the previous and next states in order to approximate the state of an object at any moment between these two points in time. The Havok physics engine maintains the previous and current state of every rigid body in the simulation for just this purpose.

The downside of state caching is that it consumes twice the memory of the update-in-place approach. It also only solves half the problem, because while the previous states at time $t_1$ are fully consistent, the new states at time $t_2$ still suffer from potential inconsistency. Nonetheless, the technique can be useful when applied judiciously.

### 14.6.3.5. Time-Stamping

One easy and low-cost way to improve the consistency of game object states is to time-stamp them. It is then a trivial matter to determine whether a game object's state vector corresponds to its configuration at a previous time or the current time. Any code that queries the state of another game object during the update loop can assert or explicitly check the time stamp to ensure that the proper state information is being obtained.

Time-stamping does not address the inconsistency of states during the update of a bucket. However, we can set a global or static variable to reflect which bucket is currently being updated. Presumably every game object "knows" in which bucket it resides. So we can check the bucket of a queried game object against the currently updating bucket and assert that they are not equal in order to guard against inconsistent state queries.

## 14.6.4. Designing for Parallelism

In Section 7.6, we introduced a number of approaches that allow a game engine to take advantage of the parallel processing resources that have become the norm in recent gaming hardware. How, then, does parallelism affect the way in which game object states are updated?

### 14.6.4.1. Parallelizing the Game Object Model Itself

Game object models are notoriously difficult to parallelize, for a few reasons. Game objects tend to be highly interdependent upon one another and upon the data used and/or generated by numerous engine subsystems. Game objects communicate with one another, sometimes multiple times during the update loop, and the pattern of communication can be unpredictable and highly sensitive to the inputs of the player and the events that are occurring in the game world. This makes it difficult to process game object updates in multiple threads, for example, because the amount of thread synchronization that would be required to support inter-object communication is usually prohibitive from a performance standpoint. And the practice of peeking directly into a foreign game object's state vector makes it impossible to DMA a game object to the isolated memory of a coprocessor, such as the PLAYSTATION 3's SPU, for updating.

That said, game object updating *can* theoretically be done in parallel. To make it practical, we'd need to carefully design the entire object model to ensure that game objects never peek directly into the state vectors of other game objects. All inter-object communication would have to be done via message-passing, and we'd need an efficient system for passing messages between game objects even when those objects reside in totally separate memory spaces or are being processed by different physical CPU cores. Some research has been done into using a distributed programming language, such as Ericsson's Erlang (http://www.erlang.org), to code game object models. Such languages provide built-in support for parallel processing and message passing and handle context switching between threads much more efficiently and quickly than in a language like C or C++, and their programming idioms help programmers to never "break the rules" that allow concurrent, distributed, multiple agent designs to function properly and efficiently.

### 14.6.4.2. Interfacing with Concurrent Engine Subsystems

Although sophisticated, concurrent, distributed object models are theoretically feasible and are an area of extremely interesting research, at present most game teams do not use them. Instead, most game teams leave the object model in a single thread and use an old-fashioned game loop to update them. They focus their attention instead on parallelizing many of the lower-level engine systems upon which the game objects depend. This gives teams the biggest "bang for their buck," because low-level engine subsystems tend to be more performance-critical than the game object model. This is because low-level subsystems must process huge volumes of data every frame, while the amount of CPU power used by the game object model is often somewhat smaller. This is an example of the 80-20 rule in action.

Of course, using a single-threaded game object model does not mean that game programmers can be totally oblivious to parallel programming issues. The object model must still interact with engine subsystems that are themselves running concurrently with the object model. This paradigm shift requires game programmers to avoid certain programming paradigms that may have served them well in the pre-parallel-processing era and adopt some new ones in their place.

Probably the most important shift a game programmer must make is to begin thinking *asynchronously*. As described in Section 7.6.5, this means that when a game object requires a time-consuming operation to be performed, it should avoid calling a *blocking function*—a function that does its work directly in the context of the calling thread, thereby blocking that thread until the work has been completed. Instead, whenever possible, large or expensive jobs should be requested by calling a *non-blocking function*—a function that sends the request to be executed by another thread, core, or processor and then immediately returns control to the calling function. The main game loop can proceed with other unrelated work, including updating other game objects, while the original object waits for the results of its request. Later in the same frame, or next frame, that game object can pick up the results of its request and make use of them.

Batching is another shift in thinking for game programmers. As we mentioned in Section 14.6.2, it is more efficient to collect similar tasks into batches and perform them en masse than it is to run each task independently. This applies to the process of updating game object states as well. For example, if a game object needs to cast 100 rays into the collision world for various purposes, it is best if those ray cast requests can be queued up and executed as one big batch. If an existing game engine is being retrofitted for parallelism, this often requires code to be rewritten so that it batches requests rather than doing them individually.

One particularly tricky aspect of converting synchronous, unbatched code to use an asynchronous, batched approach is determining *when* during the game loop (a) to kick off the request and (b) to wait for and utilize the results. In doing this, it is often helpful to ask ourselves the following questions:

- *How early can we kick off this request?* The earlier we make the request, the more likely it is to be done when we actually need the results—and this maximizes CPU utilization by helping to ensure that the main thread is never idle waiting for an asynchronous request to complete. So for any given request, we should determine the earliest point during the frame at which we have enough information to kick it off, and kick it there.

- *How long can we wait before we need the results of this request?* Perhaps we can wait until later in the update loop to do the second half of an operation. Perhaps we can tolerate a one-frame lag and use last frame's results to update the object's state this frame. (Some subsystems like AI can tolerate even longer lag times because they update only every few seconds.) In many circumstances, code that uses the results of a request can in fact be deferred until later in the frame, given a little thought, some code re-factoring, and possibly some additional caching of intermediate data.

## 14.7. Events and Message-Passing

Games are inherently event-driven. An *event* is anything of interest that happens during gameplay. An explosion going off, the player being sighted by an enemy, a health pack getting picked up—these are all events. Games generally need a way to (a) notify interested game objects when an event occurs and (b) arrange for those objects to respond to interesting events in various ways—we call this *handling* the event. Different types of game objects will respond in different ways to an event. The way in which a particular type of game object responds to an event is a crucial aspect of its behavior, just as important as how the object's state changes over time in the absence of any external inputs. For example, the behavior of the ball in *Pong* is governed in part by its velocity, in part by how it reacts to the event of striking a wall or paddle and bouncing off, and in part by what happens when the ball is missed by one of the players.

### 14.7.1. The Problem with Statically Typed Function Binding

One simple way to notify a game object that an event has occurred is to simply call a method (member function) on the object. For example, when an explosion goes off, we could query the game world for all objects within the explosion's damage radius and then call a virtual function named something like OnExplosion() on each one. This is illustrated by the following pseudo-code:

```
void Explosion::Update()
{
    // ...

    if (ExplosionJustWentOff())
    {
        GameObjectCollection damagedObjects;
        g_world.QueryObjectsInSphere(GetDamageSphere(),
                                     damagedObjects);

        for (each object in damagedObjects)
        {
            object.OnExplosion(*this);
        }
    }
    // ...
}
```

The call to OnExplosion() is an example of *statically typed late function binding*. Function binding is the process of determining which function implementation to invoke at a particular call location—the implementation is, in effect, bound to the call. Virtual functions, such as our OnExplosion() event-handling function, are said to be *late-bound*. This means that the compiler doesn't actually know *which* of the many possible implementations of the function is going to be invoked at compile time—only at runtime, when the type of the target object is known, will the appropriate implementation be invoked. We say that a virtual function call is *statically typed* because the compiler *does* know which implementation to invoke given a particular object type. It knows, for example, that `Tank::OnExplosion()` should be called when the target object is a `Tank` and that `Crate::OnExplosion()` should be called when the object is a `Crate`.

The problem with statically typed function binding is that it introduces a degree of inflexibility into our implementation. For one thing, the virtual `OnExplosion()` function requires all game objects to inherit from a common base class. Moreover, it requires that base class to *declare* the virtual function `OnExplosion()`, even if not all game objects can respond to explosions. In fact, using statically typed virtual functions as event handlers would require our base `GameObject` class to declare virtual functions for *all possible events* in the game! This would make adding new events to the system difficult. It precludes events from being created in a data-driven manner—for example, within the world editing tool. It also provides no mechanism for certain types of objects, or certain individual object instances, to register interest in certain events but not others. Every object in the game, in effect, "knows" about every possible event, even if its response to the event is to do nothing (i.e., to implement an empty, do-nothing event handler function).

What we really need for our event handlers, then, is *dynamically typed late function binding*. Some programming languages support this feature natively (e.g., C#'s delegates). In other languages, the engineers must implement it manually. There are many ways to approach this problem, but most boil down to taking a data-driven approach. In other words, we encapsulate the notion of a function call in an object and pass that object around at runtime in order to implement a dynamically typed late-bound function call.

## 14.7.2. Encapsulating an Event in an Object

An event is really comprised of two components: its *type* (explosion, friend injured, player spotted, health pack picked up, etc.) and its *arguments*. The arguments provide specifics about the event (How much damage did the explosion do? Which friend was injured? Where was the player spotted? How much health was in the health pack?). We can encapsulate these two components in an object, as shown by the following pseudocode:

```
struct Event
{
    const U32 MAX_ARGS = 8;

    EventType m_type;
    U32       m_numArgs;
    EventArg  m_aArgs[MAX_ARGS];
};
```

Some game engines call these things *messages* or *commands* instead of *events*. These names emphasize the idea that informing objects about an event is essentially equivalent to sending a message or command to those objects.

Practically speaking, event objects are usually not quite this simple. We might implement different types of events by deriving them from a root event class, for example. The arguments might be implemented as a linked list or a dynamically allocated array capable of containing arbitrary numbers of arguments, and the arguments might be of various data types.

Encapsulating an event (or message) in an object has many benefits:

- *Single event handler function.* Because the event object encodes its type internally, any number of different event types can be represented by an instance of a single class (or the root class of an inheritance hierarchy). This means that we only need *one* virtual function to handle *all* types of events (e.g., `virtual void OnEvent(Event& event);`).

- *Persistence.* Unlike a function call, whose arguments go out of scope after the function returns, an event object stores both its type and its arguments as data. An event object therefore has persistence. It can be stored in a queue for handling at a later time, copied and broadcast to multiple receivers, and so on.

- *Blind event forwarding.* An object can forward an event that it receives to another object without having to "know" anything about the event. For example, if a vehicle receives a Dismount event, it can forward it to all of its passengers, thereby allowing them to dismount the vehicle, even though the vehicle itself knows nothing about dismounting.

This idea of encapsulating an event/message/command in an object is commonplace in many fields of computer science. It is found not only in game engines but in other systems like graphical user interfaces, distributed communication systems, and many others. The well-known "Gang of Four" design patterns book [17] calls this the Command pattern.

## 14.7.3. Event Types

There are many ways to distinguish between different types of events. One simple approach in C or C++ is to define a global `enum` that maps each event type to a unique integer.

```
enum EventType
{
    EVENT_TYPE_LEVEL_STARTED,

    EVENT_TYPE_PLAYER_SPAWNED,
```

```
        EVENT_TYPE_ENEMY_SPOTTED,

        EVENT_TYPE_EXPLOSION,

        EVENT_TYPE_BULLET_HIT,
        // ...
    }
```

This approach enjoys the benefits of simplicity and efficiency (since integers are usually extremely fast to read, write, and compare). However, it also suffers from two problems. First, knowledge of *all* event types in the entire game is centralized, which can be seen as a form of broken encapsulation (for better or for worse—opinions on this vary). Second, the event types are hard-coded, which means new event types cannot easily be defined in a data-driven manner. Third, enumerators are just indices, so they are order-dependent. If someone accidentally adds a new event type in the middle of the list, the indices of all subsequent event ids change, which can cause problems if event ids are stored in data files. As such, an enumeration-based event typing system works well for small demos and prototypes but does not scale very well at all to real games.

Another way to encode event types is via strings. This approach is totally free-form, and it allows a new event type to be added to the system by merely thinking up a name for it. But it suffers from many problems, including a strong potential for event name conflicts, the possibility of events not working because of a simple typo, increased memory requirements for the strings themselves, and the relatively high cost of comparing strings next to that of comparing integers. Hashed string ids can be used instead of raw strings to eliminate the performance problems and increased memory requirements, but they do nothing to address event name conflicts or typos. Nonetheless, the extreme flexibility and data-driven nature of a string- or string-id-based event system is considered worth the risks by some game teams.

Tools can be implemented to help avoid some of the risks involved in using strings to identify events. For example, a central database of all event type names could be maintained. A user interface could be provided to permit new event types to be added to the database. Naming conflicts could be automatically detected when a new event is added, and the user could be disallowed from adding duplicate event types. When selecting a preexisting event, the tool could provide a sorted list in a drop-down combo box rather than requiring the user to remember the name and type it manually. The event database could also store meta-data about each type of event, including documentation about its purpose and proper usage and information about the number and types of arguments it supports. This approach can work really well, but we should not forget to account for the costs of setting up such a system, as they are not insignificant.

## 14.7.4. Event Arguments

The arguments of an event usually act like the argument list of a function, providing information about the event that might be useful to the receiver. Event arguments can be implemented in all sorts of ways.

We might derive a new type of Event class for each unique type of event. The arguments can then be hard-coded as data members of the class. For example:

```
class ExplosionEvent : public Event
{

    float       m_damage;
    Point       m_center;
    float       m_radius;
};
```

Another approach is to store the event's arguments as a collection of *variants*. A variant is a data object that is capable of holding more than one type of data. It usually stores information about the data type that is currently being stored, as well as the data itself. In an event system, we might want our arguments to be integers, floating-point values, Booleans, or hashed string ids. So in C or C++, we could define a variant class that looks something like this:

```
struct Variant
{
    enum Type
    {
        TYPE_INTEGER,
        TYPE_FLOAT,
        TYPE_BOOL,
        TYPE_STRING_ID,
        TYPE_COUNT // number of unique types
    };

    Type        m_type;

    union
    {
        I32     m_asInteger;
        F32     m_asFloat;
        bool    m_asBool;
        U32     m_asStringId;
    };
};
```

The collection of variants might be implemented as an array with a small, fixed maximum size (say 4, 8, or 16 elements). This imposes an arbitrary limit on the number of arguments that can be passed with an event, but it also side-steps the problems of dynamically allocating memory for each event's argument payload, which can be a big benefit, especially in memory-constrained console games.

The collection of variants might be implemented as a dynamically sized data structure, like a dynamically sized array (like `std::vector`) or a linked list (like `std::list`). This provides a great deal of additional flexibility over a fixed-size design, but it incurs the cost of dynamic memory allocation. A pool allocator could be used to great effect here, presuming that each `Variant` is the same size.

### 14.7.4.1. Event Arguments as Key-Value Pairs

A fundamental problem with an *indexed* collection of event arguments is order dependency. Both the sender and the receiver of an event must "know" that the arguments are listed in a specific order. This can lead to confusion and bugs. For example, a required argument might be accidentally omitted or an extra one added.

This problem can be avoided by implementing event arguments as key-value pairs. Each argument is uniquely identified by its key, so the arguments can appear in any order, and optional arguments can be omitted altogether. The argument collection might be implemented as a closed or open hash table, with the keys used to hash into the table, or it might be an array, linked list, or binary search tree of key-value pairs. These ideas are illustrated in Table 14.1. The possibilities are numerous, and the specific choice of implementation is largely unimportant as long as the game's particular requirements have been effectively and efficiently met.

| Key | Value | |
|---|---|---|
| | Type | |
| "event" | stringid | "explosion" |
| "radius" | float | 10.3 |
| "damage" | int | 25 |
| "grenade" | bool | true |

Table 14.1. The arguments of an event object can be implemented as a collection of key-value pairs. The keys help to avoid order-dependency problems because each event argument is uniquely identified by its key.

## 14.7.5. Event Handlers

When an event, message, or command is received by a game object, it needs to respond to the event in some way. This is known as *handling* the event, and it is usually implemented by a function or a snippet of script code called an *event handler*. (We'll have more to say about game scripting later on.)

Often an event handler is a single native virtual function or script function that is capable of handling all types of events (e.g., OnEvent(Event& event)). In this case, the function usually contains some kind of switch statement or cascaded if/else-if clause to handle the various types of events that might be received. A typical event handler function might look something like this:

```
virtual void SomeObject::OnEvent(Event& event)
{
    switch (event.GetType())
    {
    case EVENT_ATTACK:
        RespondToAttack(event.GetAttackInfo());
        break;

    case EVENT_HEALTH_PACK:
        AddHealth(event.GetHealthPack().GetHealth());
        break;

    // ...
    default:
        // Unrecognized event.
        break;
    }
}
```

Alternatively, we might implement a suite of handler functions, one for each type of event (e.g., OnThis(), OnThat(), ...). However, as we discussed above, a proliferation of event handler functions can be problematic.

A Windows GUI toolkit called Microsoft Foundation Classes (MFC) was well-known for its *message maps*—a system that permitted any Windows message to be bound at runtime to an arbitrary non-virtual or virtual function. This avoided the need to declare handlers for all possible Windows messages in a single root class, while at the same time avoiding the big switch statement that is commonplace in non-MFC Windows message-handling functions. But such a system is probably not worth the hassle—a switch statement works really well and is simple and clear.

## 14.7.6. Unpacking an Event's Arguments

The example above glosses over one important detail—namely, how to extract data from the event's argument list in a type-safe manner. For example, `event.GetHealthPack()` presumably returns a `HealthPack` game object, which in turn we presume provides a member function called `GetHealth()`. This implies that the root `Event` class "knows" about health packs (as well as, by extension, every other type of event argument in the game!) This is probably an impractical design. In a real engine, there might be derived `Event` classes that provide convenient data-access APIs such as `GetHealthPack()`. Or the event handler might have to unpack the data manually and cast them to the appropriate types. This latter approach raises type safety concerns, although practically speaking it usually isn't a huge problem because the type of the event is always known when the arguments are unpacked.

### 14.7.7. Chains of Responsibility

Game objects are almost always dependent upon one another in various ways. For example, game objects usually reside in a transformation hierarchy, which allows an object to rest on another object or be held in the hand of a character. Game objects might also be made up of multiple interacting components, leading to a star topology or a loosely connected "cloud" of component objects. A sports game might maintain a list of all the characters on each team. In general, we can envision the interrelationships between game objects as one or more *relationship graphs* (remembering that a list and a tree are just special cases of a graph). A few examples of relationship graphs are shown in Figure 14.17.

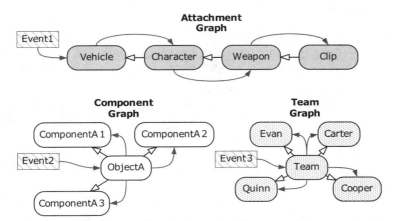

**Figure 14.17.** Game objects are interrelated in various ways, and we can draw graphs depicting these relationships. Any such graph might serve as a distribution channel for events.

It often makes sense to be able to pass events from one object to the next within these relationship graphs. For example, when a vehicle receives an event, it may be convenient to pass the event to all of the passengers riding on the vehicle, and those passengers may wish to forward the event to the objects in their inventories. When a multicomponent game object receives an event, it may be necessary to pass the event to all of the components so that they all get a crack at handling it. Or when an event is received by a character in a sports game, we might want to pass it on to all of his or her teammates as well.

The technique of forwarding events within a graph of objects is a common design pattern in object-oriented, event-driven programming, sometimes referred to as a *chain of responsibility* [17]. Usually, the order in which the event is passed around the system is predetermined by the engineers. The event is passed to the first object in the chain, and the event handler returns a Boolean or an enumerated code indicating whether or not it recognized and handled the event. If the event is consumed by a receiver, the process of event forwarding stops; otherwise, the event is forwarded on to the next receiver in the chain. An event handler that supports chain-of-responsibility style event forwarding might look something like this:

```
virtual bool SomeObject::OnEvent(Event& event)
{
    // Call the base class' handler first.
    if (BaseClass::OnEvent(event))
    {
        return true;
    }

    // Now try to handle the event myself.
    switch (event.GetType())
    {
    case EVENT_ATTACK:
        RespondToAttack(event.GetAttackInfo());
        return false; // OK to forward this event to others.

    case EVENT_HEALTH_PACK:
        AddHealth(event.GetHealthPack().GetHealth());
        return true; // I consumed the event; don't forward.

    // ...
    default:
        return false; // I didn't recognize this event.
    }
}
```

When a derived class overrides an event handler, it can be appropriate to call the base class's implementation as well if the class is augmenting but not replacing the base class's response. In other situations, the derived class might be entirely replacing the response of the base class, in which case the base class's handler should not be called. This is another kind of responsibility chain.

Event forwarding has other applications as well. For example, we might want to multicast an event to all objects within a radius of influence (for an explosion, for example). To implement this, we can leverage our game world's object query mechanism to find all objects within the relevant sphere and then forward the event to all of the returned objects.

## 14.7.8. Registering Interest in Events

It's reasonably safe to say that most objects in a game do not need to respond to every possible event. Most types of game objects have a relatively small set of events in which they are "interested." This can lead to inefficiencies when multicasting or broadcasting events, because we need to iterate over a group of objects and call each one's event handler, even if the object is not interested in that particular kind of event.

One way to overcome this inefficiency is to permit game objects to *register interest* in particular kinds of events. For example, we could maintain one linked list of interested game objects for each distinct type of event, or each game object could maintain a bit array, in which the setting of each bit corresponds to whether or not the object is interested in a particular type of event. By doing this, we can avoid calling the event handlers of any objects that do not care about the event. Calling virtual functions can incur a non-trivial performance hit, especially on consoles with relatively primitive RAM caches, so filtering objects by interest in an event can greatly improve the efficiency of event multicasting and broadcasting.

Even better, we might be able to restrict our original game object query to include only those objects that are interested in the event we wish to multicast. For example, when an explosion goes off, we can ask the collision system for all objects that are within the damage radius *and* that can respond to Explosion events. This can save time overall, because we avoid iterating over objects that we know aren't interested in the event we're multicasting. Whether or not such an approach will produce a net gain depends on how the query mechanism is implemented and the relative costs of filtering the objects during the query versus filtering them during the multicast iteration.

## 14.7.9. To Queue or Not to Queue

Most game engines provide a mechanism for handling events immediately when they are sent. In addition to this, some engines also permit events to be queued for handling at an arbitrary future time. Event queuing has some attractive benefits, but it also increases the complexity of the event system and poses some unique problems. We'll investigate the pros and cons of event queuing in the following sections and learn how such systems are implemented in the process.

### 14.7.9.1. Some Benefits of Event Queuing

*Control Over When Events are Handled*

We have seen that we must be careful to update engine subsystems and game objects in a specific order to ensure correct behavior and maximize runtime performance. In the same sense, certain kinds of events may be highly sensitive to exactly when within the game loop they are handled. If all events are handled immediately upon being sent, the event handler functions end up being called in unpredictable and difficult-to-control ways throughout the course of the game loop. By deferring events via an event queue, the engineers can take steps to ensure that events are only handled when it is safe and appropriate to do so.

*Ability to Post Events into the Future*

When an event is sent, the sender can usually specify a delivery time—for example, we might want the event to be handled later in the same frame, next frame, or some number of seconds after it was sent. This feature amounts to an ability to post events into the future, and it has all sorts of interesting uses. We can implement a simple alarm clock by posting an event into the future. A periodic task, such as blinking a light every two seconds, can be executed by posting an event whose handler performs the periodic task and then posts a new event of the same type one period into the future.

To implement the ability to post events into the future, each event is stamped with a desired delivery time prior to being queued. An event is only handled when the current game clock matches or exceeds its delivery time. An easy way to make this work is to sort the events in the queue in order of increasing delivery time. Each frame, the first event on the queue can be inspected and its delivery time checked. If the delivery time is in the future, we abort immediately because we know that all subsequent events are also in the future. But if we see an event whose delivery time is now or in the past, we extract it from the queue and handle it. This continues until an event is found whose delivery time is in the future. The following pseudocode illustrates this process:

```
// This function is called at least once per frame. Its
// job is to dispatch all events whose delivery time is
// now or in the past.
void EventQueue::DispatchEvents(F32 currentTime)
{
```

```
    // Look at, but don't remove, the next event on the
    // queue.
    Event* pEvent = PeekNextEvent();

    while (pEvent && pEvent->GetDeliveryTime() <=
        currentTime)
    {
        // OK, now remove the event from the queue.
        RemoveNextEvent();

        // Dispatch it to its receiver's event handler.

        pEvent->Dispatch();

        // Peek at the next event on the queue (again
        // without removing it).

        pEvent = PeekNextEvent();
    }
}
```

*Event Prioritization*

Even if our events are sorted by delivery time in the event queue, the order of delivery is still ambiguous when two or more events have exactly the same delivery time. This can happen more often than you might think, because it is quite common for events' delivery times to be quantized to an integral number of frames. For example, if two senders request that events be dispatched "this frame," "next frame," or "in seven frames from now," then those events will have identical delivery times.

One way to resolve these ambiguities is to assign *priorities* to events. Whenever two events have the same timestamp, the one with higher priority should always be serviced first. This is easily accomplished by first sorting the event queue by increasing delivery times and then sorting each group of events with identical delivery times in order of decreasing priority.

We could allow up to four billion unique priority levels by encoding our priorities in a raw, unsigned 32-bit integer, or we could limit ourselves to only two or three unique priority levels (e.g., low, medium, and high). In every game engine, there exists some minimum number of priority levels that will resolve all real ambiguities in the system. It's usually best to aim as close to this minimum as possible. With a very large number of priority levels, it can become a small nightmare to figure out which event will be handled first in any given situation. However, the needs of every game's event system are different, and your mileage may vary.

### 14.7.9.2. Some Problems with Event Queuing

*Increased Event System Complexity*

In order to implement a queued event system, we need more code, additional data structures, and more-complex algorithms than would be necessary to implement an immediate event system. Increased complexity usually translates into longer development times and a higher cost to maintain and evolve the system during development of the game.

*Deep-Copying Events and Their Arguments*

With an immediate event handling approach, the data in an event's arguments need only persist for the duration of the event handling function (and any functions it may call). This means that the event and its argument data can reside literally anywhere in memory, including on the call stack. For example, we could write a function that looks something like this:

```
void SendExplosionEventToObject(GameObject& receiver)
{
    // Allocate event args on the call stack.

    F32    damage = 5.0f;
    Point centerPoint(-2.0f, 31.5f, 10.0f);
    F32    radius = 2.0f;

    // Allocate the event on the call stack.
    Event event("Explosion");
    event.SetArgFloat("Damage", damage);

    event.SetArgPoint("Center", &centerPoint);

    event.SetArgFloat("Radius", radius);

    // Send the event, which causes the receiver's event
    // handler to be called immediately, as shown below.
    event.Send(receiver);
    //{
    //    receiver.OnEvent(event);
    //}
}
```

When an event is queued, its arguments must persist beyond the scope of the sending function. This implies that we must copy the entire event object prior to storing the event in the queue. We must perform a *deep-copy*, meaning that we copy not only the event object itself but its entire argument payload as well, including any data to which it may be pointing. Deep-copying the event ensures that there are no dangling references to data that exist only in the sending function's scope, and it permits the event to be stored indefinitely. The example event-sending function shown above still looks basically the same when using a queued event system, but as you can see in the italicized code below, the implementation of the Event::Queue() function is a bit more complex than its Send() counterpart:

```
void SendExplosionEventToObject(GameObject& receiver)
{
    // We can still allocate event args on the call
    // stack.

    F32    damage = 5.0f;
    Point centerPoint(-2.0f, 31.5f, 10.0f);
    F32    radius = 2.0f;

    // Still OK to allocate the event on the call stack.
    Event event("Explosion");
    event.SetArgFloat("Damage", damage);

    event.SetArgPoint("Center", &centerPoint);

    event.SetArgFloat("Radius", radius);

    // This stores the event in the receiver's queue for
    // handling at a future time. Note how the event
    // must be deep-copied prior to being enqueued, since
    // the original event resides on the call stack and
    // will go out of scope when this function returns.
    event.Queue(receiver);
    //{
    //     Event* pEventCopy = DeepCopy(event);
    //     receiver.EnqueueEvent(pEventCopy);
    //}
}
```

*Dynamic Memory Allocation for Queued Events*

Deep-copying of event objects implies a need for dynamic memory allocation, and as we've already noted many times, dynamic allocation is undesirable in a game engine due to its potential cost and its tendency to fragment memory. Nonetheless, if we want to queue events, we'll need to dynamically allocate memory for them.

   As with all dynamic allocation in a game engine, it's best if we can select a fast and fragmentation-free allocator. We might be able to use a *pool allocator*, but this will only work if all of our event objects are the same size and if their argument lists are comprised of data elements that are themselves all the same size. This may well be the case—for example, the arguments might each be a

Variant, as described above. If our event objects and/or their arguments can vary in size, a *small memory allocator* might be applicable. (Recall that a small memory allocator maintains multiple pools, one for each of a few predetermined small allocation sizes.) When designing a queued event system, always be careful to take dynamic allocation requirements into account.

*Debugging Difficulties*

With queued events, the event handler is not called directly by the sender of that event. So, unlike in immediate event handling, the call stack does not tell us where the event came from. We cannot walk up the call stack in the debugger to inspect the state of the sender or the circumstances under which the event was sent. This can make debugging deferred events a bit tricky, and things get even more difficult when events are forwarded from one object to another.

Some engines store debugging information that forms a paper trail of the event's travels throughout the system, but no matter how you slice it, event debugging is usually much easier in the absence of queuing.

Event queuing also leads to interesting and hard-to-track-down *race condition* bugs. We may need to pepper multiple event dispatches throughout our game loop, to ensure that events are delivered without incurring unwanted one-frame delays yet still ensuring that game objects are updated in the proper order during the frame. For example, during the animation update, we might detect that a particular animation has run to completion. This might cause an event to be sent whose handler wants to play a new animation. Clearly, we want to avoid a one-frame delay between the end of the first animation and the start of the next. To make this work, we need to update animation clocks first (so that the end of the animation can be detected and the event sent), then we should dispatch events (so that the event handler has a chance to request a new animation), and finally we can start animation blending (so that the first frame of the new animation can be processed and displayed). This is illustrated in the code snippet below:

```
while (true) // main game loop
{
    // ...

    // Update animation clocks. This may detect the end
    // of a clip, and cause EndOfAnimation events to
    // be sent.
    g_animationEngine.UpdateLocalClocks(dt);

    // Next, dispatch events. This allows an
    // EndOfAnimation event handler to start up a new
    // animation this frame if desired.
    g_eventSystem.DispatchEvents();
```

```
        // Finally, start blending all currently-playing
        // animations (including any new clips started
        // earlier this frame).
        g_animationEngine.StartAnimationBlending();

        // ...
}
```

## 14.7.10. Some Problems with Immediate Event Sending

Not queuing events also has its share of issues. For example, immediate event handling can lead to extremely deep call stacks. Object A might send object B an event, and in its event handler, B might send another event, which might send another event, and another, and so on. In a game engine that supports immediate event handling, it's not uncommon to see a call stack that looks something like this:

```
...
ShoulderAngel::OnEvent()
Event::Send()
Characer::OnEvent()
Event::Send()
Car::OnEvent()
Event::Send()
HandleSoundEffect()
AnimationEngine::PlayAnimation()
Event::Send()
Character::OnEvent()
Event::Send()
Character::OnEvent()
Event::Send()
Character::OnEvent()
Event::Send()
Car::OnEvent()
Event::Send()
Car::OnEvent()
Event::Send()
Car::Update()
GameWorld::UpdateObjectsInBucket()
Engine::GameLoop()
main()
```

A deep call stack like this can exhaust available stack space in extreme cases (especially if we have an infinite loop of event sending), but the real crux of the problem here is that every event handler function must be written to be fully *re-entrant*. This means that the event handler can be called recursively without any ill side-effects. As a contrived example, imagine a function that increments the value of a global variable. If the global is supposed to be incremented only once per frame, then this function is *not* re-entrant, because multiple recursive calls to the function will increment the variable multiple times.

## 14.7.11. Data-Driven Event/Message-Passing Systems

Event systems give the game programmer a great deal of flexibility over and above what can be accomplished with the statically typed function calling mechanisms provided by languages like C and C++. However, we can do better. In our discussions thus far, the logic for sending and receiving events is still hard-coded and therefore under the exclusive control of the engineers. If we could make our event system data-driven, we could extend its power into the hands of our game designers.

There are many ways to make an event system data-driven. Starting with the extreme of an entirely hard-coded (non-data-driven) event system, we could imagine providing some simple data-driven configurability. For example, designers might be allowed to configure how individual objects, or entire classes of object, respond to certain events. In the world editor, we can imagine selecting an object and then bringing up a scrolling list of all possible events that it might receive. For each one, the designer could use drop-down combo boxes and check boxes to control if, and how, the object responds, by selecting from a set of hard-coded, predefined choices. For example, given the event "PlayerSpotted," AI characters might be configured to do one of the following actions: run away, attack, or ignore the event altogether. The event systems of some real commercial game engines are implemented in essentially this way.

At the other end of the gamut, our engine might provide the game designers with a simple scripting language (a topic we'll explore in detail in Section 14.8). In this case, the designer can literally write code that defines how a particular kind of game object will respond to a particular kind of event. In a scripted model, the designers are really just programmers (working with a somewhat less powerful but also easier-to-use and hopefully less error-prone language than the engineers), so anything is possible. Designers might define new types of events, send events, and receive and handle events in arbitrary ways.

The problem with a simple, configurable event system is that it can severely limit what the game designers are capable of doing on their own, without the help of a programmer. On the other hand, a fully scripted solution has its own share of problems: Many game designers are not professional software engineers by training, so some designers find learning and using a scripting language a daunting task. Designers are also probably more prone to introducing bugs into the game than their engineer counterparts, unless they have practiced scripting or programming for some time. This can lead to some nasty surprises during alpha.

As a result, some game engines aim for a middle ground. They employ sophisticated graphical user interfaces to provide a great deal of flexibility without going so far as to provide users with a full-fledged, free-form scripting language. One approach is to provide a flow-chart-style graphical programming language. The idea behind such a system is to provide the user with a limited and controlled set of atomic operations from which to choose but with plenty of freedom to wire them up in arbitrary ways. For example, in response to an event like "PlayerSpotted," the designer could wire up a flow chart that causes a character to retreat to the nearest cover point, play an animation, wait 5 seconds, and then attack. A GUI can also provide error-checking and validation to help ensure that bugs aren't inadvertently introduced.

### 14.7.11.1. Data Pathway Communication Systems

One of the problems with converting a function-call-like event system into a data-driven system is that different types of events tend to be incompatible. For example, let's imagine a game in which the player has an electromagnetic pulse gun. This pulse causes lights and electronic devices to turn off, scares small animals, and produces a shock wave that causes any nearby plants to sway. Each of these game object types may already have an event response that performs the desired behavior. A small animal might respond to the "Scare" event by scurrying away. An electronic device might respond to the "TurnOff" event by turning itself off. And plants might have an event handler for a "Wind" event that causes them to sway. The problem is that our EMP gun is not compatible with any of these objects' event handlers. As a result, we end up having to implement a new event type, perhaps called "EMP," and then write custom event handlers for every type of game object in order to respond to it.

One solution to this problem is to take the event type out of the equation and to think solely in terms of *sending streams of data* from one game object to another. In such a system, every game object has one or more *input ports*, to which a data stream can be connected, and one or more output ports, through which data can be sent to other objects. Provided we have some way of wiring these ports together, such as a graphical user interface in which ports can be connected to each other via rubber-band lines, then we can construct arbitrarily complex behaviors. Continuing our example, the EMP gun would have an output port, perhaps named "Fire," that sends a Boolean signal. Most of the time, the port produces the value 0 (false), but when the gun is fired, it sends a brief (one-frame) pulse of the value 1 (true). The other game objects in

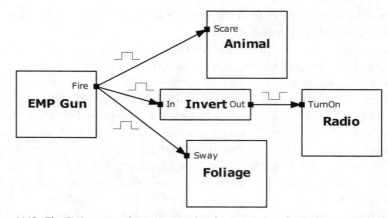

**Figure 14.18.** The EMP gun produces a 1 at its "Fire" output when fired. This can be connected to any input port that expects a Boolean value, in order to trigger the behavior associated with that input.

the world have binary input ports that trigger various responses. The animals might have a "Scare" input, the electronic devices a "TurnOn" input, and the foliage objects a "Sway" input. If we connect the EMP gun's "Fire" output port to the input ports of these game objects, we can cause the gun to trigger the desired behaviors. (Note that we'd have to pipe the gun's "Fire" output through a node that *inverts* its input, prior to connecting it to the "TurnOn" input of the electronic devices. This is because we want them to turn off when the gun is firing.) The wiring diagram for this example is shown in Figure 14.18.

Programmers decide what kinds of port(s) each type of game object will have. Designers using the GUI can then wire these ports together in arbitrary ways in order to construct arbitrary behaviors in the game. The programmers also provide various other kinds of nodes for use within the graph, such as a node that inverts its input, a node that produces a sine wave, or a node that outputs the current game time in seconds.

Various types of data might be sent along a data pathway. Some ports might produce or expect Boolean data, while others might be coded to produce or expect data in the form of a unit float. Still others might operate on 3D vectors, colors, integers, and so on. It's important in such a system to ensure that connections are only made between ports with compatible data types, or we must provide some mechanism for automatically converting data types when two differently typed ports are connected together. For example, connecting a unit-float output to a Boolean input might automatically cause any value less

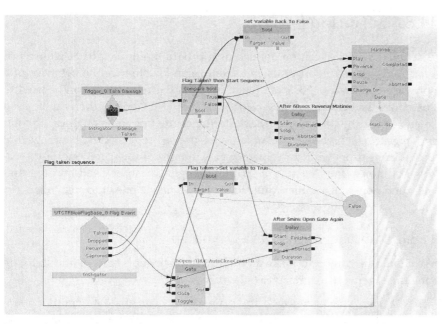

**Figure 14.19.** Unreal Engine 3's Kismet.

than 0.5 to be converted to false, and any value greater than or equal to 0.5 to be converted to true. This is the essence of GUI-based event systems like Unreal Engine 3's Kismet. A screen shot of Kismet is shown in Figure 14.19.

### 14.7.11.2. Some Pros and Cons of GUI-Based Programming

The benefits of a graphical user interface over a straightforward, text-file-based scripting language are probably pretty obvious: ease of use, a gradual learning curve with the potential for in-tool help and tool tips to guide the user, and plenty of error-checking. The downsides of a flow-chart style GUI include the high cost to develop, debug, and maintain such a system, the additional complexity, which can lead to annoying or sometimes schedule-killing bugs, and the fact that designers are sometimes limited in what they can do with the tool. A text-file based programming language has some distinct advantages over a GUI-based programming system, including its relative simplicity (meaning that it is much less prone to bugs), the ability to easily search and replace within the source code, and the freedom of each user to choose the text editor with which they are most comfortable.

# 14.8.  Scripting

A *scripting language* can be defined as a programming language whose primary purpose is to permit users to control and customize the behavior of a software application. For example, the Visual Basic language can be used to customize the behavior of Microsoft Excel; both MEL and Python can be used to customize the behavior of Maya. In the context of game engines, a *scripting language* is a high-level, relatively easy-to-use programming language that provides its users with convenient access to most of the commonly used features of the engine. As such, a scripting language can be used by programmers and non-programmers alike to develop a new game or to customize—or "mod"—an existing game.

## 14.8.1.  Runtime versus Data Definition

We should be careful to make an important distinction here. Game scripting languages generally come in two flavors:

- *Data-definition languages.* The primary purpose of a data-definition language is to permit users to create and populate data structures that are later consumed by the engine. Such languages are often declarative (see below) and are either executed or parsed off-line or at runtime when the data is loaded into memory.
- *Runtime scripting languages.* Runtime scripting languages are intended to be executed within the context of the engine at runtime. These languages are usually used to extend or customize the hard-coded functionality of the engine's game object model and/or other engine systems.

In this section, we'll focus primarily on using a runtime scripting language for the purpose of implementing gameplay features by extending and customizing the game's object model.

## 14.8.2.  Programming Language Characteristics

In our discussion of scripting languages, it will be helpful for us all to be on the same page with regard to programming language terminology. There are all sorts of programming languages out there, but they can be classified approximately according to a relatively small number of criteria. Let's take a brief look at these criteria:

- *Interpreted versus compiled languages.* The source code of a *compiled* language is translated by a program called a compiler into machine code, which can be executed directly by the CPU. In contrast, the source code of an *interpreted* language is either parsed directly at runtime or is pre-compiled into platform-independent *byte code,* which is then executed by a *virtual machine* at runtime. A virtual machine acts like an emulation of an imaginary CPU, and byte code acts like a list of machine language instructions that are consumed by this CPU. The benefit of a virtual machine is that it can be quite easily ported to almost any hardware platform and embedded within a host application like a game engine. The biggest cost we pay for this flexibility is execution speed—a virtual machine usually executes its byte code instructions much more slowly than the native CPU executes its machine language instructions.

- *Imperative langages.* In an imperative language, a program is described by a sequence of instructions, each of which performs an operation and/or changes the state of data in memory. C and C++ are imperative languages.

- *Declarative languages.* A declarative language describes *what* is to be done but does not specify exactly *how* the result should be obtained. That decision is left up to the people implementing the language. Prolog is an example of a declarative language. Mark-up languages like HTML and TeX can also be classified as declarative languages.

- *Functional languages.* Functional languages, which are technically a subset of declarative languages, aim to avoid state altogether. In a functional language, programs are defined by a collection of functions. Each function produces its results with no side-effects (i.e., it causes no observable changes to the system, other than to produce its output data). A program is constructed by passing input data from one function to the next until the final desired result has been generated. These languages tend to be well-suited to implementing data-processing pipelines. Ocaml, Haskell, and F# are examples of functional languages.

- *Procedural versus object-oriented languages.* In a procedural language, the primary atom of program construction is the *procedure* (or *function*). These procedures and functions perform operations, calculate results, and/or change the state of various data structures in memory. In constrast, an object-oriented language's primary unit of program construction is the *class*, a data structure that is tightly coupled with a set of procedures/functions that "know" how to manage and manipulate the data within that data structure.

- *Reflective languages.* In a reflective language, information about the data types, data member layouts, functions, and hierarchical class relationships in the system is available for inspection at runtime. In a non-reflective language, the majority of this meta-information is known only at compile time; only a very limited amount of it is exposed to the runtime code. C# is an example of a reflective language, while C and C++ are examples of non-reflective languages.

### 14.8.2.1. Typical Characteristics of Game Scripting Languages

The characteristics that set a game *scripting* language apart from its *native* programming language brethren include:

- *Interpreted.* Most game scripting languages are interpreted by a virtual machine, not compiled. This choice is made in the interest of flexibility, portability, and rapid iteration (see below). When code is represented as platform-independent byte code, it can easily be treated like data by the engine. It can be loaded into memory just like any other asset rather than requiring help from the operating system (as is necessary with a DLL on a PC platform or an IRX on the PLAYSTATION 3, for example). Because the code is executed by a virtual machine rather than directly by the CPU, the game engine is afforded a great deal of flexibility regarding how and when script code will be run.

- *Lightweight.* Most game scripting languages have been designed for use in an embedded system. As such, their virtual machines tend to be simple, and their memory footprints tend to be quite small.

- *Support for rapid iteration.* Whenever native code is changed, the program must be recompiled and relinked, and the game must be shut down and rerun in order to see the effects of the changes. On the other hand, when script code is changed, the effects of the changes can usually be seen very rapidly. Some game engines permit script code to be reloaded on the fly, without shutting down the game at all. Others require the game to be shut down and rerun. But either way, the turnaround time between making a change and seeing its effects in-game is usually much faster than when making changes to the native language source code.

- *Convenience and ease of use.* Scripting languages are often customized to suit the needs of a particular game. Features can be provided that make common tasks simple, intuitive, and less error-prone. For example, a game scripting language might provide functions for finding game objects by name, sending and handling events, pausing or manipulating the passage of time, waiting for a specified amount of time to pass, implementing finite state machines, exposing tweakable parameters to the world editor for use by the game designers, or even handling network replication for multiplayer games.

### 14.8.3. Some Common Game Scripting Languages

When implementing a runtime game scripting system, we have one fundamental choice to make: Do we select a third-party commercial or open-source language and customize it to suit our needs, or do we design and implement a custom language from scratch?

Creating a custom language from scratch is usually not worth the hassle and the cost of maintenance throughout the project. It can also be difficult or impossible to hire game designers and programmers who are already familiar with a custom, in-house language, so there's usually a training cost as well. However, this is clearly the most flexible and customizable approach, and that flexibility can be worth the investment.

For many studios, it is more convenient to select a reasonably well-known and mature scripting language and extend it with features specific to your game engine. There are a great many third-party scripting languages from which to choose, and many are mature and robust, having been used in a great many projects both within and outside the game industry.

In the following sections, we'll explore a number of custom game scripting languages and a number of game-agnostic languages that are commonly adapted for use in game engines.

#### 14.8.3.1. QuakeC

Id Software's John Carmack implemented a custom scripting language for *Quake*, known as *QuakeC* (QC). This language was essentially a simplified variant of the C programming language with direct hooks into the *Quake* engine. It had no support for pointers or defining arbitrary structs, but it could manipulate *entities* (*Quake*'s name for game objects) in a convenient manner, and it could be used to send and receive/handle game events. QuakeC is an interpreted, imperative, procedural programming language.

The power that QuakeC put into the hands of gamers is one of the factors that gave birth to what is now known as the *mod community*. Scripting languages and other forms of data-driven customization allow gamers to turn many commercial games into all sorts of new gaming experiences—from slight modifications on the original theme to entirely new games.

#### 14.8.3.2. UnrealScript

Probably the best-known example of an entirely custom scripting language is Unreal Engine's *UnrealScript*. This language is based on a C++-like syntactical style, and it supports most of the concepts that C and C++ programmers have become accustomed to, including classes, local variables, looping, arrays and structs for data organization, strings, hashed string ids (called `FName` in

Unreal), and object references (but not free-form pointers). In addition, UnrealScript provides a number of extremely powerful game-specific features, which we'll explore briefly below. UnrealScript is an interpreted, imperative, object-oriented language.

### Ability to Extend the Class Hierarchy

This is perhaps UnrealScript's biggest claim to fame. The Unreal object model is essentially a monolithic class hierarchy, with add-on components providing interfaces to various engine systems. The root classes in the hierarchy are known as *native classes*, because they are implemented in the native C++ language. But UnrealScript's real power comes from the fact that it can be used to derive *new classes* that are implemented entirely in script.

This may not sound like a big deal until you try to imagine how you would implement such a thing! In effect, UnrealScript redefines and extends C++'s *native object model*, which is really quite astounding. For native Unreal classes, the UnrealScript source files (normally named with the extension .uc) take the place of C++'s header files (.h files) as the primary definition of each class—the UnrealScript compiler actually *generates* the C++ .h files from the .uc files, and the programmer implements the classes in regular .cpp source files. Doing this allows the UnrealScript compiler to introduce additional features into every Unreal class, and these features permit new script-only classes to be defined by users that inherit from native classes or other script-only classes.

### Latent Functions

*Latent functions* are functions whose execution may span multiple frames of gameplay. A latent function can execute some instructions and then "go to sleep" waiting for an event or for a specified amount of time to pass. When the relevant event occurs or the time period elapses, the function is "woken up" by the engine, and it continues executing where it left off. This feature is highly useful for managing behaviors in the game that depend upon the passage of time.

### Convenient Linkage to UnrealEd

The data members of any UnrealScript-based class can be optionally marked with a simple annotation, indicating that that data member is to be made available for viewing and editing in Unreal's world editor, UnrealEd. No GUI programming is required. This makes data-driven game design extremely easy (as long as UnrealEd's built-in data member editing GUI suits your needs, of course).

### Network Replication for Multiplayer Games

Individual data elements in UnrealScript can be marked for replication. In Unreal networked games, each game object exists in its full form on one particular machine; all the other machines have a lightweight version of the object known as a *remote proxy*. When you mark a data member for replication, you are telling the engine that you want that data to be replicated from the master object to all of the remote proxies. This allows a programmer or designer to easily control which data should be made available across the network. This indirectly controls the amount of network bandwidth required by the game.

### 14.8.3.3. Lua

Lua is a well-known and popular scripting language that is easy to integrate into an application such as a game engine. The Lua website (http://www.lua.org/about.html) calls the language the "leading scripting language in games."

According to the Lua website, Lua's key benefits are:

- *Robust and mature.* Lua has been used on numerous commercial products, including Adobe's *Photoshop Lightroom*, and many games, including *World of Warcraft*.
- *Good documentation.* Lua's reference manual [21] is complete and understandable and is available in online and book formats. A number of books have been written about Lua, including [22] and [43].
- *Excellent runtime performance.* Lua executes its byte code more quickly and efficiently than many other scripting languages.
- *Portable.* Out of the box, Lua runs on all flavors of Windows and UNIX, mobile devices, and embedded microprocessors. Lua is written in a portable manner, making it easy to adapt to new hardware platforms.
- *Designed for embedded systems.* Lua's memory footprint is very small (approximately 350 kB for the interpreter and all libraries).
- *Simple, powerful, and extensible.* The core Lua language is very small and simple, but it is designed to support meta-mechanisms that extend its core functionality in virtually limitless ways. For example, Lua itself is not an object-oriented language, but OOP support can and has been added via a meta-mechanism.
- *Free.* Lua is open source and is distributed under the very liberal MIT license.

Lua is a dynamically typed language, meaning that variables don't have types—only values do. (Every value carries its type information along with it.) Lua's primary data structure is the *table*, also known as an associative array. A table is essentially a list of key-value pairs with an optimized ability to index into the array by key.

Lua provides a convenient interface to the C language—the Lua virtual machine can call and manipulate functions written in C as easily as it can those written in Lua itself.

Lua treats blocks of code, called *chunks*, as first-class objects that can be manipulated by the Lua program itself. Code can be executed in source code format or in precompiled byte code format. This allows the virtual machine to execute a string that contains Lua code, just as if the code were compiled into the original program. Lua also supports some powerful advanced programming constructs, including *coroutines*. This is a simple form of cooperative multitasking, in which each thread must yield the CPU to other threads explicitly (rather than being time-sliced as in a preemptive multithreading system).

Lua does have some pitfalls. For example, its flexible function binding mechanism makes it possible (and quite easy) to redefine an important global function like `sin()` to perform a totally different task (which is usually not something one intends to do). But all in all, Lua has proven itself to be an excellent choice for use as a game scripting language.

### 14.8.3.4. Python

Python is a procedural, object-oriented, dynamically typed scripting language, designed with ease of use, integration with other programming languages, and flexibility in mind. Like Lua, Python is a common choice for use as a game scripting language. According to the official Python website (http://www.python.org), some of Python's best features include:

- *Clear and readable syntax.* Python code is easy to read, in part because the syntax enforces a specific indentation style. (It actually parses the whitespace used for intentation in order to determine the scope of each line of code.)

- *Reflective language.* Python includes powerful runtime introspection facilities. Classes in Python are first-class objects, meaning they can be manipulated and queried at runtime, just like any other object.

- *Object-oriented.* One advantage of Python over Lua is that OOP is built into the core language. This makes integrating Python with a game's object model a little easier.

- *Modular.* Python supports hierarchical packages, encouraging clean system design and good encapsulation.

- *Exception-based error handling.* Exceptions make error-handling code in Python simpler, more elegant, and more localized than similar code in a non-exception based language.

- *Extensive standard libraries and third-party modules.* Python libraries exist for virtually every task imaginable. (Really!)

- *Embeddable.* Python can be easily embedded into an application, such as a game engine.

- *Extensive documentation.* There's plenty of documentation and tutorials on Python, both online and in book form. A good place to start is the Python website, http://www.python.org.

Python syntax is reminiscent of C in many respects (for example, its use of the = operator for assignment and == for equality testing). However, in Python, *code indentation* serves as the only means of defining *scope* (as opposed to C's opening and closing braces). Python's primary data structures are the *list*—a linearly indexed sequence of atomic values or other nested lists—and the *dictionary*—a table of key-value pairs. Each of these two data structures can hold instances of the other, allowing arbitrarily complex data structures to be constructed easily. In addition, *classes*—unified collections of data elements and functions—are built right into the language.

Python supports *duck typing*, which is a style of dynamic typing in which the functional interface of an object determines its type (rather than being defined by a static inheritance hierarchy). In other words, any class that supports a particular interface (i.e., a collection of functions with specific signatures) can be used interchangeably with any other class that supports that same interface. This is a powerful paradigm: In effect, Python supports polymorphism without requiring the use of inheritance. Duck typing is similar in some respects to C++ template meta-programming, although it is arguably more flexible because the bindings between caller and callee are formed dynamically, at runtime. Duck typing gets its name from the well-known phrase (attributed to James Whitcomb Riley), "If it walks like a duck and quacks like a duck, I would call it a duck." See http://en.wikipedia.org/wiki/Duck_typing for more information on duck typing.

In summary, Python is easy to use and learn, embeds easily into a game engine, integrates well with a game's object model, and can be an excellent and powerful choice as a game scripting language.

### 14.8.3.5. Pawn / Small / Small-C

*Pawn* is a lightweight, dynamically typed, C-like scripting language created by Marc Peter. The language was formerly known as *Small*, which itself was an evolution of an earlier subset of the C language called *Small-C*, written by Ron Cain and James Hendrix. It is an interpreted language—the source code is compiled into byte code (also known as P-code), which is interpreted by a virtual machine at runtime.

Pawn was designed to have a small memory footprint and to execute its byte code very quickly. Unlike C, Pawn's variables are dynamically typed. Pawn also supports finite state machines, including state-local variables. This unique feature makes it a good fit for many game applications. Good online documentation is available for Pawn (http://www.compuphase.com/pawn/pawn.htm). Pawn is open source and can be used free of charge under the Zlib/libpng license (http://www.opensource.org/licenses/zlib-license.php).

Pawn's C-like syntax makes it easy to learn for any C/C++ programmer and easy to integrate with a game engine written in C. Its finite state machine support can be very useful for game programming. It has been used successfully on a number of game projects, including *Freaky Flyers* by Midway. Pawn has shown itself to be a viable game scripting language.

## 14.8.4. Architectures for Scripting

Script code can play all sorts of roles within a game engine. There's a gamut of possible architectures, from tiny snippets of script code that perform simple functions on behalf of an object or engine system to high-level scripts that manage the operation of the game. Here are just a few of the possible architectures:

- *Scripted callbacks.* In this approach, the engine's functionality is largely hard-coded in the native programming language, but certain key bits of functionality are designed to be customizable. This is often implemented via a *hook function* or *callback*—a user-supplied function that is called by the engine for the purpose of allowing customization. Hook functions can be written in the native language, of course, but they can also be written in a scripting language. For example, when updating game objects during the game loop, the engine might call an optional callback function that can be written in script. This gives users the opportunity to customize the way in which the game object updates itself over time.

- *Scripted event handlers.* An event handler is really just a special type of hook function whose purpose is to allow a game object to respond to some relevant occurrence within the game world (e.g., responding to an explosion going off) or within the engine itself (e.g., responding to an out-of-memory condition). Many game engines allow users to write event handler hooks in script as well as in the native language.

- *Extending game object types, or defining new ones, with script.* Some scripting languages allow game object types that have been implemented in the native language to be extended via script. In fact, callbacks and event handlers are examples of this on a small scale, but the idea can be extended even to the point of allowing entirely new types of game objects to be defined in script. This might be done via *inheritance* (i.e., deriving a class written in script from a class written in the native language) or via *composition/aggregation* (i.e., attaching an instance of a scripted class to a native game object).

- *Scripted components or properties.* In a component- or property-based game object model, it only makes sense to permit new components or property objects to be constructed partially or entirely in script. This approach was used by Gas Powered Games for *Dungeon Siege* (http://www. drizzle.com/~scottb/gdc/game-objects.ppt). The game object model was property-based, and it was possible to implement properties in either C++ or Gas Powered Games' custom scripting language, *Skrit* (http:// ds.heavengames.com/library/dstk/skrit/skrit). By the end of the project, they had approximately 148 scripted property types and 21 native C++ property types.

- *Script-driven engine systems.* Script might be used to drive an entire engine system. For example, the game object model could conceivably be written entirely in script, calling into the native engine code only when it requires the services of lower-level engine components.

- *Script-driven game.* Some game engines actually flip the relationship between the native language and the scripting language on its head. In these engines, the script code runs the whole show, and the native engine code acts merely as a library that is called to access certain high-speed features of the engine. The Panda3D engine (http://www. panda3d.org) is an example of this kind of architecture. Panda3D games can be written entirely in the Python language, and the native engine (implemented in C++) acts like a library that is called by script code. (Panda3D games can also be written entirely in C++.)

## 14.8.5. Features of a Runtime Game Scripting Language

The primary purpose of many game scripting languages is to implement gameplay features, and this is often accomplished by augmenting and customizing a game's object model. In this section, we'll explore some of the most common requirements and features of such a scripting system.

### 14.8.5.1. Interface with the Native Programming Language

In order for a scripting language to be useful, it must not operate in a vacuum. It's imperative for the game engine to be able to execute script code, and it's usually equally important for script code to be capable of initiating operations within the engine as well.

A runtime scripting language's virtual machine is generally embedded within the game engine. The engine initializes the virtual machine, runs script code whenever required, and manages those scripts' execution. The unit of execution varies depending on the specifics of the language and the game's implementation.

- In a functional scripting language, the *function* is often the primary unit of execution. In order for the engine to call a script function, it must look up the byte code corresponding to the name of the desired function and spawn a virtual machine to execute it (or instruct an existing VM to do so).

- In an object-oriented scripting language, *classes* are typically the primary unit of execution. In such a system, objects can be spawned and destroyed, and methods (member functions) can be invoked on individual class instances.

It's usually beneficial to allow two-way communication between script and native code. Therefore, most scripting languages allowing native code to be invoked from script as well. The details are language- and implementation-specific, but the basic approach is usually to allow certain script functions to be implemented in the native language rather than in the scripting language. To call an engine function, script code simply makes an ordinary function call. The virtual machine detects that the function has a native implementation, looks up the corresponding native function's address (perhaps by name or via some other kind of unique function identifier), and calls it. For example, some or all of the member functions of a Python class or module can be implemented using C functions. Python maintains a data structure, known as a *method table*, that maps the name of each Python function (represented as a string) to the address of the C function that implements it.

### Case Study: Naughty Dog's DC Language

As an example, let's have a brief look at how Naughty Dog's runtime scripting language, a language called DC, was integrated into the engine.

DC is a variant of the Scheme language (which is itself a variant of Lisp). Chunks of executable code in DC are known as *script lambdas*, which are the approximate equivalent of functions or code blocks in the Lisp family of languages. A DC programmer writes script lambdas and identifies them by giving them globally unique names. The DC compiler converts these script lambdas into chunks of byte code, which are loaded into memory when the game runs and can be looked up by name using a simple functional interface in C++.

Once the engine has a pointer to a chunk of script lambda byte code, it can execute the code by calling a function in the engine and passing the pointer to the byte code to it. The function itself is surprisingly simple. It spins in a loop, reading byte code instructions one-by-one, and executing each instruction. When all instructions have been executed, the function returns.

The virtual machine contains a bank of registers, which can hold any kind of data the script may want to deal with. This is implemented using a *variant* data type—a union of all the data types (see 14.7.4 for a discussion of variants). Some instructions cause data to be loaded into a register; others cause the data held in a register to be looked up and used. There are instructions for performing all of the mathematical operations available in the language, as well as instructions for performing conditional checks—implementations of DC's (if ...), (when ...), and (cond ...) instructions and so on.

The virtual machine also supports a *function call stack*. Script lambdas in DC can call other script lambdas (i.e., functions) that have been defined by a script programmer via DC's (defun ...) syntax. Just like any procedural programming language, a stack is needed to keep track of the states of the registers and the return address when one function calls another. In the DC virtual machine, the call stack is literally a stack of register banks—each new function gets its own private bank of registers. This prevents us from having to save off the state of the registers, call the function, and then restore the registers when the called function returns. When the virtual machine encounters a byte code instruction that tells it to call another script lambda, the byte code for that script lambda is looked up by name, a new stack frame is pushed, and execution continues at the first instruction of that script lambda. When the virtual machine encounters a return instruction, the stack frame is popped from the stack, along with the return "address" (which is really just the index of the byte code instruction in the calling script lambda after the one that called the function in the first place).

The following pseudocode should give you a feel for what the core instruction-processing loop of the DC virtual machine looks like:

```
void DcExecuteScript(DCByteCode* pCode)
{

    DCStackFrame* pCurStackFrame =
        DcPushStackFrame(pCode);

    // Keep going until we run out of stack frames (i.e.,
    // the top-level script lambda "function" returns).
    while (pCurStackFrame != NULL)
    {
```

```
// Get the next instruction. We will never run
// out, because the return instruction is always
// last, and it will pop the current stack frame
// below.

DCInstruction& instr
    = pCurStackFrame->GetNextInstruction();

// Perform the operation of the instruction.
switch (instr.GetOperation())
{

case DC_LOAD_REGISTER_IMMEDIATE:
    {
        // Grab the immediate value to be loaded
        // from the instruction.
        Variant& data = instr.GetImmediateValue();

        // Also determine into which register to
        // put it.
        U32 iReg = instr.GetDestRegisterIndex();

        // Grab the register from the stack frame.
        Variant& reg
         = pCurStackFrame->GetRegister(iReg);

        // Store the immediate data into the
        // register.
        reg = data;
    }
    break;

// Other load and store register operations...

case DC_ADD_REGISTERS:
    {
        // Determine the two registers to add. The
        // result will be stored in register A.
        U32 iRegA = instr.GetDestRegisterIndex();
        U32 iRegB = instr.GetSrcRegisterIndex();

        // Grab the 2 register variants from the
        // stack.
        Variant& dataA
            = pCurStackFrame->GetRegister(iRegA);
        Variant& dataB
            = pCurStackFrame->GetRegister(iRegB);

        // Add the registers and store in
        // register A.
        dataA = dataA + dataB;
    }
    break;
```

```
        // Other math operations...

    case DC_CALL_SCRIPT_LAMBDA:
        {
            // Determine in which register the name of
            // the script lambda to call is stored.
            // (Presumably it was loaded by a previous
            // load instr.)
            U32 iReg = instr.GetSrcRegisterIndex();

            // Grab the appropriate register, which
            // contains the name of the lambda to call.
            Variant& lambda
                = pCurStackFrame->GetRegister(iReg);

            // Look up the byte code of the lambda by
            // name.
            DCByteCode* pCalledCode
                = DcLookUpByteCode(lambda.AsStringId());

            // Now "call" the lambda by pushing a new
            // stack frame.
            if (pCalledCode)
            {
                pCurStackFrame
                    = DcPushStackFrame(pCalledCode);
            }
        }
        break;

    case DC_RETURN:
        {
            // Just pop the stack frame. If we're in
            // the top lambda on the stack, this
            // function will return NULL, and the loop
            // will terminate.
            pCurStackFrame = DcPopStackFrame();
        }
        break;

    // Other instructions...

    // ...

    } // end switch
  } // end for
}
```

In the above example, we assume that the global functions DcPushStack
Frame() and DcPopStackFrame() manage the stack of register banks for us

in some suitable way and that the global function `DcLookUpByteCode()` is capable of looking up any script lambda by name. We won't show implementations of those functions here, because the purpose of this example is simply to show how the inner loop of a script virtual machine might work, not to provide a complete functional implementation.

DC script lambdas can also call native functions—i.e., global functions written in C++ that serve as hooks into the engine itself. When the virtual machine comes across an instruction that calls a native function, the address of the C++ function is looked up by name using a global table that has been hardcoded by the engine programmers. If a suitable C++ function is found, the arguments to the function are taken from registers in the current stack frame, and the function is called. This implies that the C++ function's arguments are always of type `Variant`. If the C++ function returns a value, it too must be a `Variant`, and its value will be stored into a register in the current stack frame for possible use by subsequent instructions.

The global function table might look something like this:

```
typedef Variant DcNativeFunction(U32 argCount,
    Variant* aArgs);

struct DcNativeFunctionEntry
{
    StringId            m_name;
    DcNativeFunction*   m_pFunc;
};

DcNativeFunctionEntry g_aNativeFunctionLookupTable[] = {
    { SID("get-object-pos"), DcGetObjectPos },

    { SID("animate-object"), DcAnimateObject },
    // etc.
    // ...
};
```

A native DC function implementation might look something like the following. Notice how the `Variant` arguments are passed to the function as an array. The function must verify that the number of arguments passed to it equals the number of arguments it expects. It must also verify that the types of the argument(s) are as expected and be prepared to handle errors that the DC script programmer may have made when calling the function.

```
Variant DcGetObjectPos(U32 argCount, Variant* aArgs)
{
    // Set up a default return value.
    Variant result;
    result.SetAsVector(Vector(0.0f, 0.0f, 0.0f));
```

```
    if (argCount != 1)
    {

        DcErrorMessage("get-object-pos:
            Invalid arg count.\n");
        return result;
    }

    if (aArgs[0].GetType() != Variant::TYPE_STRING_ID)
    {

        DcErrorMessage("get-object-pos: Expected
            string id.\n");
        return result;
    }

    StringId objectName = aArgs[0].AsStringId();

    GameObject* pObject = GameObject::LookUpByName
        (objectName);

    if (pObject == NULL)
    {

        DcErrorMessage(
            "get-object-pos: Object '%s' not found.\n",
            objectName.ToString());
        return result;
    }

    result.SetAsVector(pObject->GetPosition());
    return result;
}
```

### 14.8.5.2. Game Object Handles

Script functions often need to interact with game objects, which themselves may be implemented partially or entirely in the engine's native language. The native language's mechanisms for referencing objects (e.g., pointers or references in C++) won't necessarily be valid in the scripting language. (It may not support pointers at all, for example.) Therefore, we need to come up with some reliable way for script code to reference game objects.

There are a number of ways to accomplish this. One approach is to refer to objects in script via opaque numeric *handles*. The script code can obtain object handles in various ways. It might be passed a handle by the engine, or it might perform some kind of query, such as asking for the handles of all game objects within a radius of the player or looking up the handle that corresponds to a particular object name. The script can then perform operations on the game object by calling native functions and passing the object's handle as an argument. On the native language side, the handle is converted back into a pointer to the native object, and then the object can be manipulated as appropriate.

Numeric handles have the benefit of simplicity and should be easy to support in any scripting language that supports integer data. However, they can be unintuitive and difficult to work with. Another alternative is to use the names of the objects, represented as strings, as our handles. This has some interesting benefits over the numeric handle technique. For one thing, strings are human-readable and intuitive to work with. There is a direct correspondence to the names of the objects in the game's world editor. In addition, we can choose to reserve certain special object names and give them "magic" meanings. For example, in Naughty Dog's scripting language, the reserved name "self" always refers to the object to which the currently-running script is attached. This allows game designers to write a script, attach it to an object in the game, and then use the script to play an animation on the object by simply writing `(animate "self"` *name-of-animation*`)`.

Using strings as object handles has its pitfalls, of course. Strings often occupy more memory than integer ids. And because strings vary in length, dynamic memory allocation is required in order to copy them. String comparisons are slow. Script programmers are apt to make mistakes when typing the names of game objects, which can lead to bugs. In addition, script code can be broken if someone changes the name of an object in the game world editor but forgets to update the name of the object in script.

Hashed string ids overcome most of these problems by converting any strings (regardless of length) into an integer. In theory, hashed string ids enjoy the best of both worlds—they can be read by users just like strings, but they have the runtime performance characteristics of an integer. However, for this to work, your scripting language needs to support hashed string ids in some way. Ideally, we'd like the script compiler to convert our strings into hashed ids for us. That way, the runtime code doesn't have to deal with the strings at all, only the hashed ids (except possibly for debugging purposes—it's nice to be able to see the string corresponding to a hashed id in the debugger). However, this isn't always possible in all scripting languages. Another approach is to allow the user to use strings in script and convert them into hashed ids at runtime, whenever a native function is called.

### 14.8.5.3. Receiving and Handling Events

Events are a ubiquitous communication mechanism in most game engines. By permitting event handler functions to be written in script, we open up a powerful avenue for customizing the hard-coded behavior of our game.

Events are usually sent to individual objects and handled within the context of that object. Hence scripted event handlers need to be associated with an object in some way. Some engines use the game object type system for this purpose—scripted event handlers can be registered on a per-object-type basis. This allows different types of game objects to respond in different ways to the same event but ensures that all instances of each type respond in a consistent and uniform way. The event handler functions themselves can be simple script functions, or they can be members of a class if the scripting language is object-oriented. In either case, the event handler is typically passed a handle to the particular object to which the event was sent, much as C++ member functions are passed the `this` pointer.

In other engines, scripted event handlers are associated with individual object instances rather than with object types. In this approach, different instances of the same type might respond differently to the same event.

There are all sorts of other possibilities, of course. For example, in Naughty Dog's *Uncharted* engine, scripts are objects in their own right. They can be associated with individual game objects, they can be attached to regions (convex volumes that are used to trigger game events), or they can exist as standalone objects in the game world. Each script can have multiple states (that is, scripts are finite state machines in the *Uncharted* engine). In turn, each state can have one or more event handler code blocks. When a game object receives an event, it has the option of handling the event in native C++. It also checks for an attached script object, and if one is found, the event is sent to that script's current state. If the state has an event handler for the event, it is called. Otherwise, the script simply ignores the event.

### 14.8.5.4. Sending Events

Allowing scripts to handle game events that are generated by the engine is certainly a powerful feature. Even more powerful is the ability to generate and send events from script code either back to the engine or to other scripts.

Ideally, we'd like to be able not only to send predefined types of events from script but to define entirely new event types in script. Implementing this is trivial if event types are strings. To define a new event type, the script programmer simply comes up with a new event type name and types it into his or her script code. This can be a highly flexible way for scripts to communicate with one another. Script A can define a new event type and send it to Script B. If Script B defines an event handler for this type of event, we've implemented a simple way for Script A to "talk" to Script B. In some game engines, event- or message-passing is the only supported means of inter-object communication in script. This can be an elegant yet powerful and flexible solution.

### 14.8.5.5. Object-Oriented Scripting Languages

Some scripting languages are inherently object-oriented. Others do not support objects directly but provide mechanisms that can be used to implement classes and objects. In many engines, gameplay is implemented via an object-oriented game object model of some kind. So it makes sense to permit some form of object-oriented programming in script as well.

*Defining Classes in Scripts*

A class is really just a bunch of data with some associated functions. So any scripting language that permits new data structures to be defined, and provides some way to store and manipulate functions, can be used to implement classes. For example, in Lua, a class can be built out of a table that stores data members and member functions.

*Inheritance in Script*

Object-oriented languages do not necessarily support inheritance. However, if this feature is available, it can be extremely useful, just as it is in native programming languages like C++.

In the context of game scripting languages, there are two kinds of inheritance: deriving scripted classes from other scripted classes and deriving scripted classes from native classes. If your scripting language is object-oriented, chances are the former is supported out of the box. However, the latter is tough to implement even if the scripting language supports inheritance. The problem is bridging the gap between two languages and two low-level object models. We won't get into the details of how this might be implemented here, as the implementation is bound to be specific to the pair of languages being integrated. UnrealScript is the only scripting language I've seen that allows scripted classes to derive from native classes in a seamless way.

*Composition/Aggregation in Script*

We don't need to rely on inheritance to extend a hierarchy of classes—we can also use composition or aggregation to similar effect. In script, then, all we really need is a way to define classes and associate instances of those classes with objects that have been defined in the native programming language. For example, a game object could have a pointer to an optional component written entirely in script. We can delegate certain key functionality to the script component, if it exists. The script component might have an Update() function that is called whenever the game object is updated, and the scripted component might also be permitted to register some of its member functions/methods as event handlers. When an event is sent to the game object, it calls the appropriate event handler on the scripted component, thus giving the script programmer an opportunity to modify or extend the behavior of the natively implemented game object.

### 14.8.5.6. Scripted Finite State Machines

Many problems in game programming can be solved naturally using finite state machines (FSM). For this reason, some engines build the concept of finite state machines right into the core game object model. In such engines, every game object can have one or more states, and it is the states—not the game object itself—that contain the update function, event handler functions, and so on. Simple game objects can be created by defining a single state, but more-complex game objects have the freedom to define multiple states, each with a different update and event-handling behavior.

If your engine supports a state-driven game object model, it makes a lot of sense to provide finite state machine support in the scripting language as well. And of course, even if the core game object model doesn't support finite state machines natively, one can still provide state-driven behavior by using a state machine on the script side. An FSM can be implemented in any programming language by using class instances to represent states, but some scripting languages provide tools especially for this purpose. An object-oriented scripting language might provide custom syntax that allows a class to contains multiple states, or it might provide tools that help the script programmer easily aggregate state objects together within a central hub object and then delegate the update and event-handling functions to it in a straightforward way. But even if your scripting language provides no such features, you can always adopt a methodology for implementing FSMs and follow those conventions in every script you write.

### 14.8.5.7. Multithreaded Scripts

It's often useful to be able to execute multiple scripts in parallel. This is especially true on today's highly parallelized hardware architectures. If multiple scripts can run at the same time, we are in effect providing *parallel threads of execution* in script code, much like the threads provided by most multitasking operating systems. Of course, the scripts may not actually run in parallel—if they are all running on a single CPU, the CPU must take turns executing each one. However, from the point of view of the script programmer, the paradigm is one of parallel multithreading.

Most scripting systems that provide parallelism do so via *cooperative multitasking*. This means that a script will execute until it explicitly yields to another script. This is in contrast with a *preemptive multitasking* approach, in which the execution of any script could be interrupted at any time to permit another script to execute.

One simple approach to cooperative multitasking in script is to permit scripts to explicitly go to sleep, waiting for something relevant to happen. A script might wait for a specified number of seconds to elapse, or it might wait until a particular event is received. It might wait until another thread of execution has reached a predefined synchronization point. Whatever the reason, whenever a script goes to sleep, it puts itself on a list of sleeping script threads and tells the virtual machine that it can start executing another eligible script. The system keeps track of the conditions that will wake up each sleeping script—when one of these conditions becomes true, the script(s) waiting on the condition are woken up and allowed to continue executing.

To see how this works in practice, let's look at an example of a multi-threaded script. This script manages the animations of two characters and a door. The two characters are instructed to walk up to the door—each one might take a different, and unpredictable, amount of time to reach it. We'll put the script's threads to sleep while they wait for the characters to reach the door. Once they both arrive at the door, one of the two characters opens the door, which it does by playing an "open door" animation. Note that we don't want to hard-code the duration of the animation into the script itself. That way, if the animators change the animation, we won't have to go back and modify our script. So we'll put the threads to sleep again while the wait for the animation to complete. A script that accomplishes this is shown below, using a simple C-like pseudocode syntax.

```
function DoorCinematic
{
    thread Guy1
    {

        // Ask guy1 to walk to the door.
        CharacterWalkToPoint(guy1, doorPosition);
        WaitUntil(ARRIVAL); // go to sleep until he gets
                            // there

        // OK, we're there. Tell the other threads via a
        // signal.
        RaiseSignal("Guy1Arrived");

        // Wait for the other guy to arrive as well.
        WaitUntil(SIGNAL, "Guy2Arrived");

        // Now tell guy1 to play the "open door"
        // animation.
        CharacterAnimate(guy1, "OpenDoor");
        WaitUntil(ANIMATION_DONE);
```

```
                // OK, the door is open. Tell the other threads.
                RaiseSignal("DoorOpen");

                // Now walk thru the door.
                CharacterWalkToPoint(guy1, beyondDoorPosition);
        }

        thread Guy2
        {
                // Ask guy2 to walk to the door.
                CharacterWalkToPoint(guy2, doorPosition);
                WaitUntil(ARRIVAL); // go to sleep until he gets
                                    // there

                // OK, we're there. Tell the other threads via a
                // signal.
                RaiseSignal("Guy2Arrived");

                // Wait for the other guy to arrive as well.
                WaitUntil(SIGNAL, "Guy1Arrived");

                // Now wait until guy1 opens the door for me.
                WaitUntil(SIGNAL, "DoorOpen");

                // OK, the door is open. Now walk thru the door.
                CharacterWalkToPoint(guy2, beyondDoorPosition);
        }

}
```

In the above, we assume that our hypothetical scripting language provides a simple syntax for defining threads of execution within a single function. We define two threads, one for Guy1 and one for Guy2.

The thread for Guy1 tells the character to walk to the door and then goes to sleep waiting for his arrival. We're hand-waving a bit here, but let's imagine that the scripting language magically allows a thread to go to sleep, waiting until a character in the game arrives at a target point to which he was requested to walk. In reality, this might be implemented by arranging for the character to send an event back to the script and then waking the thread up when the event arrives.

Once Guy1 arrives at the door, his thread does two things that warrant further explanation. First, it raises a signal called "Guy1Arrived." Second, it goes to sleep waiting for another signal called "Guy2Arrived." If we look at the thread for Guy2, we see a similar pattern, only reversed. The purpose of this pattern of raising a signal and then waiting for another signal is used to synchronize the two threads.

In our hypothetical scripting language, a *signal* is just a Boolean flag with a name. The flag starts out false, but when a thread calls RaiseSignal(*name*),

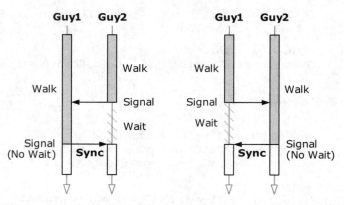

**Figure 14.20.** Two examples showing how a simple pattern of raising one signal and then waiting on another can be used to synchronize a pair of script threads.

the named flag's value changes to true. Other threads can go to sleep, waiting for a particular named signal to become true. When it does, the sleeping thread(s) wake up and continue executing. In this example, the two threads are using the "Guy1Arrived" and "Guy2Arrived" signals to synchronize with one another. Each thread raises its signal and then waits for the other thread's signal. It does not matter which signal is raised first—only when both signals have been raised will the two threads wake up. And when they do, they will be in perfect synchronization. Two possible scenarios are illustrated in Figure 14.20, one in which Guy1 arrives first, the other in which Guy2 arrives first. As you can see, the order in which the signals are raised is irrelevant, and the threads always end up in sync after both signals have been raised.

## 14.9. High-Level Game Flow

A game object model provides the foundations upon which a rich and entertaining collection of game object types can be implemented with which to populate our game worlds. However, by itself, a game object model only permits us to define the kinds of objects that exist in our game world and how they behave individually. It says nothing of the player's objectives, what happens if he or she completes them, and what fate should befall the player if he or she fails.

For this, we need some kind of system to control high-level game flow. This is often implemented as a finite state machine. Each state usually represents a single player objective or encounter and is associated with a particular locale within the virtual game world. As the player completes each task, the state machine advances to the next state, and the player is presented with a new set of goals. The state machine also defines what should happen in the event of the player's failure to accomplish the necessary tasks or objectives. Often, failure sends the player back to the beginning of the current state, so he or she can try again. Sometimes after enough failures, the player has run out of "lives" and will be sent back to the main menu, where he or she can choose to play a new game. The flow of the entire game, from the menus to the first "level" to the last, can be controlled through this high-level state machine.

The task system used in Naughty Dog's *Jak and Daxter* and *Uncharted* franchises is an example of such a state-machine-based system. It allows for linear sequences of states (called *tasks* at Naughty Dog). It also permits parallel tasks, where one task branches out into two or more parallel tasks, which eventually merge back into the main task sequence. This parallel task feature sets the Naughty Dog task graph apart from a regular state machine, since state machines typically can only be in one state at a time.

# Part V
# Conclusion

# You Mean There's More?

Congratulations! You've reached the end of your journey through the landscape of game engine architecture in one piece (and hopefully none the worse for wear). With any luck, you've learned a great deal about the major components that comprise a typical game engine. But of course, every journey's end is another's beginning. There's a great deal more to be learned within each and every topic area covered within these pages. As technology and computing hardware continue to improve, more things will become possible in games—and more engine systems will be invented to support them. What's more, this book's focus was on the game engine itself. We haven't even begun to discuss the rich world of gameplay programming, a topic that could fill many more volumes.

In the following brief sections, I'll identify a few of the engine and gameplay systems we didn't have room to cover in any depth in this book, and I'll suggest some resources for those who wish to learn more about them.

## 15.1. Some Engine Systems We Didn't Cover

### 15.1.1. Audio

I mentioned in Section 1.6.13 that audio often takes a back seat to other aspects of game development, much to the chagrin of the audio engineers, sound designers, voice actors, and composers who work so hard to add that all-too-critical fourth dimension to the virtual game world. And yet, sadly, the same thing has happened in this book—I am out of room and out of time, so a full treatment of audio will have to wait until the second edition. (In keeping with a long and painfully unfortunate tradition in game development, once again audio gets the shaft!)

Thankfully, a number of other books and online resources do provide a wealth of information on audio development. First off, I recommend reading the documentation for Microsoft's XACT sound authoring tool and runtime API, located on the MSDN website under *XACT: Tutorials and Samples* (http://msdn.microsoft.com/en-us/library/bb172329(VS.85).aspx). XACT supports virtually every audio feature the average game programmer would want, and its documentation is quite easy to digest. The *Game Programming Gems* book series also includes a plethora of articles on audio—see [7] Section 6 and [40] Section 6.

### 15.1.2. Movie Player

Most games include a movie player for displaying prerendered movies, also known as full-motion video (FMV). The basic components of the movie player are an interface to the streaming file I/O system (see Section 6.1.3), a codec to decode the compressed video stream, and some form of synchronization with the audio playback system for the sound track.

A number of different video encoding standards and corresponding codecs are available, each one suited to a particular type of application. For example, video CDs (VCD) and DVDs use MPEG-1 and MPEG-2 (H.262) codecs, respectively. The H.261 and H.263 standards are designed primarily for online video conferencing applications. Games often use standards like MPEG-4 part 2 (e.g., DivX), MPEG-4 Part 10 / H.264, Windows Media Video (WMV), or Bink Video (a standard designed specifically for games by Rad Game Tools, Inc.). See http://en.wikipedia.org/wiki/Video_codec and http://www.radgametools.com/bnkmain.htm for more information on video codecs.

### 15.1.3. Multiplayer Networking

Although we have touched on a number of aspects of multiplayer game architecture and networking (e.g., Sections 1.6.14, 7.7, and 14.8.3.2), this book's coverage of the topic is far from complete. For an in-depth treatment of multiplayer networking, see [3].

## 15.2. Gameplay Systems

A game is of course much more than just its engine. On top of the gameplay foundation layer (discussed in Chapter 14), you'll find a rich assortment of genre- and game-specific gameplay systems. These systems tie the myriad game engine technologies described in this book together into a cohesive whole, breathing life into the game.

### 15.2.1. Player Mechanics

*Player mechanics* are of course the most important gameplay system. Each genre is defined by a general style of player mechanics and gameplay, and of course every game within a genre has its own specific designs. As such, player mechanics is a huge topic. It involves the integration of human interface device systems, motion simulation, collision detection, animation, and audio, not to mention integration with other gameplay systems like the game camera, weapons, cover, specialized traversal mechanics (ladders, swinging vines, etc.), vehicle systems, puzzle mechanics, and so on.

Clearly player mechanics are as varied as the games themselves, so there's no one place you can go to learn all about them. It's best to tackle this topic by studying a single genre at a time. Play games and try to reverse-engineer their player mechanics. Then try to implement them yourself! And as a very modest start on reading, you can check out [7] Section 4.11 for a discussion of Mario-style platformer player mechanics.

### 15.2.2. Cameras

A game's camera system is almost as important as the player mechanics. In fact, the camera can make or break the gameplay experience. Each genre tends to have its own camera control style, although of course every game within a particular genre does it a little bit differently (and some very differently!). See [6] Section 4.3 for some basic game camera control techniques. In the following paragraphs, I'll briefly outline some of the most prevalent kinds of cameras in 3D games, but please note that this is far from a complete list.

- *Look-at cameras.* This type of camera rotates about a target point and can be moved in and out relative to this point.
- *Follow cameras.* This type of camera is prevalent in platformer, third-person shooter, and vehicle-based games. It acts much like a look-at camera focused on the player character/avatar/vehicle, but its motion typically lags the player. A follow camera alos includes advanced collision detection and avoidance logic and provides the human player

with some degree of control over the camera's orientation relative to the player avatar.

- *First-person cameras.* As the player character moves about in the game world, a first-person camera remains affixed to the character's virtual eyes. The player typically has full control over the direction in which the camera should be pointed, either via mouse or joypad control. The look direction of the camera also translates directly into the aim direction of the player's weapon, which is typically indicated by a set of disembodied arms and a gun attached to the bottom of the screen, and a reticle at the center of the screen.

- *RTS cameras.* Real-time strategy and god games tend to employ a camera that floats above the terrain, looking down at an angle. The camera can be panned about over the terrain, but the pitch and yaw of the camera are usually not under direct player control.

- *Cinematic cameras.* Most three-dimensional games have at least some cinematic moments in which the camera flies about within the scene in a more filmic manner rather than being tethered to an object in the game.

### 15.2.3. Artificial Intelligence

Another major component of most character-based games is *artificial intelligence* (AI). At its lowest level, an AI system is usually founded in technologies like basic path finding (which commonly makes use of the well-known A* algorithm), perception systems (line of sight, vision cones, knowledge of the environment, etc.) and some form of memory.

On top of these foundations, character control logic is implemented. A character control system determines how to make the character perform specific actions like locomoting, navigating unusual terrain features, using weapons, driving vehicles, taking cover, and so on. It typically involves complex interfaces to the collision, physics, and animation systems within the engine. Character control is discussed in detail in Sections 11.11 and 11.12.

Above the character control layer, an AI system typically has goal setting and decision making logic, emotional state, group behaviors (coordination, flanking, crowd and flocking behaviors, etc.), and possibly some advanced features like an ability to learn from past mistakes or adapt to a changing environment.

Of course, the term "artificial intelligence" is a bit of a misnomer when applied to games. Game AI is usually more smoke and mirrors than it is an attempt at true artificial intelligence. It's important to realize that, in a game, all that really matters is the player's perception of what is going on. A classic example comes from the game *Halo*. When Bungie first implemented their AI system, they included a simple rule that stated that the small "grunt" aliens would all run away when their leader had died. In play test after play test, no one realized that this was *why* the little guys were running away. Even after the Bungie team had made various adjustments to the animations and AI behaviors in the game, still no one got the connection. Finally, the developers resorted to having one of the grunts say, "Leader dead! Run away!" This just goes to show that all the AI logic in the world doesn't amount to anything if the player doesn't perceive the meaning behind it.

AI programming is a rich topic, and we certainly have not done it justice in this book. For more information, see [16], [6] Section 3, [7] Section 3, and [40] Section 3.

### 15.2.4. Other Gameplay Systems

Clearly there's a lot more to a game than just player mechanics, cameras, and AI. Some games have drivable vehicles, implement specialized types of weaponry, allow the player to destroy the environment with the help of a dynamic physics simulation, let the player create his or her own characters, build custom levels, require the player to solve puzzles, or... Of course, the list of genre- and game-specific features, and all of the specialized software systems that implement them, could go on forever. Gameplay systems are as rich and varied as games are. Perhaps this is where your next journey as a game programmer will begin!

# References

[1]    Tomas Akenine-Moller, Eric Haines, and Naty Hoffman. *Real-Time Rendering (3rd Edition)*. Wellesley, MA: A K Peters, 2008.

[2]    Andrei Alexandrescu. *Modern C++ Design: Generic Programming and Design Patterns Applied*. Resding, MA: Addison-Wesley, 2001.

[3]    Grenville Armitage, Mark Claypool and Philip Branch. *Networking and Online Games: Understanding and Engineering Multiplayer Internet Games*. New York, NY: John Wiley and Sons, 2006.

[4]    James Arvo (editor). *Graphics Gems II*. San Diego, CA: Academic Press, 1991.

[5]    Grady Booch, Robert A. Maksimchuk, Michael W. Engel, Bobbi J. Young, Jim Conallen, and Kelli A. Houston. *Object-Oriented Analysis and Design with Applications*, third edition. Reading, MA: Addison-Wesley, 2007.

[6]    Mark DeLoura (editor). *Game Programming Gems*. Hingham, MA: Charles River Media, 2000.

[7]    Mark DeLoura (editor). *Game Programming Gems 2*. Hingham, MA: Charles River Media, 2001.

[8]    Philip Dutré, Kavita Bala and Philippe Bekaert. *Advanced Global Illumination (Second Edition)*. Wellesley, MA: A K Peters, 2006.

[9]    David H. Eberly. *3D Game Engine Design: A Practical Approach to Real-Time Computer Graphics.* San Francisco, CA: Morgan Kaufmann, 2001.

[10]   David H. Eberly. *3D Game Engine Architecture: Engineering Real-Time Applications with Wild Magic.* San Francisco, CA: Morgan Kaufmann, 2005.

[11]   David H. Eberly. *Game Physics.* San Francisco, CA: Morgan Kaufmann, 2003.

[12]   Christer Ericson. *Real-Time Collision Detection.* San Francisco, CA: Morgan Kaufmann, 2005.

[13]   Randima Fernando (editor). *GPU Gems: Programming Techniques, Tips and Tricks for Real-Time Graphics.* Reading, MA: Addison-Wesley, 2004.

[14]   James D. Foley, Andries van Dam, Steven K. Feiner, and John F. Hughes. *Computer Graphics: Principles and Practice in C,* second edition. Reading, MA: Addison-Wesley, 1995.

[15]   Grant R. Fowles and George L. Cassiday. *Analytical Mechanics (7th Edition).* Pacific Grove, CA: Brooks Cole, 2005.

[16]   John David Funge. *AI for Games and Animation: A Cognitive Modeling Approach.* Wellesley, MA: A K Peters, 1999.

[17]   Erich Gamma, Richard Helm, Ralph Johnson, and John M. Vlissiddes. *Design Patterns: Elements of Reusable Object-Oriented Software.* Reading, MA: Addison-Wesley, 1994.

[18]   Andrew S. Glassner (editor). *Graphics Gems I.* San Francisco, CA: Morgan Kaufmann, 1990.

[19]   Paul S. Heckbert (editor). *Graphics Gems IV.* San Diego, CA: Academic Press, 1994.

[20]   Maurice Herlihy, Nir Shavit. *The Art of Multiprocessor Programming.* San Francisco, CA: Morgan Kaufmann, 2008.

[21]   Roberto Ierusalimschy, Luiz Henrique de Figueiredo and Waldemar Celes. *Lua 5.1 Reference Manual.* Lua.org, 2006.

[22]   Roberto Ierusalimschy. *Programming in Lua, 2nd Edition.* Lua.org, 2006.

[23]   Isaac Victor Kerlow. *The Art of 3-D Computer Animation and Imaging (Second Edition).* New York, NY: John Wiley and Sons, 2000.

[24]   David Kirk (editor). *Graphics Gems III.* San Francisco, CA: Morgan Kaufmann, 1994.

[25]   Danny Kodicek. *Mathematics and Physics for Game Programmers.* Hingham, MA: Charles River Media, 2005.

[26]  Raph Koster. *A Theory of Fun for Game Design*. Phoenix, AZ: Paraglyph, 2004.

[27]  John Lakos. *Large-Scale C++ Software Design*. Reading, MA: Addison-Wesley, 1995.

[28]  Eric Lengyel. *Mathematics for 3D Game Programming and Computer Graphics, 2nd Edition*. Hingham, MA: Charles River Media, 2003.

[29]  Tuoc V. Luong, James S. H. Lok, David J. Taylor and Kevin Driscoll. *Internationalization: Developing Software for Global Markets*. New York, NY: John Wiley & Sons, 1995.

[30]  Steve Maguire. *Writing Solid Code: Microsoft's Techniques for Developing Bug-Free C Programs*. Bellevue, WA: Microsoft Press, 1993.

[31]  Scott Meyers. *Effective C++: 55 Specific Ways to Improve Your Programs and Designs (3rd Edition)*. Reading, MA: Addison-Wesley, 2005.

[32]  Scott Meyers. *More Effective C++: 35 New Ways to Improve Your Programs and Designs*. Reading, MA: Addison-Wesley, 1996.

[33]  Scott Meyers. *Effective STL: 50 Specific Ways to Improve Your Use of the Standard Template Library*. Reading, MA: Addison-Wesley, 2001.

[34]  Ian Millington. *Game Physics Engine Development*. San Francisco, CA: Morgan Kaufmann, 2007.

[35]  Hubert Nguyen (editor). *GPU Gems 3*. Reading, MA: Addison-Wesley, 2007.

[36]  Alan W. Paeth (editor). *Graphics Gems V*. San Francisco, CA: Morgan Kaufmann, 1995.

[37]  C. Michael Pilato, Ben Collins-Sussman, and Brian W. Fitzpatrick. *Version Control with Subversion*, second edition. Sebastopol , CA: O'Reilly Media, 2008. (Commonly known as "The Subversion Book." Available online at http://svnbook.red-bean.com.)

[38]  Matt Pharr (editor). *GPU Gems 2: Programming Techniques for High-Performance Graphics and General-Purpose Computation*. Reading, MA: Addison-Wesley, 2005.

[39]  Bjarne Stroustrup. *The C++ Programming Language*, special edition (3rd edition). Reading, MA: Addison-Wesley, 2000.

[40]  Dante Treglia (editor). *Game Programming Gems 3*. Hingham, MA: Charles River Media, 2002.

[41]  Gino van den Bergen. *Collision Detection in Interactive 3D Environments*. San Francisco, CA: Morgan Kaufmann, 2003.

[42]  Alan Watt. *3D Computer Graphics (3rd Edition)*. Reading, MA: Addison Wesley, 1999.

[43]  James Whitehead II, Bryan McLemore and Matthew Orlando. *World of Warcraft Programming: A Guide and Reference for Creating WoW Addons*. New York, NY: John Wiley & Sons, 2008.

[44]  Richard Williams. *The Animator's Survival Kit*. London, England: Faber & Faber, 2002.

# Index

## Symbols

#pragma pack. See class, packing
2D graphics. See overlay
3D model. See model
3ds Max, 52, 447
80-20 rule, 86, 772
90-10 rule. See 80-20 rule

## A

A* algorithm, 824
abstract construction. See class
abstract factory. See design pattern
acceleration
  angular, 642
  linear, 634
accelerometer. See human interface
    device
ACP. See asset conditioning pipeline
action state machine, 568, 680
  layered, 580
  *Uncharted*, 580

actor
  collision. See collidable
  game. See game object
  in-game cinematic, 585
  resource (*Uncharted*), 278
  Unreal, 722
additive blending. See animation
Ageia, 602
agent. See game object; collision
aggregation, 96, 721, 723, 803, 812
AI. See artificial intelligence
aiming, 541, 626
air lock, 743
albedo. See texture; reflection, diffuse
algorithmic complexity. See big-O
    notation
aliasing. See antialiasing
Alienbrain. See version control
alignment, 123, 187, 210
allocation
  chunky, 232, 293
  delete operator (C++), 119

double-buffered, 214
dynamic, 119, 206
heap memory, 119, 290
new operator (C++), 119
optimization, 206
placement new (C++). See placement
    new
pool, 209, 217, 292, 747
resource chunk allocator, 294
single-frame allocator, 213
small memory allocator, 747
stack-based, 207, 217, 291
alpha, 402, 413
blending function, 453
testing, 453
Altivec
single instruction multiple data, 104
ALU. See arithmetic logic unit; light-
    ing, ambient occlusion
analytical geometry, 613
analytical solution, 637
animation, 42
2D, 492
action state machine. See action state
    machine
attachment, 583
blending, 553, 764
    additive, 537, 563
    binary, 561
    blend mask, 536
    blend tree, 560, 565, 569, 582
    complex, 531
    compound node, 570
    control parameter, 581
    Delaunay triangulation. See Delau-
        nay triangulation
    flat weighted average, 557, 564, 582
    generalized, 562
    LERP, 524, 561
    limitations, 539
    one-dimensional, 531, 561
    partial-skeleton, 536
    rag doll. See rag doll
    specification, 556, 569

    triangular, 533, 562
    two-dimensional, 532, 562
    *Uncharted*, 570
    Unreal, 574
camera, 517
cel, 492
channel, 514, 516
    event trigger, 517
    floating-point, 518
    meta, 517
clip, 505, 555
    difference, 537
    format, 514
    reference, 537
    source, 537
    state, 556
clock
    global, 512, 556
    local, 511, 556
compression, 496, 546
    curve-based, 551
constraint, 583
controller, 593
cross-fade. See animation, transition
death, 683
decompression, 553
end effector, 544
film, 504, 506
forward kinematics, 544
frame, 492
full-body, 536
grabbing, 588
hand-drawn, 492
Havok Animation, 33
idle, 492
instancing, 522
interobject registration, 584
    reference locator, 585
inverse kinematics, 543, 553
    foot, 591
    hand, 588
job. See multitasking
libraries, 33
loading, 551

look-at, 541, 592
looping, 492, 505, 508
morph target, 494
motion capture, 6
motion extraction. See locomotion
optimization, 566
particle, 482, 517
per-instance state, 556
per-vertex, 494
pipeline, 553
playback rate, 510, 556
playing, 509
post-processing, 542, 553
procedural, 543, 553, 660
rag doll. See rag doll
retargeting, 515
rigid hierarchical, 493
shared resource data, 554
skinned. See skinning
start time, 511
state, 569
streaming, 551
synchronization, 512
temporal interpolation. See interpo-
        lation, temporal
texture, 493, 518
time scaling, 507, 510
traditional, 492
transition, 527, 564, 575
    ease curve, 528, 576
    frozen, 527
    matrix, 577
    *Medal of Honor*, 577
    smooth, 527
    transitional state, 576
    *Uncharted*, 578
    window, 576
updating, 759
anisotropic reflection. See reflection
ANSI. See character set
antialiasing, 441
    full-screen, 442
    multisample, 442
anti-commutative, 149

antiportal. See culling
application programming interface,
        31, 34
architecture runtime, 28
arithmetic logic unit, 103
array of structs, 732. See also struct of
        arrays
artificial intelligence, 47, 305, 320, 373,
        384, 512, 553, 593, 599, 626, 677,
        701, 716, 730, 734, 737, 773, 790,
        824
    character control, 824
    decision making, 824
    goal, 824
    group behaviors, 824
    Halo, 825
    Kynapse, 33, 47, 48
    path finding, 824
    perception, 824
ASCII. See character set
ASM. See action state machine
aspect ratio. See screen
assertions, 8, 35, 72, 131, 132, 133, 134,
        135
asset. See resource
asset conditioning pipeline, 50, 51,
        278, 281, 445, 449
    Quake, 709
    Source, 709
asset conditioning pipline
    Unreal, 708
asset manager. See resource manager
asynchronous programming. See mul-
        titasking
atomic data type. See data type
attribute. See game object; vertex
audio, 44, 821
    human interface device, 349
    Scream, 44
    upating, 759
    USB, 349
    XACT, 44
authority. See multiplayer
automatic variable. See variable

`auto_ptr`, 751
axis+angle rotation, 178

# B

back buffer. See frame buffer
barycentric coordinates, 534
batched updating. See game object
behavior. See game object
Bézier. See patch; spline
Bézier triangle, 402
bicubic patch. See patch
bidirectional reflection distribution
     function. See BRDF
big-endian. See endian
big-O notation, 227
billboard, 39, 482
binary, 98
binary search tree. See container
binary space partitioning tree, 38, 467,
     623, 692
Bink Video, 822
biomechanics, 33, 525, 661, 684
bitmapped image. See image
bits per pixel. See image
blend factor. See animation, blending
blending. See animation; rendering
     pipeline, merging
blend time, 527
Blinn-Phong. See lighting
bloom. See lighting
Bluetooth, 342
BMP. See Windows Bitmap
body space. See coordinate system
bone, 495, 497. See also joint
Boost, 31, 231
   smart pointer, 752
bounding box
  axis-aligned, 184, 609, 616. See
     also sweep and prune
  oriented, 184, 610
bounding sphere tree, 467, 623
bounding volume, 460
brawler. See genre

BRDF, 429
break point. See debugger
brush geometry, 51, 692
BSP tree. See binary space partitioning
     tree
BSSRDF. See lighting
BSS segment. See executable file
bubble-up effect. See class hierarchy
build configurations. See compiler
build dependencies. See resource
build rules, 282
Bullet, 602
bullet through paper. See tunneling
bullet tracing, 676
bump mapping. See lighting
byte code. See script

# C

C4 Engine, 27
cache
  level 1. See level 1 cache
  level 2. See level 2 cache
cache coherency, 408
cache miss, 220, 222, 566
callback function, 269, 272, 308, 629
  scripted, 802
call stack. See debugger
camera, 14, 17, 21, 37, 39, 400, 433, 823
  animation. See animation
  collision. See collision
  debug, 383
  imaging rectangle, 433
  zoom, 681
camera-relative control, 681
cast. See collision, query
*Castle Wolfenstein 3D*, 25, 403, 450
Catmull-Clark. See subdivision surface
caustics. See lighting
CCD. See collision, continuous colli-
     sion detection
cel. See animation
Cell Broadband Engine, 326
center of mass, 633, 644

Cg. See shader
CgFX. See shader, effect file
chain of responsibility, 782
change of basis, 163
channel. See animation; color; logging
character, 491
character mechanics. See gameplay
character set, 249
  ANSI, 248
  multibyte, 249
  wide, 249
cheats, 384
check point. See game, load/save
chord. See human interface device
chunky allocation. See allocation
circular dependency. See dependency
      cycle
class, 91, 119
  abstract construction, 714, 736
  constructor, 299
  instance, 92, 119
  memory layout, 121
  mix-in, 94, 721
  packing, 122
  pure virtual function, 126
  reflection, 714, 736
  scripted, 812
  virtual function, 125, 717
  virtual function table, 125
class diagram
  static, 92
class factory. See design pattern
class hierarchy, 718
  bubble-up, 722
  monolithic, 719
  Unreal, 719
class static variable. See variable
ClearCase. See version control
client-on-top-of-server. See multiplayer
client-server. See multiplayer
clip. See animation
clipping, 184, 437, 452
  clipping plane, 37
clip space. See coordinate system

clock. See time
closed hash table. See container
cloth, 684
clouds, 484
CM. See center of mass
codec
  video, 822
code reuse, 28
coding standards, 97
coefficient of restitution, 651, 652
coherency. See cache coherency; tem-
      poral coherency
COLLADA, 459
collection. See container
collidable, 604
collision, 3, 11, 14, 17, 32, 41, 42, 48,
      51, 96
  agent, 619
  and game loop, 305
  broad phase, 623
  camera, 628, 681
  cast. See collision, query
  continuous collision detection, 622
  data, 734
  detection, 11, 41, 42, 595, 603, 613.
      See also intersection
    libraries, 33
  dispatcher, 620
  elastic, 651
  enabling/disabling. See collision,
     filtering
  filtering, 629
    callback, 629
  inelastic, 651
  material, 630
  midphase, 613, 623
  narrow phase, 624
  optimization, 622
  phantom, 628, 671
  plastic, 651
  primitive. See primitive
  query, 624, 671, 679
    asynchronous, 674
    closest point, 629

parallelizing, 773
ray cast, 624, 773
shape cast, 626
sphere cast, 626
when to run, 672
response, 631, 650, 651
shape-shape combinations, 619
single-sided, 683
support, 603, 657
updating, 759
world. See physics, world
collision (hashing), 239, 241, 245
color, 400, 412
channel, 412
log-LUV, 413, 473
model, 412
RGB, 412
space, 412
spectral, 411
colorization, 490
command line arguments, 257
command line options, 253
command list. See graphics processing
    unit
commutative, 145, 149
compiler, 66
build configurations, 69
debug build, 72
debugging information, 71
GNU compiler, 71
hybrid build, 73
optimizations, 69, 71
production build, 72
project configuration tutorial, 74
project files, 68
release build, 72
solution files, 68
tools build, 72
warnings, 69
component. See object model
composition, 96, 721, 723, 803, 812
compression
quantization, 345, 547
concave, 608

conditional break point. See debugger
configuration file, 252
configuration space, 544
conservative advancement, 622
console
gaming platform, 8
in-game, 40, 382
constraint
and degrees of freedom, 180
animation. See animation
physics. See physics
contact, 603, 607, 626, 654
earliest, 625, 627
multiple, 627
container, 223
array, 223
binary heap, 224
binary search tree, 224, 239
building custom, 228
DAG, 224
deque, 224
dictionary, 224, 239
dynamic array, 223, 232
graph, 224
hash table, 224, 239
closed, 239
open, 239
list, 224, 233
circular, 236
doubly-linked, 233
extrusive, 235
singly-linked, 238
map, 224
priority queue, 224
queue, 224
set, 224
stack, 224
tree, 224
vector (STL), 223
context-sensitive controls. See human
    interface device
continuity
C0, C1, C2, 526
motion, 526

controller
  game. See human interface device
controller mapping. See human inter-
    face device
convergence. See integration, numeri-
    cal
convex, 608
  hull, 617
convolution kernel, 489
cooperative multitasking. See multi-
    tasking
coordinate space
  hierarchy, 163
coordinate system, 159
  body space, 643
  Cartesian, 138
  cylindrical, 138
  homogeneous clip space, 436
  joint space, 519
  left-handed, 139
  light space, 476. See also shadow
  model space, 160, 409, 520
  right-handed, 139
  screen space, 439, 486
  spherical, 138
  tangent space, 413
  texture space, 419
  view space, 162, 433
  world space, 161, 409
copy-back cache, 220
copy on write, 243
couple. See physics
coupling, 28
cover
  entry and departure, 592
  registration, 592
__cplusplus, 70
CPU-dependent game, 314
CPU utilization. See processor utiliza-
    tion
crash report, 371
Crystal Space, 28
CSV file, 251, 392
cube map. See texture

culling, 15, 17, 37
  antiportal, 462
  back face, 405
  frustum, 37, 460
  occlusion, 15, 17, 38, 461
  portal, 15
  portals, 461
  potentially visible set, 461
  visibility determination, 460
cut-scene. See in-game cinematic
CVAR, 254
CVS. See version control

D

damping, 636, 653, 660
  physics, 657
  viscous, 636
dashpot. See damping
data break point. See debugger
data cache (D-cache), 222
data-driven, 11, 569, 698, 732. See
    also event
  cost, 698
data pathway, 791
data segment. See executable file
data type, 110
  atomic, 103
  F32, 104
  I32, 104
  I32F, 104
  __int32, 103
  TCHAR, 249
  U32, 104
  U32F, 104
  wchar_t, 249
  wstring, 249
DCC. See digital content creation tool
deadline. See simulation, real-time
deadly diamond. See inheritance
dead zone. See human interface device
_DEBUG, 70
debug build. See compiler
debug drawing, 40, 372

debugger
  break point, 79
    conditional, 83
    data break point, 82
    hit count, 84
  call stack, 80, 116, 388
  debugging optimized builds, 84
  single-step, 79
  stack frame, 116
  watch window, 80
debugging information. See compiler
debugging tools, 40
debug memory. See memory
decal, 483
decal system, 38
decimal, 98
declaration (C/C++), 110
decoupling, 724
dedicated server. See multiplayer
deep copy, 786
deferred rendering, 481
  G-buffer, 481
definition (C/C++), 110
deformable. See physics
degrees of freedom, 180, 633, 658
Delaunay triangulation, 535, 562
delegate, 309, 775
delete operator (C++). See allocation
delta time. See time
dependency cycle, 28
depth buffer, 441, 443, 475
  shadow mapping, 476
  testing, 453, 486
  z testing, 453
    early, 453, 465
    z prepass, 465
depth of field blur, 490
derivative, 526, 634
  approximate, 639
  of a vector, 634
design pattern, 96
  abstract factory, 96
  callback. See callback function

chain of responsibility, 782
class factory, 736
command, 776
iterator, 96, 225
singleton, 96, 198
destructible objects, 678, 692
development kit, 247, 395
dictionary. See container
diff. See version control
difference clip. See animation
diffuse. See lighting
diffuse reflection. See reflection
digital content creation application,
    49, 50, 52, 447
Digital Molecular Matter, 603, 678, 684
direct memory access, 327, 567
DirectX, 32, 36, 44, 77
  perspective projection matrix, 437
  view space, 163
  XACT, 44
disassembly, 84
discrete oriented polytope. See shape
display device, 400
distributive, 145, 149
division by w, 156
DivX, 822
DLL. See dynamic link library
DMA. See direct memory access
DMM. See Digital Molecular Matter
Doom, 11, 403, 450, 699
DOP. See shape, discrete oriented
    polytope
double dispatch, 619
doubly-linked list. See container
DrawIndexedPrimitive(), 463
Dual Shock. See human interface de-
    vice
duck typing, 801
DXT. See texture, compression
dynamic allocation. See allocation
dynamically typed, 775
dynamic link library, 68
dynamics. See physics

# E

early z test. See depth buffer
ease-in/out. See animation, transition
Edge, 32. See PlayStation Edge
effect file. See shader
ELF. See executable and linking format
emergent behaviors, 599
encapsulation, 92, 725
end effector. See animation
endian, 106
  big, 106
  little, 106
  swapping, 107
Endorphin, 33, 34
energy, 650
  conservation, 650
  kinetic, 650
  loss due to collision, 651
  potential, 650
engine configuration, 252
  Ogre3D, 255
  Quake, 254
  *Uncharted*, 255
engine subsystem dependencies, 763
entity. See game object
environment map. See texture
environment variable, 253
equations of motion
  analytical solution, 637
  angular, 644, 648
  linear, 635
  numerical solution, 637
equilibrium, 657, 661
Erlang language, 772
error conditions, 128
Euler angles, 161, 177, 646
Euphoria, 33, 34
event, 47, 309, 758, 773
  arguments, 775, 778, 781, 786
    key-value pair, 779
  data-driven, 790
  debugging, 788
  forwarding, 776

future, 784
GUI-based, 793
  pros and cons, 793
handling, 774, 776, 780, 802, 810
input. See human interface device
memory allocation, 787
persistence, 776
priority, 785
queuing, 783
registering interest, 783
sending, 811
system, 712
type, 775, 776
event-driven, 47
event system, 47
event trigger. See animation, channel
exception. See structured exception
    handling
exclusive check-out. See version con-
    trol
executable and linking format, 115
executable file, 67, 115
  BSS segment, 115
  data segment, 115
  read-only data (rodata) segment, 115
  segment, 115
  text segment, 115
explosion, 677
exporting. See resource
expression tree, 560. See also anima-
    tion, blending
extrusive list. See container
EyeToy. See human interface device

# F

F32. See data type
face normal. See triangle
facing, 147, 530
far plane. See view volume
field of view, 37
fighting game. See genre
file I/O
  asynchronous, 269, 743
  buffered, 266

deadline, 271
   synchronous, 268
file system, 262
   path, 244, 262
      absolute, 264
      relative, 264
   search path, 265
   wrapping, 267
finite difference, 639
finite state machine, 552, 714, 757, 813,
      816
fixed-function pipeline, 450
fixed-point, 99
fix-up table. See pointer fix-up
FK. See animation, forward kinematics
flashlight. See lighting
floating-point
   exponent, 100
   infinity, 101
   magnitude, 101
   mantissa, 100
   not-a-number, 101
   precision, 101
   significant digits, 101
FLT_MAX, 101
fluid mechanics, 486, 596, 685
FMV. See full-motion video
FName. See string id
font. See text rendering
foot sliding, 591
force, 150, 635
   application, 662, 671
   as a function, 636
   penalty, 653
force feedback. See human interface
      device
fork/join. See multitasking
forward kinematics. See animation
FPS. See frame rate, genre
fragment, 441
frame (animation), 507
frame buffer, 440
   back buffer, 316
   double buffering, 440

front buffer, 316
   swapping, 316
   triple buffering, 440
frame rate, 312, 506
   frames per second, 10
frame rate governing, 315, 316
frames per second. See frame rate
frame-to-frame coherency. See tempo-
      ral coherency
framework, 308
free store. See allocating, heap memory
friction, 651, 652, 654
   coefficient of, 655
   constraint, 654
   due to collision, 654
   dynamic, 654
   rolling, 654
   sliding, 654
   static, 654
front buffer. See frame buffer
frustum, 35, 37. See view volume
frustum culling. See culling
FSAA. See antialiasing, full-screen
full-motion video, 39, 505, 694, 822
Fx Composer, 447

## G

game
   definition, 8
   load/save, 714, 748
      check point, 749
   world, 3, 9, 46, 53, 690, 759
      element, 690, 734
      optimization, 692
      visualization, 701
   world chunk, 693, 701
      data formats, 734
      loading, 741
   world editor, 49, 53, 485, 695, 697,
      699, 712, 715, 737, 746, 750, 790,
      798
      alignment, 705
      free-form property, 704

integrated asset management, 707
layer, 703
load/save, 706
multiobject selection, 703
navigation, 702
object placement, 705
property grid, 703
selection, 702
game asset. See resource
game development team
  artist, 5
  composer, 6
  engineer, 5
  game designer, 7
  producer, 7
  publisher, 8
  sound designer, 6
  voice actor, 6
  writer, 7
game engine, 11
  line between engine and game, 11,
    711
  reusability gamut, 12
game loop, 304, 672, 757, 761
  client-server, 334
  multiplayer, 333
  multithreaded, 674
  parallelizing, 329
  pausing, 383
  *Pong*, 305
  *Quake*, 336
  single-stepping, 310, 322, 383
  sleep, 315
  slow motion, 383
game object, 695
  attribute, 696
    default values, 739
  batched updating, 761
  behavior, 696, 713
  dependencies, 763
  destroying, 712, 741
  game-driven. See physics, rigid body
  *Hydro Thunder*, 716
  instance, 696

linkage to engine, 713
linkage to physics/collision, 666, 670
physics-driven, 631, 668, 671, 676,
  683
query, 714, 750, 755
reference, 714, 750
representations, 604
spawning, 712, 741
  dynamic, 746
  memory management, 745
  preallocated, 746
state, 757
  caching, 770
  inconsistency, 769
type, 696
  defining, 713
type schema, 738
unique id, 244, 713, 728, 750, 753, 756
updating, 305, 512, 712, 757
  asynchronous, 772
  bucketed, 766
  phased, 764
game object model. See object model
game object state
  time-stamping, 771
gameplay, 48, 689
  character mechanics, 679
  flow, 689, 694, 712, 816
  hub, 694
  linear, 694
  objectives, 689, 694, 712, 817
  open world, 694
  player mechanics, 45, 593, 679, 689,
    823
  region, 705
  task, 694
  water, 486
gameplay foundations layer, 46, 711
game state, 690
game studio. See studio
gamma
  correction, 488
  response curve, 488
Gaussian elimination, 154

G-buffer, 481
gcc. See compiler
generic browser. See UnrealEd
genre, 13
  brawler, 18
  fighting, 17
  first-person shooter, 13
  goal-based, 598
  massively multiplayer online game, 23
  other, 24
  physics puzzle, 597
  platformer, 15, 598
  racing, 19
  real-time strategy, 21
  sandbox, 598
  sim, 597
  story-driven, 598
gesture. See human interface device
G-factor, 690
gimbal lock, 177, 178, 646
git. See version control
GJK, 617
glDrawArrays(), 463
Glide, 32
global illumination. See lighting
globally unique identifier, 244, 286, 296
global namespace. See namespace
global varible. See variable
gloss map. See texture
GLSL. See shader, OpenGL shader language
_GNUC_, 71
GNU compiler. See compiler
GO. See game object
goal-based game, 598
Google Code. See version control
Gouraud shading, 416
GPU. See graphics processing unit
grammar, 560
Granny, 4, 33, 286, 295, 551, 560
graphical shading language, 447

graphical user interface. See overlay
graphics accelerator. See graphics processing unit
graphics processing unit, 326, 450
  command list, 464
  pipeline. See rendering pipeline
gravity, 632, 650, 655, 662
grenade physics, 677
GUI. See overlay, graphical user interface
GUID. See globally unique identifier

H

H.261, 822
H.263, 822
Hadamard product, 142, 454
hair, 426, 452, 481, 684
half4. See shader
Half-Life 2, 26
Hammer, 54, 699
handle, 219, 714, 750, 752, 809
  stale, 753
  table, 754
hardware break point. See debugger, break point, data break point
hardware state. See render state
hardware transformation and lighting (T&L), 450
hashed string id. See string id
hash function, 240
Havok, 32, 41, 602
Havok Animation, 33
HDR. See lighting
header file, 67
heads-up display. See overlay
heap memory. See allocation
Hertz, 312
hexadecimal, 98
hex editor, 89
HID. See human interface device
high-level flow. See gameplay, flow
high-level shader language. See shader
high-resolution timer. See time

high water mark, 233, 394
HLSL. See shader, High-Level Shading
    Language
homogeneous clip space. See coordi-
    nate system
homogeneous coordinates, 154
Houdini, 53
hub. See gameplay
HUD. See overlay, heads-up display
human input device
    camera-relative control, 681
human interface device, 43, 339
    abstract control indices, 363
    accelerometer, 346
        detecting orientation with, 347
    actuator, 349
    analog axis, 345
    analog input, 344
    and game loop, 305
    audio, 349
    button
        analog, 345
        digital, 343
    chord, 354
    context-sensitive controls, 364
    control mapping, 363
    cross-platform, 361
    dead zone, 350
    disabling, 365
    DualShock, 342, 346
    EyeToy, 348
    force feedback, 43, 349
    gesture, 356
    infrared sensor, 347
    input event, 353
    interrupt, 342
    mouse, 346
    multiplayer, 361
    polling, 341
    relative axis, 346
    rumble, 348
    sequence, 356
    signal filtering, 351

Sixaxis, 346
system requirements, 350
WiiMote, 339, 346
XInput, 342, 343
hybrid build. See compiler

I

I18N. See localization
I32. See data type
I-Collide, 601
IDE. See integrated development envi-
    ronment
IEEE-754. See floating-point
IGC. See in-game cinematic
IK. See animation, inverse kinematics
image
    bitmapped, 412
    bits per pixel, 412
    sampling, 442
image-based lighting. See lighting
impulse, 651, 652, 669
    application, 663, 671
#include, 67, 112
index buffer, 407
indexed strip/fan, 408
inertia. See moment of inertia
inertia tensor, 645, 670
infinity. See floating-point
infrared sensor. See human interface
    device
in-game cinematic, 40, 505, 694
in-game menu. See menu
in-game sequence. See in-game cin-
    ematic
inheritance, 92, 125, 696, 739, 812
    deadly diamond, 93, 721
    multiple, 92, 125, 721, 722
    script, 803
    virtual, 93
initialization order (C++), 198
inline function, 71, 112
instance. See class instance; mesh in-
    stance; game object

instanced geometry, 692
instruction cache (I-cache), 222
__int32. See data type
integer
  signed, 99
  unsigned, 99
integrated development environment,
    66
integration
  backward Euler, 640
  explicit Euler, 144, 313, 638, 644, 648
  implicit Euler, 640
  midpoint Euler, 640
  numerical, 10, 313, 637, 644, 648
    convergence, 639
    order, 639
    stability, 639
  Runge-Kutta, 640
  velocity Verlet, 640, 645
  Verlet, 640
intensity. See lighting
interface, 97
internationalization. See localization
inter-object communication. See event
interpenetration. See collision
interpolation
  animation. See pose
  linear, 150, 174, 524
    parallelizing, 328
    swept shapes, 621
  pose. See pose
  spherical linear interpolation, 175,
      569
  temporal, 525, 538
  vertex attributes. See vertex
interrupt service routine, 342
intersection, 607
  AABB versus AABB, 616
  moving bodies, 620
  point versus sphere, 614
  sphere versus sphere, 614
  testing, 603. See also collision
intrusive. See container
inverse kinematics. See animation

Irrlicht, 28
island. See simulation island
ISR. See interrupt
iterator. See design pattern

J

job. See multitasking
joint, 495, 496. See also bone
  attach point, 584
  coordinate axes, 501
  index, 498
  name, 499
  parent, 499, 500
  root, 498
  scale, 502
joint space. See coordinate system
joypad. See human interface device
joystick. See human interface device

K

kd-tree, 38, 467, 623
keyboard. See human interface device
key frame, 506
key-value pair, 239, 287, 703, 705, 737,
      740, 779
Killzone 2, 481
Kynapse, 33, 47

L

lamina, 642
language
  characteristics, 794
  compiled, 794
  declarative, 795
  functional, 795
  imperative, 795
  interpreted, 794
  object-oriented, 91, 795
  procedural, 795
  reflective, 795. See also class, reflec-
      tion
late function binding, 774

latent function, 798
leak. See memory
left-hand rule, 149
level. See game, world chunk; game-
    play, objectives
level 1 cache (L1), 221
level 2 cache (L2), 221
level of detail (LOD), 404, 485, 486
level streaming, 712, 744. See also file
    I/O, asynchronous
libgcm, 32
library, 67, 307
lifetime
    debug primitive, 376
    object, 723, 725
    resource, 283
lighting, 411, 424
    absorption, 411
    ambient, 427, 431
    ambient occlusion, 477
    area light, 432
    Blinn-Phong lighting model, 429
    bloom, 432, 473
    BSSRDF, 478
    bump mapping, 471
    caustics, 478
    diffraction, 411
    diffuse, 427
    direct, 426
    directional, 431
    emissive object, 432
    emissive texture, 432
    environment mapping. See texture,
        environment map
    flashlight, 432
    gamut
        visible, 411
    global illumination model, 426, 474
    high dynamic range, 413, 432, 473
    image-based, 470
    indirect, 426, 474
    intensity, 411
    interactions with matter, 411
    light mapping. See texture, light map
    light source, 400, 430

local illumination model, 426
medium, 411
normal mapping. See texture, normal
    map
omni-directional light. See lighting,
    point light
parallax mapping, 471
per-pixel, 416
Phong reflection model, 427
point light, 431
precomputed radiance transfer, 479
radiosity, 427
ray tracing, 427
reflection, 411, 477. See also reflec-
    tion
refraction, 411
relief mapping, 471
scattering, 412
    subsurface, 412, 478
specular, 427
spot light, 432
static, 431, 449
transmission, 411
transport model, 400
transport models, 426
viewing direction, 428
wavelength, 411
light space. See coordinate system;
    shadow, mapping
Lightwave, 447
line, 181
linear
    approximation, 403, 516
linear algebra, 137
linear cast. See collision, query, shape
    cast
linear probing, 241
line of sight, 332, 372, 625
line segment, 182, 624
linkage, 113
    external, 113
    internal, 113
linked list. See container, list
linker, 66
Lisp language, 257, 570, 804

list
  intrusive, 235
little-endian. See endian
load-hit-store, 222, 566
local illumination. See lighting
localization, 242, 247, 250
local store (SPU), 326
local variable. See variable
locator
  animated, 517
  attach point, 584
  reference, 585
locomotion, 599, 626, 628, 679
  cycle, 492, 505, 590
  motion extraction, 589
  noise, 541
  pivotal, 530
  targeted, 530, 532
  traversal aids, 592
logging, 367
  channel, 370
  to file, 371
  verbosity, 369
log-LUV. See color
Loki, 31, 232
look-at. See animation
look-up table (LUT), 296, 300, 301, 419,
    451
low-pass filter, 351
LU decomposition, 154

# M

__m128. See single instruction,
    multiple data
make, 73
manager, 198
mantissa. See floating-point
map. See game, world chunk
mass, 633
material, 11, 37
  collision. See collision
  editor, 447
  visual, 424, 447
math library, 35

matrix, 151
  4 × 3, 159
  affine, 151
  column matrix, 152
  conversion to quaternion, 173
  identity, 153
  in-memory representation, 167
  inverse, 153
  isotropic, 151
  joint-to-model, 521
  model-to-world, 147, 165, 410, 522
  orthographic projection, 439
  orthonormal, 151
  palette, 522, 554, 557
  perspective projection matrix, 437
  product, 151
  pure rotation, 178
  row matrix, 152
  skinning. See skinning
  special orthogonal, 151
  transpose, 154
  view-to-world, 434
  world-to-view, 434
Maya, 52, 447
MBCS. See character set
mechanics. See physics
MEL language, 281, 794
member variable. See variable
memory
  access patterns, 206
  cache coherency, 220, 732, 762
  debug memory, 247
  defragmentation, 218
  fragmentation, 215, 744, 745
  in-game statistics, 393
  leak, 393
  management, 205, 289, 745
  relocation, 218, 748
  virtual, 217, 393
memory card, 349
memory corruption, 87
memory leak, 87
memory management, 35
memory stick, 268

menu
  in-game, 40, 255, 379
merging. See version control; rendering pipeline
mesh, 13, 42, 49, 51, 52, 53, 130, 403
  constructing, 405
  instance, 409, 734, 761
  progressive, 404
  skeletal, 52, 554
  static, 692, 701, 716
  submesh, 424
mesh-material pair. See primitive
message. See event
message map, 780
message pump, 37, 307, 336
mfspr instruction, 317
mftb instruction, 317
MI. See inheritance, multiple
Microsoft Excel, 251, 392
Microsoft Visual SourceSafe, 59
Microsoft Visual Studio, 59, 66
Minkowski sum/difference, 617. See also GJK
mipmapping, 421, 457
mix-in class. See class
MKS system of units, 632
MMOG. See genre
mod community, 11
model
  3D, 51
  analytic, 10, 632, 637
  closed-form, 10
  mathematical, 9
  numerical, 10
moiré pattern, 421
moment of inertia, 643, 646
momentum
  angular, 647, 650
  conservation, 647, 648
  linear, 635, 650
monolithic class hierarchy. See class hierarchy
Moore's Law, 325
motion blur, 489

motion capture. See animation
motion type (Havok), 670
mouse. See human interface device
movement. See locomotion
movie capture, 385
movie player, 822
moving average, 315, 351
MPEG, 822
MSAA. See antialiasing, multisample
_MSC_VER, 71
multi-byte quantity, 105
multicore, 215
multiplayer, 44, 600
  authority, 335
  client-on-top-of-server, 334
  client-server, 334
  dedicated server, 334
  human interface devices, 361
  networked, 44, 333, 822
  network replication, 714, 799
  peer-to-peer, 335
  proxy, 336, 799
  *Quake*, 336
  split-screen, 44
multiple check-out. See version control
multiple inheritance. See inheritance, multiple
multiply defined symbol error, 110
multitasking, 318, 329
  asynchronous programming, 331
  cooperative, 800, 813
  fork/join, 328, 674
  game objects, 771
  GPU, 450
  hardware, 324
  interfacing with game object update, 772
  job, 330, 567, 675
  physics, 673
  pipeline, 444
  pre-emptive, 30
  pthreads, 329
  script, 813
  sleep, 272, 315, 329

SPURS, 329
  job model, 329
  task model, 329
  thread, 267, 272, 325, 329, 334, 674,
      743, 757, 771
  thread synchronization, 674

# N

namespace
  global, 97
NaN. See floating-point, not-a-
      number
NDEBUG, 70
near plane. See view volume
negative number. See two's comple-
      ment
networking. See multiplayer
new operator (C++). See allocation
Newtonian mechanics. See physics
Newton's law of restitution, 651
Newton's laws of motion. See physics
NIS. See noninteractive sequence
noninteractive sequence, 505
non-player character, 512, 593
nonuniform rational B-spline.
      See patch
nonuniform scale. See transformation
normalized screen coordinates.
      See overlay
normal map. See texture
not-a-number. See floating-point
Novodex, 602
N-patch. See patch
NPC. See non-player character
NTSC, 312, 320, 440
numerical method. See integration
NURBS. See patch

# O

object. See class, instance; game object
object file, 67
object id. See game object

object model
  C++, 696
  component, 724, 731
    creation, 725
    generic, 727
    ownership, 725
    pure, 728
  Excel, 696
  game, 46, 696, 712
    parallelizing, 771
  Hydro Thunder, 716
  interface, 696
  object-centric, 716
  OMT, 696
  property-centric, 730
    pros and cons, 732
  runtime, 697, 715
  software, 46, 696
  tools-side, 697
object persistence. See serialization
observer. See callback function
occlusion. See triangle
occlusion culling. See culling
occlusion volume. See culling, anti-
      portal
octree, 38, 467, 623
ODE. See Open Dynamics Engine; or-
      dinary differential equation
Ogre3D, 4, 28, 35, 38, 77, 104, 105, 558
Ogre::Real, 105
one-frame-off lag, 770
opacity, 401
Open Dynamics Engine, 32, 42, 601,
      665
OpenGL, 32, 36
  perspective projection matrix, 437
  view space, 163
  view volume, 437
open hash table. See container
OpenTissue, 603
operating system, 30, 31, 34, 67, 68,
      115, 116, 119
  DOS, 263
  Mac OS, 263

Microsoft Windows, 263
UNIX, 263
operator (C++)
  postincrement, 226
  preincrement, 226
order. See integration, numerical
ordinary differential equation, 636,
        638, 644, 648
  analytical solution, 637
orphan, 750
orthogonal, 141
orthographic. See projection
OS. See operating system
OutputDebugString(), 368
overdraw, 465
overlay, 39, 434, 486
  graphical user interface, 9, 26, 28, 39,
        68, 96
  heads-up display, 28, 39, 434, 716
  normalized screen coordinates, 487
  relative screen coordinates, 487

**P**

package file, 277, 279, 286
painter's algorithm, 443
PAL, 313, 320, 440
Panda3D, 28, 803
parallax mapping. See lighting
parallelogram
  area of, 148
parallel programming. See multitask-
        ing
parametric equation, 181, 625
  surface, 402
Pareto principle, 86
partial-skeleton blending. See anima-
        tion
particle animation. See animation
particle system, 38, 39, 482, 716
  particle, 37, 38, 53
  updating, 759
pass. See shader

patch, 402
  Bézier, 402
  bicubic, 402
  nonuniform rational B-spline
        (NURBS), 402
  N-patch, 402
path finding. See artificial intelligence
pause. See game loop
peer-to-peer. See mulltiplayer
penalty force, 653
penumbra, 432, 474
perception. See artificial intelligence
Perforce. See version control
perspective. See projection
perspective-correct. See vertex, attri-
        bute interpolation
per-user options, 253
phantom. See collision
phase (animation), 508
Phong. See lighting
photorealism, 400
physics, 452, 595
  and fun, 597
  and game loop, 305
  angular dynamics, 633
    2D, 642
    3D, 645
  applications, 596, 675
  constraint, 631, 654, 658, 671
    breakable, 660, 668
    chain, 660
    hinge, 659
    limited, 659
    planar, 660
    point-to-point, 658
    powered, 661, 683
    prismatic, 659
    pulley, 660
    rag doll, 660, 684
    rod, 658
    solver, 664
    stiff spring, 658
    wheel, 660
  control, 662
    loss of, 600

couple, 663
deformable body, 596, 603, 678, 684
friction. See friction
Havok, 4, 32, 33, 41
impacts on game, 598
integration into game, 666
island. See simulation island
linear dynamics, 633, 634
mechanics, 630
  analytical, 632
middleware, 601
motion type (Havok), 670
Newtonian mechanics, 630
Newton's laws of motion, 630, 635
Open Dynamics Engine, 32, 42
PhysX, 32, 41
puzzle, 597
rag doll. See rag doll
rigid body, 496, 545, 595, 606, 631
  fixed, 670
  game-driven, 669, 671, 679, 682
  key framed, 669
  linkage to game object, 666, 670
  physics-driven. See game object
rigid body dynamics, 41, 595, 630,
      632
  classical, 630
sleep, 657
stepping, 663, 671
updating. See physics, stepping
vehicle, 626
water, 486
world, 605, 631
Physics Abstraction Layer, 603
physics libraries, 32
PhysX, 32, 41, 602
piece-wise linear. See linear
pipeline, 444, 763
  animation. See animation
  GPU. See rendering pipeline
  latency, 445
  rendering. See rendering pipeline
  throughput, 445
pitch, 161

pixel, 400, 433
placement new, 299
plain old data structures, 299
plane, 148, 183, 435
  distance to origin, 183
  point-normal form, 183, 435
plan view, 434
platformer. See genre
platform independence layer, 34
playback rate. See animation
player I/O, 43. See human interface
      device
player mechanics. See gameplay
player prediction, 334
PLAYSTATION 3
  architecture, 326
PlayStation Edge, 32, 33
PlayStation Network, 262, 268
PNG. See Portable Network Graphics
PODS. See plain old data structure
point, 138
  adding and subtracting, 143
pointer
  invalid, 751
  stale, 750
pointer fix-up, 297
polling. See human interface device
polygon
  collision, 607
  rendering, 402, 403
polygon soup, 630, 734
  shape welding, 656
polyhedron
  collision, 607
  convex, 185
polymorphism, 94, 125
polytope, 610, 617
Portable Network Graphics, 420
portal, 38
portals. See culling
pose, 499
  as change of basis, 503
  bind, 499, 500, 519
  current, 500, 519

difference, 538
extraction, 553
global, 503, 553, 557
in-memory representation, 502, 504
interpolation, 506, 524
inverse bind, 499
key. See key frame
local, 501, 553, 557
matching, 684
matrix, 501
parent-relative. See pose, local
reference. See pose, bind
rest. See pose, bind
T-pose. See pose, bind
position vector. See vector
post effect, 489. See visual effects, post
postincrement. See operator (C++)
post-load initialization, 300
potentially visible set, 37
PowerPC, 325
power processing unit, 326
PPU. See power processing unit
precision. See floating-point
precomputed radiance transfer.
         See lighting
preincrement. See operator (C++)
preprocessor, 67
primitive
    collision, 608
    debug drawing, 375
    geometric, 36, 37, 424
    mesh-material pair, 424
primitive submission, 463
printf debugging, 367
private:, 113
probe. See collision, query
processor utilization, 330, 567, 773
production build. See compiler
product of inertia, 646
profiling tools, 40, 86
    exclusive execution time, 389
    hierarchical, 387
    inclusive execution time, 389
    in-game, 385

instrumentation, 389
instrumenting, 87
statistical, 86
projectile tracing, 676
projection, 146, 434
    orthographic, 22, 39, 434, 439, 486,
         702
    perspective, 22, 434, 437, 702
        attribute interpolation. See vertex,
             attribute interpolation
        division by z, 438
        perspective foreshortening, 434, 438
        separating axis, 614
property grid, 703
property object, 730, 731
    scripted, 803
proxy. See multiplayer
PRT. See lighting, precomputed radi-
         ance transfer
pseudovector, 140
pthreads. See multitasking
public:, 113
punning. See type punning
pure virtual function. See class
Purify. See Rational Purify
PVS. See potentially visible set
Python language, 794

Q

QTE. See quick time event
quadratic probing, 242
quadtree, 38, 466
*Quake*, 11, 25, 692, 699
    game loop, 336
Quake Engine, 4, 11, 13, 25, 26, 27, 35,
         44, 54
    Radiant, 54
quantization. See compression
quaternion, 169, 179
    concatenation, 172
    conjugate, 171
    conversion to matrix, 173
    dual, 180

inverse, 171
  physics, 646, 649
  product, 170
  rotating vectors with, 172
quick time event, 505

# R

racing game. See genre
Radiant, 54, 699
radiosity. See lighting
radius vector. See vector
rag doll, 545, 553, 600, 660
  blending with animation, 683
  getting up from, 684
  integration into game, 682
  mapping to skeleton, 661
  pose matching, 684
  powered constraints, 661
random number, 192
  Diehard tests, 194
  linear congruential, 192
  Mersenne Twister, 193
  Mother of All, 194
  Xorshift, 194
RAPID, 601
rapid iteration, 570, 698
  *Uncharted*, 573
rasterization, 441, 453
raster operations. See rendering pipe-
    line, merging
Rational Purify, 88
ray, 182, 624
ray cast, 332. See collision, query
ray tracing. See lighting
RCS. See version control
rdtsc instruction, 317
read-only data segment. See execut-
    able file
real-time. See simulation
record and play back feature, 40, 316,
    600
rectangle invalidation, 303
reference clip. See animation

reference counting, 289
referential integrity, 275, 277, 283, 295
reflection. See class
  anisotropic, 412
  diffuse, 412
  specular, 412
reflectivity, 428
region. See gameplay
register, 117. See also shader
registry (Microsoft Windows), 253
relative screen coordinates. See overlay
release build. See compiler
relief mapping. See lighting
rendering engine, 36
  graphics device interface, 37
  low-level renderer, 36, 37, 38, 39
  render packet, 37
  scene graph, 38
rendering equation, 400, 427
rendering pipeline
  application stage, 446, 460
  asset conditioning stage, 445, 449
  blending. See merging
  data transformation, 446
  geometry processing stage, 446
  GPU pipeline, 450, 451
  merging, 453
  rasterization stage, 446
  raster operations. See merging
  stream output, 452
  tools stage, 445
  triangle setup, 452
  triangle traversal, 453
render loop, 304
render packet. See primitive, geometric
render state, 463, 464
  leak, 464
render target, 441
render to texture. See texture
replication. See multiplayer, network
    replication
repository. See version control
resolution. See screen

resource,  49
  binary,  299
  chunk allocator. See allocation
  compiler,  282
  composite,  295, 300
  database,  274, 707
  dependencies,  282, 295
  directory organization,  284
  exporting,  279, 281
  file formats,  286
  Granny,  286
  GUID,  286
  lifetime. See lifetime
  linker,  282
  memory,  289
  meta-data,  274
  registry,  287
  sectioned files,  294
  source asset,  49, 275, 281
resource conditioning pipeline. See as-
      set conditioning pipeline
resource management,  35
resource manager,  35, 261, 272
  Ogre3D,  280
  runtime,  283
  Uncharted,  278
  Unreal,  276
  XNA,  281
restitution. See coefficient of restitution
return address,  117
revision control. See version control
RGB. See color
right-hand rule,  149, 170
rigid body. See physics
  game-driven,  631
rigid body dynamics. See physics
RK4. See integration, Runge-Kutta
rodata segment. See executable file
roll,  161
ROP. See rendering pipeline, merging
RTS. See genre
RTTI. See runtime type identification
rumble. See human interface device
run cycle. See locomotion

Runge-Kutta. See integration
runtime type identification,  714

**S**

S3 Texture Compression (S3TC).
          See texture, compression
sample (animation),  507
sampling,  507
sandbox game,  598
save anywhere,  714, 749. See
          also game, load/save
scalar,  140
SCCS. See version control
scene,  400
scene graph,  38, 466
  choosing,  469
schema. See game object
Scheme language,  257, 570, 804
scope,  116
scratch pad,  567
Scream. See audio
screen
  aspect ratio,  436, 439
  resolution,  436
screen mapping,  440, 452
screen shot,  384
screen space. See coordinate system
script,  712
  byte code,  795, 805
  callback,  802
  data definition,  257
  data-definition,  794
  defining classes,  812
  driven engine,  803
  event handler,  802, 810
  extending game object types,  802
  interface to native language,  804
  multithreaded,  813
  property object,  731, 803
  runtime,  794
  virtual machine,  795, 804
scripting language,  47, 794
  Lua,  799
  object-oriented,  812

Pawn, 801
Python, 281, 800
    method table, 804
QuakeC, 11, 797
Small / Small C. See scripting lan-
        guage, Pawn
    typical characteristics, 796
    UnrealScript, 797
script lambda, 804
SDK. See software development kit
search path. See file system
SECAM, 313, 320, 440
segment
    executable file, 115
SEH. See structured exception han-
        dling
separating axis theorem, 614
separating vector, 607
serialization, 735
    binary image, 734
service object. See object model, com-
        ponent
shader, 447, 450
    architecture, 454
    Cg, 457
    constant register. See shader, uni-
        form declaration
    effect file, 459
        CgFX, 459
    fragment. See shader, pixel
    geometry, 451
    half4, 456
    High-Level Shading Language, 455
    memory access, 455
    OpenGL shader language, 457
    pass, 459
    pixel, 453
    pixel shader, 37
    register, 455
    semantic, 457
    shader model 4.0, 455
    technique, 459
    texture access, 457
    texture sampler, 458

    uniform declaration, 458
    vertex, 408, 451
shading, 426. See also lighting
shading equation. See rendering equa-
        tion
shadow, 432, 474
    contact, 477. See also lighting, ambi-
        ent occlusion
    mapping, 475
    volume, 474
shadows, 28, 39
shape
    bounding box. See bounding box
    box, 604
    capsule, 604, 608
    collision, 603, 606
    compound, 612
    convex volume, 611. See also convex
    discrete oriented polytope, 610
    polygon soup, 612
    sphere, 182, 608, 614, 626
    swept, 620
    swept sphere, 608
    tetrahedron, 617
shape cast. See collision, query
shlwapi.dll, 266
SID. See string id
signed integer. See integer
significant digits. See floating-point
silhouette edge, 404, 462, 474
sim, 597
SIMD. See single instruction, multiple
        data
simplex, 617
simulation, 9, 10, 24, 41, 46
    agent-based, 9, 713, 758
    discrete event, 758
    game loop. See game loop
    interactive, 9, 303
    physics. See physics
    real-time, 4, 9, 10, 12, 13, 18, 24, 34,
        303, 310, 713, 758
        deadline, 10
        hard, 10
        soft, 9, 10

rigid body dynamics. See physics
temporal, 9
updating. See game object
simulation island, 657, 679
single instruction, multiple data, 103,
185, 327, 566
Altivec, 104
intrinsics, 187
__m128, 104, 187
streaming SIMD extensions, 104
vector-matrix product, 189
VF32, 104
single instruction, single data, 327
single-stepping. See debugger; game
loop
singleton. See design pattern
singly-linked list. See container
SISD. See single instruction, single
data
Sixaxis. See human interface device
skeletal mesh. See mesh
skeleton, 447, 495, 496, 554, 661
in-memory representation, 498
root joint. See joint
SketchUp, 447
skinning, 52, 447, 495, 518
matrix, 521
to multiple joints, 523
weights, 414, 495, 518, 554, 557
sky, 484
box, 484
dome, 484
sleep. See game loop; multitasking;
physics
slope
of a function, 638
slow motion. See game loop
small memory allocator. See allocation
smart pointer, 219, 714, 750, 751
smoothing, 417
Softimage/XSI, 52, 447
software development kit, 3, 31
software object model. See object
model

sorting, 225
for rendering, 464
Sound Forge, 53
source clip. See animation
source control. See version control
Source engine, 26
source file, 67
SourceSafe. See version control
spatial hash, 466, 622, 757
spatial partitioning, 466
collision, 623
spawner, 737
pros and cons, 740
spawning. See game object
spectral color. See color
spectral plot, 411
specular. See lighting
specular power map. See texture
specular reflection. See reflection
speed, 313
angular, 642
sphere. See shape
sphere cast. See collision, query
sphere hierarchy, 38
sphere map. See texture
sphere tree. See bounding sphere tree
spherical harmonic basis, 479
spline, 402, 682, 706
Bézier, 402
B-spline, 402, 551
split-screen. See multiplayer
spring, 653, 660
constant, 636
rotational, 661
stiff, 658
sprite, 492
SPU. See synergistic processing unit
SPURS. See multitasking
SQL Server, 278
SQT, 179, 500, 524
SSE. See single instruction, multiple
data; streaming SIMD extensions
stability. See integration, numerical

stack frame
  debugger, 116
stage. See game, world chunk
stance variation, 540
standard C library, 34, 76
standard template library, 31, 229
  STLport, 31
start-up and shut-down
  construct on demand, 198
  engine subsystem, 197
  manual, 200
  Ogre3D, 202
  *Uncharted*, 204
*Star Wars: The Force Unleashed*, 603
state layer. See action state machine
statically-typed, 774
static (C/C++), 113, 121
static class diagram. See class diagram
static geometry. See mesh
static variable. See variable
stencil buffer, 441, 475
  testing, 453
stepping. See physics
STL. See standard template library
STLport, 31
story-driven game, 598
strafe. See locomotion
streaming. See file I/O, asynchronous;
    level streaming
streaming SIMD extensions. See single
    instruction, multiple data
stream output. See rendering pipeline
strict aliasing, 108
  type punning, 108
string, 242
string class, 243
string database, 250
string hashing. See hash function
string id, 244, 797, 810
struct. See class
struct of arrays, 732. See also array of
    structs
structured exception handling, 132
studio, 5
  first-party developer, 8

subdivision surface, 402
subsurface scattering. See lighting,
    scattering
Subversion. See version control
support. See collision
  function, 618, 619
surface, 400, 401
  collision, 607
  visual properties, 400, 410
sweep and prune, 624
SWIFT, 601
symbolic link, 274
synergistic processing unit, 326, 329,
    567
syntax tree, 560. See also animation,
    blending

T

Tagged Image File Format, 420
tangent space. See coordinate system
Targa, 420
target hardware, 30
targeting. See aiming
Target Manager, 368
taxonomy, 720
TCHAR. See data type
tearing, 316, 440
technical requirements checklist, 366
technique. See shader
temporal coherency, 315, 623, 624
terrain, 485, 716
  height field, 485
tessellation, 403, 452
  dynamic, 404, 485
testability, 74
texel, 418
texel density, 421
  world space, 422
text rendering, 487
text segment. See executable file
texture, 37, 42, 49, 52, 129, 417, 447,
    455, 457
  1D, 419
  3D, 473

addressing modes,  419
albedo map,  418
animation. See animation
compression,  421
coordinates,  419
cube map,  472
diffuse map,  418
emissive. See lighting
environment map,  472, 477
filtering,  423, 457
    anisotropic,  423
    bilinear,  423
    nearest neighbor,  423
    trilinear,  423
formats,  420
gloss map,  471
height field. See terrain
height map,  470
light map,  38, 39, 431, 449
normal map,  470
rendering to,  457, 478
sampler. See shader
scrolling,  463
shadow map. See shadow
specular map,  471
specular power map,  472
sphere map,  472
texture space. See coordinate system
TGA. See Targa
thread. See multitasking
three-way merge. See version control
TIFF. See Tagged Image File Format
time
    abstract time line,  310
    clock,  310
        animation. See animation
    clock class,  322
    clock drift,  318
    clock variable,  318
    delta,  313, 314, 315, 336, 351, 637
    floating-point,  319
    game,  303, 310
    global,  509
    high-resolution timer,  317
    index,  505

local,  311, 505
    measuring,  317
        and break points,  320
    real. See simulation
    units,  318
        animation,  507
        frames. See frame (animation)
        phase. See phase (animation)
time of impact,  622. See also collision,
            continuous collision detection
TOI. See time of impact
Tokamak,  603
tone mapping,  473
tool chain. See asset conditioning pipe-
            line
tools,  vii, 49
tools build. See compiler
torque,  150, 643, 661
    3D,  648
    application,  663, 671
Torque,  28
TortoiseSVN. See version control
trace. See collision, query
transformation,  151
    coordinate axes,  159, 165
    rotation,  151, 157, 177
    scale,  151, 158
        nonuniform,  142, 502, 525
    translation,  151, 157
transformation matrix,  151
translation unit,  67, 108
translucency,  401, 682
transparency,  401, 682
    alpha. See alpha
TRC. See technical requirements
            checklist
tree
    $k$d-tree,  38
    octree,  38
    quadtree,  38
    sphere hierarchy,  38
triangle,  403
    area of,  148
    face normal,  405
    fan,  407

indexed list, 406
list, 406
occlusion, 443
strip, 407
winding order, 405
triangle mesh. See mesh
triangulation, 403
trigger region. See gameplay
TrueAxis, 602
TTY, 368
tunneling, 620
turbo button, 314
two's complement, 99
type punning
   strict aliasing. See strict aliasing

U

U32. See data type
UDN. See Unreal
umbra, 432
UML. See Unified Modeling Language
UNC. See universal naming conven-
       tion
Unicode, 248
unified memory architecture, 325, 568
Unified Modeling Language, 92
universal naming convention, 263
Unreal, 11, 26
   Unreal Developer Network, 26
UnrealEd, 54, 276, 707, 798
Unreal Engine, 3, 4, 11, 13, 26, 27, 35,
       41, 44, 54
   UnrealEd, 54
unresolved symbol error, 108, 110
unsigned integer. See integer
updating. See game object
UTF-8, 248
UTF-16, 248
u, v. See texture

V

variable
   automatic, 117
   class static, 121

global, 115
local, 117
member, 119
static, 115
variant, 778, 805
V-Collide, 601
vector, 140
addition, 142
basis, 141
   extracting from matrix, 165
cross product, 145, 148, 643
direction, 141, 156
dot product, 145
front, left and up, 160, 409
magnitude, 143
multiplication by scalar, 141
normal, 145
   transforming, 166
normalization, 145
position, 141, 633
projection, 146
quaternion form, 172
squared magnitude, 144
subtraction, 142
unit, 141, 144
vector processor. See single instruction,
       multiple data
vector unit. See single instruction, mul-
       tiple data
velocity, 144, 306, 313
angular, 642
   3D, 646
animation, 526
linear, 634
relative, 654
screen space, 489
verbosity. See logging
Verlet integration. See integration
version control, vii, 57
Alienbrain, 59, 273
assets, 273
checking in, 63
checking out, 63

ClearCase, 59
committing, 63
CVS, 58
deleting files, 66
diff, 64
exclusive check-out, 64
git, 59
Google Code, 60
history, 62
locking, 64
merging, 64
multiple check-out, 64
Perforce, 59, 273
RCS, 58
repository, 60
resources, 273
SCCS, 58
SourceSafe, 59
submitting, 63
Subversion, 59
three-way merge, 65, 89
TortoiseSVN, 61
updating, 63
vertex, 413
    attribute interpolation, 416, 453
        perspective-correct, 439, 453
    attributes, 413
    binding to skeleton. See skinning,
        weights
    binormal, 414
    bitangent, 413
    cache optimization, 408, 456
    formats, 414
    normal, 413
    skinning weight. See skinning
    tangent, 413
vertex buffer, 407
vertical blanking interval, 316, 440
VF32. See single instruction, multiple
        data
VGA, 450
view matrix. See matrix, world-to-view
viewport, 37

view volume, 435, 452
    far plane, 435
    frustum, 184, 435, 452
    near plane, 435
vignette, 490
virtual function. See class
virtual function table. See class
virtual inheritance. See inheritance
virtual machine. See script
visibility. See culling
    determination, 20, 37, 121
visual effects, 38, 39, 53
    anti-aliasing, 39
    bleach bypass, 39
    bloom, 28, 39
    environment mapping, 38, 39
    post, 38
    post effects, 38, 39
visual properties. See surface
Visual SourceSafe. See Microsoft
        Visual Studio SourceSafe
Visual Studio. See Microsoft Visual
        Studio
voice over IP (VOIP), 349
Voodoo, 450
vtable. See class, virtual function table

W

walk cycle. See locomotion
watch window. See debugger
water, 404, 411, 426, 427, 451, 478, 481,
        486, 629, 685, 691, 701, 716
wavelength. See lighting
w buffer, 444. See also depth buffer
wchar_t. See data type
WCS. See character set, wide
weighted average, 151, 414, 454, 518,
        523, 534, 557, 633
welding, 656
WiiMote. See human interface device
_WIN32, 71
winding order. See triangle
Windows Bitmap, 420

Windows Media Video, 822
WMV, 822
work, 650
world. See collision; physics; game
world matrix. See matrix, model-to-
      world
write-back cache, 220
write-through cache, 220
wstring. See data type

## X

XACT, 822. See audio
Xbox 360
  architecture, 325
Xbox Live, 27, 253, 262, 268
XInput. See human interface device
XNA, 26, 27

XNA Game Studio, 26
XSI, 447

## Y

Yake, 28
yaw, 161

## Z

z-bias, 483
ZBrush, 52
z buffer. See depth buffer
z-fighting, 443, 483
ZIP file, 285
zlib, 285
z-prepass. See depth buffer
z-testing. See depth buffer